P

THE JEWISH PEOPLE

· PAST AND PRESENT

DETAIL FROM MOSAIC FLOOR IN THE SYNAGOGUE AT BETH ALPHA
(EARLY 6TH CENTURY)

The design represents the Sun, its chariot drawn by four galloping horses

THE JEWISH PEOPLE

PAST AND PRESENT

VOLUME 1

JEWISH ENCYCLOPEDIC HANDBOOKS

CENTRAL YIDDISH CULTURE ORGANIZATION (CYCO)

NEW YORK

PRINTED IN THE UNITED STATES OF AMERICA

By MARSTIN PRESS, New York, N. Y.

I. LONDON, *President*

PREFACE

THE IDEA of publishing a series of volumes in English under the title *Jewish People:* PAST AND PRESENT was conceived before the United States entered the war. After this country was drawn into the world conflict, the contact with a number of Jewish scholars in other lands was almost completely severed. This and a number of other contingencies were responsible for the belated appearance of the first volume.

This initial volume makes its appearance at a time when the magnitude of the tragedy which has befallen the Jews as a people is beginning to grow clear for us Jews as well as for the world in general. Two-thirds of European Jewry has been annihilated and the Old World's most important centers of Jewish culture and spiritual creative forces are no longer in existence. At so tragic a moment in the three-thousand-year old history of our people, it is of greater importance than ever before to acquaint the readers of the English-speaking world — the present home of the majority of the Jews — with the past and the present of the Jewish people as well as with its achievements in the various fields of cultural life and with the complex problems of Jewish life in our times.

The Jewish community in America — the greatest and most influential today — is the bearer of the heaviest responsibility, of the keenest duty to save and preserve the cultural treasures of our people and to keep up our spiritual creative work.

The aim of the publication *Jewish People:* PAST AND PRESENT is to provide the utmost possible comprehensive and objective data prepared by outstanding authorities in the respective fields of scientific endeavor.

The present work is based principally on the three volumes *Yidn,* issued in the years 1939-1942 as an integral part of the *General Encyclopedia* (in Yiddish). The particular virtue of these volumes is that the contributors and editors who have compiled them were both intimately connected with the throbbing Jewish life and actively participated in the cultural and spiritual creative work of East European Jewry. A considerable number of outstanding scholars of Europe, America and Palestine are represented in the present work.

This first volume contains monographs on anthropology, archæology, Jewish history, the origin and development of Jewish religion, Jewish religious philosophy, Jewish mysticism and Kabbala, the Messianic movements, as well as Jewish statistics, economic development and migration movements.

The subsequent volumes will comprise monographs and articles on Jewish demography, the development and evolution of social and national movements, anti-Semitism, the history of Jewish literature, art, theater, music, languages, etc.

We deem it a duty to express our sincerest gratitude to the Editors, the Editorial Advisory Board, the Associate Editors, Contributors, and Translators for their devoted work.

The appearance of this volume has been made possible by the generous support given by various sympathizing organizations and public-spirited individuals. Recognition is due the following for permission to use valuable material: American Schools of Oriental Research; Oxford University Press; Oriental Institute, University of Chicago; University Museum of Pennsylvania; Bibliothèque Nationale, Paris; Czechoslovak Government Information Bureau; American Jewish Historical Society; Netherlands Information Bureau; Dr. Chester C. McCown. Particular acknowledgment is gratefully made for the numerous courtesies extended by Professor Alexander Marx, Miss Anna Kleban and Mr. Morris Lutzki of the Library of the Jewish Theological Seminary in New York, and to the American Bible Society for permitting the use of the maps of Ancient Palestine which appear in this volume.

THE PUBLISHERS

CONTENTS

ILLUSTRATIONS

RACE THEORY IN THE LIGHT OF MODERN SCIENCE

M. F. Ashley Montagu

I. THE HISTORY OF THE CONCEPT OF RACE

"RACE" IS A TERM which is now generally understood to embrace the concept which holds that a "something" called "race" is the prime determiner of all the important traits of body and soul, of character and personality, of human beings and nations. It is further alleged that this "something" called "race" is a fixed and unchangeable part of the germ plasm which, transmitted from generation to generation, unfolds in each people in a typical expression of personality and culture.

This conception of "race" is relatively new in the world, for it first made its appearance in the middle of the 19th century. Before that time, while there had been a considerable amount of discussion in the preceding seventy years for and against the equality of races of man, there had been no formalization or codification of a racist viewpoint. Men might fight others in order to gain some economic advantage, as the Crusaders did the "infidels" in the name of religion, they might discriminate against others on the ground of religious differences; as Lord Bryce put it: "They fought for land. They plundered one another . . . But strong as patriotism and national feeling might be, they did not think of themselves in terms of ethnology, and in making war for every other sort of reason never

made it for the sake of imposing their own type of civilization . . . In none of such cases did the thought of racial distinctions come to the front."

Within any society men might be persecuted or made the object of discrimination on the grounds of differences in faith, culture, politics or class, but never on any biological grounds such as are implied in the idea of racial differences.

In Europe during the Middle Ages and also during the Renaissance the Jews, for example, were singled out for discrimination and persecution, but this was always done on social or cultural or religious grounds. The Jews, it was urged, had killed Christ, they were accused of murdering Christian children and using their blood for ritual purposes, they were infidels, anti-Christians, usurers, they were almost everything under the sun, but whatever they were held to be they were never considered to be so for biological reasons. The biological basis for racial discrimination is a modern "discovery," and that is the important point to grasp. The objection to any people on "racial" or biological grounds is a purely modern innovation, and that is the basic sense in which modern group antagonism differs from that which prevailed in earlier periods.

It was not until the latter part of the 18th century when voices began to make themselves heard in Europe and America against the inhuman traffic in slaves, and when these voices assumed the shape of influential men and organizations that, on the defensive, the supporters of slavery were forced to look about them for reasons of a new kind to controvert the dangerous arguments of their opponents. The abolitionists argued that those who were enslaved were as good human beings as those who had enslaved them. To this, by way of reply, the champions of slavery could only attempt to show that the slaves were most certainly not as good as their masters. And in this highly charged emotional atmosphere there began the recitation of the catalogue of differences which were alleged to prove the inferiority of the slave to his master.

The idea of "race" was not so much the deliberate creation of a caste seeking to defend its privileges against what was regarded as an inferior social caste as it was the strategic elaboration of erroneous notions which had long been held by many slaveholders. In order to bolster up those rights the superior caste did not have far to seek for reasons which would serve to justify its conduct. The illiteracy and spiritual benightedness of the slaves supplied plenty of material for elaboration on the theme of their essential inferiority. The difference in physical appearance provided a convenient peg upon which to hang the argument that this represented the external sign of more profound ineradicable mental and moral inferiorities. It was an easily grasped mode of reasoning, and in this way the obvious difference in *social* status, in caste status, was equated with the obvious difference in *physical* appearance which, in turn, was taken to indicate a fundamental *biological* difference. Thus a culturally produced difference in *social* status was converted into a difference in biological status. What was once a social difference was now made to function as a biological difference which would serve, it was hoped, to justify and maintain the social difference.

This was a most attractive idea to many members of a society in which the classes were markedly stratified, and it was an idea which had a particular appeal for those who were beginning to take an active interest in the scientific study and classification of the "races" of mankind. For the term "race" had by this time become established. It was with this tremendous handicap of a

term in which the very question they were attempting to ask had from the outset already been begged that the anthropologists of the 19th century set out on their researches. The question they had begged was the one which required to be proved, namely, that mental and moral differences were associated with "racial" external physical differences.

It was not, however, the scientific student of the variety of man who influenced European thought along these lines, but an aristocrat of the Second Empire, an amateur orientalist and professional diplomat, Count Joseph Arthur de Gobineau. Gobineau rejected the principles of the French Revolution, and looked upon the egalitarian philosophy of the Revolution as the hopelessly confused expression of a degraded rabble. If the founders of the First Republic had believed in the liberty, equality, and fraternity of mankind, he would show that, on the contrary, a man was not bound to be free, that the idea of the brotherhood of man was a vain and empty dream, a repugnant dream which could never be realized because it was based upon a fallacious belief in the equality of man. These views were fully set out by Gobineau in his four-volume work *Essai sur l'inégalité des races humaines,* Paris, 1853-1855. Gobineau never attempted to disguise the motives which led him to write the *Essai.* He wrote it as a contribution towards the great struggle against equality and the emancipation of the proletariat. As Finot says: "Imbued with aristocratic ideas . . . he thought it useful to oppose to the democratic aspirations of his time a number of considerations on the existence of natural castes in humanity and their beneficial necessity."

In 1856 an American translation of the first two volumes of Gobineau's work was published at Philadelphia under the title *Moral and Intellectual Diversity of Races.* This translation was the work of H. Hotz, the Alabama pro-slavery propagandist. Ever since their publication Gobineau's works have enjoyed a great reputation among reactionaries and demogogues of every kind, and forty-five years later the views expressed in these works were taken over lock, stock and barrel by Houston Stewart Chamberlain and elaborated in his *Grundlagen des neunzehnten Jahrhunderts*. This work, which has been accurately described as "one of the most foolish books ever written," enjoyed an enormous popularity in Germany. Kaiser Wilhelm II called it "my favorite book."

Both Gobineau's and Chamberlain's works may be regarded as the spiritual progenitors of Hitler's *Mein Kampf,* a work in which the concept of "race" reaches its final theoretic development, in preparation for that dreadful consummation of its principles which has led to the deliberate murder of more than 5,000,000 Jews, millions of Poles, and millions of others throughout the continent of Europe.

II. THE CRITIQUE OF THE RACE CONCEPT

The fact that the popular conception of "race" has no basis in scientific fact, nor in any other kind of demonstrable fact, that it is, indeed, a pure myth, has not prevented it from acquiring a firm hold upon the minds of men. The earlier anthropologists contributed to the development of the erroneous concept of "race" in no unsubstantial manner. Their classificatory schemes were pretentious and for the most part speculative. They had no basis for their attempts to link up certain physical characters with particular behavioral characters other than anecdotal and travellers' accounts. Where, as in America, they wrote out of personal experience of the Negro and the American Indian they were usually moved more by emotion than by reason. In short, the anthropologists themselves took very much for granted what required to be proved, namely, that "race" corresponded to a reality rather than to a fiction.

In the Darwinian period, when evolution **was** conceived as a process involving con-

tinuous materials which, without the operation of natural selection, would remain unchanged, it was possible for anthropologists to think of "races" as groups which could be classified upon the basis of the fact that they possessed an aggregate of common physical characters, and as Darwin later postulated, as groups which varied only under conditions of natural selection, but which otherwise remained unchanged.

That many differences exist between different groups of human beings is obvious, but the older anthropological conception of these is erroneous, and it is now coming to be fairly clearly understood that the older anthropological approach to the study of their relationships is unscientific and pre-Mendelian. Taxonomic exercises in the classification of assemblages of phenotypical (visible or apparent) characters will never succeed in elucidating the relationships of different groups of mankind to one another for the simple reason that it is not assemblages of characters which undergo change in the formation of the individual and of the group, but single units which determine those characters. One of the great persisting errors involved in the anthropological conception of "race" has been due to the steady refusal to recognize this fact. The fact is that it is not possible to classify the various groups of mankind by means of the characters which anthropologists have customarily used, for the simple reason that those characters do not behave as pre-Mendelian anthropologists think they should behave, namely, as complexes of characters which are relatively fixed and are transmitted as complexes, but behave instead in a totally different manner as the expressions of many independent units, linked and unlinked, which have entered into their formation.

The parallel in the history of biology is very striking here and has been well illustrated by Dobzhansky, who writes: "Many studies on hybridization were made before Mendel, but they did not lead to the discovery of Mendel's laws. In retrospect, we see clearly where the mistake of Mendel's predecessors lay: they treated as units the complexes of characteristics of individuals, races, and species, and attempted to find rules governing the inheritance of such complexes. Mendel was the first to understand that it was the inheritance of separate traits, and not complexes of traits, which had to be studied. Some of the modern students of racial variability consistently repeat the mistakes of Mendel's predecessors." (*Genetics and the Origin of Species*, Columbia University Press, New York, 2nd Ed., 1941, p. 78).

It is now known that the materials of evolution are not represented by continuous aggregates of characters but by discontinuous packages of chemicals, each of which is more or less independent in its action, and may be only partially responsible for the form of any character. These chemical packages are the genes situated within the chromosomes, and they retain both their independence and their individual character more or less indefinitely, although they are probably all inherently variable and, in time, may undergo mutation.* For these reasons any conception of "race" which operates as if inheritance were a matter of the transmission of gross aggregates of characters is both erroneous and meaningless. To quote Dobzhansky once more: "The difficulty . . . is that . . . the concept of race as a system of character-averages logically implies a theory of continuous, rather than of particulate, germ plasm. Such a concept is obviously outmoded and incapable of producing much insight into the causative factors at work in human populations. Although the genic basis of relatively few human traits is known it seems that following up the distribution of these few traits could tell us more about the 'races' than a great abundance of measurements" (Ibid., p. 359).

The principal agencies of evolutionary change in man are primarily gene varia-

bility and gene mutation. Evolutionary changes are brought about through rearrangements in the combinations of genes (in consequence of the operation of many secondary factors, physical and social) and change in the character of the genes themselves. In order to appreciate the meaning of the variety presented by mankind today it is indispensably necessary to understand the manner in which these agencies work. Thus, in man, it is practically certain that some forms of hair, and skin color, are due to mutation, while still other forms are due to various combinations of these mutant forms with one another, as also with non-mutant forms.

In view of these facts it has become obvious that if anthropologists are ever to understand how the differing groups of mankind came to possess such characters as distinguish the more geographically isolated of them, and those of the less isolated more recently mixed, and therefore less distinguishable groups, they will never succeed in doing so if they continue to make omelettes of the very ingredients, the genes, which it should be our purpose to isolate and map. What must be studied are the frequencies with which such genes occur in different groups or populations. The gene frequency method for the study of the distribution of human genes is a very simple one and has now been available for some time, as likewise has been the method for the study of genetic linkage in man. If, roughly speaking, one gene be assigned to every component of the human body, it should be fairly clear that as regards the structure of man we are dealing with many thousands of genes. If we consider the newer concepts which recognize that the adult individual represents the end point in the interaction between all these genes, the complexities become even greater. The morphological characters which anthropologists have relied upon for their "racial" classifications have been very few indeed, involving a minute fraction of the great number of genes which it would actually be necessary to consider in attempting to

---

* Mutation defines the condition in which a particular gene undergoes a permanent change of some sort, and whose action expresses itself in the appearance of a new form of an old character.

make any real—that is to say, genetically analytic—classification of mankind.

The indictment against the older anthropological conception of "race" is (1) that it is artificial, (2) that it does not correspond with the facts, (3) that it leads to confusion and the perpetuation of error, and finally, that for all these reasons it is meaningless, or rather more accurately, such meaning as it possesses is false. Based as it is on unexamined facts and unjustifiable generalizations, it were better that the term, being so weighed down with false meaning, were dropped altogether than that any attempt should be made to give it a new meaning.

It is today universally agreed by all competent students of the subject that there exists but a single human species, and that this species consists of a group of populations which, more or less, replace each other geographically or ecologically and of which the neighboring ones intergrade or hybridize wherever they are in contact, or are potentially capable of doing so. It should be clear that the task of the student interested in the character of these populations must lie in the study of the frequency distribution of the genes which characterizes them—and not in the study of entities which are purely imaginary. As Dr. G. M. Morant, England's most distinguished anthropologist, said at the centenary meeting of the Royal Anthropological Institute in 1944: "It seems to me that the time has come when anthropologists must fully recognize fundamental changes in their treatment of the problem of racial classification. The idea that a race is a group of people separated from all others on account of the distinctive ancestry of its members, is implied whenever a racial label is used, but in fact we have no knowledge of the existence of such populations today or in any past time. Gradations between any regional groups distinguished, and an absence of clear-cut divisions, are the universal rule. Our methods have never been fully adapted to deal with this situation." ("The Future of Physical Anthropology," *Man*, XLIV 1944, p. 17).

Many of the younger generation of anthropologists are already taking active steps to exorcise the monster of "race" and deliver the thought and conduct of mankind from its evil influence.

III. THE CONCEPT OF ETHNIC GROUP

Since the term "race" has been responsible for so much confused thinking, and, what is worse, has rendered possible much confused and confusing action, it has been urged, with much reason, that the term "race" be altogether dropped from the vocabulary. Words have a tyrannous and awful power, and if we do no more than resign this term to the oblivion to which it properly belongs, this would in itself serve as a contribution towards clear thinking, for what is implied in the anthropological and popular conceptions of race represents an egregious and dangerous congeries of errors.

Huxley has suggested that "it would be highly desirable if we could banish the question-begging term 'race' from all discussions of human affairs and substitute the non-committal phrase 'ethnic group.' That would be a first step toward rational consideration of the problem at issue." This suggestion has met with wide support, and the term "race" promises to make way for the phrase "ethnic group."

An ethnic group may be defined as one of a number of populations, which together comprise the species *Homo sapiens*, and which individually maintain their differences, physical and cultural, by means of isolating mechanisms such as geographic and social barriers. These differences will vary as the power of the geographic and social barriers vary. Where these barriers are of low power, neighboring ethnic groups will intergrade or hybridize with one another. Where these barriers are of high power such ethnic groups will tend to remain distinct from each other or replace each other geographically.

From this definition of an ethnic group it will be seen that the problem of ethnic variation is really an ecological problem, and may ultimately to a considerable extent be resolved into the problem of the physical mobility of populations and the consequences resulting therefrom. Thus, the problem of ethnic variation falls very definitely within the purview of the student of the social life of man.

One of the important advantages of the term "ethnic group" is that it eliminates all question-begging emphases on physical factors or differences, and leaves that question completely open, while the emphasis is now shifted to the fact—though it is not restricted to it—that man is predominantly a cultural creature. The change in emphasis is a highly desirable one. It does not exclude the consideration of the possible significance of physical characters, but it leaves the question of the latter open for further dispassionate analysis, omitting any suggestion that the physical factors are determined, fixed or definable, or that they are in any way connected with mental or cultural factors. This is not simply to replace one term by another, but represents a definite shift in emphasis based upon a fundamental difference in point of view.

The frequency with which certain genes occur within a population, which serve more or less to distinguish one ethnic group from another for the most part represent the effects of the action of different isolating agents upon a common stock of genetic materials. Such agencies as natural and sexual selection result in different frequency distributions of genes among local groups and populations.

From the definition of an ethnic group already given it will be perceived that so-called "racial" differences simply represent more or less temporary expressions of variations in the relative frequencies of genes in different parts of the species population, and rejects altogether the all-or-none conception of "race" as a static immutable process of fixed differences. It denies the unwarranted assumption that there exist any hard and fast genetic boundaries between any groups of mankind and asserts their common genetic unity. Such a conception of "race" cuts across all national, linguistic, religious and cultural boundaries, and thus asserts their essential independence of genetic factors.

IV.   THE CLASSIFICATION OF MANKIND

From the standpoint of a classificatory view of mankind which has a due regard for the facts, it is possible to recognize four distinctive stocks or divisions of mankind. These are the Negroid or black, the Archaic White or Australoid, the Caucasoid or white, and the Mongoloid stocks or divisions of mankind.

It is preferable to speak of these four large groups of mankind as *divisions,* and to speak of the varieties of men which enter into the formation of these divisions as *ethnic groups.* The use of the term "division" emphasizes the fact that we are dealing with a major group of mankind sufficiently distinguishable in its physical characters from the three other major groups of mankind to be classified as such. Nothing more is implied in the term than that.

Within the four divisions of mankind there exist many local types, but most of these local types are very much mixed, so that it is only in a relatively small number of cases possible to distinguish unequivocally clear local types or ethnic groups among them. Every honest attempt to discuss such types or ethnic groups within the larger parent groups or divisions deserves the fullest encouragement. Truth will not be advanced by denying the existence of large groups of mankind characterized, more or less, by distinctive inherited physical traits. Such physical differences are found in geographical and genetic races of animals and plants in a state of nature, and in many races of domestic animals and cultivated plants. They are, to a certain extent, also found in the human species, but in a much more fluid condition, since the biological development and diversification of mankind has proceeded upon very different lines from that which has been characteristic of animals and plants. No animal or plant has had anything like an equal history of migration and hybridization, and that is the fundamentally important fact to be remembered when any comparisons are made between man and other living forms. Not one of the great divisions of man is unmixed, nor is any one of its ethnic groups unmixed; all are, indeed, much mixed and of exceedingly complex descent. Nor is there any scientific justification for over-zealous or emotional claims that any one of these is in any way superior to the other.

In biological usage a race is conceived to be a subdivision of a species which inherits the *physical* characteristics serving to distinguish it from other populations of the species. This, however, is not the sense in which the racists and many of the race classifiers employ the term. For them "race" represents a compound of physical, mental, personality, and cultural traits which determines the behavior of the individuals inheriting this alleged compound. We have already traced something of the history of the racist viewpoint and it has already been indicated that the evidence of science is unequivocally opposed to it.

There can be little doubt that in many parts of the world most children are early emotionally conditioned to a belief in the existence of "race" differences. In many parts of Europe, for example, where the larger number of troubles of state and person have traditionally been attributed to the Jews, such attributions can hardly have failed to escape the attention of most children. Indeed, they usually become aware very early that hostility towards Jews is a socially sanctioned, even required, form of behavior. Such children grow up to accept the existence of imputed "race" differences as real, and act upon such belief almost automatically. Prejudices early acquired are notoriously difficult to eradicate.

"Race" prejudice is socially sanctioned and socially learned. It is a ready-made and culturally accepted outlet for various forms of hostility and feelings of frustration.

Education in the facts of anthropology will not solve the "race" problem, but as societies are organized today, such education provides the best means of bringing about a more rational attitude than at present prevails towards that problem. It is not sufficiently realized that "racism" offers the greatest threat to democracy, and that from its very earliest beginnings this is exactly what it was calculated to do. Education in the practice of democracy and above all in the art of being a human being should, therefore, be our greatest safeguard and bulwark against the growth of this nefarious doctrine.

The anthropological status of the Jewish people provides a good illustration of the kind of difficulties with which the anthropologist is faced.

The Jews are almost always referred to in popular parlance as a "race" or ethnic group, and this common belief is shared by many Jews, as well as publicists of various sorts, politicians, philosophers and other professional men. This common belief is not, however, shared by the anthropologist.

What then has the anthropologist to say in answer to the question "Are the Jews a 'race' or any other kind of ethnic entity?" Do they possess distinguishable physical and behavioral traits? If they do, why do they? Are any of these traits inborn or acquired? These are the questions which shall be answered in what follows.

V. THE PHYSICAL HISTORY OF THE JEWS

The early history of the Jews is one of mixture with the neighboring peoples, the Canaanites, the Amorites, the Horites, Hittites, and others. Archaeology supports this statement, as does the Old Testament. Most of these groups were characterized by varying frequencies of one or more distinctive physical characters.

During the Diaspora the Jews have been dispersed to practically every part of the earth and have intermixed with numerous peoples. In the 6th century B.C.E., during the Babylonian captivity, there was some intermixture with many Mesopotamian peoples. During the Hellenistic period which began in the 4th century B.C.E., Jews followed Alexander the Great into the Hellenistic world—into Egypt, Syria, Asia Minor, and Macedonia, to mention a few of the more important regions into which they penetrated and settled. In the 2nd century B.C.E., at the time of the Maccabees, there commenced the movement of the Jews into the Roman world which carried them to the farthest corners of the Roman Empire, especially to Western Europe, and particularly to Spain, Italy, France, and to the Rhineland of Germany. During the 11th century, at the time of the First Crusade, the plunder and massacre of the Jews by the Christian knights started a Jewish migration eastward which was accelerated into a mass migration after the 13th century. The large majority of these Rhineland Jews settled in what is now Poland, Lithuania, and the Ukraine.

A list of the peoples with whom the Jews have at one time or another intermixed would include a very large proportion of the populations of the world. This does not mean that the Jews as a whole have undergone such mixture, but—and this is the important point—that different populations of Jews have undergone independent, and different kinds and degrees of intermixture, with differing populations. Now, the result of such differing biological experiences would be, even if the Jews had started off as a homogeneous group—which they did not—that a certain amount of diversification in physical characters would eventually be produced between different local groups of Jews. That this is actually what has occurred is proven both by historical facts and the analysis of anthropological characters. Some of the evidence will be found in the works of Fishberg, Kautsky, and in the Brutzkus article published in the present volume. The figures for shape of head, eye and hair color, stature, and so on, tend to follow the population trends for these characters as a whole, depending, as a rule, upon the length of time during which the Jews have lived among these populations.

The anthropological findings indicate that the Jews are very mixed and very variable both in their ancestry and in their physical characters. From the standpoint of anthropology there is no such thing as a Jewish type, and there is not, nor was there ever, anything even remotely resembling a Jewish "race."

There undoubtedly exists a certain quality of looking Jewish, but this quality is not due to any inherited characters of the persons in question, but rather to certain culturally acquired habits of expression, facial, vocal, muscular, and mental. Such habits do to a very impressive extent influence the appearance of the individual and determine the impression which he makes upon others.

It is extremely difficult to define the "quality of looking Jewish," even though it is doubtful whether anyone could be found who would deny that such a quality exists. This quality is exhibited not only in the facial expression, but in the whole expression of the body, in its movement, and in its gesticulations. No attempt will be made here to define this quality, because it defies definition, but that it exists in many Jews, and that it is culturally determined there can be little doubt. This quality gradually disappears in persons whose recent ancestors have abandoned Jewish culture for several generations and who have themselves been raised in a non-Jewish culture.

What makes certain persons or communities of persons visible or distinguishable as Jews is neither their physical appearance, nor the fact of their adherence to the religion of Judaism, but certain cultural traits which they have acquired in a Jewish cultural environment.

We see then, that it is membership in Jewish culture which makes a person a Jew, and nothing else, not even his adherence to Judaism.

Just as there is such a thing as an English, German, French, Italian, and even American cast of face, so there is such a thing as a Jewish cast of face. This cast of face is often taken to be biologically determined, but the fact is that it is culturally determined.

Add to the culturally determined cast of face traditionally determined gesticulations of the face and body, character of speech, together with certain likewise culturally determined preferences for color-combinations in clothes, style and total ensemble of clothes, and we have a powerful association of traits which readily enables one to distinguish certain persons as Jews from non-Jews.

All the traits which Jews exhibit as Jews are culturally determined and in not the slightest degree biologically determined. Efron has shown that Jews lost their traditional gestures in America with the degree of their Americanization.

The facts then, lead to the following conclusions:

Owing to the original mixed ancestry of the Jews and their subsequent history of intermixture with many of the peoples among whom they have lived and continue to live, the Jews of different regions are neither genetically nor physically equivalent. Where they have lived for long periods of time the Jews frequently closely resemble the general population in their physical characters, but many Jews may differ from that population in behavioral characters because they have been primarily educated in a Jewish cultural environment rather than in that of the general population.

A Jewish physical type has neither been preserved nor transmitted down to the present day because such a type never existed, and if such a type had existed it would long ago have been dissolved as a result of the subsequent intermixture of Jews with other peoples. What the Jews have preserved and transmitted have been neither physical nor mental "racial" traits, but religious and cultural traditions and modes of conduct.

BIBLIOGRAPHY

M. F. Ashley Montagu, *Man's Most Dangerous Myth: The Fallacy of Race.* Columbia University Press, 2nd edition, New York, 1945.

M. F. Ashley Montagu, *An Introduction to Physical Anthropology,* Charles C. Thomas, Springfield, Ill., 1945.

R. Benedict, *Race, Science and Politics.* Viking Press, New York, 1943.

F. Boas, *Race, Language and Culture.* Macmillan, New York, 1940.

Th. Dobzhansky, *Genetics and the Origin of Species.* Columbia University Press, 2nd edition, New York, 1941.

M. Fishberg, *The Jews,* Scribner's, New York, 1911.

J. Huxley and A. C. Haddon, *We Europeans.* Harper, New York, 1936.

K. Kautsky, *Are the Jews a Race?* International Publishers, New York, 1926.

O. Klineberg, *Race Differences,* Harper, New York, 1935.

THE ANTHROPOLOGY OF THE JEWISH PEOPLE

J. D. Brutzkus

In the early days of scientific research, the terms people, race and language were often used indiscriminately. Since Hebrew, the language of the Israelites from whom the present Jews are descended, belonged to the linguistic group designated by philologists as the Semitic languages, it was assumed that the Jews belonged to the Semitic race, while the other European peoples, again because of their linguistic characteristics, were regarded as members of the Indo-European or Aryan race.

In the course of later scientific evolution, other and more precise designations were found for the various races. But independent of terminology, the question was posed as to whether all Jews descended from a single original Jewish race whose prototype should be sought in ancient Palestine, or whether the Jews were a mixture of several different races. If the latter were the case, there arose the questions—from which races are the modern Jews descended, and where,

when and how did this race-mixing take place, in Palestine or in the Diaspora, in ancient or in modern times?

These questions were the subject of heated scientific discussions, especially at the end of the 19th and the beginning of the 20th century. Besides its purely scientific character, the controversy had a political and national aspect. In the specific racial origin of the Jews the partisans of the newly introduced "scientific" anti-Semitism sought evidence of ethnic, mental and moral inferiority in the Jewish people. On the other hand, the protagonists of Jewish emancipation and assimilation contested the idea of a "Jewish race" and spent a good deal of energy in trying to prove that the Jews differed anthropologically very little, if at all, from the surrounding populations.

In 1895 and later the Jewish anthropologist S. Weissenberg enumerated the following hypotheses about the origin of the Jews:

1. The Jews are pure Semites; in which case North African Jews are direct descendants of the original stock, while European Jews are the result of a mixture with members of the "Alpine race" from Italy, Gaul and Southern Germany.

2. The Jews were never, in fact, pure Semites, having already lost their Semitic character in Palestine through intermarriage with the native non-Semitic populations (Hittites, Philistines, etc.). If so, European Jews have preserved unchanged the characteristics of ancient Israel, while North African Jews are the result of a mixture with the long-headed Mediterranean race.

3. Both types, the European as well as the North African Jews, developed in the

Diaspora through subsequent mixtures. Neither is thus a pure racial type, and both differ from the old Israelitic prototype.

To these problems, stated by Weissenberg, the scientists have provided different answers. The concept of the purity of the Jewish race in Palestine was maintained by Graetz, Jacobs, Nott, Judt and others, who rejected the idea that alien ingredients were a substantial factor of Jewish racial inheritance. Some of them believed that the crystallization of the Jewish prototype dated back to the epoch of the patriarch Abraham; others assigned it to the epoch of the Babylonian exile; Jacobs suggested the epoch of the destruction of the Second Temple. The anthropologists Vogt (1863) and Broca (1865) divided the Jewish people into two separate branches: the Sephardim, descendants of the pure Semitic prototype, and the Ashkenazic Jews who had become intermixed with Celts, Germans and Slavs. Other scientists differentiated also between the Spanish-Sephardic Jews and the Berber and Yemenite Jews, thus proposing three different branches. Many scientists and some scholars—among them Renan, Ripley, and Krzywicki—discerned a whole series of mixed types, according to the character of the peoples among whom the Jews lived.

The anthropologist Ikoff (1884) was the first to assert, on the basis of skull measurements, that modern Jewry included both "Semitic" dolichocephals (especially among the Jews of the Mediterranean countries) and non-Semitic brachycephals (particularly among the Jews of Russia and Poland). In 1892, on the basis of his own investigations, the anthropologist and ethnographer von Luschan established the mixed character of the Jewish race. In his opinion the predominating elements among the Israelites in Palestine were not the purely Semitic (Oriental), but the "Hittite" or "Western Asiatic," as they are now termed (Luschan himself coined the term "Armenoid;" the type in question has been preserved chiefly by the Armenians). The variety of hypotheses was due chiefly to the low level of scientific research. The number of books dealing with the subject was very large, but the array of morphological and biological investigations was quite insignificant and embraced in general small groups of individuals.

The meager and insufficiently scientific preparation of the material with which the anthropologists have to operate in dealing with the Jewish racial problem, was pointed out by F. Kahn as early as 1922. It is true that some younger scientists, for example, Czortkower, maintain that in the last few years science has recorded great achievements in this field, and that we now possess enough exact scientific material to answer all questions posed by the Jewish racial problem. Nevertheless there is reason to doubt strongly that the general state of the science of anthropology and particularly of

HITTITE TYPES. From Hittite monuments

Jewish anthropology, presents sufficient data to enable us to arrive at safe conclusions.

With reference to anthropological research among modern peoples, who from the racial viewpoint represent a mixture of different ingredients, it must be further

SEMITE WAR-PRISONERS
From Egyptian bas-reliefs

borne in mind that by virtue of the laws of heredity established by Mendel the hybrid type becomes partly dissolved in subsequent generations into the component primitive types which had served to produce it. Thus it can happen that a mongrel type, in whose case the characteristic features of the original types have become practically obliterated, can evolve those characteristic traits in a very marked form in a later generation. A number of scientists, including Professor Czekanowski of Lwow, tried to formulate a mathematical law which would permit the determination of the frequency of such phenomena. Whether these laws can be directly applied to human races and types, and not only to animals and plants, is a question which has not yet been scientifically answered. But the fact cannot be denied that among Jews we find, in a particularly telling form, heads which appear strikingly similar to antique Assyrian bas-reliefs (the purely Semitic-Oriental type), as well as Egyptian-Semitic profiles resembling copies of Egyptian mural paintings, and pronounced Hittite or Armenoid types, and types of other races (Negroid, Slav, Nordic).

While confirming the mixed character of the Jewish people this phenomenon, on the other hand, must make difficult the numerical analysis of its various component parts, since the quantity of each type varies from generation to generation. Above all, however, there remains unsolved the paramount problem in the whole racial controversy, namely, the question as to whether physical (anatomical and physiological) racial characteristics really determine the mental and moral individuality of a given people. Does dolichocephaly or brachycephaly, do light or dark eyes, straight or curly hair, a hooked or a flat nose, determine the spiritual and mental qualities of an ethnic group, the trend and moral value of its social disposition, etc?

It goes without saying that no serious scholar will assert anything of the sort; nor are anthropology and racial research at all qualified to pose or solve such problems. This belongs to the sphere of the social sciences, but even these are not, at the present stage of research, able to provide an adequate answer. So far as an answer can be given, it is in the negative (See later).

TYPES OF ISRAELITE WAR-PRISONERS
From Assyrian monument

I. ANATOMICAL CHARACTERISTICS OF THE JEWISH POPULATIONS

At first the peoples of the earth were classified into five races, according to the color of their skin: the White or Caucasian race, the Yellow or Mongolians, the Black or

Negro race, the "Red" (Indian) and the Brown (Malayan). Not all scientists recognize the last two as independent racial types. The color of the skin is also connected with certain other anthropological characteristics, such as head-form, hair-color and hair-texture, eye-color, nose-form, etc. All these characteristics often—but not always—accompany a particular skin-color. Thus among members of the white Caucasian race we find the most varied cranial forms, different colors of the eyes and hair, different statures. The white race is, therefore, subdivided into a number of subsidiary lines, such as the Nordic, Alpine, Dinaric (East European and Western Asiatic), Mediterranean, Oriental (Semitic), Slav (Eastern), Baltic, Phalic races. Though each nation speaks one language, it comprises several different physical types or ethnic groups. Among the Germans we find six physical or ethnic types: the Nordic, Dinaric, Alpine, Atlanto-Mediterranean, Neo-Danubian and East-Baltic. Among the French we find three principal physical types: the Alpine, Mediterranean and Nordic. Among the Italians, we find the Mediterranean, Alpine and Dinaric types. The majority of the European peoples are mix-

TYPES OF JUDAEAN WAR-PRISONERS
From Assyrian monument

tures of different white ethnic groups. Many scientists also regard the Jews as made up of similarly mixed ethnic groups, but others with somewhat slim scientific evidence, insist on considering them a "pure race" because of their comparative isolation for 2,000 years. For a clearer light on this matter, let us turn to the results of the anthropological investigations and measurements undertaken among the Jewish populations in various countries.

1. CRANIAL FORM

Until very recently cranial form was regarded as one of the most stable hereditary

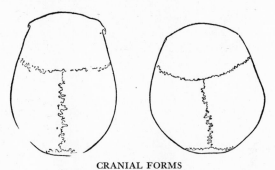

CRANIAL FORMS
The left cranium has an index of 72.9; right, 88.3

ethnic characteristics. Anthropology divides the various ethnic types into long-headed, medium-headed, and short-headed, according to the so-called cephalic index (percentage ratio of breadth to length). If the index is under 75.0, the type is called long-headed (dolichocephalic); if it is from 75.0 to 80.0, medium-headed (mesocephalic); if it is over 80.0, broad-headed (brachycephalic). By taking the cranial measurements of a great number of people belonging to a particular ethnic group, the average cranial index of that group may be obtained, although it may vary considerably among its individual members.

Among the Jewish population of the world only very few long-headed types have been found, as will be seen from the table on p. 17, except in Yemen and the Sahara where we may assume the admixture of Arabs and Berbers; indeed, from history we know that a Jewish kingdom of Arab proselytes existed in Yemen in the 6th century and a Jewish-Berberic state in the Sahara in the 7th. The majority of the Jewish populations, both Sephardic and Ashkenazic, belong to the broad-headed (brachycephalic) type, while there is only an insignificant difference between German, Italian or

WESTERN SEMITE WAR-PRISONERS IN ANCIENT EGYPT
From the Haremheb bas-relief, 14th century B.C.E.

CRANIAL INDEX OF JEWS OF VARIOUS COUNTRIES

Country (Origin)	Cranial Index	Number Measured	Anthropologist	Remarks
Sahara, Africa	72.9	10	Higet	
Yemen	74.3	92	Weissenberg	In Palestine
Tunisia	77.56	332	Fishberg	School Children
Palestine (Sephardim)	78.1	130	Weissenberg	
Palestine (Samaritans)	78.1	35	Huxley	
Constantine, Algeria	79.2	170	Fishberg	
England	80.0	263	Jacobs	
Algiers	80.1	104	Fishberg	
Bosnia (Sephardim)	80.1	55	Glueck	
Syria	80.9	40	Weissenberg	
Western Russia	81.05	275	Fishberg	
Romania	81.82	150	Fishberg	Immigrants in the U.S.A.
Poland	81.9	200	Elkind	
Polish Immigrants in U.S.A.	81.91	315	Fishberg	
Turin, Italy	82.14	112	Lombroso	
Ukraine	82.2	438	Talko-Hryncewicz	
Southern Russia	82.5	100	Weissenberg	
Southern Russia	83.45	219	Fishberg	Immigrants in the U.S.A.
Lithuania	83.11	100	Bleichman	
Galicia	83.33	305	Fishberg	Immigrants in the U.S.A.
Galicia	83.6	413	Meier—Kupernicki	
Baden, Germany	83.5	86	Amman	
United States of America	83.0	764	Boas	
Georgia, Caucasus	85.9	33	Weissenberg	
Daghestan, Caucasus	86.35	160	Kurdov	

EYE-COLOR AND HAIR-COLOR

(The percentage referring to the female sex is indicated in brackets)

Country and Anthropologist	EYES		HAIR			Dark Type	Fair Type	Mixed Type
	Dark	Light	Dark	Fair	Red			
Poland— Elkind	55.0 (56.8)	45.0 (43.2)	96.8 (86.4)	0.5 (8.0)	2.6 (5.6)	57.9 (58.5)	0.5 (8.5)	41.5 (33.0)
Galicia—Meier and Kupernicki	53.8 (60.0)	46.1 (40.0)	74.0 (76.0)	21.5 (20.0)	4.3 (4.0)	44.0 (51.0)	13.0 (16.0)	43.0 (33.0)
Ukraine—Talko-Hryncewicz	56.7 (61.8)	43.3 (38.1)	76.4 (83.1)	19.3 (14.0)	4.3 (2.9)	51.3 (68.6)	16.2 (6.9)	31.0 (24.3)
Southern Russia— Weissenberg	64.8 (75.6)	35.2 (24.4)	81.7 (82.0)	14.8 (14.6)	2.4 (3.4)	59.1 (69.3)	11.5 (4.9)	28.9 (24.4)
Lithuania— Talko-Hryncewicz	65.2	34.8	68.1	29.9	2.0	50.7	13.0	36.2
Romania—Fishberg	48.7	51.3	82.3	14.7	2.8	47.0	11.0	42.0
Hungary—Fishberg	50.7	49.3	77.1	17.9	5.0	46.0 (62.0)	12.0 (5.0)	42.0 (33.0)
Baden—Amman	48.8	51.2	84.9	12.8	2.3	——	——	——
England—Jacobs	61.3 (66.8)	38.7 (33.2)	77.6 (88.1)	20.4 (11.9)	2.0 (0.0)	——	——	——
Italy—Levy	67.6	32.3	88.2	11.8	——	60.2	14.7	25.0
Bosnia—Glueck	69.1	30.9	80.0	18.2	1.8	——	——	——
North Africa—Fishberg	83.1	16.9	92.2	5.2	2.6	76.4	4.6	19.0
Daghestan—Kurdov	93.0	7.0	97.0	0.5	2.5	97.0	——	3.0
Georgia, Caucasus— Weissenberg	89.0	11.0	93.0	5.0	2.0	82.0	3.0	15.0
Turkestan—Ushanin	85.0	15.0	98.0	2.0	——	85.0	2.0	13.0
Samaritans— Szpidboim	88.9 (88.9)	11.1 (11.1)	96.3 (92.6)	3.7 (0.0)	0.0 (7.4)	——	——	——
Karaites—Weissenberg	74.0	26.0	94.0	2.0	4.0	70.0	6.0	24.0
Yemen—Weissenberg	100.0	——	100.0	——	——	100.0	——	——

SCULPTURE PORTRAIT OF A SEMITE WOMAN
Approximately 1300 B.C.E. (*Louvre Museum, Paris*)

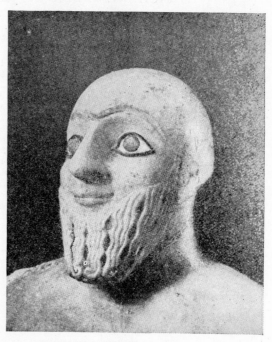

SCULPTURE PORTRAIT OF A SEMITE
Approximately 1300 B.C.E. (*Louvre Museum, Paris*)

TYPES OF JUDAEAN WAR-PRISONERS
From Assyrian monument

EASTERN SEMITIC TYPE
Assyrian king. From Assyrian bas-relief

ing urban populations in Europe, hardly ever leads to the establishment of a difference in their relative stature. The notion that Jews are of small stature is due to comparisons made between the Jews and the rural populations. Given good nutrition and care, Jewish children grow very quickly. Statistical investigations in Tel-Aviv prove that the Jewish school children in that city are not inferior in stature and weight to the children of Sweden, who are regarded as the tallest in Europe. The same process of improvement was registered in Lithuania before the Second World War. Comparing the stature of immigrants and native Jews in North America, the anthropologist Fishberg obtained the following figures:

STATURE OF JEWS
(In percentage)

Stature (in Centimeters)	Immigrant Jews in U.S.A.	Jews Born in New York	Jews in Eastern Europe*
Very short (Under 160 cm.)	24.57	8.77	35.46
Medium short (160 to 165 cm.)	30.63	24.19	32.48
Medium tall (165 to 170 cm.)	26.99	33.07	21.41
Very tall (Over 170)	17.81	33.87	10.65
	100.0	100.0	100.0

*The figures in these columns are based on investigations carried out in various countries.

The above table shows how quickly the stature of the Jews changes under the better conditions of American life. We find also a great diversity of stature among the Sephardic Jews in many countries. The Jews of Morocco are of small stature; on the other hand, the Jews of Salonika are very tall. The evidence suggests that the Jews have inherited from their ancestors a biological disposition to a tall stature, and that it was only poverty and distress that led to a diminution of their height in various countries. The average stature of females among the Jews, as among most peoples, is considerably smaller than that of the males.

4. FACIAL FORM

Some anthropologists believe that the narrow face is a characteristic of the Jewish type. Innumerable caricaturists have exploited this feature. Professor Luschan attributes it to the fact that the Western Asiatic type of the ancient Hittites, charac-

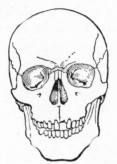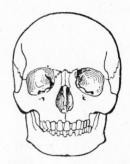

SKULL TYPES

terized by a narrow face and long nose, is very largely represented among the Jews. This "Hittite" type, however, is much rarer among the Jews of Eastern Europe. Some figures relating to the average width of the face may be cited for comparison.

	Centimeters
Yemenite Jews	12.7
Ukrainian Jews	13.4
Jews of Baghdad	13.4
Caucasian Jews	14.0

5. FORM OF THE NOSE

The "Jewish nose" has always been considered a prominent characteristic of the "Jewish" racial type. The anthropologist Fishberg examined the nose-form of 4,120 Jews, with the following results:

Form of the Nose	Men (percent)	Women (percent)
Straight nose (Greek form)	57.26	59.42
Short snubbed nose	22.07	13.86
Hooked nose	14.25	12.70
Broad flat nose	6.42	14.02

The hooked long nose among the Jews is much rarer than among the Armenians, Italians or Bavarians. But the general descriptions contained in Fishberg's table do not convey a sufficiently precise idea of the variety of nose types. Not every curved nose is regarded as a Jewish nose. It depends on the point where the curve begins, as well as on the form of the wings, and whether the tip of the nose is thin or fleshy. An entire literature has sprung up, particularly through the efforts of the new anti-Semitic racial researchers, about the characteristics of the "Jewish nose." The truth is, how-

JEWISH NOSE TYPES
From Fishberg

ever, that what is meant by the Jewish nose is the Western Asiatic, Hittite nose. We have already noted that not only the Jews, but a number of other Asiatic, Caucasian and even European peoples have a good deal of Western Asiatic ancestry and show a substantial number of "Hittite" noses. This nose-form, however, continues to be described as the "Jewish nose," because it is rarely found among the Nordic and Slav nations among whom the majority of the Jewish people have lived.

6. OTHER MORPHOLOGICAL CHARACTERISTICS

In the past there was a trend to see among the Jews some other anatomical characteristics, such as narrow-breastedness, shortness of the extremities in relation to the body, etc. All these characteristics, however, are generally present among town-dwellers who do not perform much hard physical work, undergo no physical strain, do not indulge in sports and lead a sedentary life. This specific mode of living, of course, is particularly characteristic of the Jews, who have been town-dwellers for untold generations, whereas the immediate forebears of other urban people lived mostly in the rural regions, devoting themselves to agriculture and other outdoor work.

II. PHYSIOLOGICAL CHARACTERISTICS OF THE JEWISH POPULATIONS

Besides the anatomical (morphological) differences among the ethnic individual groups there are also physiological differences, *i.e.* differences due to the functioning of the internal organs of the human body. The Negroes, for example, have more sweat-glands and exude much more perspiration than the white or yellow races. (The secretion of sweat is a regulative function designed to cool the body in a hot environment and is, naturally, of great importance in the climatic zones where the Negroes live.) In recent years a certain difference has also been discovered in different ethnic groups, namely, as regards the distribution of the ratio of the so-called "blood groups" (See later).

1. THE FOETOR JUDAICUS

The idea has been prevalent since the Middle Ages that the Jews have a peculiar smell or "bad odor" (Foetor Judaicus). It is a well known fact that some peoples find the smell of other peoples unpleasant, and even repulsive. White people visiting China maintain that the Chinese have a sickening odor. The Japanese, on the other hand, assert that the Europeans, especially European women, have a bad odor. Many African Negro tribes believe that the Whites "stink."

The specific odor of different peoples, and even of particular classes of the same people, may be due to various causes rooted in the peculiarities of cultural or hygienic conditions and of their general mode of life. Food (*e.g.* abundant consumption of garlic, onions, or various sharp spices; the eating of sea food, especially of tainted fish, habitual among certain northern peoples, etc.), lack of cleanliness, filthy and badly aired slum dwellings, hard manual labor causing excessive perspiration, clothing of a particular character (*e.g.* fur garments used by certain peoples), the rubbing of certain oils and fats into the skin and scalp, and a series of other social and cultural conditions may engender a specific, characteristic odor among certain populations, mostly among the poor and hardworking classes.

This, however, has nothing to do with physiological or biological peculiarities which could be described as characteristic of certain peoples or ethnic groups. The German anthropologist Guenther believes that different peoples may, indeed, have a different chemical composition of the sebaceous acids and etheric oils secreted by the sweat-glands and sebaceous glands of the human body, and he thinks that it may be possible to ascertain the chemical formula of the specific racial odors by means of careful chemical analyses. However, for the present it is nothing but a superficial assumption.

2. MORBIDITY

As regards morbidity as a characteristic racial feature, the problem is to find out whether belonging to this or that race leads to greater incidence of various sorts of diseases under similar climatic, sanitary and social conditions. Has the fact been recorded that particular diseases are entirely absent among certain peoples, while, conversely, other peoples are subject to specific maladies with which the former are never afflicted? Such phenomena do exist, but they always refer to peoples living in entirely different climatic zones, in different parts of the world. In tropical colonial areas such differences are often observed between the white settlers and the natives. However, until now it has been impossible to establish similar differences between the Jews and the surrounding populations among which they live.

It is true that the statistics of morbidity and mortality in many European towns show certain differences between Jews and Gentiles.

To what extent such differences (e.g. lower mortality from tuberculosis and typhus among Jews, and their greater susceptibility to afflictions of the circulatory system, etc.) are the results of racial peculiarities or, respectively, due to differences of occupation, hygiene, social and cultural conditions, is a problem which scientific research has not solved so far. The same is true of mental diseases.

3. BLOOD GROUPS AMONG THE JEWS

Many anthropologists now attribute much greater importance to the frequency of the different blood groups among races and peoples than to other physiological phenomena. Landsteiner was the first to discover (in 1900) the variations in blood types. He classified human blood into four main groups, designated as groups O, A, B, and AB, and showed that the blood characteristics of the individual remain constant throughout his lifetime and are inherited according to the well-known heredity laws of Mendel.

During World War I the biologists L. and H. Hirszfeld, serving as army physicians in the Balkans, were able to test blood samples of soldiers and civilians of various peoples and they found that the distribution of the four main groups varied and was to a certain extent conditioned by geographical location. They were able to establish and to illustrate graphically the curious phenomenon, that in the blood of the European races there is a relatively high percentage of group A, while group B predominates in the blood of the Eastern, i.e. Asiatic populations. Generally speaking, the farther we move from the European shores of the Atlantic eastward to the Asiatic shores of the Pacific, the more the frequency of group A decreases, while at the same time the frequency of group B increases in the respective populations. Thus the frequency of the main blood groups in a given people can yield a clue as to its geographical origin.

In order to simplify the analysis of the blood group distribution the Hirszfelds introduced a "biochemical index" ($I = \frac{A + AB}{B + AB}$) for typing the blood characteristics of every race on the earth. For the European populations this index (I) was established as 2.5 or more; for the Asiatic races as 1.0 or less, and for all intermediary peoples from 1.8 down to 1.3.

Since the epoch-making work of the Hirszfelds countless studies have been made all over the world and the distribution of the blood groups among practically every people of the earth has been examined.

The study of the frequency of the blood groups (not only of the four main groups but of the various sub-groups as well) has made a valuable contribution to our knowledge of the human races in Europe and North Asia. To begin with, the investigation of the blood groups established the interesting fact that in a given ethnic unit the proportion of blood groups remains constant from generation to generation, if there is no intermarriage with other populations. The studies of Verzar and Weszeczky on Gypsies and the German colonists in Hungary supply a striking illustration of this phenomenon. The Gypsies came to Hungary from India many centuries ago and lived as a segregated tribe, only infrequently intermarrying with the local population. The same is true of the German colonists in the Hungarian region of Transylvania who immigrated from Germany at the beginning of the 13th century and have lived there as an exclusive group, ethnically and culturally separated from the surrounding population. The result, from the point of view of blood distribution, is shown in the following table:

various countries. This is shown in the tables on page 24, which include data on the Gentile neighbors of the Jews (marked by an asterisk).

Two important facts can be deduced from these tables. First, they show that in almost every country there is a difference in blood group distribution between Jews and Gentiles. This can be seen in Holland as well as in Macedonia, in Poland and in Turkestan, in Russia and in Palestine. This is a clear indication and a confirmation, if such a confirmation were needed, of the well-known historical fact that the Jews constituted and always remained in every land a distinct ethnic group segregated from their non-Jewish neighbors not only in religious life but generally speaking also in respect to intermarriage.

The second conclusion to be drawn from the analysis of these tables is that there are very large differences between the Jewish communities of different countries. In many cases these differences between Jews and Jews are far greater than between Jews and Gentiles. The proof of this can be found, for example, by comparing the blood group distribution of Russian Jews with that of the Daghestan Jews or the Crimean Jews on the one hand, and on the other with that of the Russian or Polish Slavs.

People	Number of Tests	Percent in Groups			
		O	A	B	AB
Gypsies in Hungary	385	34.2	21.1	38.4	8.5
Hindus	1000	31.3	19.0	41.2	8.5
Hungarians	1500	31.0	38.0	18.8	12.2
Germans in Hungary	476	40.8	43.5	12.6	3.1
Germans (Heidelberg)	500	40.0	43.0	12.0	5.0

It is obvious that the difference between the émigrés and the domestic stock, even after centuries of geographic separation, remains relatively very small.

In the light of these general observations we shall now examine the blood group distribution among the Jewish population of

If we use the original Hirszfeld index not as a yardstick of racial characteristics, but only as a simplified method for defining the predominance of the "Eastern" (B group) type of blood in a given population we can establish the following table of the Jewish communities in the Eastern hemisphere:

BLOOD TYPE OF THE JEWS OF VARIOUS COUNTRIES

(According to the Hirszfeld Index)

Place	Index	Group B
Germany	2.70	11.9
Holland	2.50	13.4
Poland	1.94	17.4
Romania	1.94	17.5
Russia	1.89	19.6
Georgia	1.83	19.01
Morocco	1.63	19.9
Syria	1.50	20.0
Daghestan	1.10	24.1
Crimea	1.04	32.6
Samarkand	0.97	30.5

In accordance with the original Hirszfeld classification of races the above table would indicate that the Western European Jews belong to the European race (index above 2.5), the Jews of the Caucasian Mountains, the Crimea and Turkestan to the Asiatic race (index around 1 and less), and all the other Jewish groups to the "intermediary race" (from 1.8 down to 1.3).

The farther we proceed from Holland and Germany to the East and the Southeast, to Eastern Europe, Asia and the Caucasus, the more does the blood type of the Jewish population become "Eastern," *i.e.* showing a higher percentage of B and a smaller percentage of A. This phenomenon can be explained only by assuming that during the centuries of their wandering there was some admixture of alien Eastern blood in the Jewish bloodstream despite their rigorous segregation from the other peoples.

This is the same general West-East trend which was established for the whole of the European peoples by many anthropologists, from the Hirszfelds to Candela and Haldane. It is extremely interesting that the explanation of this phenomenon proposed by Candela and Haldane, namely, that the gene B was introduced into Europe from Asia through the Mongolian invasions and the ensuing crossing with the Europeans, applies, with some modifications, to the European Jews as well.

In the Caucasus and the Crimea the Jews (and this is also true of the Karaites) have apparently absorbed a substantial admixture of Turco-Mongolian ethnic elements through intermarriage with the Khazars. This people, as we know from history, for about a thousand years, from the 2nd to the 12th century, inhabited the steppes region between the Caspian, Azov and Black Seas and constituted a large empire. In the first half of the 8th century the upper classes of the Khazars adopted the Jewish religion. Thus the Jewish immigrants from other countries who found refuge in this Judaeo-Khazarian empire could practice intermarriage with the Khazars without any religious restriction. The result of the Khazar influence may be seen not only in the blood characteristics of the Jewish mountaineers and the Crimean Jews and Karaites, but also probably in the blood type of the Eastern European Jews in general, which differs from the blood type of the Western European Jews. Since the Russian, Ukrainian and Polish Jews never intermarried with the Slavs, at least not in substantial numbers, a good deal of blood group B which flows in the veins of the Eastern Jews must have originated with the Turco-Mongolian Khazar-Jews, who lived in the region of Kiev from times immemorial, and who also influenced the Jewish cranial form in the direction of the brachycephalic type.

III. JEWISH PHYSIOGNOMY JEWISH GESTURES

Apart from anatomical and physiological peculiarities, some anthropologists claim to have found pronounced racial characteristics in the facial expressions, the carriage and the gestures of the Jews. They maintain that a Jewish face is easily distinguishable, and that one can recognize the gait of a Jew or his gestures. This is partly true in Northern Europe, where the dark-haired, dark-eyed, fidgety, nervous, gesticulating Jews contrast with the surrounding blond, sedate, calm, placid populations. But this is not valid at all in the southern countries, *e.g.* in France (especially in the south of

France), Italy, Spain, Greece, etc. It is further believed that the Jews are distinguished by greater mobility of their facial muscles and, consequently, a more pronounced facial expressiveness. However, if such characteristics exist, they are the result of special historical conditions, certain cultural traits, and some degree of mental unrest and nervousness, and these are to be found in varying forms, as writers have shown, among certain strata of every people. An agitated gait and violent gesticulation ("speaking with their hands") are often regarded as characteristic of the Jews. These features, however, are not due to anatomical peculiarities of the muscles, but are the result of a restless mentality, i.e. of the sum total of economic, legal, social and psychological conditions in which the Jewish masses have had to live in various countries. Among those classes of the Jewish people whose position is safe and stable, the facial muscles and extremities work quietly and normally; they have no "Jewish physi-

BLOOD GROUPS AMONG THE EUROPEAN JEWS

People	Number of Tests	Percent in Group			
		O	A	B	AB
Jews, Russian	3,333	32.2	41.7	19.6	6.5
Russians	*10,151	33.9	36.7	22.7	6.7
Ukrainians	*2,075	31.0	39.4	22.0	7.6
Lithuanians	*1,582	36.8	40.0	19.5	3.7
Jews, Polish	818	33.1	41.5	17.4	8.1
Poles	*11,488	32.5	37.6	20.9	9.0
Jews, Romanian	1,135	38.2	39.0	17.5	5.3
Romanians	*2,740	41.4	39.4	13.8	5.2
Jews, Berlin	230	42.1	41.1	11.9	4.9
Germans	*2,500	35.0	44.0	15.0	6.0
Jews, Amsterdam	705	42.6	39.4	13.4	4.5
Hollanders	*14,483	46.3	42.1	8.5	3.1

BLOOD GROUPS AMONG THE JEWS IN THE MEDITERRANEAN COUNTRIES

Country or Town	Number of Tests	Percent in Group			
		O	A	B	AB
Macedonia (Monastir), Jews	500	38.8	33.0	23.2	5.0
Greeks	*4,398	40.0	41.6	13.7	4.7
Tunis, Jews	200	41.0	31.0	15.0	12.5
Syria (Aleppo), Jews	173	38.0	34.0	20.0	8.0
Aleppo (Arabs)	*933	35.7	37.0	20.8	6.5
Persia, Jews	116	19.9	46.5	25.0	8.6
Yemenites	1,000	56.0	26.1	16.1	1.8
Palestine (Arabs)	*347	32.5	39.7	20.4	7.4
Morocco, Jews	642	36.9	35.9	19.9	7.3

BLOOD GROUPS AMONG THE JEWS IN THE CAUCASUS, CRIMEA AND TURKESTAN

Country or Town	Number of Tests	Percent in Group			
		O	A	B	AB
Jewish Mountaineers (in Daghestan)	87	40.2	26.6	24.1	9.1
Georgia, Jews	1,236	26.29	43.93	19.01	10.76
Georgia, Christians	*2,177	46.6	37.11	10.93	4.82
Samarkand (Bokhara), Jews	616	32.3	29.2	30.5	7.9
Uzbek, Turkestan	*1,159	29.4	33.9	27.0	10.6
Kirgiz	*914	36.76	23.96	31.4	7.87
Crimea, Jews	500	20.8	34.4	32.6	12.2
Crimea, Tatars	*1,631	20.7	43.3	25.3	10.7

TYPES OF JEWS

1. Lithuanian; 2. Russian; 3. Ukrainian; 4. Polish; 5. Polish Jewess; 6. Mummy-portrait of a Jewess (2nd century) 7. German; 8. German Jewess.

TYPES OF JEWS

1. White Jew from Cochin, British India; 2. Yemenite; 3. Samaritan; 4. Caucasian (Daghestan);
5. Moroccan; 6. Moroccan Jewess; 7. Bokharian girl; 8. Iranian; 9. Iranian Jewess.

ognomy" and no "Jewish gait." Nor does one notice among them that specific melancholy or frightened look which many anthropologists and writers regard as "typically Jewish," but which can be found also among many other oppressed peoples, and not only among the Jews.

IV. MENTAL PROPERTIES

Books without number have been written about the mental qualities of the Jewish people and its culture. That literature consists mostly of nebulous, tendencious and anti-Semitic theories without any scientific foundation. In England objective measurement tests were made with a view of gauging the intellectual ability of the Jewish children; the result led some research workers to the conclusion that Jewish children are inferior to Gentile children. Others established that the children of Jews were more gifted than Gentile children. Nor are any conclusive indications supplied by the statistics of mental afflictions among the Jews. The mental state of a people depends chiefly on its historical evolution, its environment, and the social conditions in which it lives—and these are not hereditary factors. The fact, for example, that 20 percent of the Nobel prize-winners in Germany were Jews, although the latter constituted no more than one percent even among the urban population, belongs to the sphere of sociology, but not to that of anthropology. The psychology of the Jewish populations is strongly influenced by their economic or social status and their occupations, but the peculiarities thus acquired are neither durable nor hereditary, and cannot, therefore, be regarded as anthropological racial characteristics. The vast publicistic literature about "race and culture" has very little to do with science in general and with anthropology in particular.

V. BASIC TYPES OF THE JEWISH PEOPLE

On the strength of manifest morphological (anatomical) and physiological charac-

teristics we come to the conclusion that the Jewish populations of the various countries are derived from a common Palestinian stock. Modern Jews have inherited and preserved many features of the ancient inhabitants of their old homeland, but during their wanderings for over 2,000 years the Jews intermarried with various other peoples. As we know from history, the Jews spread their religion among neighboring peoples, such as the Philistines, Idumeans and Syrians. Later they made many proselytes in Mesopotamia, Greece and Rome. Part of them were subsequently converted to Christianity, but the others have clung to their Judaism. In addition, intermarriages were frequent until the 6th and 7th centuries, as can be seen from the resolutions adopted by various councils of the Christian Church. Besides, the Jews often converted their alien slaves to Judaism and admitted them into the Jewish communities. (The fact of racial mixture is often very conspicuous, for example, among the Jews in India. Similar evidence can be seen in Abyssinia, Daghestan and Bokhara).

Notwithstanding the many alien elements which the Jews absorbed, we find two basic types, the Semitic-Oriental and the Western Asiatic, everywhere among them in considerable numbers.

The Oriental type may be characterized as follows: mesocephalic head, straight or somewhat curved nose, strongly developed cheek bones, round cheeks, rather thick lips, large almond-shaped eyes, curved eyebrows. This type is very frequent: 34 per cent among the Polish Jews, and up to 35 per cent among the Yemenites.

The second type, the Western Asiatic (Armenoid, Hittite), shows a greater resemblance to the peoples of Western Asia —Armenians, Kurds and cognate peoples in Europe, such as the Croats, Bavarians, Albanians, etc. This type is characterized by a round skull, sloping hindhead, a large hooked nose, a small mouth and a longish narrow face. Although these characteristic features are present among the Jews in a less pronounced form than among the above-mentioned Armenoid or **Dinarian** peoples, they are nevertheless often exploited by the anti-Semites and caricaturists. In the last 2,000 years, in different countries and in different degrees, these two basic types received an admixture of Mediterranean, Alpine, Eastern, Mongolian and Nordic elements. In this way the hybrid types came into existence. Since every biological characteristic is inherited independently of other characteristics, we find among the Jews only rarely the pure types of a particular race. All efforts to ascertain the percentage of the various racial components of the Jewish people are, therefore, unreliable.

Attempts to draw an anthropological distinction between the Sephardic and the Ashkenazic Jews have likewise failed. The so-called Sephardim have no common origin, being a mixture of Spanish, Berber, Balkan or Syrian Jews, etc., who became only partly intermixed after the expulsion from Spain. Nor are the so-called Ashkenazic Jews all of the same stock, although almost all of them have the same language.

Since, however, the physical evolution of the Jewish populations is influenced not only by anthropological factors, but also by a number of other factors, environmental, economic, social, etc., it is possible to establish in different areas, historically, geographically and economically separated from each other, a different composition of the physical ethnic elements among the respective Jewish populations. From this point of view, we may divide the Jews (geographically), into the following four large groups:

1. *The Jews of the Mediterranean Countries.* These Jewries, Sephardic and Arab, have mostly preserved their Oriental and Western Asiatic (Armenoid) character, except for the admixture of native Berbers in North Africa and of pure Arabs in Yemen.

2. *The Jews of Western Europe.* These have preserved their oriental character to a lesser extent, since they have absorbed many proselytes in the first centuries of their habitation in Western Europe. This fact is responsible for the high blood index and the great number of blond (up to 15 percent) in this group.

3. *The Judaeo-Khazar Groups in the Crimea, Caucasus and Central Asia,* who are descended from a mixture of Jews with Turco-Mongolian Khazar tribes. They have inherited a very broad skull and a high percentage of blood group B.

4. *The Eastern European Jews of Poland, Lithuania, Russia and Romania,* who came mostly from Western Europe, but however, have absorbed, besides the admixture of Western Europe ethnic elements, also a considerable number of Khazar Jews. Therefore, according to their cranial index, hair-color, eyes and blood structure, they occupy a position intermediate between the German and Khazar Jews.

BIBLIOGRAPHY

F. BOAS, *Changes in Bodily Form of Descendants of Immigrants,* New York, 1912.

F. BOAS, *Race, Language and Culture,* Macmillan, New York, 1940.

J. BRUTZKUS, *Les groupes sanguins parmi les populations juives.* Races et Racisme, No. 3. Paris 1937.

J. CZORTKOWER, *Di farsheidene rassen-elementen bai yidden* (Sociale medicin, 1937, Nos. 3, 4, 5, 6, 9, 10, Yiddish).

M. FISHBERG, *The Jews.* Scribner's, New York, 1911.

F. VON LUSCHAN, *Voelker, Rassen, Sprachen.* Berlin, 1922.

A. RUPPIN, *Soziologie der Juden.* Berlin, 1930.

R. N. SALAMAN, *Racial Origins of Jewish Types* (Transactions of the Jewish Historical Society). London, 1922.

J. TALKO-HRYNCEWICZ, *Charakterystyka fizyczna ludnosci Zydowskiej Litwy i Rusi* (Zbior wiadomosci do Antropologii Krajowej, T. XVI). Cracow, 1892.

S. WEISSENBERG, *Die suedrussischen Juden* (Archiv fuer Anthropologie XXIII, 1895).

S. WEISSENBERG, *Die syrischen Juden* (Zeitschrift fuer Ethnologie, B. 43, 1911).

S. WEISSENBERG, *Zur Anthropologie der deutschen Juden* (Zeitschrift fuer Ethnologie, B. 44, 1912).

S. WEISSENBERG, *Die Juden in Mesopotamien* (Archiv fuer Anthropologie, B. X.).

ALEXANDER S. WIENER, *Blood Groups and Transfusion.* 1943.

I. ZOLLSCHAN, *Das Rassenproblem.* Vienna, 1925.

ISRAEL IN THE FRAMEWORK OF THE ANCIENT NEAR EAST

William Foxwell Albright

Though the beginnings of Near-Eastern archaeology go back over a hundred years, it is only within the past fifteen years that it has become possible to combine all the scattered finds into a plastic whole. For a half century and more after the initial decipherment of hieroglyphics and cuneiform it remained impossible to find any data illustrating the links which must have connected the cultures and the political lives of Egypt and Babylonia. Up to about 1890 practically all competent biblical scholars, including Julius Wellhausen himself, were convinced that Palestine was still a land of primitive savages in early Hebrew times, and that no community of civilization existed between it and neighboring lands. The discovery of the Amarna Tablets in 1887 and the first authentic information about its contents in 1888 struck these scholarly isolationists such a stunning blow that certain anachronistic survivors have not recovered from it yet. The beginning of scientific excavations in Palestine, in 1890, was followed by a long series of similar undertakings in ancient Palestinian sites, in the course of which many thousands of imported objects from Egypt, the Aegean, Syria, and Mesopotamia were discovered. Yet so few biblical philologians were able to grasp the significance of such finds, and the chronological picture was so obscure, that isolationism still remained dominant, despite the steady accumulation of data opposed to it.

In 1929 the ancient Canaanite city of Ugarit was discovered by Schaeffer at the site of Ras Shamrah on the coast of northern Syria, and rich finds of tablets and artistic objects of Canaanite origin were almost immediately made. Two years later the new script in which most of the tablets were inscribed, was deciphered, and the language of nearly all documents proved to be closely related to biblical Hebrew. Since then every year has witnessed many striking new parallels and points of comparison between Hebrew and Canaanite literature. It is not too much to say that the recovery of the long-lost Canaanite literature marks an entirely new epoch in biblical studies, which has already rescued them from the doldrums and made them intensely vital and productive. Not only has it become certain that Hebrew literature was throughout profoundly influenced by the literature of Israel's Hebrew-speaking neighbors, but hundreds of obscure lines in Hebrew poetry have been clarified and our picture of the development of the Bible as a whole has become more plastic. Moreover, the culture of Ugarit is found to have been exceedingly mixed, reflecting elements of the cultures of all surrounding peoples. It is thus an extremely good illustration of the situation throughout Syria and Palestine, whose cultures, both material and mental, have always been highly composite.

Scarcely had scholars recovered from the impact of Ras Shamrah when new, hardly less sensational, finds were made at Mari on the Middle Euphrates. In 1935-1936, two years after Parrot began to dig at this site, he discovered more than twenty thousand tablets from a period several centuries before the Amarna Age; moreover, these tablets were written in Semitic Accadian by a people whose native tongue was that of the Hebrew Patriarchs. Most surprising of all, these documents from the Age of the Patriarchs demonstrated extraordinary international activity in trade and social intercourse. Palestine now turned out to have been one end of an ethnic and cultural continuum which extended as far as the mountains of southern Armenia, the Zagros mountains of Iran and the Persian Gulf. Most important of all single gains were synchronisms between ancient princes of different lands which made it possible to reduce Mesopotamian chronology drastically and to establish a new system which agrees perfectly with all the relevant facts from different parts of the Near East. Egyptian chronology was astronomically fixed as long ago as 1900, though it took several decades to convince various "die-hards" of this fact; so far as I know there is not a single competent Egyptologist who still rejects the clear evidence that the Twelfth Dynasty began about 2000 B.C.E. The publication of the great Assyrian list of kings by Poebel in 1942-43 combines with the Mari evidence to make Mesopotamian chronology almost as precise as Egyptian in the early centuries of the second millenium. Not all scholars have accepted the astronomical pegging of Babylonian dates by means of early records of the movements of Venus, but the narrowness of the chronological scope within which the historian must move, is vividly illustrated by the fact that we have at least one continuous synchronism: Nefer-hetep of Egypt was contemporary with Entin of Byblus (Gebal), who was contemporary with Zimri-Lim of Mari, the contemporary of Hammurabi of Babylon!

These outstanding discoveries have only been made possible by the continuous work of scores of industrious scholars, who have labored in the analysis of languages and in the interpretation of documents, in the exhuming and recording of millions of individual artifacts, as well as in their comparative study. Without all this intellectual labor, the significance of Amarna, Ugarit and Mari, to say nothing of scores of minor sites, would have been unrecognized and the two last sites might have remained undiscovered for centuries. No new scripts nor tongues can be read until philologists have laboriously gathered the materials out of which the decipherer constructs his edifice. The interpretation of every text rests upon the arduous grammatical, lexical, and comparative work of previous scholars. The dating of every object of art or piece of pottery is made possible only by the patient inductive research of precursors. There is no master key to the solution of the myriad problems which confront the student of the ancient Near East; systematic collection of everything significant from the forgotten past, precise recording and comparing, methodical deduction, balanced critical interpretation—these are the instruments which must be employed.

I.   THE PATRIARCHAL AGE
(C. 2000—1500 B.C.E.)

The extraordinary finds at Mari on the Euphrates (see page 27) have demonstrated that this period was intensely cosmopolitan. The people of Mari had constant intercourse with their neighbors for hundreds of miles on all sides; letters reached the court of Mari from Elam in the far southeast and Cappadocia in the far northwest. Objects of Egyptian manufacture were abundant in contemporary Ugarit on the Syrian coast (see page 27). Pottery made in Crete was exported to Egypt and Syria; Assyrian textiles flooded Asia Minor; Egyptian scarabs and figurines turn up constantly in Syria and the Aegean. A few years ago an untouched royal burial deposit was discovered at Tod in Upper Egypt. When it was opened, quantities of precious metal and jewelry appeared, among the objects being a number of Babylonian cylinder seals of superior workmanship. Had these objects been found a decade or two ago, historians would have been at a loss because of the apparent chronological discrepancy; the recent reduction and stabilization of dates (to which we referred above) remove all difficulty, since the deposit was made in the late 20th century while the seals were cut in the preceding century, just as we should have expected *a priori*.

The most striking historical phenomenon of this period of five centuries is the Amorite expansion. Beginning, as far as we can tell, in the 21st century B.C.E., the nomadic and semi-nomadic Semites of the region west of the Euphrates began to move into adjacent settled lands and to settle down in turn. This movement reached one crisis in the course of the 20th century, when it flooded Transjordan and put an end to sedentary life there; for more than six centuries, as Nelson Glueck's explorations have demonstrated, most of Eastern Palestine was occupied only by semi-nomads. About 1960 B.C.E. related tribes swarmed into Babylonia, and during the next two hundred years practically every new dynasty of local princes in all parts of Mesopotamia was of West-Semitic origin, as shown by the known names of its members. These nomadic intruders were called *Amurru*, "Westerner (s)," by the Accadians of Mesopotamia, who were by this time rather sharply differentiated from them both in speech and in social organization. The invaders had little culture of their own; they adopted Sumero-Accadian civilization for themselves and transmitted it to their kindred in Syria and Palestine.

What was the Sumero-Accadian civilization of Mesopotamia, which was given a fresh lease of historical life by the Amorites? From the earliest centuries of recorded history we now know that there were two principal ethnic groups in the valleys of the Euphrates and Tigris: the non-Semitic folk called by the Semites "Sumerians" and the East-Semitic people who called themselves "Accadians." "Sumerian" is derived from the native non-Semitic name of southern Babylonia, whereas "Accadian" is derived from the capital of the first known Semitic empire, Akkadu in northern Babylonia (biblical אַכַּד). The Sumerians probably settled down in the great river valleys at the time of the early painted-pottery cultures which have been brought to light by archaeologists during the past twenty years; when we meet them in their own inscriptions and literary works more than a thousand years later, we already find that their language (unlike any other known tongue, living or dead) had broken down phonetically and was broken up into sharply distinct dialects. It was the Sumerians who invented the pictographic script from which cuneiform developed, and who developed most of later Babylonian religion, magic and mythology. Probably not less than one-fifth of the Accadian vocabulary was of Sumerian origin. Sumerian remained the language of religion and learning through the second millennium and far down into the first. It is extremely interesting to note that the most active period of the study of Sumerian literature was precisely during the Amorite occupation of Babylonia, between 1900 and 1600 B.C.E. Our knowledge of this early Sumerian literature has been greatly enlarged during the past few years, thanks to the industry and ability of Dr. Samuel N. Kramer of Philadelphia, working on the tablets from Nippur excavated by the University of Pennsylvania between 1889 and 1900. It is now certain that the Hebrew stories of Creation, the Flood, the Antediluvian Patriarchs, Paradise, etc., either were derived from Sumerian originals, handed down through Accadian and Amorite intermediation, or were profoundly influenced by the Sumerian versions of them. In addition to such obvious influences there were many less obtrusive borrowings and adaptations from Sumerian sources to be found in Hebrew literature. Among them we may mention the literary formulation of the cosmogonic narratives of Genesis; the formulation of the oldest juristic documents of Israel, including the Book of the Covenant; the didactic form in which much of Proverbs is couched. The extent to which Sumerian material culture influenced the Canaanites and Hebrews is illustrated by many cultural loan-words in the Bible, as well as in Ugaritic literature: typical examples are היכל , "temple," from Sum. *egal*, literally "great house"; מורג , "threshing sled," from Sum. *mar-ragh,* etc.

As we have pointed out in our introductory remarks, the Amorite phase reached its climax in the time of the Mari archive, when Amorite princes ruled over all Mesopotamia, Syria and Palestine. The most important states of the 18th century B.C.E., such as Babylon, Ashnunnak, Assyria, Mari, Harran, Aleppo, Qatna and Damascus, were all under kings bearing Northwest-Semitic names. Nomenclature was the same in Palestine (as shown by the Execration Texts, of which more below), Syria and Mesopotamia, as far as the Zagros Mountains. Even when we find exceptions they are only apparent: thus, for example, we find several good Accadian names borne by kings of the Dynasty of Hammurabi whose ancestors and descendants bore Amorite names; two kings of Larsa in Babylonia have Accadian names while their father and grandfather had Elamite names, though heads of a tribe whose very name is characteristically Amorite. I mention these facts merely to illustrate the amount of mixture of peoples and cultures which was going on in the Age of the Patriarchs. It is a great pity that we lack the Amorite documents necessary to enable us to reconstruct their tongue in detail. However, the thousands of tablets written by scribes of Mari whose native language was Northwest-Semitic, show a great many Amorite words and grammatical forms as well as idioms, which the imperfect knowledge of Accadian possessed by the scribe was not able to conceal. After several thousand of these priceless documents have been published (assuming that they are not destroyed by enemy action) we shall have many thousands of Amorite proper names, and scores, perhaps hundreds of native words, besides many grammatical constructions and expressions, which will enable us to gain an excellent idea of the language spoken by the Patriarchs. Among the Amorite proper names are such good biblical names as Abram, Jacob, Benjamin, Zebulun. Among the most flourishing towns of the age are the cities of Harran and Nahor, both mentioned in Genesis. The patriarchal flavor of the tablets from Mari is, in fact, so great that the excavator, M. Parrot, wrote me once in great excitement: "Nous n'avons pas encore trouvé la mention d'Abraham, mais presque . . ." (We have not yet found any mention of Abraham, but almost . . .)

All of this is naturally very striking when we compare the clear-cut Israelite tradition about the Patriarchs: they were semi-nomadic Western Semites, related to the nomadic peoples west of the Euphrates and to the Aramaeans of the Harran region, east of the Great River; their original home was in Mesopotamia, where they founded flourishing settlements in the region of Harran and Nahor, other towns in which also bear the same names as relatives of Abraham, such as Serug and Terah; the cosmogonic stories told by the Hebrews, now imbedded in the early chapters of Genesis, go back to Sumero-Accadian sources (in part to clear North-Mesopotamian origins) and diverge very sharply indeed from later Canaanite cosmogony (see below). It follows that no serious scholar can treat the early Hebrew historical tradition with anything but respect. This respect is enhanced when we study the Patriarchal narratives in the light of such recently published material as the Nuzu archives, from a North-Mesopotamian town of the 15th century B.C.E. These tablets reflect the customary law and social practice of a Hurrian (Horite) colony which probably illustrates life in other parts of this region not long after the Patriarchs had migrated westward. As Speiser, Gordon, and other scholars have shown, there are a number of striking parallels between the social and legal practices of the Nuzians and those of the narratives of Genesis—parallels which are all the more striking because they were no longer true in the

SPECIMEN OF A TABLET FOUND AT NUZI
15th century B.C.E.

time when Mosaic law was codified, and because in at least two instances our present narrative shows clear ignorance of the motive behind the episodes in question: the unmotivated reference to Abraham's heir, Eliezer, in Gen. 15:2, and the equally unmotivated allusion to the theft of Laban's gods in Gen. 31: 19, 30. Now we know that all childless folk were expected to adopt an heir, and that possession of one's father's gods was *prima facie* evidence of right to inherit.

We have mentioned the Horite colony of Nuzu (or Nuzi) north of Babylonia; this introduces us to the fascinating story of the Horites. Until recently the biblical Horites were just as obscure as the Hittites had been fifty years earlier. Until the discovery and publication of the Hittite archives from Boghazköy in Asia Minor, no one had any idea of the true character or importance of the Hurrian people. It is only, in fact, during the past decade that the Hurrian problem has been clarified, thanks to discoveries at Mari and Ugarit. We now have an elaborate study of Hurrian grammar, made by Speiser on the basis of tablets discovered in Babylonia and Assyria, in Egypt, Syria and Asia Minor—an unusual instance of the elaborate puzzle patterns which must sometimes be put together from widely scattered fragments. Speiser's monograph appeared in 1941 and was followed within two years by an elaborate thesaurus of Horite personal names, edited by Gelb of Chicago.

The Horites (note that חרי comes from older *Hurriyu* just as אמרי is derived from older *Amurriyu*) spoke a language not related to Semitic, Indo-European or Sumerian; it was at home in the mountains of Armenia and northwestern Iran, where the people of Urartu (אררט) spoke a related tongue a thousand years later. Their prevailing physical type was hyper-Alpine; that is, they were extremely short-headed, with exceptionally prominent curved noses, closely resembling types now common among Armenians and Kurds inhabiting the same mountainous region. They made their appearance on the stage of written history about the 24th century B.C.E., in the time of the Semitic Empire of Accad. At that time, however, they were still restricted to the northern and northeastern mountains, and no Hurrian names occur on the business documents from northern Mesopotamia. Horite names became more frequent on Babylonian documents of the 21st-18th centuries B.C.E., and there is good reason to believe that the Amorites settled in Mesopotamia not long after a period of Hurrian migration and settlement. However this may be, it is now certain, thanks

UPPER PART OF THE STELE WHICH BEARS THE CODE OF HAMMURABI
About 1690 B.C.E.

to the finds at Mari, that the Hurrian princes of the 18th century were again restricted to the mountainous regions around the edge of the plains of Mesopotamia and northern Syria.

Before the death of Hammurabi, king of Babylon, about 1686 B.C.E., there was a great irruption of barbarians into the northern part of his empire; in 1692 and 1690 B.C.E. the great Amorite king claims to have vanquished the northern hordes, but in the last two years of his reign he had to build tremendous fortifications along the northern boundary of Babylonia proper to keep the northern hordes from inundating his own land. For two centuries silence settled over northern Mesopotamia; there is not a single Assyrian document from the period 1715-1515 B.C.E. which is known to us, though a mass of documentary Assyrian material before and after these dates has been discovered. At the end of this period we find Horites settled over all northern Mesopotamia, around the tiny state of Assyria to the east and down to the Middle Euphrates on the west. In Syria we find them settled as far south as Lebanon, with scattered enclaves in Palestine.

From the 16th-13th centuries B.C.E. we have decisive evidence for a most curious symbiosis between the Hurrians and the Indo-Aryans. Not long after the publication of the Amarna letters written in Hurrian and Accadian by a king of Mitanni in the early fourteenth century, it was pointed out that the royal Mitannian names looked Sanskrit or Old Iranian. Many similar names then turned up among contemporary names of chieftains in Palestine and southern Syria. In 1907 Winckler discovered a group of names of absolutely certain Indo-Aryan gods—Indra, Mithra, Varuna and the Nasatyas—named together among the deities of Mitanni. Still more recently was discovered a Hittite tablet, translated from Hurrian, which described the training of horses for chariot-racing, and wrote out the names of the odd digits in a dialect almost identical with Sanskrit. To avert possible

error, each name of a cardinal number was accompanied in the same context by the correct ideogram of the number. Since then more words and particularly many more personal names of obvious Indo-Aryan character have been found, proving beyond the slightest doubt that there was a large Indo-Aryan element in the mixed migration that swept over Mesopotamia and Syria in the 17th century B.C.E. But the most curious fact, illustrated by finds in many different places, is that the Hurrians were generally ruled, not by men bearing Horite names, but by persons with Indo-Aryan names. This was true in Palestine as well as in Mesopotamia and Syria; in Accho and Achshaph, Taanach and Shechem, as well as probably in Hebron, we find in the 15th and 14th centuries princes or nobles with good Indo-Aryan names; at Taanach we can demonstrate from cuneiform records that the population was partly of Hurrian origin. At Shechem and Gibeon, where the Hebrew Bible locates Hivites, the Greek Bible more correctly places Horites; evidently *resh* was corrupted to *waw* after the 3rd century B.C.E., when the Greek translation was made. In Hebron Israelite tradition calls this element "Hittite," probably because from about 1375 B.C.E. onward Syria became part of the Hittite Empire and so all the non-Semitic elements with Syrian ties which had settled in Palestine became known as "Hittite." This fact explains why the prophet Ezekiel says that Jerusalem sprang from Hittite and Amorite stock. It must also be remembered that these names did not necessarily imply ethnic affiliation in the racial or linguistic sense; the name "Hittite" was originally applied to a non-Semitic, non-Indo-European group, which occupied the town of Khatti in northern Asia Minor. At a very early period, certainly before the 16th century, an Indo-European tongue known as Nesian or Nasian (generally called "Cuneiform Hittite" today) replaced the strange Khatti language as the medium in which their documents were written. After the fall of the Hittite Empire in the early 12th century B.C.E. the term "Hittite" became restricted to the southeast of Asia Minor and northern Syria, to which both language and culture were again shifted.

It was this survival of the Hittites into the Iron Age (after C. 1200 B.C.E.) which preserved the memory of them among the Hebrews, almost completely displacing the culturally far more important Horites. Our knowledge of the Hittites goes back to the documents of the Assyrian colonists in Asia Minor, settled among the non-Semitic na-

purview in the late 16th century B.C.E., suffering an almost complete eclipse for more than a century. Hittite civilization was indebted to the Horites for many of its higher elements, and Hittite scribes wrote Accadian rather than Hittite much of the time, filling even their Nasian documents with so many Sumero-Accadian ideograms and words that decipherment of their language was an easy job for the Czech Assyriologist Hrozny. The Hittite (Nasian) tongue has proved to be one of a number of related Indo-European languages, most

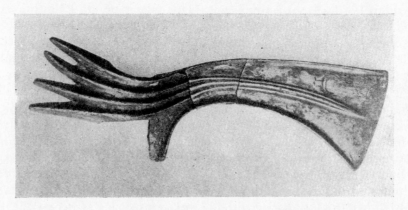

Courtesy of the University Museum, Philadelphia

HITTITE BRONZE AXE-HEAD FOUND AT BETH SHAN
Beginning of 14th century B.C.E.

tives of Cappadocia in the 19th century B.C.E. Thousands of these tablets have been recovered, and they have been admirably interpreted by Julius Lewy (now in Cincinnati), who has demonstrated their significance for biblical study, especially in the Patriarchal Age. At that time the Hittites were only one of numerous small groups, each occupying the region around its capital (see page 33). About 1600 B.C.E., a king of Khatti named Labarnas was able to conquer all eastern and central Anatolia (Asia Minor); his son extended his gains, and his grandson Mursilis I, about the middle of the 16th century B.C.E., captured and destroyed Aleppo and even Babylon. It appears from our source-material that most of these conquests were soon lost, and the Old Hittite Empire vanishes from our

closely akin (according to the latest research) to modern Armenian and more remotely to Greek, Latin and Slavonic.

During the Patriarchal Age Egypt was the wealthiest and, in general, the most cultivated land of the Near East. From about 2030 B.C.E., when the Theban prince Mentuhotpe II (so with Winlock, 1943) conquered northern Egypt and reunited the country, to about 1730 B.C.E., the Nile Valley remained continuously under Theban domination. The pharaohs erected a mighty empire, which extended in the 19th century from south of the Second Cataract of the Nile in Nubia to northern Phoenicia, a distance of over a thousand miles (almost half again as far by boat). Until within the past few years it was generally not believed by historians that the kings of the Twelfth

Dynasty (about 1992-1789 B.C.E.) had controlled Palestine and southern Syria. In 1940 a French Jewish scholar, G. Posener, published a series of Egyptian magical texts, execrating a long list of Canaanite princes, in order to prevent them from rebelling against the Egyptian crown or to assure their death if they ventured to revolt. M. Posener's inscriptions date from about 1825 B.C.E., nearly a century after a body of similar documents published fourteen years previously by Sethe. They prove that Palestine had become much more intensively settled during the lapse of a century: towns replace tribes and tribes are broken up into sections; moreover, the proportion of place-names which can be identified has been multiplied several times. This situation is entirely in accord with the evidence from study of archaeological remains in Palestine, where excavations and surface explorations (especially the investigations in Transjordan carried out by Nelson Glueck) have shown that sedentary occupation reached the nadir of its downward course in the period about 1900 B.C.E., and that settlement in Western Palestine increased rapidly during the 18th and 17th centuries, while in Transjordan sedentary occupation ceased almost entirely for many centuries.

Until recently there was little material to illustrate the closeness of relations between Egypt and Syria-Palestine, which has now been proved by the discovery of the execration texts. The most important document was the Story of Sinuhe, an Egyptian prince who fled to Syria for political reasons after the death of Amenemmes I (about 1960 B.C.E.). In spite of the fact that our oldest manuscript of this popular narrative dates from the following century, it has commonly been considered as pure romance. The Mari finds, combined with a critical analysis of the text of the story on the basis of numerous variants, have demonstrated that personal names and other details are correct for the period and region, so the Sinuhe Story now takes its place beside the Wen-Amun Report (see page 43) as a reliable narrative; it thus becomes an invaluable description of conditions prevailing in Syria during the early part of the Patriarchal Age. Another priceless long-known source was the pictorial account of the arrival of a group of Semites from Palestine at a town in Middle Egypt about 1890 B.C.E. The group included thirty-seven persons, men, women, and children; it was a party of traveling smiths, tradesmen and musicians, as illustrated by the statement that they brought with them presents of stibium and by the fact that they carried portable bellows and musical instruments with them. The light this sheds on Gen. 4: 20-22 is evident; it also helps to explain the frequent visits of the Patriarchs to Egypt.

During the past quarter-century much more light on relations between Egypt and Syria in this period has been cast by excavations at Byblus, Ugarit and Qatna. Byblus (Gebal) was not only the most important Egyptian port on the Asiatic coast; it was also a link through which poured influences in both directions. The principal goddess of Byblus, called Baalath ("The Lady"), was identified with the Egyptian Hathor, whose cult was profoundly influenced by that of her Canaanite counterpart. When a native Byblian dynasty arose toward the end of the 19th century, its princes entitled themselves vassals of Pharaoh; they imported Egyptian articles of use and luxury and even wrote their names regularly in hieroglyphics. The last of these native princes whose name is known to us was a certain Entin, who seems to have become quite powerful; immediately after his reign (about 1725 B.C.E.) a still unknown Syrian prince or confederation of chieftains invaded Egypt itself and turned it into a Canaanite or Amorite state. This solution of the long obscure Hyksos problem has been imposed by the finds at Mari and elsewhere, thanks to which the hitherto enigmatic names of several Hyksos princes have proved to be good Northwest-Semitic names of the period. It may well be that there were Horite and Indo-Aryan elements among them, but the plain fact is that not a single Hyksos name has been demonstrated to be anything but "Amorite." One prince bore the name "Jacob" (in full, *Ya'qob-Har*); an important official was named "Hur." In short, the Hyksos movement so well represents the background necessary to understand the migration of the Hebrews into Egypt under Joseph that a close connection has become obvious and is accepted by nearly every scholar, however details may be interpreted.

II. THE AGE OF MOSES
(C. 1500—1200 B.C.E.)

The age into which we now come, (the Late Bronze of archaeologists), has been styled "the First Internationalism" by the late James Henry Breasted. This appellation was essentially correct, though it should be modified to "the Final Phase of the First Internationalism." During it much closer diplomatic relations were set up between the courts of Egypt, Mitanni, Khatti and Babylonia than were ever before known in comparable cases. On the other hand, the Amorite phase of Sumero-Accadian culture, in which a single dialect was employed for oral communication throughout most of Western Asia, had died out with the assimilation of the Amorites settled in Mesopotamia and elsewhere beyond Palestine, southern Syria and the desert. To what extent Accadian cuneiform had become the medium of written culture and inter-communication before the 15th century we do not know; we may surmise that the Syrian Semites who established the Hyksos Empire with its capital at Tanis (Zoan) in the northeastern Delta brought the cuneiform script along with them from the north, where it was regularly employed during the 18th century. At all events, Egyptian scribes now studied Accadian cuneiform in school and used Sumero-Accadian vocabularies and dictionaries, phonetically spelled Accadian epics and myths, and other helps as textbooks. That these scribes were themselves native Egyptians is

certain, because their Accadian swarms with Egyptian phonetic and idiomatic peculiarities, which no person but an Egyptian would use.

This age was thus one of extraordinary learned activity, in which scribes had to learn different languages and when experts in the arts and professions might wander far and wide. At Ugarit on the north-Syrian coast, for example, four languages are represented in the excavated tablets, of which two were actually spoken locally, while the two others were learned in school. At Boghazköy, ancient Khatti in northern Asia Minor, eight languages were employed in tablets from the period 1400-1200 B.C.E. There was great activity on the part of translators, who rendered Assyro-Babylonian texts in Horite, Hittite, Egyptian and probably in Canaanite, who put Canaanite texts into Egyptian and presumably Egyptian into Canaanite. Expert Egyptian physicians and architects were in demand in Syria and Asia Minor; learned Babylonian diviners and magicians were sought for everywhere. There was not only a definite tendency to codify international custom into a kind of *corpus juris,* as we know from comparison of numerous treaties which have been discovered, but also a more surprising movement toward common jurisprudence. Of course, each of the countries of Western Asia had its own customary law, which was fast being put into formal codification, but the Sumerian code of Babylonia enjoyed such prestige among jurists that it became a standard norm to which all other legal codes were formally assimilated. This Sumerian law is known partly from later copies of Sumerian originals, and partly from its latest standard codification, which we happily possess intact in the Code of Hammurabi (now dated about 1690 B.C.E.). All other bodies of Asiatic jurisprudence which date in substantially their present form from our period—Babylonian, Assyrian, Hittite and Canaanite (in its Hebrew form of the Book of the Covenant)—have carefully copied the original Sumerian formulation and, despite

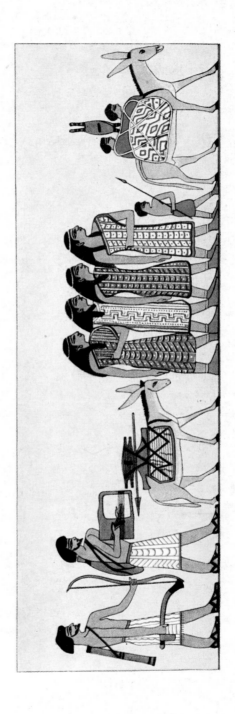

A PARTY OF SEMITES FROM PALESTINE ON A VISIT TO EGYPT

From a wall painting in a tomb at Beni-Hasan, approximately 1890 B.C.E.

many differences in detail, all show surprising general resemblance in conceptions of ethics and legal practice.

When we turn to the religious sphere in its narrow sense, there are parallel phenomena of the greatest possible interest to students of Hebrew history. We shall limit ourselves to two general phases: the systematization, classification and canonization of religious literatures; the unifying and syncretizing movements in theology. By 1500 B.C.E. the major categories of religious literature had been reduced to canonical form in both Egypt and Babylonia; thenceforth the chief activity of priestly scholars was to copy and interpret documents whose basic content was fixed. In Egypt, as is well known, the principal body of religious literature was composed of the Book of the Dead and related compilations from earlier sources, some of which are preserved in the much earlier Pyramid Texts and the Coffin Texts of the Twelfth Dynasty. Our earliest manuscripts of the Book of the Dead belong to the 15th century B.C.E., and from that time onward for over a millennium and a half the basic text remained substantially unchanged except for scribal errors and the expansion of commentators. A similar situation seems to prevail elsewhere in Egyptian religious literature, though our evidence is still spotty. In Babylonia, on the other hand, we have exceedingly clear-cut documentation which shows that nearly all the important epics, grammatical and lexical texts, magical series, etc., were given their canonical Accadian form during the period 1800-1500 B.C.E., *i.e.*, in the time of the First Dynasty of Babylon. Thereafter there were revisions of spelling and grammar, occasional modifications in detail, as well as the inescapable mistakes of scribes; but both form and content remained substantially without change. The other lands of Western Asia followed suit during the next four hundred years. The Hittite cuneiform tablets of the 14th and 13th centuries seem to indicate the same tendency several centuries later than in Egypt and Babylonia, though the destruction of the Hittite Empire at the beginning of the 12th century put at end, so far as we know, to scribal activity along the old lines. The recently recovered Ugaritic tablets in Canaanite cuneiform (see page 39) seem to indicate a very active period of reduction of Canaanite literature to writing with consequent canonization of form in the first quarter of the 14th century. Unfortunately, there is still no evidence indicating corresponding activity elsewhere in Canaan.

The theological movements to which we referred, are illustrated in numerous ways. Naive association and combination had in previous centuries given rise to elaborate pantheons of the gods in all foci of Near-Eastern civilization. In each country or region one god tended to be the recognized head of the pantheon, but all deities of cosmic function were recognized as controlling their respective domains on a cosmic basis. The deities of sun and moon, of storms and of reproduction, of heaven and the underworld, were at home in their respective domains throughout the visible universe. Babylonian, Canaanite, Hittite and Homeric religious epics and hymns agree absolutely in this. Hence there was constant identification of the storm-god of Egypt (Sutekh) with that of Hurrian and Hittite lands (Teshub) and of Semitic lands (Baal or Hadad, Accadian Adad). Similarly the Hittites believed that the goddess of reproduction, whose holiest shrine they located in the distant city of Nineveh, later capital of Assyria, was at home in innumerable sanctuaries of Asia Minor, Syria and Mesopotamia. Many examples of this strong syncretistic tendency of the Age of Moses can be given. At the same time there were local tendencies in Babylonia, Canaan and Egypt to identify deities of similar or related function until all important figures were combined into one. The only absolutely clear-cut illustration of the emergence of a monotheistic system from this demonstrable tendency is in the sudden appearance and extinction of the Aten heresy in Egypt, during the first half of the 14th century.

It should be scarcely necessary to point out how perfectly this picture provides the necessary background for the traditional activity of Moses. In evaluating the contrary views of the Wellhausen and related schools of biblical scholarship, we must remember that their positions were developed and systematized during the decades before the discovery of the Amarna Tablets (see page 27), when it was perfectly possible to hold to a theory of cultural isolation. Not until it became possible to paint a comprehensive, plastic picture of this background could the Wellhausen school be called "anachronistic." Certain Assyriologists, including especially Hugo Winckler, saw long ago how absurd its premises were; today, there are too few endowed with Winckler's breadth of knowledge and creative imagination to make the necessary deductions from our wealth of factual data. It is precisely in or about the early 13th century that we should expect the Mosaic system to have been set up, since all parallel phenomena outside of Israel before the 6th century B.C.E. belong to the period be-

EGYPTIAN WORSHIP OF THE CANAANITE GODDESS ASHERAH
On Egyptian stele of the age of the Exodus; about 1300 B.C.E.

tween the 16th and the 12th century B.C.E. This does not, of course, prove that the Pentateuch is Mosaic in its present form; in fact, external parallels would rather suggest that it was only the normative elements of Mosaism and a certain amount of detail which were then fixed, other matter of suitable nature being added and expanded from time to time until the canonical form of the Mosaic tradition was defined. How carefully later elements were excluded from the canonical form of this tradition needs no illustration for the scholar who knows the historical evolution of civilization in the ancient Near East.

By far the most important single chapter in the history of archaeological discovery bearing on the Age of Moses has been written by the excavator and translators of the Canaanite cuneiform tablets of Ugarit (see page 37). These tablets, put into writing about the beginning of the 14th century, have preserved for us the form of the most important Canaanite mythical epics as they were told in northern Phoenicia during the last century or two before the Israelite conquest of southern Canaan. The contents of the Baal Epic, of the epics of Keret and Danel, not to mention other significant texts, square so completely with all that we know of Canaanite mythology from other sources—earlier, contemporary and later—that Canaanite origin is quite certain. Moreover, the language in which they are written is only dialectically different from the language native to the scribes who wrote the Canaanite Amarna Letters. Ancestral Hebrew resembled Ugaritic and South Canaanite more closely than Castilian resembled Aragonese, or Provençal Parisian in the Middle Ages, and more nearly than Syrian Arabic resembles Egyptian Arabic today. We must, therefore, expect far-reaching parallels between biblical Hebrew style and vocabulary on the one hand, and Ugaritic on the other, especially in poetry (since we have scarcely any Ugaritic prose at all). This parallelism we actually do find, especially in Psalms, Job, and the prophets of the 7th and 6th centuries. Moreover, our new knowledge of what Canaanite language and poetic style were in the age immediately preceding the Conquest, makes it possible to show that such early poems as the Oracles of Balaam fit perfectly into the picture of that age and need not be dated in the period of the Monarchy, much less in the Persian or Greek periods. The discovery of the Ugaritic tablets revolutionizes our historical perspective of Hebrew literature, since we can no longer reduce dates just because evi-

THE ISRAEL STELE; 1230 B.C.E.

An Egyptian monument of Pharaoh Merenptah. The text makes reference to a victory over "the people of Israel," thus giving evidence that the Israelites had already settled in Palestine at that time

dence for earlier literary activity is wanting. In particular, this discovery compels us to reconsider earlier arguments for dating all researches of such Jewish scholars as H. L. Ginsberg, C. H. Gordon, U. Cassuto and T. H. Gaster.

From *The Cuneiform Texts of Ras Shamra Ugarit* by Claude F. A. Schaeffer; published for the British Academy by Humphrey Milford, Oxford University Press, London 1939.

FIRST OF THREE TABLETS RELATING THE LEGEND OF KERET
Cuneiform text of Ugarit; 15th to 14th century B.C.E.

or nearly all of the Psalms in post-exilic times, since many Psalms now prove to be adaptations of Canaanite originals or, at least, to swarm with reminiscences of Canaanite literary forms and expressions. It is gratifying to note that our knowledge of this material is largely due to the recent

III. THE AGE OF THE JUDGES AND UNITED MONARCHY

(C. 1200—925 B.C.E.)

In the period of the Judges we are hampered by an almost complete cessation of inscribed objects in Palestine and Syria. It was a period in which new, relatively primitive, immigrants without high culture almost completely replaced the Canaanites, forcing the latter into a narrow strip of the Phoenician coast. In Syria the Aramaeans, in Palestine Philistines and Israelites took

Conquest. In the Amarna Tablets from Canaanite towns and in roughly contemporary cuneiform tablets dug up at Taanach, Shechem, Tell el-Hesi and other biblical sites in Palestine, we find remarkably vivid hints about the life of the times.

From *The Cuneiform Texts of Ras Shamra Ugarit* by Claude F. A. Schaeffer;
published for the British Academy by Humphrey Milford,
Oxford University Press, London 1939.

GODDESS OF FERTILITY CARVED ON COVER OF IVORY BOX
Ugarit, 14th century B.C.E.

up the heritage of the Canaanites; but it was some time before any of them regained the level of material culture attained by the Canaanites. In addition to the striking picture of the fall in material culture painted by the excavator of early Israelite sites, we have some external information which illustrates this point. Thanks again to outside sources we are able to obtain a good idea of conditions in Palestine before the

Studied in the perspective sketched for us by contemporary documents from Egypt and Syria, and firmly anchored in the solid results of excavation in Canaanite sites, we can now obtain an exceedingly clear idea of the culture and social organization of pre-Israelite Palestine.

Against this background the narratives of the Judges fit perfectly: we are able to recognize striking similarities along with

From *The Cuneiform Texts of Ras Shamra Ugarit* by Claude F. A. Schaeffer;
published for the British Academy by Humphrey Milford,
Oxford University Press, London 1939.

GOLDEN PATERA SHOWING A CANAANITE WARRIOR IN A CHARIOT
HUNTING DEER AND WILD CATTLE
Ugarit, 15th or first half of 14th century B.C.E.

Courtesy of the Oriental Institute, University of Chicago
RETURN OF SETHOS I FROM A CAMPAIGN IN PALESTINE
About 1318 B.C.E.

even more remarkable differences. Foreign control was replaced by tribal autonomy, but at the same time the protection against aggression which was generally provided by Egyptian garrisons was taken completely away, and the Israelites had none but themselves and their God on whom to rely. The cult of foreign deities similarly vanishes in large part from the scene, but with them went the art and probably much of the music of the Canaanites. Slavery, serfdom and the *corvée*, all thoroughly characteristic of Canaanite society, disappeared (except as a result of occasional foreign incursions), but the art of building was neglected and such public works as city-walls, temples and palaces ceased to be built. The Canaanite emphasis on schools and on teaching the scribal art and the arts of divination and magic was replaced by nearly complete illiteracy and by reliance on the simplest types of oracles. On the other hand, there were changes which were all to the good. We need only contrast the extreme sexual

and modifying this or that crudity, but the spirit of Israelite religion was opposed to drastic change. Just as the scribes and scholars of Israel described the defeats and humiliations of Israel along with its triumphs and glories, just as they pictured the sins of Jacob and Judah, of David and Solomon, as well as their virtues, so they preserved a few crude bits from the past along with edifying passages, whenever there was some historical or ethical lesson to be drawn from them.

Our most striking external sources for the period of the Judges are Egyptian; among them we may single out particularly the inscriptions and reliefs of Ramesses III (1195-1164 B.C.E.) and the Report of Wen-Amun, from about 1070 B.C.E. The former are extremely important because of their elaborate portrayal of the invasion of Palestine and Egypt by the Peoples of the Sea, including particularly the Philistines, who reached the shores of Palestine in 1187. About a century and a half after their first

Courtesy of the Oriental Institute, University of Chicago

CIRCUMCIZED CAPTIVES BEING LED BEFORE A CANAANITE KING
SEATED ON THE CHERUB THRONE
About 1200 B.C.E.

depravity and the sadistic brutality of Canaanite mythology and ritual with the high moral tone of Israelite religious faith and practice to recognize this fact. Those scholars who insist on treating the biblical sources as though they represented only a final exilic or post-exilic revision of crude polytheistic originals have no parallel for their postulated process among the literatures of the ancient Near East. Naturally there was a certain amount of revision, bringing the reader up to date, so to speak,

settlement on the Coastal Plain came their decisive victory at Eben-ezer, followed by the destruction of many Israelite towns, some of which we have identified through traces of general destruction by fire about the third quarter of the 11th century B.C.E. The latter is an authentic account (no doubt colored in various places by the author's desire to put himself in the most favorable light) of the experiences of an Egyptian envoy to Byblus (Gebal), who was robbed when he stopped at the Palestinian port of Dor and treated contemptuously by the prince of Byblus, no longer afraid of the powerless authorities of Egypt. All in all, this is one of the most instructive documents which have come down to us from the ancient Near East. For example, we read here the earliest account of the activity of an ecstatic prophet, a description which is very pertinent to any analysis of the nature and age of Israelite prophetism.

Strangely enough, at first thought, there is even less extra-biblical material bearing on the century of the United Monarchy than on the preceding period of the Judges. Besides the external epigraphic and literary data to which we referred above, the time of the Judges is greatly illuminated by the results of excavations at Megiddo and Bethshan, Tell Beit Mirsim, Beth-shemesh and Bethel, to mention only a few of many excavated sites in Palestine. It is only recently that our data for the United Monarchy have been appreciably increased until we now have building remains of Saul at Gibeah, of David at Tell Beit Mirsim and Beth-shemesh, and of Solomon at Megiddo, Gezer and elsewhere. But not a single scrap of writing in Palestine except the Gezer Calendar can be referred even probably to this century. And owing largely to the fact that the military power of Egypt and Assyria shrank in the 10th century to the lowest level in fifteen centuries of history, we have almost no light at all from hieroglyphic or cuneiform sources. Inscriptions of 9th century Assyrian kings tell us about Aramaean victories over the Assyrians in

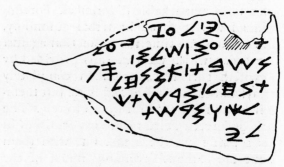

Courtesy of the American Schools of Oriental Research

**A HEBREW LETTER FROM THE
11TH CENTURY B.C.E.**
Inscription on copper from Byblus

the Euphrates Valley under Asshur-rabi II (1012-972 B.C.E.), which illustrate the events described in II Sam. 8 and 10. Still later Assyrian documents prove that Zobah was further north than was believed by Winckler and Guthe, entirely confirming the traditional interpretation of the extent of David's control of Syria. The famous Karnak List of towns in Judah, Edom and Israel which were conquered by Shishak immediately after Solomon's death is immensely valuable to the topographer because of the light it sheds on details of occupation at the close of the United Monarchy. Otherwise there is little direct light, though indirect light continues to accumulate from every direction.

A very interesting example of such indirect light is the rapidly expanding evidence for the substantial correctness of the Chronicler's attribution of the origin of Israelite temple music to David. Though my detailed study on this subject has not

Courtesy of the American Schools of Oriental Research

CHERUBIM GUARDING THE "TREE OF LIFE"

Courtesy of the Oriental Institute, University of Chicago

SOLOMON'S STABLES AT MEGIDDO
Present condition

Courtesy of the Oriental Institute, University of Chicago

SOLOMON'S STABLES AT MEGIDDO
Partially restored

yet appeared, I have discussed it at some length elsewhere. A few remarks must suffice here. Musical instruments, hymns and litanies played a very great place in the Egyptian and Mesopotamian temple worship of the third and especially of the second millennium. The Accadian *kalu* and the Canaanite *shar* were organized as temple guilds; myths and legends about the divine origin of music figure largely among both peoples. Profane music was perhaps equally popular among the Canaanites, as we know mainly from Egyptian sources, where Canaanite musicians frequently appear. The Greeks borrowed several musical instruments from the Canaanites (Phoenicians), and their legends show that this influence went far beyond the mere borrowing of instruments. Sennacherib carried male and female musicians from Jerusalem to Nineveh as part of the tribute he forced Hezekiah to pay. Most interesting of all these facts is the recent proof that the famous wise men, Ethan, Heman, Chalcol and Darda, the first two of whom were also considered as founders of two guilds of temple musicians, were of Canaanite origin and may even antedate the Conquest. Furthermore, it is scarcely accidental that the most archaic Psalms, such as 18, 29, 45, 68, swarm with words, expressions and entire lines which already appear in Ugaritic religious poetry as far back as the 15th century (see page 39).

The construction and decoration of the Temple of Solomon, together with details of the temple furniture, are now being illuminated by archaeological finds. Since the architect of the Temple and chief craftsman in its construction was himself a Tyrian, we must look to Phoenicia for our best parallels. Unfortunately, scarcely anything has hitherto been found in Phoenician cities of this age, aside from Byblus. In particular, we have no ruined buildings of the period. Hence we are dependent upon building remains and objects of Phoenician origin or inspiration which have been discovered in surrounding lands—in Syria and Palestine, in Cyprus and Assyria, etc. At Ta'yinat in northern Syria the University of Chicago excavators have unearthed a 9th century temple with the same plan as Solomon's Temple (though considerably smaller), thus proving that later occurrences of this temple-plan in archaic Greek sites go back to Phoenician inspiration and may be legitimately adduced as parallels to Solomon's Temple. We now know the general appearance of the decorative elements described in the Book of Kings, thanks to rich finds of Phoenician ivories at Megiddo (12th century), Calah of Assyria (10th century), Samaria and Arslan Tash (9th century), etc. We know that the long-obscure cherubs were winged sphinxes; we can explain the conceptual imagery of "YHWH enthroned on the cherubim" from contemporary representations of divine and royal thrones supported by two flanking cherubs.

In a similar way much light has been cast on the commercial ventures of Solomon, as well as on the material organization of his state. Thanks to recent finds in Cyprus and Byblus it has become possible to interpret the long-enigmatic Phoenician inscription of the 9th century from Nora in Sardinia, and to show that the Tarshish mentioned there was in Sardinia, which possessed extraordinarily rich copper deposits, worked from the late second millennium onward. Solomon's own metallurgical activity, mentioned in Kings, has become far clearer since Glueck's excavation of unique refining works at Eziongeber on the Red Sea, dating back to the time of Solomon. His horse-trading has been illustrated by several scattered documentary finds, but especially by the clearance of elaborate stables for chariot horses at Megiddo. The Queen of Sheba has not yet been identified, but the early importance of Sheba in South Arabia is attested by Assyrian inscriptions of the 8th century, while the dominance of Arab political life by queens is emphasized in the Assyrian texts from the 8th and 7th centuries.

BIBLIOGRAPHY

ALBRIGHT, W. F., *The Archaeology of Palestine and the Bible* (New York, Revell, 1932-33-35). Out of print and somewhat antiquated in detail.

ALBRIGHT, W. F., *From the Stone Age to Christianity* (Baltimore, Johns Hopkins Press, 1940-41-42). Comprehensive survey with particular attention to the dominant religious ideas.

ALBRIGHT, W. F., *Archaeology and the Religion of Israel* (Baltimore, Johns Hopkins Press, 1942).

BLACKMAN, AYLWARD M., *The Literature of the Ancient Egyptians* (London, Methuen, 1927). A translation of Adolf Erman's authoritative book by one of the ablest British Egyptologists, and still by far the best available collection of translations from Egyptian.

BURROWS, MILLAR, *What Mean These Stones?* (New Haven, American Schools of Oriental Research, 1941). The best general introduction to biblical archaeology.

CHIERA, EDWARD, *They Wrote on Clay* (Chicago, University of Chicago Press, 1938). The latest authoritative popular sketch of Mesopotamian archaeology.

GINSBERG, H. L., *Kitve Ugarit* (*The Ugarit Texts*, Jerusalem, Vaad Halashon, 1936). Still the best collection of translations, though antiquated in detail.

GLUECK, NELSON, *The Other Side of the Jordan* (New Haven, American Schools of Oriental Research, 1940). A vivid popular account of his archaeological explorations.

GORDON, C. H., *The Living Past* (New York, John Day, 1941). A vivid sketch of explorations and discoveries in the ancient Near East.

GORDON, C. H., *The Loves and Wars of Baal and Anath* (Princeton, Princeton University Press, 1943). The latest popular survey of the finds at Ugarit, with a number of translated passages.

HEIDEL, ALEXANDER, *The Babylonian Genesis* (Chicago, University of Chicago Press, 1942). The most up-to-date translation and interpretation of the Babylonian Epic of Creation and related literature.

KRAMER, S. N., *Sumerian Mythology* (Philadelphia, American Philosophical Society, 1944). The only popular account of Kramer's epochal work on Sumerian mythological texts.

MAISLER, BENJAMIN, *Toldot Erets Yisra'el* (*History of Palestine*, Vol. I; *From the Most Ancient Times to the Hebrew Monarchy*, Tel-Aviv, Mizpah, 1938). The latest historical survey of the history of Palestine as such, with full attention to archaeological data.

MAISLER, BENJAMIN, *Israel in Biblical Times* (Theilhaber, *The Graphic Historical Atlas of Palestine*, Tel-Aviv, Szapiro, 1941). A good compact atlas.

MCCOWN, CHESTER C., *The Ladder of Progress in Palestine* (New York, Harper, 1943). The latest and best popular account of excavations in Palestine and their results.

OLMSTEAD, A. T., *History of Palestine and Syria to the Macedonian Conquest* (New York, Scribner, 1931). Still the most complete survey, though antiquated by the rapid progress of archaeology.

SCHAEFFER, *The Cuneiform Texts of Ras Shamra-Ugarit* (London, Humphrey Milford, 1939). An authoritative survey by the excavator of Ugarit. The interpretations of texts are antiquated.

STEINDORFF, GEORGE AND SEELE, KEITH C., *When Egypt Ruled the East* (Chicago, University of Chicago Press, 1942). An authoritative account of the history and civilization of Egypt in the second millenium B.C.E., vividly described and beautifully illustrated.

WRIGHT, G. ERNEST AND FILSON, FLOYD V., *The Westminster Historical Atlas to the Bible* (Philadelphia, The Westminster Press, 1945). An authoritative and up-to-date historical atlas, accompanied by a historical and archaeological sketch of biblical history. Superbly executed, at a low price.

HISTORY OF JEWISH ARCHAEOLOGY

E. L. Sukenik

I. HISTORY OF JEWISH ARCHAEOLOGY

Archaeological excavations in Palestine were begun as early as 1863. In that year the French scholar de Saulcy uncovered the "Tombs of the Kings" (the mausoleum of Helena of Adiabene). A few years later the English archaeologist, Sir Charles Warren, began his researches of the region around the Temple Area. Up to the end of the 19th century many other excavations were undertaken in Jerusalem. A significant date in archaeological research in Palestine is the year 1890, when the English archaeologist Flinders Petrie began excavations in the Tell el-Hesi in the Shefelah. Although the belief that this was the site of ancient Lachish later proved to be erroneous, these excavations nevertheless established the foundations for research on ruins of ancient cities of Palestine.

A series of excavations were made by British archaeologists in the Shefelah; in the Jezreel valley and in Jericho by the Germans; and in ancient Samaria by American scholars. In addition to these should be mentioned the systematic research and excavation of ancient synagogues carried out by German scholars in the years 1905-1906. All these excavations were conducted by non-Jewish institutions, although they were frequently financed by Jews; the funds for the excavations at Samaria, for example, were provided by Jacob Schiff, the American philanthropist. An exception was the excavation on Mount Ophel in Jerusalem in the year 1913 which was carried out by the French-Jewish archaeologist Raymond Weill with funds provided by Baron Edmond de Rothschild.

After the First World War, when England was given the Mandate over Palestine, a new period of archaeological excavations began. Several countries participated in the work; much greater funds than before the war were put at the disposal of archaeologists, the methods employed were in time perfected, and much more fruitful results were achieved.

After the war the government control over the country's antiquities became more stringent and better organized than it had been under Turkish rule. As a result many important objects were saved from damage and disappearance.

1. RESEARCH SOCIETIES

Among the various organizations which took part in archaeological research in Palestine the oldest is the English Palestine Exploration Fund which carried on extremely valuable work in geographical surveying, excavations, and research in the various ruins. The *Palestine Exploration Fund*

Quarterly Statement, founded in 1869 (now called *Palestine Exploration Quarterly*) contains a vast storehouse of information concerning Jewish Palestine and Jewish antiquities.

The next oldest society is the *Deutscher Palaestina Verein* which is responsible for important research and excavations in Palestine. The results of its work are published in its journal, *Zeitschrift des Deutschen Palaestina Vereins,* which was founded in 1878, and in various other publications.

In Jerusalem itself there are several institutions devoted to archaeological research. The oldest of them is the *École Biblique* of the Dominican Order, which is the official French archaeological school. The number of excavations which the *École Biblique* undertook is small but its researches, the results of which are published in its *Revue Biblique,* founded in 1891, are of great importance. The second institution in order of importance in Palestine is the American School of Oriental Research, founded in 1900. Its most important undertakings were begun after the First World War and the results of its researches and excavations, as well as of the work it performs in collaboration with other American institutions, are published in the quarterly *Bulletin of the American Schools of Oriental Research* and in the *Annual of the American Schools of Oriental Research.* There are other organizations, as, for instance, the German Evangelical Institute for Research in the Holy Land, which was founded in 1898. In the last-named organization's *Palaestina Jahrbuch* there is extremely interesting material on Palestine and on biblical history. There are, too, the British School of Archaeology which was established after the First World War and undertook a series of excavations in Jerusalem and Samaria, and the Pontifical Biblical Institute which devotes itself to research on the biblical period.

The Department of Antiquities of the Government of Palestine, besides controlling and preserving antiquities, is also doing research work in connection with antiquities discovered by chance, and undertaking excavations of ancient sites. The results of these investigations are published in the *Quarterly of the Department of Antiquities in Palestine,* which was founded in 1932.

Before the First World War various attempts were made to establish a Jewish society for archaeological research in Palestine, but it was only in 1919 that such a society was founded under the name of החברה העברית לחקירת ארץ-ישראל ועתיקותיה (Jewish Palestine Exploration Society). In spite of its limited means the Society managed to conduct several important excavations, notably on an ancient synagogue at Tiberias which was accidentally uncovered by Jewish laborers while building a road. The Society also did the research in the neighborhood of the Tomb of Absalom and in the vicinity of the Tomb of Zechariah near Jerusalem.

A particularly important task which the Society carried out in collaboration with the Hebrew University was the excavation of the Third City Wall of ancient Jerusalem. The Society also conducted research on ancient tombs in the neighborhood of Jerusalem and undertook the excavation of a large Jewish cemetery and an ancient synagogue in Beth Shearim (Sheikh Abreiq) at the foot of Mount Carmel, near the entrance to the Jezreel Valley. The Society published the results of its work in קובץ החברה העברית לחקירת ארץ-ישראל ועתיקותיה. In recent years the Society issues a quarterly bulletin ידיעות החברה העברית לחקירת ארץ-ישראל ועתיקותיה.

In 1926, two years after the official opening of the Hebrew University in Jerusalem, an archaeological department was established in the University, its chief interest being research concerning Jewish antiquities in Palestine as well as in the Diaspora.

The department conducted research on a number of ancient Jewish synagogues in Palestine, as well as in other countries. Excavations were made which uncovered ancient synagogues of the Byzantine period in Hammath by Gadara, Beth Alpha, on the island of Aegina, and other places. In the neighborhood of Jerusalem a number of old tombs were uncovered dating from the time of the Second Temple. Numerous inscriptions of the period were among the objects discovered.

In collaboration with other learned societies and universities excavations were undertaken by the archaeological department of the Hebrew University in the ancient City of David in Jerusalem, and also in Samaria. In Samaria valuable remains of the palaces of the kings of Israel, inscriptions, etc., were found, and ruins of buildings erected by King Herod. The department publishes the results of its work in various periodicals in Hebrew and other languages. In connection with the new Museum of Jewish Antiquities, a Hebrew periodical dealing with Jewish antiquities, *Kedem,* is published, two volumes having already appeared.

2. MUSEUMS

Collections of Jewish antiquities are to be found in museums all over the world. In the Lateran Museum and the Thermae Museum in Rome there are large numbers of inscriptions from the Jewish catacombs in Rome. Various museums in the Italian provinces, in Naples, Venosa and Taranto, for example, have material relating to the ancient Jewish settlements in Italy.

In the Louvre Museum in Paris there are sarcophagi which were discovered by de Saulcy in the "Tombs of the Kings" in Jerusalem, the Mesha Stone and much other important material relating to the Jewish past.

A small collection of Jewish antiquities is in the British Museum, including inscriptions from the time of the First Temple, the ossuary of Nikanor the Alexandrian, who presented the famous Nikanor Gate to the restored Temple of Herod, and the famous Black Obelisk of King Shalmaneser III. In addition, the British Museum has the relief representing King Sennacherib at the conquest of Lachish and important Chaldaic inscriptions and paintings bearing a relationship to Jewish history.

A larger collection of Jewish antiquities is in the Museum of Istambul where can be seen the famous Siloam inscription, the Greek tablets from Herod's temple, and various other important inscriptions. In addition, the museum has the largest collection of the materials uncovered in archaeological excavations undertaken in Palestine before the First World War.

In the Cairo Museum there is the so-called "Israel Stele" of the Egyptian king Merneptah (13th century B.C.E.) containing the first mention of the name Israel. In the same museum is a large collection of Jewish papyri found in Elephantine (some of them are in the Berlin Museum).

There is a small number of relics of the large, ancient Jewish community of Alexandria in the Museum of Alexandria. A few clay lamps bearing Jewish symbols and several inscriptions from Jewish catacombs are all the objects that have been found relating to the Jewish past in that one-time large center of Jewry.

In the museum recently founded in Damascus there is a unique relic of the Jewish past: the mural paintings from the synagogue in Dura-Europos. The American archaeologists who uncovered the synagogue brought the paintings and the remains of the building to the museum and performed an excellent job of reconstruction on them.

Before the First World War there was no archaeological museum in Palestine, but after the war preparations were made by the Palestine government for the establishment of an appropriate institution. A large financial subsidy from the Rockefeller Foundation made possible the erection of an imposing building in which are being gathered the most important archaeological finds uncovered by excavation or discovered through various accidental circumstances.

Recently the Hebrew University made preparations for the founding of a museum for Jewish antiquities with funds bequeathed to the University by the Russian Jew, Gedaliah Moshe Kutscher, who had settled in South Africa. The museum aims to be a center for gathering the relics of the Jewish past and of research not limited to Palestine. By arrangement with the Jewish Palestine Archaeological Society in Jerusalem the latter's collection has passed over to the Museum.

II. JEWISH ARCHAEOLOGICAL MATERIAL

1. PERIOD OF THE FIRST TEMPLE
(12th to 6th century B.C.E.)

The excavations which have been made in the ruins of ancient towns in Palestine

PART OF THE FORTIFICATION WALL AT GIBEAH OF SAUL
Dating from the beginnings of the Period of the Kings

give a more or less general picture of living conditions in the biblical period.

a large open square at the main gate which served as an assembly place and a Court of

PART OF THE PALACE WALL OF THE ISRAELITE KINGS IN SAMARIA

A. *Ancient Cities and Buildings*: The principal cities, as well as the large provincial towns, were surrounded by walls. In the walls were gates, flanked with towers, which opened into the city and from which connecting roads led to other settlements. The city walls were built of stone or brick. The dwellings, of which many were two stories high, usually contained rectangular rooms, in most cases not large. In addition to the dwelling rooms the houses contained kitchens, various chambers for products, wine-cellars, etc. The entrance to the rooms was through a courtyard opening onto the street. The streets were very narrow and the entire city presented a crowded, constricted appearance. Inside the city itself there was practically no open space. There was usually

IVORY PLAQUE WITH THE REPRESENTATION OF A SPHINX
From the "ivory house" of Ahab in Samaria

Justice, where the elders sat to dispense justice to the townspeople. Sanitary arrangements were not too primitive; cattle were kept outside the city walls. Often there were installations of a primitive drainage system, the principal purpose of which was to make it possible for rain water to be carried outside of the city. In those settlements which were not near streams, rain was gathered in cisterns hewn out of rock near the houses themselves and in large reservoirs. Similar cisterns have been found in towns adjoining springs; here the purpose was to insure a supply of water in case of a siege, and to serve as a reserve supply in normal times.

The inhabitants occupied themselves chiefly with farming and cattle raising. Spinning wheels and weaving looms, which are found in practically all houses, indicate that each family took care of its own needs in matters of clothing, linen, etc. However, there were communities which developed complete industries—dyers, potters, etc.

In addition to the usual dwellings, in various places were found larger buildings which served as residences for the royal officials and in general for the wealthier sections of the population. These houses are of a superior type of construction and contain larger rooms. Similar palaces have been uncovered in Taanach and Megiddo. In the last-named city were also found the ruins of large stables with enough room for several hundred horses. The Bible records that King Solomon maintained horses and chariots in special places; one of these appears to have been Megiddo.

Up to now no trace has been uncovered of the Temple which Solomon built in Jerusalem. Outside of small sections of the city walls and a few ancient tombs, no important remains have been found of the buildings in Jerusalem of the First Temple period.

We have much more material from Samaria, the principal city of the kingdom of Israel. The excavations which have been made in the mountain near the Arab village of Sebaste, not far from Shechem, uncovered under the ruins of the later Herodian and Roman buildings imposing remains of the capital which was built by Omri and his successors. Up to now remains have been uncovered of a group of palaces which occupy an area of more than 220 meters in length and over 100 meters in width. The entire group was surrounded by thick walls built of fine ashlar masonry showing an extraordinary technical skill.

Within the palace area was found a number of small ivory plaques decorated with various figures in relief and in *à jour* work. Tiny bits of gold still adhering to them reveal that many of them were covered with a thin layer of gold-foil and inlaid with glass of various colors. It is related in I Kings, 22, 39 that Ahab, king of Israel, built an "ivory house." The name בית השן

as the latest excavations indicate, probably derives from the fact that the furniture and the walls of the building were decorated with ivory ornaments similar to those which were found in the palaces of the Assyrian kings of the same period.

The excavations have not yet definitely determined the dimensions of the city area or of its walls. One wall section was discovered with an extremely interesting gate, reminiscent of the Lion Gate of Mycenae.

Outside of the city, near the later Roman stadium, a number of old tombs of the period were found. These were caves dug out of the rock and consisting of ante-chambers and small burial chambers. In the walls of the ante-chambers were bottle-shaped niches full of fragments of clay vessels and bones of animals, no doubt the remains of sacrifices offered to the dead, the זבחי מתים against which the prophets fought so sternly. Not far from the tombs was found a sort of sanctuary which appears to have been dedicated to the cult of the dead.

B. *Inscriptions*: There is no doubt that the kings of Judah and Israel left inscriptions on monuments which told of their wars and recorded their victories and buildings. Up to this time, however, very few of them have been discovered. In 1935 a small fragment of such a monument inscription was uncovered in Samaria. On the fragment, which dates from the 8th century B.C.E., unfortunately only a single word is preserved.

The famous Siloam inscription was found in 1880 in the Siloam tunnel near Jerusalem and reads as follows:

1 . . . . הנקבה . וזה . היה . דבר .
. . . הנקבה . בעוד .
2 הגרזן . אש . אל . רעו . ובעוד .
שלש . אמת . להנק [ב. נשמ]ע . קל .
אש . ק
3 רא . אל . רעו . כי . הית . זדה .
בצר . מימן . . . . . א . ובים . ה
4 נקבה . הכו . החצבם . אש . לקרת .
רעו . גרזן . על . [ג.]רזן . וילכו
5 המים . מן . המוצא . אל . הברכה .
במאתים . ואלף . אמה . ומא
6 ת . אמה . היה . גבה . הצר . על .
ראש . החצבם

(. . . *the boring through. And this was the story of the boring through: whilst yet . . . the pick, each towards his fellow, and whilst yet there were three cubits to be bored [through, there was hear]d the voice of each calling to his fellow, for there was a split in the rock on the right hand. . . . And on the day of the boring through the diggers struck, each to meet his fellow, pick upon pick; and the waters flowed from the source to the pool for two hundred and* a thousand cubits; and a hundred cubits was the height of the rock above the head of the diggers.)

The tunnel was constructed for the purpose of conducting the water of the Gihon Spring which was outside the city walls of old Jerusalem, to the Pool of Siloam, which was inside the city. According to the Bible record it appears that the tunnel was constructed in the time of King Hezekiah, around 700 B.C.E. In the tunnel can still

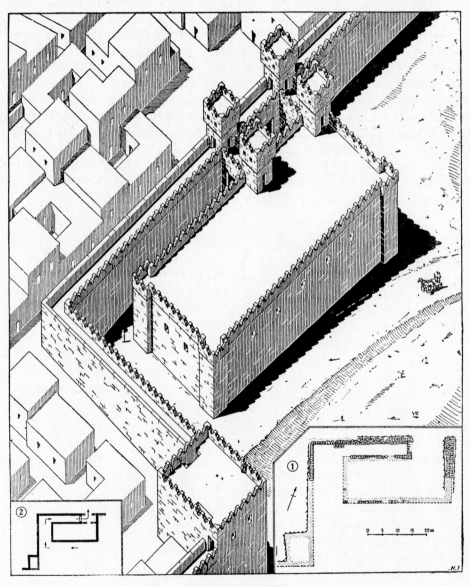

EAST GATE OF THE CITY OF SAMARIA
Reconstructed drawing

be seen the site where the two groups of laborers, digging from opposite ends, met.

The oldest Jewish inscription discovered up to the present time is the so-called Farm-

taxes. It appears that these taxes were paid by the lessees of the private estates of the king. The inscriptions are very brief, as is appropriate for such records. Most of them

THE SILOAM INSCRIPTION

er's Calendar of Gezer which dates from the 9th century B.C.E. The Calendar is inscribed on a small stone tablet and indicates the divisions of farm labor according to the months of the year.

The ostraca from Samaria date from the 8th century B.C.E. They were found in some side rooms in the palace of the kings of Israel. The inscriptions, written in red ink on fragments of pottery, are accounts of receipts by the royal officials of wine and oil

begin with a date, probably the number of years of the king's reign; then follows the name of the place from which the taxes were paid, the name of the tax-payer, the name of the tax-officer and the number of jars of oil or wine delivered. Among the places listed are many which are not mentioned in the Bible, but which seem like names of Arab villages in the neighborhood of Samaria. The following is an example of one of these inscriptions:

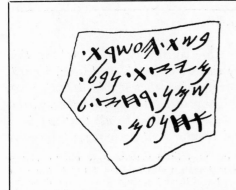

בשת העשרת

מיצת נבל

שמן רחץ ל

אחנעם

(In the tenth year: from Yazot a jar of purified oil through Ahinoam.)

OSTRACON FROM SAMARIA

The name of the place, Yazot, indicates a somewhat altered form of Yazid, an Arab village still in existence eight kilometers north-east of Sebaste.

An ostracon with an Old Hebrew inscription was found on Mount Ophel near Jerusalem. The largest number of ostraca have been found since the beginning of 1935 in Tell ed-Duweir which, it is conjectured, is situated on the site of the ancient city of Lachish. Several more ostraca were found there in 1938, in a gate-room in the town wall. They date from the last years before

and Azekah, still resisted the Babylonians.* The orthography of these ostraca differs from that used in the Masoretic texts. In addition, the sign which usually separates one word from another in the Old Hebrew inscriptions, is frequently omitted. This makes an exact interpretation of the letters extremely difficult and has led to various interpretations of several sentences. The following is one of the letters inscribed on both sides of a sherd. There are thirteen lines of inscription, eight on one side and five on the other:

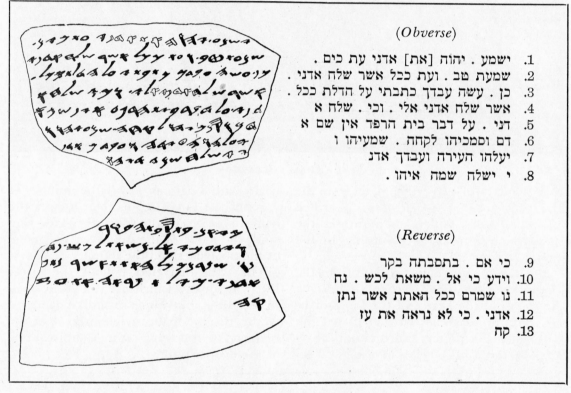

(Obverse)

1. ישמע . יהוה [את] אדני עת כים .
2. שמעת טב . ועת כבל אשר שלח אדני
3. כן . עשה עבדך כתבתי על הדלת ככל .
4. אשר שלח אדני אלי . וכי . שלח א
5. דני . על דבר בית הרפד אין שם א
6. דם וסמכיהו לקחה . שמעיהו ו
7. יעלהו העירה ועבדך אדנ
8. י ישלח שמה איהו .

(Reverse)

9. כי אם . בתסבתה בקר
10. וידע כי אל . משאת לכש . נח
11. נו שמרם ככל האתת אשר נתן
12. אדני . כי לא נראה את עז
13. קה .

OSTRACON FROM LACHISH

the destruction of the First Temple at the beginning of the 6th century B.C.E.

They consist of letters which an officer of the Jewish army, Hoshayahu, sent to his superior, Yaush, who is addressed as "my lord Yaush," or, frequently, simply "my lord." The letters give a vivid picture of the period when the Babylonian army had already conquered the larger part of Judaea, and only a few fortified cities, Jerusalem, Lachish

(*May God cause my lord to hear this very day tidings of good. And now, according to everything that my lord hath sent, thus hath thy servant done. I have written on the door according to all that my lord hath sent to me. And with regard to what*

* "When the king of Babylon's army fought against Jerusalem, and against all the cities of Judah that were left, against Lachish, and against Azekah: for these defenced cities remained of the cities of Judah" (Jeremiah, XXXIV, 7).

my lord hath sent about the matter of Beth Harefed, there is nobody there. And as for Semachiah, Shemaiah hath taken him and hath brought him up to the city. And thy servant, my lord, will send there to inquire where he will be, tomorrow at dawn. And may my lord know that we will watch for the signals from Lachish according to the instructions which my lord hath given, if we do not see [the signals from] Azekah.)

The letter is a good example of the letter writing style of the times. It is brief, begins with a greeting, reports on the carrying out of the orders received, and ends with a communication from the writer who, it appears, is stationed at a post between Lachish and Azekah.

C. *Seals*: In addition to the above inscriptions, mention should be made of the old Hebrew seals of which more than 150 have been found up to the present time. The number is constantly increasing, however, as a result of new excavations and accidental discoveries. For the most part the seals are engraved on hard, semi-precious stones, but

are the seals on which are engraved the titles of the owner, as, for instance, the seal which was found in Megiddo and which bears the inscription לשמע עבד ירבעם (belonging to Shema the servant of Jeroboam). The seal apparently belonged to one of the important officials of King Jeroboam. On other seals the title reads simply עבד המלך (the king's servant), or נער המלך (the king's page), the king's name not being given. On several seals there appears the title בן המלך (the king's son). This, however, is probably a title rather than an actual reference to a son of a king. On one seal which was found several years ago in Tell ed-Duweir, there is the inscription לגדליהו אשר על הבית (belonging to Gedaliah who is over the House). This is the title of a high official encountered several times in the Bible.

Recently a seal was published (below, No. 1) bearing the inscription לאשנא עבד אחז (belonging to Ashna the servant of Ahaz). Another seal (below, No. 2) is divided into three registers; the two upper contain the inscription ליאזניהו עבד המלך

THREE ANCIENT HEBREW SEALS

1. Impression of the seal לאשנא עבד אחז
2. Impression of the seal ליאזניהו עבד המלך
3. Impression of the seal לחנניהו נריהו

occasionally on a hard paste. The seals belonged to private individuals or officials who carried them on rings and used them for stamping their letters or clay vessels, as well as for signing various official documents. In most cases the owner's name and that of his father were engraved on the seal; often there was a picture of a flower, an animal or a legendary creature. Of special interest

(belonging to Yeazanyahu the king's servant); in the lower register is portrayed the likeness of a fighting cock. This seal was found not far from Jerusalem in a tomb near the ruins of an ancient city which several scholars have identified with Mizpah. It may have belonged to the Jewish army officer יאזניהו בן המעכתי or יאזניהו בן הושעיהו who is mentioned in the Bible as an officer

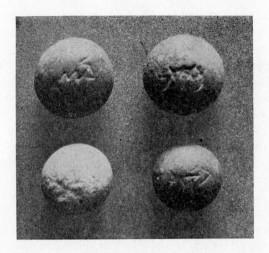

ANCIENT JEWISH WEIGHTS

A separate group of inscriptions of the period is represented by the stamps on handles of jars which were found in large numbers in various mounds of ruins in Judaea. They can be divided into two groups: the first group, in addition to the inscription, contains the likeness of a four-winged scarab; the second, a flying sun symbol. The inscriptions are as follows: למלך שוכה, למלך ממשת, למלך זיף, למלך חברון The word למלך indicates that the stamps had an official character. Some scholars believe that the jars were made in royal potteries located in the four cities named, Hebron, Zif, Memshat and Shochah, all situated in the southern part of Judaea. Other scholars believe that the jar stamps were official confirmations of measures according to which the people paid taxes in kind to the king, and that the four cities mentioned were administrative centers where the taxes were collected. There remains to be mentioned the stamped weights which were made of stone, flat at the bottom and with

during the time of the destruction of the First Temple. On the seal (page 57, No. 3) there is only the inscription לחנניהו נריהו (belonging to hananyahu the son of Neryahu). The omission of the word *ben* (son) between the two names is not infrequent on seals.

RUINS OF HOUSES AT ELEPHANTINE IN WHICH PAPYRI HAVE BEEN FOUND

domed back. The upper surface bore a weight symbol or an inscription such as פים (a weight mentioned in I Samuel, XIII, 21), חמש, שלשת, בקע, נצף.

2. THE PERIOD OF THE SECOND TEMPLE
(5th century B.C.E. to 1st century C.E.)

A. *Materials and Documents*: A sensational discovery relating to this period were the archives of a Jewish military garrison on the small island of Elephantine in Upper Egypt, near the first cataract. Some papyri inscribed in Aramaic, which were found in a heap of rubble by Egyptian fellaheen, led to an excavation on the island in 1907. Many documents, inscribed on papyri and

sian government, individual and communal legal documents, private letters, etc. They are all written in Aramaic characters and in the Aramaic language. Through these documents various facts were substantiated which up to then had been known only from literary-historical sources concerning Jewish mercenaries under the Egyptian and Persian governments in Egypt. A specially interesting document is the petition which the representatives of the Jewish community of Elephantine sent to Bagohi, the Persian satrap in Jerusalem. The letter contains a petition that he use his influence with the Persian officials known to him so that the Jews would be permitted to rebuild their

PAGE FROM A LETTER SENT BY THE JEWS OF ELEPHANTINE TO
THE PERSIAN SATRAP BAGOHI IN JERUSALEM

sherds, belonging to the 5th century B.C.E. were found. They consist of literary texts, such as the history of Ahikar the Wise, official notices, proclamations of the Per-

sanctuary which was destroyed by the Egyptian and Persian officials while the Persian satrap was away from Egypt. In the letter the Elephantine Jews relate how they had previously approached the High Priest Ye-hohanan and his colleagues in Jerusalem on the matter but had received no answer from him. What makes the letter particularly surprising is the statement that the affair was also being reported to the sons of Sanbalat, the governor (פחה) of Samaria, whom Nehemiah mentions as an enemy of the Jews. This petition, of which two copies were found in Elephantine, was probably sent to Jerusalem by a special messenger who brought back the satrap Bagohi's letter with a recommendation to the Persian satrap in Egypt.

Another document which was found in Elephantine, and dated the fifth year of the reign of king Darius (419 B.C.E.), is addressed to the representative of the Jewish garrison by a certain Hananiah. This Hananiah brought an order from the Persian king to the satrap Arsham dealing specifically with the Passover celebration of the Jewish soldiers in Elephantine. It is not known who this Hananiah was but it is quite possible that he came as a messenger of the Jewish community in Judaea.

So far as the religious ideas of the Elephantine Jewish community are concerned, a list of the donations which the members of the community gathered for their temple is informative. There is first a statement that the list indicates the names of Jewish soldiers who made donations for יהו אלהא (the god Yahu). Then follow the names of more than a hundred donors, men and women, with the specific amounts of their donations. The seventh column of the list begins with the total of the donations which Yedoniah bar Gemariah, the elder of the community, collected. There is then a statement that the money was divided among Yahu, אשמביתאל (Ashambethel) and ענתביתאל (Anathbethel). This would indicate that the Jews of Elephantine, in addition to their loyalty to the belief in יהוה (as is indicated by their names, the majority of which possessed the ending *yahu*) also believed in various other gods and goddesses. Recent research, however, has raised

doubts as to whether this interpretation is correct.

The archives of a Jewish merchant in Babylonia dating from approximately the same period as the Elephantine papyri were uncovered in Nippur (the biblical Calneh), near the Kebar river. The archives contained more than a hundred clay bricks with cuneiform writing in Chaldaic. They record the business transactions which were carried on in the course of several generations by a Jewish business firm named Murashu. From these records it can be seen that the Jews in Babylonia during this period were prosperous. Many of them owned land and capital and took a prominent part in the country's trade. Jews were government officials, tax collectors, etc. Their position was much better than that of the Jews in Elephantine, and they lived at peace with the surrounding population.

A JAR-HANDLE BEARING THE STAMP יהד

There is very little information concerning the province of Judaea before this period. There are no historical sources and up to now archaeological excavations have not succeeded in yielding much information. From silver coins bearing the inscription Yahud and from stamped jar handles bearing the inscription Yerushalaim and Yahud which served as official units of measure, it can be inferred that under Persian rule the province of Judaea had certain autonomous rights.

RUINS OF THE HASMONAEAN FORTRESS AT BETH-ZUR

GREEK INSCRIPTION CONTAINING A WARNING FOR GENTILES NOT TO
ENTER THE TEMPLE OF HEROD

There are some records of the Hasmonaean period: coins issued by the Hasmonaeans, and a few buildings.

B. *Buildings*: It is definite that the fortress of Beth-zur was partly built in this period. Macalister, the British archaeologist, discovered another large structure during his excavations in Gezer. It is also likely that the imposing tombs in Jerusalem, such as the Tomb of Absalom, the tomb of Zechariah, and others belong to this period.

It is clear that the majority of ancient buildings in Palestine of the last period of the Second Temple belong to the time of King Herod (37—4 B.C.E.), who in his long reign developed an extraordinary building activity. The remains of the ancient city walls in Jerusalem give evidence of this. But his activity was not limited to Jerusalem. Very important remains of his buildings were found in Caesarea and Sebaste (Samaria). Both these cities, where the majority of the population was non-Jewish, were completely rebuilt by Herod in honor of the Roman emperor Augustus to whom he was indebted for his throne. The ruins of Caesarea have not yet been investigated. The excavations in Sebaste which began before the First World War and were continued in recent years, throw a good deal of light on the imposing structures which were built by this "Edomite slave."

The remains in Caesarea and Sebaste convey an impression of the appearance of Jerusalem during that period. Apart from the Temple which was rebuilt by Herod and the magnificence of which was admitted even by the Pharisees, his enemies, and the magnificent fortifications with which he surrounded the city, he built in the city itself a number of public and private buildings. Beginning with the Hasmonaean period and later, Jerusalem was not only the principal city of the relatively small kingdom, but also the center for the large and wealthy surrounding Jewish Diaspora. Donations poured into Jerusalem from all Jewry, increasing the welfare of the population and undoubtedly helping to develop the building activity in the city. The magnifi-

cent mausoleum of Queen Helena of Adiabene who settled in Jerusalem during this period still arouses great admiration. On Mount Ophel, not far from the Temple Mount, were found remains of a synagogue together with a guest-house which Roman Jews built for the use of Jewish pilgrims. Unfortunately, no trace remains of other buildings of the period.

C. *Burial Caves and Ossuaries*: Important for the knowledge of Jewish life in those days are the hundreds of burial caves which were hewn out of the rock. The caves served as family burial places. As a rule they consisted of a small courtyard from which a few steps led down to the burial chamber. In the chamber benches were cut around the walls. Above the benches niches were cut into the walls, usually only in three walls of the chamber, and not in the entrance wall.

STONE TABLET FROM THE HASMONAEAN PERIOD

Bearing an Aramaic inscription which relates that the bones of King Uzziah had been transferred

Bodies of the dead were placed in the niches. In time, when the number of niches no longer sufficed, the bones of corpses buried earlier were removed (this custom is known in the Talmud under the name ליקוט עצמות). The probability is that originally they were put in a corner of the cave or in a specially hewn opening in the wall. Later it became the custom to place the accumulated bones into a chest made of wood, stone or clay. Naturally no trace remains of the wooden chests apart from their

STONE OSSUARY BEARING THE INSCRIPTION
שלום אשת אלעזר

iron nails. In Talmudic writings these chests, known to us as ossuaries, are called גלוסקמאות ; according to a Greek inscription found on one of the chests they were known as ostophagoi.

Several hundred of these stone ossuaries have been found during the last century. For the most part they were uncovered in the immediate neighborhood of Jerusalem; a small number was found in other sections of the country. The stone chests are rectangular, hewn out of a single block, about 70-80 centimeters long, 30-40 centimeters high and 20-30 centimeters wide, covered with a stone lid, flat, gabled or semi-cylindrical. Frequently the outside of the chest is painted with red or yellow color, and rosettes are carved on one of the sides, the majority of them set in frames of leaves, line borders or other ornaments.

The inscriptions on the ossuaries are of great interest. They are in one of the languages which were used in Palestine at the time: Hebrew, Aramaic and Greek; frequently they were bi-lingual, Hebrew-Greek or Aramaic-Greek.

The majority of the inscriptions consist of the names of the deceased whose bones the chest contained. Frequently their titles and kinship and sometimes the place of their origin were included. Some of them are designated as proselytes.

There is reason to believe that the chests were made in workshops in Jerusalem. On two of the flat chest-covers found there appear the names of the workers and certain figures indicating either the number of

PART OF AN OSSUARY BEARING THE INSCRIPTION
יהועזר בר שמעון בר קלון

days of work performed, or the number of completed chests.

FAÇADE OF A JEWISH TOMB TO THE NORTH OF JERUSALEM
Reconstructed drawing

D. *Jewish Coins*: The largest number of Jewish coins also belongs to the Second Temple period. The opinion held up to now that Jewish coins date exclusively from the Hasmonaean period has been shown to be erroneous. We know that during the time of the Persian rule in Palestine—in the 5th century B.C.E.—there were various coins of the then province of Judaea. The silver coins, which bear the inscription Yahud, *i.e.* Judaea, are very similar in appearance to other coins which were in circulation in all the Persian provinces. Their type was similar to Greek coins. On one side there was the representation of an owl, on the other side the head of a man. On one coin, in the possession of the British Museum, instead of an owl there is the representation of a god seated in a winged chariot and holding a bird in his hand. For a long time the inscription Yahud on the coins was mistakenly interpreted by many scholars as indicating the word Yahu, the name of God. As a matter of fact, the legend should not be read Yahu, but Yahud, meaning Judaea.

Following the issue of these Jewish coins there comes a long pause and it is only some centuries later, during the reign of the Hasmonaeans, that Jewish coins again begin to appear. The first among them were the small copper coins with two horns of plenty engraved on one side with a poppy head between them, and on the other side the inscription יהוחנן הכהן הגדל וחבר היהודים (Jehohanan the High Priest and the Assembly of the Judaeans), or sometimes the words יהוחנן הכהן הגדל ראש חבר היהודים (Jehohanan the High Priest, head of the Assembly of the Judaeans). The coins of his son, Judas Aristobulus, have a similar appearance.

Of an entirely different type are the coins of Alexander Jannaeus. He was the first Hasmonaean prince to take the title of king. His later coins, which bear the inscription

יהונתן המלך also bore a similar Greek inscription, Alexandru Basileos. The favored interpretation of the anchor on the coins is that it is a symbol of the expansion of the Jewish kingdom to the shores of the Mediterranean during his reign.

The coins of Mattathias Antigonus bring to an end the series of Hasmonaean coins. On these coins the inscriptions are also bilingual. Those discovered are in a very bad condition owing to the poor metal from which they were minted. To this period belongs the small copper coin with a seven-branched menorah on which are characters that appear to be the first letters of the name Antigonus. If this opinion is correct this would be the first known representation of the menorah which later became a Jewish emblem.

On the coins of Herod and his dynasty Hebrew inscriptions are no longer found; only Greek ones: Herodu Basileos in the case of Herod and the titles Tetrarchu and Ethnarchu in the case of his sons. Even in the reign of his grandson, Agrippa I, who was much closer to the people and their customs than the other rulers of the dynasty, we find only Greek inscriptions on the coins.

The coins of the Herodian dynasty are richer than the earlier ones and are imitations of the coins of other nations. On coins from Jewish provinces under Herodian rule, no royal portraits were found, but in non-Jewish provinces portraits of Roman emperors are found on the coins and occasionally portraits of the rulers of the Herodian dynasty.

The coins which were issued in Palestine at the time of the Roman procurators after the banishment of Herod Archelaus are beyond the scope of this article, but it is interesting to note that they did not contain portraits of Roman emperors; apparently the feelings of the Jews were taken into consideration.

Hebrew inscriptions on coins appear again in the last years before the destruction of Jerusalem—and again as in the time of the first Hasmonaeans without Greek addition—at the time of the uprising against the Romans. To this period belong the silver shekels and half-shekels. On one side of these coins there is a chalice and the words שקל ישראל and on the other side a stem with three flowers or pomegranates and the words ירושלים הקדושה. In addition to these inscriptions an abbreviation for the year is given. On the half-shekels, instead of the words שקל ישראל appear the words חצי השקל.

The date of these coins formed the subject of a long discussion. Some scholars would assign them to Simeon the Maccabee, basing their assumption on the fact that he had been granted the right to strike coins by Antiochus Sidetes. But some hoards of coins recently found established beyond any doubt that these "thick shekels" were struck during the war against the Romans, shortly before the destruction of Jerusalem.

An echo of the popular feeling of rebellion can be found in the inscriptions on the copper coins of this period which are dated according to the deliverance of Zion, e.g. שנת ארבע לגאלת ציון. The coin types are a vine leaf, date palm, citron and fruit basket. It is obvious that these figures represent purely Jewish symbols, baskets of first fruits, *lulab* and *ethrog*.

After the destruction of Jerusalem there is an interval in the minting of Jewish coins. In Palestine as in Rome various coins were minted in commemoration of the Roman victory over the Jews. They bear the familiar figure of a weeping woman in bonds seated under a palm tree, or of a woman with hands tied seated and a man standing on either side of a palm. The inscriptions on these coins in Roman or Greek characters tell of "captured Judaea" (Judaea Capta).

The second uprising against the Romans (the Bar-Kochba rebellion) brings with it the last series of independent Jewish coins. Probably because of the shortage of metal those in charge of the mint in many cases stamped over Roman coins, as is indicated by traces of Roman letters, frequently also traces of a Roman emperor's head.

Apart from symbols and designs familiar from the first uprising, some new designs appear; various musical instruments and a building with a four-pillared front. It appears that the new designs on the coins were connected with the hope for the rebuilding of the Temple. These aspirations can also be seen in the purely Hebrew inscriptions which date the years as the first or second of the deliverance of Israel.

The name Simeon, frequently with the addition נשיא ישראל on the coins of the period, undoubtedly indicates the then Nasi Simeon ben Gamaliel, who was the legal heir to the office of Nasi in the Hillel family. On some coins there is also found the name אלעזר הכהן whom we are unable to identify definitely.

It should be mentioned that there are also a number of spurious coins struck in the Middle Ages. Some of them are copies of the silver shekels and carry the inscription Shekel Israel on one side and Yerushalaim Hakedoshah on the other, in square Hebrew characters. There are coins with the inscription דוד המלך ובנו שלמה המלך (King David and his son King Solomon). There is also a coin with the Hebrew inscription לא יהיה לך אלהים אחרים על פני (Thou shalt have no other gods before me) on one side and the head of Moses on the other side. Nor are there lacking coins with the head of Jesus of Nazareth and appropriate inscriptions in this collection of spurious coins.

3. ROMAN—BYZANTINE PERIOD
(1st to 6th century c.e.)

A. *Catacombs, Cemeteries and Tombstones*: Important remains from this period have been found in Italy, principally in Rome. Near Rome are several large Jewish burial places hewn out of the rock: the so-called Catacombs. They usually consist of a small courtyard from which steps lead to underground galleries, often on several levels. Niches were carved into the walls to serve as burial places. The corpse was put inside and the niche closed with a marble or brick plate. The inscriptions on the plate usually gave the name, the family connection and often the title of the deceased. Up

to now these catacombs have yielded several hundred tombstones on the majority of which the inscriptions are in Greek. A smaller number are in Latin and very few in Aramaic. Occasionally at the end of a Greek inscription appears the Hebrew word שלום or שלום על ישראל. Besides the inscriptions the tombstones often carry pictures of Jewish sacred objects to indicate the religious affiliation of the deceased. The seven-branched menorah takes first place among these symbols. Aside from the menorah the tombstones often carry representations of a citron and palm branch, a ram's horn, a Holy Ark, Scrolls of the Law, and other ritual objects. The same ritual objects are pictured on the so-called gilt glasses

BOTTOM OF A GLASS VESSEL WITH GILT PICTURES

which are found in the Jewish catacombs. On the walls and ceilings of the catacombs, too, these motifs are frequently represented. It is characteristic of the religious feeling of the Jews in Rome, however, that quite often mythological heathen motives are found in the catacombs.

The large number of inscriptions on the tombstones are extremely important as a source of information concerning the social structure of the Jews in Rome. Although no dates appear on the tombstones, there are nevertheless various indications which

WALL PAINTING FROM THE TORLONIA CATACOMB IN ROME

prove that the oldest tombstones date from the 2nd century B.C.E. and the latest from the 4th century C.E. It can be seen from the inscriptions that the Jews in Rome were organized into individual communities grouped around separate and independent synagogues which had their own officers.

Up to now we know of thirteen such communities in Rome with individual names such as Augustesian, Herodian and Agrippian, named after the rulers. Others again bear the names of various Roman sections, probably the places where the Jews lived. Still others are named after the countries

WALL PAINTING FROM THE TORLONIA CATACOMB IN ROME

from which the Jews came. Among these it is particularly interesting to note the community known as Hebraei, probably indicating Jews who had recently come from Judaea. A number of titles of community officials are mentioned on the tombstones, as, for instance, Elders, Archisynagogoi, Administrators, etc.

them consist of long corridors which lead to various chambers where the burial places are situated. The chambers are closed with stone doors which in many cases were still in position when found and still swung on their hinges. All types of graves were found, such as kokhim, arcosolia and ordinary rock-hewn graves. There were also found remains

INTERIOR OF A CATACOMB IN BETH-SHEARIM

In recent years the Jewish Palestine Exploration Society succeeded in uncovering a large ancient Jewish cemetery in Beth Shearim (Sheikh Abreiq) in the mountains of Lower Galilee near the entrance to the Valley of Jezreel. As is known from Talmudic literature, on this spot, which was at one time the seat of the Sanhedrin, there was a large cemetery which served as the burial place not only for Jews of Palestine but also for Jews of various neighboring countries such as Palmyra, Arabia, etc. The excavations have uncovered a number of large catacombs hewn out of the rock. Some of

of wooden, leaden, stone and clay sarcophagi.

The walls of the chambers were decorated with various pictures, reliefs and engravings. Among the decorations the largest number represented traditional Jewish symbols, the menorah, the Holy Ark, palm branch and citron, ram's horn, etc. Also plants and animals, ships, and geometrical ornaments served as motifs in the decorations. In some cases representations of human figures were also found.

Of special importance are the large number of inscriptions uncovered there, painted or engraved on the soft rock. The inscriptions are found on the doors, ceilings and also inside the tombs. There were uncovered, in addition, several marble tablets bear-

ARAMAIC TOMBSTONE
From the ancient Jewish cemetery near Jaffa

ing inscriptions. There is evidence that the number of marble tablets was much greater, but many of them were stolen. The number found up to now amounts to two hundred. For the most part the inscriptions are in Greek; a small number are in Hebrew and

TOMBSTONE FROM THE ANCIENT JEWISH
CEMETERY NEAR JAFFA
With Greek inscription and Hebrew monogram שלום

Aramaic and still fewer in Palmyrene. The inscriptions consist mostly of the names of the deceased, with or without the name of the deceased's father, accompanied in some cases with brief blessings. Some of the deceased are identified as Ribi (Rabbi), Scholar, etc. On the ceiling of one chamber there was the inscription Kohanim in Hebrew and Greek, indicating that this was a special burial chamber for priests. The style of the inscriptions, and also various objects which were discovered, indicate that the catacombs of Beth Shearim were built in the first centuries after the destruction of the Second Temple.

From about the same time date the old cemeteries near Jaffa which were uncovered some seventy years ago and where a number of marble tablets was found with inscriptions in Hebrew, Greek and Aramaic. Some of the names mentioned on these tablets are well-known from Talmudic literature. A number of other tombs with inscriptions were uncovered in Caesarea, Sepphoris, etc.

B. *Ancient Synagogues in Palestine, Asia Minor and Greece*: Up to now there have been uncovered remains of a large number of synagogues in various countries of Asia, Africa and Europe. The majority of them, more than forty, are in Palestine, but the most ancient synagogue, dating from the 3rd century B.C.E. was found in Egypt.

Architecture: We know little about the architecture of the oldest synagogues. It is more or less certain that the synagogue consisted of one large, undivided main hall, which served as prayer room, and of a number of side rooms which served as school rooms for children, lodgings for strangers and guests, etc. In addition there was probably a courtyard and an entrance hall.

The basilica form of synagogue probably made its appearance in the 3rd century C.E.: the prayer hall was divided in length by two rows of columns into three naves, the middle one wide and the two side ones narrower. The columns supported a gallery which was reserved for the women's section. This style of architecture, with some slight changes, is typical of the ancient synagogues in Palestine of the later Roman period and after. In other countries, however, the earlier and later types of architecture are found together. The orientation of the ancient synagogues was towards Jerusalem. In Palestine itself the synagogue buildings north of Jerusalem faced south, those south of Jerusalem faced north; in Transjordan, east of Jerusalem, they faced west. There are some synagogues which face towards the east.

This orientation of Palestinian synagogues of the later Roman period is emphasized by the façade which faced Jerusalem. In the wall are usually found three entrances corresponding to the three divisions of the prayer room.

A change appears in the architecture of the synagogues in the Byzantine period; in the wall facing Jerusalem there appears a rounded or square apsis in which the Holy Ark was kept.

In the prayer hall, along the length of the wall, there were benches, often in two sections, on which the worshippers sat. The leaders of the community sat on either side of the Holy Ark. In some synagogues in Palestine there were found stone cathedrae which served as seats for the oldest members of the community. These seats, as we learn from the Midrash, were called קתדרה של משה.

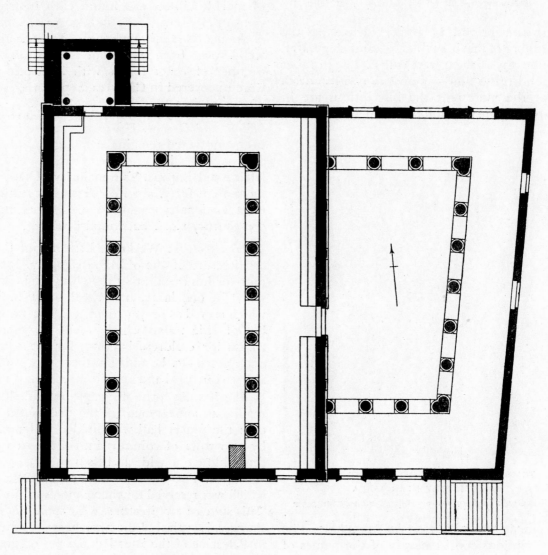

PLAN OF THE SYNAGOGUE AT CAPERNAUM

RECONSTRUCTED NORTH WALL OF THE SYNAGOGUE AT CAPERNAUM

WEST WALL WITH BENCHES IN THE SYNAGOGUE AT CAPERNAUM

RECONSTRUCTED DRAWING OF THE ANCIENT SYNAGOGUE IN KEFAR BIRIM

MOSAIC PAVEMENT OF THE SYNAGOGUE
IN BETH ALPHA

They are mentioned also in the New Testament.

In a few of the ancient synagogues there were found the remains of a platform (בימה) which, it would seem, had no definitely fixed position in those times. As a rule the platform seems to have been placed near the wall facing Jerusalem.

Unfortunately no remains of an ancient Ark of the Law have been found up to the present time. It can be seen from frequent pictures on old Jewish gilt glasses, mosaics, etc., that the Ark was in most cases made of wood, rectangular in shape and with two doors. Of other ritual objects there has been preserved only a stone menorah in the synagogue near the Hot Springs of Tiberias.

Synagogue Art: Research of ancient synagogues reveals that there was no tendency to refrain from decorating the synagogues with figures of animals and even of human beings. Such figures in relief are found, for example, in the stone friezes of the synagogues in Capernaum and Chorazin, dating from the later Roman period. Even more important are the motifs which are found

JEWISH COINS

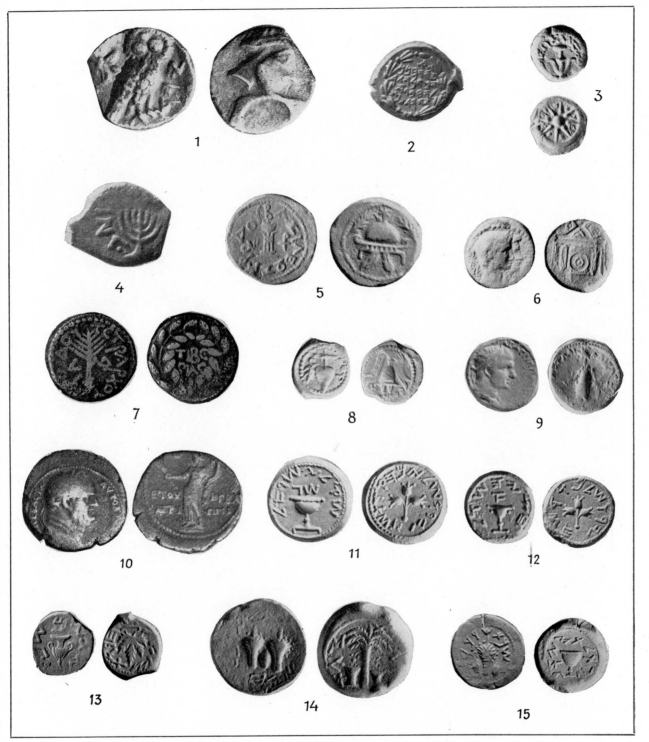

1. Silver coin of the Persian period, inscribed "Yahud" in Hebrew; 2—4. Bronze coins of the Hasmonaean dynasty: 2. John Hyrcanus; 3. Alexander Jannaeus; 4. Antigonus Mattathias; 5—10. Bronze coins of the Herodian dynasty: 5. Herod I; 6. Herod Philip II; 7. Herod Antipas; 8. Herod Archelaus; 9. Agrippa I; 10. Agrippa II; 11—15. Coins struck during the war against the Romans: 11. Silver shekel of the year three of the war; 12. Silver half-shekel of the year one; 13, 14, 15. Bronze coins.

JEWISH COINS

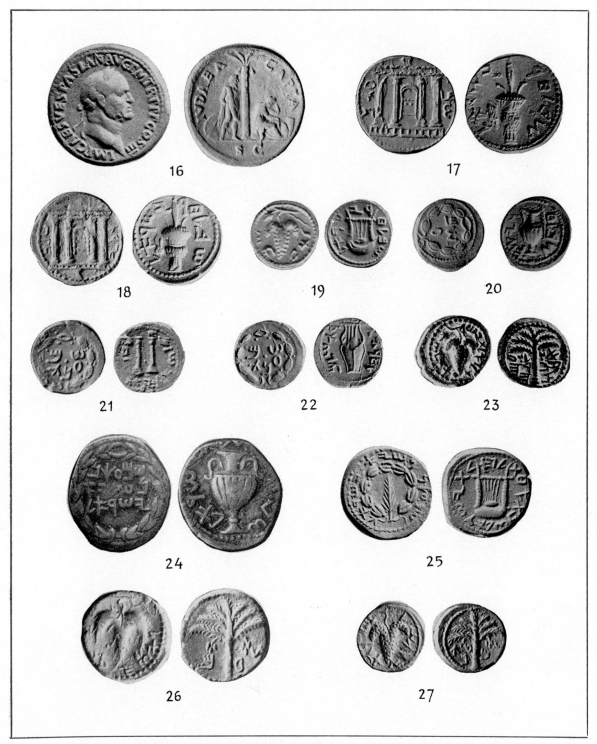

16. Bronze coin struck by Vespasian at Rome after his victory over the Jews; 17—27. Coins struck during the revolt of Bar-Kochba; 17—22. Silver coins; 23—27. Bronze coins.

The coins on this and the preceding page are reproduced in their natural size, except 1, 2 and 4 which are enlarged. All these coins, except 1, are in the possession of the Museum of Jewish Antiquities of the Hebrew University in Jerusalem.

PART OF THE MOSAIC FLOOR IN THE SYNAGOGUE OF JERASH
Animals leaving Noah's Ark

FRESCO FROM THE SYNAGOGUE OF DURA-EUROPOS
The Purim story

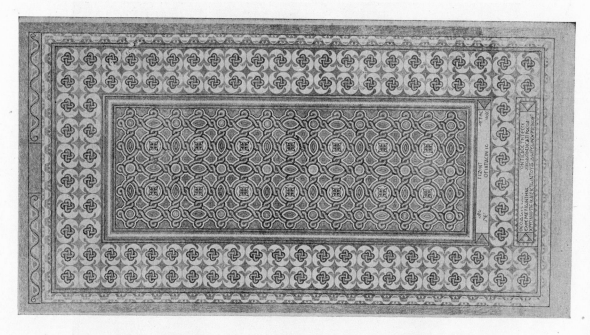

MOSAIC PAVEMENT IN THE ANCIENT SYNAGOGUE OF AEGINA (GREECE)

MOSAIC PAVEMENT IN THE ANCIENT SYNAGOGUE OF HAMMAM-LIF (TUNIS, NORTH AFRICA)

FRESCO FROM THE ANCIENT SYNAGOGUE OF DURA-EUROPOS
Ezekiel's vision of the resurrection of the dry bones

in the mosaics of the Byzantine period. The most important of these were found in Naaran (near Jericho) and Beth Alpha (in the Valley of Jezreel), and in Jerash in Transjordan.

From fragments of painted plaster which were found during the excavations in Palestine, as well as from information from Talmudic sources, it can be seen that the interior walls of the synagogues of the period were also decorated with pictures and designs.

Surprising records concerning the themes of these decorations were found in recent years in the synagogue of Dura-Europos on the Euphrates, in northern Syria. According

FRESCO FROM THE ANCIENT SYNAGOGUE
OF DURA-EUROPOS

Moses with the scroll of the law

MOSAIC INSCRIPTION FROM THE ANCIENT
SYNAGOGUE OF JERASH

Probably mentioning Jewish mosaic workers

to an Aramaic inscription which was uncovered on a ceiling tile, the synagogue dates from 245-246 C.E. By a fortunate circumstance a large part of the walls of the synagogue and all its pictures were preserved in good condition. Of greatest interest is the west wall which was left standing to a height of six meters. At the right of the Holy Ark were representations of Moses at the burning bush and descending from Mount Sinai, and at the left Joshua, the son of Nun, at Jericho and at Gibeon.

The other section of the wall was divided into three panels picturing various biblical stories, among them, for example, the Exodus from Egypt, the Purim story, the childhood of Moses, the anointing of David by Samuel, Aaron and his sons, Moses striking the stone, Jacob blessing his children, and the Ark captured by the Philistines. On the other walls, which were in a less satisfactory state of preservation, there are pictures representing the miracles of the prophet Elijah, etc. There is a specially interesting series of pictures on the north wall representing the prophecies of Ezekiel. Outstanding among them is Ezekiel's vision of the resurrection of the dry bones.

The remains of this ancient synagogue show without doubt that there existed a Jewish popular art in those times. It seems that illuminated Bible manuscripts later served as models for wall decorations and mosaics. This shows that a liberal interpretation prevailed of the biblical ban against the making of images, actually a law forbidding the worship of idols. Later, however, at the end of the Byzantine period, the interpretation changed; as a religious reaction following the persecutions of the Jews in the Byzantine period there developed a stricter

MOSAIC INSCRIPTION IN THE SYNAGOGUE OF HAMMATH BY GADARA

Showing a list of donors to the synagogue

interpretation of the biblical ban and an iconoclastic movement began which destroyed all figures and pictures in the synagogues of Palestine. In Beth Alpha, which was probably destroyed by an earthquake at about the end of the 6th century C.E., the figures of animals and human beings in the mosaic remained intact. In Naaran near Jericho all figures of people and animals were later destroyed by the Jews themselves.

The same is true for the friezes of the synagogue in Capernaum; the sculptures there were later destroyed. It seems that the reaction against sculptured decoration took place before the destruction of mosaics, because the attitude of the Jews was much more strongly opposed to sculpture than to painting.

Inscriptions: In many ancient synagogues inscriptions were found in Hebrew, Aramaic and Greek. The inscriptions were sometimes engraved on the stones in various parts of the building, sometimes incorporated into the mosaics, sometimes also painted on the walls and ceiling. The inscriptions usually consisted of texts which mentioned the names of donors, embellished with various benedictions on their behalf.

Particularly interesting inscriptions of this kind were found on the mosaic floor in the synagogue at Hammath by Gadara. Inscriptions in the local synagogue which dates from the 4th century C.E. give the names of donors and a record of the amount of money they gave. The record of places of origin of the donors is very valuable, since it gives an idea of the distribution of the Jewish settlements nearby. In a few of the synagogues the names of the builders or artists have been preserved. For example, a special inscription in the mosaic floor in Beth Alpha mentions a father and son (Marianos and Chanina) who completed the work.

Brief inscriptions also accompany the pictures on the mosaics. They give the names of the Zodiac signs, the contents of various biblical stories, etc. A few inscriptions contain chronological information. The first inscription of this kind was found in Beth Alpha; it dates the mosaic from a year (the actual date is destroyed) in the reign of the emperor Justinian. More definite is the inscription in Dura-Europos which contains a double date, according to the Seleucid era and the reign of the Roman emperor Philippus.

BIBLIOGRAPHY

A. G. BARROIS, *Manuel d'archéologie biblique*, t. I., Paris, 1939.

THÉODORE REINACH, *Les Monnaies Juives.* Paris, 1888.

L. H. VINCENT, *Canaan d'après l'exploration récente.* Paris, 1907.

W. F. ALBRIGHT, *The Archaeology of Palestine and the Bible.* New York, 1935.

W. F. ALBRIGHT, *From the Stone Age to Christianity.* Baltimore, 1940.

W. F. ALBRIGHT, *Archaeology and the Religion of Israel.* Baltimore, 1942.

F. J. BLISS, *The Development of Palestine Exploration.* London, 1906.

M. BURROWS, *What Mean These Stones?* New Haven, 1941.

A. E. COWLEY, *Aramaic Papyri of the 5th Century* B.C. Oxford, 1923.

S. DAICHES, *The Jews in Babylonia in the Time of Ezra and Nehemiah.* London, 1910.

GEORGE FRANCIS HILL, *Catalogue of the Greek Coins of Palestine.* London, 1914.

H. V. HILPRECHT, *Explorations in Bible Lands.* Edinburgh, 1903.

F. W. MADDEN, *Coins of the Jews.* London 1881 (1903).

C. C. McCOWN, *The Ladder of Progress in Palestine.* New York, 1943.

G. A. REISNER, C. S. FISHER, D. G. LYON, *Harvard Excavations at Samaria*, 1908-1910. Cambridge, Mass., 1924.

E. L. SUKENIK, *Paralipomena Palaestinensia: I. The Oldest Coin of Judea*, in "Journal of the Palestine Oriental Society," 1934, pp. 178-184.

E. L. SUKENIK, *Ancient Synagogues in Palestine and Greece.* Oxford, 1934.

E. L. SUKENIK, *The Ancient Synagogue of El-Hammeh.* Jerusalem, 1935.

H. W. BEYER, H. LIETZMANN, *Die jüdische Katakombe der Villa Torlonia in Rom.* Berlin, 1930.

K. GALLING, *Biblisches Reallexikon.* Tübingen, 1937.

KOHL UND WATZINGER, *Antike Synagogen in Galilaea.* Leipzig, 1916.

S. KRAUSS, *Synagogale Altertümer.* Berlin, Wien, 1922.

M. A. LEVY, *Geschichte der jüdischen Münzen.* Leipzig, 1862.

N. MÜLLER, *Die jüdische Katakombe am Monteverde zu Rom.* Leipzig, 1912.

E. L. SUKENIK, *Jüdische Graeber Jerusalems um Christi Geburt.* Jerusalem, 1931.

E. L. SUKENIK, *Die Wand-Malereien der Synagoge in Dura-Europos.* Schocken Verlag.

G. WATZINGER, *Denkmaeler Palaestinas.* Leipzig, 1933-1935.

J. B. FREY, *Corpus inscriptionum judaicarum.* Roma, 1936.

ב. מייזלר : תולדות המחקר הארכיאולוגי בארץ - ישראל, ירושלים, תרצ"ו.

ב. מייזלר: עונת החפירות השניה בבית שערים (שיך אבריק) — "ידיעות החברה העברית לחקירת ארץ־ ישראל ועתיקותיה", שנה ה', חוברת ג', תשרי תרצ"ח.

מ. נרקיס: מטבעות ארץ - ישראל. ספר ראשון : מטבעות היהודים, ירושלים, תרצ"ו.

א. ל. סוקניק : בית־הכנסת העתיק בבית־אלפא, ירושלים, תרצ"ב.

שמואל רפאלי : מטבעות היהודים. ספר הכולל תולדות המטבעות בישראל ירושלים, 1913.

מ. שובה : הכתובות היווניות מבית שערים, — "ידיעות החברה העברית לחקירת ארץ-ישראל ועתיקותיה", שנה ה', חוברת ג', תשרי תרצ"ח.

THE HISTORY OF THE JEWS IN ANCIENT TIMES

A. Menes

I. THE FIRST THOUSAND YEARS OF JEWISH HISTORY

1. INTRODUCTION

The period of Jewish Antiquity embraces a span of over two thousand years—from about 1500 B.C.E. to the beginning of the 7th century C.E. The rise of Islam and the downfall of the Sassanian empire in the first half of the 7th century had the same significance for the Near East as did the downfall of the Roman empire for Christian Europe. In Jewish history, too, the rise of Islam constitutes that historical turning point which marks the boundary between Antiquity and the Middle Ages, since the overwhelming majority of the Jewish people, up to almost the end of the first millennium of the Common Era, lived in the countries of the Near East.

The history of Israel, however, constitutes more than merely a chapter of the history of the ancient Orient. From its very beginnings the Jewish people was destined to play its own unique part in the history of mankind.

The people of Israel has its origin, according to biblical tradition, in the land between the Tigris and Euphrates, in Mesopotamia. After a considerable period of wanderings, the Israelites enter the land of Canaan, the "Promised Land," which now becomes the land of Israel. In the course of some fifteen centuries the history of the Jewish people is bound up with the destiny of this land—Palestine. However, just as the God of Israel became in time the God of all the peoples of the world, so did the people of Israel, as early as in the time of the Second Commonwealth, take on the character of a world people.

The name "Hebrew," as it is frequently used in the earlier sections of the Bible, had a broad connotation, including also many neighboring peoples of the Israelites—Ammonites, Moabites, Edomites and particularly the nomadic desert tribes such as Ishmaelites, Midianites, etc. The Hebrews were thus connected from the earliest times with the simple and relatively primitive world of the desert as well as with the centers of the most advanced civilization in the ancient world. The name "Israel," which designates the Jews as a separate people, indicates a new period in Jewish history; it began with the events of the exodus from Egypt when the separate Hebrew tribes formed the commonwealth of Israel, and ended with the fall of Samaria, the capital of the kingdom of Northern Israel, at the end of the 8th century B.C.E. After the fall of Samaria the political and spiritual hegemony shifted southward, to the kingdom of Judah, which managed to preserve its political independence until the beginning of the 6th century B.C.E. The name "Judah" (Greek *Ioudaios*; Latin *Iudaeus*) from which the term "Jew" is derived, originally designated only the inhabitants of the territory of Judah; later it assumed a more general meaning and was used in the same sense as the older "Israel." These three designations reflect three separate periods in the history of the Jewish people.

The people of Israel appeared on the stage of world history at a time when the older centers of civilization in Mesopotamia and Egypt had behind them a past of more than two thousand years of advanced cultural life. Although the Israelites learned a good deal from these older cultures, Jewish development was distinguished by the fact that from the very beginning it stood opposed to the dominating cultural currents of the ancient world. The chief task that confronts the historian, therefore, is to determine not only the influence of these foreign cultures, but also the unique and distinctive features which Jewish history presents.

Evidences of human habitation have been found in Palestine and other countries of the ancient Near East dating from as early as the Paleolithic Age. Evidences of a more advanced civilization—such as the beginnings of the art of writing and monumental buildings—make their first appearance in the so-called Chalcolithic Age when copper began to replace stone as the material for tools and weapons. The transition from stone to metal created the basis for the emergence of a highly developed civilization in Mesopotamia and Egypt. The creation of the great Oriental empires in the beginning of the third millennium B.C.E. coincided with the beginning of the Bronze Age. It was in this Bronze Age, 3000 B.C.E. to 1200 B.C.E., that ancient Oriental civilization reached its highest development.

The last half of the second millennium B.C.E. brought with it a number of profound changes in the political, social and spiritual life of Western Asia, changes which marked a radical turning point in the history of civilization. One of the most significant events in this period was the introduction of iron as the principal material for weapons and implements. The most important result of this "industrial revolution" was the fact that it opened up for intensive agricultural use regions which were previously inaccessible and thus drew into the orbit of the advanced cultural life of the times new elements which had formerly lived on the edge of the ancient Oriental civilization.

In the Chalcolithic Age and even later in the Bronze Age, a higher civilization developed, principally in the fertile valleys of the Tigris, Euphrates and Nile rivers. The well-advanced system of irrigation, which made use of the seasonal flooding of these rivers, was the foundation of the entire economic and political life. Water is the key to the entire history of civilization in the countries of North Africa and Western Asia which were blessed with plenty of sun but little moisture. The fertile, watered sections were no more than tiny oases in the almost limitless expanse of desert. The necessary and timely supply and distribution of water was thus the central problem not only for the individual tiller of the soil but for the people as a whole. In these countries the maintenance of the complicated system of canals and dikes had to be taken over by the state. Only a well-organized and centralized government was able to discharge such a task. The individual had no choice other than to become part of a government-controlled system of "planned economy." This led naturally to the development of an administrative and religious bureaucracy which decisively determined the economic, political and spiritual life of the country.

The higher forms of civilization gradually extended to those regions where the only water supply came from the rainfall. A series of technical innovations and improvements during the course of the second millennium B.C.E. made it possible to expand substantially the area of sedentary culture. The greatest achievements in this sphere were made at the close of the Bronze Age and at the beginning of the Iron Age. As a number of archaeologists have properly pointed out, the Israelite settlements in Canaan covered a greater area than was the case with the previous inhabitants. A number of regions which, in the middle and late Bronze Age, had seen no human settlements, were now dotted with a thick network of agricultural communities. The march of civilization proceeded further and further from the fertile valleys to the less fertile mountainous regions. In these newly-opened territories there was plenty of room for individual pioneering initiative; the main problem was how to gather, conserve and properly distribute the heaven-sent rainfall. The art of constructing reservoirs and water cisterns, in such mountainous regions as Syria and Palestine, played perhaps a no smaller role than the art of irrigation in Mesopotamia and Egypt. (Up to very recent times even such a city as Jerusalem was to a large extent dependent on water stored in cisterns.) Fresh spring-water, "living water" as the Bible refers to it, was a rare phenomenon in many sections of Palestine. The well-known archaeologist W. F. Albright in his *From the Stone Age to Christianity* properly points to the importance of the technical advance in the building of cisterns in enabling the Israelites to settle in a number of new regions: "Thanks to the rapidly increasing diffusion of cisterns which were lined with true lime plaster (previously not used) the area of settlement was vastly extended."

The peculiar nature of Palestine from the point of view of its agricultural possibilities is clearly indicated in the Bible:

> For the land, whither thou goest in to possess it, is not as the land of Egypt, from whence ye came out, where thou sowedst thy seed, and wateredst it with thy foot, as a garden of herbs:
> But the land, whither ye go to possess it, is a land of hills and valleys, and drinketh water of the rain of heaven:
> A land which the Lord thy God careth for: the eyes of the Lord thy God are always upon it, from the beginning of the year even unto the end of the year. (Deuteronomy xi, 10-12).

In contradistinction to Mesopotamia and Egypt, where the entire welfare of the country as well as of the individual inhabitant was dependent on the extent to which the state was able to carry out its functions, the governments in Syria and Palestine had much more modest responsibilities. In these latter countries it was even possible for the idea to emerge that a governmental apparatus was not absolutely necessary at all, the welfare of the people depending primarily on whether or not God would send down timely rains. Thus, in times of trial, the eyes of the Israelite peasant were constantly turned towards the heavens.

Next to the peasant it was the shepherd who played the most important part in the development of the unique civilization of Israel. The tiny country of Palestine was characterized by sharp contrasts of terrain and climate, which led to sharp contrasts in the mode of living of its inhabitants. In a number of regions, as for example in Transjordan and the Negeb, animal husbandry

EXAMPLES OF ANCIENT CANAANITE POTTERY PAINTING
Late Bronze Age

was more important even than agriculture. The space devoted in the Bible to the desert traditions and the life of the shepherd illustrates the important part which the semi-nomadic groups played in the ancient history of Israel. It is necessary, however, to avoid giving undue emphasis to the role of this element in Jewish history. The entire question regarding the character and the way of life of the Hebrews in ancient times must now be reconsidered in the light of the newest archaeological discoveries (See *Origin and History of the Jewish Religion* in this volume).

Palestine, the small country on the Mediterranean Sea, which was the principal arena of Jewish history in ancient times, lies at the borders of Asia and Africa. Together with Syria it formed a bridge between Mesopotamia and Egypt, the most important centers of civilization in the world of the ancient Orient. Through its western boundary, the Mediterranean Sea, Palestine was connected with the Aegean world; in the east and northeast it came in constant contact with the nomadic tribes of the desert. Thus this small and fertile region between the Euphrates and the Nile, was, by reason of its geographical situation, in close contact with several distinct civilizations. In trade and commerce this region, the natural meeting place of the three continents of the old world, Asia, Africa and Europe, played a significant role. The most important trade routes between Western Asia and Egypt and the roads which led from Mesopotamia and Arabia to the Mediterranean Sea, cut across Syria or Palestine.

In spite of the strategic central situation of the country, Palestine never became the nucleus of a large empire; its human and material resources were inadequate for such a role. Neither did the geographical configuration of the country favor the development of a central government in the land itself. As is characteristic of many mountainous countries, the dominating tendency in Palestine was towards political fragmentization and particularism. Because of this in-ternal weakness Palestine was almost always politically and to a large extent even culturally dependent on the great neighboring countries. In the so-called Amarna period, in the 14th century B.C.E., Palestine was divided into a number of small city-states which were under the protection of Egypt, although in some parts of the country Egyptian rule was very little in evidence. A similar picture of the political fragmentization of the country is given in the accounts in the Book of Joshua concerning the time of the conquest in the 13th century B.C.E.

Among the various ethnic groups which inhabited the land of Canaan, the dominating population, both in number and influence, were the Canaanites. By language and probably by descent they were closely related to the Israelites. The Canaanites played an extremely important role as the intermediaries between the various cultural spheres of the ancient world. According to the most recent archaeological findings the contribution of the Canaanites, or Phoenicians as they were later called by the Greeks, to civilization in general and their influence on the development of Israel, was a good deal more important than has been hitherto supposed. With some reservations, the Canaanites can be considered as pioneers of a new Western Semitic civilization. This civilization, which encompassed all of Syria and Palestine, is marked by the kinship of language, a common script and to some extent similar living conditions. A characteristic of the Western Semitic peoples during the period under discussion (second millennium B.C.E.) was the "quest for an alphabet," to use the felicitous phrase of the archaeologist C. C. McCown—an expression of the urge to emancipate themselves from the spiritual hegemony of the Babylonian script and civilization which, as late as the 14th century B.C.E., exerted the dominating influence in all of Western Asia. Even the correspondence between the various Asiatic rulers and the Egyptian royal court was carried on in the Babylonian language and the Babylonian cuneiform, as we

Courtesy University Museum, University of Pennsylvania

BASALT PANEL FROM THE MEKAL TEMPLE AT BETH-SHAN, NORTHERN PALESTINE,
15TH CENTURY B.C.E.

The mythological figure of a lion engaged in combat with the
mythological Temple-guardian in the form of a dog

know from the Amarna Letters. In the second half of the second millennium B.C.E., in the Canaanite-Hebrew language sphere, there were developed at least two alphabetical systems: the Ras Shamra script and the so-called Phoenician alphabet. The latter, in a more or less modified form, is the alphabet now in use by most of the civilized world. The invention of the alphabet enormously simplified the art of reading and writing. Instead of the hundreds of characters employed in the highly complicated writing system of the previous time, a system was now evolved which made it possible to give expression to all the richness of human language with a couple of dozen characters. This led in time to a strong democratization of spiritual life. Writing and reading gradually ceased to be the monopoly of the professional scribes; more and more the common people mastered the

Courtesy American Schools of Oriental Research

PAINTED JAR FROM LACHISH
Late Bronze Age

art of reading. It is probably not purely accidental that up to a hundred years ago the biblical writings and the works of Graeco-Roman literature (written in the Greek and Latin variants of the Canaanite-Hebrew alphabet) were the only literary mementos remaining from the ancient world. The entire literary treasures of Mesopotamia and Egypt, on the other hand, were forgotten. It was only the archaeological discoveries of the 19th and 20th centuries which re-

vealed for us the spiritual life of the countries which were the cradle of our present civilization. The invention of the alphabet introduced a continuity in spiritual life uninterrupted up to the present time. Not only the ideas but also the literary works of the great writers and thinkers of Israel, Greece and Rome were thus able to become an integral part of Western civilization.

It was in this transition period—at the end of the Bronze Age and the beginning of the Iron Age—that it fell to Israel's destiny to take its first step on the stage of world history, and it was given to no other people to give expression in such classical form to the tendencies of the new era.

2. EARLY HISTORY

The beginning of Jewish history—the period of the wandering of the Hebrews—which embraces the era from Abraham to Moses, falls entirely within the Bronze Age. The history of the patriarchs, the sojourn of the Israelites in Egypt and their wanderings in the desert are narrated in great detail and with unusual warmth in the Pentateuch. The authors, however, were more concerned with conveying the story of the faith of Israel than of the people of Israel. Religious ideas and motifs, therefore, are given a much greater place in the Pentateuch than in the other historical works of the Bible. Abraham, for example, is not only the forefather of the people of Israel, but he is also—or rather more properly—a prophet. The same emphasis can be found in the narratives of the Exodus, the Sinai events, and the wanderings in the wilderness. In addition, elements of folklore occupy considerable place in many of the tales and narratives of the Pentateuch. For this reason it is frequently difficult to separate the historical kernel from the purely legendary and folkloristic trappings.

It is natural, therefore, that there are marked differences of opinion concerning the interpretation of the biblical accounts dealing with the time of the patriarchs and the exodus from Egypt. Some scholars, indeed, dismiss completely the historical validity of many of the events recounted in the Bible. These critics point to the fact that the biblical narratives were not put into written form until approximately the 9th or 8th century B.C.E. and that there was thus a time-span of five or six hundred years between the events themselves and their recording. Although this extreme criticism is largely disproved by recent archaeological research, it is nevertheless true that the modern scholar must exercise extreme caution in attempting to reconstruct a picture of the early history of Israel on the basis of the narratives in the Bible.

The history of Israel in ancient times, that is, up to the conquest of Canaan, can be divided into three periods: 1) the period of the Patriarchs; 2) the Egypt period; 3) the Mosaic period.

The period of the Patriarchs is narrated in the Bible in the form of a family chronicle. The first eleven chapters of Genesis recount the story of mankind from the creation of the world to the division of peoples according to races, countries and languages. This imposing, universal-historical introduction prepares the Bible reader for the main theme—the history of the people of Israel. According to the popular conceptions of ancient times, each individual nation was considered as an expanding family group, stemming from a common ancestor. The Ishmaelites, for example, were the descendants of a man called Ishmael; the Canaanites, of Canaan, etc. The forefather of the Israelites, according to the biblical tradition, is Israel (Jacob), the grandson of Abraham, who, at God's command, left his home and family in Haran (Northwestern Mesopotamia) in order to settle in the land of Canaan. Most of the narratives in Genesis describe the personal and family life of the three ancestors of the Israelites: Abraham, Isaac and Jacob. The history of the adventures and wanderings of the patriarchs, which ends with the migration of the "children of Israel" into Egypt, was naturally much more than merely a family chronicle to the authors of the biblical accounts.

In some narratives it is quite clear that the patriarchs were considered not only as family heads but as leaders of much larger groups. Most of the modern scholars assume, therefore, that the biblical narratives contain elements of folk recollections mirroring the wanderings of the Hebrews in the early times. The Israelites thus constituted part of a greater Hebrew-Aramaic group which in the second half of the second millennium B.C.E. occupied most of Syria and Palestine. The first migration of the Hebrews into Canaan—in the main a peaceful movement—probably took place about the middle of the second millennium B.C.E. Some of these Hebrews migrated further into Egypt.

We have only scant material from non-biblical sources which might corroborate or supplement the biblical traditions. In many cases, therefore, it is difficult to obtain a clear picture of the historical background as well as of the chronological order of the events which are recounted in the Bible. Of particular importance is the question of the connection between the Habiru (Khapiru), who are mentioned in the cuneiform texts of the beginning of the second millennium B.C.E. and especially in the Nuzi and Amarna texts of the 15th and 14th centuries B.C.E., and the Hebrews of the Bible. In the Amarna texts the Habiru frequently appear as raiders and rebels against the old-established rulers of the Canaanite city-states and the Egyptian authorities. It is recognized by many scholars that the name Habiru refers to a social status rather than to an ethnic group. They appear mostly as landless mercenaries, day-laborers, servants and other socially and economically disoriented or dependent elements, who lived mostly as tolerated aliens in foreign lands. Most competent scholars now consider that the Hebrews were in one way or another related to the Habiru of the cuneiform texts. We are thus justified in revising somewhat the previously held point of view which considered the early Hebrews as an exclusively ethnic group.

It was not primarily their mode of life as much as their social position that distinguished the Habiru, and, as we shall see later, the Hebrews. Nor was it the contrast between the settled peasant and the semi-nomadic shepherd, but the opposition between the independent, self-sustained peasant or town-dweller and the dependent day-laborer, servant, etc. In this connection it is appropriate to note that the anomalous socio-economic status of the early Hebrews can be clearly traced in a large measure in the traditions which are found in the Pentateuch. The patriarchs, for example, were everywhere accepted only as tolerated strangers and were frequently compelled even to leave their new homes as a result of the enmity of the old-established population. Specially illuminating in this connection is the story of Jacob, the "lost Aramaean," as he is designated in Deuteronomy XXVI,5, who was compelled to toil for Laban for years as a bonded servant. Such sojourns of individuals in foreign lands, far from their homes and families, is a characteristic motif in the history of the patriarchs. This motif is by no means typical of genuine nomadic or semi-nomadic tribes. The narrative of Joseph's unique rise to power as well as the accounts of the later enslavement of the children of Israel in Egypt also mirror similar conditions. Much can be learned, too, from the fact that the expression "Hebrews" is frequently used in the Pentateuch to indicate individuals or groups in a socially dependent position.

In addition to the Hebrew tribes in Canaan, most of whom lived in the southern parts of the country, a number of Hebrews settled in Egypt, as has previously been noted. It is hardly likely, as would appear from the biblical tradition, that all the children of Israel left Canaan. As is true in so many other cases, events which concerned only a part of the people have been generalized and applied to the entire people. On the other hand, however, there is no ground to doubt the substance of the account regarding the sojourn of the Israel-ites in Egypt. From time immemorial the fertile soil of the Nile attracted various elements from the poorer neighboring countries—especially in times of famine. This is the reason for the sharp admonitions in various parts of the Pentateuch directed against those desiring to "return" to Egypt. In some cases such aliens even managed to reach positions of importance. Many of them, however, were compelled sooner or later to perform slave labor for the rulers of the country. Thus, for the writers of the Bible, Egypt was a "house of bondage."

The first chapter of Exodus describes in particularly bold colors the misery and heavy labor of the Hebrews in Egypt. The biblical writer then goes on to recount how God heard the lamentations and sighs of the Hebrews, remembered His covenant with Abraham, Isaac and Jacob, and sent a redeemer to them.

But the God who heard the cries of the Hebrews was a God completely unknown to the Israelites at that time; a God whose name they had never even heard. Yahweh, who later became the God of Israel, was originally, it would appear, merely the God of the Hebrew shepherd tribes in the neighborhood of Sinai and Kadesh. But there, too, the Hebrews were not exclusively nomads in the accepted sense of the term. The desert was often a refuge for all discontented and persecuted people for whom there was no longer any place in the "civilized" lands. As can be gathered from the ancient biblical traditions there was in the Sinai area a sanctuary of Yahweh which was generally considered as an asylum and a place of refuge. Yahweh was thus the God-protector of all outcast, persecuted and homeless people, and this is probably the reason that He also became the God of the Hebrews. If it is permissible to draw such conclusions from the laws concerning the Sabbath, the seventh year and the jubilee (the 50th year), which were put into writing considerably later, it would appear that the Yahweh festival, which already at that time had a social character, attracted pilgrims from distant lands. Thus the Yahweh cult began to spread beyond the region of Sinai proper quite early. There is further reason to assume that one of the characteristic features of the Yahweh festival was a temporary dropping off of all social differentiations. We find festivals of a similar nature among other ancient peoples: the Kronia in Greece, the Saturnalia in Rome, etc.

The accounts of the exodus from Egypt and the events of Sinai are dominated by the grandiose figure of the leader and teacher, Moses. Although there are no definite grounds to doubt the historicity of Moses it must be admitted that many of the details concerning his life and accomplishments belong to the field of folklore. For this reason it is possible to reconstruct only in general terms the story of the exodus from Egypt and the wanderings in the desert, and great care must be taken to avoid reconstructions which aim to fill the gaps in the traditions with the products of modern "scientific" phantasy.

According to the Bible, Moses was compelled as a young man to flee from Egypt because of his intercession in behalf of his enslaved brethren. He fled to the desert, to the neighborhood of Sinai, where he met his wife-to-be, Zipporah, the daughter of the Kenite Jethro. This contact between Moses and the semi-nomadic Kenites, a group which played an important part in the history of the Yahweh faith, is especially illuminating. It was at Mount Sinai that God revealed himself to Moses, and entrusted him with the mission of redeeming the people of Israel from Egypt.

These traditions illustrate the great historic role which the Sinai sanctuary played in the fight for liberation of the Hebrews from Egypt. Moses goes to Egypt on his mission, and brings to his brethren the news of their imminent redemption. Accompanied by the elders of the Israelites he conveys to Pharaoh God's demand that the Hebrews be given permission to go to the desert to celebrate the festival of Yahweh, "the God of the Hebrews." Pharaoh denies the demand and orders his overseer to heap more work on the Hebrew slaves:

Ye shall not diminish ought thereof; for they be idle; therefore they cry, saying: Let us go and sacrifice to our God; Let there be more work laid upon the men, that they may labor therein; and let them not regard vain words (Exodus v, 8-9).

Pharaoh's stubborn refusal to give the Hebrews their freedom leads to a direct divine intervention. The struggle between Moses and Pharaoh ends in a series of plagues visited by God on Egypt and the resultant victory of God's messenger. After the last of the plagues the powerful ruler of the Nile empire comes to Moses with the request that he lead the Israelites out of Egypt as soon as possible.

There are important differences of opinion concerning the time of the Exodus. The most probable date, according to the opinion of the majority of scholars, is the first half of the 13th century B.C.E. The decline of the Egyptian empire created a particularly favorable situation for the Hebrew tribes in Egypt itself as well as in the desert of Sinai. The leading role was taken, as we have seen, by the Hebrews of the Sinai Peninsula, and this explains the strong religious element in the tradition of the Exodus as well as of the wanderings in the desert. The central figure here is Moses, the redeemer, leader and teacher of the people. At Sinai he established a religious-national commonwealth which united the tribes of Israel in a common holy covenant with Yahweh. Over the years a chain of legends developed around the Sinai events which completely obscured the true historical picture. The Sinai events did not constitute the completion—as is suggested by the biblical tradition—but rather the beginning of the religious development of Israel. But the very fact of the creation of a religious-national entity and the particular social character of the Yahweh faith had an enormous influence on the entire further development of Jewish history.

Through the Sinai covenant Yahweh became the God of Israel. The confederation of the twelve tribes of Israel, brought about by Moses in the desert, had more of a religious than a political character. Israel's unity found its greatest expression in a common belief in Yahweh and in a number of common observances and rituals. But precisely for this reason the political effects of the Sinai covenant were of far-reaching extent. How far-reaching the political results of a common religious faith could be is illustrated by the history of the Arab tribes in the time of Mohammed, a history which is in many respects similar to the history of the Israelite tribes, in the time of Moses. The confederation of the Israelite tribes or the Yahweh Amphictyony, as it is termed by several modern scholars, from its very inception held its own periodic national festivals. At these festivals, which were held annually, singers and prophets would recite the story of the exodus from Egypt and the divine commandments which God had handed down to Moses at Sinai. A special solemnity characterized the seventh-year festival (Deuteronomy xxxi, 10-13). These celebrations were the sources of the rich literary treasures which, in the course of time, were gathered together in the Torah, the Books of Moses.

The holy covenant between Yahweh and the people of Israel is the first example in recorded history of an entire people adopting a new religious faith. In the biblical traditions the events of Sinai are evaluated in their full significance. According to the Pentateuch God revealed Himself to the patriarchs under the name of Elohim; it was only to Moses that he first disclosed himself as Yahweh. The new divine name is here a symbolical expression of the new era in the history of the manifestation of God to Man. The relations between Yahweh and Israel were not the result of a natural bond, as was the case with other peoples where God and Man always belonged together, but of a holy covenant. It was only after the solemn conclusion of the Sinai covenant that Yahweh became the God of Israel and Israel the

people of Yahweh. The covenant idea therefore occupies a central place in all biblical literature; it is the cornerstone on which rests the entire structure of the religious, ethical and social ideas of Yahwism. The "Book of the Covenant" or the "Words of the Covenant" are terms frequently used for parts of the Pentateuch or for the entire Torah of Moses. The Holy Ark, which, according to biblical tradition, accompanied the Israelites in their wanderings, is often referred to as the "Ark of the Covenant." The Israelites, as we have seen, adopted the Yahweh faith as a voluntary act of free choice. With this act Yahwism lost its primitive qualities of a nature faith and took on a social-ethical character. More and more Yahweh became the God of righteousness and justice, the protector of the weak and helpless and the guardian of the sanctity of covenants. The Torah took on more and more the significance of a sacred constitution, of a divine Magna Charta, which embodied not only man's duties to God but also guaranteed the sacred rights of the common man.

3.   CONQUEST OF CANAAN AND THE PERIOD OF THE JUDGES

The conquest of Canaan was not accomplished as quickly as is to be inferred from the accounts in the Book of Joshua, but was a long-continuing process which began with the first settlements of the Hebrews in the 15th and 14th centuries B.C.E. and ended only in the time of David and Solomon, at the beginning of the 10th century B.C.E. The main phase of the conquest, however, took place around the middle of the 13th century B.C.E., that is, after the Exodus, when the Hebrew tribes were welded together by Moses as a religious and national unity. After a period of wanderings in the desert the Israelites invaded the land of Canaan and occupied a considerable portion of the country by force of arms. At first this occupation was confined mainly to the hill country which was very sparsely populated. However, most of the fortified cities in the fertile valleys and plains remained for a long time in the hands of the Canaanites. The account of the conquest in Judges 1 enumerates a number of places which the Israelites had not succeeded in capturing: "And the Lord was with Judah, and he drave out the inhabitants of the mountain; but could not drive out the inhabitants of the valley, because they had chariots of iron." The same was true of the northern tribes, Ephraim, Manasseh and the others, which were unable to subdue such places as Gezer, Megiddo, Beth-shan, etc. This account of the conquest is in contrast to the standard tradition in Joshua which states: "So Joshua took the whole land, according to all that the Lord said unto Moses; and Joshua gave it for an inheritance unto Israel." (Joshua XI, 23).

In the valleys and plains, where the iron chariots of the Canaanites were able to maneuver freely, the poorly armed Israelites were unable to overcome their adversaries; their military superiority was confined to the hills. Centuries later we find the officers of the Aramaean army explaining to their king, Ben-hadad, the reason for their defeat at the hands of the Israelites: "And the servants of the king of Syria said unto him, their gods are gods of the hills; therefore they were stronger than we; but let us fight against them in the plain, and surely we shall be stronger than they." (I Kings XX, 23). Some of the Canaanite cities concluded peaceable agreements with the Israelites, but there were also cases where the Canaanites retained their dominant positions and even compelled the Israelite peasants to pay tribute. On the whole, however, the Israelites strengthened their positions more and more and continued to expand into wider areas. This expansion was, for the most part, not a result of military victory, but of peaceful colonization. It was not the sword, but the plough which finally decided who the rulers of the land were to be. Large areas of idle land and forest regions were for the first time brought under cultivation by Israelite peasants.

Joshua XVII; 16-18 vividly describes the nature of this peaceable expansion:

And the children of Joseph said, The hill is not enough for us: and all the Canaanites that dwell in the land of the valley have chariots of iron; both they who are of Beth-shan and her towns, and they who are of the valley of Jezreel.

And Joshua spoke unto the house of Joseph, even to Ephraim and to Manasseh, saying, Thou art a great people, and hast great power: thou shalt not have one lot only:

But the mountain shall be thine; for it is a wood, and thou shalt cut it down ...

The conquest of Palestine by the Israelites coincides, as already noted, with the beginning of the Iron Age (1200-1000 B.C.E.) and the consequent introduction of iron implements and other technical improvements which made it possible to cultivate areas previously inaccessible for agriculture. The technically backward Israelites were quick to learn from their neighbors, the Canaanites and the Philistines, and made good use of the new technical advantages to expand the area of agricultural settlement.

The assumption, based mainly on the account in the Book of Joshua, that the Israelites, at the time of the conquest, exterminated all of the previous population, is completely at variance with the well-attested historical facts known to us from other parts of the Bible. There were undoubtedly cases, during the conquest and after, when the entire populations of particular places were annihilated. These, however, were exceptions. On the whole the Canaanite element gradually disappeared not through physical annihilation but through a process of assimilation. There is documentary evidence, for example, that the Canaanite population of Jerusalem, which was occupied in the time of David, not only remained in the country but even retained their land holdings. Many foreigners served in David's army, among them Uriah the Hittite. Even in the time of Solomon a substantial number of Canaanites lived in Palestine; it may be mentioned that Hiram, who designed and executed all the elaborate metal work in the Holy Temple,

IVORY RELIEF CARVINGS FROM MEGIDDO, PROBABLY PART OF CHAIR-FRAME, ABOUT 1300-1200 B.C.E.

Above: Human figures and ducks

Below: Battle scene with chariots

was the son of a Jewish mother and a Phoenician father (I Kings VII, 13, 14).

At the same time as the Israelites occupied most of Canaan other Hebrew-Aramaic tribes occupied neighboring territories: Edomites, Moabites, Ammonites settled in Transjordan, and Aramaean tribes in Syria. The Canaanites, who had previously constituted the ruling group in all the territory of Syria and Palestine, were now confined to a comparatively small area on the seacoast and in a few inland points. At the same time, about the beginning of the 12th century B.C.E., a wave of migration from the west, from the Aegean Islands, brought to Palestine the Philistines, who occupied the southern coastal plain.

In the first half of the 12th century B.C.E., at the beginning of the period of the Judges, the situation in Palestine was approximately as follows: The tribes of Simeon and Judah were settled in the south; north of Judah there was a chain of Canaanite cities, Gezer, Jerusalem, Gibeon and others, separating the southern part from the center of the country, the region of Ephraim and Manasseh, which, however, was not entirely occupied by the Israelites. Farther to the north, the Canaanites occupied the region of the Jezreel valley, while even farther, in the region north later known as Galilee, the tribes of Asher, Zebulun, Dan, Naphtali and Issachar, settled. In Transjordan the tribes of Reuben, Gad, and a part of the tribe of Manasseh settled. Their neighbors to the east and south were the Ammonites and Moabites. The Edomites settled the region south of the Salt Sea. The southern part of the Mediterranean coast line was occupied by the Philistines; the northern

Courtesy Oriental Institute, University of Chicago

IVORY BOX FROM MEGIDDO, CARVED IN RELIEF, SHOWING FIGURES OF SPHINXES AND LIONS
1300-1200 B.C.E.

part of the coast line and the port cities were in the hands of the Phoenicians. The Israelites thus occupied the greater part of the country, but most of the economically and strategically important points were still controlled by the Canaanites and Philistines.

It is clear, therefore, that the Israelites were not the sole masters in the country. The position of the various ethnic groups was far from being stabilized. At the same time as the Israelites were encountering the resistance of the Canaanites, they had from time to time to defend themselves against the attacks of the newcomers in the east, Ammon and Moab, and of the Philistines in the west. These difficulties were intensified by the fact that precisely at the time they were occupied in settling the country the tendency towards political particularism significantly increased. The territory which the Israelites occupied was, as we have seen, geographically divided into four practically isolated parts. The various tribes, therefore, lived separately from one another and it was only rarely that they engaged in common military or political undertakings. From time to time individual figures appeared on the scene, whose boundless energy, heroism and moral authority managed to achieve a temporary unification of large sections of the people for the purpose of warding off threatening dangers. These "Judges," as they are called in the Bible, were naturally unable to carry out the functions of a well-organized central government. They were "charismatic" leaders, their power depending exclusively on their personal influence and on the extent to which they were able to arouse the people and to lead them.

It is not to be wondered at, therefore, that the Canaanites, thanks to their better developed military technique, were able from time to time to strengthen their positions. This was especially true of the militarily powerful Canaanite group in the Valley of Jezreel. The end of the 12th century B.C.E. witnessed an alliance between the Israelite tribes in Central and Northern

Palestine for the purpose of overthrowing the yoke of the Canaanites. The great battles of Taanach and Megiddo, which are so eloquently celebrated in the Song of Deborah, one of the oldest of the biblical documents, decisively determined who was to remain the master of the country.

The Song of Deborah praises the tribes, Issachar, Zebulun, Naphthali, Ephraim, Manasseh and Benjamin, who responded to the call of Deborah and Barak, the leaders of the Jewish army, and went out to battle against the oppressors. It bitterly reproaches the other tribes, Reuben, Gad, Asher and Dan, for not supporting the fight for freedom. In this decisive battle at Taanach "by the waters of Megiddo" in the Valley of Jezreel, the Israelite peasants destroyed the Canaanite army and thus became the dominating power in Palestine. The Canaanites were now doomed to disappearance as an independent national group and as time went on became absorbed among the Israelites.

From this time on the Israelites had to defend themselves chiefly against external enemies. Under the leadership of Ehud of the tribe of Benjamin and Jephthah of the tribe of Gilead, the Israelites fought successfully against Moab and Ammon. Gideon, of the tribe of Manasseh, put an end to the plundering attacks of the nomadic Midianites who laid waste the fields and flocks of the Israelite peasants. During this time of "charismatic" leaders, the so-called Judges, Gideon's son Abimelech was the first to attempt to introduce a personal rule into Israel and to establish a hereditary dynasty. He set up his own guard of mercenaries, killed off all of his brothers, and became ruler of a large area in the center of the country with Shechem as his capital. His support came mainly from the declassed elements among the Israelites and from the older Canaanite aristocracy. The new regime was not destined to last long. Sharp internal conflicts broke out, and Abimelech fell in battle during the siege of the city of Thebez.

4. THE RISE OF THE MONARCHY

At the end of the 12th century B.C.E. a new and dangerous enemy appeared in the western part of Palestine. The Philistines, who, since the beginning of the century, had occupied the southern coastal plain, began to penetrate more deeply into the country. The Israelites resisted, but the Philistines, whom the biblical accounts describe as well-trained and heavily armed, were much more advanced in military techniques. As a result the Israelites were often compelled to give ground and some areas of the country were completely subjugated. The struggle against the foreign masters frequently took on the character of partisan uprisings, as can be gathered from the legends concerning Samson who is described as fighting alone and unarmed against the enemy. The first attempt at a united Israelite action against the Philistines ended in catastrophe. The national shrine, the "Ark of the Covenant," was captured and the religious center of Shiloh, the site of the Yahweh Amphictyony, was destroyed. The victors now became the rulers of the entire country. To prevent uprisings they quartered their garrisons at strategic points. That they took steps to deprive the people of weapons is also indicated in I Samuel XIII:19.20: "Now there was no smith found throughout all the land of Israel: for the Philistines said, Lest the Hebrews make them swords or spears. But all the Israelites went down to the Philistines, to sharpen every man his share, and his coulter, and his axe and his mattock." This compulsion for the Israelites to go to the Philistines to have their agricultural implements sharpened was also a form of tribute which they were compelled to pay to the rulers.

The yoke of the Philistines greatly weakened the tribe organization with its innate particularistic tendency, and helped to forge the national unity which, under the existing conditions, was possible only under a monarchy. It became clear that only a common policy would serve to free Israel from alien rule and secure national independence.

This feeling was maintained through the patriotic circles of the so-called Sons of the Prophets and also received the sanction of the old seer or prophet, Samuel. The decisive event which resulted in the establishment of the monarchy was the war with the Ammonites who sought to take advantage of the weakness of Israel in order to occupy the key fortress of Jabesh-gilead in Transjordan. In this war all of the Israelites came

POTTERY FRAGMENT FROM MEGIDDO,
SHOWING ISRAELITE WARRIORS
From period of the Judges

to the aid of their brethren across the Jordan and the victory that followed over the Ammonites evoked a spirit of national enthusiasm. Saul ben Kish, of the tribe of Benjamin, who had particularly distinguished himself in the relief of Jabesh-gilead, was crowned king, about 1030 B.C.E., and under his leadership Israel began its war of freedom against the Philistines.

The Philistines suffered a severe defeat in the battle near Michmash and for a time the land was cleared of its foreign rulers. Saul now also occupied the territory of the Gibeonites, a number of Canaanite cities which, according to the biblical tradition, as early as the time of Joshua had concluded a sacred peace treaty with the Israelites. As a result the southern and the central regions of Palestine were now united.

During his entire reign Saul remained a man of war; in spite of his earlier victories the struggles with the Philistines did not abate. This was probably the reason that he was unable to consolidate his authority in Israel. In the later years of his reign an open rebellion broke out. David, a young hero from Judah, who had distinguished himself in the war against the Philistines, became the leader of all the discontented elements. He stayed for some time in the Negeb but was finally compelled to abandon the territory of Israel and, together with his followers, went over to the territory of the Philistines. The Philistines took advantage of the favorable situation and again began a war against Israel. This time they attacked from the north, and concentrated their military forces in the Jezreel region. The Israelites suffered an overwhelming defeat near the mountain of Gilboa; Saul took his own life so as not to fall alive into the hands of the enemies. His three sons fell in the battle and the remnants of the Israelite army fled (1010 B.C.E.). Again the Philistines became the rulers of the country; only the region of Transjordan remained free.

5. DAVID AND SOLOMON
1010-930 B.C.E.

The catastrophic defeat at Gilboa did not entirely obliterate the results of Saul's reign. The tribal particularism of the time of the Judges was liquidated and after a relatively short period of internal wars the national unity was re-established. This is the more remarkable inasmuch as the Philistines made all possible efforts to strengthen the centrifugal currents in Israel. In spite of this no serious attempt was made to abolish the institution of the monarchy. After the tragic death of Saul his young son Ishbaal was proclaimed king at Mahanaim in Transjordan, apparently the only region in Israel which was free from Philistine interference. In the southern part of the country, however, David, with probably the consent of the Philistines, established a separate kingdom, Judah, with Hebron as its capital. In the struggle which followed between Ishbaal and David the latter strengthened his position continually not only through military victories but to a large extent through skilful diplomacy. The steadily growing influence and popularity of David led to defections in Ishbaal's own court. After several years of internecine wars the weak heir of Saul was assassinated by two of his own servants. The representatives of all the tribes now gathered at Hebron, signed a treaty with David, and anointed him king over all of Israel.

The re-unification of Israel and Judah, under the leadership of so strong a personality as David, was a life-and-death challenge to the domination of the Philistines in Palestine. Their reaction was immediate. They attacked David's army but could not prevail against the united strength of all of Israel. After a long struggle David won the upper hand and cleared the enemy from the territory of Israel.

After defeating the Philistines and securing his western borders, David turned to the task of destroying the last strongholds of the Canaanites. Jerusalem, the powerful fortress of the Jebusites, which stood in the way of the unification of the south with the north, was captured and, turning northward, David occupied the region of the Jezreel valley. With these victories the entire territory of Israel from Dan to Beersheba became united.

Hebron, which lay far in the south, could no longer serve as the center of a kingdom which extended to the sources of the Jordan. As his principal city, therefore, David chose Jerusalem, which served at the same time as an important strategic point and a junction between the south and the north. In order to enhance the significance of Jerusalem as a spiritual center, the Ark of the Covenant, the symbol of the Yahweh Amphictyony, was brought to the capital, which in this way also became the religious center for all of Israel.

By territorial extent as well as by the size of its population, Israel was now the largest kingdom in the region between the Nile and the Euphrates, a circumstance which gave David the possibility for further expansion. The entire region from Eziongeber, the port on the Gulf of Aqabah in the south, up to Damascus in the north, was conquered. As a result David acquired control of the important trade routes which led from Arabia and Mesopotamia to the Mediterranean Sea. In Palestine proper only the coastline remained in the hands of the Philistines and the Phoenicians. The national unity, which, up to the time of Samuel had been hardly more than an abstract concept and which during the reign of Saul was never realized to its full extent, now became a political reality. The kingdom of Israel now reached its highest power and its widest geographical extent. Later generations properly evaluated the enormous accomplishments of David, and it is not surprising that he became one of the most beloved figures of Jewish tradition and that the David dynasty managed to survive even the downfall of the kingdom of Judah.

David was less fortunate in his internal policies. In the early years of his reign, and especially while he still led the struggle against Saul, he found his principal support among the lower sections of the population. Gradually, however, he began to organize the government after the pattern of other Oriental kingdoms, with a standing army, a ramified governmental apparatus, taxes, etc. For military and tax purposes David ordered a general census of the population to be taken, over the strong protests of the people who had never been accustomed to the type of bureaucratic supervision and regimentation common in the ancient Orient. The growing dissatisfaction of large sections of the people prepared the soil for a series of internal conflicts culmi-

Courtesy Oriental Institute, University of Chicago

WATER TANK MADE OF MUD-BRICKS IN STABLE COURTYARD AT MEGIDDO

About 950 B.C.E.

nating in the uprising of Absalom, David's favorite son and heir-presumptive to the throne, and in the rebellion of the Benjaminite, Sheba ben Bichri. Shortly before David's death sharp conflicts arose in the royal court over the succession to the throne. David's battle comrades of his earlier years, with the old general Joab and the priest Abiathar at their head, supported the candidacy of David's eldest son Adonijah. Another faction, consisting mainly of the new dignitaries who had risen to high office during David's reign, supported the king's favorite son, Solomon. This latter group, supporters of the new political tendencies, prevailed, and Solomon, with David's blessing, was crowned king of Israel.

results not only of court intrigues and court revolutions. The general political and economic development of Israel since the rise of the monarchy and especially since the advent of the David empire had to lead irrevocably to the crystallization of a centralized autocratic regime on the pattern of the other Oriental countries. In this period of Antiquity a form of popular democracy could not be realized except within the framework of a comparatively small country, as is evidenced by the development of ancient Greece and Rome.

In various passages the Bible describes the period of Solomon as a golden age when the Jews lived each under his own grapevine and under his own fig tree. Externally,

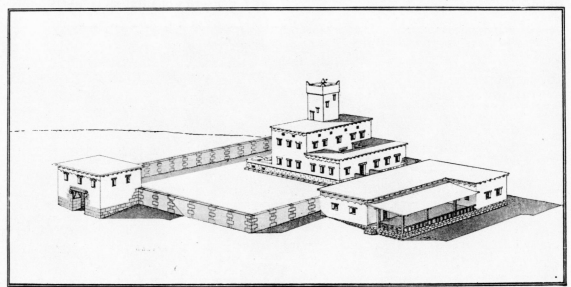

Courtesy Oriental Institute, University of Chicago

RECONSTRUCTION OF GOVERNOR'S PALACE AT MEGIDDO
About 950 B.C.E.

The centralized autocratic tendency, which had emerged strongly in the second half of David's reign, now reached its zenith. The supporters of the old traditions, who wanted to continue to guard the popular institutions of the previous eras, were deposed from office; some, among them Joab and Adonijah, even forfeited their lives. Control over the country's affairs now passed into the hands of the royal administration. These events were, naturally, the

Solomon's reign was such a golden age. Israel occupied a highly important place in the world and entered into the circle of the great Powers. The friendly political and economic relations with Tyre which had been established in the time of David, were now developed further. An alliance was concluded with Egypt, and Solomon even married one of the daughters of the Egyptian king, receiving as a dowry the important city of Gezer, which had a short time

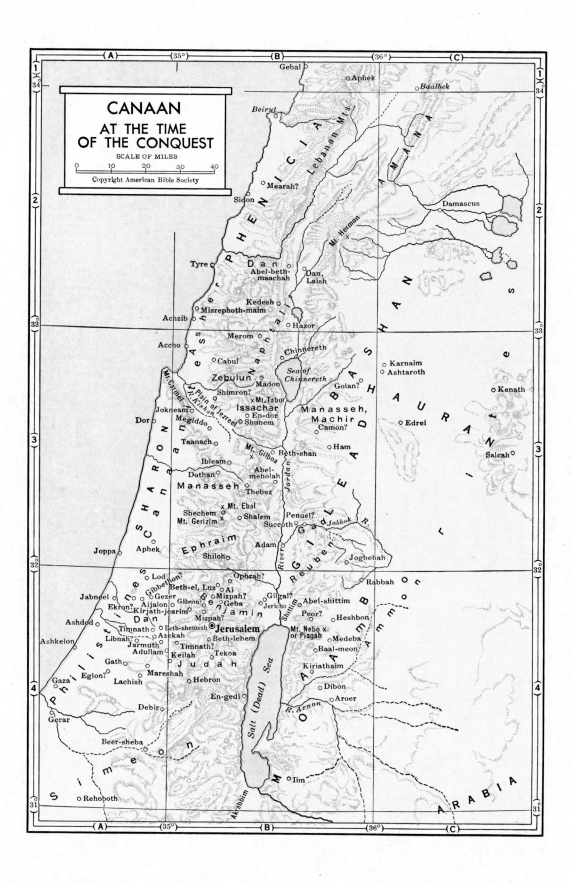

CANAAN
AT THE TIME OF THE CONQUEST
SCALE OF MILES

0   10   20   30   40

Copyright American Bible Society

(A)   (35°)   (B)   (36°)   (C)

Gebal

Aphek

Baalbek

Beirut

P H E N I C I A

Lebanon Mts.

A M A N A

Mearah?

Sidon

Damascus

Mt. Hermon

Tyre   Dan   Dan, Laish

Abel-beth-maachah

Kedesh

B A S H A N

Misrephoth-maim

Achzib   Hazor

Merom

Accho   Chinnereth

Cabul   Sea of Chinnereth

Karnaim

Ashtaroth

Zebulun   Madon   Golan?   H A U R A N   Kenath

Shimron?   x Mt. Tabor

Mt. Carmel   Plain of Jezreel   Issachar   Manasseh,   Edrei

R. Kishon   En-dor   Machir

Jokneam   Shunem   Camon?

Dor   Megiddo   G I L E A D

Taanach   Mt. Gilboa   Ham   Salcah

x   Beth-shan

Ibleam

Dothan   Abel-meholah

Thebez

M A N A S S E H

x Mt. Ebal

Shechem   Shalem   Penuel?

Mt. Gerizim x   Succoth   Jabbok R.   Gad

Ephraim   Adam   Reuben

Joppa   Aphek

Shiloh   Jogbehah

Ophrah?   Rabbah

Lod   Gibbethon?   Beth-el, Luz   Ai   River Jordan

Jabneel   Gezer   Mizpah?   Gilgal?   Abel-shittim

Ekron?   Aijalon   Gibeon   Geba   Jericho   Peor?   Heshbon

Ashdod   Kirjath-jearim   Benjamin   Shittim

Dan   Mizpah?   A M M O N

Ashkelon   Timnath   Beth-shemesh   Jerusalem   Mt. Nebo x   Medeba

Libnah?   Azekah   Beth-lehem   or Pisgah

Jarmuth?   Timnath?   Baal-meon

Gath   Adullam   Keilah   Tekoa   Kiriathaim

Gaza   Eglon?   Mareshah   Judah   Hebron   Dibon

Lachish   M O A B

En-gedi   Aroer

Gerar   Debir   R. Arnon

Salt (Dead) Sea

Beer-sheba

S i m e o n   Iim

Rehoboth   Akrabbim   A R A B I A

Sharon   Canaan   Philistines

(A)   (35°)   (B)   (36°)   (C)

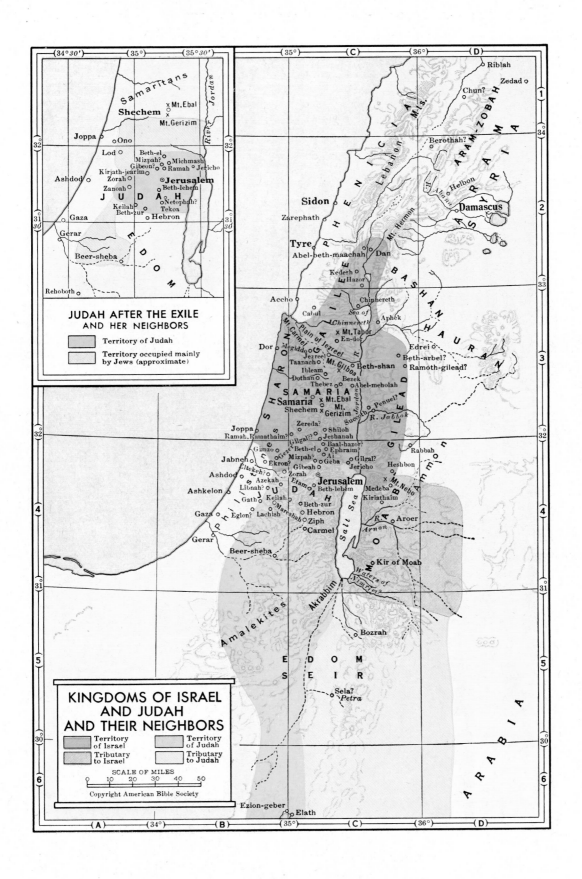

JUDAH AFTER THE EXILE
AND HER NEIGHBORS

Territory of Judah

Territory occupied mainly
by Jews (approximate)

Inset map labels: Samaritans, Shechem, x Mt. Ebal, Mt. Gerizim, Joppa, Ono, Lod, Beth-el, Mizpah?, Gibeon?, Michmash, Kirjath-jearim, Ramah, Jericho, Zorah, Jerusalem, Zanoah, Beth-lehem, JUDAH, Ashdod, Keilah, Netophah?, Beth-zur, Tekoa, Gaza, Hebron, Gerar, Beer-sheba, EDOM, Rehoboth, River Jordan

KINGDOMS OF ISRAEL
AND JUDAH
AND THEIR NEIGHBORS

Territory
of Israel

Tributary
to Israel

Territory
of Judah

Tributary
to Judah

SCALE OF MILES

0   10   20   30   40   50

Copyright American Bible Society

Main map labels: Riblah, Zedad, Chun?, ARAM-ZOBAH, ASSYRIA, Berothah?, Sidon, PHOENICIA, Lebanon Mts., Mt. Hermon, Helbon, Abana, Damascus, Zarephath, Tyre, Abel-beth-maachah, Dan, BASHAN, HAURAN, Kedesh, Hazor, Accho, Chinnereth, Sea of Chinnereth, Aphek, Cabul, Edrei, Beth-arbel?, Dor, Mt. Carmel, Plain of Jezreel, Mt. Tabor, En-dor, Megiddo, Jezreel, Beth-shan, Ramoth-gilead?, Taanach, Mt. Gilboa, Ibleam, Bezek, Dothan, Thebez, Abel-meholah, SAMARIA, Samaria, Mt. Ebal, Mt. Gerizim, Shechem, Penuel?, Succoth, R. Jabbok, GILEAD, SHARON, Joppa, Zereda?, Shiloh, Jeshanah, Ramah, Ramathaim?, Gilgal?, Baal-hazor?, Gimzo, Gezer, Beth-el, Ephraim, Rabbah, Jabneh, Ekron?, Mizpah?, Ai, Gilgal?, AMMON, Eltekeh?, Gibeah, Geba, Heshbon, Ashdod, Zorah, Jericho, Azekah, Etam?, Jerusalem, Ashkelon, Libnah?, Keilah, Beth-lehem, Medeba, Mt. Nebo, Gath, JUDAH, Kiriathaim, PHILISTIA, Eglon?, Mareshah?, Beth-zur, MOAB, Gaza, Lachish, Hebron, Ziph, Aroer, Gerar, Carmel, Arnon, Salt Sea, Kir of Moab, Beer-sheba, Waters of Nimrim, Akrabbim, Amalekites, EDOM, SEIR, Bozrah, Sela?, Petra, ARABIA, Ezion-geber, Elath

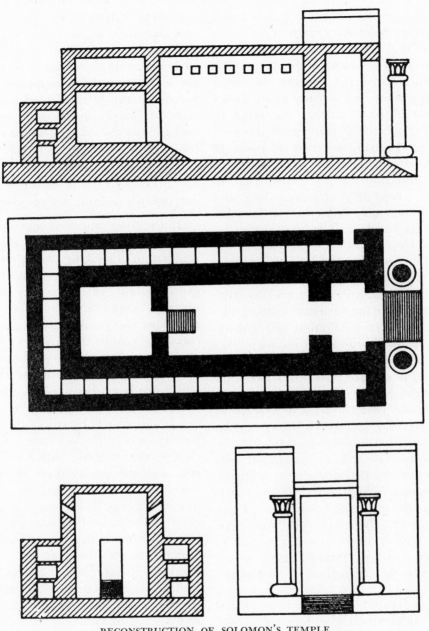

RECONSTRUCTION OF SOLOMON'S TEMPLE
By C. Watzinger

before been conquered by the Egyptians. With the help of Phoenician artisans and architects a magnificent royal palace and various administrative buildings were constructed and Jerusalem took on the imposing appearance of a royal capital. Of particular importance was the erection of the Temple of Jerusalem, known also as the Temple of Solomon, which inaugurated a new epoch in the history of the Yahweh cult. The military organization of Israel was also thoroughly modernized, the most striking innovation being the introduction of war chariots. Solomon also constructed a number of fortresses and built stables and storehouses for his garrisons in many parts of the country. Recent excavations have brought to light at Megiddo remnants of these stables which were large enough to accommodate about 450 horses.

The long period of peace which Israel enjoyed under Solomon's reign enormously stimulated the economic development of the country. The most important trade routes which traversed western Palestine and Transjordan had already been under the control of Israel during the reign of David. Through the port of Ezion-geber on the Gulf of Aqabah, Solomon, in cooperation with Hiram, king of Tyre, was now able to send out trading expeditions to Ophir, the "land of gold." According to I Kings, Solomon also carried on a lucrative trade in horses and chariots.

This, however, was only one side of the picture. The imposing but excessively costly building program, the standing army, the elaborate royal administration, and the large royal harem after the Oriental fashion (according to tradition Solomon had a thousand wives) burdened the people with taxes and corvees which were beyond the resources of the country. In order to obtain 120 talents of gold Solomon was even compelled to cede twenty cities in Galilee to his ally, Hiram, a fact which illustrates the severe financial troubles which beset Solomon's administration. For taxation purposes Israel was now divided into twelve administrative regions which only partly corresponded to the old tribe boundaries. Thus, in the space of two generations, Israel traversed the road from the popular monarchy of the first years of David's reign to the typical Oriental despotism of Solomon's rule.

The burdensome political and social pressure undermined the prestige of the David dynasty and shook the political unity of Israel to its foundations. The situation became even more critical since in neighboring Egypt a new dynasty had come to power which radically changed the prevailing political orientation towards Israel. The new rulers on the banks of the Nile were not disposed to tolerate a too-strong neighbor in Palestine and therefore in every manner possible they gave support to the particularist currents in Solomon's empire. The first uprising broke out in the outlying regions of Palestine, in Edom to the south and Damascus to the north, through which the most important trade routes ran. Also in Israel itself there was an uprising under the leadership of Jeroboam ben Nebat, who was in charge of the forced laborers of the tribe of Joseph. Jeroboam's attempt failed and he was forced to flee the country and find a place of refuge in Egypt.

6. INTERNAL LIFE IN ISRAEL IN THE PERIOD OF THE JUDGES AND THE UNITED MONARCHY

In the three hundred years that followed the exodus from Egypt, the people of Israel underwent a striking evolution. The semi-nomadic Hebrew shepherds and the Habiru groups—most of them day-laborers and servants, depending for their elementary rights on the protection of patrician landowners—became the masters of a country with an ancient culture and passed over to new forms of economic and social life. More and more Israel became an agricultural nation, and although in some places—in Southern Judah and in Transjordan—animal husbandry was still dominant, this did not change the general character of the country; agriculture played the most important role and stamped its impress on the entire mode of living. The average Israelite of the time of David and Solomon was a peasant who felt himself attached to the soil and saw agriculture and the peasant's life as the natural condition of man. The oldest biblical traditions of the creation of man and his expulsion from Paradise are summed up in the passage in Genesis:

> In the sweat of thy face shalt thou eat bread, till thou return unto the ground; for out of it wast thou taken: for dust thou art, and unto dust shalt thou return.

The verses reflect the pessimism of a people toiling unceasingly to cultivate the unyielding soil and dreaming of the lost Paradise. The annual Israelite festivals and the commandments of the Torah, too, are practically all bound up with the life of the peasant and with the rhythm of agricultural labor.

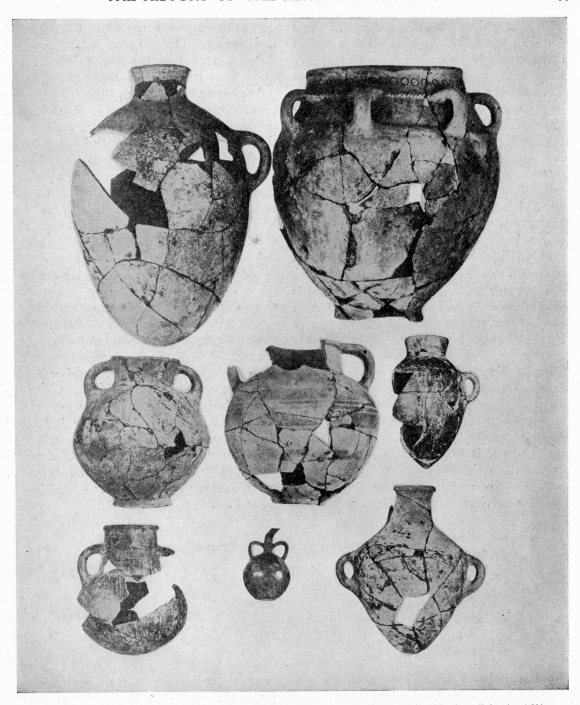

TYPES OF JARS FOUND AT MEGIDDO
About 1000 B.C.E.

In the course of time the Israelites also became masters in the towns. These were small settlements, into which no more than a few hundred families could be crowded. The more important centers—the principal cities—were, of course, considerably larger both in area and population.

The first period of the Israelite occupation of Palestine brought with it a visible decline in the field of technical culture. It took a long time for the Israelites to catch up with the old Canaanite civilization in this respect. Israelite pottery and masonry were considerably inferior, and the same was true of the city fortifications. This was largely due to the fact that whereas the Canaanite city-states had a feudal organization, so that labor could be commandeered for the construction of patrician palaces and public buildings, the entire social order in Israel functioned on a more democratic basis, and it was not easy to compel the peasant to pay high taxes or to work for the rulers. In the time of the Judges "there was no king in Israel; every man did that which was right in his own eyes."

Agricultural technique, however, advanced considerably in the early Iron Age, so that the area of cultivated land greatly increased and a number of new settlements sprang up, especially in the hill country and in Transjordan. The comparatively large natural increase of the peasant population in the hill country was the most important factor in giving the Israelites dominance over the Canaanites and Philistines. The Song of Deborah, composed about the end of the 12th century B.C.E., makes reference to 40,000 adult Israelite men fit for military service; the total Israelite popula-

tion at the time can therefore be estimated as approximately 200,000. In the time of David and Solomon the population of Palestine was at least four to five times greater.

We have comparatively little information concerning urban industry in Palestine for this period. The earliest crafts to be mentioned in the Bible are tinkers, potters, smiths, and musicians. A large number of industrial articles were manufactured for their own use by the peasants themselves, and various luxury and metal articles were brought in from outside the country. This situation changed radically in the time of David and Solomon, when not only the general development of the Near East but the development of Israel itself created the necessary conditions for substantial economic progress. The rapid development of trade during Solomon's reign took place at the same time as the phenomenal expansion of the Phoenicians in trade and seafaring activities in the 10th century B.C.E. The extensive building activity of the period was a strong stimulus to the entire industrial life of Israel. Recent excavations at Eziongeber on the Red Sea have revealed a new aspect of Solomon's activity—an extensive ore refinery, the largest ever found in the Near East.

Courtesy Oriental Institute, University of Chicago

FRAGMENT OF COLUMN FROM BUILDING IN MEGIDDO
Proto-Ionic capital, probably 10th century B.C.E.

6942

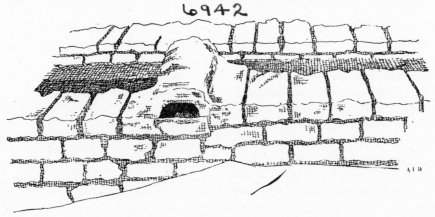

Courtesy American Schools of Oriental Research
WALL OF ORE REFINERY AT EZION-GEBER
About 950 B.C.E.

This ramified industrial activity in Israel was made possible with the help of Phoenician artisans. Tradesmen also were for the most part Phoenicians or, as they are called in the Bible, Canaanites. Exports from Palestine consisted mainly of agricultural products: grain, wine, oil, spices, etc. It was with grain and wine that Solomon paid for the various building materials sent to him by Hiram.

According to the biblical tradition, after the conquest of Canaan the land was divided by lot into equal parts among all the tribes of Israel. This, of course, is an idealistic interpretation by later social utopians, but it is true that, although we encounter wealthy land owners in the time of the Judges and the first kings, the dominant class was the free and independent peasant on his own land. The military organization of the tribe, too, was based on the economically independent peasants who were able to provide themselves with the necessary weapons. A series of laws concerning inheritance and family life were intended to prevent a diminution of the number of independent peasant families, in order to preserve the potential military strength of the people.

The tribes and clans formed the organic base of the entire folk-life not only in the period of the Judges but also later in the time of the Kings. The frequent mention in the Scriptures of the twelve tribes of Israel indicates that the system was based on a fixed number which had to be represented at important national councils or religious celebrations. The gathering of the twelve tribes or the gathering of Israel, as the event is referred to in some parts of the Bible, was usually connected with the Yahweh Amphictyony which has been previously mentioned. Thus the Commonwealth of Israel is frequently referred to in the Bible as the "Congregation of the Lord."

The tribe organization was a mixture of primitive democracy and patriarchal aristocracy. In principle all Israelites were considered equal and the assembly of all adult men suitable for military service served as the highest governing body. The administration of current affairs, on the other hand, was controlled by the so-called elders, who belonged mainly to the wealthiest and most respected families. A new element in the patriarchal-democratic system was introduced with the emergence of a centralized monarchy. At first this centralized government did not depart from the old democratic traditions and the first rulers were supported by the poorer classes and were enthroned by the People's Assembly or by the elders. Their rights and functions were agreed on through solemn covenant. At the same time the king stood apart from and often above the tribe organization. In time there developed a body of royal officers, a standing army of mercenaries and a number of central state institutions which narrowed the authority and functions of the older bodies. Nevertheless the People's Assembly remained—at least theoretically—the highest authority. No new basic law could be adopted without its consent. Even the divine laws which had been handed down at Mount Sinai required—according to biblical tradition—the approval of the assembled people. They were given force, as we have already noted, only after their solemn ratification as a covenant between the people of Israel and God. The great importance of the People's Assembly is corroborated in the account in Joshua xxiv. The historical value of this account is by no means diminished even though there is good reason to doubt the actual historicity of the events described. Joshua, the leader of the people at the time of the conquest of Canaan, we are told, gathered all the tribes of Israel at Shechem and exhorted them to

follow in the ways of Yahweh and heed His commandments. The account closes with these words:

And if it seem evil unto you to serve the Lord, choose you this day whom ye will serve; whether the gods which your fathers served that were on the other side of the flood, or the gods of the Amorites, in whose land ye dwell: but as for me and my house, we will serve the Lord.

And the people answered and said, God forbid that we should forsake the Lord, to serve other gods. . . .

And Joshua said unto the people, Ye are witnesses against yourselves that ye have chosen you the Lord to serve him. And they said, We are witnesses. . . .

So Joshua made a covenant with the people that day, and set them a statute and an ordinance in Shechem.

And Joshua wrote these words in the book of the law of God and took a great stone and set it up there under an oak that was by the sanctuary of the Lord.

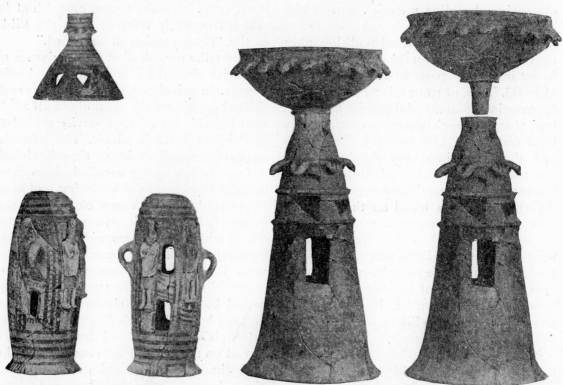

Courtesy Oriental Institute, University of Chicago

RITUAL AND CULT OBJECTS FROM MEGIDDO
Early Iron Age

There can be no doubt that this account, as well as similar accounts in other parts of the Bible, is based on actual occurences in Israel during the period of the Judges and the United Monarchy.

The transition from a semi-nomadic existence, to a sedentary agricultural life considerably increased the internal tensions and social cleavages. What was of particular importance was the emergence of a declassed group which became a factor in political life as early as the time of Abimelech and Jephthah. The peasant who owned only a small patch of ground could not divide it among all his children. According to the custom the oldest son was the chief heir; the remaining sons were therefore frequently compelled to leave their homes and seek their fortunes elsewhere. In earlier times, as long as there were new areas to be colonized, these younger sons often established new settlements and at the same time founded new clans, but in time this became more and more difficult and most of them were compelled to seek work as day laborers or hire themselves out as bonded workers. But even these possibilities were barred to many of them, and thus there developed a class of social outcasts who could find no place for themselves in the economy of the country. The struggles between brothers for the birthright—Isaac-Ishmael, Jacob-Esau, etc.—as well as the adventures and experiences of the disinherited sons, are the themes of many popular legends of biblical literature and indicate the role these factors played in the early history of Israel.

With the growth of the cities the number of the socially and economically unabsorbed classes increased. These disinherited and declassed groups were the strongest supporters of the tyrants and the kings against the clan and tribe organizations. These elements also constituted the reserves from which the kings drew the manpower for their standing armies.

This social differentiation, however, went along parallel with a process of national unification. In the period of the United Monarchy (1030-930 B.C.E.) a unified Israel was welded together from the various ethnic elements which composed the population of Palestine. The difficult political crises which the country went through no longer placed the very existence and the spiritual unity of the people in jeopardy. Nor did the split in the kingdom after Solomon's death and the frequent wars between Israel and Judah have any effect on this unity. Biblical writers talk of two kingdoms but recognize only one people and never abandon their dreams of the re-union of Israel and Judah.

7. THE DIVIDED MONARCHY: FROM JEROBOAM TO JEHU (930-843 B.C.E.)

The internal antagonisms and tensions which had evidenced themselves strongly during Solomon's reign, took on the form of an open and sharp conflict between the people and the David dynasty immediately after Solomon's death. Apart from the deep dissatisfaction over the onerous taxation and the forced labor which Solomon had imposed on the people, other factors contributed to the unrest, particularly the continuous antagonism—sometimes open, sometimes concealed—between the north and the south, between Israel and Judah. There was considerable discontent, too, in the Yahwist circles over Solomon's religious policies. When the time came for Solomon's son, Rehoboam, to seek the sanction of the People's Assembly before ascending the throne, the people were at last in a position to present their demands and conditions.

The national assembly gathered at Shechem, the site of the Yahweh Amphictyony in the time of Joshua. The rebel, Jeroboam, who had now returned from his exile in Egypt, was the spokesman for the people. When Rehoboam arrogantly refused the demands of the people to "lighten the heavy burden and loosen the yoke" an open revolt broke out, which resulted in a split in the monarchy. Jeroboam, the leader of the assembly, was crowned king over the ten tribes of northern Israel, Judah and a part of Benjamin remaining loyal to the David **dynasty.**

In the kingdom of Judah the David dynasty was securely established and this assured a certain stability and continuity in the political life of the people. In Israel the situation was different; there in the space of less than half a century two kings were assassinated and two dynasties—the house of Jeroboam and the house of Baasha—were liquidated. The collapse of the em-

SHISHAK RELIEF FROM THE TEMPLE AT KARNAK,
ABOUT 920 B.C.E.

Containing a list of Palestine cities
conquered by the Egyptians

pire of David and Solomon also brought a radical change in the balance of power in the Palestine-Syria area. Israel and Judah were both weakened and their strength was being more and more dissipated as a result of the unceasing fratricidal struggle. On the other hand, the strength of the newly arisen power in the north, the kingdom of Aram (Damascus), which in time became

Israel's most dangerous neighbor, considerably increased.

Shortly after the division of the kingdom Shishak (Sheshonk), the founder of the 22nd Egyptian dynasty, invaded the territory of Judah and Israel, attacked Jerusalem, and carried away all the treasures of the royal palace and of the Temple.

About 882 B.C.E. Omri became king of Israel. His dynasty, too, was not destined to last long. The "House of Omri," the first Israelite dynasty to be mentioned in the cuneiform records, distinguished itself by a sounder handling of external political problems and a proper appraisal of the international situation as well as the special situation of Israel and Judah. Close and friendly relations were established with Phoenicia, and Jezebel, the daughter of the king of Tyre, was given in marriage to Ahab, Omri's son. A reconciliation was reached with Judah, thus putting an end to the fratricidal wars, which were exhausting both kingdoms, and leaving Omri free to deploy his military forces to the east and subjugate Moab. The most notable accomplishment of Omri's reign was the establishment of a new, strongly fortified capital, Samaria, which remained the principal city of Northern Israel until the downfall of the Kingdom of the Ten Tribes.

During the reign of Ahab, Omri's son, a treaty of mutual assistance was concluded between Israel and Judah. This was probably a favorable factor in enabling Jehoshaphat, king of Judah, to re-occupy Edom. Jehoshaphat's attempt to follow the example of Solomon in utilizing the port of Ezion-geber for extensive seafaring expeditions failed, the kingdom lacking the financial and especially the technical resources for such a huge undertaking.

Israel's most dangerous enemy during the entire 9th century B.C.E. was the Aramaean kingdom on the northeastern boundaries of Palestine. Omri was compelled to cede to the king of Aram a number of cities in Israel and to grant trade privileges in Samaria to Damascus merchants. His son Ahab was successful in recovering the lost terri-

THE MESHA STONE, DATING FROM THE 9TH CENTURY B.C.E.

On it Mesha, King of Moab, tells of the liberation of
the country from Israelite rule

tory and for a time even friendly relations between the two kingdoms were established. It was during this period that Ahab and King Ben-hadad of Aram headed a coalition against Assyria, the new world power which was just emerging in Western Asia. In the battle fought at Karkar (853 B.C.E.) between the Syria-Palestine coalition and King Shalmaneser III of Assyria, the Israelite army, according to the Assyrian records, numbered 10,000 foot soldiers and 2,000 chariots. This account of the first encounter between Israel and Assyria, makes it possible for us to fix the time of Ahab's reign and to verify the chronology of the Books of the Kings. Some years later war broke out anew between Israel and Aram. In the battle at Ramoth-gilead, in which an army of Judah, headed by Jehoshaphat, also took part, Ahab fell.

The wars with Aram took their toll of the military strength of Israel and to some extent of Judah. The vassal states of Moab and Edom were quick to take advantage of the situation, proclaimed their independence and stopped paying tribute. Moab went so far as to annex a part of the territory of Israel in Transjordan. The city of Libnah, which belonged to Judah, also declared its independence.

Ahab's reign also witnessed a violent increase in the internal conflicts and tensions in Israel. The prophets, the leaders of the opposition, fought bitterly against the internal policies of Ahab in which his Phoenician wife, Jezebel, played an influential part. The attempt to introduce alien cults into Israel and to install Oriental methods of government aroused the strong protest of the Yahwistic circles. The opposition of the prophets became even more pronounced during the reign of Ahab's son, Jehoram. Taking advantage of the aggravated external situation the prophetic party inspired and supported a military revolt, as a result of which Jehu, the leader of the army, was proclaimed king of Israel.

8. SOCIAL AND RELIGIOUS CRISIS IN THE PERIOD OF THE OMRI DYNASTY

The ninety-year period between Solomon's death and the Jehu revolution saw a series of grave internal crises leading to frequent changes of dynasty in the kingdom of Israel. The monarchy, which during the period of the United Kingdom had symbolized the idea of the unification of all of Israel, lost this national function and necessarily, after the division of the kingdom, a great deal of its moral prestige. At the same time the conflicts with neighboring peoples lost the character of a struggle for national freedom, as had been the case in the time of Saul and David. New problems began to occupy the forefront of the national scene,—problems of religion and social justice which now filled the hearts and minds of the people.

Profound changes in all fields of social, economic and spiritual life had taken place in Israel since David's and Solomon's times. The most significant symptom of the new period was the continually increasing importance of the money economy. It is true that money had been frequently used as a medium of exchange in earlier periods, when, however, most of the trade was done by barter. As late as Solomon's reign, when Israel's trade had already reached considerable proportions, taxes were paid in kind. This method of payment was also used in the case of the Phoenician artisans employed by Solomon. The expanding trade and building activities during Solomon's reign were based mainly on barter economy and forced labor. As a consequence there were very few free, skilled workers. This situation changed completely in the course of the hundred years following Solomon's death. In the middle of the 9th century B.C.E.—as can be seen from the account in II Kings xii—a substantial part of the voluntary contributions for the Temple in Jerusalem was paid in money. The workers employed in the repair of the Temple were also paid in money. The laws in the Book of the Covenant, which stem from this period, reflect a fairly well developed money economy, fines and indemnities for damages being reckoned in money. Money became not only the most important medium of exchange but also the accepted standard in public life. This, of course, had necessarily led to deep changes not only in the economic structure but also in the social relations between the various groups and classes. At the same time it resulted in a significant strengthening of the political and spiritual influence of the Phoenicians, the pioneers of international trade in the ancient world. It was not by chance, therefore, that the Phoenician princess Jezebel, Ahab's wife, set the standards for the political—and to some extent the religious— life of Israel. The chief resentment of the people as well as of the prophets was directed not towards King Ahab but towards his Phoenician wife, who appeared to them the very personification of sin and injustice.

The growth of the money economy brought the moneylender in its wake. The needy peasant was often compelled to seek help from his more prosperous neighbor, sometimes as a result of personal misfortune, sometimes due to a general catastrophe such as drought, war, etc. As a rule such mutual help during a time of trouble was considered as a brotherly act or as a form of collective social security within the framework of the clan or tribe. The relationship between borrower and lender changed completely with the development of a money economy. Now borrowing and lending took on more and more of a commercial character. It gradually became clear that the business of lending money offered the opportunity to increase one's own wealth. At the same time, however, the money economy caused large sections of the peasant population to become more and more impoverished or to sink deeper and deeper into debt, so that they were often compelled to surrender their land-holdings or to sell their children into slavery. This development did not occur overnight, but in the time of the Omri dynasty it reached such proportions as to confront the people and the leading circles with an entire series of new problems and responsibilities. We know of social antagonisms and even social struggles as early as in the time of the Judges and the first kings. At that time, however, social oppression was concealed under a veil of paternalism and a system of social distinctions sanctified by tradition. The money economy, on the contrary, in principle dissolved all social distinctions; as seller and purchaser all persons were equal. At the same time, however, it eliminated all social and ethical motives which to a large extent regulated the economic relationships within the old clans and tribes. Social oppression lost its patriarchal disguise and social antagonisms became more pronounced. The evils and injustices became the more noticeable, since they were mainly attributed to the recently emerged class of the *nouveaux riches,* and since they occurred at a time when the processes of social ascendancy and social downfall were clearly evident.

The money economy shook the foundations of the traditional mode of life in Israel, but did not lead to the establishment and consolidation of a new social order with a system of laws and rights based chiefly on the principles of private ownership and government authority, as had been the case in similar circumstances among other peoples in the ancient Near East. It was characteristic of Israel that it lacked a dominating social group, a circumstance which permitted a relative equilibrium among the various social forces. Parallel with the royal administrations there functioned the old clan and tribe organization which survived even the downfall of the kingdom of Judah. The highest authority in questions of constitution and legislation was the People's Assembly which, however, did not have its own executive organ. The people could also be represented through delegates, through the leaders of the tribes and families. In the economic life of the country the small peasant was still the most important element, but there was a substantial growth of the urban population. Whereas a hundred years earlier Solomon was obliged to have recourse to Phoenician artisans, the class of skilled craftsmen in Jerusalem now was an important factor. This is clear from the fact that in the time of Jehoash (837-798 B.C.E.) the government was confronted with the entirely new problem of finding work for unemployed skilled laborers.

The proletarian element, too, formed an important segment of the population in Israel and Judah and played a part in public life. Even the Israelite *ebed* (servant), frequently mentioned in the Bible, was not a disenfranchised slave; he was most often a bonded worker who earned his freedom after a specified term. There was therefore no sharp distinction between the proletarian class and the economically independent citizen.

In this manner there developed in Israel and Judah a mixture of royal bureaucracy and democratic organization the competencies or functions of neither of which were clearly defined. Apart from the People's Assembly—which, however, met only rarely —there was no permanent authority with the power to make final decisions. But where the people were not able to agree among themselves the decision was left to the word of God, the continual internal disputes and conflicts thus creating the basis for the ever-growing influence of the prophets. Reliance on God's word was especially intense among the socially weak and oppressed; Yahweh had been from earlier times the Protector of the downtrodden and the Father of the orphans and the widows. The Yahweh prophets thus became the champions of the social ideals of equality, righteousness and justice.

Differing from the priests, whose position as religious functionaries was hereditary, the prophets occupied no official position in the sanctuary. The priests were paid for their services in the form of definitely fixed "priestly gifts"; the prophets, on the other hand, had no fixed income from their religious activities and for the most part even refused to accept voluntary gifts from their friends and followers. This material independence was the mark of the so-called true prophets who thus had to limit their needs to the bare essentials. The Yahweh prophets constituted a free religious order and were distinguished by a strictly puritanical, often ascetic mode of life. It was primarily their great moral prestige which earned for them an important position in public life as the champions of the rights of the common man.

The prophets appeared as a decisive political factor for the first time during the reign of Ahab. The majestic figure of the prophet Elijah was the central religious and political personality of the period, and his disciple Elisha was the initiator of the Jehu revolution which brought the Omri dynasty to an end. As can be seen from the accounts in Kings there were two basic demands for which Elijah carried on the struggle: 1) The recognition of monotheism—Yahweh as the one and only God of Israel; 2) Absolute respect for the rights of the common man even on the part of the rulers.

These demands were of course not entirely new, but they had never before been so clearly and sharply formulated and had never been regarded as the basic principles of religious and social life. King Ahab, for example, committed no greater sins and perpetrated no worse evils than David; it is sufficient to recall David's seduction of Bath-sheba and his murder of her husband, Uriah the Hittite, which surpasses in perfidy even the judicial murder of Naboth by Ahab. Nor was Ahab the first king in Israel to tolerate the cult of foreign gods. In spite of this he remained a loyal worshipper of Yahweh, as is shown by the fact that all his children bear typical Yahweh names—Ahaziah, Jehoram, Athaliah. That his activities aroused vehement protest and deeply disturbed public opinion in Israel is the best evidence that in those new times higher demands were made even on the rulers and that the stern morality of the prophets found a strong popular echo.

The struggle against the foreign gods, especially against the Phoenician Baal, also had a social background. The Baal cult symbolized the newly-introduced Phoenician *mores* of sophisticated luxury so close to the hearts of the upper classes of Israel. Belief in Yahweh as the one and only God was thus an expression of protest against all the abuses and social evils which were bound up with the money economy. In some Yahwist circles the opposition to the Canaanite-Phoenician civilization took an extreme form. It was in these radical Yahwist circles that there arose the so-called nomadic ideal, which called on all faithful Yahweh worshippers to renounce the established social order and everything connected with it and to return to the ideal way of life of the desert period. One of the leading figures in the Jehu uprising, Jehonadab ben Rechab, was the founder of the strict Yahwistic religious order of the Rechabites which had for its goal the realization of the "nomadic ideal" in daily life. The Rechabites drank no wine, built no houses, and did not even work the fields, but lived in tents, like the shepherds. Not everyone in the Yahwist circles, it is true, went so far; the Nazirites contented themselves with abstention from wine; the prophets did not abandon a settled life. But even those who did not go so far as the Rechabites were deeply influenced by the nomadic romanticism of the Yahwistic desert traditions.

It would be an error, however, to regard the prophets as reactionaries whose only goal was the restoration of the old social and economic order. On the contrary, the prophets were radical reformers and Utopians whose arguments were based not on the actual but on an ideal past. Nor was it narrow nationalism which induced the Yahweh zealots to fight against the foreign gods. The prophet Elisha, for example, maintained contact with highly placed persons in Aram (Naaman) and was even involved in the Hazael revolt in Damascus. Yahwism was from its very beginnings more than a national creed and sought to spread its teachings beyond the boundaries of the place of its origin. Yahwistic monotheism has therefore never lost its universalistic aspect. The representation in Genesis of Adam as the father of all peoples, the biblical traditions concerning mankind's common language in ancient times, and the radical pacifism of the prophets are the best evidences of Yahwistic universalism.

The social, economic and religious program of the prophetic reform movement is contained, as several scholars agree, in the so-called Book of the Covenant (Exodus XXI-XXIV). The democratic character of the laws in the Book of the Covenant is especially evident in the provisions concerning the freeing of slaves after six years of service, the prohibition against usury and the ban against receiving interest on loans in general, and in the other regulations favoring the poor sections of the population, especially the wageworkers and slaves. The concept of the Sabbath as a day of rest is given particular emphasis in the Book of the Covenant. As far as we know this is the first instance in history that an obligatory day of rest is provided for slaves, hired workers, and even for work animals. Closely connected with the institution of the Sabbath and displaying the same social tendency are the laws concerning the Sabbatical year as well as the above-mentioned provision that a Hebrew slave must be set free after six years of service.

The puritanical ideology of the prophetic movement also evolved rigid standards in the field of sexual morality. Beginning with the reign of King Asa of Judah, a stern struggle was waged against the various forms of sacred prostitution and licentiousness in general. According to the prophetic conception sexual transgressions were the gravest of sins and threatened to bring about the complete downfall of mankind. Earlier generations had been much less rigorous in this respect, as is clearly shown by the story of Judah and Tamar in Genesis xxxviii, one of the oldest narratives of the Pentateuch. This rigorous and puritanical attitude of the Yahwistic circles in matters of sexual morality put its special impress on Israelite family life and on Israelite moral standards in general and greatly influenced the course of Jewish history.

9. THE JEHU DYNASTY: DECLINE AND DOWNFALL OF ISRAEL
(843-721 B.C.E.)

The propaganda of the prophets paved the way for the downfall of the house of Ahab and brought a new dynasty to the throne. This dynasty—the Jehu dynasty—reigned over Israel for more than a hundred years. As soon as he came to power Jehu destroyed the Temple of Baal in Samaria and wiped out the supporters of the old regime. The accounts in II Kings give us inconclusive information as to the extent to which the social and economic demands of the prophets were carried out. The Yahwistic movement was not limited to North Israel only. Six years after the Jehu revolution in Israel the Yahwist party came to power in Judah, at the time when Ahab's daughter, Athaliah, who seized the throne after the death of her son, Ahaziah, reigned in Jerusalem. The priest Jehoiada, the leader of the uprising against Athaliah's reactionary regime, won over the support of the garrison of the Temple, and the seven-year-old prince, Jehoash, was proclaimed king. As the crowning act of the popular revolution a covenant was concluded "between the Lord and the king and the people, that they should be the Lord's people: between the king also and the people." The covenant with Yahweh clearly implies the removal of all foreign gods and the account actually relates that "all the people of the land went into the house of Baal and brake it down." The covenant between the people and the king was aimed at re-establishing and securing the rights of the people.

The account in II Kings xii is highly illuminating of the situation in Jerusalem at that time. It relates that by decision of King Jehoash all the money paid into the Temple funds had to be reserved exclusively for the maintenance and repair of the building. The control of these funds had been in the hands of the priests; now it was turned over to the representatives of the construction workers—a striking illustration of the influence of the class of the artisans and skilled laborers in the Yahwistic movement in Jeru-

salem. The plebeian-democratic spirit which dominated the newly established regime in Jerusalem is clearly indicated in the following passage in II Kings xii, 11-15.

And they gave the money, being told, into the hands of them that did the work, that had the oversight of the house of the Lord: and they laid it out to the carpenters and builders, that wrought upon the house of the Lord,

And to masons, and hewers of stone, and to buy timber and hewed stone to repair the breaches of the house of the Lord, and for all that was laid out for the house to repair it.

Howbeit there were not made for the house of the Lord bowls of silver, snuffers, basons, trumpets, any vessels of gold, or vessels of silver, of the money that was brought into the house of the Lord.

But they gave that to the workmen, and repaired therewith the house of the Lord.

Moreover they reckoned not with the men, into whose hand they delivered the money to be bestowed on workmen: for they dealt faithfully.

Externally the reign of Jehu brought new difficulties for Israel. The elimination of

RELIEF FROM THE OBELISK OF SHALMANESER III, 841 B.C.E.
Showing Israelites bringing tribute to the Assyrian king

From W. F. Albright: *The Excavation of Tell Beit Mirsim*

OLIVE-PRESSING PLANT EXCAVATED AT TELL BEIT MIRSIM

Period of the Divided Monarchy

From W. F. Albright: *The Excavation of Tell Beit Mirsim*

REMAINS OF DYE-PLANT FOUND AT TELL BEIT MIRSIM

Period of the Divided Monarchy

the Omri dynasty created strained relations with Tyre and put an end to the military alliance with Judah. Shortly after his accession to the throne Jehu sent a large tribute of gold and silver to Shalmaneser III, attempting in this way to gain the support of the Assyrians against Damascus. The renewed expansionist policy of Assyria in Western Asia, however, was short-lived. Internal difficulties prevented the Assyrian kings for a long time from interfering in Syria and Palestine. Hazael, the king of Damascus, was now free to concentrate his entire strength against Israel and to occupy all the Israelite territory in Transjordan. The situation became even more critical under Jehoahaz, the son of Jehu, when Israel lost practically all of its independence and Jehoahaz was compelled to reduce his armed forces "to 50 horsemen, 10 chariots, 10,000 foot soldiers." The situation took a more favorable turn at the beginning of the 8th century B.C.E. Damascus, weakened by defeats suffered in resisting the overwhelming might of the Assyrian empire, was not in a position to maintain its supremacy in Palestine. King Jehoash of Israel (802-787 B.C.E.), son of Jehoahaz, succeeded in recovering a large part of the old territory of Israel. Even greater successes were scored by Jehoash's son, Jeroboam II (787-747 B.C.E.), who freed the entire territory of Israel from foreign yoke and restored the ideal boundaries of North Israel "from the entering of Hammath unto the sea of the plain." Israel now again became the strongest power in the Syria-Palestine area.

After many years of exhausting wars and foreign bondage the people could breathe freely and give more attention to the tasks and problems of their internal life. The results were apparent in the blossoming of prophecy which now surpassed even the high level it had attained in the time of Elijah and Elisha. The first representative of the so-called literary prophets (who left their prophecies in written form) was Amos, the herdsman from Tekoa in Judah, who during the prosperous reign of Jeroboam ben Jehoash, came to Northern Israel to preach the word of Yahweh to the people and their rulers.

The weakening of Aram, which made possible the resurgence of Israel, at the same time removed the last buffer between Palestine and Assyria. With the accession of Tiglath Pileser III (745-727 B.C.E.) there began the great Assyrian expansionist policy which in a comparatively short time established the hegemony of the Mesopotamian empire over the ancient Orient.

Immediately after the death of Jeroboam II a rapid decline set in which, a score of years later, resulted in the downfall of the kingdom of Israel. After a reign of only six months Jeroboam's son, Zechariah, was assassinated by Shallum ben Jabesh who then seized the throne. A month later the new ruler was dethroned by a second usurper, Menahem ben Gadi. In the short space of barely a quarter of a century no less than six rulers occupied the throne of Israel, only one of them dying a natural death. In 738 B.C.E. Menahem ben Gadi paid a tribute of a thousand talents of silver to Tiglath Pileser. A few years later an anti-Assyrian coalition was formed under the leadership of Aram and Israel. The attempt to stem the onslaught of the Assyrians ended in a sharp defeat for the coalition. Israel lost the entire region of Transjordan and Galilee, Aram disappeared as an independent kingdom (732 B.C.E.), and the kings and princes of Palestine—Ammon, Moab, Edom, Judah, etc.—went to Damascus to pay homage to the victor. The entire region between the Euphrates and the borders of Egypt was now at the feet of the mighty ruler.

After the death of Tiglath Pileser in 727 B.C.E. a new anti-Assyrian coalition was formed. On this occasion, too, Israel participated in the coalition, King Hoshea suspending the payment of tribute. The successor of Tiglath Pileser, Shalmaneser V, thereupon invaded Israel and laid siege to Samaria. After a heroic but hopeless resistance which lasted for three years the capital of North Israel was taken (721 B.C.E.).

With these events the kingdom of Israel disappeared from the political map of the ancient Orient and the territory of central and northern Palestine became an Assyrian province. A substantial part of the population—according to Assyrian records, 27,290 inhabitants—was deported to the eastern regions of the Assyrian empire and their place taken by colonists forcefully deported from other countries. The majority of the deported Israelites came from the upper classes; the large mass, especially the peasants, remained in Palestine and held fast to the old national traditions. The influence

CAPTURED ISRAELITE MUSICIANS IN ASSYRIA

of the newly arrived foreign element made itself felt only in a few important localities. The territory of the Ten Tribes, which had up to then been the center of Israelite life, and where the overwhelming majority of the people lived, where the first great prophets (Elijah, Elisha, Amos, Hosea) flourished and where probably by far the largest portion of the earlier biblical literature was composed and written down, remained essentially an Israelite land. But the heavy blow had struck Israel in the very bloom of its spiritual development—this was the period of the beginning of the literary prophecy—and the people were not yet fully prepared to carry on an autonomous cultural life without political independence. The spiritual leadership passed over to Judah which had been able to save its political independence and which thus became the heir of the great national cultural heritage. As in the time of David and Solomon the eyes of all Israel were now turned to Jerusalem to which the inhabit-

ants of Shechem and Samaria came to bring their sacrifices. The hope for the recovery of political independence and national hegemony was nevertheless not entirely extinguished in North Israel. An echo of these aspirations has come down to us in the post-biblical traditions concerning the two Messiahs: one from the House of David (Messiah ben David) and the other from the House of Joseph (Messiah ben Joseph).

10. HEZEKIAH AND MANASSEH (725-642 B.C.E.)

Judah, which under the reign of Ahaz, had yielded to Assyrian rule, salvaged whatever political independence and freedom was possible under the circumstances. The successor to Ahaz, his son Hezekiah (725-697 B.C.E.), at first maintained the policy of loyalty towards Assyria. It was only after the death of Sargon II in 705 B.C.E., when unrest and revolt broke out in various parts of the Assyrian empire, that Hezekiah made an attempt to shake off the Assyrian yoke. The fortifications of Jerusalem were put in order and it was probably at that time that the Siloam tunnel was constructed for the purpose of assuring a supply of water to the city in case of siege. In 701 B.C.E. Sennacherib advanced on Palestine with his army. Edom, Moab and a number of Phoenician cities yielded, Ascalon was subdued, and the land of Judah, with the exception of Jerusalem, was occupied. Hezekiah had no alternative other than to accept the terms of the victor and to pay the imposed tribute of thirty talents of gold and three hundred talents of silver. It was not long before Sennacherib increased his demands and called for the complete capitulation of Judah and the opening of the gates of Jerusalem. On the advice of the prophet Isaiah, Hezekiah refused to yield. Again the people of Jerusalem, exhausted as they were, faced an imminent attack, but at this precise moment Sennacherib—for reasons not entirely clear—was compelled to withdraw his armies from Palestine and the threat to Jerusalem was removed. This wholly unexpected de-

The long reign of Hezekiah's son, Manasseh (697-642 B.C.E.), was, according to the accounts in II Kings, the darkest period in all of Judah's history. Assyria's power had now reached its highest peak and there was no alternative for Manasseh other than to be a loyal vassal of the great Assyrian king. It was probably this difficult external situation which was responsible for the sharp reaction in internal policies. Manasseh revoked all the religious reforms previously introduced in Jerusalem and re-established the worship of foreign gods in the Temple of Jerusalem. He also ruthlessly suppressed the prophetic movement, so that for a period of more than half a century the voices of the prophets were no longer heard. The accounts indicate that Manasseh's regime provoked strong opposition and Jerusalem was deluged with innocent blood "from one end to another." There is a post-biblical tradition that Isaiah himself fell victim to Manasseh's bloody regime.

11. THE DECLINE OF THE ASSYRIAN EMPIRE AND THE REFORM MOVEMENT UNDER JOSIAH
(641-609 B.C.E.)

The second half of the 7th century B.C.E. witnessed the decline and subsequent collapse of the Assyrian empire. The first blow came from Egypt, where Psammetichus I (664-610 B.C.E.), the founder of the 26th Dynasty, threw off the Assyrian yoke. Then came the devastating invasions of the wild Scythians. With the death of Ashurbanipal in 625 B.C.E. a revolt broke out in Babylonia and the entire edifice of the mighty Assyrian empire began to crumble. In less than two decades the Assyrian empire vanished from the world scene and the sway over Western Asia was taken over by the rising power of the new Babylonian empire.

It was natural that these events should have their reverberations in Judah. After the death of King Amon, the victim of a palace revolution in 639 B.C.E., the "people of the land" arose against the conspirators, killed the king's murderers and crowned the eight-year-old prince, Josiah, as king over Judah. As later events proved, the ap-

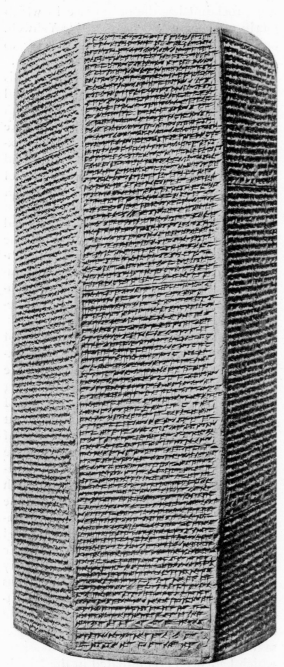

Courtesy Oriental Institute, University of Chicago

ROYAL ANNALS OF SENNACHERIB, KING OF ASSYRIA

Containing an account of his expedition against Judah and the siege of Jerusalem

liverance made a profound impression on the population of Judah and added to Jerusalem's reputation as a holy city under divine protection.

pearance of the "people of the land" as the decisive political factor, signified the end of the reactionary regime of the time of Manasseh. The power of Judah now passed over to the plebeian democratic elements.

The groups which now arose to power had as their goal the carrying out of a series of radical reforms intended to introduce deep changes into the political, economic and religious life of the people. At first, however, the supporters of the new regime had to proceed with the utmost caution; the power of Assyria was still far from broken. It was not until the death of Ashurbanipal that the party which had put Josiah on the throne dared to come out in the open with its entire program.

A detailed account in II Kings xxii, xxiii, relates that in the eighteenth year of the reign of King Josiah, in 621 b.c.e., a copy of a Book of the Law was accidentally discovered while some repair work was being done on the Temple. Its contents aroused great dismay and consternation. At the request of King Josiah the prophetess Huldah confirmed it as the authentic Torah of Moses which the people and their rulers had forgotten and which was now, by divine will, again revealed. A general People's Assembly was summoned by the king and a solemn agreement was made to observe and carry out all the commandments and laws which the newly-discovered Torah contained.

On the basis of this Torah, sanctioned by the People's Assembly, the Yahwistic party proceeded to put into effect a far-reaching program of political, social and religious reforms. The first goal of the reform movement was to rid the country of everything related to Assyrian rule and the reactionary, ruthless regime of Manasseh. The Temple of Jerusalem was cleared of all foreign cult objects and idols. At the same time the reformers attempted to implant the ideas of the prophets in the daily life of the people and to remove from the Yahweh cult itself all traces of the Canaanite pagan practices and symbols. All local sanctuaries and altars

were abolished. The Temple in Jerusalem was proclaimed as the only place in which sacrifices could legally be offered to Yahweh, and the people were required to come to Jerusalem to celebrate the great festivals.

Besides its purely religious aspect this centralization of worship had great political significance. The collapse of the Assyrian empire made it possible for Josiah to take over important sections of Israel and to extend his religious reforms. There is special mention in II Kings of the destruction of the altar in Beth-el which had been built by Jeroboam i at the time Israel had broken away from Judah. This removal of the local sanctuaries and altars, the centers of the particularistic religious and political tendencies, became a symbol of the reunification of Israel and Judah and of the restoration of national unity and political independence.

In all of these activities the leaders of the reform movement proceeded with extreme care, so as to give no ground for the impression that they were strengthening the position of Judah at the expense of Israel. This is the explanation for the fact that Shechem, the old religious center of Israel and for a long time the seat of the Yahweh Amphictyony, where the great national celebrations were held, occupied such an important place in the literature of the Josiah period. The program of the reformers was the restoration of a Greater Israel within the boundaries of the old Davidic empire on the basis of complete equality for all elements of the population. It was this interest in the common spiritual heritage of Israel and Judah on the part of the reformists that was responsible for the saving of the extensive literary treasures which had been accumulated in the Northern kingdom.

In addition to the religious reforms, a number of very significant social and economic provisions were carried out for the benefit of the poor and unprotected elements of the population. Deuteronomy, the Fifth Book of Moses, which is generally identified with the Book of the Law discovered in the

Temple, is permeated with a deep feeling of sympathy for the needs and concerns of the common people. All Israelites were brothers. Even the criminal and law-breaker was not outside the pale; provision was made for the preservation of his human dignity:

> And it shall be, if the wicked man be worthy to be beaten, that the judge shall cause him to lie down, and to be beaten before his face, according to his fault, by a certain number.
>
> Forty stripes he may give him, and not exceed: lest, if he should exceed, and beat him above these with many stripes, then thy brother should seem vile unto thee (Dueteronomy xxv, 2-3).

Particular attention was given to the rights of day-laborers, widows and orphans. The humane treatment demanded for slaves in the laws of Dueteronomy is of conspicuous significance. The same is true of the laws concerning the right of asylum for fugitive slaves, and the laws concerning the Sabbatical year, freeing debtors from their indebtednesses every seventh year. The laws laid down a well-developed system of social care and protection of the needy: all crops remaining in the fields or in the vineyards belonged to the poor; every third year a tenth of the harvest had to be given to the poor; part of the sacrifices and offerings in the Temple were reserved for the day-laborers, widows and orphans.

The economic development which took place in the 8th and 7th centuries B.C.E. had intensified all the negative aspects of social life produced by the money economy. The independent peasantry had become more and more impoverished as a result of the constantly growing debts and the tributes which had to be paid to the foreign conquerors. There had been a marked increase in the size of the proletarian class and particularly in the number of the declassed. Therefore the laws concerning usury, debtors and creditors were given a place of special importance. Also—for the first time in the history of Israel—there was an attempt to solve the problem of agricultural reform and the more equitable division of land holdings.

The Josiah reform also made an attempt to put into practice the social demands of the prophets. Not all of the reform program could be realized and many of the laws in Dueteronomy were probably never enforced. Nevertheless the mere fact that these demands were formulated and fixed in the Torah was extremely significant. The religious reforms carried out in the time of Josiah were of even greater historic consequence. The abolishing of the local sanctuaries and altars and the total ban against pagan images and symbols signify a radical revolution in the religious thinking of Israel. Sacrificial offerings became progressively less important, and the "holy book," the Torah, now occupied the center of religious life. The consequences of the spiritualization of religious life were enormous. It laid the ideological foundations for the transition from an independent state to a religious community, and thus brought into being that single factor which was of overwhelming importance in enabling the Jewish people to maintain their existence and identity under the hardships of their exile in later generations.

12. THE DOWNFALL OF JUDAH

Judah was not destined to enjoy for long the political independence it had achieved after the decline of the Assyrian empire. In 609 B.C.E. Josiah fell in battle near Megiddo, where he had gone to oppose the Egyptian army advancing through the Jezreel valley to the aid of its Assyrian ally. A few years later, however, the Egyptian army was decisively defeated at Carchemish (605 B.C.E.) and the hegemony over the ancient oriental world passed to Babylonia. Judah at first surrendered to the unavoidable fate, but later attempted to recover its independence and stopped paying tribute. In 597 B.C.E. Nebuchadnezzar, at the head of a large army, entered Palestine and laid siege to Jerusalem. King Joiachin, who had just ascended the throne of Judah, offered no opposition and, together with a large number of officials, officers, soldiers and skilled craftsmen, was carried away to Babylonia. Nebuchadnezzar then named Joiachin's uncle, Mattaniah, as king of Judah, giving him the name of Zedekiah (597-586 B.C.E.).

The leading elements of Judah continued unceasingly to cherish the idea of throwing off the yoke of Babylonia, hoping for the support of Egypt. The pro-Egyptian orien-

After a stubborn resistance which lasted for a year and a half, the Babylonian army smashed the city's fortifications on the 9th of Tammuz, 586 B.C.E. The garrison, headed by Zedekiah, stole out of the beleaguered city at night, but near Jericho the king fell into the hands of the enemy. A month later, on the 7th of Ab, Nebuzaradan, a high Babylonian official, was sent to Jerusalem

From THE LACHISH LETTERS. *Courtesy Oxford University*

THE FORTIFIED CITY OF LACHISH
Showing double fortifications constructed by Rehoboam. Destroyed in 588-587 B.C.E.
Drawn by H. H. McWilliams

tation was supported by the adherents of the religious and political reaction. The prophet Jeremiah, on the other hand, sternly opposed any kind of political alliance with Egypt, emphasizing the military weakness of the Nile empire—the "broken reed." Finally the pro-Egyptian policy won the upper hand and in the ninth year of Zedekiah's reign Judah rebelled against Babylonia. As Jeremiah had foretold, the promised help of Egypt did not materialize and Nebuchadnezzar was able to lay siege to Jerusalem without any outside opposition.

to liquidate whatever remained of Judah's independence. He destroyed the fortifications around Jerusalem, burned the Temple, the royal palace and all large buildings, and deported a large part of the population to Babylonia. Only the poorest classes were left.

We have very little information of conditions in Judah during the following fifty years of Babylonian rule. It is certain that, in spite of the enormous losses through the war, deportations and voluntary emigration, Judah did not become a wilderness. Religious and cultural life did not entirely disappear, and it is quite probable that fragments of the literary creations of the period were preserved and have come down to us in various parts of the Bible. The fact that several years after the catastrophe Nebuzaradan carried off to Babylonia an additional group of 745 prisoners (Jeremiah lii, 30) indicates that the spirit of resistance had not completely died out in Judah.

II. THE PERIOD OF THE SECOND COMMONWEALTH

(6th century B.C.E. to 1st century C.E.)

1. BABYLONIAN EXILE
(586-538 B.C.E.)

The state fell but the people remained, and in different ways and under different conditions continued to weave the fabric of its history. The leading classes had been deported to Babylonia; the poorer sections of the population, which had remained in Judah, lived in great want. Lamentations v, gives a somber account of the conditions in the country during this period. In addition to the disastrous devastation of the war, the people had to endure the onslaughts of their neighbors, the Ammonites, Moabites, Edomites and Philistines, who took advantage of the collapse of the Davidic kingdom to occupy Judaean territory.

Apart from the two large Jewish centers in Babylonia and Judah there was a number of smaller Jewish settlements in the neighboring countries, especially in Egypt and Syria. The Jewish Diaspora did not begin with the downfall of Judah. Even before the destruction of Jerusalem there had been Jewish settlements in many neighboring countries . These, however, were only of small consequence in comparison with the large and compact Jewish community in Palestine. Even the exiles from Northern Israel who had been deported in comparatively large numbers as early as 721 B.C.E. had not managed to develop an autonomous community life. It was only after the destruction of the First Temple that the Diaspora became a substantial, and for a long time, even the dominating factor in Jewish life and that the Jews became a "world people."

Among the widely scattered Jewish communities, the colony of the exiles in Babylonia held the leadership. According to the accounts in Jeremiah and Ezekiel the exiles in Babylonia lived in comparatively normal circumstances. They were able to engage in agricultural and urban pursuits and were permitted to settle in compact groups and colonies. The Babylonian government did not interfere in their internal life and they were free to observe the traditions of their forefathers and to gather together for the observance of the Sabbaths and holy days. Various passages in Ezekiel make it clear that from time to time a council of elders assembled in order to discuss important community affairs. The *Golah,* as the community of exiles in Babylonia was called, also maintained close contact with the mother country, from which messengers and letters arrived from time to time. There is evidence, too, that other Jewish communities in the Diaspora were not entirely cut off from contact with the homeland.

No definite information has come down to us as to the number of people deported from Judah. The figures given in Kings and Jeremiah, besides showing many inconsistencies, deal only with the number of adults. The best estimate is, that beginning with 597 B.C.E. *(Galut Joiachin),* approximately 30,000 to 40,000 persons were carried off to Babylonia. The Jewish population increased considerably in exile and it is not unlikely that some of the exiles from Judah in the outlying provinces of Babylonia were joined by the survivors of the exiles from North Israel. Less than a century later, when about 50,000 exiles had returned to the homeland, a very large Jewish community still remained in Babylonia and for a long time continued to play a leading role in Jewish life.

It was not only in numbers that the exiles in Babylonia advanced. All available evidence indicates that their economic situation was not unfavorable and that a few of them even managed to attain elevated stations in life. For the most part, following their mode of life in the homeland, they engaged in agricultural pursuits. However, there was, in addition, a large number of merchants, artisans, and even state officials among them. Thus they were later in a position to make substantial contributions towards the restoration of Judah and Jerusalem.

The cultural and spiritual heritage which the exiles from Judah brought along with them to Babylonia was much greater than had been the case with those who had been exiled from North Israel five or six generations earlier. That time interval had witnessed the full flowering of literary prophecy and had seen the emergence of the prophets Isaiah, Micah, Jeremiah and Zephaniah. It was at the end of the 7th century B.C.E. that the great Dueteronomic reform had been introduced, a reform which so radically changed the religious life of the people. Thus the exiles from Judah were able to carry along with them a large number of holy writings, books of the prophets and sections of the Torah, which made it possible for them to establish the forms of a Jewish life in a non-Jewish land.

In that alien land the exiles organized themselves according to family and regional groups and cherished their family traditions. Most of the exiles lived with the hope that sooner or later they would return to their old homes, and thus held fast to the memory of their origin. "By the rivers of Babylon, there we sat down, yea, we wept, when we remembered Zion ... If I forget thee, O Jerusalem, let my right hand forget her cunning. If I do not remember thee, let my tongue cleave to the roof of my mouth; if I prefer not Jerusalem above my chief joy."

It was precisely here, in an alien land, that the old traditions and customs were observed and fostered with particular devotion and loyalty. The Sabbath and the rite of circumcision became national religious symbols which distinguished the Jews from the surrounding world, and the system of religious ritual which was developed to a considerable extent influenced the further evolution of specific Jewish ways of life. This ritual was in part a result of the strong influence of the priests, who constituted a large number of the exiles. What is most remarkable is that, although the priests lost their most important function with the destruction of the Temple, their influence among the exiled Jews increased considerably. It was in exile that the Jews began to consider themselves as a chosen and separate group, distinct from the rest of the world. It was in Babylonia that there emerged the concept of the Jews as a "kingdom of priests and a holy nation." In this way, the ritual, previously reserved for the priests, became the property of the people, and the demands of ritual purity and cleanliness became obligatory for all classes alike.

A central place in Jewish life in Babylonia was taken by an institution which had its roots in the reforms of Josiah, but which was fully developed only in exile. On the Sabbaths and holy days the loss of the Temple and the absence of the solemn sacrificial celebrations were keenly felt by the exiles. The problem of continuing the sacrificial services in their old form or substituting a new form for them gave deep concern to the leading groups. A way out was found in the form of the prayer house, the synagogue, which served as a substitute for the Temple. In the synagogue there was no altar, and prayer and the reading of the Torah took the place of the sacrifice. In addition the prayer house performed an important social function. As is implied by its name in ancient literature—Bet ha-Keneset, Bet Moed—it was a gathering point and a meeting place where the people could congregate whenever it was necessary to take council over important community affairs. The synagogue became the cradle of an entirely new type of social and religious life and established the foundation for a religious community of universal scope. For the first time Jewish monotheism emancipated itself in religious practice from its bonds to a specific and designated site. God was now brought to the people wherever they dwelt. The Jew in exile was no longer compelled to serve the "gods of the country."

The period of the Babylonian exile was not only a time of preservation of the national values; it was also a period of creative spiritual achievement. A very important part of the biblical literature was written during the Babylonian exile and it was in Babylonia that the older collections were put into the form in which they have come down to us. It was in Babylonia, after the destruction of the First Commonwealth, that the Jews properly became the "People of the Book." The holy writings now occupied a central place in the life of the people, and, as a consequence, the teacher and the scribe grew in prestige. Interest in the nation's past increased and the events of its history were presented as object lessons for the present and future. It was to this end that the old folk traditions were revised and the older literary creations edited and interpreted. The central theme which permeated the entire literature of exile was the idea of the coming redemption of Israel and the restoration of Zion.

The most significant figure of the period of the Babylonian exile was the prophet Ezekiel, whose writings present a vivid picture of the conditions which prevailed in the colonies of the deportees. Large numbers of the exiles lost their hope and belief in the possibility of a continued existence in a strange land and brought their doubts and fears to the prophet. In the first years of his prophetic activity, Ezekiel constantly addresses words of warning to the people and prophesies the downfall of Jerusalem because of the people's sins. But immediately after the catastrophe Ezekiel changes his prophetic note. He becomes the preacher of consolation, faith and hope. The most eloquent example of this phase of his activity is the vision of the valley of dried bones which, by God's command, took on flesh and sinew and were restored to life.

So I prophesied as I was commanded: and as I prophesied, there was a noise, and behold a shaking, and the bones came together, bone to his bone.

And when I beheld, lo, the sinews and the flesh came up upon them, and the skin covered them above: but there was no breath in them.

Then said he unto me, Prophesy unto the wind, prophesy, son of man, and say to the wind, Thus saith the Lord God; Come from the four winds, O breath, and breathe upon these slain, that they may live.

So I prophesied as he commanded me, and the breath came into them, and they lived, and stood up upon their feet, an exceeding great army.

Then he said unto me, Son of man, these bones are the whole house of Israel: behold they say, Our bones are dried, and our hope is lost: we are cut off for our parts.

Therefore prophesy and say unto them, Thus saith the Lord God; Behold, O my people, I will open your graves, and cause you to come up out of your graves, and bring you into the land of Israel.

It was from among the circles supporting Ezekiel that there emerged the reform program for a restored and united Israelite commonwealth (Ezekiel XL-XLIII). Although this reform program chiefly concerned itself with religious ceremonials, the Temple, the priests and the sacrifices, it must not be overlooked—as has frequently been the case —that the program included a number of important social and ethical demands of exceptional significance. For example, the detailed plan for the division of the land in the restored Israel made no differentiation between native born and aliens:

And it shall come to pass, that ye shall divide it by lot for an inheritance unto you, and to the strangers that sojourn among you, which shall beget children among you and they shall be unto you as born in the country among the children of Israel; they shall have inheritance with you among the tribes of Israel.

And it shall come to pass, that in what tribe the stranger sojourneth, there shall ye give him his inheritance, saith the Lord God.

Jerusalem was to remain a holy city and its soil was never to be sold. The princes of the restored commonwealth were enjoined to observe the dignity of the people:

Let it suffice you, O princes of Israel: remove violence and spoil, and execute judgment and justice, take away your exactions from my people, saith the Lord God.

It can thus be seen that the idea of national restoration was from the beginning bound up with the idea of a religious and socio-ethical renaissance.

2. RESTORATION OF JUDAH

For Babylonia, too, the time came to drink of the bitter cup, as the prophets expressed it, and the hopes of the exiled people were fulfilled much sooner than many of them expected. In 549 B.C.E. Cyrus, king of Persia, conquered the kingdom of Media and a few years later overran the kingdom of Lydia in Asia Minor. Thus a new and formidable power appeared at the borders of the Babylonian empire, speeding the process of internal decay which had begun after the death of Nebuchadnezzar in 562 B.C.E. The Persian ruler was farsighted enough to take advantage of the grievances of the dissatisfied elements in the Babylonian empire, and when the unavoidable conflict broke out and Cyrus won the initial battles, the Babylonians themselves opened the gates of their capital city to the victor (539 B.C.E.). In this way Cyrus became the founder of a world empire which in extent and duration was never equalled in the ancient Orient.

Even before his conquest of Babylonia Cyrus had been hailed by the anonymous prophet, the so-called Second Isaiah, as Yahweh's anointed who had been chosen to redeem the people of Israel and restore the Temple. These expectations undoubtedly had some grounds. In contrast to the Assyrian and Babylonian rulers whose policies of mass deportations were aimed at destroying the old national boundaries and obliterating all national characteristics, Cyrus conducted his propaganda on the policy of national restoration. The Persian ruler showed the greatest tolerance toward the national and religious traditions of the various peoples in his empire. In particular he supported the efforts towards religious restoration and conducted himself as the appointed protector of the religious beliefs of his subjects.

The decree issued by Cyrus in 538 B.C.E., permitting the Jews in Babylonia to return to Judah and rebuild the Temple, is indicative of that policy. The decree aroused intense enthusiasm among the exiles and under the leadership of Sheshbazzar, a son of King Joiachin, the first of the exiles to return reached Jerusalem in the autumn of the same year.

In a comparatively short time a large number of the exiles had again settled in Judah. Those who remained in Babylonia, mostly belonging to the more prosperous classes, helped the settlers with substantial contributions of money and goods. In their first enthusiasm the returned exiles immediately built an altar on the site of the Temple and began to prepare for its rebuilding. However, the hard struggle for daily existence forced the pioneers to abandon the plan for a period of almost two decades.

After the death of Cambyses, the successor to Cyrus, in 522 B.C.E., unrest and insurrections broke out in various parts of the empire. Although Darius I soon succeeded in crushing all separatist rebellions, the impetus of the insurrectionist movement exerted an influence for a long time. In Judah, too, where affairs did not reach the stage of open rebellion, the events in the outside world had strong repercussions. National aspirations revived, finding expression in the prophecies of Haggai and Zechariah, who reproached the repatriates for neglecting the rebuilding of the Temple: "Is it time for you, O ye, to dwell in your ceiled houses, and this house lie waste? . . . Go up to the mountain and bring wood and build the house." There were willing ears for these words of Haggai, and the leaders of the people, Zerubbabel, the grandson of Joiachin, who was at that time governor of Judah, and the High Priest, Joshua, resumed the work on the Temple. But the restoration of the Temple was not the limit of the people's national ambitions;

Haggai and Zechariah proclaimed Zerubbabel as the anointed of the Lord, a veiled intimation that the Davidic dynasty would soon be restored and the independence of Judah achieved. Zechariah even went so far as to have a crown made for Zerubbabel out of the offerings sent by the exiles in Babylonia.

The Persian administration took strong steps against the movement for political independence, although it permitted the work on the Temple to continue. (Four years later, in 516 B.C.E., the Temple was completed.) Zerubbabel disappeared from public life in Judah, and with him the last representative of the David dynasty. The High Priest Joshua remained the only representative leader recognized by the Persian government. Under these conditions, prophecy, which had emerged and developed within the framework of national independence and political freedom, could no longer function. The period of prophecy thus gradually drew to its close, the later prophets not even having the spirit to act and write under their own names.

3. EZRA AND NEHEMIAH

For a long time conditions in Judah remained difficult and insecure. Most of the cities were in ruins and the small, weak settlements of the returned exiles had to rely on outside help. Archaeological research verifies in general the picture of the period given in the Bible. In addition to the purely material difficulties other factors played a part. It would appear that little harmony existed between the returned exiles from Babylonia and the population which had remained in Judah. There were also cleavages and conflicts between the new settlers and the neighboring populations, who looked with distrust at the attempts to rebuild Jerusalem. This enmity was especially intense on the part of the leaders of the community of the Samaritans. Added to these difficulties were tensions of a religious character. The Jews who had remained in Judah had not gone through the same evolution which had taken place

in Babylonia. In Babylonia the exiles had had to maintain a continuous struggle against the dangers of assimilation and their religious life had to become more intensive in order to compensate for the absence of its native environment. The chief emphasis was on national and religious integrity. It was for this reason that the exiles in Babylonia lived their internal life apart from the Gentile population, in order to safeguard their individual customs and traditions. Great importance was also placed on the purity of the family, since intermarriage was a grave threat to the very existence of the Jewish people. In Judah the situation was entirely different. The poor peasants who had remained there were lax in their observance of religious rituals and ceremonies, and they maintained intimate contact with the neighboring peoples, who were closely related to them by descent and culture. Intermarriage among Jews and Samaritans, or even among Jews and the neighboring Ammonites and Moabites, was by no means rare. The result was that foreign customs and foreign languages began to infiltrate into Judah, the danger of assimilation thus becoming particularly acute on the very soil of the Jewish homeland.

The prosperous communities in Babylonia still held the leadership in Jewish life. They considered themselves the guardians of the spiritual heritage of all Jewry and it was on them that the government relied in all questions of internal Jewish life, not only in Babylonia itself but in the other countries of the Persian empire. It was thus natural that the exiles who had returned to Judah should turn for help in times of difficulty to the Babylonian settlement, whose leaders were greatly concerned over the news of the troubled conditions in the mother country. In 458 B.C.E., early in the year, a caravan of a few thousand Jews left Babylonia under the leadership of Ezra the Scribe, and reached Jerusalem four months later. Ezra brought with him donations for the Temple and, what was more important, a royal rescript which gave him full authority to establish the rule of the

Torah in Judah and Jerusalem, to appoint judges for the Jews in the province "beyond the River"—the entire region between Euphrates and Egypt—and to punish all those who did not obey the "commandments of God's Torah."

Ezra's first struggle was against intermarriage which was prevalent among the upper sections of the population. He found support in the circles of the Haredim, "Those who tremble at the word of the Lord," and four months after his arrival in Jerusalem, a People's Assembly of all of Judah and Benjamin was summoned to the open place before the Temple, and all mixed marriages were declared annulled. But it was easier to promulgate the measure than to carry it into effect. The attempt to enforce it met with strong opposition and Ezra's mission, which had begun with such high promise, ended in complete failure.

In order to prevent any further outside interference, especially from the Samaritans, the Haredim decided to proceed with the strengthening and repair of the fortifications of the city. The opponents of the orthodox Jews denounced this move as an act of rebellion against the Persian government: "If this city is builded, and the walls finished, they will not pay tribute, impost or toll." As a consequence King Artaxerxes I ordered the work halted "until another commandment shall be given from me," and, supported by the royal order, the opponents of the Haredim proceeded to Jerusalem "unto the Jews, and made them to cease by force of arms."

The bad news from Jerusalem was disquieting to the Jewish settlement in Babylonia. One of the leaders, Nehemiah ben Hachaliah, an important official in the royal court, obtained the King's permission to continue with the reconstruction of the walls around Jerusalem, and with the King's authority went to Jerusalem as governor of Judah.

The opposition did not subside, however, and under the leadership of Tobiah the Ammonite and Sanballat, the governor of Samaria—both of them related to leading Jewish families in Jerusalem—the campaign against securing the city's fortifications went on. In spite of the various intrigues and conspiracies against him—internal as well as external—Nehemiah went on with his task, and the restoration of the walls—which probably had been only partially destroyed —was brought to completion in the short space of fifty-two days. This unique achievement was made possible only through the enthusiastic support given to Nehemiah by large sections of the people. All the clans of Judah and Benjamin were mobilized for the work and armed for the defense of the city. "They which builded on the wall and they that bare burdens, with those that laded, every one with one of his hands wrought in the work, and with the other hand held a weapon."

Now at last it was possible for Ezra and Nehemiah to return to their main task: the reorganization of Jewish community life in Judah in accordance with the laws of the Torah. On the first day of the month of Tishri the people gathered into the street before the Water Gate and Ezra the Scribe "brought the Law before the Congregation . . . and he read therein from the morning until midday, before the men and the women, and those that could understand . . . And all the people answered, Amen, Amen, with lifting up their hands: and they bowed their heads and worshipped the Lord with their faces to the ground." Three weeks later, after the Feast of Tabernacles was celebrated according to what was "found written in the Law," the people again assembled in order to ratify the Book of the Law. On the twenty-fourth day of Tishri the solemn ceremony of the covenant was carried out. The account in Nehemiah ix,x of the ratification of the Book of the Law makes particular mention of the obligations taken by the people to abstain from intermarriage "with the people of the land," to pay strict observance to the Sabbath laws, to hold fast to the rules of the Sabbatical year—"to leave the seventh year (the seventh-year harvest), and the exaction of every debt,"—and to observe the ordinances regarding the donations and gifts for the Temple.

With Ezra the Scribe and his school, the collecting and editing of the rich Torah literature which had been accumulated during the first thousand years of Jewish history was completed. The Written Torah, which now became the theocratic constitution of Israel, and which was even accepted by the Samaritans, regulated not only the public life but also the private life of the individual. It would be an error to assume, however, that Ezra was the first to establish the so-called religious legalism or normative Judaism. The entire history of Jewish religious thought is permeated with the idea that there is no substantial difference in principle between the duties of man to God and of man to man. It is appropriate to mention that even in the Book of the Covenant no differentiation is made between the religious commandments and the laws regulating the relationships between people. According to Jewish tradition Moses was both prophet and law giver. Thus the fundamental difference between prophecy and the Torah mistakenly assumed by many critics, simply does not exist. The fact is that even the sections of the Torah composed in the time of Ezekiel and Ezra are permeated with the prophetic spirit. This is especially evident in the so-called Code of Holiness (Leviticus XVII-XXVII). The cornerstone of this code of laws is: "Ye shall be holy, for I am holy." However, this was by no means only a demand to observe the regulations that had to do with religious ritual, as is clearly shown in Leviticus XIX which contains a large number of socioethical commandments of an extremely elevated character. There is evidence of an attempt towards a radical social reform intended to guarantee the freedom of the Jewish peasants in the laws concerning the jubilee year (Leviticus XXV):

And ye shall hallow the fiftieth year and proclaim liberty throughout all the land unto all the inhabitants thereof: it shall be a jubilee unto you; and ye shall return every man unto his possessions, and ye shall return every man unto his family.

The accounts in the Books of Ezra and Nehemiah also support the view that social demands occupied an important place in their program.

With the reforms of Ezra and the reconstruction of Jerusalem the intellectual hegemony of the community of exiles in Babylonia comes to an end. Through Ezra and Nehemiah Jerusalem again became the center of the Jewish world. But the Babylonian period left deep traces and strongly influenced the entire future development of Jewish life.

The inhabitants of the province of Samaria considered themselves an organic part of the Commonwealth of Israel and many of them looked to Jerusalem as the spiritual center of all Israel. For a long time they brought their sacrifices there and even offered to participate in the reconstruction of the Temple. Their political leaders, however, regarded with displeasure the revival of Judah and tried in every way possible to block the attempt to fortify Jerusalem. The old differences between Israel and Judah arose in a new guise and even became intensified as a result of the unbending attitude of Ezra and Nehemiah and their followers who considered the Samaritans as half-Jews. Nevertheless the authority of Jerusalem was so great that the Samaritans adopted the text of the Torah in the form fixed by Ezra and his adherents. It was not until the 4th century B.C.E. that the Samaritans built their own temple on Mount Gerizim near Shechem and completely separated themselves from Jerusalem. The remnants of the Israelites in Transjordan and Galilee, however, maintained their loyalty to Jerusalem, although administratively they were separated from Judah. Even in Samaria proper there were many who continued to make pilgrimages to Jerusalem and felt themselves bound to the Jewish community in Judah in all religious matters. The Samaritan schism did not succeed in turning away the majority of the Israelite communities from Jerusalem, and the holy city retained its spiritual leadership in Jewish life.

At the center of religious life in Judah stood the Temple, uniting the Jewish communities of the entire world. The sacrifices brought to the Temple were offered on behalf of the entire Jewish people and all Jews voluntarily paid taxes for the support of the national sanctuary. This strengthened considerably the economic and social position of the priests who were also the recipients of the favor of the Persian government which feared the political aspirations of the more worldly leaders. The priesthood thus became a source of political power and great material wealth. The High Priest was the recognized religious and secular head of the Jewish people; the scribes and Levites fulfilled the role of folk teachers and interpreters of the law. Notwithstanding the veneration in which the Temple was held, the scribes and Levites enjoyed a great deal more moral prestige than the priests. The Persian administration confined itself to the collection of taxes and the general supervision of the province. In local affairs Judah enjoyed a comparatively broad autonomy. As in pre-exilic times the People's Assembly functioned as the highest authority in religious and secular affairs. There is mention in Talmudic literature of the *Keneset ha-Gedolah*, the General Assembly, as standing at the head of the autonomous Jewish community in the time of Ezra.

Regarding Jewish communities outside of Palestine we have detailed information of the military colony of the Judaeans in Elephantine on the southern boundaries of Egypt (See *History of Jewish Archaeology*, in this volume). Jewish communities also existed in other parts of Egypt. It was in these communities that the last prophecies of Jeremiah were recorded and preserved. In addition, we have evidence of Jewish settlements in Syria and on some of the islands in the Mediterranean.

As was the case in other countries, the Jewish communities in Palestine included a substantial number of proselytes. Some of the Jewish leaders strongly disapproved of them and sought to strengthen the barrier between the Jews and the non-Jewish world. The frequent mention of the proselytes in the later parts of the Bible clearly indicates the part they played in Jewish life in the post-exilic period. Among the Haredim there was also a universalist faction which carried on an intensive religious propaganda among the Gentiles and maintained that the Temple should be a house of prayer for all peoples. The account of the loyalty of the Moabite Ruth to her adopted faith and people is quite apparently a veiled polemic against the purists of the period. The same universalistic tendency is present in the Book of Jonah.

The historic parts of the Bible, which are practically our only sources for ancient Jewish history, end with Ezra and Nehemiah. The books and fragments of the biblical literature dating from the end of the Persian or even the beginning of the Hellenistic period, contain no historical accounts regarding the contemporary period. A time span of about two hundred and fifty years of Jewish life is thus completely obscure and it is only from time to time that a ray of light falls to illuminate another moment of Jewish history. Reliable information from Jewish sources begins to flow again only in the time of the Hasmonaeans. Nevertheless, this period, known to have been poor in great historical occurrences, was distinguished by a deep spiritual life which has bequeathed to us such treasures of biblical literature as Job, Proverbs, a large part of Psalms, etc.

4. GREEK RULE
(332-167 B.C.E.)

The Persian empire had for long been suffering from internal decay and was ripe for collapse. But there was no other power in the oriental world to take over the inheritance. The aggregate of ethnic groups in the provinces which made up the empire as a result of four-hundred years of foreign sway, had long before ceased its struggle for national independence. And they were just as indifferent towards the struggles being carried on between the court groups and satraps. That was the internal situation. Externally, outside the borders of the Persian empire, there was no power strong enough to match itself with the Persian might. Although the Greeks had continually strengthened their position in Asia and Africa through peaceful penetration and had dotted the entire Mediterranean basin with Greek colonies, Greece itself was politically torn apart, and the competing city-states were in no position to challenge the Asiatic empire. This situation underwent a radical change when all of Greece became united under the leadership of Philip of Macedon in 338 B.C.E. Four years later his son, Alexander the Great, crossed the Hellespont and invaded the Persian territory in Asia. Alexander inflicted a crushing defeat on the Persian army in the battle at Issus in 333 B.C.E. and opened the way to Syria, Palestine and Egypt. A later victory of the Greek army at Gaugamela near Arbela in 331 B.C.E. spelled the doom of the Persian empire and cleared the way for Greek rule over the Orient.

After Alexander's death, 323 B.C.E., a long series of struggles began among his generals for control of the empire. A compromise was reached after the battle of Ipsus in 301 B.C.E., as a result of which two great Greek states emerged on the borders of Palestine—the Syrian-Mesopotamian empire under the rule of the Seleucids, and the Hellenized Egyptian empire under the Ptolemies. In some respects this was like the resurrection of the old empires of Mesopotamia and Egypt, and the age-old conflict between the two competitors for the rule over the Orient was renewed. Once again Palestine was a bridge in times of peace and a battleground in times of war. Throughout the 3rd century B.C.E. Palestine found itself under the control of the Ptolemies; it was only after the great victory of the Syrian king, Antiochus III, at Panium in 198 B.C.E., that Judah became a part of the Syrian empire.

Under the rule of the Ptolemies the Jews enjoyed the same rights of autonomy as under the Persians. The central government concerned itself only with seeing that taxes were collected, but interfered very little in internal affairs. Antiochus, too, recognized the autonomous rights of the Jews "to live according to the laws of their own country." The people of Judah, who had earlier reconciled themselves to the rule of the Persians and Ptolemies, were just as loyal in their relations to the Seleucids.

The situation in the Syrian empire, however, changed considerably after the defeat of Antiochus III in the critical battle with the Romans at Magnesia in 190 B.C.E. Rome was now actually the ruler over the oriental world and the prestige of the Syrian rulers deteriorated steadily. Syria therefore began to carry out a policy of planned Hellenization of the various populations composing the Syrian empire in order to sidetrack any particularistic tendencies within the framework of the Syrian kingdom. The policy was by no means as short-sighted as it might seem at first glance. As early as at the beginning of the 3rd century B.C.E. the process of Hellenization had made substantial progress.

In contrast to the Persians, who confined themselves to a political overlordship, the Greeks were colonizers and cultural missionaries even before they became the political masters of the ancient world. After the victories of Alexander of Macedon these activities were considerably widened. In almost all the countries of Alexander's empire the Greeks formed the leading element not only in the administrative apparatus but also in economic and cultural life. The upper classes of the local populations adopted Greek culture and Greek customs and gave their children a Greek education. It was impossible for the Jews to remain unaffected by this circumstance; Greek influence was particularly strong in the Jewish communities in the Diaspora. In the 3rd century B.C.E. the Jews in Egypt spoke Greek and even translated the Torah into Greek. In Palestine, too, the Greek element was prominent. The Philistine and Phoenician cities on the coast were almost completely Hellenized. Even in the interior there was a number of completely Hellenized cities: Scythopolis, Samaria, Pella, Philadelphia, and others. Thus Greek culture penetrated into the very heart of Palestine.

Chief among the Hellenized elements were the upper classes—the secular and priestly nobility, and the wealthy. But whereas among other oriental peoples the national culture was practically a monopoly of the upper classes—whose assimilation would mean, to all intents and purposes, the disappearance of national individuality—the situation in Judah was entirely different. From the time of the prophets it was the broad masses that were the strongest supporters of Jewish monotheism and the staunchest opponents of foreign influences. Jewish culture was from its very beginnings a folk culture, in the truest sense of the word. The prophets, the scribes, and later the Pharisees were all close to the common people. Therefore the desertion of the upper classes did not put the national life in jeopardy. Their assimilation and their adoption of Greek manners and "worldly" living simply served to widen the breach between them and the masses who remained loyal to traditional Jewish conduct and the strict Jewish way of living. Nevertheless, there was undoubtedly a very strong kinship between Jewish and Greek culture. Jewish monotheism, too, was essentially universalistic, with aspirations to expansionism. The absence of cult images and of the primitive forms of ritual, the entire structure of Jewish life and especially biblical literature and biblical ideas concerning religion and morality, made a strong impression on many Gentiles who came in contact with the Jewish world. Some Greek writers, for example, considered the Jews as a philosophic sect. "Besides the Greeks," wrote Megasthenes, "the Jews and the Brahmans are the only philosophers." This universalistic character of Jewish monotheism explains the great influence of Jewish religious propaganda in Greek and later in

Roman times. It also accounts for the strong resistance of the Jews to the spiritual domination of Hellenism. Although the Jews lacked political independence, they were nevertheless a world people who considered it their mission to disseminate their unique philosophy among all the peoples of the world. Thus there could not develop among them any feeling of inferiority in the presence of Greek culture.

Although the so-called Hellenists in Judah were a very small group, they nevertheless occupied a very important social position. The large majority of the people supported the Hasidim, the faithful, who now continued the traditions of the prophets and the Haredim. As a minority the Hellenists had to seek the support of the Syrian government. "In those days," we read in I Maccabees, "came there forth out of Israel transgressors of the law and persuaded many, saying, Let us go and make a covenant with the Gentiles that are round about us, for since we were parted from them, many evils have befallen us."

King Antiochus IV (called Epiphanes, 175-163 B.C.E.) welcomed the movement and found ready tools to promote the Hellenization of the country. One of these was Yeshua, brother of the High Priest Onias. On his promise to pay higher taxes and to promote Greek culture in Judah, Yeshua was given the office of High Priest, his own brother being removed to make place for him. Yeshua changed his name to the Hellenic form, Jason, and diligently applied himself to his task. He established a gymnasium where young Jews exercised naked, in the Greek manner, and introduced Greek civil rights for the citizens of Jerusalem which in this way became a Greek municipality. Three years later Jason, in his turn, was ousted from office by a stronger competitor, Menelaus, who was not even a priest by descent. The appointment of Menelaus was a flagrant violation of the Jewish law and aroused bitter dissatisfaction in Judah. The aggressive Hellenist party now met with strong opposition, and serious disturbances broke out in Jerusalem. The situation

REMAINS OF BUILDING IN ARAK IL-EMIR, TRANSJORDAN
Greek period

Drawing by H. C. Butler

RECONSTRUCTION OF BUILDING IN ARAK IL-EMIR, TRANSJORDAN
Greek period

in Judah became even more strained when Antiochus IV, after a successful invasion of Egypt, was compelled to bow to a peremptory Roman order and evacuate the land of the Nile. On his return to Syria Antiochus vented his fury on the Jews. He felt it all the more necessary to put an end to the stubborn resistance of the orthodox Jews towards Hellenization since the opponents of the Hellenist party began to show a pronounced political orientation towards Egypt.

On the orders of Antiochus the fortifications of Jerusalem were dismantled and the "City of David" on the eastern hill, south of the Temple, was garrisoned with Syrian soldiers in order to hold Jerusalem in check. A systematic and ruthless campaign to stamp out the Jewish religion was initiated. On the 25th of Kislev (December), 167 B.C.E. the Temple was converted into a sanctuary for Zeus Olympios, Jewish sacrificial offerings were suspended, and the observance of Jewish laws, such as the keeping of the Sabbath and festivals and the practice of circumcision, was sternly prohibited. Even the possession of a copy of the Torah was made punishable by death. Heathen altars were erected in various parts of the country and the Jews were forced to offer pagan sacrifices.

5. THE MACCABAEAN REVOLT
(167-142 B.C.E.)

Although the people of Judah had for a long time been reconciled to the loss of political independence, they bitterly opposed the attack against their religion and their national culture. Some, it is true, resigned themselves to the inevitable and bowed before the ruling power. The faithful, however, were ready to sacrifice themselves for their faith. Many fled, to hide in the desert or in the caves of the hills, but it soon became apparent that passive resistance alone was not enough, and a number of the faithful decided to start an active struggle against the Syrian rule.

The banner of open revolt was raised by the aged priest, Mattathias the Hasmonaean,

in Modein, in the hill country of Lydda. He called the people to rise against the oppressors: "Whosoever is zealous for the law and maintaineth the covenant, let him come after me." Mattathias died soon after and the leadership of the revolt was taken over by his son Judah, who had been given the name Maccabaeus (probably "the Hammerer"). The first encounter with Syrian troops ended with a victory for the Jewish rebels. After a series of hard fights the Hasmonaeans succeeded in capturing Jerusalem, only the newly constructed citadel, the so-called Akra, remaining in the hands of the Syrian garrison. The Temple was cleansed of all pagan objects, and on the 25th of Kislev, 164 B.C.E., exactly three years after the altar had been desecrated and pagan worship introduced, the Temple was rededicated amid wild rejoicing. The commemoration of this event is observed up to the present day as the Festival of Dedication, Hanukkah.

But the war was far from over. There was a vast inequality between the forces of the opposing armies. The tiny Judah numbered no more than 150,000 to 200,000 inhabitants, and no aid could be looked for from outside. In this situation the small forces of the Jewish rebels were no match for the great Syrian might. Fortune favored the rebels in that continuous internal and external conflicts absorbed the attention of the Syrian rulers. But when sufficient Syrian forces could be marshalled against the Jewish patriots, they were compelled to retreat before the overwhelming power of the enemy. However, the Syrians were never able to control the land permanently, since they found very little support within Judah itself.

After the death of Antiochus IV, the regent, Lysias, guardian of the young king, invaded Judah anew. A pitched battle was fought at Beth Zacharia, where Eleazar, the brother of Judah, lost his life. Judah Maccabaeus was compelled to withdraw his forces to Jerusalem where he made preparations to withstand a siege. Again fortune favored the rebels. The appearance of a rival claimant to the regency forced Lysias to make terms with the revolutionary party of the Hasmonaeans. Religious freedom was granted, the decrees of Antiochus against the Jewish religion were annulled and the High Priest Menelaus was deposed.

The primary aim of the Hasmonaean revolt, the restoration of Jewish autonomy, was thus achieved, but the ambitions of the Jewish patriots went a good deal further. What they now sought was complete political independence. With this end in view Judah concluded an alliance with Rome, the powerful republic in the west. This alliance, however, brought no immediate results; Rome saw no advantage at the time in interfering in the internal troubles of the Syrian empire. The conflict broke out anew. A Syrian army advanced into Judah in order to make it possible for the newly appointed High Priest, Alkimus, a moderate Hellenist, to take office. In the battle at Adasa the Syrians were decisively defeated and Nicanor, the Syrian commander, was killed. The date of the battle, the 13th of Adar, was decreed a national holiday.

Soon after, the Syrian commander Bacchides marched into Judah at the head of an army of 20,000 foot soldiers and 2,000 horsemen. Resistance was now hopeless, the Hasmonaean forces numbering no more than 3,000 warriors. Many of the followers of Judah Maccabeus, seeing the formidable forces of the enemy arrayed against them, deserted. With only 800 men left Judah refused to retreat and, after a heroic fight, fell on the battlefield.

Now the rule of the Syrians extended over the entire country and the Hellenists lifted their heads again. But the spirit of revolt was not extinguished. The remnants of the Hasmonaean forces, under the leadership of Jonathan (160-142 B.C.E.), fled to the desert region of Tekoa and launched a guerrilla war. Bacchides finally agreed to conclude peace with Jonathan, who thereupon established himself in Michmash. For a time Jerusalem, where a strong Greek garrison was stationed, remained in the hands of the Hellenists, but a few years later Jonathan, taking advantage of the internal conflicts raging in Syria, gained control of the city. He even managed to obtain from Alexander Balas, one of the rival pretenders to the Syrian throne, the appointment to the office of High Priest. The leadership of the Hasmonaeans was now generally acknowledged, and the Hellenists disappeared as a political factor from public life in Judah.

6. THE INDEPENDENT JEWISH STATE UNDER THE HASMONAEANS
(142-63 B.C.E.)

Jonathan was treacherously murdered by the Syrian general, Trypho, and the succession passed to Simon, his brother and the last surviving son of Mattathias the Hasmonaean. Demetrius II, Trypho's rival as claimant to the Syrian throne, granted Simon immunity from taxation, an act which brought to a successful culmination Judah's long struggle for its political freedom. Simon's rule was designated as beginning a new era—"And the people of Israel began to write in their instruments and contracts: In the first year of Simon the great High Priest and captain and leader of the Jews." Simon also succeeded in getting rid of the Syrian garrison at the citadel of Jerusalem, the last remnant of Syrian rule in Judah. He also captured Gazara, Bethsura and Joppa, incorporating them into Judah.

Their great political achievements and successful military exploits enormously enhanced the prestige of the Hasmonaeans, but their rule still lacked the sanction of the highest national authority, the People's Assembly. Jonathan had been made High Priest not by the people but by the favor of the Syrian ruler. It was not until 140 B.C.E., after the long and bitter struggle for independence that had lasted for more than a quarter of a century, that "In a great congregation of priests and people and leaders of the nation and elders of the country" Simon was ratified as "their leader and High Priest forever until a true prophet should appear."

As had been the case with the other sons of Mattathias the Hasmonaean, Simon was not destined to end his days in peace. He was murdered by his son-in-law, Ptolemy, but the assassin's attempt to seize the throne was frustrated by John Hyrcanus, Simon's son. In the early years of the reign of John Hyrcanus (135-104 B.C.E.) Antiochus VII Sidetes, the ruler of Syria, renewed the war against Judah and laid siege to Jerusalem, compelling John Hyrcanus to sue for peace and to recognize Syrian overlordship once more. Several years later, in 129 B.C.E., when Antiochus Sidetes fell in a battle against the Parthians, Judah recovered its freedom and John Hyrcanus was even able to extend considerably the borders of the Jewish state. Edom, the province of Medeba in Transjordan and the entire territory of Samaria were incorporated into the country.

Aristobulus, John Hyrcanus's son and successor, reigned for only a single year. He occupied the territory of Galilee and, according to Flavius Josephus, assumed the title of King, although the coins minted during his reign bear only the title High Priest. During the reign of his brother, Alexander Jannaeus (103-76 B.C.E.), the Hasmonaean state reached the peak of its territorial extent. Alexander Jannaeus was the first of the Hasmonaeans to issue coins with Greek inscriptions and to designate himself on the coins as King. The expansionist policy of his regime, and its worldly and autocratic character, evoked a strong movement of opposition in the country and a long and bloody civil war ensued which ended with the defeat of the rebels. Alexander exacted bitter revenge. Eight hundred of his prisoners were crucified and about eight thousand of his political opponents fled the country, returning only after the king's death.

Alexander was succeeded by his widow, Alexandra Salome. The expansionist policy of the Hasmonaeans, which had succeeded in a comparatively short time in restoring the boundaries of the former Greater Israel, was now over. An internal political reversal took place and the democratic party of the Pharisees came to power. When the queen died, in 67 B.C.E., a bitter struggle broke out between her two sons, Hyrcanus and Aristobulus, both of whom appealed for help to the Roman triumvir, Pompey, who had won a great victory over the Pontian king, Mithridates, in Asia Minor and had liquidated the last remnants of the Seleucid kingdom. In addition, a people's delegation pleaded with him to abolish the Hasmonaean monarchy and to permit a return to the old theocratic constitution. Thereupon Pompey moved into Jerusalem and took over the

THE "TOMB OF ABSALOM" NEAR JERUSALEM
Hasmonaean period

control of the city. The party of Aristobulus, however, led by the priestly aristocracy, resolved to resist and barricaded themselves on the Temple hill. After a three-month siege the Temple area fell into the hands of the Romans in 63 B.C.E. and thousands of the defenders and priests were killed. This marked the collapse of the Jewish independence which the first Hasmonaeans had achieved at the cost of so much sacrifice and which their own descendants had helped to destroy.

The uprising of the Hasmonaeans marks the beginning of a new period in the history of the Jewish people. Out of the

THE HISTORY OF THE JEWS IN ANCIENT TIMES

small religious community within the restricted bounds of the Jerusalem area there
arose again a nation with intense national
awareness and with an overwhelming desire
for political independence. The Hasmonaeans succeeded in reuniting all the living
sinews of ancient Israel. The Jewish settlements in Northern Palestine and Transjordan became organic parts of Greater
Judah, with the exception of the small
group of Samaritans who constantly declined in number and importance. The persecutions of Antiochus IV and the heroic
resistance of the Hasidim also had a strong
influence on the religious thought of the
Jews. For the first time in recorded history
an entire people rose up to fight for its
faith, and not only individuals but large
masses suffered martyrdom for their belief.

This struggle gave birth to a rich religious literature which dealt with the moral
order of the world, the problem of theodicy;
it sought in particular the explanation for
the undeserved well-being of the wicked
and the sufferings of the righteous. It was in
the circles of the Hasidim, too, that the
doctrine of retribution after death and the
belief in resurrection became vital principles of the Jewish faith.

The Hasmonaeans gradually turned
away from the Hasidim, with whose help
they had risen to power, and allied themselves with the priestly aristocracy and the
owning classes, the party of the Sadducees.
The masses of the people, and especially
the population of Jerusalem, supported the
Pharisees, who were at the same time a political party, an order, and a religious movement. It was the Pharisees who continued
the traditions of the Hasidim with their
zeal for the law. The Pharisees and their
opponents, the Sadducees, emerge on the
scene of history for the first time under the
reign of John Hyrcanus.

The principal controversy between the
Pharisees and the Sadducees centered
around the question of the Oral Torah.
Many of the laws and regulations contained
in the Bible were of a fragmentary character and hence problems often arose for

decision which were not anticipated in the
Torah. In addition, it was necessary to ad-
just many of the laws and ordinances of
the Pentateuch to the new conditions. As a
result a rich oral tradition had accumulated
which reflected the political, social and
spiritual development of the Jewish people
during the period of the Second Commonwealth. The Pharisees and the Scribes, the
teachers and interpreters of the Law, sup-
plemented the Written Torah with an un-
written law which was transmitted orally
from generation to generation. The Sadducees, on the other hand, rejected the oral
tradition and held that all religious evolution had ended with the Written Torah.
To quote Josephus:

> The Pharisees had passed on to the
> people certain regulations handed down
> by former generations and not recorded
> in the Laws of Moses, for which reason
> they are rejected by the Sadducean group,
> who hold that only those regulations
> should be considered valid which were
> written down and that those which had
> been handed down by former generations
> need not be observed.

According to the constitution adopted in
140 B.C.E., during Simon's reign, the right
to summon a People's Assembly was vested
in the head of the Jewish Commonwealth.
The struggles between the different parties
and schools took place, therefore, in and
around the Sanhedrin, the *Gerousia,* which
had the function of a national council and
supreme court. The social and political attitude of the party of the Pharisees, which
was recruited in the main from the intellectual classes—the scribes, the Levites, and
the teachers of the Law—was thoroughly
democratic and was strongly opposed to
the expansionist policy of the last Hasmonaeans and their "royal" ambitions. The
Pharisees were just as strongly opposed to
the Hellenistic influences which began
again to penetrate into Judah, especially
in the royal court. Nevertheless, in spite of
their democratic outlook, the party of the
Pharisees was a closed order, a fact which,

in time, led to a cleavage between them and the large mass of the agricultural population, especially in Galilee. The results of this cleavage became apparent only in later generations (See *Origin and History of the Jewish Religion* in this volume).

7. JUDAEA UNDER ROMAN RULE

Pompey reduced drastically the territory of the Jewish state, taking away from it the Hellenized cities of the coastline, Samaria, and the non-Jewish cities to the east of the Jordan. Hyrcanus II was left as the nominal ruler of the Jews with the title of Ethnarch. The driving force behind the weak-willed Hyrcanus was the shrewd Edomite, Antipater, who was the actual master of the reduced Jewish realm. Antipater also showed himself to be an adroit diplomat in his dealings with the Romans on behalf of Hyrcanus II, a fact of particular significance at a time when Rome was passing through a severe crisis and when the great world empire was undergoing frequent changes of rulers.

The pressure of the new masters let itself be felt quickly. "Within a short time," says Josephus, "the Romans exacted from us ten thousand talents." When the taxes did not suffice the treasures of the Temple were plundered. As a result a new series of rebellions broke out in Judaea. In 57-55 B.C.E. there were three uprisings under the leadership of Aristobulus II and his two sons, Alexander and Antigonus, who had escaped from Roman imprisonment. The uprisings were crushed, but in 53 B.C.E. another rebellion broke out in Galilee. This, too, was suppressed with the greatest brutality.

After Julius Caesar's overwhelming victory over Pompey at Pharsalus in 48 B.C.E., Antipater immediately changed his allegiance and went over to the side of the victor. The Jewish reinforcements sent by Antipater were of great help to Caesar during his war in Egypt and the Roman ruler showed his gratitude by enlarging the Jewish territory which Pompey had so drastically reduced. Caesar also recognized the

importance of the Jewish Diaspora for Rome's external policies and confirmed the old privileges of the Jewish communities in all the places of Jewish settlement within the Roman empire.

Meanwhile Antipater, whom Caesar appointed as procurator of Judaea, did everything he could to buttress his own position. He made his oldest son, Phasael, governor of Jerusalem, and his second son, Herod, governor of Galilee.

The influence of Rome in Western Asia extended only as far as the Euphrates. Farther to the east, in Mesopotamia and Persia, the kingdom of Parthia had been established ever since the time of the Seleucids. In 41-40 B.C.E. the Parthians defeated the Roman garrisons and managed to occupy all of Syria and Palestine. With the help of the new rulers, the Hasmonaean Mattathias Antigonus, the surviving son of Aristobulus II, established himself as king and High Priest, Hyrcanus II being deposed from the latter office and deported by the Parthians. Herod, the son of Antipater, escaped to Rome to seek help against Antigonus and the Parthians. The reign of Antigonus, however, did not last long. Temporary setbacks could not stop Rome's ever-mounting power and the Parthians were soon forced to abandon the territory of Syria and Palestine. In the meantime Herod, the friend of the Romans, was declared king of Judaea by Senatorial decree; but it took a long and difficult war before he was able, with the help of the Roman forces, to establish his rule over Judaea. During the siege of Jerusalem Herod married the Hasmonaean princess, Mariamne, a grand-daughter of Hyrcanus II, attempting in this way to legitimatize his claims to the throne of Judah.

By the grace of the Roman rulers the Edomite usurper gradually extended his territory until Herod's kingdom surpassed the boundaries of Greater Judah in the time of the last Hasmonaeans. In spite of his political successes, the external grandeur of his reign, and his grandiose building activities, Herod remained a stranger in his own country. His entire reign was filled with court intrigues and conspiracies. The Edomite tyrant executed large numbers of the Jewish aristocracy and many of the members of the Sanhedrin. Among Herod's victims were his own wife, the Hasmonaean princess, Mariamne, her brother Aristobulus, and her children, whom the people considered the heirs presumptive to the throne. At the same time Herod made several gestures intended to conciliate the people, for that reason showing surprising tolerance towards the leaders of the Pharisees, Shemayah and Abtalion. In 20 B.C.E. he began his most ambitious project, the rebuilding of the Temple in Jerusalem. But only the main edifice was completed in his lifetime; the surrounding courts and buildings were not finally completed until 64 C.E. Herod's Temple was of dazzling beauty: "When the morning sun burst upon the white marble of the Temple, Mount Moriah glittered like a hill of snow" (Josephus).

In spite of Herod's attempts to win the confidence of the people the chasm between them grew wider and wider. It was only with the help of Rome and a regime of terror and espionage that Herod was able to maintain his power over Judaea for over thirty years.

Immediately after the death of Herod disturbances broke out in Jerusalem and quickly spread all over the country. In Galilee, Judaea and Transjordan there arose leaders of guerrilla groups and religious visionaries who called on the people to rise against the hated dynasty and the Roman overlords. The revolutionary movement was mercilessly crushed and the kingdom, according to the terms of Herod's will, was divided among his three sons, Archelaus, Herod Antipas, and Philip. To Archelaus was assigned the territory of Samaria, Judaea and Idumaea; to Herod Antipas, Galilee and Peraea; and to Philip, the northern region of Transjordan.

The reign of Archelaus was brief. As a result of the bitter complaints against his rule by the Jews and Samaritans, the Emperor Augustus deposed him and sent him to Gaul, Judaea being placed under the rule of a Roman procurator who made his residence in Caesarea and was directly responsible to the emperor.

On the whole the Roman authorities respected the Jewish traditions, and the Jews in Judaea, as well as in the Diaspora, were able to live according to their own laws and customs. The Jews were also permitted to abstain from taking part in the emperor worship which was obligatory for all subjects of the empire. But this did not satisfy the Jewish patriots. They found unbearable the foreign yoke which other peoples accepted with resignation. The Roman officials, for their part, could not understand the "obstinacy" of the Jews and their fanatical adherence to the traditions of their forefathers, and thus, even with the best will in the world, it would have been impossible to avoid conflicts. Any sort of good will, however, was for the most part lacking; many of the Roman procurators used their power mostly for their personal interests. Traffic in the office of High Priest was particularly good business for the procurators. The pressure of foreign rule was therefore more intensely felt at this time than in the time of Herod.

The attempt of the Roman emperor, Gaius Caligula, to impose the imperial cult on the Jews, and his order to the Syrian legate Petronius to erect a statue of the Caesar in the Temple, brought Judaea to the brink of catastrophe. Petronius did all he could to postpone the fulfilment of the order, so as to ward off an open uprising, and he finally approached Gaius Caligula with the request to rescind the order. But before Caligula was able to make his final decision he was assassinated by a conspirator and the rule of the insane emperor came to an end.

Claudius, Caligula's successor (41-54 C.E.), confirmed the ancient rights and privileges of the Jews in Palestine as well as in the Diaspora. In addition he named his friend Herod Agrippa, the grandson of Herod and the Hasmonaean princess, Mariamne, king

From THE THIRD WALL OF JERUSALEM *by E. L. Sukenik and L. A. Mayer. Courtesy Oxford University Press*

PART OF THIRD WALL AROUND JERUSALEM
Construction begun by Agrippa, completed during the Judaeo-Roman war

over all of Judaea. For a short time, from 41 to 44, the entire Jewish territory was again united under the rule of a prince of the Herod-Hasmonaean stock. But in marked contrast to his grandfather's rule, Herod Agrippa made efforts to win the confidence of the people and, during his stay in Jerusalem, scrupulously observed all the religious ordinances and commandments and acceded to the demands of the Pharisees. He even commenced the construction of a wall around Jerusalem, but orders from Rome compelled him to abandon the work.

8. CULTURAL AND ECONOMIC LIFE IN THE ROMAN PERIOD

During the Roman period Palestine remained, as before, essentially an agricultural country. The industrious Jewish peasant was tireless in getting the greatest possible yield out of the soil. Josephus describes Galilee, for example, as one great garden: "Every inch of the soil has been cultivated by the inhabitants; there is not a parcel of waste land." Agricultural technique was comparatively far advanced and the peasant in Palestine utilized the peculiar configuration of the hill country as well as all available water resources with the utmost skill. As a result, by the end of the Second Commonwealth, the country was thickly populated. Its Jewish population numbered close to 1,500,000.

Trade, too, occupied an important place in the country's economy. The Jewish literature of the period makes mention of a great number of crafts. Greek influence probably played an important role here as is indicated by many terms in the Mishnah borrowed from the Greek to designate various crafts. There were many villages and towns which were known for their particular industries. Many of the leaders of the Pharisees as well as many of the early followers of Jesus were craftsmen; Jesus himself was a carpenter. Commerce did not play an outstanding part in the life of the country, although Palestine was by no means isolated commercially from the rest of the surrounding world. On the contrary many of the great international trade routes, which bound the countries of the east with the countries of the west, now as in earlier days passed through Syria and Palestine. However, in a number of important trade centers and port cities the population was largely non-Jewish.

Jerusalem, with a population of 80,000 to 100,000, was not only the capital of Judaea but the religious and cultural center for the widely scattered Jewish communities all over the world. The political and religious development of the Jewish people in the period of the Second Commonwealth was to a large extent determined by the dominating influence of Jerusalem in Jewish life as a whole. Within the population of Jerusalem the laboring classes, the artisans and unskilled workers, occupied a conspicuous place. Shortly before the outbreak of the Judaeo-Roman war, according to Josephus, when construction work on the Temple had been completed 18,000 workers were left without employment: "So when the people saw that the workmen were unemployed, and that they, receiving no wages, were in want," the funds of the Temple were applied to the repair of the streets of the city in order to provide work for the needy population.

Courtesy Ewing Galloway

"TOMBS OF THE KINGS" IN JERUSALEM
1st century

Since the time of the last Hasmonaeans profound changes had taken place in Jewish spiritual life. The widespread elation over the recovery of their political independence gradually cooled. The autocratic regime of the last Hasmonaeans, and especially the sanguinary civil war following the death of Queen Alexandra intensified the feeling of opposition towards every form of worldly government. This feeling gradually increased during the rule of Herod and the procurators. Worldly power came to be considered more and more as evil and ungodly. Among the pacifist-minded Pharisees of the Hillel school there were many supporters of the tendency which preached the idea of political abstinence: to ignore political life as far as possible and to have as little as possible to do with mundane government. Although they showed no opposition to alien rule they categorically refused to swear loyalty to a rule not decreed by God. Another wing of the Phari-

families. The Sadducees gradually made peace not only with the foreign rule but also with the foreign rulers and became "friends" of the Romans, while their opposition to the national revolutionary movement grew steadily. Thus the conflict between the conquered and the conquerors was complicated by the sharp cleavage between the upper classes and the masses of the people in Judaea itself.

Notwithstanding the heavy political pressure, Jewish life in the Roman period was characterized by great spiritual freedom and creativity. Among the Pharisees there were divergent political tendencies, nation-

DEDICATION STONE WITH GREEK INSCRIPTION FROM SYNAGOGUE IN JERUSALEM

The dedication reads in part: "Theodotos, son of Vettenos, Priest and Archisynagogos, son of an Archisynagogos, grandson of an Archisynagogos, built the Synagogue for the reading of the Law and for the teaching of the Commandments; furthermore, the Hospice and the Chambers, and the water installation for lodging of needy strangers . . ."

sees, principally the supporters of Shammai, argued for unyielding resistance and uncompromising struggle against the alien rule.

Nor did the Sadducees remain unaffected by the storms of the period. A large part of the old Hasmonaean nobility had perished during the reign of Herod. In their stead there arose a new nobility belonging to worldly as well as to priestly

alist and extreme pacifist, and various theological schools, Bet Hillel and Bet Shammai. Close to the Pharisees were the Essenes, a religious and social community, who had as their aim the realization of the social and ethical ideas of the prophets. The Essenes were celibates. They renounced private property, recognized no distinctions between the social classes, and were extreme pacifists. They lived in communes, ate their meals in common and practiced communal ownership. A stern ritual asceticism and a striving for social justice were the characteristics of the Essene way of life. The Zealots, who were extreme patriots, were also connected with the Pharisees. The founders of the national revolutionary Zealot movement were Judah the Galilean, the son of the "robber leader" Hezekiah, and the Pharisee Zadok. The Zealots recognized no ruler other than God and refused to reconcile themselves to the Roman rule. They carried on the struggle not only through open rebellion and terroristic attempts, but by passive resistance through the non-payment of taxes and refusal to obey the orders of the foreign power.

The period of Roman rule over Judaea witnessed the birth of Christianity, which, at its outset, played only a minor role, but in time became a powerful factor in world history. Jesus of Nazareth came from Galilee, then under the rule of Herod Antipas. It was in Galilee, some time before, that the ascetic and preacher, John the Baptist, who paid with his life for his open opposition to the ruler, had been active. At first the Christians were close to the Zealots—one of the apostles bears the name Simon Zelotes—and found most of their supporters among the common people of Galilee. Many even regarded the first Christians as an anti-Roman group. The social reformist aspects in Christianity—opposition to the existing social order and renunciation of personal property; practice of the common purse and common table of the early Christian community—stem from the Zealots as well as from the Essenes.

At the same time Jesus was an opponent of the rigid asceticism of John the Baptist and the strict observances of the Pharisees. The first Christians arose in the tense mood of the eve of the Messianic period. The expectation of imminent redemption, of the advent of the Kingdom of Heaven, was the chief theme of the Christian message. Gradually this changed. As more and more non-Jews joined the movement, Christian propaganda had to conform to the Greek-Roman world and thus depart further from its Jewish roots. With this development Christianity lost its original Utopian character and made a compromise with the existing social order. Christian missionaries spoke more and more about the Messiah as having already arrived and less and less about redemption still to come. In the great Judaeo-Roman war the Christian communities played no part whatsoever.

As early as in the Hellenistic period the large majority of the Jewish people lived outside the borders of Palestine. As is emphasized by many Jewish, Greek and Roman writers of the time, there was practically no part of the then known world without its Jewish community, large or small. The Jews settled mostly in the large trade centers and port cities such as Alexandria, Antiochia, Cyrene, Damascus, Palmyra, etc. In Europe, too, and especially in

RELIEF FROM SYNAGOGUE IN PRIENE, ASIA MINOR

Greece and Italy, the number of Jewish settlements constantly increased. At the end of the Second Commonwealth the population of the Diaspora, according to the best estimates, numbered approximately 3,000,-000, about two-thirds of whom lived in Babylonia and Egypt. In the countries to the east of Palestine the Jews spoke Aramaic; in the western countries in Asia Minor,

Africa and Europe they spoke Greek. The increase in the Diaspora population was the result not only of emigration but was to a large extent caused by the conversion to Judaism of members of the local populations. From the time of the Persian empire the number of proselytes to Judaism increased considerably in all Jewish settlements. In addition to the proselytes who accepted all the Jewish ordinances there was a large number of semi-proselytes who observed only part of the Jewish ordinances. These proselytes were known by the name of *Sebomenoi*—"those who fear God." In the Roman world the custom of celebrating the Sabbath was extremely widespread. Other Jewish ordinances and customs, too, were adopted by many Gentiles. The intensive Jewish religious propaganda in the Diaspora, which went hand in hand with a certain separateness from the Gentile population—"Jewish exclusiveness" as it was termed even then—evoked strong dissatisfaction in many circles and even fomented open hatred toward the Jews. An important factor in this enmity was economic competition. The Jews in the Greek-speaking parts of the Diaspora settled mostly in the cities and were thus the natural competitors of the Greek urban population.

In Alexandria, the capital city of Egypt, Jews had their autonomy and their own judicial courts. The Senate *(Gerousia)* and the Ethnarch were at the head of the community. In most of the other cities of the Roman Diaspora the situation was the same. In Rome, however, there was no unified Jewish community; the population was organized into small synagogue congregations. In Babylonia agriculture was the most important element in the Jewish economy, and in several sections Jews constituted the majority of the population. They exerted a profound influence on the surrounding populations; in Adiabene, a vassal kingdom of the Parthian empire, the entire royal family and a large part of the population went over to Judaism. Spiritually, Babylonian Jewry maintained continuous close contact with the Jewish center in Palestine. A favorable circumstance was that the Jews in Babylonia spoke Aramaic, studied the holy books in Hebrew and thus shared a common language with the Jews in Palestine.

9. THE LAST PROCURATORS AND THE JUDAEO-ROMAN WAR

After the death of Agrippa I the rule over all of Judaea passed again to the Roman procurators. The pressure of the Roman yoke became heavier and heavier, increasing the will for resistance among the Jewish population. The leading circles of the Sadducees, as well as of the Pharisees, both of whom had made constant efforts to restrain the people from revolutionary action, found their influence steadily declining. At the same time the influence of the revolutionists and Zealots grew. Around them were gathered all the dissatisfied elements—all those who awaited the coming of "the end of the days."

The tyranny and misrule of the Roman administration reached its peak under the procurator Florus (64-66) who, according to Josephus, far exceeded all his predecessors in brutality and corruption and who, in order to cover up his excesses, deliberately provoked the people to revolt. At a great assembly held in the Temple the Zealots forced through a decision to reject all sacrifices offered by Gentiles. This meant, in effect, the suspension of the daily sacrifices in behalf of the emperor and was tantamount to an open declaration of war against the Roman empire. The peace party again made desperate efforts to quiet the people in order to avoid open conflict. But now it was too late. The enmity of the Zealots towards the "appeasers" and "Romanophiles" was no less intense than towards the Romans themselves. A bitter and bloody civil war followed. Street by street the rebels captured the entire city, burning a number of houses and palaces of the aristocracy.

In many Palestinian cities with mixed populations, the news of the revolution in

Jerusalem set off bitter encounters and massacres. In Caesarea, according to Josephus, 20,000 Jews were slain; in other towns the Jews avenged themselves on the Gentile inhabitants. The unrest carried over to neighboring countries; in the great center of Alexandria thousands of Jews were killed.

At last the Roman legate in Syria, Cestius Gallus, marched into Judaea at the head of a large military force. His attempt to take Jerusalem by storm failed, and he retreated with his army. On its march through the narrow mountain pass at Beth-horon the Roman troops were attacked and defeated by the rebels, losing many men and immense quantities of supplies.

The defeat of Cestius Gallus aroused wild enthusiasm among the Jewish population. The peace party ceased to exist as a political factor and even the moderate elements joined in the revolutionary movement. Feverish preparations were made for the war against Rome. A government of national defense was formed; it consisted, characteristically enough, almost exclusively of representatives of the aristocracy and the moderate Pharisees. The former High Priest, Hanan, and Joseph ben Gurion, were chosen commanders of Jerusalem; and the command of Galilee was entrusted to the young priest, Joseph ben Matthias, who was later to become famous as the historian Flavius Josephus.

In the spring of the year 67 the Roman general Vespasian entered Palestine with an army of approximately 60,000 men. There could be no thought of the rebels matching themselves against so formidable an enemy in the open field, where Roman superiority was indisputable. The Jewish warriors had plenty of courage but they lacked military technique and experience. Most of all they lacked skilled military leaders, and they therefore had to rely on defensive warfare. These circumstances placed the Roman army in an advantageous position from the very beginning. Vespasian was able to place his entire force at the most strategic points while the Jewish

forces were scattered all over the country. Within a few months all of Galilee was subdued. The main fortress, Jotapata, fell after a forty-seven-day siege and the commander of the Jewish army in Galilee, Joseph ben Matthias, surrendered to the victors. Vespasian met more stubborn resistance at Gamala in Northern Transjordan and at Gish-halab in Galilee. A large number of the Zealots in Gish-halab, together with their leader, Johanan, succeeded in escaping to Jerusalem.

In Jerusalem the extremists were utterly dissatisfied with the conduct of the war by the moderates. The loss of Galilee, followed by the arrival in Jerusalem of the surviving Zealots and refugees, strengthened the position of the extremists. An open rebellion against the moderate government broke out. The Zealots, who controlled the Temple area, decided to choose a new High Priest by lot; as a result Phinehas, a simple priest, was elevated to the highest office in the country. This action amounted to a declaration of war against the priestly aristocracy. The bitter civil strife which ensued ended with a victory for the Zealots.

After their victory over the moderate elements, contention and division of opinion developed in the camp of the Zealots themselves. The revolutionists had shown miracles of strength and heroism in the struggle against the Romans, but they were far from being adequate to the task of organizing the people and gathering together all the national energies for a war against so mighty an enemy as Rome.

While these internal disputes were going on Vespasian did not remain idle. Deliberately avoiding Jerusalem, he occupied the greater part of Judaea. The internal strife among the Zealots was worth a military victory to him; he had no intention of letting his presence interfere with the process of internal weakening. An interruption in the campaign came with the confused situation in Rome following the death of Nero in 68. When, in 69, Vespasian was proclaimed emperor, the leadership of the Roman armies

THE WAILING WALL IN JERUSALEM
Part of the wall around the Temple Mount

in Judaea was given to Titus, Vespasian's son.

In the spring of the year 70, the Roman armies, under Titus, approached Jerusalem. Even at this critical moment, with the enemy at their gates, the leaders of the opposing factions of the Zealots, Johanan of Gish-halab and Simon bar Giora, kept up their civil strife. It was only when the Romans began to storm the fortified walls of the city that the internal dissension ended. Soon another enemy, hunger, came to torment the defenders. In spite of this they fought furiously.

After the fall of the Third Wall the battle shifted to the upper city and the Temple hill. On the fifth day of the month of Tammuz, the Tower of Antonia, the fortress near the Temple, fell. For more than a month the battle raged about the Temple area with unrestrained ferocity. On the tenth of Ab the Temple was in flames. Some of the defenders managed to break through to the upper city where Simon bar Giora still held out. Less than a month after the burning of the Temple the last Jewish positions in Jerusalem were lost. The city was completely destroyed and most of its people and its defenders killed during the siege and in the final battles. Those who survived were either slaughtered or sold into slavery. Seven hundred of the survivors, among them Simon bar Giora and Johanan of Gish-halab, and some of the sacred objects of the Temple were taken by the Romans to enhance the triumphal march of the victorious Titus.

After the fall of Jerusalem there still remained in the hands of the Zealots the fortresses of Herodium, Machaerus and Masada. The defenders of Masada, headed by Eleazar ben Yair, a descendant of Judah the Galilean, held out the longest. When further resistance was impossible the embattled warriors killed their wives and children and then took their own lives so as not to fall alive into the hands of the enemy. When the conquering Romans entered the fortress, they found a city of the dead.

RELIEF DETAIL FROM THE ARCH OF TITUS ERECTED IN ROME AT
THE END OF THE 1ST CENTURY
Representing Jewish captives carrying holy objects from the Temple

III. FROM THE DAWNFALL OF THE SECOND COMMONWEALTH TO THE RISE OF ISLAM

(1st-7th century C.E.)

1. YABNEH AND THE PATRIARCHATE

Jerusalem lay waste; the entire country was in ruins. Small groups of the Zealots who had managed to save themselves attempted again to light up the flame of rebellion against Rome in the large Jewish settlements in North Africa—Alexandria and Cyrene. The attempt was destined to fail; nevertheless Rome, as a matter of caution, closed up the Temple of Leontopolis, the Jewish religious center in Egypt. The Roman government also took steps to make sure that the Jews would never forget the destruction of Jerusalem. Instead of the earlier shekel payment for the Temple the Jews were now compelled to pay a special head tax, the "Fiscus Judaicus," which went to the sanctuary of Jupiter Capitolinus in Rome. A large area of Jewish territory in Palestine was confiscated and leased to Gentile colonists. Amidst the rubble of the ruined Jerusalem there was left only a Roman garrison. The administrative center of Judaea remained in Caesarea. Palestine, however, remained a Jewish country, although with the destruction of Jerusalem and the abolition of the office of High Priest and the Sanhedrin, the most conspicuous symbols of Jewish autonomy disappeared.

Profound changes had been wrought in the social and spiritual life of the people by the political catastrophe which had overwhelmed the country. The priestly aristocracy lost its function and, as a consequence, its dominating position. The worldly nobility, unable to survive the downfall of Jerusalem, almost completely disappeared from the Jewish scene. For the Sadducees this meant the loss of their social basis and the reason for their existence. In addition the Sadducees were completely unsuited ideologically to the new situation. As for the Zealots most of their number had perished in the war; the few survivors were spiritually broken. For the immediate future, at any rate, there were no material possibilities for carrying on the war against the Romans. The Pharisees alone remained as the guardians of Jewish traditions and national hopes. They were the only group able to give comfort to the individual and hope to the masses. Within their ranks it was the pacifist wing, the school of Hillel, which now came to the fore. They were the element which had constantly urged the people to avoid an unequal war against the Roman might and to wait with patience for God's mercy to become manifest. Now, in any event, no other hope remained.

There is a Talmudic tradition which relates that during the Judaeo-Roman war Johanan ben Zakkai, the leader of the moderate Pharisees, stole out of beleaguered Jerusalem and went to the camp of the Romans. There he secured Vespasian's promise to spare Yabneh and its sages and the family of Rabbi Gamaliel, the grandchildren of Hillel. We do know that immediately after the destruction of Jerusalem the Romans consented to the establishment at Yabneh of a Bet-din (high court) and a Talmudic academy. These institutions took over the leadership of the people and many of the functions of the Sanhedrin, and were headed by Johanan ben Zakkai. He was succeeded by Gamaliel II, the grandson of Gamaliel I. The head of the Bet-din, the Nasi, or Patriarch, as he was called by the Romans, was also recognized by the Roman authorities as the representative of the Jewish people. The office of head of the Bet-din or Sanhedrin remained hereditary in the Hillel family for more than three centuries.

Religion was now the only force which, under the existing circumstances, was able to keep together the Jews in Palestine as well as in the Diaspora. Consequently the Bet-din of Yabneh occupied itself mainly with regulating and coordinating religious life. With the discontinuance of the Temple services, the reorganization of divine worship on the basis of synagogal services and individual prayer was of primary importance. The sacrificial service in the Temple was replaced by "service with the heart" and, especially for the common man, prayer became the most important aspect of religious life.

The comparatively wide spiritual freedom of the period before the destruction was gradually replaced by the principle of strict discipline and authority in matters of law and ritual and eventually even in affairs of religious dogma. Gamaliel I had been able to show the greatest tolerance toward the Christian apostles who were brought before the Sanhedrin; his grandson, Gamaliel II, authorized the inclusion of a special prayer against the apostates and heretics in the daily synagogue service, for the purpose of making it impossible for them to participate in Jewish communal religious worship. He even rigorously disciplined his opponents in the Sanhedrin itself and imposed a religious ban on the great teacher and sage, Eliezer ben Hyrcanus.

The authoritarian policies of the head of the Bet-din aroused a great deal of dissatisfaction, the result of which was that Gamaliel II was deposed and replaced by Eleazar ben Azariah. That frictions and conflicts of a social character played a part in the disputes within the Bet-din is indicated by a Talmudic tradition which relates that when Eleazar was appointed to the office of Nasi, the gates of the academy were opened wide to all who sought admittance. The family of the Patriarch seems to have held itself aloof from the common people. One of the most venerated members of the Sanhedrin, Joshua ben Hanania, a renowned teacher and sage but a poor, hard-working artisan, is reported to have said to Gamaliel: "Woe to the generation whose leader thou art, seeing thou knowest not the sorrows of the scholars, nor how they maintain their life." Later on a reconciliation was reached and Gamaliel was reinstated as the head of the Bet-din.

2. THE BAR KOCHBA UPRISING (132-135)

In the year 114 the emperor Trajan set out to conquer the East, and began his campaign against the Parthian empire. For this purpose the Romans withdrew a large part of the forces stationed in the province of Africa. Taking advantage of the difficulties in which the Romans found themselves, the Jewish Zealots in Egypt, Cyrene, and Cyprus rose up against Rome (115-117). At the same time, in the rear of the Roman army in Mesopotamia, the Babylonian Jews, too, raised the banner of revolt. The struggle, conducted on both sides with great energy and ferocity, ended in the defeat of the Jews and the utter destruction of a large number of Jewish communities in Africa and Western Asia.

Barely fifteen years later war broke out anew, this time in Palestine itself. Trajan's successor, Hadrian, ordered that Jerusalem be rebuilt as a Roman city to be named Aelia Capitolina. A more menacing threat to Jewish survival came with his second decree reviving an ancient Roman law forbidding any physical mutilation. The decree was interpreted as including a ban on the Jewish custom of circumcision, and this attack on Jewish religious beliefs gave birth to the revolutionary-messianic movement of Bar Kochba (132-135), who is also referred to in the Talmud as Bar Koziba. The suddenness of the movement, which soon reached formidable proportions. caught the Romans unaware and unprepared. Discipline among the Jews, as well as the military and political leadership of the uprising, was better than in the time of the destruction of the Temple. The spiritual leader of the people, the renowned sage, Rabbi Akiba, joined the movement and gave his moral support to Bar Kochba. In the first year of the revolt the rebels succeeded in driving out the Roman garrisons and freeing the country. The messianic expectations of the people were reawakened and the revolutionary government issued coins stamped with the inscriptions "In the year of the liberation of Jerusalem" and "Simon the Prince of Israel" (See *History of Jewish Archaeology*). For a long time Bar Kochba fought successfully against the Roman armies but finally the superior military tech-

Courtesy THE LADDER OF PROGRESS IN PALESTINE *by C. C. McCown, published by Harper and Brothers*

MENORAH CARVED ON WALL OF CATACOMB IN BETH-SHEARIM
The seven-branched lamp was a common Jewish religious symbol
at the close of the period of Antiquity

nique and the unlimited reserves of the Roman empire prevailed. In 135, three-and-a-half years after the beginning of the uprising, Bether, the fortress in which Bar Kochba had entrenched himself with the remnants of his forces, fell to the Romans. The Romans paid a heavy price for the victory; in his report to the Senate announcing the end of the Judaeo-Roman war, Hadrian omits the usual introductory formula: "I and my armies are well."

The defeat of Bar Kochba was a national disaster as crushing as the destruction of Jerusalem. The enormous loss of life and the countless thousands sold into slavery led to a sharp reduction of the Jewish population. The suffering in the territory of Judaea was severe. Jerusalem was rebuilt as a Roman city under the name of Aelia Capitolina. On the site of the Temple a sanctuary for Jupiter Capitolinus was erected and entrance to their one-time principal city was forbidden to the Jews under the penalty of death.

After his military victories Hadrian issued a number of oppressive decrees with the aim of destroying the Jewish faith. These included strict bans on the observance of the Sabbath, on circumcision and the study and teaching of the Torah. Any violation of the decrees was punishable by death. Religious martyrdom was thus added to the national catastrophe. Talmudic literature designates the period as the "time of annihilation" in which the "ten martyrs," among whom was the sage Akiba, openly defied the Roman decrees and died for the "Sanctification of the Name."

3. THE SANHEDRIN IN USHA: THE REDACTION OF THE MISHNAH

The successor of Hadrian, Antoninus Pius (138-161), revoked the oppressive decrees against the Jews. The country began to recover but the center of Jewish life shifted to Galilee, which had suffered least during the recent events. The disciples of Akiba again began to organize Jewish religious life. In the city of Usha, in Galilee, the supreme religious body, the Sanhedrin, was reestablished and ordinances were adopted, most of them aimed at enforcing Jewish family discipline, which had been violently shaken by the national catastrophe and the economic collapse.

Since the time of Yabneh the Sanhedrin had been more of an academic than a political institution. Under the restricted conditions the leaders of the people occupied themselves more and more with the study and teaching of the Torah. After the destruction of the Temple a large number of religious laws and commandments lost their practical meaning and became only matters for theoretical study. Others had to be adjusted to the changed circumstances brought about by the national catastrophe. In addition, various new ordinances and practices were introduced. The scope of the Oral Torah thus steadily increased and the accumulation of traditions and laws grew greater, making it imperative to collect and systematize the material which had been gathered for generations. That task was commenced in Yabneh by the great sage, Akiba, continued by his pupil, Meir, and completed by Judah ha-Nasi (approximately 135-200). The patriarch Judah ha-Nasi, or Rabbi, as he is most frequently referred to in Talmudic literature, took over the office of Nasi from his father, Simon ben Gamaliel, and his authority was widely recognized not only as teacher and sage but also as leader. He had all the necessary personal qualifications for undertaking so colossal a task as the codification of the Oral Torah, and since the Romans were more tolerant towards autonomous Jewish institutions, external circumstances favored the work. The systematizing and editing of the Mishnah, as the collection of oral laws and traditions was called, was Judah's life work and was accomplished with the help of a large number of his colleagues and students. From then on the Oral Torah became a second Written Torah and the redaction of the Mishnah, from the point of view of its historical influence, can be compared without exaggeration to the epoch-making work of Ezra the Scribe more than six hundred years before.

The completion of the Mishnah marks more than merely a date in literary history. Among the Jews literature and life were closely interwoven. In its written form the Oral Torah could more easily be spread beyond the borders of Palestine and was thus able to strengthen the spiritual unity of the dispersed Jewish people. At the same time it made possible the emergence of a new spiritual center which, in course of time, diminished to a large extent the authority of Palestine. Judah ha-Nasi's disciple, Rab, was now able to take the new Torah along with him and plant it in the fertile soil of Babylonia, whose Jewish population, dating from the time of the deportation of King Joiachin, about eight hundred years before, now far surpassed in number the Jewish settlement in Palestine. The political catastrophe and the accompanying oppressions and persecutions in

From SEFER HA-YISHUB, *Jerusalem*

MARBLE TOMBSTONE WITH GREEK INSCRIPTION AT BETH-SHEARIM
Probably 3rd century

Palestine had started a fresh stream of emigration into the territory of the Parthians, where the Jews lived in comparative security. Thus the Babylonian settlement received a significant and continuous increase of valuable spiritual energies and became ready for the historic role which it was soon called upon to assume.

4. THE JEWS IN CHRISTIAN ROME
(4th-7th century)

The reign of Constantine the Great (306-337), during which Christianity became the predominant religion in the Roman empire, marks the beginning of a new chapter in Jewish history. Up to this period the causes which had led to the conflicts and wars between Rome and Judah were almost invariably national and political in character. The Roman rulers, with the exception of Hadrian, had never made war against the Jewish faith. Now there came a radical change. Christianity, differing from ancient polytheism which knew very little of religious wars, from its very beginnings showed a strong tendency toward expansion. In common with Judaism, Christianry was neither willing nor able to recognize any other God or any other belief. But while Christianity had up to this time carried on its battles with purely ideological weapons, there was now brought to its aid the powerful state apparatus of the great Roman empire. The worship of pagan gods gradually began to disappear and it fell to the lot of the Jewish people to stand alone against the overwhelming coalition of worldly and religious might which came into being in the Roman empire. The struggle was especially hard for the reason that Christianity was ideologically close to Judaism; it accepted the holiness of the Bible and to a large extent the principles of the Jewish faith. The Jewish people had never before been confronted with such a threat and even the oppressions of Antiochus and Hadrian were not much more than minor historical episodes in comparison. Fortunately the Roman might did not reach as far as Babylonia, the largest Jewish settlement of the period, and Jewish life there continued to develop under more or less tolerable conditions.

As a matter of fact Judaism had the status of a permitted and tolerated faith (*religio licita*), but Jewish rights were continually narrowed; as citizens Jews were more and more degraded. Jewish religious propaganda was severely punished, as was conversion to Judaism, whereas converts to Christianity were placed under the protection of the ruling power. The Church conducted a systematic and purposeful policy of separating the Christian population from their

ARAMAIC LETTER ON PAPYRUS
FROM PALESTINE
About 5th century

Jewish neighbors. Christians were prohibited from joining in Jewish meals, or observing the Sabbath—which was at that time practiced by many Gentiles—or attending Jewish religious gatherings, etc. Marriage between Christians and Jews was strictly forbidden and Jews were prohibited from owning Christian slaves.

The situation thus created could not help worsening the relationship between the Jews and the Christians in Palestine. On the site of the Temple in Jerusalem a Christian church was now erected. The constant stream of newcomers who wanted to settle in the Holy Land augmented the Christian community and as a result the Jewish population of the country steadily decreased.

After the death of Theodosius I in 395, the Roman empire was finally divided into two completely separated States, the Western Roman empire with Rome as its capital, and Byzantium—the Eastern Roman empire—which embraced the Hellenized areas, with Constantinople as its capital. By far the greater number of Jewish settlements remained in Byzantium, where the influence of the Church was especially great. During the reign of Theodosius II (408-450) a new series of repressive laws was issued against the Jews. The building of new synagogues was forbidden, Jews were excluded from all public office, and Jewish religious-national autonomy was drastically limited. After the death of Gamaliel VI in 425, the institution of the Patriarchate was completely abolished.

The treatment of the "infidels" by the government as well as by the Church bodies and the Christian population in time became even harsher. The repressive decrees of the emperor Justinian (527-565) led to a revolt among the Samaritans which was ruthlessly put down, resulting in the almost complete extermination of this branch of ancient Israel. Justinian also undertook to regulate the internal religious life of the Jewish communities and even issued orders on the manner in which the Torah should be read and interpreted in the synagogue.

In the later Roman period the Jewish Diaspora expanded and many new Jewish colonies appeared. In Asia Jewish settlements were established as far as Northern and Southern Arabia. In Africa, Jewish settlements spread to the neighborhood of the present-day Algiers and Morocco. In these areas the Jews joined with the descendants of the ancient Phoenician inhabitants who, a thousand years earlier, had colonized the important port cities of the North Africa coastline. In Europe, too, in spite of the collapse of the Western Roman empire, Jewish settlements spread further and further. There were Jewish settlements in various parts of Italy as well as in Gaul (France) —mostly in the southern provinces—and in Spain where the West Goths settled in the 5th century. At the end of the 6th century the conditions under which the Jews in Spain lived began to show considerable deterioration; a wave of persecutions and forced conversions culminated in the almost total ruin of the Jewish settlements during the 7th century. The earliest record of Jews within the boundaries of what is now Germany, places Jewish settlements in the Rhine area at the beginning of the 4th cen-

Jewish population at the close of the period of Antiquity and the beginning of the Middle Ages. This was in part a consequence of the decline of the general economy—especially the urban economy—during this period, but no small part was played by the increasing repressions and persecutions on the part of the Christian rulers.

The Jewish settlements which suffered most severely were the ones in Palestine and Egypt. The Jewish homeland was losing its Jewish character more and more and in the first half of the 7th century only small rem-

TOMBSTONE FROM NARBONNE, FRANCE, DATING FROM 689
With Latin inscription and Hebrew phrase "Shalom al Yisrael"

tury, in the year 321. Within the borders of present-day Hungary, too, traces have been found of Jewish settlements in the later Roman period, and in the Balkans such settlements date from an even earlier time.

In spite of this geographical expansion the number of Jews in the Christian countries continually declined. All available evidence supports the assumption that there was a catastrophic decline in the size of the

nants were left of the once great Jewish center; its spiritual leadership over Jewish life had been lost by Palestine as early as the 4th century. In Egypt, too, the Jewish population was greatly reduced. Of the approximately three million Jews who, in the period of the Second Temple, lived within the borders of the Roman empire, no more than half a million were left at the end of the period of Antiquity. Parallel with these catastrophic events was the evolutionary process through which the Jews, who had previously enjoyed full civil rights, became transformed into an "alien" and disfranchised people.

Even more important was the profound change in the social-economic structure of the Jewish settlements. The Jews in the Roman Diaspora had from the beginning

TOMBSTONE FOUND IN TORTOSA, SPAIN, WITH TRI-LINGUAL INSCRIPTION IN HEBREW, LATIN AND GREEK
6th century

been, for the most part, an urban element. However, at least in the cities, there was no sharp distinction between their means of earning a livelihood and those of the Gentile population. At the beginning of the Middle Ages, however, the Jews became a separate social-economic group sharply differentiated from the surrounding world. Trade began to play a dominant role in Jewish life and the Jewish merchant began to fulfill an important function in the economy of the Christian states. There can be no doubt that both internal and external

factors played a part in this evolution. The limitation of their rights and, most of all, the frequent persecutions to which they were subjected, undoubtedly contributed toward forcing the Jews to abandon those means of livelihood which were bound up with the soil and helped to intensify the one-sidedness of the Jewish economic structure. In addition, it can be assumed that their religious ethics and their rigidly regulated way of life stimulated among the Jews in exile the qualities necessary to fulfill specific economic functions, especially at the time when the old Greek-Roman world was collapsing and new peoples and nations were beginning to emerge. The very fact of Jewish dispersion all over the world—a circumstance which gave Jewish merchants ready-made contacts with their brothers in many countries—was without doubt an important factor in the growth of Jewish trade in the early Middle Ages.

5. THE JEWISH SETTLEMENT IN THE SASSANIAN EMPIRE

The great majority of the Jewish people now lived in Babylonia, which, in the spiritual sphere, too, had become the heir of Palestine. The so-called Talmudic period in Babylonia coincides approximately with the period of the Sassanian empire (226-641). Although the Jews suffered frequent persecutions and oppressions during this period the actual existence of the Jewish people was, on the whole, not imperilled. The Sassanians nursed the ambition to restore the former Persian empire as well as to renew and strengthen the ancient Persian religion: Zoroastrianism. As a result the priests obtained wide influence in the State and frequently utilized the State apparatus against their opponents to advance their own interests. During the reign of the first ruler of the Sassanians, Ardashir I, the situation of the Jewish population deteriorated. This did not last very long, however, and during the reign of Ardashir's successor, Shapur (242-272), the country's internal policies underwent a change.

The Jews were not the only religious minority in the Sassanian empire, as was the case in the majority of the Christian countries. The Persian religion and Persian culture in general did not manifest a particularly strong urge toward expansion, nor did it have the cultural strength to assimilate the foreign minorities. There were some outbreaks of fanatical persecutions against minority religious groups, including the Jews, under Sassanian rule during the reign of Yezdigird II (440-457), and especially during the reign of Firuz (459-484) when repressions against the Jewish population reached a degree reminiscent of the persecutions of Hadrian. By royal decree the synagogues and Talmudic academies were closed, Jewish laws were annulled, and Jewish children were compelled to be reared in the Persian faith. Among the victims of Firuz were several important Talmudic scholars and the Exilarch, Huna Mari. There is evidence that a Jewish uprising took place under the leadership of Mar-Zutra ben Huna. The rebels even succeeded in establishing a small Jewish kingdom, which, after a seven-year struggle, collapsed. The eventful reign of Kovad (490-531), when the revolutionary sect of the Mazdak came to power, was a period of extreme suffering for the Jews.

On the whole, however, the situation of the Jews in the Sassanian empire was much more favorable than in the Christian world. They lived in compact masses and some regions even had a purely Jewish appearance. For this reason Jewish traditions and Jewish culture could be better preserved and fostered. For the second time in Jewish history it was the destiny of Babylonia to become the home of large Jewish masses and the center of Jewish spiritual life. Just as in the time of Ezra, a type of Jewish community life developed which was able to insure the existence of the Jewish people in the Diaspora, serving that function for the last fifteen centuries. In the 5th century the Babylonian *Amoraim,* the rabbinical scholars and interpreters of the Mishnah, completed the collecting and editing of the unusually rich traditional material which, in the course of nearly three hundred years, had accumulated in the Talmudic academies and which, in the form of the Babylonian Talmud, became the authoritative code of Jewish life. The important role played by the Babylonian center led to the acceptance of the Babylonian Talmud as the final authority in all religious matters for Jews all over the world. The intensive spiritual life of Babylonian Jewry was built on a firm economic and social base. It might even be said that the Babylonian exile was in actuality only a semi-exile. Some Talmudic authorities even considered Babylonia a Jewish land, like Palestine. Jews participated in all spheres of economic life, had their autonomous institutions, and spoke Aramic, which became in fact the national Jewish language. At the head of the Jewish community stood the Exilarch, who was recognized by the government as the representative of the Jews. The office was hereditary and was held by a family which claimed its descent from King David.

Thus it was that Babylonian Jewry, which at the end of antiquity comprised at least two-thirds of the entire Jewish people, constituted the greatest reservoir of Jewish physical and spiritual power. But at the same time Babylonian Jewry was chiefly occupied with its own internal affairs and exerted little influence on the Jewish settlements in distant countries, especially in Africa and Europe. This state of affairs was radically changed when the newly arisen Islam again released the energies of the Eastern world and the Arab-Moslem conquerors brought to an end the rule of Byzantium over most of Western Asia and North Africa.

THE HISTORY OF THE JEWS IN THE MIDDLE AGES AND MODERN TIMES

A. Steinberg

I. THE MIDDLE AGES

The term "Middle Ages" was introduced into modern European historiography chiefly for the purpose of systematizing the material relating to European history exclusively. Nevertheless it is not without significance in the history of the Jewish people. For it is in this period of almost a thousand years, from the 7th to the 16th century, that the Oriental people of Israel becomes progressively Europeanized. At first this Europeanization was only geographical, but its immediate consequence was to identify Jewish destiny to an increasing extent with the destiny of Europe as a whole in both the political and economic as well as the cultural sense.

It is true that during the first half of this period we find the essential and sole center of the Jewish people shifted back again to its historic place of departure, Mesopotamia, in the very center of the Near East. One of the main factors leading to this temporary assumption of leadership of the entire Jewish people by the Jews of Mesopotamia-Babylonia was the rise of Islam, the new world power that was destined to play a decisive part in determining the complexion of medieval Europe. Just as the Arab Moslems accumulated in the Near East the strength that afterwards enabled them to stride up to the Atlantic Ocean and with the aid of the Berbers right into Europe (711), so the Jewish people retreated to the East in order afterwards, in the wake of the Arabs, to reach the most western point in Europe, Spain.

In both instances we are confronted with one and the same historic process—the collapse of the Western Roman empire, the continued disruption of all its territorial fragments, the material and spiritual stagnation of Eastern Rome—which left a void, so to speak, in both the political and the economic sense, and so almost spontaneously engendered new organizing and unifying forces. In making themselves the masters of this disintegrating world the heirs to Mohammed's sword built a vast bridge from one end of the Mediterranean Sea to the other, and by this means a new road— or more correctly a system of new roads— not only into the interior of Europe but into the very heart of the European-Christian ecclesiastical-feudal medieval world. Though small groups of Jews (in Byzantium, Italy, the Frankish empire etc.) had previously lived in a Christian environment, the Jewish people as a whole joined company with the Christian nations on their road only after the waves of Islam had thrown them up against the West European shores. And just as was the case with Islam's early victories, so its defeats at the hands of the Christian nations and States were also destined to make a deep impress on the course of Jewish history.

1. THE JEWS IN THE MOSLEM WORLD
(7TH TO 11TH CENTURIES)

Islam's first encounter with the Jewish people forebode no good. As soon as Mohammed, "Allah's Prophet," found that it was futile to expect the "Guardians of God's Word" to confirm his claim of a divine mission he turned against them with the full force of his fury. In four years (624-628) he destroyed several Jewish communities in his native Arabia. The Jews of Yathrib (Medina) had to emigrate to Transjordan. In the adjoining area of the Banu-al-Nadir he ordered the destruction of all their date palms, and of another Jewish tribe, the Banu Kuraiza, he ordered 600 Jews to be beheaded before his own eyes—all deeds recorded in the Koran (suras 33 and 59). Mohammed's chief motive, however, was that he wanted to make Arabia a land with one single religion. And as soon as this purpose had been more or less achieved and the Arab generals set out after Mohammed's death (632) to vanquish the world, they had of necessity, according to their own Law, to differentiate sharply in the newly-conquered countries (Syria and Palestine, Egypt, Persia and Mesopotamia, etc.) between the monotheists, the Jews and the Christians, on the one hand, and the heathen, the idolaters, on the other. The second caliph (the Prophet's deputy on earth) Omar (634-644), the real founder of the Arab empire, reopened Jerusalem to the Jews (638) immediately after he had wrested Palestine from Byzantium. When the Arabs seized Alexandria about three years later they made a special point of securing in their treaty with the local Greeks the right of residence of the Jewish inhabitants. Yet Moslem tolerance was at first limited by the explicit command in the Koran that Jews and Christians, since they denied Mohammed's prophetic mission, must remain permanently subjected tribute-payers ("Dhimmi") and consequently on a much lower level than the True Believers, the Moslems (Koran, suras 2, 7, 9, 29). Thus Islam from the beginning adopted a two-sided policy with regard to the Jews, liable to develop into either a favorable or unfavorable direction. And various historical factors, political, economic, social and cultural, resulted in the later emphasis of one or the other.

A. *Babylonia:* Arab rule was undoubtedly an improvement for the Jews in all those lands in which they had till then languished under the yoke of Byzantium (besides Syria and Palestine, Egypt and "Moghrabi," the Western part of North Africa). Even in Persia, especially in that section lying within the territory of ancient Babylonia (the modern Iraq) where the Jews under the Sassanids had built up a powerful autonomous center, the Jews found the rise of Islam beneficial to them. Persia had not yet been completely conquered when Omar helped to elevate the local Exilarch to his former high political rank. The legitimate heir to the title at that time was Bostanai, who claimed to be descended from the House of David, and it is said that the caliph himself arranged his marriage to a sister of the last Sassanid king of Persia. Later, when Kufa became the capital of the Arab empire, under Mohammed's son-in-law Ali (656-661), Jewish autonomy in Babylonia acquired an even greater degree of national significance. The new caliph was an adherent of the Shiite sect, which introduced elements into Islam from Jewish-Christian Messianism. It may have been this new spiritual atmosphere in Mesopotamian Islam that was responsible for the emergence now in Babylonia, side by side with the Exilarch, of the Gaon, a leader of the people with purely spiritual authority. The Gaon was usually the head of the Yeshibot of Sura or Pumbedita. During the rule of the Omayyads (661-749), when the political and military center of the Arabic caliphate was shifted to Damascus, in Syria, the Jewish community in Babylonia had to stand aside temporarily in the general life and affairs of the nation. But when the new Abbasid dynasty (750-1040) restored the center to Mesopotamia and made Baghdad the capital (about 763), the local Jews, headed by their Exilarchs and Geonim, again played a unifying and therefore a predominant part in Jewish life.

B. *Moslem Expansion; Extension of Jewish Settlement:* The Arab empire reached its widest expanse about 750. It extended from India in the east to the shores of present-day Portugal in the west, and from Turkestan, Caucasus and the Pyrenees in the north to the Indian Ocean and the Sahara Desert in the south. And within this huge area ruled by one central government, with one dominant language and script, one identical Moslem calendar and an almost uniform legal code, the ancient Jewish communities of the East suddenly found vast opportunities opened up for them both for economic initiative and for territorial expansion. Wherever the Moslem Power established itself new Jewish settlements immediately arose. Jewish Palestine had already revived at the time of the Omayyads. Now important Jewish communities (Kairwan, Fez, Cairo-Fostat, etc.) came into existence in North Africa. And simultaneously the foundations were laid of the great Jewish center in Spain. Though we lack precise statistical data it may be assumed that it was at this period that the Jewish population began to increase rapidly in number. It is true that the Jews found the poll-tax and land-tax which they had to pay in common with all the "Dhimmi," a heavy economic burden. The Jewish landowners seem to have suffered particularly under this oppression and this may have been the reason that a number of them turned to trade or artisanship or went westward, away from the center of government. But in a general way we may say that the legal and economic status of the Jewish population in the first centuries of the caliphate was secure and stabilized, and provided all facilities for favorable development.

It was very different, however, during the period of Abbasid rule. The soil that the Arabic warriors of old had ploughed up with their swords had borne rich fruit, material and spiritual. But as the material and cultural life of Islam developed and became more refined so its military strength declined. Here and there the seams of the hastily constructed empire began to give way. And at the same time the political status of the Jewish communities became differentiated in certain parts of the Islamic world (Palestine, Egypt and North Africa generally; Spain in particular). But culturally they still remained for a considerable time (till the 11th century), a fairly compact unity, like their Moslem environment. Yet it was this same intimate relationship with it that proved to be one of the main causes gradually leading—like European assimilation a thousand years later—to the collapse of the foundations on which the friendly protectorate of the people of Ishmael over the people of Israel had for so long been established.

C. *Internal Effects:* The lightning victories of Islam impressed the Jewish people like real miracles of God. At a very early stage, by the end of the 7th century, there were already Jewish sects (Isavites, Yudghanites) who recognized Mohammed and his Koran as God's Prophet and God's Law, but intended only for "his own nation." Similar views are met with among the early Karaites. But the essential fact that there were again new religious sects springing up among the Jews was, like the revival of Jewish religious-philosophic, philological, mathematical, natural-scientific and especially medical research and thought in the 9th and 10th centuries (Isaac Israeli, Saadia Gaon, David al-Mukammas and many others) a direct result of the close contact between Jews and Arabs. The Arabic language, which is at its roots connected with Hebrew, easily penetrated into the life of the Jewish people and also into its literature. The community of language thus led to community of thought. A contributing element was the fact that Arab culture in course of time became a development of Hellenism which had always attracted Jewish thinkers, especially in Egypt. And things had very soon gone so far that it was hard to tell where Arab-Moslem culture ended and Jewish culture began. An educated Jew and an educated Moslem understood each other perfectly. In Baghdad, Basra and many other places there arose a class of ambitious Jewish magnates (bankers, export-merchants, diamond dealers, etc.) with a desire to play a part in the life of the State. The Exilarchs, who were recognized at the caliph's court as the Princes of the Jewish people, and who lived like princes, on Jewish national taxation, became the ideal of all the wealthy Jews. That put the thought into the minds of the guardians of Islam that the Jews might now be ripe for conversion. And at the same time, to prevent any dangerous intermingling of the two faiths, they decided to erect a visible wall to separate the Jews who still adhered to Judaism from the True Believers, who were privileged under the Koran. Political enmity and trade competition intensified the motives of religious persecution, more especially since the time when the dominant class in Islam had abandoned warfare as a profession, engaging like those of other faiths in business and international trade, by means of which goods were exchanged among almost all the countries of the then known world. Baghdad, it should be remembered, stood at the cross-roads of world-trade, leading to China and India on the one side, and to Europe on the other.

D. *Persecutions:* It was in the time of the first of the Abbasids, the renowned Harun al-Rashid (786-809), that on the proposal of Abu Yusuf, his legal adviser, Jews and other "Dhimmi" were compelled to wear distinguishing clothing and forbidden to ride horses or build new houses of worship—surely an echo of the old similar Byzantinian prohibition. The caliph's adviser based his action on an alleged "Pact of Omar" with the "non-Believers" after the capture of Jerusalem. The result of this new attitude was that even the Caliph al-Mamun (813-833), although he was a great friend of learning and culture, deprived all Jews of their State offices. In 850 a law was enacted under the reactionary Caliph al-Mutawakkil (847-861) compelling Jews to wear a yellow patch on breast or back "so that they should be immediately recognizable." This was the origin of all the patches, yellow, red or whatever color they were, that Jews were required to wear later on among the Christian peoples. It is true that such legislation was not enforced for long in the Moslem lands. Under the Abbasid Caliph al-Radi (934-940) we again hear of Jews and Christians holding very high Government positions. Baghdad's international trading connections branched out in so many directions and the Jews occupied such a very strong position in the economic life of the world that the State simply couldn't dispense with their services by a stroke of the pen.

Very similar was the status of the Jews in those countries which successively broke away from the Baghdad caliphate, primarily in Egypt under the Fatimite caliphs (910-1171), the dynasty which in addition to North Africa also wrested Syria and Palestine from Baghdad.

E. *Spain:* The evolution of the old Jewish community in Spain constitutes a chapter in itself. The 7th century, the last under Christian-Visigothic rule, was simply a hell for them. On top of all their other troubles the rise of Moslem power had added the suspicion that the Jews were secret allies of the Moslems, the country's most dreaded foes. Throughout the century, the last preceding the destruction of their State, the Visigothic rulers one after the other proclaimed war against Jews and secret Jews. In 653 King Recceswinth, emulating the example of the Byzantine State, proclaimed at the Eighth Council of Toledo that "the God-insulting sect of Jews must either be made to accept the true faith or be beaten to the ground by the rod of vengeance." Thus the anti-Jewish policy of Byzantium yielded a rich harvest on this side of the Mediterranean. Consequently it was simply salvation for those Jewish refugees who escaped from the Visigothic conversionist persecutions to North Africa, and so it was for the secret Jews and for the rest of the unbaptized Jews in Spain itself when the Moslem armies in a few years seized almost the entire Pyrenean Peninsula (711-714).

F. *The Center of Jewish Unity:* Though the chains that connected the Moslem provinces in the far west of Europe to the center of Islam in the east were very loose and the Omayyad Abd-ar-Rahman 1 had already in 756 declared himself in Cordova as the independent "Emir of Spain," for a number of centuries the country remained economically and culturally part of the Moslem world. This was a fact of the utmost importance to the Jewish world. During the period that the star of Baghdad waned and the star of Cordova waxed, the real center of Jewish national unity shifted as if by deliberate intention further away from the Near East to the west, to that part of Europe from which the road was destined to open at the end of the Middle Ages for the Jews across the Atlantic to the new American world. In addition to the general political, economic and cultural causes that brought this about there was also the effect of the determination of the Jews to remain an independent social unit in the surrounding world, a unit in which membership was not only a divine injunction but also a powerful guarantee of social and economic security. The Babylonian Yeshibot and their Geonim (from Mar Isaac in the 7th century to Sherira and Hai in the 10th) were more than the crowning glory of the Jewish autonomous structure in the land between the rivers Tigris and Euphrates: their supervision insured the uniform application and development of the Jewish-national biblical-talmudic legislative code which, of course, embraced the entire traditional religious mode of life. It was entirely due to this code that business dealings between Jews, no matter how distant their places of habitation from each other, acquired that strictly normalized and consequently normal and consistently uniform character that converted the entire Jewish merchant world into a kind of closed world-wide guild, and enabled it, by means of the business contacts existing among its members, to compete with non-Jews for nearly fifteen centuries in all the markets of the world. Every other section of the migratory Jewish people enjoyed the advantages of this national Jewish code, the most settled and secure of those days. No matter where a Jew might find himself, the local Jewish community was bound to assist him to create a new means of livelihood for himself or to find a suitable place where he could do so. It was therefore, if only for this reason, in the interests of all of them that this state of affairs should be perpetuated and extended. And when the foundations of its principal institutions in Abbasid Babylonia began to totter on account of outside political factors—invasion by Mongolian tribes—efforts were immediately made to provide a new place of refuge for them, first of all in the 10th century and also later, in Palestine, but also in the Egypt of the Fatimites (where from the 11th century they even had their own "Exilarchs," the so-called Nagidim), and almost simultaneously further to the west, in Kairwan in Africa, and still further, in Spain. That this was not merely an attempt at creating new institutions but was definitely intended to continue the old traditions is evident from the fact that the Rabbis of Kairwan, Jacob ben Nissim, his son Nissim, and Hananel ben Hushiel (about 970-1050) immediately received from the younger generations the title "Geonim." Incidentally, according to later information, the fathers of Talmudic teaching, which now became "Rabbinical," both in Egypt and the western part of North Africa and even in Spain, had arrived straight from Babylonia. They were said to be "redeemed captives": for, as was the case with the Christian merchant corporations later on in the Middle Ages, the Jewish communities were already at this time fighting with combined forces against the perils of piracy on the Mediterranean trading routes.

G. *Jewish Culture in Spain:* The first flowering of the newly-established Jewish community in Islamized Spain, or Sepharad, as the Jews called it, was at the time of Abd-ar-Rahman III (912-961) who assumed the title of caliph and, like his successor al-Hakim II (961-976), conceived it to be his function to make Cordova the actual center not only of the Moslem world but of the entire civilized world. Both appointed as their adviser the Jewish sage Hasdai ibn Shaprut who made use of the opportunity provided by the tolerance of his powerful friends to create a State-recognized basis for the Jewish national autonomy. He himself became the "Nasi" of the Jews in the new caliphate while the spiritual authority was carried out in Spain by the Rabbi of Cordova, Moses ben Enoch, who was at the same time the head of the new Yeshibah founded there as well as the spiritual leader of all the Sephardic communities. Spain was now overtaking and even surpassing Babylonia in respect both of its bright and its shady sides. On the one side men like Samuel ha-Nagid, Isaac Alfasi and Solomon ibn Gabirol (11th century) demonstrate to what an extent Jewish creative thought which, thanks to the Arabs, had been revived in the east, had developed in the west. But on the other side, there were already Sephardic "Nasis" and "Nagidim" who secured the right of taxing the Jewish population and exploited their power to impose their will even in purely spiritual matters. Relations between them and the great Rabbis were no better in Spain than they were between the Exilarchs and the Geonim in Babylonia. As in Babylonia national interests got entangled with the purely selfish interests of a small wealth and power seeking minority of financial magnates (palace lords, tax farmers, owners of capital), who ruthlessly exploited the broad masses of the people,—artisans, shopkeepers, fruit and vine growers, cattle breeders, etc., irrespective of whether they were Jews, Christians or Moslems. And when Cordova lost its predominance at the beginning of the 11th century and Granada, the new center of Moslem and Jewish life in Andalusia, proved incapable of holding together the crumbling Spanish Caliphate, the Jewish population suffered a great deal because of the sins of its own aristocracy. In 1066 a Moslem dynastic war was accompanied by a terrible massacre of Jews in Granada, and the Jewish refugees from the Granada emirate fled to Seville, most of them settling in or around Seville.

H. *Beginning of Christian Expansion:* At this moment of steadily increasing Moslem anarchy the Sephardic section of the Jewish people found a new road open to them, leading northward, to that part of the Pyrenean Peninsula where the Christian power, as a direct consequence of the chaos in the south, was now beginning to re-consolidate itself. Connected previously with the non-Moslem world by their participation in the international markets, and politically neutral, the Jews at the time of the Christian reconquest of Spain were a considerable power whose support was valuable. And consequently Alphonso VI (1072-1109), the ruler of the new Central Spanish Christian Kingdom of Castile, disregarding the formal existence in his kingdom of the Visigothic anti-Jewish legislation, displayed a most magnanimous tolerance towards his Jewish population, in accordance with the best Moslem precedents. In this way the Sephardim or Spanish Jews found themselves provided with the historic conditions that enabled them in the period following to assume the leadership of the whole Jewish people (in conjunction with the Jews on the other side of the Pyrenees, the French Jews, or Zarfatim).

Both the expansion of Islam and the later diminution of its power worked in one and the same direction: to shift the main center of the Jewish people to Europe.

2. JEWS IN THE CHRISTIAN WORLD
(7TH TO 11TH CENTURIES)

The center of gravity of Jewish national life could not have been completely transferred to Europe by such gradual stages unless the Jewish communities that had grown up here all along the line of Graeco-Roman civilization had survived and begun to increase in numbers just towards the end of the period of Islamic glory.

This was a period of consolidation and expansion of new historic forces in the European world, the young Roman Catholic States in the West, the Byzantine Greek Orthodox Kievian Russia in the East, and above all the Papacy in the South. Maintaining their own existence among the European Christians was not an easy task for the Jewish communities. Immediately after the first successes that attended Mohammed's armies—so it is said—the emperor of Byzantium, Heraclius, instigated Dagobert, the Frankish king (629-639), to force all the "circumcised" under his rule to accept baptism or emigrate. They must have been, for the most part, Jewish refugees from the Visigothic inferno who now became pseudo-Christians in order to retain their livelihoods in the harbor cities of Marseilles, Arles and Bordeaux, where they were engaged, often also as ship-owners, in the import of Oriental goods (perfumes and spices, gold and silver, silks, papyrus, and also slaves), and, it would appear, investing part of their profits in land. To such an extent had the struggle between the Koran and the Evangel gone, and so natural to Christians from one end of Europe to the other was a confusion of Jews with Moslems.

A. *Byzantium:* The military victories of Islam placed the Jews of Byzantium in a very perilous plight. Emperors and Church Councils were prepared to exterminate the Oriental element in their midst. Throughout the 7th century there was no end to the expulsion orders and the forcible baptism decrees. Things grew worse still at the time of Leo III (717-741) when the Moslem army which had appeared before the gates of Constantinople was driven far back into Asia Minor (718). The Jews who had here, like those in Spain under the Visigoths, placed all their hopes in an Islamic victory were plunged into such despair by the Moslem defeat that great numbers of them followed the false Messiah, Serenus, to Syria. Throughout the period of temporary stabilization (8th-11th centuries) the Eastern Roman empire hardly ceased to wage war against its "internal Asiatics," the Jews. It did not even spare the ancient traditional autonomy of the Jewish communities. In economic life, where they occupied a high place both as merchants and as manufacturers (especially of fine silks), they suffered grievously from the powerful and aggressive Greek competition. Yet in spite of their difficulties they never lost contact with the Jewish people as a whole. There were times, of course, when they were shut out from the common national sources of strength behind the Christian-Moslem world and it may have been for this reason that they provided the most fertile soil for the spread of Karaism. Nevertheless, the Jews in the Balkans and on the eastern shores of the Black Sea (in the Crimea) always found new roads and devious paths by means of which they managed to keep within the framework of the Jewish legal and cultural system. Hebrew was still a vital factor in their spiritual life, and in the 9th century an important Yeshibah was founded in Apulian Oria, in Southern Italy, which belonged to Byzantium, providing a powerful new stimulus in the life of Byzantine Jewry.

B. *Italy:* Those areas which until the Norman invasion (9th-11th centuries) were for a long time under Moslem rule, constituted during this period, except for Spain, the most important route between the Jewish center within the circle of Moslem civilization and its periphery, which kept expanding in the medieval Christian world. The main stream of Jewish migration moved direct from east to west, but a lesser stream branched off from it just half-way, from the shores of Africa, and proceeded north. Though it partly returned to the east, to Byzantium, it ascended past the frontiers of the Apennine Peninsula, and not only penetrated into the region of present-day France but even into the German Rhine district, to meet there again in time the main stream from Africa and Spain. With all its other arteries and veins this route constituted a kind of natural blood circulation in the body of Jewish

history and we must admit that its pulse would inevitably have stopped had Papal Catholic Rome, the Church State in the heart of Italy, obstructed this historic process at the start. But as it happens the Popes, from Gregory I (590-604) to Gregory VII (1073-1085), did not hinder this march of events but on the contrary encouraged it, as though they considered it their duty to continue the pro-Jewish policy of the first Roman dictator, Julius Caesar. The result was that a very important autonomous Jewish community grew up in the capital of the pontiffs, the spiritual Caesars, which soon became the principal intermediary between the people of Israel and the entire Catholic world. A number of other Jewish communities in more or less independent towns in Southern, Central and Northern Italy (above all in Venice) benefited directly or indirectly from the Levantine trade which had flourished since the 9th century. The only restrictions were against Jewish ownership of land, under the old Christian policy prohibiting Jews from owning Christian slaves. Nevertheless, the Italian Jews in the 10th and 11th centuries felt so secure that they even appeared in public religious disputations.

C. *France and Germany:* Next to the Italian sphere the most important sphere of influence of the Roman Church at that time was the land of the Franks, known today as France. After Charles Martel had rolled back the tide of Moslem conquest which had swept across the Pyrenees (732), and when his son, Pepin the Short, had finally broken the Arab power at Narbonne and stabilized the political situation of the Frankish empire, the status of the new Jewish communities became strengthened both at its center (Paris, Orleans, Tours) and in the south, where the Jews now reappeared in their old places of residence. In the year 800 Charles Martel's grandson, Charlemagne (768-814), was crowned by the Pope as emperor of a new Roman Christian empire comprising almost the whole of Western Europe and large parts of Central Europe, and throughout his domains he spread the Catholic faith, the Latin tongue and culture, and the old Roman spirit of tolerance to the Jewish population. Christian Europe was now strong enough to be the equal of Islamic might. The two centers of civilization were almost balanced. In international trade they converged towards a common center and the Jewish people, which still stood with one foot in the Christian West and the other in the Moslem East, was the natural mediator between these two worlds. Arab and Latin sources are unanimous in testifying to the fact that the Jewish merchants were the vital force at that time in promoting world trade. At almost every point of contact there were Jews, bound together by ties of religion and culture and business interests: at the Strait of Gibraltar and in Marseilles, in Sicily and on the Adriatic Sea, in Alexandria and Cairo, in Antioch, Aleppo and Baghdad, whence the trade routes continued across the Red Sea, the Persian Gulf and Central Asia to India and China. Much of this international trade was river-borne, on the Rhone and the Rhine, the Danube and the Dnieper. And the gold and the luxury-articles that the Jews brought from the East helped to refine West European civilization and influenced the whole system of Western urban economy.

The rulers of the new Roman Catholic empire protected the creative powers of the Jewish population in every possible way. They even employed Jews in political life. About 801, for instance, Charlemagne sent a Jew named Isaac, who probably knew Arabic and the Moslem world, to accompany his two Ambassadors to the Caliph Harun al-Rashid in Baghdad. Just as in the Moslem world about the same time, the guardians of the Christian faith, Popes, bishops and Church Councils, had to keep reminding the temporal rulers that the differences between Jews and Christians must not be wholly obliterated. "I almost die with fright," Pope Stephen III writes in 770 to the Bishop of Narbonne, "because

the Jews, the rebels against God, own with as much right as Christians large tax-free estates and employ on them Christian serfs." Jewish landownership apparently developed at this time no less than Jewish trade by land and sea. Under Charlemagne's son, Louis the Pious (814-840), Jewish influence in the Carolingian empire grew still further. The new emperor regarded himself as the protector of the Jewish people, and bestowed privileges not only on individuals but on entire communities, so that their autonomy was once more given a State-legalized basis. Christians began to look up to the Jews as a higher social class and there were proselytes to Judaism even at the Imperial Court.

After Louis' empire was divided among his sons and Germany was separated from France (843), the Carolingian tradition still lingered on for a long time in both countries. The principal clients of the Jewish merchants, the princes and the bishops, the spiritual and the temporal pillars of feudalism which was now beginning to emerge in Western and Central Europe, looked upon the Jews for the most part as a group that had to perform a specific function in economic life; they had to develop the newly-founded towns and especially the system of exchange. For this reason the feudal lords deliberately perpetuated the system of Jewish legal autonomy (10th - 11th centuries). But it was a central principle of feudalism that the land must belong exclusively to themselves. And this though very slowly at first, gradually tended to bring about the discriminatory legislation which from the 11th century was destined to lead the Jewish population of medieval Europe ever downward. But till then the Jewish people would have ample time to consolidate the foundations of its own internal autonomous life in the Christian feudal world.

Due to their close ties through Southern France with the Jewish spiritual centers in Spain and North Africa and along the broad track of Italy with the ancient Jewish East, Babylonia, Egypt and Palestine, the young Jewish communities in France and Germany, in those places where they lived in close proximity to each other, in Lorraine and in the Rhine regions, suc-

OLD SYNAGOGUE AT WORMS, GERMANY

ceeded in creating a common cultural center which became a beacon of light for all the Jewish communities in Western Europe and beyond. In the 11th century they already produced a legislator like the head of the new Mayence Yeshibah, Rabbenu Gershom, and a commentator of the national legal codes—the Torah, Mishna and Gemara—like Rashi. Together with the leaders of the older Narbonne Yeshibah these were now the "Geonim" of the West, the peers of the declining Geonim of the East.

D. *Eastern Europe:* During this period the only Jewish communities that stood somewhat apart from the rest of the Jewish world were those in the various countries of Eastern Europe, from Bohemia and Hungary to Poland and Kievian Russia. Just as in the pre-Carolingian era some venturesome Jewish merchants had managed to find their way from the Frankish lands to Britain, so now Jews went from the German East and South (Lower Saxony and Bavaria)—where judging by the documents of the 10th century the terms Jew and merchant were almost synonymous—to the Slavic countries, from which they brought to their protectors, the feudal

lords, principally furs and slaves. Some who had settled in the new places (Magdeburg, Naumburg, Meissen, Prague, etc.) also took part in the development of local industry. Possibly these pioneers of East European trade might not have ventured so far into the dense forests around the Danube and the Vistula had they not known at the outset that a little further to the south they would strike the road that had for centuries linked the Jewish Orient with the Crimea, the peninsula in which there had never ceased to be a Jewish community, even during the Moslem-Byzantine era.

At the very time of the persecutions in Byzantium (8th-10th centuries) the Crimea had come under the rule of the Khazars, a Turkish tribe that had spread from Central Asia to the Dnieper, and whose princes had in the 8th century adopted the Jewish or Karaite faith. The consequence was that the Crimean Jews, who were able merchants, came into close contact with the Jewish communities in the farthest east of the Moslem world—in the Caucasus and on the Caspian Sea. And in this way the cycle of the blood circulation in the organism of the Jewish people was completed. Evidence of the fact that it really was an organic unity is provided in the correspondence between the Nasi of Cordova, Hasdai ibn Shaprut, and the Jewish king of the Khazars, Joseph. There is even more conclusive proof in the fact that at the very time when the German Jews were cutting a path through the Bohemian and Polish forests they encountered the Jews of Khazaria, who had established themselves in Russian Kiev.

Afterwards, when Poland was Christianized as a part of the Roman Catholic Church, and Russia was Christianized as a branch of the Byzantine Church (10th century), the ground was prepared not only for an all-European unification but for a firm bond between the main trunk of the Jewish people in the western half of Europe and its still rather frail branches in the eastern half.

3. THE SECOND HALF OF THE MIDDLE AGES (12TH TO 15TH CENTURIES)

The first Crusade at the end of the 11th century (1096) with the aim of conquering the Holy Land, is a turning point in European history. The Roman Catholic Church had now consolidated itself so successfully that it was able to unite its followers in France and Germany, and soon after also in England, for a joint attack on the Moslem infidels, who were then concentrated around the Turkish Seljuk empire, the new master of Palestine. As soon as the armies of the Crusaders began to gather along the Rhine they vented their fury first of all on the local "infidels," meaning the Jewish communities.

There were very deep-lying causes behind Europe's march against Asia, and in time they were bound to undermine completely the position occupied by the Jewish people in the Christian world in Western Europe. To begin with, there were signs of over-population in the west, especially in the Rhineland. From the middle of the 11th to the middle of the 12th century the number of inhabitants in the most important part of Germany rose from about 5-6 million to 7-8 million. As long as this increase kept pace with the whole process of economic development the Jews were able to increase unhindered like the rest. But there was a complete change as soon as economic expansion reached its natural limits in relation to the production possibilities of the time. The population was compelled to live under more congested conditions or to emigrate.

The wars for the liberation of "God's Tomb" in Jerusalem and the almost simultaneous colonization of the forest and marshland tracts in Central and Northern Germany as well as the growth of the cities of Western Europe are all symptoms of the same crisis. And though in the end the world benefited from it, for the Jews it was inevitably the beginning of one of the most frightful transition periods in the whole course of their history. It was just then that the feudal system took final shape.

And the Jews crossed over its threshold mostly as a segregated social class without roots among the broad peasant masses, connected only more or less with the noble

HOME OF A 12TH CENTURY JEW IN LINCOLN, ENGLAND

and ecclesiastical apex of the social pyramid. So when the Christian masses had to crowd together and a growing middle class emerged from the lower classes—merchants and artisans who were organized in purely Christian guilds—and the nobles and the Church were the monopoly owners of the land, there was little left for the Jewish population to do. It had to live on its accumulated capital and engage to a large extent in money-lending. The Catholic Church, which had now become the supreme legislator of the Western Christian world, allowed the Jews to exercise this function—ostensibly a "privilege"—that was to become in time the worst possible curse, the origin of countless libels, outrages and massacres.

A. *Decline and Downfall of the Jewish Communities in Western Europe:* This, it is obvious, was only the general scheme. Feudalism had a distinct character of its own in each separate country, so that the status of the Jews varied in different places. The need of concentrating on monetary transactions became during the 12th century, the century of the second and third Crusades, more apparent in France and England (the young Jewish community of Angevin England was essentially a part of the French community) than in Germany, where we still encounter ordin-

EARLY GERMAN JEWISH POET AND
MINSTREL, SUSSKIND VON TRIMBERG,
IN POINTED JEWISH HAT

ary Jewish traders even in the 13th century. This is particularly understandable in regard to England, where the Jews were brought over towards the end of the 11th century for the specific purpose of developing the money market. France was the classic land of West European feudalism. In Germany where the feudal system consolidated itself much more slowly, the Jews, especially in the eastern parts, still had time to do for economic progress what their brothers in the West had previously accomplished. But sooner or later the Jewish communities were doomed to be the victims of feudalism all along the line.

Even before that, the Jews of Western Europe had been regarded as "foreigners" whose hearts were really in the East, in their old home in Palestine, and they themselves always considered the eastern wall in their synagogues as paramount. But whereas previously their association with the Orient, derived from their connection

with the Oriental trade and the part played by that Oriental trade in the life of Europe, gave them added prestige, now, during and after the Crusades, they were almost superfluous even in this respect. Normans, Italians and the new French, English, Flemish and German trading companies (Hanseatic League, etc.) dominated the world market; they still needed only the Jewish money. The upper classes, headed by the kings and princes, thereupon attempted to transform the Jewish population into a kind of pumping machine from which they could extract not only coin but also—in the form of pledges—every other kind of valuables. Thus the Jews became dependent not only in the matter of their possessions but even of their bare lives upon the protection which they might purchase at great expense from the German emperors, the French and English kings and their armies of higher and lesser lords.

When Frederick Barbarossa declared during the second half of the 12th century that Jews "belong" to the Imperial Treasury he merely supplied the legal form for a state of affairs that in actual practice already existed. Thus the Jews as far down as Spain gradually became *servi camerae*, in other words, the property of the State. Great and respected merchants now became merchandise themselves. From Norman Sicily right into the interior of Ger-

SYNAGOGUE IN ERFURT, GERMANY
14th century

GATE LEADING TO THE JEWISH QUARTER IN
CARPENTRAS, FRANCE

Spain, since the time of the Arab invasion, had lived side by side with another very important section of the population that was politically, economically, socially and culturally more or less in the same position as themselves. First it had been the Christians under Moslem rule, and then after the Christian re-conquest, the Moslems. Thus the attitude of the dominant class towards the Jews and the attitude of the Jews in relation to the authorities were both influenced to a great extent by the reaction of their neighbors, first the Christians and then the Moslems, to the same historic circumstance. The persecutions in England, France and Germany utterly failed to break the Jewish spirit. In spite of all their afflictions the Jews in these countries held fast to their religious traditions, and their calamities only served to confirm them in their conviction that Israel was a unique people. They let themselves be killed, or they killed themselves,

many the kings and dukes, bishops and cities started to trade "their" Jewish communities, bartering them or pawning them to each other against whatever might be extorted from them. And then when native finance developed so far that it could dispense with the Jews they were simply kicked out. This is the most significant economic aspect of the Jewish expulsion from England (1290), from France (1306-1394), and from a number of German areas in the 13th-15th centuries. That the victims of this economic development were well aware of their situation is evident from the fact that in 1254 (about the time when the first Christian money-lenders, the so-called "Papal usurers," made their appearance in Western Europe) the English Jews were begging to be allowed to leave the country.

B. *The Catastrophe in Spain:* The events preceding the expulsion from Spain in 1492 are much more complicated. Unlike in the Catholic lands where they were the sole non-Christian element, the Jews in

OLD SYNAGOGUE IN CAVAILLON, FRANCE

WEST WALL OF 14TH CENTURY SYNAGOGUE,
CORDOVA, SPAIN

JEWS' GATE IN CORDOVA, SPAIN
Leading to the Jewish quarter

STONE INSCRIPTION FROM 14TH CENTURY SYNAGOGUE IN CORDOVA, SPAIN
The inscription identifies the builder of the synagogue as Isaac Moheb and the year as 1315

or they fled, anywhere—but they would not stoop to baptism.

It was different in Spain. There the Christian and later the Moslem readiness

From Bibliotheque Nationale, Paris

FRENCH JEWS IN THE 14TH CENTURY

to submit to the powers that be made things more difficult for the Jews. And when the wave of violent persecutions arose at the end of the 14th century thousands of Jews accepted baptism. Side by side with those who went to the stake for their faith, there were large numbers of Marranos, the counterpart of the Moslem "Moriscos," pseudo-Christians but, most of them, no longer real Jews. In a land which had fought hard for religion, it was natural that doubtful Christians should be considered a greater menace than avowed Jews. When Aragon and Castile were united (1469) and Spain became an entirely Christian kingdom, it was on account of these semi-converts that the Jewish community as a whole in Spain was later (1492) destroyed. There were very important economic and social factors that also contributed to this course of development. The fact that the Jews in the Pyrenean Peninsula were an organic part of both the economic life of the country in all its branches and of the surrounding culture, and that they were prepared to make all kinds of religious concessions as long as they might maintain their important economic and political positions, not only

failed to weaken the anti-Jewish feeling, but actually intensified it. Nationalist suspicions and religious enmity were reinforced by social and economic envy.

C. *The Catholic Church:* The complete destruction of the Jewish center in Spain (expulsion of 1492) and of its branch in Portugal (1498) was the supreme achievement of the Church militant and its propagandist and suppressive machinery—the religious orders and the Inquisition—in the long struggle waged against Judaism. Since the first Crusades, and especially since the Fourth Lateran Council (held in Rome in 1215) which under the influence of Pope Innocent III confirmed all the previous anti-Jewish Church legislation and added, along the lines of the old Moslem regulations, the ordinance compelling all Jews and Moslems to wear a distinguishing sign (a yellow patch or something similar) to mark them out from the rest of the popula-

THE SYNAGOGUE OF TOLEDO, SPAIN
13th (?) century

tion, Church policy had been directed towards one aim, to segregate the Jewish population from the Christian population and to keep them so placed that each "be-

EL TRANSITO SYNAGOGUE DEDICATION
INSCRIPTION, TOLEDO, SPAIN
14th century

liever" might see with his own eyes how much the heretic has to suffer on this earth. This policy also included the need of maintaining the existence of the people of Israel as the living confirmation of the historic side of Christian tradition and consequently the protection of the Jews against physical extermination.

The Church was lenient even in the matter of forced conversions. For while there must always be a stream of converts, to show that Christianity is able to break down the resistance of even "the stiff-necked race," there must at the same time be no spiritual extermination of the entire Jewish people by conversion any more than there may be physical extermination. So that the Church protected not only Jews but also Judaism, as for example against the blood libel. Yet it was not easy for the prelates in the dioceses and for the minor clergy to steer an exact middle course between the simultaneously anti-Jewish and pro-Jewish policies of the Church. In almost every place where the anti-Jewish feeling of the Christian population had its origins in secular motives (political, social, or economic), the clergy joined with the enemies of Israel and hallowed their worst deeds, making them appear to be religious

virtues, thus creating a religious ideology to cover up the most brutal instincts.

And where the real incentive behind the anti-Jewish feeling among the clergy themselves—as in Spain, since the rise of the Inquisition—was avarice and arrogance, there could be no other result than the total destruction of the Jewish community.

D. *Italy:* It was simplest for the Roman Catholic Church to practice its dual policy with regard to the Jews in its native Italy, most of all in Rome, the capital of the Church-State. The Curia, the Papal Government, was on the one hand strictly concerned to see that the Synagogue should be properly submissive to the Church lest the world might for a moment forget that the Jewish glory had for ever departed. But on the other hand the Jewish community in Rome was recognized as a completely autonomous body. Its representatives were never absent from the great ceremony of enthroning the new Pope, to whom they were required to present a Scroll of the Law. Even during the reign of so anti-Jewish a Pope as Innocent III (1198-1216), when the power of the Church was supreme, the anti-Jewish laws, including the new decree prescribing the wearing of the yellow patch, were left practically unenforced in Rome and in Italy generally. Pope Gregory I's Bull protecting the Jews was constantly reaffirmed and many of the Popes during this entire period appointed Jewish physicians at their Court (in the Middle Ages Jews already held a high place in medicine) or employed Jewish financial advisers. In this way the Jews of Rome, and thus the Jews of the entire Roman Catholic world, were almost always able to approach the Papal Throne and obtain, at whatever cost, such protective Church pronouncements as that, for instance, of Pope Calixtus II (1119-1124) against pogroms, or Pope Innocent IV's famous Bull against the blood libel (1247).

This policy continued in Rome till the middle of the 16th century.

Its influence was felt in other parts of Italy that lay outside the Papal territories.

In conjunction with the legal status of the autonomous Jewish communities it was also effective everywhere in stabilizing the normal economic activities of their members. In South Italy where the Norman princes were considered for a long time as Papal vassals, silk production in the 12th century became almost a Jewish industry, as was the case at a later date, too, when the German Emperor Frederick II of Hohenstaufen be-

Jews being both excellent craftsmen and occupying an important place in commerce and banking. From the early part of the 14th century the trading Republic of Venice used to conclude a contract with its Jewish community every ten years, suggesting in a way a treaty as between States. When Jewish competition grew too powerful for the Venetians, however, they demanded that the Jews should at least live

JEWISH MERCHANTS IN NORTHERN ITALY
From a 13th-14th century manuscript

came the ruler of Naples and Sicily. Till the late Middle Ages the Jews of Sicily, like the Spanish Jews, did not cease to engage—besides sea-trading—in agriculture, especially the cultivation of the date palm. It was not till the catastrophe in Spain to which Sicily belonged at this time that this flourishing community came to an end.

Jewish economic life in Central and Northern Italy was considerably variegated,

segregated from their Christian environment. Though the Christian trading companies in Italy were also closed to Jews it was not unusual for Christian merchants, money changers, agents, etc. to have Jewish business partners. There was in particular a very broad tolerance in respect of Jewish commercial and industrial initiative in Florence, both at the time of the Republic and under the Medicis, from

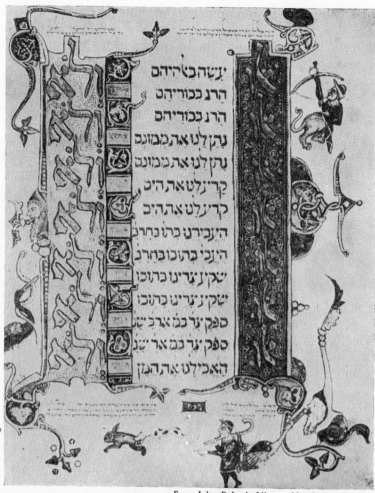

From John Rylands Library, Manchester, England
13TH CENTURY HAGGADAH

the second half of the 15th century. The only exception was the trading Republic of Genoa where Jews were not generally admitted. But even the Genoese had nothing against Jews in the Genoese colony in the Crimean Peninsula (from 1260 till the middle of the 15th century).

E. *Spiritual Culture:* The second half of the Middle Ages was not only a transition period in regard to places of Jewish domicile and the economic existence of the greater part of the Jews, it was also a time of great changes in the spiritual and cultural life of the people. Broad and creatively daring, at first, especially in Spain (where it will suffice to mention the names of Moses and Abraham ibn Ezra, Judah ha-Levi and Maimonides), as time went on

it became even among the Sephardim narrower, one-sided and conservative-mystic (Nahmanides, Rosh, Hasdai Crescas, Joseph Albo, the Kabbala). Creative work was concentrated on retaining at least that which had always held the Jewish communities together, the Jewish Law, the traditional legal code inherited from past generations. Contact between the different Jewish communities took the form of combining the legal and the religious foundations on which the unity of the scattered people was based.

This new road had already been indicated by Maimonides (1135-1204). While France and Germany still continued for some time along the road laid down by the Tosaphists (Rashbam, Rabbenu Tam, etc.)

who like Rashi were only commentators on the national-legal original sources, Maimonides considered it his duty to set up at the side of the Talmud a second, more accessible code compiled on his own system. A pathfinder for the Posekim (Rosh's

leadership of the people in the Christian part of Spain and the strict guardianship of Jewish self-administration devolved upon such a Posek as Rosh (1250-1327), the pupil of one of the last of the German Tosaphists, together with his friend, the Rabbi

ILLUSTRATION FROM 13TH CENTURY LATIN MANUSCRIPT

The manuscript is a translation by a Sicilian Jew of an Arabic work on medicine. The illustration on the right, shows the presentation of the original Arabic work by the Oriental ruler, and that on the left, King Charles of Anjou receiving the translation

son, the Baal Haturim and others) he sought moreover in face of the spiritual disturbance of the time to draw a sharp distinction in his "Guide for the Perplexed," written in Arabic, between the Graeco-Arab (in other words, the European-Moslem) mode of thought on the one hand and the purely Jewish conception on the other. In this way he prepared the ground for the dissolution of the Jewish-Arabic cultural bond in his Spanish homeland. It is a sign of the times that immediately after him the

of Barcelona, Solomon ben Adret (1235-1310) who fought hard against religious liberty and for the restoration of a barrier against all forms of alien teaching.

By the end of the Middle Ages the only places where any interest in secular affairs still existed in Jewish cultural life were Provence in Southern France, and Italy, where the Renaissance was spreading. There were Jewish students and even professors, mostly of medicine, in a number of universities (Montpellier, Salerno, Padua).

Latin became for many Jewish scholars what Arabic had been previously. And the decline of Arabic also helped to raise the prestige of Hebrew. Whole families of scholars (like the Tibbons) translated into Hebrew the works that had been written in Arabic by the Jewish theologians, philosophers and scholars, and in this way made of the Hebrew language a vessel that could in time take in the most polished products of European culture. It was during this time that Jewish thinkers began to exercise a powerful influence upon Christian scholasticism and philosophers such as Albertus Magnus, Thomas Aquinas, Meister Eckhart.

The conservative, conserving spirit of the Jewish autonomous legislation during this entire period was most evident in the northern part of Western Europe, where the Jewish communities lived in constant peril. There the Rabbinical Synods were concerned primarily through their various Takkanot or regulations, as in the famous Takkanot Shum for the communities of Speyer, Worms and Mayence, in the 13th century, to preserve internal Jewish discipline and to see that Jewish relations with non-Jews would give no ground for the desecration of God's Name (Hillul ha-Shem). We can see how close the ties were that bound all Jews together at that time in the matter of their traditional spiritual life (a parallel to the Roman Catholic world with its Latin), from the fact that a commentary to the Talmud written in London by a London scholar before the expulsion (in the middle of the 13th century) soon became known as far away as Palestine and even Russia. And this was also the extent of contemporary Rabbinical jurisdiction in regard to the rulings or responsa of the rabbis in questions of religious law. So that when the disaster came in Germany, especially in the years that followed the period of the Black Death (about 1348) and the remnants of the Jewish communities there had to find new places of domicile, they went into the unknown as into a new province of the same empire, for in the sphere of their own social life they were everywhere subject to their own laws. This is how they colonized Eastern Europe.

F. *The Migration from West to East:* For a considerable majority of Jewish refugees from Western Europe the road was marked out from the first by definite historical factors. Its main direction, which had at the beginning of the Middle Ages been from east to west, was now the other way around, from west to east, from England to France, from Germany (and Austria) to Poland, from Spain and Portugal to the Turkish Empire. But till the consolidation of Ottoman power (Byzantine Constantinople became Turkish only in 1453) the ancient Jewish dwelling places in the Near East including Palestine and Iraq were almost cut off from the West European communities. Jerusalem was under the rule of the Crusaders for almost a century (1099-1187). And after that a number of Moslem dynasties fought among themselves for the possession of Palestine and the neighboring countries. Jewish creative activity there was paralyzed. Something of a revival occurred in the 12th century in Baghdad and also in Persia where Exilarchs appeared again, as did a Gaon (Samuel ben Ali ha-Levi) and a pseudo-Messiah, David Alroy. But it was only a last dying gleam. The Mongolian invasions (about 1258) thrust Baghdad and its Jewish community away from the broad path of history. Byzantium was all this time in its death-throes.

In Eastern Europe this was a period of rapid political and economic expansion, mainly in Hungary, Poland and Lithuania, beyond which lay the broad lands of Russia and the new center, Moscow. Consequently the Jews who were driven out of Germany turned in increasing numbers in the same direction as the German artisans and merchants who were driven from their native towns by poverty and want—to the new towns in the young Hungarian, Polish and Lithuanian lands. The privileges which the Jews obtained in 1251 from the

Hungarian King Bela IV served as a model for the Polish rulers, Boleslav of Kalisz (1264), Casimir the Great (1333-1370), and Casimir Jagiello (1447-1492), who was also Grand Duke of Lithuania. The Jews came to Poland with their own system of autonomous law, just as the Germans had done with their "Magdeburg Rights" and the consequence was that at the end of the Middle Ages there was a repetition there both materially and culturally of the same process as had taken place in Western Europe at the beginning of the Middle Ages.

II.   THE EARLY MODERN ERA

1. THE JEWISH PEOPLE UP TO THE CRITICAL YEAR 1648

The history of the Jewish people flows on, like the stream of general human history, without interruption. The collapse of the feudal system in Western Europe and the split in the Roman Catholic Church, the rise of separate national cultures in the Christian world and the transformation that took place in the entire outlook and conception of the European peoples—the result of revolutionary changes

SILVER COINS FROM POLAND, WITH HEBREW INSCRIPTIONS
12th and 13th centuries

The Sephardim, direct inheritors of the Jewish-Arabic Orient, were no longer predominant in Jewish collective national life. The hegemony passed to the Ashkenazim.

in science, of the great geographical discoveries and the various technical inventions—all these indications of a new epoch were quietly in preparation long before the

16th century, though their full import was not realized until the very threshold of the new historic epoch. At the same time vestiges of the Middle Ages, especially the medieval view of life with its religious conceptions in regard to truth and falsehood, right and wrong, did not cease to influence the course of history in general and of Jewish history in particular, even when the new epoch had already reached its climax.

Nevertheless we may regard the 16th century as being in a way a dividing line not only in European history generally but also in Jewish history. Just as the main factors that determined the character of both the Christian-European and the European-Jewish Middle Ages became evident in the 7th century, so now there came into operation those factors that would in time place the entire structure of Europe—from England to Russia—on a sounder political, economic and cultural basis, would transform European history in such a way that for the first time it would become real world history, and would thus weave together the future of the Jewish world-people with the destiny of mankind as a whole.

It was in the Middle Ages that the fundamental conditions for the Europeanization of the Jewish people were created; the new epoch would make the Jewish people ripe for universalization.

A. *New Expulsions:* The further development of the feudal-Catholic social order in Western Europe displaced almost the entire Jewish population and compelled them, both there and in Central European Germany, to emigrate during the 14th and 15th centuries mostly further to the east, if not across the Polish frontier then at least to the border countries, Austria, Bohemia, Silesia and Hungary. At the end of the 15th century, just before and more so after the expulsion from Spain, this process of displacement involved, besides a number of Central German provinces and towns (Mecklenburg, Brandenburg including Berlin, Nurnberg, etc.), even the Austrian and their associated semi-Slavic

countries. Right at the beginning of the 16th century it was simply touch and go with the whole Jewish community in Bohemia. In conjunction with the impression of the Spanish example, the same causes operated there as had previously operated in the West: an urban Christian middle-class becoming increasingly self-

Courtesy Czechoslovakia Government Information Bureau

THE FAMOUS ALT-NEU SYNAGOGUE IN PRAGUE, CZECHOSLOVAKIA

conscious wanted to monopolize trade and industry, to degrade the Jewish competitors to the lowest level of social existence, and at the first suitable opportunity, by means of some sort of libel, to get rid of them completely—by fire and sword, by bloodshed, pogroms, or by a special decree of expulsion. That is why the citizens of Prague, for instance, induced the Bohemian Court to forbid Jews to sell goods at wholesale, restricting them to retail trade (about 1502). Other Bohemian towns, like Pilsen, following the German example, obtained a "privilege not to tolerate Jews."

B. *The Time of the German Reformation:* Such repressive edicts and persecutions

were repeated throughout the German Reformation period (from 1517) till its most
important political event, the Thirty Years'
War (1618-1648). At the beginning of this
period what Jews were left in Western Germany were almost everywhere shut away in
narrow streets. The number of those who
had money and the amount of money they
had kept dwindling. Unless they were
small money-lenders or old-clothes dealers
they were mostly poor people, who had to
depend on each other for a living. Economically things were better with the Jews of
the Austrian countries (since 1526 the Austrian sovereigns were also the rulers of
Bohemia and Hungary). They traded here
with Poland, Italy and Turkey, and inside
the country they linked together the town
and the village, and sometimes there emerged among them a magnate whose wealth
brought him in touch with the powers that
be. Yet here too they never knew what the
morrow might bring. The great events
taking place in the outside world that were
destined also to alter the whole of internal
Jewish life meanwhile flitted by like a
dream so far as the great majority of the
Jewish population in Germany was concerned.

About a hundred years previously, during the Hussite Reformation in Bohemia,
the Jews do appear to have played some
part. There were several reasons why the
Jews were so indifferent to the latest and
most severe clash within the Catholic
Church. Luther, the Protestant leader, had
soon realized, like Mohammed, the founder
of Islam before him, that the Jews were not
to be won for his new faith, and the result
was that he became their implacable foe.
Materially the Jews of Central Europe were
everywhere badly off, but they could not
look forward to anything better from that
section of the population which had adopted Protestantism; if anything they might
expect it from the Catholic princes and
bishops. Jewish approval of the Protestant
movement would indeed have been of importance for those Christians who had se-
ceded from Rome, for it was just then that

the Humanists, like Reuchlin, had raised
Hebrew to equal dignity with Latin and
Greek, so that the Jews again became, as
they were in Mohammed's time, "the People
of the Book," called upon to interpret the
Scriptures to their neighbors and to act
as referee in the quarrel between the rival
Christian camps. Luther had himself translated the Bible into German, so that it became the Book of the People. But all this
was not enough to rouse the Jews from their
unconcern, and soon the growing anti-
Jewish feeling among the Protestants in the
German countries proved to them the ad-
visability of looking for protection rather
to the power of the Catholic emperor.

The Roman emperor at that time was
Charles v (1520-1556). It is true that the
Jewish spokesman, Yosel Rosheim, did on
several occasions intervene on behalf of the
German Jews with the Protestant rulers,
e.g. as at the "Frankfurter Anstand," held
in Frankfort on the Main in 1539, which
simultaneously with the renewal of the
edict compelling the Jews to wear the yellow patch also condemned the blood libel,
largely through the efforts of the Protestant
theologian, Melanchthon. Yet Rosheim's
greatest achievements were the letters of
protection for the whole of German Jewry
which he obtained from the emperor in
1544 and 1546, not only prohibiting unjust
persecution of the Jews, but also permitting
them to charge higher rates of interest on
loans "because they are more highly taxed
than the Christians." These protective decrees are indicative of certain changes in the
economic life of the German Jews, who
after the terrible decline of the 15th century
were now again beginning to accumulate
capital. This tendency was promoted by
the wars which followed in the train of the
Reformation. Jewish financiers became
army contractors, mostly on the Imperial
and Catholic side, and several of them attained high social positions.

It is characteristic of the new epoch of the
struggle for a more liberal Christian conscience and a greater degree of human dignity that even the Catholic emperors now

raised their Jewish agents to the rank of Court Jews. It is no less characteristic of the tenacity of the old Jewish system of law that these new Jewish notables of the 17th century everywhere (especially in Vienna) elevated their own trusted Jewish friends. They did this not only out of compassion nor even out of a mere sense of solidarity, but because there was no other class of people upon whom they could rely so implicitly in their various hazardous war-transactions as on their fellow-Jews. The result was that this social elevation of a few individual Jews or of a few Jewish families became the basis of the economic elevation of an entire class.

C. *The Jews of Poland:* The intimate connection between the autonomous Jewish legal system and the social-economic processes in which the Jews took part was nowhere so much in evidence at this time as in Poland, where the Jewish community gradually absorbed not only the majority of the German Jews, including a considerable number of Bohemian Jews, but through Poland's union with Lithuania (1569) also elements of such ancient communities as the Karaite colonies in South Russia (in the 14th century Lithuania extended to the shores of the Black Sea). So far as its social-economic basis was concerned this community was probably more firmly established than even the Babylonian or the Spanish Jewish centers at their peak. There was not a single branch of Polish economic life, from agriculture to tax-farming, which did not provide Jews with a means of livelihood. Owing to their favorable economic position their numbers were almost quintupled during the 16th century, from less than 25,000 to more than 100,000 souls, when outside immigration had already subsided.

Though the Polish Jews were not a self-contained class from the point of view of their means of livelihood, they were, however, a separate social group within the framework of the feudal State, more so by virtue of their separate laws and customs than on account of the separate "rights and privileges" guaranteed to them repeatedly by the Crown. Being in principle all equal under Jewish law and unhampered by any barriers so far as internal Jewish life was concerned, with the result that they were

SYNAGOGUE IN LEMBERG, POLAND
Built in 1582

all closely knit together by the most intricate family ties, the Jews with their many different kinds of economic activities had better opportunities of economic success than any of the other minorities in Poland, such as the Germans, for instance. And in this way, important Jewish communities grew up in Posen, Cracow, Lemberg, Lublin, Brest-Litovsk, Vilna and many other Polish and Lithuanian towns, whose members, mostly merchants and artisans, were the core of the urban middle-class in Poland. Their chief competitors were the Germans who previously had the same economic function as the Jews in the towns of Western Poland. The German guilds and corporations in Poland fought against Jewish trade and artisanship in the same way as in Germany. And since the German right of self-administration in the towns was formally recognized in Poland (the

Magdeburg Rights) the German-Jewish relationship in Poland assumed the regular medieval forms. Jews had to live in segregated quarters, were often forced to trade only in particular goods, were in some places forbidden to engage in certain industries, were not allowed to charge more than a fixed rate of interest, etc. But the German towns in Poland were only islands in a great sea. It was a big country, capable of much development, and consequently also big with opportunities for Jewish economic expansion.

D. *Jewish Self-Administration and Cultural Life in Poland:* It was on this economic foundation that the autonomy of the Jewish communities evolved in the 16th century into a self-administrative organization embracing the whole of the Jewish population of Poland and Lithuania. First the Kahal in one town (Cracow or Posen) linked up with the neighboring communities in the same province. Then the provinces or "lands" united, till there emerged their central body, a periodical assembly, the "Council of the Four Lands," with a central Bet Din and machinery for allocating among the different "lands" their share of the heavy State taxation levied upon the Jews. They also promulgated new Takkanot or regulations which were binding upon all Jews, and found the funds for various communal needs (to secure alleviation of unfavorable decrees, obtain the release of persons innocently imprisoned, etc.).

As a corollary of this new organized system in Polish Jewry there now began a flourishing period of Talmudic Rabbinical study. The number of Yeshibot kept increasing with each generation. The fame of their great men, Rabbi Moses Isserles (Rema), Rabbi Solomon Luria, Rabbi Mordecai Jaffe (the Baal Lebushim), Rabbi Samuel Edels (Maharsha) and others spread far beyond the Polish frontiers. Though the Shulhan Aruk, the most important of all the Jewish codes of that time, was introduced to Poland from Sephardic Palestine, it nevertheless acquired its enormous

hold on world Jewry only through the efforts of its Ashkenazic interpreters in Eastern Europe. The great practical value of contemporary Rabbinical teaching which at bottom corresponded to the study of Law in a modern State, did not restrain the Jewish sages of Poland from studying for the sake of studying and often descending to casuistry. It may have been the fault of their having taken their method of study from Western Germany, by way of the Yeshibot of Prague, etc., at a time of decline in these centers.

The Kabbala and the new literature in Judaeo-German or Yiddish, which was the vernacular of all the Ashkenazim, the two branches that were destined to flower later on, first in Hasidism and then in the secular democratic movement, had already begun to flourish in Poland. Here appeared the pride of Yiddish literature, the Zeena u-Reena. The very fact that in Poland the Judaeo-German speech had become an independent Yiddish language and that the Reformation in Germany gave a kind of religious sanction to the linguistic separation from Christian creative work, was of great benefit to Yiddish literature, as was another new manifestation, the printing of books. In the face of the flood of anti-Jewish writings that were being circulated at that time in both Germany and Poland in the languages of the credulous masses the Jews could not properly appreciate whether this new invention was a blessing or a curse. In spite of that the printer soon came to occupy among the People of the Book the place that had previously been held by the scribe.

E. *Indications of the Coming Decline:* Chief guardian of all the spiritual treasures of the people, fortified within its organically evolved autonomous organization and with a more or less firm economic basis, the Ashkenazic community in Eastern Europe seemed in the 16th century to be secure against all the troubles that had overtaken its forerunners in the West at the end of the Middle Ages. But even during this favorable period there were already indications of the coming catastrophe. The same old story was to be repeated here under different conditions.

The Jagiellon dynasty which lasted for almost 200 years, came to an end in 1572. The main decision in the Parliaments that had to elect the future kings of Poland now belonged to the Shlachta, the upper-middle-class, who had long grudged the Jewish land-and-tax-farmers the important positions they held. And in the towns there had never been any cessation of enmity on the part of the German merchants and guilds. Thus the Jews gradually had to move away from the towns and from the more economically developed areas, primarily to the Ukraine and White Russia, where only the large landowners and the aristocracy were Poles and Catholics. Caught in a vise between the Polish Roman-Catholic lord and the Russian Greek-Catholic peasant the Jewish land-farmer in Eastern and Southern Poland in the first half of the 17th century found himself inevitably cast for the part of the first victim of any uprising of the oppressed against the oppressors. Earlier uprisings in the German towns of the plebeians against the patricians had often begun or ended in the same way with a pogrom in the Jewish quarter (as, for instance, in Frankfort on the Main in 1614).

F. *Persecutions in Poland:* The foundations of Jewish life in Poland were gradually being shaken also at their strongest points. The Catholic clergy, who were closely allied with the urban and aristocratic middle-class, lost no opportunity of inciting the masses against the economically, socially and culturally higher placed Jewish population. The Reformation's penetration into Poland, till then the most important country Rome had in Eastern Europe, was a powerful contributing factor. The fear of Jewish influence was spreading throughout the Catholic world. The old anti-Jewish libels were now reinforced by the new allegation that Jews were in alliance or were ready to ally themselves with Moslem Turkey, at that time Christendom's most dangerous foe. Already in 1530

Yosel Rosheim had to answer this charge before the famous Protestant Reichstag held at Augsburg. In 1547 the Inquisition in Portugal where there were only a few Marranos still left suddenly "discovered" that they were all supposed agents of a secret Jewish organization in Constantinople, the new Turkish capital. The more Turkish rule was consolidated in Central Europe, up to Hungary, and the better the Turks treated the Jewish population under their rule, the stronger became the suspicion in almost all the Christian countries—in Bohemia under Ferdinand I (about 1541) just as much as two years earlier in Poland under Sigismund I (1539)—that Jews in reality were a kind of disguised Turks. This provided fresh soil for anti-Jewish feeling, and the result was a long series of mass persecutions. From the end of the 16th century the inhabitants of the Jewish quarters in the towns of Western Poland had to endure a great deal at the hands of the Jesuits, who were in charge of the education of the younger nobility and taught them to despise the Jews and to embitter their lives.

G. *Italy During the Counter-Reformation:* The Jesuit Order was from its foundation (1534) the vanguard of the Counter-Reformation, of the reaction in the Catholic Church against the Protestant heresy. It is one of the ironies of Jewish history that the new Order received its sanction from Pope Paul III (1534-1549), a typical representative of the Renaissance spirit in Italy, even in the matter of tolerance towards the Jews. Things began to get difficult for the Jews in Italy about the beginning of the 16th century, from the time of the arrival not only of the Ashkenazim from the north but also of a considerable number of refugees, Sephardim, from the west. In addition to the Jews who had been expelled from Spain and Portugal there was a constant influx of part-Jews, Marranos. Some of these returned to Judaism in their places of refuge in Italy, but some kept up the pretense that they were Christians. This masquerade infuriated the Christian merchants who had no wish to lose the opportunity of controlling all outside competition.

So it is not surprising that in 1497 there was already a specific expulsion of Marranos from the Venetian trading Republic and that it was precisely there that the word ghetto first came into common use. Jewish migrants always settled everywhere without any compulsion as near to each other as possible. The Jewish quarters which were created in that way over the whole expanse of the medieval Christian world, in Spain or England, Germany or Poland, therefore answered an inner Jewish need. But as soon as the powers began to fear the influence of the Jews upon their non-Jewish environment, the privilege of living among their own people behind the protective walls of their own "town" was immediately transformed into a compulsion, and the Jewish quarter became converted into a kind of prison, a "ghetto."

At times when the Jews inclined to closer contact with their environment, as, for example, in Italy during the Renaissance period when there was a sudden rise in the number of converts in Rome, this compulsory confinement to the Jewish quarter was a terrible hardship to a considerable section of its inhabitants. After the death of Pope Paul III, during the Catholic reaction under such Pontiffs as Julius III (1550-1555) and Paul IV (1555-1559) the compulsory ghetto spread over almost the whole of Italy. From the simultaneous persecution directed against Jewish religious books (primarily the "anti-Christian" Talmud), the intensification of conversionist propaganda and the importance which was now attached to the House of Catechumens, a special institution in Rome for preparing Jews for baptism, it is evident that the real intention was to counteract the danger of Judaization. The result was that Italian Jewry, which during the Renaissance and Humanist period was capable of becoming the pioneer of a new Humanist Renaissance in Jewish spiritual life, once again had to retreat into the background. And there it was destined to remain till the

present day. Independent thinkers like Judah Modena (1571-1648) had to conceal their doubts. A Jewish censorship was introduced by the Rabbis themselves in order

GHETTO IN SIENA, ITALY
16th century

to keep on the right side of the Papal Sanctum Officium (the Holy Office), the Italian Inquisition Tribunal. All the Jewish communities were swept by mysticism, which had already previously taken hold of the Sephardic Jews at the time of the pseudo-Messiahs David Reubeni and Solomon Molko (1524-1532). Sephardic Marranos returning to Judaism were now in constant danger of being burned at the stake, in the same way as Christian heretics, and consequently they gradually made their way abroad, to the neighboring countries under Turkish rule.

H. *Turkey:* In the Near East, the Marranos could return to their Jewish faith without concealment. Ever since the expulsion from Spain Turkey had been receiving Sephardim with open arms, both Jews and half-Jews, and very soon the number of them there exceeded a hundred thousand. When the Sultan Bayezid II (1481-1512) heard of the Spanish King's decree he is said to have remarked: "He is destroying his own land in order to build up ours." This was more or less the way the Turkish monarchs felt about the Sephardic immigration. Some of them (besides Bayezid II, Selim I, Soliman the Magnificent and Selim II) would have none but Jewish physicians, like many of the medieval and later Popes. They also employed the diplomatic skill of such great Jewish merchants as Joseph Nasi. It was only natural, for the expulsion from the Pyrenean Peninsula brought into existence a new connecting factor in contemporary international life, especially in world-trade which the discovery of America revived. The Sephardim, scattered and dispersed throughout almost the entire world, yet bound together firmly by the bond of their unique historic destiny, their common language (Spanish and Portuguese) and even their inextinguishable love of their old home, Spain, where there still lived many of their friends and kin (Marranos), constituted a kind of nation within the nation, and were almost one single huge family. They could be found in England and America, in Holland and the south of France, as well as Hamburg, in Germany, and even Hungary and Poland. If a country was closed to the Jews, like France, they came in under the guise of Catholics.

I. *Holland:* The Sephardic refugees were the first Jews to benefit by the Reformation. It came as good news to the anti-Papists in a country like Holland when they found (end of 16th century) that the merchants who had recently arrived there from Spain and Portugal and went about whispering among themselves like conspirators, were not secret agents of the Inquisition but its victims and foes. They were not many in number but they were extremely able in the art of utilizing and developing the new openings for sea-borne or more properly ocean-borne trade. They provided a good deal of the capital of the big West Indian and East Indian trading companies, and they played a part in making the Amsterdam stock exchange one of the chief financial markets of the world. The fact that they maintained relations with their relatives, the pseudo-Christians living in the Catholic countries, and the further fact that they held on to their own distinctive language and tradition, led to their segregation from the Ashkenazic Jews. The consequence was that a gulf came into existence between the Sephardic and Ashkenazic Jews not less wide than that which had once existed between the kingdoms of Judah and Israel. And, indeed, within a few generations the fragments of Spanish Jewry were considering themselves a kind of Jewish aristocracy, the veritable perpetuation of the tribe of Judah. But in the interval the exceptionally powerful internal bond that united the Sephardim had enabled their eastern branch not only to assume a leading part in the Levant trade, to increase Turkish power and to develop the arms industry in the East, but even to influence Jewish national spiritual life in a creative form.

J. *The New Spiritual Center in Palestine:* Sephardic spiritual influence was shown chiefly in Palestine. Not a few in that great stream of refugees, mostly not Marranos, who from 1492 made their way from the western to the eastern shores of the Mediterranean, had immediately identified their personal tragedy with a complete change of destiny of the entire people of Israel throughout the world, with the beginning of the Messianic era. They hastened to attach themselves to the "Holy Soil" so that they might there speed the redemption and be the advance guard for the return of the exiled Presence of God. And the most intellectually active among them began to develop these elements of Judaeo-Spanish culture that were adapted to the new mystic conception of the world. Poetry, thought, scholarship all became mystical, a means of bringing nearer the redemption. Mysticism itself, the Kabbala, became practical, no longer theory aiming to recognize the mysteries of the world, but the teaching of methods by which the world might be transformed.

This feeling which animated the spiritual leaders of the Sephardim in contemporary Palestine expressed itself no less characteristically in Joseph Caro's (1488-1575) code, the Shulhan Aruk, than in Solomon Alkabez's mystic Sabbath hymn "Leka Dodi," as well as in the works of his brother-in-law, Moses Cordovero, and of Rabbi Isaac Luria's disciple Hayim Vital. Joseph Caro, the new legislator, a Kabbalist like almost all his circle, was convinced that he was proclaiming to the world only what had been put in his mouth by an angel from heaven. In this way the son of Spanish exiles became the prophet of Rabbinical legislation, even to the Ashkenazim outside Palestine, while his relative by marriage, Rabbi Isaac Luria, who was himself of Ashkenazic origin, became the founder of a Kabbalistic movement that was destined to develop in Eastern Europe, and there rise to be a real movement of the people—Hasidism.

2. FROM THE MASSACRES OF 1648 TO THE FRENCH REVOLUTION

The year 1648 (5408-5409 according to Jewish reckoning) is the chronological border-line dividing the first half of the modern era from its second half, which is essentially the prelude to our own period. As in European history generally so in Jewish history too it is only now that the real foundations upon which the new epoch was evolving became visible. In this year 1648 the consequences of the Thirty Years' War between the Catholics and Protestant ar-

mies were drawn in the Peace of Westphalia, and the Christian West was more or less stabilized. Reason finding itself released to a considerable extent from its spiritual fetters made big strides forward not only in the realm of creative thought and philosophy, but also in material production, which came to be as rationalized as the conception of the world held by the people of Europe who were progressively liberating themselves from the Church dogmas. They were becoming more interested in this world than in the world to come, in all that concerned the betterment and the beautifying of life on earth.

And that inevitably involved a change of attitude towards the Jews. If the Jew could show that he was capable of co-operating in the rationalization of human life he might within his own four walls hold whatever belief he wished and there would always be a place for him in the newly-discovered world of reason. The Jews themselves had always considered that they were rationalists in the Christian world, representatives of common sense in religion, so that really the spirit of the times was coming to meet them and inevitably, sooner or later, both sides would have to realize their cultural and historic kinship. These were the general conditions that once more opened a road for the Jewish masses from east to west, as previously in the heyday of Islam, though no longer from Asia to Europe but rather from Eastern Europe to Western Europe.

A. *The Massacres of 1648-1649:* However, the Jewish people was to receive its most powerful stimulus to make use of these new opportunities not from any inward natural urge but—as at the time of the Crusades—from a catastrophe coming from outside, the terrible persecutions and massacres in Polish Ukraine. The rising of the Greek-Catholic cossacks and peasants under Chmielnicki (afterwards the Haidamacks) in 1648 against the Catholic-Polish State authority headed by the big landowners, was the beginning of the end both of the greatest and most significant of all the

Jewish settlements of that time and of the Polish State itself, with the result that the frontier between Western and Eastern Jewry was shifted further east. While the Jewish population of those parts of Poland that at the end of the 18th century came under Austrian and Prussian rule took their place in West European Jewish history, both influencing and being influenced by it, the future of the bulk of the Jews of Poland, Lithuania and the Ukraine was linked up with the historic destiny of the youngest world power at that time, with Russia, the empire that inherited the legacy of Byzantium, and its czars (an abbreviation of Caesar) who had already by the end of the 16th century begun to dream of elevating their capital Moscow to the dignity of a "Third Rome."

Thus the century and a half between the catastrophe of 1648 and the beginning of our own epoch which still continues the traditions of the great French Revolution is, in Jewish history, simultaneously a period of decline for the great Jewish community in Poland and a period of construction and reconstruction both to the west and east of Poland. Once again there is a cross-current in the history of the Jewish people, a process of decline concurrent with a complicated process of new upward growth. This simultaneous descent and ascent is the second, the positive aspect of the Jewish dispersion, which ensures that at all times of great change in the world in which it is living, the people as a whole not only gets its share of troubles in the declining part of the world but also benefits from the rising trend in the progressive part of the world. In less than ten years (1648-1656), the years of the Chmielnicki rising and its direct results, the Russo-Polish and Swedish-Polish war, more than six hundred Jewish communities were destroyed in the Ukraine, White Russia (the eastern part of Poland), Lithuania, and the old Polish areas. But the stream of refugees who succeeded in escaping from the disaster poured westward, into Bohemia, Moravia, Austria, Germany, Italy and even Turkey, where they were for the most part captives brought there by the Crimean Tartars who were Chmielnicki's allies, and were afterwards ransomed there by Jewish funds.

The immediate effect was the same as after the expulsion from Spain. Like the Sephardim at that time the East European Ashkenazim now formed a firm bond between the various Jewish communities in the different countries (primarily in Western and Southern Europe), intensified the sense of national solidarity everywhere, enhanced appreciation of the specifically Jewish historical destiny, and thus created the atmosphere for the great movement of the year 1666, the center of which was the pseudo-Messiah Sabbatai Zebi (1626-1676), himself a follower of the practical Kabbala and thus an inheritor of the traditions of the Sephardic refugees.

B. *Holland, England and France:* The catastrophe which had now overwhelmed the chief Ashkenazic center in Poland led to a temporary revival of the Sephardic section of the Jewish people. Several positive factors contributed to this as well. Whatever advantages the Jewish people derived from the new epoch in Europe, especially from the changes that accompanied the Reformation, were at first entirely in favor of the Sephardim.

The first victims of the Church Militant they were also, of course, among the first to benefit when the Catholic Church had to abandon attack and concentrate on defense. It was during the worst period in Poland that after an interruption of three and a half centuries the road opened again for them that led from Protestant Holland to Protestant England (1650-1656). Manasseh ben Israel (1604-1657), who was the leader of this return movement among the Dutch Sephardim and conducted the negotiations with Oliver Cromwell, the revolutionary dictator of the English Puritans, was incidentally one of the chief representatives of contemporary Jewish "realpolitik," which was based on the mystical foundations of the Kabbala. It was because he interpreted the Polish disaster as a sign of the approach of the Messianic era that he considered it so essential to establish quickly in all parts of the world points of firm support for the coming redemption.

Of course, there would have been no restoration of the Jewish settlement in the British Isles unless it had happened to coincide with the interests of British international trade, in the same way as its establishment during the Norman Conquest centuries previously had been in accordance with the interests of the English economy of the time. Yet it is a historical fact that the Sephardim reopened the doors of England to Jewish immigration on the basis of a clearly-formulated Jewish national program, and thus constructed a bridge for the Ashkenazim as well. The same thing had happened previously in Holland. In the German trading city Hamburg the Senate permitted Ashkenazim, including Polish Jews, to live there only as "servants to the Portuguese," meaning the Sephardim (decision of the year 1654). It was not till 1697 that independent "German-Jewish communities" were recognized there.

In the same way the Sephardim acted as the advance guard in the restoration of the ancient ruined Jewish settlements in France. The Marranos who penetrated there (chiefly in the great port city of Bordeaux) under the guise of Christians, but who were at heart loyal Jews, obtained in 1732 from Louis xv the right to describe themselves openly as Jews. Half a century before that the famous French statesman Colbert had already indicated that "the cause of the anti-Jewish persecutions is business jealousy." In France the Sephardim became a driving force in international trade, as they were in Northern Europe, especially in the trade with America and the East (India and China). But the French Sephardim had played a dual role too long to be able to find their way back completely to their people when there was no longer any need for them to conceal the fact that they were Jews. That is why even after 1789 they repudiated all connection with other Jewish elements in France, including what was left of the ancient Franco-Jewish community in Avignon. Those Ashkenazim who were already in France at that time owed their presence, not as in England to their wealthy Sephardim, but to France's military victories which had made French provinces of Alsace and Lorraine, with their old-established and religiously observant Jewish population (Metz had already been annexed in 1552 and Alsace only in 1648 under the Peace of Westphalia).

C. *The Culture of the Sephardim:* The highly advanced standard of economic life among the West European Sephardim was accompanied, both as cause and effect, by a high level of culture. It was precisely for this reason that they were in both respects far in advance of the average of contemporary European achievement, that they were able to build the road that again led their people into the West European world, with all its various offshoots down to South America. For the first time in Jewish cultural history they created a literature in languages (Portuguese and Spanish) which, though they were non-Jewish, were nevertheless not the languages of their non-Jewish environment. It was an expression of deep and abiding affiliation with their former homeland such as is probably never again encountered in all world history. Even the rigorously orthodox Manasseh ben Israel wrote in Spanish, to say nothing of heretics like Spinoza's predecessor, Uriel da Costa, whose "Theses Against the Tradition" (1616) was written in Portuguese. The Sephardim couldn't possibly have retained the languages of the Pyrenean Peninsula in their private and social life had they not been extremely assimilated from the start. Marranoism itself was evidence of this.

The same ability to adapt themselves to their environment and at the same time perpetuate their own cultural tradition which for centuries was consciously a tradition of adaptation, was now manifested by the Sephardim who became Dutch, English, French, yet remained "Portuguese" or

DISPUTATION BETWEEN CHRISTIAN AND
JEWISH THEOLOGIANS
16th century

after the Peace of Westphalia and the Polish catastrophe. The refugees from the east brought from Poland (chiefly to Bohemia and Moravia), their own scholarship and the basic principles of Jewish centralized self-administration. But at the same time the economic and spiritual decline of Polish Jewry—consequent on the repeated Haidamack insurrections in the Polish part of the Ukraine (Volhynia, Podolia, etc.) and a long chain of terrible ritual murder trials—in the course of the 18th century, undermined the former prestige of the principal Ashkenazic center and its achievements in the cultural sphere. Meanwhile the Jews of Central Europe had again found their way back into the process of capital-accumulation.

This rise of a new Jewish class of capitalists, essentially the result of the general progress in production and international trade, had also its specific causes. As previously in the Thirty Years' War, so now

"Spanish," in other words, the children and grandchildren of Jewish refugees, avowed Jews or secret Jews, from the Pyrenean Peninsula. Even their Messianism at the end of the 17th century (during the Sabbatian movement) was much influenced by contemporary Christian Messianism. The result was that after the collapse of their Messianism the Sephardim of Western Europe became the parents of a new Marranoism, the assimilation of the 19th century, whose first stage was the Haskalah.

D. *Germany and the Haskalah Movement:* The new cultural movement manifested itself especially among the German Jews in the 18th century, though the historic foundations for its development had been laid much earlier. The Jews in the German cultural area (including Austria and Bohemia, Moravia and Hungary) fell under a dual influence from the west and the east

ENTRANCE TO JEWISH GHETTO IN VIENNA
17th century

EXPULSION OF JEWS FROM VIENNA IN 1670

OLD AND NEW SYNAGOGUE IN FÜRTH, GERMANY
Beginning 18th century

again (in the wars against the Turks and in the Silesian wars) Jewish contractors distinguished themselves chiefly through their purely Jewish international contacts in

ROTHSCHILD HOUSE IN
FRANKFORT-ON-THE-MAIN,
GERMANY

organizing the war-economy. The sons of the abnormal migrant-people seemed as though born for those abnormal times and their abnormal economic conditions. All the Central European Courts were only too glad to avail themselves in those lean years of the services of Jewish purveyors, financial agents and general advisers, like the Court factors, Samuel Oppenheimer of Heidelberg or Samson Wertheimer of Worms, who attained a high position in Imperial Vienna (1674-1724). True enough, in 1670 there was an expulsion of Jews from Vienna due to pressure from below. But it was one of the signs of the times that these Jews who were expelled from Vienna easily found a new refuge by formal agreement in Prussia, which was just beginning to emerge very rapidly, and some of them were soon able to return to Austria.

This class of Jews whom the German Government found so useful allied themselves, particularly in the West German territories (Cleve, etc.) commercially at first, then culturally as well, with the Sephardic magnates in neighboring Holland, thus becoming the social basis of Jewish Haskalah. German became to these enlightened

Ashkenazim, led by Moses Mendelssohn (1729-1786) and his followers, like David Friedlaender or Lazarus Bendavid, what Spanish and Portuguese were to the Sephardim. Even Hebrew to the German-Jewish Haskalah was primarily the Hebrew of old classical Sepharad (Spain). The cosmopolitan spirit of the "world citizen" which dominated the contemporary French and German educated world (the Encyclopedists, Lessing, Herder, etc.) was also, as far as the Jewish Haskalah was concerned, essentially a matter of external adjustment of the old Judaism to the new cosmos rather than an inner spiritual revolution; so strong was the Sephardic assimilation in the Ashkenazic Haskalah—the need of the newly-rising wealthy class to find a common language with "enlightened" mercantile absolutism and with the young growing capitalism that

HOLIDAY COSTUME OF JEWESS IN
NURNBERG, GERMANY

18th century

HOLIDAY COSTUME OF JEW IN
NURNBERG, GERMANY
18th century

to their ears in debt and that their creditors were very often their former debtors, the Catholic monasteries. Hardly safe with their lives and their possessions the Polish Jews suffered during the 18th century more than anywhere else, more than at any other time, from the blood libel—for this was how the clergy took revenge for the growing influence of the anti-Catholic Christians, the Russians and the Prussians, in this Catholic land. This must have demoralized the Polish Jews but for the fact that when the danger was most acute externally and internally, a great movement arose among them, Hasidism, which created a new synthesis of all the main positive factors of Jewish life: roots in the broad masses of the people, faith in the historic eternity of the Jewish microcosm, and the thoroughly optimistic conviction that the weakest of the Zaddikim was according to his metaphysical substance incomparably more powerful than the strongest oppressors.

There had to be a combination of several circumstances in order to make it possible for this trend of joyful piety that is associated with the name of Israel Baal Shem Tob (1700-1760) to constitute the foundation of a new social and economic

meanwhile still stood under the tutelage of the State.

E. *The Jews in Poland Before the Dissolution:* During this period the Jews in Poland travelled downhill in company with the Polish State. Like the Ukrainian rising in the middle of the 17th century, all the later wars and civil wars in Poland were incidentally always anti-Jewish wars as well. No matter how the Jews tried to restore the balance by their own efforts it always came to nothing. About the middle of the 18th century the impoverishment of the Jewish masses became simply catastrophic, and a large number of them had to depend on the charity of the handful of wealthy Jews who controlled all the Jewish social institutions. It is typical of the economic position of the Polish Jews at the time that the communities themselves were up

SYNAGOGUE MURAL IN KAMIONKA-
STRUMILOWA, POLAND
Showing Jerusalem scene

structure. Hasidic "practical Kabbala" could never have found its way down to the depths of the soul of the people unless the sparks were still smouldering there since the days of Sabbatai Zebi. And as the old traditional rabbinical teachings tended to become dry as dust, and its pillars, the rabbis, compromised themselves by their part in the decaying communal self-administration, the path was made clear for a transvaluation of religious and social values within the Jewish world. The Frankists, who derived direct from the Sabbatians and were connected with the Sephardim of Salonica, tried to use the opportunity in the direction of a neo-Marrano adjustment to the Catholic environment, this time by means of openly formulated dogmatic compromises and concessions (repudiation of the Talmud, recognition of the Trinity, etc.). But the broad masses of the people did not turn to Jacob Frank's mystical syncretism but to the warm and friendly teachings of the Baal Shem's disciples, which stimulated them to find their help in the active force of their own faith and a conscious transformation of their entire mode of living. At the very moment of its break-up Polish Jewry succeeded in creating a legacy for the coming generations, the social essence of which was to survive not only throughout the period of the French Revolution but up to the present time.

F. *Russia:* Poland's end (the partitions of 1772-1795), which broke up its Jewish community, also had the effect of bringing together the Jews of the Ukraine, White Russia and Lithuania in a new historic association under Russian rule. And this new center remained intimately connected with that section of Polish Jewry which in Galicia came under Austrian rule, as well as with the colonies of Ukrainian Jews in the eastern part of the Balkan Peninsula (afterwards Romania). On the

THE OLD MILL STREET SYNAGOGUE IN NEW YORK
Erected in 1730

other hand, that section of Polish Jewry which went to Prussia immediately responded to the powerful attraction of the West European communities. An important factor in linking together all Jews from Vilna and Vitebsk to Lemberg and Cracow was the further development of the Hasidic revolution and the conflicts it started along the whole area of what had formerly been the field of Polish-Jewish

ture of the Jewish population in this entire area remained more or less the same right up to the 19th century. The experiments made by enlightened absolutism in Austria and Russia (Joseph II and Catherine II) aiming at an economic reconstruction which would convert the Jewish innkeepers and landowners' factors into real peasants and producers generally could not possibly succeed as fast as these crowned representatives

Courtesy American Jewish Historical Society

SYNAGOGUE IN CHARLESTON, S.C.
Built in 1794

culture. The bans pronounced against the Hasidim by Rabbi Elijah, the Vilna Gaon, the leading figure among the Mitnagdim, who went in fear and trembling of any kind of change in the ancient faith, had repercussions in Brody and Lemberg no less than in the Jewish communities of Lithuania or White Russia. Another important contributing factor was that the economic struc-

of the age of reason, and their ideologists, the adherents of "enlightenment," Jewish and Christian, desired. Essentially, everything remained as it was materially and spiritually.

G. *Emancipation in America:* The first and greatest triumph of the age of reason in relation to the Jewish people was to come not in Eastern Europe but in the

To the President of the United States of America.

Sir

Permit the children of the Stock of Abraham to approach you with the most cordial affection and esteem for your person & merit— And to join with our fellow Citizens in welcoming you to NewPort.

With pleasure we reflect on those days— those days of Difficulty, & danger when the God of Israel, who delivered David from the peril of the Sword.— Shielded Your head in the day of battle:— And we rejoice to think, that the Same Spirit, who rested in the Bosom of the greatly beloved Daniel enabling him to preside over the Provinces of the Babylonish Empire, rests and ever will rest upon you, enabling you to discharge the arduous duties of Chief Magistrate in these States.

Deprived as we heretofore have been of the invaluable rights of free Citizens, we now (with a deep sense of gratitude to the Almighty disposer of all events) behold a Government, erected by the Majesty of the People.— a Government, which to bigotry gives no Sanction, to persecution no assistance— but generously affording to All liberty of Conscience, and immunities of Citizenship:— deeming every one, of whatever Nation, tongue, or language equal parts of the great governmental Machine:— This so ample and extensive Federal Union whose basis is Philanthropy, Mutual Confidence and Publick Virtue, we cannot but acknowledge to be the work of the Great God, who ruleth in the Armies of Heaven, and among the Inhabitants of the Earth, doing whatsoever seemeth him good.

For all the Blessings of civil and religious liberty, which we enjoy under an equal and benign administration, we desire to Send up our thanks to the Antient of Days, the great preserver of Men— beseeching him, that the Angel who conducted our forefathers through the Wilderness into the promised land, may graciously conduct you through all the difficulties and dangers of this mortal Life:— And, when like Joshua full of days and full of honour, you are gathered to your Fathers, may you be admitted into the Heavenly Paradise to partake of the water of life, and the tree of immortality.

Done and Signed by Order of the Hebrew Congregation in NewPort Rhode Island August 17th 1790—

Moses Seixas Warden.

LETTER OF GREETING TO GEORGE WASHINGTON
From the Jewish community of Newport, R.I., August 17, 1790

remotest west of the West European world, in America. As soon as the descendants of the English Puritan pioneer settlers across the Atlantic rose against British rule, they expressly proclaimed that "all men are created equal and are endowed by their Creator with certain inalienable rights; among these are life, liberty and the pursuit of happiness" (Declaration of Independence of 1776). Though the American Revolution was for more than a century overshadowed by the French Revolution which broke out a few years later, and but few Jews originally benefited by American emancipation (about 5,000), the new democratic Republic was destined to become the blessed land of the Jewish future.

III. THE NINETEENTH CENTURY
(1789-1914)

1. BETWEEN TWO REVOLUTIONARY EPOCHS
(1789-1848)

The Great Revolution that put an end to the degenerate feudalism in France at the same time cleared the road for gigantic creative forces, material and intellectual, that had been striving for a long time to shape the political and social-economic conditions of life that were necessary for their further development. From 1789 France made terrific efforts to catch up with England where the Industrial Revolution had come about gradually in the course of several generations. The first principle of the new order was that all the sons of France are "brothers," all equally free to take part in the coming progress of the community as a whole which thus becomes a "nation," which is to say, a natural league of citizens enjoying equal rights throughout the entire area of the State territory. In other words, their "city," their place of domicile, is now the whole country. All legal distinctions between the individual and the community, between class and class, between one social group and the other, such as, for instance, the old guilds or corporations, had to be abolished, and therefore they had to be abolished also between the Jewish community and its French environment, from

which it had always been cut off by the separate Jewish law ("Jus Judaicum").

A. *The Jews in Europe on the Eve of the Revolution:* Conditions for the Jews on the eve of this revolution in the West European conception of human rights were unendurable. The new Jewish bourgeoisie felt every day the marked and glaring contrast that existed between its position in economic life and its non-possession of citizen rights. In their own environment these Jewish magnates were told by the Jewish preachers of enlightenment that all this was contrary to reason, by which the world should be governed. Their own belief in reason derived from the general spirit of the time. First the Englishman, John Toland (1670-1722), then the Abbé Gregoire and Count Mirabeau in France, like Lessing and his circle in Germany, evolved in black and white the formula: Jew=human being. In 1777 Germany's greatest philosopher, Kant, no longer had to fear embracing in public a Jewish hunchback, Lessing's friend, Moses Mendelssohn. And soon afterwards the Germanized East European Jew, Solomon Maimon, found favor with the prince of German poets, Goethe.

Though the material and intellectual barriers between Jews and non-Jews were in this way gradually removed, there was very little change effected in the dense forest of legal proscriptions. There were roughly two-and-a-half million Jews in the world at that time and about three-quarters of them lived in Europe and only one quarter in the rest of the world (Turkey and Palestine, Persia, North Africa and both Americas). Though the political and cultural separation of the European Jews east and west of the Russian frontier was effected at this time, their status remained in most respects practically the same over the whole Continent. In point of culture Austrian Galicia was still the bridge to the east while the Jewish community in French Alsace was in economic structure reminiscent of the Jewish Ukraine. The political status of the Jews in Eastern and Western Europe showed even greater similarity. In both places, in the Russia of Catherine II or in moribund Poland, there was the same controversy, over the question of converting the Jewish middleman into a "productive" person, as there was in Joseph II's Austria and Frederick II's Prussia or Louis XVI's France. In Russia this gave the Jewish population the right to participate in the local self-administration like all the other inhabitants of the towns (1778).

But at the same time began the ejection of Jews from the villages. Till then they had been mainly innkeepers and leaseholders of land engaged in various branches of agriculture. Now they had to find new means of livelihood in the towns and cities where competition among the Jewish merchants and artisans was already severe. From 1786 they were all crammed into the borders of the annexed Polish territory (the Pale of Settlement plus the newly-acquired New Russia, or South Ukraine). This introduced the West European ghetto system into the Russian empire on a vast scale. In Western Europe it was still the most severe of all the anti-Jewish discriminations. For the most natural privilege of man, the right of free movement, the Jew had to pay a special tax ("Protection money" in Prussia, "right of domicile" tax in France). If he was not rich enough to purchase a place in the class of "tolerated" Jews in Vienna, or "Schutz-Juden" (protected Jews) in Prussia, he was denied the right to marry off his child, even when he himself was allowed to live there. This created separate classes among the Jews. Furthermore the right of domicile that Jews enjoyed in many of the European towns was tantamount to the duty to spend the night only in the Jewish quarter (in Vienna as much as in Rome, and in Venice no less than in Frankfort on the Main). And there was a number of cities that Jews were not allowed to enter, like Paris, which was barred to the Ashkenazim of Eastern France.

B. *Emancipation in France:* Some idea can be had of the rejoicing which animated the French Jews when the National Assembly on September 27th, 1791 finally abolished all anti-Jewish discriminatory legislation, and proclaimed these outcasts of yesterday, Frenchmen with equal rights, when we read the manifesto issued at the time by the Jewish leader, Berr Isaac Berr, to the Jewish communities of Alsace and Lorraine: "In the same way as God once appointed Antiochus to enslave us so He has now chosen the noble French nation to return our rights to us and to enable us to be reborn." Nevertheless, there were two points about this passage of the French Jews "from slavery to liberty" which might well have dampened their enthusiasm. In the first place, the Sephardim were conducting a separate policy of their own at the expense of the rest of the Jews in France, the result of which was that on Talleyrand's proposal they obtained citizenship rights for themselves before the general Jewish emancipation (January 1790). This created a dangerous precedent—a dispensation allowing the economically privileged section of the Jews, in the supposed interests of all Israel, to break the principle of the equality and fraternity of all Jews within their own sphere. In the second place, the Jews in France were recognized as equal citizens on the ground that in future they would not form part of the separate people of Israel but would only be members of a separate religious group, whose faith might indeed be as much spread throughout the world as, for instance, Christianity. It was the opponents of emancipation who contended that as long as Jews remain Jews they will not cease to be a national group even in France. To this the defenders of Jewish equality (Clermont-Tonnerre, etc.) had only one answer: "There certainly must not be a nation within a nation . . . If they say they are you may expel them from the country . . . All that they are obtaining they have obtained as human beings, not as a nation." Those who opposed Jewish emancipation and, for their own purpose, stressed the traditional Jewish point of view (like the Bishop of Nancy, La Fare) insisted that the Jews are a nation without a land, that they themselves consider this state of

KETUBAH, MARRIAGE CONTRACT, OF THE YEAR 1811 IN GIBRALTAR

DECREE OF THE FRENCH NATIONAL ASSEMBLY GRANTING EQUAL RIGHTS TO JEWS
September 27, 1791

affairs only temporary and look forward to their ultimate return to their former home, Palestine.

This argument was repeatedly used also in Holland as when the Batavian Republic was proclaimed there under French influence (1795). But the Dutch friends of emancipation answered the objectors by telling them that believing Christians ought not to take the Jewish Messianic hope seriously, since according to their own faith it was not realizable. The Jews themselves, wherever the French armies introduced the new system (besides Holland in Germany and Italy), kept quiet for the most part and were content to gather the fruits that fell from the tree of liberty in the social and economic field. But their silence was itself a tacit admission that the Jews were ready to compromise in return for the great gains of emancipation. The West European Ashkenazim went further still along the Sephardic road of adaptation. Since the Jewish religion and the people of Israel were always, according to Jewish belief, two aspects of the same thing, they began to propose changing this state of affairs, reforming traditional Judaism by divorcing faith from nation and in the realm of faith, too, introducing a new interpretation of the Messianic belief on the lines of an abstract universal ideal.

C. *The Reformation Under Napoleon:* The first Jewish reformation of the modern period began in the classic land of Jewish emancipation, in France. The Great Revolution had meanwhile devoured her children and had entered on the Imperialist phase. Napoleon I, following in the path of Cyrus, king of the Persians, and Julius Caesar, emperor of Rome, sought to convert the world-people Israel into an instrument of French imperialism. As General Bonaparte he had already issued a proclamation to the Jews of the Near East, promising to restore their holy city Jerusalem (1799). He seems to have come to the conclusion that under whatever conditions emancipation had been achieved in France the Jews nevertheless were a nation even though they might not be like all the other nations. When he enforced a new discriminatory law against the Jews of Alsace because their economic reconstruction and cultural assimilation were not proceeding fast enough for his liking, he explicitly declared: "We must consider the Jews as a nation, not as a sect," which is to say, not as a federation only of religious communities. And at the same time, the emperor made up his mind to compel this nation to link its historic destiny with his world-domination plans. It was by his command that the Assembly of Jewish notables (representatives of the most important Jewish communities in the empire) was convoked that same year (1806) to acknowledge that the law of the land takes precedence over the Jewish law, in principle, especially where it applies to Jewish soldiers, and the Assembly even consented to mixed marriages.

The following year (1807) a "Sanhedrin," appointed mostly by the First Assembly, formally ratified these decisions. Thus all Jews living under Napoleon's rule were defined as Frenchmen with a reformed Jewish faith. The Sephardim dominated both Assemblies. Though the "nation" of Jews was thus formally abolished the man who had, so to say, redeemed it from national existence was everywhere hailed as a Jewish "Messiah" (in Vienna, Berlin and even Petersburg), and people feared that wherever Napoleon's armies came they would now find the local Jews their loyal allies. While the French Revolution prepared the road for Jewish civic equality in all the lands under French influence, Napoleon's imperialism ploughed the soil for Jewish reformation far into Eastern Europe. The executive organs of the Jewish communities in France, Italy and also partly in Germany were converted into consistories on the Protestant model. Instead of being living cells of the national organism as they had been thereto, they became frigid bureaucratic institutions.

D. *The European Reaction:* The Vienna Congress which in 1815 put an end to Napoleon's dreams of world domination and closed the first revolutionary chapter in the modern history of Europe, could not wipe out all achievements of the previous quarter of a century, including the transformation in the legal status of the Jewish population. In those lands where the Jews owed their citizenship rights to the French victories (as in Italy and parts of Germany) they were thrust back into their pre-revolutionary

Prussian State citizens. The reason was chiefly the cultural transition which had begun long before the French Revolution and had since brought about a real spiritual revolution among a large section of German Jewry. The new Jewish schools where German was the language of instruction and the purely German secondary schools and universities produced a generation that felt nearer to the non-Jewish than to the Jewish

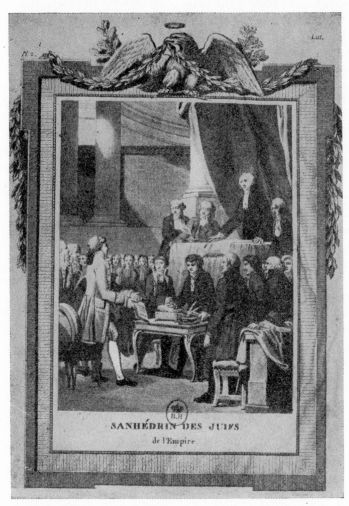

THE "SANHEDRIN" CONVENED BY NAPOLEON IN 1807

ghetto positions during the reactionary period that is bound up with the name of Metternich. But in France after the Bourbon restoration they remained Frenchmen with all their equality of rights. Prussia, too, continued to give effect to the moderately liberal edict of 1812 which made the Jews

environment. The salons of the educated Jewesses of Berlin or Vienna (Rachel Levin or Fanny Arnstein) were the meeting places of all the great men in German science and art. This intellectual alliance often resulted in mixed marriages, and baptism came to be frequent in these circles. Jews shed their blood together with Germans fighting to liberate Germany from the French yoke. Jewish bankers, principally the Rothschilds, rose to high positions and had a voice even in important political decisions. Under such conditions it seemed to be utopian to want to turn the wheel back. Jews and non-Jews alike began to think that the shortest and the most natural way of getting rid of the difficulties of being a Jew, at least in Central and Western Europe, was to hasten the process of assimilation.

A pestilent anti-Jewish literature and an outbreak of pogroms in a number of German districts four years after the Vienna Congress (1819) awakened doubts, indeed, about the possibility of getting rid of the Jewish question quickly. But except for that section of Jews who adhered to the old ways and held that till the Messiah comes Jews must be Jews and Gentiles Gentiles, and the avowed anti-Semites who were agitating for Pharaonic methods against the Jews, all who pondered the Jewish question at all were convinced that economic reconstruction and closer attachment of the Jews to their non-Jewish environment was the only proper solution.

E. *Internal Dissensions Among the Jews of Central Europe:* To the generation between the '20's and the '40's of the 19th century (including men like Heine, Marx and Lassalle) it was evident that without complete Jewish emancipation even assimilation could not accomplish as much as almost everyone desired. It was one of the results of the new wave of liberalism in Europe that even the most inveterate foes of assimilation, the orthodox Jews, demanded at conferences and in petitions their "human rights" from the Governments in every place where emancipation had got stuck half-way. The reactionary Governments in Central Europe belonging to the "Holy Alliance," in other words, the anti-revolutionary Christian league of Austria, Prussia and Russia, were thus deprived of their last pretext that the most Jewish part of the Jewish population itself opposed any change in the legal status of the Jews.

There was a very deep-lying internal reason for this new orientation among the orthodox Jews. The ancestors of Central European Jewish orthodoxy had a hard struggle for their influence in Jewish communal life and they therefore couldn't leave the responsibility of dealing with the burning questions of the day—in the first place, the improving of the legal and economic status of the Jewish masses—to the new Jewish "heretics," liberals with leanings to Reform Judaism, like Gabriel Riesser, etc. As long as the European languages and the new methods of education were forced upon the Jews from above, usually by the police, as in the early post-Mendelssohnian period (at the time of Herz Homberg), the majority of the Jews, especially in Austria, resisted it in every way possible. But when assimilation ceased to be an oppressive movement from outside and became an internal question, the conservative elements found themselves compelled to compete with it not only in the secular but even in the religious field. And the result was that parallel with the Jewish reform movement inspired by Abraham Geiger there developed in Central Europe a Jewish neo-orthodoxy—the old Jewish orthodoxy in a neo-German form—led by Rabbi Samson Raphael Hirsch.

Both movements spoke the language of modern philosophy, both were based on science, Jewish learning, and both helped to destroy the old Jewish mode of life throughout the west, as far as England and America. It was clear from the start that the victory would be for the more radical reformist movement which had evolved direct from the Franco-Jewish reformation, in other words, indirectly from the French Revolution, so that it was natural that the 1848 revolutions which placed Central and Southern Europe more or less where France had stood at the beginning of the 19th century, and brought Jewish emancipation there to a temporary conclusion (in Italy, Prussia and Austria) should lead those Jewish communities, too, along the same broad French road—the road of intensified religious assimilation.

F. *Eastern Europe:* There was a much fainter repercussion of the 1789 and 1848 revolutions in Eastern Europe under the shadow of Russian autocracy. Galicia, which was the link in the chain of European Jewish communities uniting East and West, was the advance guard of the East European Jews in the West, and was destined afterwards to become the reverse, the advance guard of West European Haskalah in Eastern Europe, especially in the Ukraine and South Russia. The change in Galicia's function in the life of the Jewish people was determined by the alterations in Poland's political fate. About twelve years after the

JEWISH OFFICERS AND SOLDIERS IN THE
POLISH NATIONAL GUARD
During uprising against Russia in 1831

Third Partition of Poland Napoleon re-created a Polish State (the Duchy of Warsaw) which included about 400,000 East European Jews, some 7 percent of the total population. The reformist assimilationist spirit from Western Europe penetrated here, too, where the German Jewish Haskalah had already found its way at the end of the 18th century. The Hasidic movement had now passed its peak, yet it continued to foster the people's trust in their own

culture and language with such effect that the modernized and denationalized Jewish-German culture failed to strike roots there. So the renewed intellectual tendencies, which were a direct sequel to the Mendelssohnian Haskalah with its essentially orthodox intentions, created their own thoroughly national medium, a modernized Hebrew and afterwards also a Yiddish literature. After the Vienna Congress, which put an end to the Polish State that had been created by Napoleon's favor, and transferred the greater part of it to the Russian czar, the frontier that divided east and west in the European Jewish world was more or less established for a century. But the new great Jewish settlement in Russia (which was to become by the end of the 19th century the largest in all Jewish history) refused to recognize any external frontiers and thus soon became the main support of the all-Jewish historic destiny.

The economic position of the Jewish masses in the Russian provinces that constituted the Kingdom of Poland (Congress Poland) was somewhat better than that of the rest of the Jewish Pale of Settlement. It was the only place where Jews were still allowed to own land. But even there they earned their living mainly as traders, artisans and by all manner of unskilled labor. But the number of Jewish manufacturers, too, steadily increased. The number of Jewish factory workers, on the other hand, was still small. The market in which they could sell their products was so restricted that the Jews, both merchants and artisans, found themselves competing now almost entirely with fellow-Jews.

Though chronologically Russia was backward she was nevertheless a part of Europe, and so here as well the Government tried to utilize the economic abilities of the Jewish population and to confer economic and cultural benefits upon them almost by force. In this regard Alexander I (1801-1825) and his brother Nicholas I (1825-1855) followed the road of the so-called "enlightened absolutism." The Jewish agricultural colonies which were established during their

reigns (for the purpose, incidentally, of settling the almost empty steppes of "New
Russia") testify that their economic reconstruction policy was in this respect at least
no less successful than that in Galicia, for
example. They encountered greater resistance in the cultural field. Though the Russian Government offered advantages to Jews
with modern education in the shape of valuable civil privileges, this "poison," as the
old religious orthodox Jews dubbed the official assimilationist school policy, brought
but little success. Nor was Nicholas I much
more successful with his experiment of
training the Jewish youth in his military
barracks. The children who were pressed
into military service (Cantonists) manifested the same spiritual tenacity as their fathers
and grandfathers. They preferred to hold
fast to their inherited Judaism, even at the
cost of degradation, rather than be equal
before the law with the Gentile population,
at the sacrifice of their precious inheritance.

This doctrine, formulated by Rabbi
Shneur Zalman, the founder of the new
Hasidic Habad movement, remained the
guiding principle of the great majority of
the Russian Jews and their ancient autonomous communities right up to the second
half of the 19th century. Rich and poor
alike displayed the same determination in
avoiding the schools specifically opened for
Jewish children, where Russian was the
language of instruction, though these
schools provided a royal road out of the
Pale. In Russia, unlike Western Europe, no
one had any doubts as to whether the Jews
were a "nation," or might perhaps be a
"sect." Here quantity passed into quality.
Scholars and illiterates, Hasidim and
Mitnagdim, modernist Maskilim and fanatical adherents of the old traditional ways,
all felt that they were children of the ancient
people of Israel. And the Russian world
regarded them in the same way—not only
the Government but even its antagonists
(like Paul Pestel, the leader of the revolutionary Decembrists).

G. *National Solidarity:* At this juncture
the excitement that was created through-

out the entire Jewish world by the ritual
murder affair in Damascus (1840) suddenly
demonstrated that the sense of national solidarity was by no means extinguished even
among the West European Jews. The terrible injustice that was being committed
against their brothers in the Orient affected
the young Lassalle in Germany as much as
the wealthy financier Moses Montefiore in
England or the future French statesman,
Crémieux in France. The Damascus affair
was an episode in the struggle of the European Great Powers for influence in the Near
East. The Eastern Question came on the international agenda and with it the problem
of the future of Palestine. There were voices
even in Western Europe urging that Palestine should revert to the Jews. This same
sense of solidarity led twenty years later to
the establishment of the Alliance Israélite
Universelle in Paris as a society for the
defense of Jewish rights throughout the
"universe."

2. THE RISE OF EUROPEAN NATIONALISM
(1848-1881)

The revolutionary wave that swept across
Europe from Paris at the beginning of 1848
to Berlin and Vienna, Prague and Budapest,
Venice and Rome, gave a powerful impetus
to the process of European democratization,
and revealed how active and deep-seated
the spirit of the great French Revolution
had been ever since 1789, even during the
reaction under Metternich. The general
social and economic causes which had
actually brought it into existence still operated. Gradually all the European nations reconstructed themselves from within, on the pattern of the French "nation"
and wished to become free societies of co-
equal members. Those that were politically
split up strove to secure both liberty and
unity, like the Germans and the Italians.
If they were under alien rule (like the
Czechs, the Hungarians, the Poles or the
Slavs in South Eastern Europe) their aim
was political independence. To all of them
the natural basis of their struggle was their
bond of association by reason of their com-

mon place of domicile, their old territory. This explains why the effect of this powerful new contemporary force upon the only inter-territorial people in Europe, the Jews, could at first be only indirect. The democratization of the surrounding political and social life, with its accompanying manifestation, Jewish emancipation, was beneficial at first primarily to individual Jews, while to the Jewish collective body it fatally implied national assimilation. Since the great French Revolution there were, indeed, plenty of nationalists among the Jews, too, including some who had come to exercise considerable influence on their non-Jewish environment. But even those among them who at the same time fought for Jewish rights did so not as Jewish nationalists, but—like Gabriel Riesser—in the name of German, French, Italian or some other non-Jewish national idea, or else it was for cosmopolitanism.

Nor was the Jewish religion—as it had been reformed in the spirit of a universalist "mission"—capable of further maintaining the existence of the people of Israel on its own distinctive national foundations. The reformed Jewish temples not only dropped many old prayers, substituting for them new invocations—generally replacing the Jewish by Christian customs—but they also gradually abandoned the holy tongue in favor of the languages of the surrounding world. Thus the concepts of nation and Jewishness continued to be one and indivisible essentially among the broad masses of the people in Eastern Europe who still walked in the ways of their fathers and never even at the worst moments of material distress lost faith in the veracity of the ancient prophecies.

A. *Political Development After* 1848: The reaction which swept over all of Europe immediately following the 1848 upheavals spared the Jews least of all, perhaps because they were so strongly represented in all the revolutionary movements, especially among the leaders (Riesser, the Vice President of the German "National Assembly" and Johann Jacoby in Prussia, Adolf Fischhof, Moritz Hartmann and Hermann Jellinek in Austria, Manin and Maurogonato in Italy, etc.). Nevertheless, wherever Jewish emancipation had been introduced in the year of the revolution, it was retained as a general rule, at least in principle (above all in Prussia and Austria, as well as in parts of Italy.) In France even Napoleon III's dictatorship could not challenge it and in England it was on the way to be carried in Parliament as one of the reforms demanded by progressive public opinion. In these two countries, the Jewish bourgeoisie was actively collaborating in the expansion of both industrial-commercial and financial capital. So that what Metternich had failed to do his later disciples were far from accomplishing.

The conception of a united and democratically organized nation gained in strength parallel with the development of capitalist economy, which was out to expand the export market everywhere and was therefore materially interested in raising the standard of living of the masses of the people—which meant stimulating the desire of the common people for new products and letting them share completely in the achievements of the modern age. Things went so far that the Governments themselves (Bismarck in Germany, Cavour in Italy) soon harnessed democratic nationalism to the State chariot. The expansion of European capitalist interests throughout the world, which simultaneously brought out the differences between the competing national economies, also intensified the danger of international conflicts and made it necessary to democratize and broaden further the basis of the State's authority.

This was all in favor of Jewish emancipation, even during the general reaction. Public opinion in England, France, Prussia and of course in the United States of America, which received a great stream of Jewish and non-Jewish immigrants from the German countries in the years of reaction that followed 1848, was scarcely interested as yet in the origin of the individual, his faith or his private convictions, so long as he did useful work within the national economy. And as no one had any doubt that the Jewish

capitalists and their entire Jewish environment, above all, the Jewish intellectuals,
were as closely identified with this order of
things as were the rest of the citizens, the
triumph of the idea of the national state
led to a new consolidation of Jewish emancipation. This was true of Bismarck's German Reich after the Franco-Prussian war
of 1870-1871, and it was equally true of
Southern Europe after Garibaldi's victories
over the Pope of Rome, the chief opponent
of a democratic united Italy. The approximately five thousand Jews who were released from the Rome ghetto at the end of
1870, were convinced that this time it was
final, that after three thousand years of fighting, Esau-Edom and Jacob-Israel were once
again brothers, as the great French Revolution had proclaimed.

B. *The Reform Period in Russia:* Even
in backward Russia things proceeded
in the same direction. After the Crimean
war (1854-1856) the czarist empire increasingly took to industrialization, which
it regarded as a matter of military security.
The emancipation of the peasants (1861)
created the necessary labor reserve and the
gradual emancipation of the Jewish population opened up new sources of enterprise
and capitalistic initiative. This was the real
purpose of the privileges (chiefly, in respect
of domicile outside the Pale for limited
groups of merchants, artisans and professionals) granted to the Russian Jews in the
reign of Alexander II (1855-1881). The important achievements of the Jews of Western Europe in the capitalist development of
their various countries proved that a progressive policy in regard to the Jews was of
value. While Nicholas I was still under the
influence of the reactionary Christianized
nationalism that dominated Western Europe during the restoration period subsequent to 1815, and therefore at first tried to
force Russification upon all his non-Russian
subjects, including the Jews, his son's policy
was directed—as in the more progressive
phases of West European history—towards
facilitating cultural assimilation through
emancipation in graduated doses, as for in-

stance, in Germany. Part of the older orthodox section of Russian Jewry therefore regarded Alexander's policy with profound
suspicion.

Nevertheless, like causes of necessity
brought more or less like results. In the
Russia that was approaching Western Europe economically, socially and politically,

JEWISH STREET (GLESER-GAS) IN
VILNA, POLAND

the demand for emancipation also made itself felt among the Jewish middle class. For
the moment the Government took fright at
its own generosity. The development of the
productive forces liberated in Russia proceeded with unexpected acceleration, and
with the development of capitalism there
also developed its inmost contradictions.
The Government tried to turn back the
clock and so roused an opposition movement among the progressive section of the
middle class, especially among the intellectuals. There were now also the beginnings
of a revolutionary socialist movement, both
in the towns and the villages. At this time
the number of Jews in Russia amounted to
millions. Here they were a people like all

the others and the bridges that Government policy, especially its educational policy, unceasingly constructed between them and their environment gradually had the effect of bringing them nearer to the progressive trends in Russian society. At the same time that we have the new Jewish financial magnates (tax-farmers, army contractors, bankers, railway -constructors and great merchants), there are also more or less Russified Jews, mostly intellectuals, fighting in the ranks of the Russian revolutionary organizations, "Land and Liberty," etc. Thus the Government's nationalist Russification policy in the same way as in Western Europe, produced, besides the desired assimilation of the upper classes, a most undesirable result: a revolutionary process which because of the poverty and destitution of the Jewish masses in the country, proved a much more serious danger to the czarist Government than anywhere at any time in the West. Nevertheless, at the Berlin Congress (1878) it still had to subscribe to Disraeli-Beaconsfield's and Bismarck's emancipation policy in respect of the Jewish populations in the Balkan countries.

C. *Romania:* The most important of these countries for our purpose is Romania, where the Jewish colony had been from a remote period a kind of settlement of Jews from the Ukraine and Galicia. The constant immigration from outside which was still going on in the third quarter of the 19th century had increased the number of Romanian Jews from about 100,000 in 1850 to more than 200,000 in 1880. It was an agrarian country, much more backward in trade and industry than even Russia, so that there were good prospects there at first for the Jewish population to become an integral part of Romanian economic life. As in Poland previously, the Jews became the most important element in the towns. But with the swift development characteristic of the 19th century it did not take long before there was a clash between the interests of the Jews and of the new rising non-Jewish urban class. While round about 1848 there was a section of the ruling Romanian caste

that had contemplated Jewish emancipation on West European lines, about twenty years later they were planning to declare the Jews in Romania "aliens," who would thus be deprived of all rights, because there was no foreign power that would regard them as its subjects and defend their interests. Russian influence played a great part in this. By the end of the '60's there were actually pogroms in Romania. The Berlin Congress had indeed made the Romanian Government "naturalize" its Jews, so that they would be citizens with equal rights, but the power of economic envy proved stronger than all the international guarantees. And the result was that, like Galicia and Russia, this land of Jewish immigration became a land of emigration.

D. *Emigration to America:* The extreme poverty and the degradation of the Jewish masses in Eastern Europe, and most of all in Russia, gave the Jews a powerful incentive to emigrate across the Atlantic, and from the '60's the United States began to receive, besides the two main elements of its existing Jewish population, Sephardim and German Jews, also a third element that was destined to play a great part in the future of American Jewry, the Ashkenazim of Eastern Europe. The Paris Alliance Israélite assisted them on their long road and as soon as they arrived in the new world they gradually rose on the crest of the wave of the incredibly rapid American industrialization and urbanization process, with the result that by 1880 there were already about a quarter of a million Jews in the North American Republic mostly distributed in the big cities (sixty thousand in New York alone). While the older Ashkenazic community reflected the spiritual tendencies among the West European Jews who were influenced by the German-Jewish reformation, the new immigrants from Eastern Europe laid the foundations of a many-sided Jewish culture on the same lines as in their old home.

3. THE DYNAMIC PERIOD (1881-1914)

The 30 years preceding World War I were a period of exceptional activity, a dynamic period without an equal in human history. Year by year there was an increase of creative forces both in production and in organizing the exchange of products. The population of the world was never before so large. Technical progress linked together East and West, North and South. All the markets of the five continents moved nearer to each other and one could perceive very soon the foundations of a united world economy. Civilization became international and the interchange of cultural values scarcely lagged behind the interchange of goods.

The Jewish people in common with all the other peoples of the world took an intensive part in this general human activity. Its energy found simultaneous outlets in all the various directions in which it had manifested itself throughout all the three thousand years of its history. Impelled by the determination to liberate itself from poverty and want the Jewish people spread into new lands, colonized virgin territories in South America, demonstrated its will to rebuild the ancient ruins in Palestine, battled for its rights and liberty in the lands of its domicile, flung itself into the great national and revolutionary movements, and at the same time strengthened the foundations of its own independent cultural existence. Jewish life became multifarious and multi-colored, of such diversity that one could hardly take it all in at a glance. The Jewish people divided up into classes, parties and cultural tendencies, creating a deep internal crisis that demanded a new synthesis, theoretical as well as practical. Though both the positive and negative factors at the bottom of this dynamic process had their historic roots partly in Western Europe, their driving force came for the most part from the Jewish masses in the Russian Empire.

A. *The Crisis of Emancipation and Assimilation:* The most important negative factor was the crisis of emancipation and its offspring, assimilation. With the increase in the number of assimilated and emancipated Jews entering economic and cultural fields hitherto barred to them, there was an increase in the effectiveness of the argument, especially among the non-Jewish middle class—who felt the Jewish competition most —that a Jew is always a Jew, no matter what language he speaks, what education he has had, or even what religion he professes.

Nationalism, like everything else, became secularized, and anti-Semitism grew. By the end of the '70's there were already in Germany the first signs of an anti-Jewish movement among the representatives of the "liberal" professions and the middle class, who were demanding that the Jews should be deprived of their newly-won citizenship rights, not because they were not Christians, but because they were of the "Semitic race," that is to say, because of their natural psycho-physical character. The new essentially a-religious State nationalism of the hyper-capitalist period could not explain the existence of the Jewish people otherwise than by some natural cause, and so it had to adopt allegedly biological racial symptoms in order to segregate the Jews.

The increasing significance of the working-class and the bourgeoisie in European life stood in the way of the petty-bourgeois ideologies, inclusive of anti-Semitic propaganda. But it nevertheless made a considerable impression on both the German people and its neighbors (Hungarians, Poles, Czechs), and here and there it sometimes led to actual restriction of Jewish citizenship rights (chiefly in the academic field and in Government service), to economic boycotts and even anti-Jewish disturbances resulting in bloodshed, and ritual murder allegations, as in Tisza-Eszlar or Konitz. It had a remarkable repercussion at the end of the 19th century in France, where the Dreyfus Affair started a fierce political struggle, in which the reactionary front, consisting of Roman Catholics, Royalists, militarists and the new-fangled anti-Semites of the school of Drumont, was opposed by a united front of all the progressive republican and socialist elements led by Émile Zola, Jean Jaurès and Georges Clemenceau, who were to be instrumental, together with the unjustly convicted Jewish officer, in saving the French Republic.

Courtesy Netherlands Information Bureau

SYNAGOGUE IN AMSTERDAM, NETHERLANDS

The new anti-Jewish wave sweeping on from Western Europe brought terrible havoc to Romanian Jewry. But its greatest significance in the further course of Jewish history was in Russia, where Jewish strength was combined with Jewish numbers.

B. *The Persecutions in Russia:* The savage wave of pogroms in 1881 and the whole pogrom policy under Czar Alexander III (1881-1894) and his son Nicholas II (1894-1917), whose chief political motive was to divert the discontent of the people from its real enemies, had their origin in a number of causes. Though the broad masses of the Jewish population throughout the Pale suffered terrible privation, the Jewish population as a whole, compared with the peasants and even with the non-Jewish unskilled workers in the towns, was a higher social and cultural class. After the Crimean War Russia became increasingly Europeanized also in the matter of economic development,

and in the Jewish Pale of Settlement (the northwestern region, White Russia, Poland and above all the Ukraine), the Jews benefited more than any others because they had so long been mainly an urban element.

Though the number of Jewish capitalists (wealthy manufacturers and merchants, trading in timber, grain and manufactured goods) was extremely small in comparison with the Jewish population, they were very much in evidence in the Jewish towns. Wherever he went, in the street, in the market place, and often even in the village itself selling his produce, the peasant met the "rich" Jew, who was almost the only man with money with whom he came in contact. Added to this, since the '70's, there was the increasing competition between Jews and non-Jews in the academic and liberal professions. The old anti-Jewish traditions still lingered on in Poland and the Ukraine and the Russian Government skillfully exploited all this to stir up the smouldering embers of anti-Jewish hostility.

C. *The Jewish Reaction Against Russian Official Anti-Semitism:* It would nevertheless have been impossible for the officialdom in Petersburg and for those educated Russian circles that stood behind the Government to enter into an open alliance with the pogromists unless they had the support of West European anti-Semitism. But while the anti-Semitic propaganda in Western Europe had a demoralizing effect on most of the Jews, putting them into a state of terror and impelling them to deny their Jewish separateness more stubbornly than ever, the most terrible outrages committed against the Jews in Russia as a rule only stiffened their resolve to fight on for the future of the Jewish people and its historic heritage. Even the great migration movement among the Russian Jews and their spiritual kin, the Galician and Romanian Jews, which began immediately after the 1881 pogroms and continued with intervals right up to the time of World War I, was not merely the result of fear. Most of the refugees regarded themselves as political emigrants and as the pioneers of a new and a more dignified mode of life from the individual as well as from the national point of view. Hundreds of thousands of Jews went to America because they hoped to find there both bread and liberty, in other words, the opportunity to live as free citizens and as loyal sons of their people. That is how the new vast settlement of East European Jews—which on the eve of World War I was the largest in the world next to the Russian—grew up, with its own literature and press in Yiddish, with "Landsmanshaften" on the same lines as in the older and oldest periods—as in Turkey, for example, after the expulsion from Spain, or in Babylonia after the destruction of Jerusalem, and with powerful organizations for mutual aid and for assisting their kin in the old home.

The emigration to the far west was accompanied at the same time by a growing movement to the east, to Palestine. The Russian Jews tried to inaugurate a new epoch in Jewish history, like the Sephardim after the expulsion from Spain and afterwards the Polish Ashkenazim during the Chmielnicki massacres.

Though political Zionism arose in the west, its founder, Theodor Herzl, would have been a politician without party had not the Hovevei Zion in Russia preceded him both in theory and in practical colonization work. Moses Hess (1812-1875) had already based his Zionist hopes mainly on the traditional-religious nationalism of the Russian Jews. It was to them, too, that Baron de Hirsch looked to realize his colonization plans in South America, and it was only among them that Territorialism became a popular movement. On the whole, we may say that wherever the Russian Jews appeared the pulse of the Jewish people began to beat once more. And in the course of the thirty-three years of their great migration movement from Eastern Europe to America they settled in a good many European centers as well, in Germany and Austro-Hungary, in France and in England, besides smaller places of Jewish settlement like Holland, Belgium, Italy, Switzerland, etc.

All this enormous emigration could not, however, destroy the basic structure of Russian Jewry, which at the beginning of the 20th century numbered about six million Jews, Russian, Polish, Lithuanian, Ukrainian and Caucasian (about half the total Jewish population of the world at the time).

The only way for these masses, who were full of creative energy, to escape from their intolerable position under the despotic czarist regime which denied them all rights, was to join in the fight for political and economic liberty with all other fighters for liberty in the Russian empire. Jews were also taking a prominent part in the socialist movement in Western Europe. But it was only in Russia that Jewish socialism came into existence. Side by side with the Jewish Social-Democratic organization, "Bund," which led the economic and political struggle of the newly-evolved Jewish working-class and included in its program the demand for cultural autonomy for the Jewish population, there grew up Zionist and Territorialist socialist parties. There were also a large number of Jews prominent among the leaders of the Russian revolutionary and opposition parties, the Social Democrats (Mensheviks and Bolsheviks), the Socialist Revolutionaries, and from 1905 the Moderate Democrats (Cadets). The only effect of the Government's attempt to intimidate the Jews through new massacres (the second wave of pogroms in 1903-1906) was to cause armed Jewish self-defense groups to spring up in every corner of the Pale, as if out of the ground, mostly organized by the Jewish socialist parties. And the more the Government tried to intimidate them, the more it learned to fear the fighting spirit of the Jewish masses. Then the Government pretended that it was willing to compromise. But now even the most moderate of the Jewish leaders demanded full equality of rights and, unlike the Jews in Western Europe, not only for Jews as individuals, but also national rights, national self-administration for the Jewish collective body. Because of the collapse of the Russian revolutionary movement in 1905-1906 the struggle brought no concrete results till 1917. The official anti-Semitic policy, on the other hand, again became aggressive and on the eve of World War I it staged a big ritual murder trial on the old model (the Beilis affair in Kiev).

Russian Jewry's tremendous power of resistance and its fighting spirit, reminiscent of the most heroic periods of Jewish history, were part and parcel of its spiritual independence. Though large numbers of Russian Jews took part in non-Jewish intellectual life, their approach to their non-Jewish environment did not as a rule lead to assimilation as it did in the West, but rather to an enrichment of their own Jewish national culture by bringing new forms of expression into it from outside. Instead of a reformed synagogue the Russian Jews developed a distinctive and rich secular literature in Yiddish and Hebrew, as well as to some extent in Russian. They also established a Yiddish theater, and the beginning of a consciously cultivated Jewish music and school of painting. In the field of science, too, the West European methods of research (especially in Jewish learning) were often adopted in order to intensify the Jewish national spirit (as in the works of Simon Dubnow, who by building further on the foundations laid down by Graetz provided the historical basis for the demand for national autonomy, or autonomism). Through these cultural achievements Russian Jewry extended its spiritual influence throughout the Jewish world, in the first place among its own children and grandchildren, and so demonstrated what the all-Jewish hegemony of a single Jewish center had meant in older times.

D. *The General Situation on the Eve of the First World War:* Scattered over almost all the earth—it was just then that the European Jews came to know of the existence of Jewish communities even in Abyssinia and deep in China—the Jewish people thus remained a real historic unit. It lacked a common soil, but there was a visible effort being made in all its various parts to create such a territorial basis of national existence. It lacked a common language, yet Jews in all the four corners of the globe, in Canada as in South Africa, in San Francisco as in Vilna, spoke, wrote and read Yiddish, and of those who prayed almost all did so in Hebrew. Though the friends of assimilation denied that the Jews are a people, the Jews crossed the threshold of World War I with their own ancient name which they had borne for three thousand years—Israel.

IV. THE FIRST WORLD WAR AND ITS RESULTS (1914-1939)

1. SEVEN YEARS OF WAR AND REVOLUTION (1914-1921)

The nearer the continents and oceans moved towards each other economically and culturally the more their different political clashes of interest conspired to produce that gigantic struggle of forces, World War I. As a catastrophic transition in the development of humanity as a whole, the war of

1914-1918 also had to be, even if for no other reason, the starting point of a new chapter in the history of the Jewish people. Before World War I came to an end the whole world realized that the Jewish people was not merely a passive subject but also an active factor in the course of world history. Thus the Jewish question became a problem of world politics, and new perspectives opened up with regard to the fundamental place of the Jewish people among the peoples of the earth.

A. *The First World War:* The Jewish problem took an entirely new direction immediately after the outbreak of the war. One of the most important battlegrounds, the East-European, where the German and Austrian armies fought the Russians, was a region of dense Jewish settlement (the Russian Pale, from the Ukraine in the south to Lithuania in the North, as well as Galicia, Bukovina, Hungary, etc.). In view of the influence of Russian Jewry throughout the Jewish world, and especially in the United States, the Central European Powers spread propaganda to the effect that their war aims included the liberation of the Russian Jews. This in turn provided Nicholas II's Government with a fresh pretext for conducting its anti-Jewish policy. As in the Russo-Japanese War of 1904-1905 the Jewish population was accused of treasonable relations with the enemies of Russia. At the beginning of 1915 cruel mass evacuations were carried out in Poland and Lithuania, as well as in the occupied Austrian territories. The result was something that the czar's ministers had least expected.

First of all, the Jews who were evacuated from the frontier zones had to be admitted to places outside the Pale, in the Russian interior. And in this way the Russian Government demolished with its own hands the walls of the Pale, the most gigantic ghetto in all Jewish history. Secondly, the anti-Jewish persecutions forced Russia's democratic allies in Western Europe, England and France, to intervene on behalf of the victims. One of the reasons that influenced their action was quite clearly their desire to gain the sympathy of the Jews of the United States, who formed a very important section of American public opinion and were still closely attached to their old homes in Eastern Europe. The rivalry between the two camps, each seeking to secure Jewish sympathies for its own side, resulted in the question of the future status of the Jews being almost imperceptibly internationalized.

Turkey's entry into the war on the side of the Central European powers made it possible for Western Europe, in the first place Great Britain, to put the Eastern question on its order of the day and so also the question of the future of Palestine. Zionism, which had long been waiting for such a conjuncture of political circumstances, hastened to submit its demand for the return of the Jewish homeland to the prospective victors who would have to decide the future destiny of the world. Once more the driving force was supplied by Russian Jews (Nahum Sokolow, Chaim Weizmann, Vladimir Jabotinsky, etc.).

A Jewish Legion was organized on the model of the Polish Legions who were fighting on the Austrian side for Polish liberation, so as to give a military backing to the Zionist demands. A further factor was the stalemate that existed for a long time between the two groups of the belligerents. And then after the Russian Revolution of 1917, which paralyzed the Russian army, Western Europe found itself suddenly faced with a catastrophe. At this critical juncture the British Government decided to mobilize the active sympathies of the Jewish masses throughout the world on behalf of the British empire, and most of all those in Russia and America, and to do this it pledged that after the war it would facilitate the establishment of a national home for the Jewish people in Palestine (Balfour Declaration of November 2, 1917).

So the development of nationalism in Europe which had gradually encompassed even the smallest nations, eventually also brought the people without a land into the circle of internationally recognized nations.

B. *The Revolutionary Years:* The great and historic Russian Revolution of 1917 gave the Jews at once complete citizenship and equality of national rights (Decree issued, April 4, 1917). The Romanoff dynasty came to an end. That same year, in 1918, the collapse of the Central Powers wrote the last chapter of the history of both the Hapsburg dynasty and the Prussian-German Hohenzollerns as well as of the Turkish Sultanate. The West-European democracies in alliance with Italy and the United States became the sole arbiters of the world. On western Russian territory, they helped to create a resurrected Poland and recognized the independence of the Baltic states, Lithuania, Latvia, Estonia and Finland. A similar process was set in motion in the Hapsburg and Ottoman empires. Both these lines of development, the external result of World War I and the internal upheavals in the defeated countries, radically altered the entire position of the Jewish people.

If a balance were drawn up of this position about 1921 (the year of stabilization of the Communist regime in revolutionary Russia, the democratic Republic in Germany, and the democratic systems generally in most of the new European States), it would show that the Jews, besides some very important gains, had suffered not a few heavy losses. From whatever point of view it is regarded, every manifest plus was offset by an equally definite minus. The triumph of the national principle, the so-called principle of "self-determination" of each nation, was incorporated in the peace treaties in the form of international guarantees covering also the rights of the Jewish minorities in Poland, Czechoslovakia, Romania, Lithuania. At first sight, this afforded the Jewish communities in a number of East European countries the opportunities of arranging their lives on an autonomous basis. But against this there was the fact that the great Russian Jewry was broken up, about half remaining behind the new Russian frontiers, while the other half was split up into smaller fractions. The union with Galicia and East Prussia had indeed created a

new big Jewry in Poland, but as a result of this there was introduced a diversity of cultural traditions and tendencies that needed merging into one stream.

In Republican Germany as in Russia the Jews became absolutely equal citizens, but again their comparatively large participation in the socialist revolutionary movements aroused against them such hostility in the Russian and the German counter-revolutionary camps as had rarely been known in Jewish history. During the Russian civil war which broke out immediately after the Bolshevik Revolution at the end of 1917, this led to massacres in South Russia more horrible than almost anything in the past, and in Germany there were the first signs of the coming anti-Semitic storm that was presently to destroy all the achievements of the great French Revolution. At the same time the British Government began to reconsider whether it might not be a dangerous thing to admit uncontrolled immigration to Palestine from Eastern Europe. Even the fact that the world had at last in principle recognized the national character of the Jewish people had as a corollary this grave disadvantage, that it became inclined to saddle the whole Jewish people once again with the entire responsibility for the actions of each individual Jew.

Thus the seven years of catastrophe that were to have brought a better world ended, for the Jewish people, with a question mark.

2. TEMPORARY STABILIZATION (1922-1932)

As soon as the political sky had cleared a little the Jewish people returned to its old optimistic confidence. The war had accelerated technical progress still more and the Jewish communities benefited from this fact. In the Soviet Union Russian Jewry was cut off from its contacts with the world, but as compensation, relations between all the other centers had become much closer. Internally, too, in the various places the bonds between the core and the assimilated periphery had also been tightened and consolidated. This was due to the international recognition of the national character of the

literature and the schools to the streets and the homes. The sacred tongue became a living language, the everyday speech of the new generation. The Hebrew University was established in Jerusalem in 1925. At about the same time an institute for scientific research in Yiddish, the Yiddish Scientific Institute (Yivo), was founded in Vilna. Similar institutions were established in Minsk and Kiev in Russia.

At the same time that Hebrew became an everyday tongue, Yiddish was increasingly adapted to the severe requirements of scientific thought. A rich literature continued to flourish in both languages. In the early 1930's the Simon Dubnow Fund, established in honor of the noted historian, enabled a group of writers and scholars to prepare and publish the *Algemeine Entsiklopedie,* a general encyclopedia in the Yiddish language.

3. THE GREAT CRISIS SINCE 1933

International unrest and disruption, a result of World War I, manifested itself most strongly in the economic world crisis at the end of the '20's. The most severe symptom was widespread unemployment. Germany was affected much sooner than the victorious countries. The enemies of the Weimar Republic, particularly the old Prussian militarist caste and the capitalist circles, were awaiting the opportunity to throw off the chains of the Versailles Treaty. They ascribed all the responsibility for the suffering and distress among the masses, more especially among the ruined middle class, to the republican parties and the so-called "international forces," the Roman Catholic Church, the Marxists, and above all, the Jews. The anti-Semitic element in their propaganda proved extremely successful.

For the most part, the German Jews regarded themselves as thoroughly German, but to the reactionary elements they remained Jews even though they were baptized. To the thoroughly secularized and materialistic German nationalism, and of course to its more shady side, anti-Semitism,

a man's feelings were not as important as his race, and when in 1933 this counter-revolutionary materialistic conception became the official attitude of the nationalist dictatorship, the Jews were its first victims.

One of the main incentives of the anti-Semitic propaganda was economic competition. Many people in the German middle class, and particularly professional men, hoped to step into the shoes of the displaced Jews. Not a few "Aryan" merchants or physicians usurped the high positions of the Jews who had been ousted. After a long series of partial discriminations, the German Jews were formally deprived of their civil rights in September, 1935. Whereas a century before they had been forcibly assimilated, German nationalism now decreed "de-assimilation," and mixed marriages became a crime under the Nuremberg laws. Not only baptized Jews, but persons who had only one Jewish parent or one Jewish grandparent were now considered Jews. After the annexation of Austria in March 1938, and the partition of Czechoslovakia in October 1938 and its annexation in March 1939, the civil degradation and legalized extermination of the Jews was extended automatically to these parts of "Greater Germany."

General disaster overwhelmed the entire Jewish population of Greater Germany when Hershel Grynszpan, a seventeen-year-old Jewish boy, assassinated a German consular official in Paris. On orders of the Nazi party thousands of Jewish businesses were completely destroyed in the course of a few days, November 9 to 11, 1938. Synagogues were burned down all over the country; masses of Jews were put into concentration camps. In addition, the Government imposed a levy of one thousand million marks upon the Jewish population, and Jews were even deprived of the right to work as artisans. World-wide protests, especially in the Anglo-Saxon countries and by the Christian churches, were ignored, and at the end of 1938, German Jewry stood on the brink of annihilation. Representatives of a committee constituted in July 1938 at a conference of over thirty governments held at Evian, France, sought to negotiate with the German Government in order to find out what the price would be for ransoming the German Jews condemned to extermination. No tangible results were achieved.

Germany's increasing military power since 1933 meant a corresponding increase of German influence in the neighboring countries to which the anti-Jewish epidemic had spread. In 1934 the Catholic dictatorship in Austria followed the German example of wiping out the opposition, and there was additional anti-Jewish legislation in Poland; in 1937 Romania was on the verge of proclaiming all Romanian Jews "aliens" without rights. In 1939 nearly a third of the Romanian Jews were actually deprived of their citizenship rights which had been internationally guaranteed them. In Hungary a quota was enforced against Jews, including even baptized Jews, in all the principal professions and industries. A further restrictive law was adopted in May 1939. But the climax was reached in Fascist Italy, which in 1938 adopted the German racial legislation and directed it against its Jewish community numbering no more than 50,000. Nazi-dominated Czechoslovakia, too, followed in Germany's footsteps. For the first time in world history a great state made anti-Semitism a main pillar of its international policy, and pro-German and anti-Jewish propaganda came to be synonymous. Anti-Semitism gradually permeated to all the corners of the world, as far away as South Africa and South America, wherever German influence extended. Thus the post-war internationalization of the Jewish question produced its counterpart, the internationalization of anti-Jewish policy, the conversion of anti-Semitism into an international organized force.

The late 1930's witnessed the rise of serious difficulties in the reconstruction of the Jewish settlement in Palestine. In the space of the first few years after Hitler's rise to power, Palestine became the most sought-after haven for the Jews able to save themselves from starvation and persecution in Eastern and Central Europe. In the four year period from 1932 to 1936 the Jewish population of Palestine almost doubled. Since 1936, the situation of the Jews in Palestine changed for the worse. The wave of Arab outbreaks, which lasted for more than three years, had a profound effect on the economic life of the country and on the continued development of the Jewish settlements. Although Jewish initiative and labor had markedly raised the well-being of the country—with the Arab population sharing in the benefits—the leaders of the Arab extremists nevertheless succeeded in winning over to their anti-Jewish campaign substantial parts of the Arab population. The movement, which was partly supported by fascist and Nazi funds, had its repercussions in the Arabic and Islamic world outside Palestine. This had the effect of strengthening the anti-Zionist elements in British policy, and in May, 1939 the British government issued the White Paper which practically negated the pledge of the Balfour Declaration, strictly limited Jewish immigration into Palestine—with its complete cessation after five years—and drastically limited the rights of Jews to purchase land in the country.

In spite of the restriction of immigration into most countries, nevertheless, in the twenty year period between the two World Wars more than 1,000,000 Jews left Europe. The largest number went to the United States and Palestine. A smaller number found haven in the Latin American countries. As a result, there was a significant increase in the size of the Jewish community in Argentina and communities of smaller size arose in Brazil, Uruguay, Mexico, Cuba, Chile, etc.

The twenty year period between the two World Wars began with great promise for the Jewish people in Europe but ended on the threshold of grave disaster. Although from time to time the Jews received pledges of support from the democratic countries they had only rarely an opportunity to witness any positive action which might serve to relieve their situation. Abandoned and forgotten by practically the entire world, the Jews, in the midst of the greatest national catastrophe in their history, did not abandon their faith that "the remnant of Israel" would not be destroyed.

Even if the democratic world failed to see that the fate of the Jewish people must react on the fate of the entire world, the Jews themselves understood that their historic destiny is bound up with the destiny of all nations, and that if there is a future for the world there is also a future for the Jewish people.

CHRONOLOGICAL TABLE
OF JEWISH HISTORY

POLITICAL CHRONOLOGY	CULTURAL CHRONOLOGY
2000-1500 B.C.E. The Middle Bronze Age: Invasion of Amorites in Mesopotamia, Syria and Palestine Beginning of wanderings of the Hebrew tribes Rise and fall of the Mari kingdom 1720-1550—Egypt under the rule of the Hyksos 1700—Reign of Hammurabi	2000-1500 B.C.E. The Middle Bronze Age: The quest for the alphabet
1500-1200—Late Bronze Age: Earliest settlements of Hebrews in Canaan Amarna Age Palestine under Egyptian rule Sojourn of the Israelites in Egypt	1500-1200—Late Bronze Age: The cuneiform alphabet or the Ras Shamrah script The Hebrew-Phoenician alphabet
13th century—Exodus from Egypt and conquest of Canaan	13th century—The Covenant at Sinai and the beginnings of Yahwism
12th-11th centuries—Expansion of Israelite settlement in the hill country The Philistines occupy southern part of Palestine sea coast	12th-11th centuries—The Song of Deborah Beginnings of the biblical writings
1100—Decisive battle between Israelites and Canaanites in Valley of Jezreel	
11th century—Wars with Philistines	
1030—Establishment of unified monarchy under Saul	
1010-970—Reign of David	
970-930—Reign of Solomon	10th century—Construction of Solomon's Temple in Jerusalem
930—Division of the monarchy, establishment of the separate states of Judah and Israel	
886-843—Omri dynasty Wars with Aram	9th century—The prophets Elijah and Elisha "Yahwist," author of the earliest sections of the Pentateuch
859-824—Shalmaneser III, beginning of Assyrian expansion southward	
853—Battle of Karkar	
843—Yehu revolution in Israel	
837—Revolution in Judah	
787-747—Reign of Jeroboam II	
745-727—Reign of Tiglath Pileser, renewal of Assyrian expansionist policy	8th century—Rise of literary prophecy: Amos, Hosea, Isaiah, Micah
721—Fall of Samaria	
701—Invasion of Judah by Sennacherib	
625—Babylonia becomes independent kingdom Disintegration of Assyrian empire	
621—Reform movement under Josiah, restoration of the Law, reunion of Northern Israel with Judah	
605—Battle of Carchemish, fall of Assyria Rise of the neo-Babylonian empire	End of 7th and beginning of 6th century—Jeremiah

POLITICAL CHRONOLOGY	CULTURAL CHRONOLOGY
597—First Babylonian deportation	6th century (first half)—Ezekiel
586—Destruction of Jerusalem, second deportation	6th century—Rise of the Synagogue
539—Cyrus, king of Persia, conquers Babylonia	6th century (second half)—The Second Isaiah
538—Cyrus permits Jews of Babylonia to return to Judah	
520—Administration of Zerubbabel Rebuilding of the Temple	520—Haggai and Zechariah
458-433—Ezra and Nehemiah in Jerusalem: Fortification of Jerusalem completed Introduction of religious reforms	5th century—Final redaction of the Pentateuch
334-330—Alexander the Great destroys the Persian empire and lays basis for Greek world domination	5th-4th centuries—Samaritan schism Construction of Samaritan temple on Mt. Gerizim
332—Alexander occupies Palestine	4th-3rd centuries—Book of Job, Proverbs, parts of Book of Psalms
320-198—Judah under the rule of the Ptolemies	
3rd-2nd centuries—Growth of large Jewish community in Egypt	3rd-2nd centuries—Song of Songs, Ecclesiastes, Ben Sira, Daniel Greek translation of the Pentateuch (Septuagint)
198-167—Judah under the rule of the Seleucids	2nd century—Beginning of Jewish-Greek literature
190—Battle of Magnesia Roman power extends to the Orient	2nd century—Rise of religio-political parties: Sadducees and Pharisees
167—Revolt of the Maccabees	
160—Judah the Maccabee falls in battle	
142—Judah regains its independence under the rule of Simon the Maccabee	
64-63—Syria becomes Roman province	
63—Pompey enters Jerusalem	
1st century—First Jewish communities in Italy	1st century B.C.E. to 1st century C.E.—The rise of the Essenes The Pharisaic schools of Shammai and Hillel
37-4—Reign of Herod the Great	
	1st century C.E.—Rise of Christianity Philo of Alexandria Josephus Flavius
26-36 C.E.—Administration of Pontius Pilate, procurator of Palestine	
38—Anti-Jewish riots in Alexandria	
66-73—Judaeo-Roman war Destruction of Jerusalem	70—Establishment of Bet Din and Academy at Yabneh
115-117—Insurrection against Rome	
132-135—Revolt of Bar Kochba	
	200—Final redaction of Mishnah
2nd-4th centuries—First Jewish communities in Spain, France, and Germany	219—Establishment of Talmudic academy in Sura, Babylonia, by Rab

POLITICAL CHRONOLOGY	CULTURAL CHRONOLOGY
306-337—Reign of Constantine the Great Christianity becomes dominant religion in the Roman empire	
350-351—Jewish insurrection in Galilee	350-400—Compilation and final redaction of the Palestinian Talmud
	352-427—Ashi, Talmudic authority in Babylonia, first compiler of Babylonian Talmud
395—Division of the Roman empire	
425—Abolition of the Patriarchate	
476—Fall of the Western Roman empire	500—Final redaction of Babylonian Talmud
	5th-7th centuries—Flowering of Midrash literature and liturgical poetry
6th century—Persecution of Jews and Samarians in Palestine	
527-565—Reign of Justinian, Byzantine emperor	
569(?)-632—Mohammed, rise of Islam	589—Beginning of period of Geonim
610-641—Reign of Heraclius, last Byzantine emperor to rule over Palestine	
Early 7th century—Persecutions of Jews in Spain	
624-628—Mohammed's war against Jews in Arabia	
628-638—Persecutions of Jews in Palestine	
629-639—Forcible conversion of Jews to Christianity in Frankish lands	
638—Jerusalem again opened to Jews	
649-711—Persecutions in Visigothic Spain	
717-741—Persecutions in Byzantium	8th century—Conversion of Khazars to Judaism Spread of Karaite sect
850—Moslem "yellow badge" edict	9th-12th centuries—Flowering of Jewish-Arabic culture
	892-942—Saadia Gaon, religious philosopher, head of Talmudic Academy in Sura, Babylonia
915-970—Hasdai ibn Shaprut, Nasi of the Jews in caliphate of Cordova	10th-12th centuries—Flowering of Talmudic learning in France and Germany
	960-1028—Rabbenu Gershom, "The Light of the Diaspora," Rabbinical authority in the Rhineland
	993-1055—Samuel ha-Nagid, poet and Talmudist, Spanish statesman
	11th century—Blossoming of Jewish culture in Spain
	1013-1103—Isaac Alfasi, Talmudic authority

POLITICAL CHRONOLOGY	CULTURAL CHRONOLOGY
	1020-1070—Solomon ibn Gabirol, poet and philosopher, Spain
	1040-1105—Rashi, the most renowned Bible and Talmud commentator, France
	1070-1138—Moses ibn Ezra, poet and philosopher, Spain
	1080-1140—Judah ha-Levi, poet and philosopher, Spain
	1092-1167—Abraham ibn Ezra, Bible commentator and philosopher
1096—First Crusade	
12th century—Jewish "royal serfdom" in the Holy Roman empire	12th-13th centuries—Peak of Jewish culture in Spain
	Rise and spread of Kabbala
	Schools of the Tosaphists in Western Europe
	1135-1204—Moses Maimonides (Rambam), philosopher and codifier
1146-1147—Second Crusade	1165-1173—Travels of Benjamin of Tudela
1189-1192—Third Crusade	
13th-15th centuries—Expulsion of Jews from Germany and migration to Eastern Europe	
1215—Fourth Lateran Council decrees wearing of yellow badge	1235-1310—Solomon ibn Adret, Rabbinical authority in Spain
	1240-1292—Abraham Abulafia, Kabbalist and mystic
1247—Papal Bull against ritual murder accusation	1250-1327—Asher ben Jehiel, Rabbinical authority and Talmud commentator
1251—Statute on Jews in Hungary	
1264—Privileges granted Jews in Poland	1269-1340—Jacob ben Asher, "Baal ha-Turim," author and codifier
1290—Expulsion of Jews from England	
1306—Expulsion of Jews from France	
1348—Black Death	
1391—Persecutions and massacres in Spain	
1394—Expulsion of Jews from France	
1413-1414—Disputation between Jews and Christians at Tortosa, Spain	1437-1508—Isaac Abravanel, philosopher, Bible commentator and statesman
	1469-1549—Elijah Levita, poet and grammarian
	1475—First Hebrew books printed in Italy

POLITICAL CHRONOLOGY	CULTURAL CHRONOLOGY
1480—Inquisition established	1481—First Hebrew books printed in Spain
1492—Expulsion of Jews from Spain	1488-1575—Joseph Caro, author of "Shulhan Aruk"
1492—Columbus discovers America	
1496—Decree on expulsion of Jews in Portugal	
1497—Expulsion of Marranos from Venice	
16th-18th centuries—Period of Jewish autonomy in Poland (Council of Four Lands)	1510-1573—Solomon Luria, Talmud commentator, Poland
	1517—Beginning of the Reformation
	1520-1523—First complete edition of the Talmud printed in Venice
	1520-1572—Moses Isserles, author and codifier, Poland
	1524—David Reubeni, Messianic adventurer, received by the Pope in Rome
1530—Yosel Rosheim at Augsburg Reichstag	
1532—Solomon Molko burned at the stake	
	1534—First Yiddish books printed in Cracow, Poland
	1534-1572—Isaac Luria ("Ari"), founder of modern Kabbala
1544-1546—"Letters of Protection" for German Jews	
1553—Burning of the Talmud in Italy	
	1567—Shulhan Aruk published
	1585-1640—Uriel da Costa, philosopher and "heretic"
17th-18th centuries—Ritual murder accusations and trials in Poland	1604-1657—Manasseh ben Israel, author, Rabbi in Amsterdam
1614—Massacre at Frankfort on the Main	
1618-1648—The Thirty Years' War	
1626-1676—Sabbatai Zebi, pseudo-messiah	1632-1677—Baruch Spinoza, philosopher
1648-1649—Chmielnicki massacres in Poland	
1649-1655—Return of Jews to England	
1654—Jews arrive in New Amsterdam (New York)	
1658—First Jews settle in Newport, R.I.	
1666—Peak of Sabbatai Zebi movement	
	18th-19th centuries—Haskalah movement in Central and Eastern Europe
	1700-1760—Israel Baal Shem Tob, founder of Hasidism
	1707-1747—Moses Hayim Luzzatto, author, Kabbalist, philosopher
	1720-1797—Elijah of Vilna, "the Vilna Gaon," most renowned of Rabbinical authorities in Eastern Europe
1726-1791—Jacob Frank, pseudo-messiah	

POLITICAL CHRONOLOGY	CULTURAL CHRONOLOGY
	1729-1786—Moses Mendelssohn, philosopher, founder of Haskalah movement
1732—Portuguese Jews' residence legalized in France by royal patent	1747-1812—Shneur Zalman of Liady, founder of Habad Hasidism
	1754-1800—Solomon Maimon, philosopher
1772-1795—Partitions of Poland	
1776—U.S.A. Declaration of Independence	
1784-1885—Moses Montefiore, philanthropist and champion of Jewish rights	1785-1840—Nachman Krochmal, philosopher
	1788-1860—Isaak Ber Levinsohn, author, leader of Haskalah movement in Eastern Europe
1789—French Revolution	
1791—Jews in France receive full citizen rights	1794-1886—Leopold Zunz, founder of the "Wissenschaft des Judentums"
	1800-1865—Samuel David Luzzatto, author, one of founders of the "Wissenschaft des Judentums"
	1803—Yeshiva founded at Volozhin, Russia
1806-1863—Gabriel Riesser, leader of Jewish emancipation movement in Germany	
1807—Grand Sanhedrin convoked in Paris	
1807-1809—Jews granted equal rights in Grand Duchy of Warsaw	1808-1867—Abraham Mapu, author, pioneer of modern Hebrew literature
	1808-1888—Samson Raphael Hirsch, founder of neo-orthodoxy in Germany
	1810-1874—Abraham Geiger, leader of German Jewish Reform movement
	1810-1883—Israel Salanter, founder of "Musar" movement
1812—Prussian Jews granted citizen rights	1812-1875—Moses Hess, author, socialist, forerunner of Zionist movement
	1815-1905—Isaak (Eisik) Hirsch Weiss, Talmud scholar
	1817-1891—Heinrich (Hirsch) Graetz, historian
1819—Pogroms in Germany	
1827—"Cantonist" edict in Russia	1830-1892—Judah Loeb Gordon, poet
1832—Political rights of Jews in Canada granted by act of Legislature	
	1835-1917—Mendele Mocher Seforim (Sholem Jacob Abramovich), author
1840—Damascus ritual murder accusation	
1843—Founding of Order Bnai Brith	

POLITICAL CHRONOLOGY	CULTURAL CHRONOLOGY
1848—Revolutions in Central and Western Europe	
	1850-1915—Solomon Schechter, Rabbi, scholar, leader of Conservative Judaism in U.S.A.
	1852-1915—Yitzhok Leibush Peretz, author
1856-1929—Louis Marshall, American-Jewish leader	1856-1927—Ahad ha-Am (Asher Ginzberg), philosopher, founder of cultural Zionism
	1859-1916—Sholem Aleichem (Sholem Rabinovich), author
1860—"Alliance Israélite Universelle" founded in France	1860-1941—Simon Dubnow, historian
1860-1904—Theodor Herzl, founder of political Zionist movement	
	1873-1934—Hayim Nahman Bialik, poet
	1875—Hebrew Union College founded at Cincinnati, Ohio
1878—Beginning of Jewish colonization in Palestine	
1880-1885—Establishment of the Jewish trade union movement in the United States	
1881—Pogroms in Russia	
1881—"Am Olam" founded in Russia	
1881-1882—"Bilu" movement founded in Russia	
1881—Beginning of mass emigration to America	
1882—Founding of the "Propaganda Verein," the first Jewish socialist organization in United States	1882—Leo Pinsker's "Auto-Emanzipation" published
1884—Founding of Hovevei Zion ("Lovers of Zion")	
	1886—Jewish Theological Seminary founded in New York
1888—United Hebrew Trades founded	
1889-1891—Beginning of Jewish colonization in Argentina	
1891—Founding of Jewish Colonization Association (JCA)	
1892—Workmen's Circle ("Arbeter Ring") founded	
1894-1906—Dreyfus affair in France	
1897—First Zionist Congress First conference of "Bund" — Jewish Workers' Party in Russia	1897—Yeshivat Rabbi Isaac Elhanan founded in New York

POLITICAL CHRONOLOGY	CULTURAL CHRONOLOGY
1900—International Ladies Garment Workers Union founded	
1904—United Hatters, Cap and Millinery Workers International Union founded	
1905—Founding of the Zionist - Socialist Workers' Party in Russia	
1906—Founding of the Jewish Socialist Workers' Party ("Sejmists") in Russia	
1906—Founding of the Poale-Zion Party	
1906—American Jewish Committee founded	
	1908—Yiddish cultural conference held in Czernowitz
1909-1910—Degania, first collective colony (kvutza), established in Palestine	1910—First Bureau of Jewish Education established in U.S.A.
	1910—Founding of First Yiddish schools in U.S.A.
1911-1913—Beilis trial in Russia	
1912—Agudat Israel founded	
1912—Jewish National Workers' Alliance founded	
1913—Anti-Defamation League (Bnai Brith) founded in Chicago, Ill.	
1914—Amalgamated Clothing Workers Union of America founded	
1914-1918—First World War	
1914—Joint Distribution Committee founded	
1917—American Jewish Congress founded	1917—Founding of the Hebrew Cultural Organization "Tarbut"
1917—Russian Revolution	
1917—Jews granted full citizen rights in Russia	
1917—Balfour Declaration	
1918—Revolution in Germany	
1918—Independence of Poland, Lithuania, Latvia and Estonia	
1918-1920—Pogroms in Ukraine	
1919—International guarantee of minority rights	
1919—Treaty of Versailles	
1919—"Comité des Délégations Juives" founded	
1920—Histadrut ha-Obedim (General Federation of Jewish Labor in Palestine) founded	
	1921—Establishment of Central Yiddish School Organization in Poland (Cysho)

POLITICAL CHRONOLOGY	CULTURAL CHRONOLOGY
	1922—Founding of Jewish Institute of Religion in New York
1924—Immigration quota established by U.S.A. Congress	
1924—National Labor Committee for Palestine ("Geverkshaften Campaign") founded	
	1925—Founding of Hebrew University in Jerusalem
	1925—Founding of Yiddish Scientific Institute in Vilna ("Yivo")
1929—Jewish Agency for Palestine constituted	
1933—Nazism comes to power in Germany	
1934—Birobidjan declared a Jewish Autonomous Region by the U.S.S.R. Government	
1934—Jewish Labor Committee founded in New York	
1934-1936—Mass emigration to Palestine	
1935—Adoption of Nurnberg laws	
1936—World Jewish Congress founded	
1938—Evian Conference	
1938—Persecutions and pogroms in Germany	
1938-1939—Anti-Jewish decrees in Italy, Hungary, Romania	
1939—White Paper issued by British Government	
1939—Second World War begins September 1	

JEWISH HISTORIOGRAPHY

E. M. Tcherikover

No other history of a people presents the difficulties which are met with in the writing of Jewish history, a history of a three thousand-year-old people which has lived in a state of dispersion, in small groups and in alien surroundings on several continents and in many lands, and yet has remained one national entity. Notwithstanding this oneness in the destiny of the Jews each separate community has been usually treated by scholars as a historical study in itself. The access to source material, too, is no easy task. The Jews in exile, unlike other peoples, had no professional chroniclers or Court historians; nor could they safely store away important documents for posterity. Owing to their enforced and continuous migration as well as to persecution, the material which had been accumulated haphazardly was, in the course of time, lost.

The result was that for eighteen hundred years, until the emergence of modern historiography, there was only a handful of serious works on Jewish history, or, rather, on chronography. Significant events in the existence of the Jewish people in the course of many centuries, the rise and decline of a number of Jewish communities, would have remained hidden in obscurity had it not been for material preserved in non-Jewish sources, although this material is all too often meager and very frequently biased. On the whole, however, we have for this period a very extensive religious literature replete with excellent historical material which reflects the life and creativeness of the Jewish people on its long historic path.

Jewish historical literature offers incomparably greater information on the period of Antiquity than it does on the later periods. This, of course, is due to the rich historical material to be found in the Bible. A number of chapters of the Books of Samuel and Kings, for instance, are among the best examples of historical literature in the ancient world. On the other hand, most of the historical narratives of the Bible are not so much concerned with the telling of history as the stressing of a religious-ethical moral. In these narratives the legendary element is very frequently intermingled with the real. The Bible, being the product of many generations, has grown by accretion into a great literary monument which affords inexhaustible material concerning the earliest history of the Jews—from its beginning to the decline of the Persian empire—in the broadest sense; it contains material relative to extraneous events, to Israel and the neighboring peoples, to genealogy and historic geography, to social and economic conditions, to law and folk-ways and, above all, to religious and spiritual development.

Among the oldest historical works mentioned in the Bible are the *Sefer Milhamot Yahweh* and the *Sefer ha-Yashar*. Later, there are the Court Chronicles and probably also the Temple Chronicles, which have not come down to us in their original text and which, in a revised form, are incorporated in the Bible. Joshua, Judges, Samuel, Kings, as well as Ezra, Nehemiah and the Chronicles, can be regarded as purely historical works.

In the post-biblical period I Maccabees

is the first work of historical importance. It has a more secular character. The account it gives of the Maccabaean wars, narrated by an anonymous author, was written not long after the events. II Maccabees, written in Greek, is the summary of a lost work by Jason of Cyrene, written some time later than I Maccabees in Alexandria. Works in Greek on Jewish history were also written in the 2nd century B.C.E. by Jewish historians in Egypt—Demetrius, Eupolemus and Artapanus. But of these only small fragments are extant.

The second great historiographic monument of the post-biblical period are the works of Josephus Flavius, written at the end of the 1st century C.E. Without his works — *Jewish Antiquities, The Jewish War,* and *Against Apion*—it would be well-nigh impossible to treat of some four centuries of the history of the Jewish people, from the period of Alexander the Great to the period which followed the destruction of the Second Temple. These works are among the finest examples of the Hellenistic historical literature. They embody a system and a method of their own, and are full of interesting material and citations from the historical literature of the period.

To the Hellenized Jewish authors, especially in Alexandria, Jewish historiography was chiefly a medium for apologetics and propaganda. Most of their works, written in Greek, have either been completely lost or are extant only in fragmentary form. Among the lost historical works are the writings of Justus of Tiberias, a contemporary of Flavius, and others. The works of Philo the Alexandrian have been preserved, but not in their entirety. Of particular interest to the historian is Philo's work on Moses' legislation (*The Life of Moses*) as well as the works which relate the persecutions of Alexandrian Jews—*Against Flaccus,* and *Embassy to Gaius* (Caligula). In the works of Greek and Roman authors of Antiquity there are frequent references to Jewish history, but these are usually written in a hostile tone: in the writings of Poly-

bius, Strabo, Diodorus of Sicily, the orations of Cicero as well as the works of Suetonius and, especially, those of Tacitus. (Appropriate excerpts from these writings are given in T. Reinach's notable work, *Textes d'auteurs grecs et romains relatifs au Judaïsme,* Paris, 1895).

In the period preceding the Mishnah only two chronographic works appeared, the *Megillat Taanit,* a calendar of holy days on which fasting is forbidden—and later, the *Seder Olam Rabba,* a chronicle of events from the day of creation until the rise of Bar Kochba—based upon biblical and oral tradition. In the Talmud and subsequent Midrashim we find only scattered references to historical events. However, the Talmud and the Midrashim in themselves have become exceedingly valuable sources of history concerning Jewish culture in late Antiquity and early medieval times. Indeed, not only the Agada but also the Halakah portions of the Talmud present a vivid picture of the legal status, economy, social and family conditions, customs, education, folk-ways, folklore, legends and, above all, the religio-ethical and philosophical ideas of the Jews of the time. On the other hand, little is found in the vast store of Talmudic literature concerning general political events, even events so crucial in the life of the people as the destruction of Jerusalem or the Bar Kochba insurrection. The post-Talmudic literature does not even mention the Arab occupation of Palestine in 638 C.E. Darkness also surrounds the migratory path of the Jews in Europe and the establishment and growth of Jewish communities. For such information the present-day historian must depend almost exclusively on non-Jewish sources, mostly biased and hostile. Material concerning this period in Jewish history is to be found partly in the works of Roman historians, Christian church chroniclers, Byzantine and Arab chronographers, in the codes of Theodosius and Justinian, in the Acts of the Church Councils, in the Roman-Visigothic law book, and in similar sources. Important data relating to Jewish history can also be gathered from archaeological finds and discoveries.

Among Jewish sources, mostly literary-historical in character, reference should be made to the chronicles of the Talmudic academies of the 8th to 10th centuries, to the *Seder Tannaim ve-Amoraim,* to the *Seder Olam Zuta* (concerning the Exilarchs) and, especially, to Sherira Gaon's *Iggeret* (Epistle), an outstanding chronicle of the sages of the Talmud, the Saburaim and the Geonim up to the second half of the 10th century. From the same period we also possess fragments of the writings of Nathan the Babylonian and the *Megillat Ahimaaz.* Important material for the study of Jewish 12th century history in the Orient may be found in Maimonides' *Iggeret ha-Shemad* (Epistle on Apostasy), *Iggeret Teman* (Epistle of Yemen), and in Spain in the *Zikron ha-Shemadot* by Profiat Duran. From the period of the Khazars in the 10th century we have the celebrated letter of Hasdai ibn Shaprut addressed to the king of the Khazars. There is valuable information on particular events of those periods in the fragments of the old Karaite literature discovered at the end of the 19th century in the Genizah of Cairo and elsewhere.

The ruthless excesses against the Jews during the Crusades are almost completely ignored in the Christian chronicles of the time. The scant information we have comes from the few Jewish chroniclers in Germany—Eliezer of Worms, Solomon ben Simon of Mayence and Ephraim of Bonn—who had themselves experienced the great ordeal, and from the communal registers of the martyrs, and the historical *Selihot.* (The chronicles of that period were collected and published in the *Quellen zur Geschichte der Juden in Deutschland,* Berlin, Vol. II.) In connection with the polemics against the Karaites there is a 12th century *Sefer ha-Kabbala* of the noted Spanish-Jewish Aristotelian Abraham ibn Daud; in it the Biblical, Talmudic and post-Talmudic authorities are enumerated chronologically and it contains in addition considerable information about the Jewish cultural renaissance in Spain. The accounts published in the 12th century by the renowned travelers, Benjamin of Tudela (in Navarra, Spain) and Petahyah of Regensburg, contain valuable source material. As to the later Middle Ages, from the 13th to the 15th centuries—the period of the most ruthless persecutions, the Black Death, the Inquisition and the mass expulsions of Jews—but little Jewish source material has been preserved. However, an abundance of official documents found in governmental and municipal archives, as well as in the archives of the Inquisition tribunals, has been examined by historians only in recent times.

With the Renaissance in Europe and the introduction of the printing press there came a marked advance in Jewish historiography. A number of works on history previously circulating in manuscript were now published. Other printed works appeared, one of the first being the *Sefer Yuhasin* by Abraham Zacuto, a historical compilation concerning Talmudic literature.

In the 15th and 16th centuries Italy became a center of Jewish historical writing, owing to the influx of Jewish refugees from Spain and Portugal. The more notable works of that period are the *Shebet Yehudah* by Solomon ibn Verga, a treatise on the persecutions of the Jews in Spain and the religious disputes in that land, and the poetical work in Portuguese, *Consolation for the Sorrows of Israel,* by Samuel Usque.

The most important Jewish historian of the 15th-16th centuries was Joseph ha-Kohen of Avignon, the author of *Dibre ha-Yamim le-Malke Zarfat ve-Otoman* (History of the Kings of France and the Ottomans), and of the celebrated work *Emek ha-Baka,* dealing with the Jewish martyrology from the destruction of Jerusalem up to 1575. Another invaluable chronicle is Capsali's *Debe Eliyahu,* the only source material for the history of the settlement of Jews in Turkey in the 16th century. The same period also saw the first Jewish historico-philosophical work, *Meor Enayim,* by Azarya de Rossi (1513-1578), a work secular in character, keenly critical of accepted traditions, and the first to acquaint the Jewish world with the writings of Philo and the Septuagint. The Rabbis of the time placed Rossi's book under the ban and it was republished only at the end of the 18th century. In keeping with the spirit of time-honored tradition was Gedaliah ibn Yahya's popular work, *Shalshelet ha-Kabbala* (1587), a literary chronicle in which commentary, fantasy and mysticism were intermingled. Dating from the early part of the 16th century is the diary of David Reubeni, an important source for the history of the Messianic movement of the period. Only few works of a historical character appeared in countries other than Italy in the 16th and 17th centuries. The most important of these is *Zemah David* (1592), by David Gans of Prague, the first Jewish historian in the German-speaking countries. The work is a record of important Jews and Jewish events from ancient times to the end of the 16th century.

In Poland, the first historical works—or rather chronicles dealing with current events—made their appearance in the 17th century, during the Chmielnicki period. The most complete record of the persecutions of 1648-1649 is the *Yeven Mezulah,* by Nathan Hanover (1653), which along with a detailed account of the Chmielnicki pogroms, presents a picture of the communal and cultural conditions among Polish Jewry. The persecutions of 1648-1649 are also treated in the chronicles *Zok ha-Ittim, Petah Teshuvah, Tit ha-Yoven,* and *Zaar Bat Rabbim.* The same period also saw the appearance of the *Megillat Ebah,* by the renowned Rabbi Yom Tob Lipmann Heller. Other material relevant to the period is found in the *Selihot* and Lamentations of the time (collected and published in S. Bernfeld's *Sefer ha-Demaot,* volume 3, Berlin, 1926); in the Responsa, in the homiletic literature and in the non-Jewish historical writings of the period. The *Seder ha-Dorot,* by the famous Rabbi Jehiel Heilprin of Minsk, is in the first part, *Yemot Olam,* a chronicle of events ranging from the biblical period down to the end of the 17th century; its second and more important part is a chronological index of the Tannaim, and the Rabbinical authorities in the post-Talmudic period, with a valuable list of the Rabbinical works and authors.

The 16th century saw the first appearance of historical works in Yiddish. These are simpler and more popular in style, from the point of view of language as well as of content. In these works history is presented with a lavish admixture of legend. The earlier writings of this type were for the most part translations from known Hebrew texts. Among original Yiddish works was the *Sheerit Yisrael* by Menahem Mann Amelander (Amsterdam, 1743), a partly fictional chronicle. Besides such chronicles, there are a great many Yiddish poetic works and songs of historical content, most of them dating back to the 17th century. The most notable of these is the *Megillat Winz* (1616), written by Elhanan Helin. Its subject is the pogrom in Frankfort on the Main instigated by Fettmilch Winz. A monumental work in Yiddish literature is the memoirs of Glueckl of Hameln which vividly describes Jewish life in Germany in the 17th-18th centuries. Solomon Maimon's autobiography, *Lebensgeschichte,* in German (1792-1793), is of great value.

The beginning of the 18th century showed a marked increase of interest in Jewish history among non-Jewish scholars. In the latter part of the 17th century Johann Christoph Wagenseil edited several selections from Hebrew and Yiddish writings of historical interest. In the early part of the 18th century the French theologian, Basnage, published his *L'Histoire et la religion des Juifs depuis Jésus-Christ jus-qu'à présent* (Rotterdam, 1706-1711). Although an objective work the treatise nevertheless showed a Christian tone. More important and more objective in character was the four-volume work of the German Orientalist, Johann Jakob Schudt, *Juedische Merckwuerdigkeiten,* published at the beginning of the 18th century. The work is a description of Jewish life in Frankfort on the Main and Hamburg. A number of other Christian historians, up to the 19th century, wrote about Jews in Denmark, England, and Germany. There is even a book on Jewish history, including material on Jews in the United States, by an American, Hannah Adams.

Modern Jewish historiography is a product of the 19th century. It was at first markedly apologetic in character. Leopold Zunz, the father of the *Wissenschaft des Judentums,* was the first to formulate the essence of Jewish history as merely that of learning and suffering, of literature and martyrology. Zunz wrote a series of brilliant studies on medieval literature and liturgy, especially in his history of synagogal poetry (1855). The real father of Jewish historiography was Jost, the author of the first comprehensive Jewish history, beginning with the Maccabaean period and ending with the 19th century (9 volumes, 1820-1829). Jost's *Geschichte der Israeliten* was an unusual achievement, especially since at that time the necessary preliminary studies were lacking. In substance, however, his *Geschichte* was more a pragmatic chronicle than a history, frequently without a critical approach, and characterized by a primitive apologetic spirit and Prussian patriotism. However, Jost has the merit of being the first systematic Jewish historian. Beginning with the 1840's and 1850's a number of serious scholars, principally in Germany and Austria, among them Zacharias Frankel, Abraham Geiger, Solomon Rapoport, and others, produced a series of classic monographs on the Bible, the Talmud, and the Geonic and Rabbinic literature. Thus modern Jewish historiography, too, was from its very outset principally the history of a literature; not the history of the people, but of its scholars and their works. Its tendency was to prove the greatness of the Jewish spirit and to express the idea of the Jewish religio-ethical mission. We find the idea of such a mission in the works and utterances of a number of men of the period: in Abraham Geiger's *Das Judentum und seine Geschichte* (1871), a purely theological system on the evolution of Judaism; in the writings of the more moderate Nachman Krochmal; in the utterances of the orthodox leader Samson Raphael Hirsch; and to a greater or lesser extent in the historico-philosophical works of the Jewish scholars almost up to the present. Among the authoritative Jewish historians in Germany only Zacharias Frankel wrote his principal works in Hebrew. The rest wrote in German. Frankel was the founder of the *Monatsschrift fuer Geschichte und Wissenschaft des Judentums* (1851), the most notable periodical for Jewish learning. He was also the director of the Breslau Jewish Theological Seminary which produced a number of prominent students of Jewish history.

The first Jewish historians in Austria were more national-minded than those in Germany. Almost all of them came from Galicia and brought with them profound Jewish learning. They wrote in Hebrew. The first historian of this type was the pioneer of the Haskalah, Solomon Rapoport, who, as early as 1828-1831 wrote a series of brilliant monographs on the Geonim. His friend, Nachman Krochmal, the author of *More Nebuke ha-Zeman,* was the first among his contemporaries to develop a novel Jewish historico-philosophical system which exercised considerable influence at a later period (his work was published after his death, in 1851, by Zunz). Krochmal was actually the first Jewish thinker to formulate philosophically the theory of a Jewish mission. Some years later Isaac Hirsch

Weiss, also of Galician origin, wrote in Hebrew his classic five-volume work on the Oral Torah, *Dor Dor ve - Dorshav.* An awakened interest in history, though to a lesser degree than in Germany and Austria, was also discernible during this period among French Jews. Joseph Salvador, an original thinker and historian, published a series of studies on Jewish history. His principal work was *Paris, Rome, Jerusalem— ou la question religieuse au 19e siècle* (1860). But all these works are rather in the domain of the philosophy of history than of history proper—as is *Rome und Jerusalem,* by Moses Hess, the German-Jewish socialist and political émigré in Paris. In the field of Jewish history proper there were in France two scholars, Adolphe Franck, who wrote on Kabbala, and the noted orientalist, Salomon Munk.

Epochal in Jewish historiography was the appearance of Heinrich Graetz's monumental eleven-volume work in German (1853-1876) which embraces the history of the Jewish people from its remotest past to the middle of the 19th century. With his keen sense of analysis, his vast erudition and universal outlook, Graetz, despite his somewhat subjective approach, reconstructed the millennial history of the Jews as a living people. In his attitude and historical outlook, Graetz is more national-minded than most of his contemporaries. He frequently assails the accepted authorities. In his general view of Jewish history, however, he is at one with Zunz—though not so one-sidedly—that this history is essentially a record of the Jewish spirit and Jewish suffering. To him, too, the Jews are a religious category. Graetz's system of historic periodicity is in keeping with this approach. Inclined toward rationalism and Haskalah, he was hostile to the Kabbala and to mysticism and to the Messianic movement; he also failed to realize the value of Jewish communal autonomy, and he dwells very little on the history of East European Jewry.

The growth of Jewish historiography

received a marked stimulus from Graetz's work. The second half of the 19th century is the high watermark of Jewish historical scholarship in all countries, especially in Germany. During this period there appeared a large number of monographs on individual phases of Jewish life in many countries. These dealt with the history of the Jewish spirit and Jewish martyrdom, as well as with the history of legislation, politics, sociology, economics, folk-ways, etc. This new generation of historians also differed from its predecessors in regard to the selection of material. Graetz and his predecessors depended almost exclusively on published source material. They seldom utilized source material contained in the various Jewish and non-Jewish archives. In the 1880's a change took place. Historians began, zealously and systematically, to work on governmental and municipal documentary records, family archives and similar sources. The first to adopt this method was a group of French-Jewish scholars, headed by Isidore Loeb, who in 1880 founded the *Société des Études Juives* in Paris, which published a periodical *Revue des Études Juives,* and which became an important center of Jewish learning in general and history in particular. In 1885 a similar society was founded in Berlin, the *Historische Kommission,* for the study of the history of Jews in Germany. This body published a large volume, *Regesten,* by Aronius, three volumes of *Historische Quellen,* and the *Zeitschrift fuer die Geschichte der Juden in Deutschland.* Research along the same lines was also followed by the previously mentioned *Monatsschrift.* In Bucharest in 1886 a society was founded for the study of the history of the Jews in Romania. In London the *Jewish Historical Society of England* was established in 1893; it published a series of monographs and the *Society Transactions.* Earlier, in 1888, there appeared in the British capital the first issue of the *Jewish Quarterly Review,* the most important English language journal concerned with Jewish studies. In 1892 the *American Jewish Historical Society* was organized in the United States. This society issues a series—"Publications of the American Jewish Historical Society." Some years later, at the beginning of the present century, a society for the study of Jewish history was established in Vienna.

Thus Jewish historiography expanded considerably and became more comprehensive and specialized. Innumerable publications were issued. Modern Jewish historiography extended into new fields. In the domain of the history of Jewish cultural life, M. Guedemann wrote his basic work in three volumes: *Geschichte des Erziehungswesens und der Kultur der abendländischen Juden* (1880-1888). This was followed by Israel Abrahams' *Jewish Life in the Middle Ages.* Later there appeared A. Berliner's *Aus dem Leben der deutschen Juden im Mittelalter.* In the field of economics the most notable contributions were *Sozial- und Wirtschaftsgeschichte der Juden in Mittelalter und der Neuzeit,* by Georg Caro, and I. Schipper's monograph on the economic history of the Jews in the early medieval period, published in German in 1907; the same work, extensively revised and expanded, was published in Yiddish in 1930. Among the works devoted to significant periods in Jewish history, mention should be made of Juster's *Les Juifs dans l'empire Romain* (2 volumes, Paris, 1914); M. Kayserling's numerous studies in German on the political and cultural history of the Jews in Spain and Portugal; Joseph Jacob's *Sources of the History of the Jews in Spain* (1895); and especially, Fritz Baer's *Die Juden im Christlichen Spanien* (2 volumes, Berlin, 1929-1936). Important source material for the study of Jews in Germany is contained in *Monumenta Germaniae Historica* (Berlin, 1877-1919). The material of the Cairo Genizah was utilized by Jacob Mann in his *The Jews in Egypt and in Palestine under the Fatimid Caliphs* (1920-1922), and in his *Texts and Studies in Jewish*

History and Literature (1931-1935). Works on the history of Jewish philosophy were written by S. Munk, D. Kaufmann, J. Guttmann, David Neumark, H. A. Wolfson, Isaac Husik, S. Bernfeld, and Z. Diesendruck.

Beginning with the present century the number of Anglo-American scholars devoting themselves to the study of Jewish history increased considerably. This was largely due to the extraordinary growth of the American Jewish community and the establishment of a number of Jewish academic institutions in the United States. Important studies in the field of Jewish history were made by Louis Ginzberg, A. Marx, Meyer Waxman, J. Morgenstern, S. Zeitlin, J. Lauterbach, Salo W. Baron, Louis Finkelstein, Jacob R. Marcus, Abram L. Sachar, Abraham A. Neuman, and others in America. In England important work was done by M. Gaster, A. Buechler, A. Marmorstein, Cecil Roth, and others.

(For further information on works on Jewish history and related subjects in English see bibliographies appended to *History of Jewish Archaeology; Origin and History of Jewish Religion; History of Jewish Religious Thought* in this volume; as well as to this article.)

A series of historical studies has been published in the *Jewish Quarterly Review,* appearing since 1910 in the United States; in the *Hebrew Union College Annual,* established in 1924; and in the *Proceedings of the American Academy of Jewish Research,* established in 1930.

One of the earlier Jewish historians in Russia was Abraham E. Harkavy, who wrote a series of monographs on the history of the Jews in Russia and Poland. Of particular importance were the works in Russian of the non-Jew, S. Bershadski, who devoted himself to Jewish history. His principal works are the *History of the Lithuanian Jews* (1883), and *The Russo-Jewish Archives,* 3 volumes (1882-1903). The outstanding Jewish historian in Eastern Europe was Simon Dubnow, who, beginning in 1891, initiated the systematic collection and publication of material concerning the history of the Jews in Eastern Europe. Valuable source material was compiled and published by the *Jewish Historic Commission* known as *Historico-Ethnographic Society* (beginning with 1908) in Petersburg. The most important periodical for studies on Jewish history in Poland and Russia was *Yevreyskaya Starina,* published under the direction of Simon Dubnow, and first issued in 1909. A collection of studies on the history of Jewish culture appeared in *Perezhitoye* (1909-1913, 4 volumes), under the direction of Saul Ginsburg. On the basis of government archives, Julius Gessen published a series of works on the political history of the Jews in Russia, and later *A History of the Jewish People in Russia* (2 volumes, 1925-1927). Significant contributions to the history of the Jews in Russia were made by I. Zinberg, M. Margolis, J. Brutzkus, M. Wischnitzer, P. Marek, and others. In the Ukraine several studies on Jewish history appeared in general historical publications. Two miscellaneous collections *(Zbirnik Prac,* Kiev, 1928-1929), issued by the Jewish Historico-Archaeographic Commission affiliated with the Ukrainian Academy, were devoted to Jewish history.

The pioneer of modern Jewish historiography in Poland was Tadeusz Czacki, a non-Jew, who in 1807 published his *Rozprawa o Zydach,* containing a series of documents on the history of Jews in old Poland. Some sixty years later other works appeared in Poland: Kraushaar's *Hystoria Zydow w Polsce* (1865-1866), and Ludwik Gumplowicz's work dealing with the history of legislation relative to the Jews in Poland. Judaeo-Polish historians for a long time principally concerned themselves with the legal status of the Jews in old Poland. Jewish historians of this type best-known are: Hilary Nussbaum, Matthias Bersohn, noted for his collection of historic documents, *Dyplomatarjusz.* Jewish historiography received a new impetus in the early part of the present century. M. Schorr and M. Balaban wrote a number of monographs on Jewish communities. I. Schipper wrote on the economic history of the Jews in Poland during the Middle Ages; his basic work on Jewish trade in Poland appeared in Polish in 1937. A series of studies on particular aspects of the history of the Jews in Poland were written, mainly in Yiddish, by J. Shatzky, F. Friedman, E. Ringelblum, Raphael Mahler, B. Weinryb, M. M. Gelber, and others.

Works on Jewish history in Hebrew—written mainly in Eastern Europe—primarily dealt with the inner religious and spiritual life of the Jews in the Slav countries. The first Kehillah monograph in Hebrew, *Kiryah Neemanah* (1860), was a history of the Jewish community in Vilna, by S. J. Finn. A number of similar monographs appeared later on the history of various Jewish communities in Russia and Poland, and on Jewish autonomy in general, especially on the Council of Four Lands. The history of Hasidism was also specially dealt with by historians writing in Hebrew. Among them were D. Kahana, S. A. Horodezky, S. Dubnow, H. Zeitlin, and others. A comprehensive work, written from a purely orthodox viewpoint, is the nine-volume history *Toledot Yisrael,* by Z. W. Yawitz; also the four-volume work, *Dorot ha-Rishonim,* by Isaak Halevy.

In recent years a wealth of important works on Jewish history has appeared in Palestine. They deal chiefly with the history of Jewish religion and religious literature, Jewish cultural life, and the history of Jewish settlement in Palestine, as well as with Zionism and modern Hebrew literature (the most important of these works are enumerated in the bibliographies to the related articles in this volume). A series of studies on subjects of historic interest was published in the collection *Reshummot* (6 volumes); in the publication *Zion,* and *Tarbitz,* a periodical issued by the Hebrew University.

Modern historiography in Yiddish is, on the whole, the product of the last few decades and is chiefly concerned with economic history, internal life, history of literature, and Jewish national and social movements. Among the outstanding Yiddish works are I. Schipper's *Economic History of the Jews in the Middle Ages* (4 volumes) and *History of the Jewish Theater and Drama* (3 volumes). I. Zinberg's *History of Jewish Literature* (8 volumes) is a monumental work. Saul Ginsburg's *Historical Writings* (4 volumes) is an important contribution to the history of Jewish culture in Russia. M. Balaban's *Jews in Poland* and E. Frank's *Jewish Converts to Christianity in Poland in the 19th Century* are important studies. In the last two decades important historical research in Yiddish has been carried on by the Yiddish Scientific Institute (Yivo) which has issued three volumes of *Historishe Shriftn; Bleter far Geshichte* (2 volumes); *Yidn in Frankraich* (2 volumes); and two volumes of *History of the Jewish Labor Movement in the United States.* In addition, articles and source material on Jewish history are published by the Yivo in its periodical, *Yivo Bleter,* and in other Yivo publications. Numerous valuable Yiddish monographs on Jewish communities in Eastern Europe have appeared in the last two decades in Eastern Europe as well as in America. In the field of contemporary history there have also appeared some important collections of documents bearing upon the Jewish situation during the First World War and the Russian Revolution. In the Soviet Union several important Yiddish works have appeared, dealing mainly with the history of the Jews in Eastern Europe. Among such works are *The Socio-Economic Status of the Russian Jews in the 19th Century,* by J. Sosis; T. Heilikman's *History of the Social Movements in Poland and Russia Among Jews;* Margolis' *History of the Jews in Russia;* and Yuditzky's *The Jewish Bourgeoisie and the Jewish Prole-*tariat in the First Half of the 19th Century. Many studies in Jewish history appeared in the *Zeitshrift,* which was published in Minsk.

Following his writings on Jewish history in Eastern Europe, S. Dubnow, the most outstanding Jewish historian after Graetz, devoted himself to general Jewish history. His major work in this field, *Die Weltgeschichte des juedischen Volkes* appeared in German, in ten volumes from 1925 to 1929. To Dubnow the Jews are not merely a religious entity; they are a national entity, a living people, which has never ceased to fight for its autonomous existence both socially and spiritually, and which has in the course of its historic path evolved its own unique forms of existence, supplanting the normal attributes of nationhood—state and land.

Moreover, in keeping with his re-evaluation of Jewish history, Dubnow advanced a new classification of the main periods of Jewish history. Traditional historiography considered Jewish history essentially as the record of the spiritual creativeness of the Jew. This viewpoint was, in substance, adopted by modern West European Jewish historians. Graetz divides Jewish history into periods of persecution and periods of religious and literary activity, *i.e.,* the periods of the First Temple, the Second Temple, the first generation of Rabbis, the second generation of Rabbis, etc. Dubnow, however, divides the early history of the Jews into two periods—that of the East (Palestine and the Orient) and that of the West (European period), the latter being subdivided into periods of centers of hegemony and organizational autonomy. Recent history Dubnow divides into the brief periods which embrace the first emancipation and reaction, the second emancipation, and the assimilationist and nationalist movements. Dubnow's approach represents a kind of synthesis of Jewish historiography in West and East.

BIBLIOGRAPHY
(In addition to the works cited in the above article)

ALBRECHT ALT, *Die Staatenbildung der Israeliten in Palaestina*. Leipzig, 1930.

SALO W. BARON, *A Social and Religious History of the Jews*. 3 vols., New York, 1937.

SALO W. BARON, *The Jewish Community*. 3 vols., New York, 1942.

E. R. BEVAN AND CH. SINGER, *The Legacy of Israel*. Oxford, 1927.

Cambridge Ancient History. 12 vols., 1923-1939.

R. H. CHARLES, *Apocrypha and Pseudepigrapha of the Old Testament*. 2 vols., Oxford 1913.

BEN ZION DINABURG, *Yisrael ba-Golah* (Israel in Dispersion). 2 vols., Jerusalem, 1926-1936.

ISMAR ELBOGEN, *A Century of Jewish Life*. Philadelphia, 1944.

LOUIS FINKELSTEIN, *The Pharisees*. 2 vols., Philadelphia, 1938.

JEAN-BAPTISTE FREY, *Corpus inscriptionum judaicarum*. Vol. 1: *Europe*. Paris, 1936.

M. GASTER, *The Samaritans*. London, 1925.

LOUIS GINZBERG, *Geonica*. 2 vols., New York, 1909.

LOUIS GINZBERG, *Genizah Studies in Memory of Dr. Solomon Schechter*. 2 vols., New York, 1928-1929.

RUDOLF KITTEL, *Geschichte des Volkes Israel*. 3 vols., Stuttgart, 1923-1929.

S. KLEIN, *Sefer ha-Yishuv*. Jerusalem, 1939.

J. LIFSCHITZ, *Zikron Yaakob*. 3 vols., Kaunas, 1929-1933.

ADOLPHE LODS, *The Prophets and the Rise of Judaism*. New York, 1937.

ADOLPHE LODS, *Israel*. New York, 1932.

BENJAMIN MAISLER, *Toledot Erets Yisrael* (History of Palestine), Tel Aviv, 1938.

JACOB RADER MARCUS, *The Jew in the Medieval World*. Cincinnati, 1938.

MAX L. MARGOLIS AND ALEXANDER MARX, *A History of the Jewish People*. Philadelphia, 1927.

ABRAM MENES, *Die vorexilischen Gesetze Israels*. Giessen, 1928.

JULIAN MORGENSTERN, *Amos Studies*. Cincinnati, 1941.

ABRAHAM A. NEUMAN, *The Jews in Spain*. 2 vols., Philadelphia, 1944.

MARTIN NOTH, *Das System der zwoelf Staemme Israels*. Stuttgart, 1930.

W. O. E. OESTERLEY AND TH. H. ROBINSON, *A History of Israel*. 2 vols., Oxford, 1932.

A. T. OLMSTEAD, *History of Palestine and Syria to the Macedonian Conquest*. New York, 1931.

JAMES PARKES, *The Conflict of the Church and the Synagogue: A Study in the Origin of Antisemitism*. London, 1934.

JAMES PARKES, *The Jew in the Medieval Community*. London, 1938.

SALOMON A. ROSANES, *Divre Yeme Yisrael be-Togarma* (A History of the Jews in Turkey). 3 vols., Jerusalem, 1931-1938.

LOUIS ROSENBERG, *Canada's Jews*, A Social and Economic Study. 1939.

CECIL ROTH, *A History of the Jews in England*. London, 1941.

ABRAM LEON SACHAR, *A History of the Jews*. 2nd ed., New York, 1940.

B. G. SACK, *History of the Jews in Canada*, in "The Jew in Canada." 1926.

EMIL SCHUERER, *Geschichte des juedischen Volkes im Zeitalter Jesu Christi*. 4th ed. 3 vols., Leipzig, 1901-1911.

A. TSCHERIKOWER, *Ha-Yehudim ve-ha-Yevanim*. Tel Aviv-Jerusalem, 1931.

MEYER WAXMAN, *A History of Jewish Literature*. 4 vols., New York, 1938-1941.

JULIUS WELLHAUSEN, *Israelitische und juedische Geschichte*. 4th ed., Berlin, 1901.

JULIUS WELLHAUSEN, *Prolegomena zur Geschichte Israels*. Berlin, 1883.

PETER WIERNIK, *History of the Jews in America*. New York, 1931.

SOLOMON ZEITLIN, *The History of the Second Jewish Commonwealth*. Philadelphia, 1939.

ORIGIN AND HISTORY OF THE JEWISH RELIGION

A. Menes

INTRODUCTION

Two of the great world religions, Christianity and Islam, derive their origin, as we know, from Judaism. Jewish monotheism has thus indirectly spread throughout the entire world, and has, in the course of centuries, deeply influenced the spiritual development of the majority of civilized peoples. But whereas the Jews have given the world new universal forms of religious life and thereby brought about the decline of the old national religions, the Jewish religion itself has remained the faith of one people, and the Jews are, in the contemporary civilized world, the only people that has preserved its old religion. For over three thousand years the Jewish religion has shared the fate of the Jewish people, and the religious universalism of the prophets, which gave Christianity and Islam their extraordinary power of expansion, was precisely the factor that has, throughout the Diaspora, held together the various parts of the Jewish people all over the world. But while it is true that Judaism has continued to be a national faith, the Jews, thanks in a large measure to their religion, have in time become a universal people. This twofold aspect of the religion of Israel—its universal radiation and influence as well as its tremendous national energy—explains the peculiar interest which attaches to the rise and history of the Jewish religion.

Despite the severe prohibitions against adding to or subtracting from the Law of

Moses, the religion of Israel has constantly developed, and the living Torah has donned a new garb in every period. Thus, although the Jewish religion, throughout the course of its history, significantly changed its original form, the organic continuity in the development of the Jewish religion cannot be denied. A critical study of the Jewish religion therefore has as its task the presentation of a historic picture of the religious life among Jews in the various periods; it must also attempt to bring to light the internal and external factors that have in every period determined the development of the Jewish faith in connection with the general conditions of Jewish life.

But is it possible to submit to analytical study such an essentially "unscientific" matter as religion? It cannot be denied that the question is a very serious one. The fact that there prevail such wide divergences of opinion regarding the most important problems of religious life, proves, at least, that religious research has to date not emerged from the embryonic stage. Precisely the most intimate phenomena of religious life often remain hidden from the eye of the student. Hence it is not sufficient to present a bald description of religious beliefs and rituals. Behind these external ceremonies and logically formulated dogmas there lies a world of emotions, experiences, and aspirations, constituting the very core of the faith.

The student of religion must, therefore, often possess the ability to be "subjective"; he must possess the aptitude not only to understand rationally the "beliefs" but also to sense and experience the feelings and emotions of the believer.

It is obvious that "subjectivity," too, has its limitations. To begin with, it is absolutely impossible to approach a solution of any historic problem without a critical analysis of the sources. This holds true in the fullest measure of the history of religious belief. The scholar must use as his foundation a set of scientifically controlled and more or less authenticated facts. Otherwise, all his conclusions are built on air. As regards the Bible—the main source for the history of the Jewish religion in ancient times—we must, to a large extent, rely on the conclusions of biblical criticism. In the treatment of several important questions, however, a new approach is required.

Such a new approach is primarily necessary in an appraisal of the early history of the Israelite tribes, the so-called nomadic period. In the literature of modern biblical criticism the "desert tradition" occupies a central place. It is accepted as axiomatic that the Yahweh cult was a product of the "simple" conditions of desert life and that the later struggle of the prophets against "alien" cults is an expression of the conflict between the traditionalists, the supporters of the old desert beliefs, and their opponents, who sought to introduce into the life of Israel the standards and concepts of the higher Canaanite civilization. This theory was based on the assumption that the nomadic life generally precedes a sedentary agricultural life. Today, however, this theory is far from being accepted. There is no conclusive evidence that animal husbandry represented an earlier stage of civilization. In many cases it was precisely the development of agriculture that created the conditions necessary for the domestication of animals. Besides, it must not be forgotten that nowhere in the biblical tradition are the patriarchs described as desert nomads. On the contrary, according to the Pentateuch, Abraham, the forefather of the people of Israel, came from Haran in Mesopotamia, which was then a center of the most advanced civilization. In addition, the most recent archaeological finds make it necessary for us to revise our earlier ideas concerning the "nomadic" period of the history of Israel (see *History of the Jews in Ancient Times* in this volume).

The theories of modern Bible scholars concerning the part played by nomadism in Jewish history have been strongly influenced by the desert romanticism which permeates many of the biblical writings. This "primitivism," the idealization of the past, of the "simple" and "happy" life of the "natural" man, is in actuality no more than an expression of the "discontents of civilization," the burden of many modern writers as well—Rousseau, Tolstoy, and others. The question as to why the Torah, which was intended to regulate the life of a civilized people, had its inception in the desert, was posed as early as the 1st century c.e. by Philo of Alexandria. The answer he gives is highly illuminating:

> To the question why he [Moses] promulgated his laws in the depths of the desert instead of cities we may answer in the first place that most cities are full of countless evils, both acts of impiety towards God and wrong doing between man and man.

The same primitivism has led a number of scholars to assume that the teachings of Mohammed were essentially a product of Bedouin life. This conclusion is now meeting with considerable doubts. In his work, *Islam*, H. Massé says:

> Mohammed did not rely on the desert folk; he wanted the support of the townfolk. His preaching of One God as opposed to the polytheism of the nomad was to take root first in the cities. Renan's formula "the desert leads to Monotheism" does not apply to Arabia.

We shall see later that Renan's formula is just as inapplicable to the history of Israel and that the profound revolution which Yahwism introduced into the life and thought of the Israelite tribes was not the result of primitive and "simple" conditions but was, on the contrary, an expression of the deep spiritual and moral conflicts of a higher civilization.

The history of Jewish religious belief cannot, of course, be isolated from the religious development among other peoples. The study of comparative religion can be of great help in understanding the many complicated phenomena in the religious history of the Jewish people. However, in this respect, too, an entirely new approach is necessary. In most discussions of religious life in Israel we are confronted with the somewhat outdated terminology of the positivist-evolutionary school of thought which flourished in the last part of the 19th century. Such terms as animism, tabu, totem,

mana, etc., contribute little towards explaining the pattern of the more highly developed religious life—and there is no doubt at all that the Yahweh faith represents one of the highest achievements in the history of the development of religion. It is, moreover, methodologically entirely erroneous to look for the "origin" of religious belief in the ceremonials and rites of the so-called primitive peoples. These "primitives" were frequently just as distant from the origin of religion as the more civilized peoples. The truth lies in quite the opposite direction. The nature of religion is more clearly revealed and is given clearer expression in the higher religions than in the literature of anthropology, which describes the religious life of primitive peoples. One of the greatest difficulties encountered by the student of religion is to find an adequate terminology to convey an idea of individual or collective feelings and experiences. The religious literature of the more highly civilized peoples is therefore a purer and more direct source of information concerning the nature of religious life and belief than the anthropological data, no matter how important they may be.

As has been observed by G. F. Moore, the terminology of the anthropologist confuses rather than clears up the problem:

> The jargon of the anthropologists (and anthropological theologians) is getting to be as portentous as that of the medieval alchemists, with this difference, that the alchemists' jargon was for the mystification of outsiders, while the anthropologists mystify not only the unlearned but themselves unawares with their Totem, Mana, Taboo, and the rest. The Sabbath as a "taboo-day" means nothing but that it was a day on which certain doings were interdicted under a supernatural sanction, which is the very definition of the Sabbath, as everybody knew before (*Judaism*, vol. II, p. 21).

The Sabbath was something more than a day on which it was forbidden to labor. Refraining from labor as well as from daily work was not an end in itself but a means of achieving an ideal aim, of establishing a day of rest and holiness. This is clearly shown in the biblical injunctions concerning the Sabbath. It is therefore methodologically incorrect to appraise the Sabbath from the viewpoint of the practices which were interdicted. For the outside observer who is more acquainted with the regulations concerning the Sabbath than with the Sabbath in actual practice it is difficult to formulate a clear conception of the highly significant role of the institution of the Sabbath in the life of the Jewish masses.

Even many modern scholars consider the Sabbath primarily as a day of restrictions and privations: one was not allowed to work or take a walk; nothing could be carried and it was even forbidden to prepare warm food. Viewed "objectively" it may appear that this contention is a sound one; we know, however, how false it is; and we know what a tremendous wealth of joyous experience the Sabbath has brought into the doleful life of the Jews of the Diaspora; we know that "Oneg Shabbat," the bliss of the Sabbath, is far from being an empty phrase.

The biblical writers did not seek out definitions from primitive peoples when they sought to designate the Sabbath as a day distinguished from all other days of the week. The Sabbath is a holy day; no other day in the Jewish calendar is so filled with holiness. As has been correctly observed by the French sociologist, Emil Durkheim, the feeling of holiness constitutes the very core of religious life. There is an even more emphatic appraisal of the central significance of the feeling of holiness in the epoch-making work of Rudolf Otto, *The Idea of the Holy*:

> There is no religion in which it does not live as the real innermost core, and without it no religion would be worthy of the name. It is pre-eminently a living force in the Semitic religions, and of these again in none has it such vigour as in that of the Bible.

There is no adequate explanation in the interpretation and definition of the concept of "holiness" by reference to such terms as "tabu" or "mana." Holiness is holiness. It is simply adding confusion to interpret it as "power." The power of the prophet Elijah in no way resembled the power of King Ahab. The power of the holy martyr is entirely different from the power of a tyrant; even the power of a Mahatma Gandhi is entirely different from the power of the leader of a modern political movement.

It is true, however, that in addition to its purely religious significance, the idea of holiness also had a paramount socio-ethical and partly even an economic function. This is given clear expression in a number of biblical regulations and institutions. The Holy Place, to which the people came to find God, frequently served as a place of refuge for the abused and persecuted. The Sabbaths and Holy Days were days of rest for all those who labored and even for work-animals. The enormous socio-ethical significance of such institutions as the Sabbath, the Sabbatical year, and the Jubilee, is generally known. As we shall later see, the sacrificial cult and the sacred meals played an equally important socio-economic role. The same was true of the holy word, the oath, and the holy covenant which regulated the relationships between individuals as between nations. There is particular illumination in the fact that in the Bible the term "kodesh" is used to designate those things which belong to the community, which have passed out of the province of private ownership. The prophet Zechariah, when he inveighed against the petty traders in the Temple who took money for the loan of utensils needed in offering sacrifices, says as follows:

> Yea, every pot in Jerusalem and in Judah shall be holiness unto the Lord of hosts: and all they that sacrifice shall come and take of them, and seethe therein: and in that day there shall be no more a Canaanite [petty trader] in the house of the Lord of hosts.

The available material is too scanty to give us a complete picture of the religious life of the Jews in earlier times. In many vital matters we must be satisfied with conjecture. We have, therefore, dwelt mainly on the central factors, and have endeavored, along general lines at least, to mark the path that led from the origin of the Yahweh faith to the complete formation of so-called Judaism—the religion of the Pharisees and of the men of the Talmud. (It remains to be observed that a number of subjects relating to our theme have been treated separately in this volume in the articles: *The History of the Jews in Ancient Times; History of Jewish Religious Thought; Jewish Mysticism and Kabbala; Messianic Movements*).

I. RISE OF YAHWISM

1. THE BIBLICAL TRADITION

The Biblical authors were aware that the Jewish religious belief, as it found expression in the Law of Moses, had a long history behind it. The first chapters of Genesis tell of tremendous moral and religious degeneration in prehistoric times. Beginning with the expulsion of the first man from Paradise, a deep chasm is formed between the Creator and His creatures, God's name is never invoked on earth, and humanity sinks deeper and deeper into sin. With God's revelation to Abraham a new period opens in world history. The forefather of the people of Israel is the first to be called prophet (Genesis xx,7), and wherever Abraham went he called on God's name. But to the patriarchs—Abraham, Isaac and Jacob —God revealed Himself only with His name of *El Shaddai* (according to another version, with the name of *Elohim*). "But by My name *Yahweh* I made Me not known to them." Not until the time of the Exodus did God make Himself known to Moses and the entire people of Israel by His actual name of Yahweh, and it was at Sinai that Yahweh gave His Torah to the people of Israel and became the God of Israel. The biblical tradition knows of yet another stage, the last stage, when the earth will be filled with knowledge and all people will worship the One God. But this consummation is relegated to the End of Days. In the meantime—according to the authors of the biblical narratives—the evolution of religious life was sealed with the revelation

at Sinai. True, the Jews were often backsliders and forgot God's commands; the Torah and its precepts, however, have remained changeless since Sinai.

This traditional representation of the evolution of religious life is contradicted by a series of historical facts preserved in the Scriptures. The narratives of Samuel and Kings indicate that not only did the people "forget the Torah," by transgressing the commandments given by God to Moses at Sinai, but that such religious heroes as Samuel, David, and Elijah themselves often failed to observe the precepts of the Torah. There can be no doubt that the Law of Moses in its present form was not known even to the later prophets (Amos, Isaiah, Jeremiah, Ezekiel, and others), and it is almost universally accepted that the final redaction of the Pentateuch was not completed until the days of the Second Commonwealth. The Sinaitic events do not, at any rate, form the end, but the beginning, of the religious development in Israel. The main stages of the religious evolution of Israel take place not in the wilderness but in the land of Canaan and are intimately related to general political and socio-economic developments in Israel. Nonetheless, it would be wrong to conclude that the biblical tradition concerning the evolution of the Yahweh faith is, historically, of little value. It has one important central point on which the scholar must dwell. The biblical tradition strongly emphasizes the fact that the name Yahweh was totally unknown to the Israelites in pre-Mosaic times. This means that for the children of Israel the Yahweh faith was something entirely new. This tradition is distinguished by its novel concept of the relationship between God and People. Among ancient peoples it was generally believed that the bond between God and People was a natural one. The tribal god is often considered the ancestor of his people, and is from of old bound up with his devotees. But in the Bible emphasis is placed on the fact that the acceptance of the Yahweh belief was a *voluntary* act on the part of the Israelites. Not until a solemn treaty, a Covenant *(Berit),* had been made, did Yahweh become the God of Israel. The history of the children of Israel as a nation thus begins, according to the biblical tradition, with a religious revolution, with the adoption of a new faith.

Almost all scholars are agreed that in this tradition, precisely because it stands in contrast with generally accepted religious concepts, there must be a historic kernel. Yahwism must have been a new form of religious belief among the Israelites, and the introduction of the Yahweh worship had evidently brought about a profound change in the life of the people and had, therefore, left such a powerful impress upon its memory. What could prevail upon the children of Israel in those ancient times to accept a new God, and what strange gods did the Hebrews worship in pre-Yahwistic times?

2. RELIGIOUS LIFE AMONG THE HEBREW TRIBES IN THE PRE-MOSAIC PERIOD

We have scant information concerning the beliefs and religious customs of the Hebrew tribes in the time of the patriarchs. All attempts to reconstruct a picture of the religious life of the ancient Hebrews are at best no more than conjectures. Scholars must rely mainly on the considerable material archaeology has unearthed and on the remnants of primitive beliefs and customs preserved in the biblical literature. Arabic folklore also throws some light on the subject. A critical examination of these materials permits us to say with certainty that the theory concerning an old Semitic monotheism, as was accepted by some scholars, is without foundation.

The assumption of the existence of an early Semitic monotheism is moreover clearly disproved by the biblical tradition itself. "Your fathers dwelt on the other side of the flood in old time," the Israelites are told, " . . . and they served other gods" (Joshua xxiv, 2).

The newest archaeological discoveries also offer a better idea of the religion of the Canaanites, the people who lived in Palestine before the Israelites came there. The Canaanites already had a highly elaborate religious ritual and a well-developed mythological system. At the head of the Canaanite pantheon was the god El, but the central figure in the religion of the Canaanites was Baal. The fertility cult was represented mostly by the goddesses Anath and Astarte. Among the Hebrew tribes, however, the fertility cult did not occupy a special place. The word *El,* which probably meant "the strong one," is also used in Hebrew to designate God. The plural form, *Elohim,* is often used in the Bible to indicate the One God. In the older sections of the Bible God is frequently designated by various names: El-elyon, El-shaddai, El-olam, etc. The present state of our knowledge about the pre-Mosaic period does not permit us to assert with certainty whether these names indicate separate gods, or are alternative names for the god El. It is, however, unlikely that such terms as "The God of the Fathers," or "The God of Abraham," reflect the religious ideas of the patriarchal times, as some scholars assume.

Traces of old god-names persisted in some personal names, as, for example, Gad—the god of good omen, and in a number of Palestinian place names: Nebo, Ashtaroth-karnaim, Baal-gad, Beth-shemesh, and others. In addition, various Semitic deities appear in biblical and post-biblical literature as angels or demons.

There is evidence that the moon cult was known among the ancient Hebrew tribes. The first day of the new moon (Hodesh) was observed as a holiday. It is also probable that the day of the full moon, the fifteenth day of the month, was celebrated in ancient times. This conjecture is supported by the fact that the festivals of the Passover and Tabernacles begin on the fifteenth day of the month. Traces of a sun myth can be discerned in the hero legends of Samson, as well as in the legend of the fiery chariot in which Elijah ascended to Heaven.

The belief in spirits and demons was apparently widespread. To this category belong the "seirim," satyrs (spirits in the form of a he-goat). Traces of the earliest forms of Semitic beliefs and ritual are preserved in many Passover rites. The night of the Passover is called a Night of Watching (a night of vigil against evil spirits). The celebration used to take place not in the sanctuary but in the home, behind closed doors —"And none of you shall go out of the door of his house until the morning." As a charm against the destroyer who was supposed to go about during the night of Passover seeking his victims, the blood of the paschal lamb would be sprinkled on the doorposts. The sacred dance, too, occupied a very important place in the religious ritual (hence the designation "Hag"—circle, dancing in a circle—for the feast days). Other characteristics of the old Semitic religion include the practice of magic and the belief in sacred numbers. These beliefs and practices did not entirely disappear even in later times.

As among the other Semitic peoples, the entire social life of the Hebrews was bound up with the religious cult. Family life, the organization of the tribes and clans, the institution of blood revenge, the right of inheritance, and other social customs and institutions, were regulated by religious injunctions and prohibitions.

There is only meager information concerning social and economic conditions among the Hebrew tribes in the period of the patriarchs. From a series of passages in the Bible it is evident that at least a portion of the Hebrew tribes had already inhabited Canaan before the time of Moses. Other Hebrew tribes lived as shepherds in the region of the wilderness of the Negeb and of the Sinai Peninsula. We also find Hebrews in Egypt, where, according to tradition, they labored "with rigor" for Pharaoh.

3. THEORIES ON THE RISE OF YAHWISM

In the narratives of the Pentateuch the Hebrews who sojourned in Egypt occupy the central position. At Sinai Yahweh appears to Moses and bids him free his brethren from Egyptian bondage. When Moses has fulfilled his mission, the entire people of Israel gathers at Sinai, the holy mount, and concludes a covenant (Berit), pledging itself to worship Yahweh and to observe all of His commandments. Moses thus appears in the biblical tradition simultaneously as the redeemer of the people and the founder of the new faith. In the opinion of most scholars we have here the historic kernel of the entire Moses tradition. In the name of Yahweh Moses frees the children of Israel from Egypt, and creates the holy Commonwealth of the Hebrew tribes under the protection of the Deity of Sinai. "Yahweh, the God of Israel; Israel, the people of Yahweh" —with these words does Wellhausen describe the achievement of Moses.

It is not, however, altogether clear how a foreign, hitherto unknown god could, in the imagination of the people, become its savior and redeemer; nor what could prevail upon Moses, and upon the children of Israel, to accept the new religion. Wellhausen's hypothesis, for that matter, does not give us an answer to the question: What was inherent in the achievement of Moses which made possible the further development of the original Yahwism into ethical monotheism? The children of Israel were not the only people in Antiquity to have a national god. Wherein did Yahweh differ from Chemosh, the god of Moab? Why did not the deity of other peoples attain to the position of a universal God?

Rudolf Kittel, one of the most eminent Bible scholars of the past generation, emphasizes correctly that Wellhausen's hypothesis tells us very little about the achievement of Moses. The great significance of the Sinai events lay, according to Kittel, not merely in the acceptance of a new god, but in a new manner of religious belief and religious ritual. The Ten Commandments, which Kittel considers the work of Moses, preserve for us the content of the Covenant at Sinai. This assumption, however, is without sufficient foundation. For a number of reasons the Ten Commandments must be considered as a work of a much later period.

Eduard Meyer, the well-known historian of Antiquity, also opposes Wellhausen's thesis. The formula "Yahweh, the God of Israel; Israel, the people of Yahweh," is, in Meyer's opinion, an empty phrase which does not explain anything. If, however, Kittel pays the biblical tradition too great a tribute, Meyer, on the other hand, believes that the biblical Sinai narratives have very little historic value. Meyer, too, does not see in Moses any historic figure, but an ideal representative of the Levites. In the narratives of Sinai and the wilderness there are reflected not historic events, but the religious way of life of the tribes of the South (mainly Judah) and their neighbors. Here, in the South, the wilderness was no subject for historic speculation, but a living reality. Yahweh, the God of Sinai, was the God of the tribes of the South and, in the conflict between Yahwism and the Baal cult, which raged in the 9th century B.C.E., the clash of the religious culture of the tribes of the South with that of the North finds expression. Whereas the South was closer to the desert and the pastoral life, the North was dominated by the agricultural economy and the Baal cult which was bound up with it. The sharp social conflicts within the kingdom of Northern Israel, however, created there, too, suitable conditions for the romanticism of the desert; the simplicity of the life of the wilderness and its mores found an echo in the masses of the population. Yahwism thus became the ideal of the leaders of the social opposition in Israel.

In the theory of Eduard Meyer there are no doubt very important and valuable elements; it does not, however, supply an answer to the main problem: What has, from the beginning, been the special distinction of Yahwism? And what led to the rise of ethical monotheism in Israel? Aside from that, it is worthwhile to note that the Yahwistic movement had its most significant representatives not in the South, but in Northern Israel, where there lived and worked the prophets Elijah, Elisha, Amos, and Hosea. To what extent the agricultural economy actually dominated the entire life of Israel is evident from the fact that the oldest laws of the Torah and almost all the commandments and festivals are bound up with agriculture. One therefore poses the question: Whence stems this idealization of the wilderness among a peasant people which in the course of centuries had to wage such bitter struggles for its land and soil?

An answer to this question may be found in the parallel versions to the Sinai story still preserved in the Pentateuch. The very fact that we have in the Bible several variants on the history of the rise of Yahwism is most instructive. In this connection it is particularly noteworthy that in two variants the beginning of the Yahweh worship is bound up not with the desert, but precisely with the most important centers of Northern Israel, Shechem and Beth-el.

Particularly instructive as a parallel to the Sinai narrative is the story of the holy covenant at Shechem. After the conquest of Canaan by the children of Israel, we are told in Joshua xxiv, all Israel assembled at Shechem. In a great address which may be considered his political testament, the leader of the people, Joshua, enumerates all the miracles wrought by Yahweh for Israel, and at the close of his speech he turns to the assembled tribes of Israel with these words: "Choose you this day whom ye will serve; whether the gods which your fathers served that were beyond the River, or the gods of the Amorites, in whose land ye dwell, or will ye serve Yahweh?" Joshua warns the people: "Know ye that Yahweh is a severe God, a jealous God." The entire people, however, replies: "Nay, but we will serve only Yahweh!" Thereupon, Joshua declares solemnly: "Ye are witnesses against yourselves that ye have chosen you Yahweh to serve Him." And now Joshua turns to the people: "Now therefore put away the strange gods which are among you . . ." The people then repeats: "Yahweh our God will we serve, and unto His voice will we hearken." The Book of Joshua further tells us:

> So Joshua made a covenant with the people that day, and set them a statute and an ordinance in Shechem. And Joshua wrote these words in the book of the law of God: and he took a great stone, and set it up

there under the oak that was by the sanctuary of Yahweh.

The well-known Hebrew writer, Micah Joseph Berdyczewski (Bin Gorion), in an interesting and valuable work which appeared in German under the title *Sinai und Garizim*, points to the extraordinary importance of this biblical account. Joshua here plays the role of Moses; he gives laws to the children of Israel, introduces the Yahweh cult through a solemn ceremony of the covenant, and records it all in the book of the law of Yahweh. We thus have in the biblical tradition a Moses-Sinai version and a parallel Joshua-Shechem version. A trace of this Joshua tradition has also been preserved in Deuteronomy xxvii, where the people are commanded after the crossing of the Jordan to inscribe the law upon stone and to perform a solemn ceremony with the participation of the twelve tribes on Mount Ebal and Mount Gerizim at Shechem.

At first sight it may appear that the two versions are contradictory, and this is, in fact, the opinion of Berdyczewski, as of some other scholars who believe that the Shechem narrative represents the tradition of the northern tribes in contrast to the tradition of the southern tribes (Judah) which was bound up with Moses and Sinai. It must, however, be observed that we have in the Pentateuch several other accounts dealing with the rise of Yahwism. It would, therefore, be more accurate to acquaint ourselves also with the other biblical traditions on the rise of the Yahweh worship, in order to obtain as complete a picture as possible of the social factors and religious elements at work in ancient Yahwism.

4. THE SOCIAL ROOTS OF YAHWISM

It is necessary at the very outset to refer to the Jacob-Beth-el narrative. When Jacob escaped from his brother, Esau, we are told, God appeared to him on the way in a dream, promising him to be with him and to protect him. Jacob then vowed a vow: "If Yahweh will be with me, and will keep me in this way that I go, and will give me bread

to eat and raiment to put on, so that I come back to my father's house in peace, then shall Yahweh be my God." These last words deserve the closest attention. Until now, accordingly, Yahweh has not been the God of Jacob. Even now Jacob pledges himself to worship Yahweh on condition that God fulfill His promise, protect him on the way and bring him home in peace. Somewhat further, in Genesis, it is indeed related how Jacob fulfilled his vow after having returned in peace to Canaan:

> Then Jacob said unto his household, and to all that were with him: Put away the strange gods that are among you, and purify yourselves, and change your garments: and let us arise, and go up to Beth-el, and I will make there an altar unto God, who answered me in the day of my distress, and was with me in the way which I went.

Yahweh having fulfilled his promise, Jacob redeems his pledge, causes the strange gods to be put away, and builds an altar unto Yahweh. Not until now is Yahweh the God of Jacob.

This Jacob narrative gives us the clue to the whole complex problem of the older Yahwism. The home, the family, the tribe, are the natural forms of social organization in ancient times. Here the individual finds protection and succor in times of need. The principle of blood revenge, the duty of help and solidarity toward the family brother, dominate the old society. Outside the pale of the family the individual is a stranger without protection; the gods, too, and the entire religious cult, are organically bound up with these primitive social organizations. In relation to this situation, Yahweh manifests Himself, not as the god of an ethnic group, of a people or tribe, but as the protecting deity of those who are compelled to leave their home and folk. The Yahweh devotees are thus recruited not according to their family or folk-affiliation, but according to their social lot.

We are led another step forward by the narrative of Ishmael, and particularly by the Cain story. Ishmael and Cain are names of nomad tribes, and the stories of Genesis seek to tell us why it is that the children of Ishmael and Cain led the life of wanderers in the desert. The answer of the biblical narrators is extraordinarily instructive: the forefathers of these nomad tribes were forced to leave their civilized habitat and to seek a place of refuge in the wild desert. The father of the children of Ishmael was the son of a rebellious bondwoman cast out by her mistress; the father of the children of the tribe of Cain was a fratricide who was compelled to leave his home. The nomadic life is thus here considered not as a natural, normal phenomenon, but as a result of social conflicts. True, this explanation does not accord with the opinion of a large number of modern scholars who consider the desert life an older cultural period preceding the peasant life. It would, however, be erroneous to consider these remarkable biblical conceptions concerning the beginning of the nomadic life as merely literary constructions. There is every reason to believe that the biblical authors drew upon reality, and the desert has in actuality, as we know it from the Bible and also from examples of modern times, often served as a place of refuge for elements which have, either voluntarily or under compulsion, withdrawn from civilized lands. All kinds of ill-used men, political and social malcontents, and revolutionary elements, were wont to go off into the desert, where the arm of the hated ruler could not reach them. "This is still the land of disoriented groups and of individual fugitives, where organized semi-nomadic Arab tribes alternate with the flotsam and jetsam of sedentary society, with runaway slaves, bandits and their descendants" (W. F. Albright). Incidentally, it is important to note that also the Habiru of the cuneiform texts were not nomads in the actual sense, but must rather be considered as groups of socially dependent and declassed persons (mercenaries, day laborers, etc.). Particularly noteworthy, however, is the fact that it was precisely the children of Cain and probably also the children of Ishmael who were the first Yahweh worshippers.

The Cain narrative is deserving of the closest scrutiny. In our present text Cain appears as a murderer whom God has placed under a curse and banished from the fertile soil (Adamah); the Cain sign must brand him, according to the accepted notion, as a murderer. One of the most eminent biblical scholars of the last century, Bernhard Stade, has shown, on the other hand, that in the present biblical text there are preserved traces of an older version, in which Cain appeared in an altogether different light. Yahweh revealed himself to Cain not with the intent of punishing him, but rather in order to protect him. The sign of Cain was not one of shame, but, on the contrary, one of protection, given him by Yahweh "lest anyone finding him should smite him." The Kenites thus bore a Yahweh sign, and, as Stade has quite correctly observed, this fact could have only one meaning, namely, that the Kenites considered themselves devotees of Yahweh. Religious signs were a widespread phenomenon in Antiquity, and were also known among Jews. Thus we read, for example, in Isaiah: "This one will write (with) his hand [make a sign] unto God." The Kenites lived in the wilderness, in the vicinity of Sinai, and maintained the friendliest relations with Israel. The Kenite Hobab or Jethro was even, according to tradition, the father-in-law of Moses, and, on his first contact with Israel, brought sacrifices to Yahweh.

Also to Ishmael's mother, Yahweh reveals Himself (according to the present text it was the angel of Yahweh) in the wilderness as a guardian, and for that reason she names her child Ishmael, "because God hath heard my affliction."

The Moses narrative is parallel to the Cain story. Moses escaped to the desert because he had slain an Egyptian. At Sinai, in the region of the Kenites, God appeared to him, and revealed His name to him. The original character of Yahweh appears here in clear outline. The sanctuary of Yahweh at Sinai—and possibly also other sanctuaries of Yahweh—was a place of refuge which afforded protection to runaway slaves, social outcasts, and even criminals (Cain and Moses were murderers). Here the fugitives became the "servants" of Yahweh, and received the Yahweh sign of protection. For that reason, too, the children of Israel had come to Sinai after escaping from Egypt, and accepted there the faith of Yahweh. The servants of Yahweh were not satisfied, however, merely with giving protection to those who had come into the sanctuary, but looked upon themselves as the appointed guardians of all the oppressed, and in particular of strangers. Yahweh is the God of all those who are without the bond of family and tribe. Yahweh sends His messenger to free the Israelites from Egypt, and it is in the name of Yahweh that the Israelite tribes in Canaan wage their wars of liberation against the oppressors.

In the story of the Exodus the redemption theme plays, as we have seen, a central role. Yahweh delivers the Israelites from bondage in Egypt and thus the Israelites become God's people. This idea of salvation and redemption occupies an extremely important place in the later biblical and post-biblical literature and is also encountered as the basic theme in early Christian literature. Adolf Deissmann, one of the most prominent New Testament scholars, in his volume *Light From the Near East*, shows how strongly the Christian idea of salvation was influenced by the popular customs of the Hellenistic times. The concept of the divine redeemer, who delivered man from sin and from servitude to evil, was illustrated by examples from daily life:

Among the various ways in which the manumission of a slave could take place by ancient law we find the solemn rite of fictitious purchase of the slave by some divinity. The owner comes with the slave to the temple, sells him there to the god and receives the purchase money from the temple treasury, the slave having previously paid it in there out of his savings. The slave is now the property of the god; not, however, a slave of the temple, but a protégé of the god. Against all the world, especially his former master, he is a completely free man.

The custom of freeing slaves or ransoming prisoners through payment of money in the temple was known in the Semitic world as early as 2000 B.C.E. In the Code of Hammurabi we find the following provisions for the freeing of captured soldiers or officials:

If a merchant ransom either an officer or a constable who has been captured on an errand of the King, and enable him to reach his city; if there be sufficient ransom in his house, he shall ransom himself; if there be not sufficient ransom in his house, in the temple of his city he shall be ransomed; if there be not sufficient ransom in the temple of his city, the palace shall ransom him.

We know also from Talmudic literature that the ransoming of a prisoner was one of the most important duties of the Jewish communities. All the resources of the treasury had to be utilized, if necessary, for such purposes, even the money collected for the building of a synagogue. In many synagogues there were special funds for the ransom of captives. There is every reason to assume that in pre-Exilic Israel the altar served as a place of refuge where runaway slaves could find safety from the abuses of their masters. This right of sanctuary is specifically stated in Deuteronomy xxiii,15: "Thou shalt not deliver unto his master the servant which is escaped from his master unto thee."

Further light on the question is supplied by the report of the Greek historian, Herodotus (5th century B.C.E.), concerning a temple in Egypt in which runaway slaves would find sanctuary:

Now there was on the coast, and still is, a temple of Heracles; where if a servant of any man take refuge and be branded with certain sacred marks in token that he delivers himself to the god, such a one may not be touched.

The Yahweh sanctuaries in ancient times were also places of refuge for the homeless, the persecuted, and the wanderer. The great antiquity of this custom is indicated by the text of Genesis xxviii, which recounts how the fleeing Jacob rested the night at the place that later became a Yahweh sanctuary. The account is undoubtedly intended to explain the custom of giving lodging to strangers in the sanctuary of Beth-el, by reference to precedent established by the patriarch Jacob. As we have seen, however, the Beth-el narrative has an additional purpose — as an expression of thankfulness to Yahweh, Jacob becomes a worshipper of the God. In the same way the Israelites, as an expression of thankfulness for their deliverance from slavery in Egypt, became the servants of Yahweh. According to this concept the Israelite should not be enslaved to other men; in the event that, out of need, he did sell himself into servitude he was to be redeemed or freed after a specified term: "For unto me the children of Israel are servants whom I brought forth out of the land of Egypt."

In the story of the Exodus the Yahweh festival plays an important part. The first demand which Moses presented to Pharaoh was that he permit the Hebrew laborers to celebrate the holiday of Yahweh in the desert:

> And afterward Moses and Aaron went in, and told Pharaoh, Thus saith the Lord God of Israel, Let my people go, that they may hold a feast unto me in the wilderness.

It is quite likely that there is a historical kernel in this tradition and that even in the most remote times the Yahweh festival had a specific social function. It had the character of a "freedom" holiday for the laborers and slaves, as is found among other peoples. During the Roman Saturnalia, for example, the slaves were freed from their labors, feasting with their masters and even being served by them.

The institutions of the Sabbath as a day of rest for all who labored and the holy Jubilee year when all bonded slaves returned to their home and their families, were probably a further development of the Yahweh festival.

It is very likely that the festival was celebrated by the Israelite tribes in the south in the spring of the year (Passover). The tribes in the north probably celebrated it in the autumn (Succot). One of the high spots of the Yahweh holiday was the dramatic enactment of the events of the Exodus from Egypt and of the Sinai Covenant. The celebration of the Feast of Tabernacles assumed, in specific cases, the character of a renewal of the Sinai Covenant. The assembled people—"all the tribes of Israel"—would pledge themselves anew to abide by the commandments which God had handed down to Moses. Such a solemn gathering was to be held every seventh year:

> And Moses commanded them, saying, At the end of every seven years, in the solemnity of the year of release, in the feast of Tabernacles.
>
> When all Israel is come to appear before the Lord thy God in the place which he shall choose, thou shalt read this law before all Israel in their hearing.
>
> Gather the people together, men, and women, and children, and thy stranger that is within thy gates, that they may hear, and that they may learn, and fear the Lord your God, and observe to do all the words of this law:
>
> And that their children which have not known any thing, may hear, and learn to fear the Lord your God, as long as ye live in the land whither ye go over Jordan to possess it (Deuteronomy xxxi).

But these solemn assemblies had much more than a religious significance. The Assembly of the People of Israel, or the gathering of the Twelve Tribes, was at the same time the highest political and legislative authority in Israel, and in this respect can be compared to the Athenian *Ecclesia*.

To summarize: In the traditions of Sinai and the wilderness there were preserved not only motifs of the religious way of life, but also historic events. Precisely in moments of profound social and national crises did Yahwism find a particularly appropriate opportunity to become effective and win adherents. Yahweh could be accepted in various ways: individually through a vow (Jacob in Beth-el), or collectively through a solemn ceremony of covenant.

5.   THE SOCIAL AND NATIONAL FUNCTIONS
OF YAHWISM

From the outset Yahwism contained the elements of a universal faith. At the same time Yahweh was concerned with the fate of the individual living apart from his clan and native community. As the God of social justice and the protector of the weak, Yahweh was, by His very nature, distinguished from other gods by His ethical character and His social functions. This ethical character of early Yahwism was further strengthened by the fact that Yahweh-worship was not a matter of tradition but of free choice, of a popular covenant or an individual vow. The Yahweh devotees must therefore have looked upon themselves as particularly obligated to observe the commandments of their God, which they had voluntarily taken upon themselves. At all rites of the covenant this element of free consent was thus emphasized.

Especially important was the fact that Yahweh, through a series of such rites, had become the God of Israel, *i.e.*, the guardian of the union of the twelve tribes or the Commonwealth of Israel. Thereby Yahweh had, on a higher plane, become again a national God. The Yahweh cult was, however, not bound up with a dynasty, or with any local sanctuaries in Palestine. Yahweh was first of all the guarantor of the rights of the people and the guardian of national unity. Elijah took twelve stones—corresponding to the number of the tribes of Israel—in order to build an altar to Yahweh on Mount Carmel. At Mount Sinai, when the entire people of Israel had pledged itself to observe Yahweh's commandments, Moses erected twelve stones representing the twelve tribes. The idea that national unity was realizable not through the royal dynasties, but in the assembly of the twelve tribes under the protection of Yahweh, received fullest expression in the introduction to the blessings of Moses: "And there was a King [Yahweh] in Jeshurun (Israel), when the heads of the people were gathered, all the tribes of Israel together." The gathering of the people was for that reason often designated by the name of Congregation of Yahweh *(Kehal Yahweh)*. This political function of the

Yahweh cult had an especially important historic significance and in a large measure protected the democratic institutions and democratic traditions in Israel against the absolutist aspirations of the kings.

6. PRIESTS AND LEVITES

To complete the picture of the old Yahwism it is still necessary to give a brief characterization of the cult personnel, the "servants of Yahweh." Besides Moses, his brother Aaron is also often mentioned in the biblical narratives and is designated as the forefather of the priests. We know that in the time of the Second Temple the "servants of Yahweh" were divided into a higher cult personnel, the Priests, and into a lower, the Levites. In the pre-Exilic period the situation had been entirely different. The priests were not considered—at any rate, in the strictly Yahwistic circles—as loyal servants of Yahweh. It was Aaron, the forefather of the priests, who made the golden calf and led the people towards idol worship. When Moses said: "Whoso is on Yahweh's side, let him come unto me," all the Levites joined him ("And all the sons of Levi gathered themselves together unto him"). That in the older time the Levites were looked upon as the only true servants of Yahweh is also evident from other biblical passages. But in contrast to the Priests, whose office was hereditary, the Levites had become servants of Yahweh in an entirely different manner. It is generally assumed that the Levites had once constituted a secular tribe. We do not find in the Bible, however, any explicit reference to such a secular tribe as Levi. The oldest information concerning the Levites is found in the blessings of Moses and Jacob. In the blessings of Moses Levi is characterized in these words: "Who said of his father, and of his mother: I have not seen them; neither did he acknowledge his brethren, nor knew he his own children; for they have observed Thy word, and keep Thy covenant."

In Jacob's blessings the Levites are designated as a group which is "divided in Jacob and scattered in Israel" (Genesis xlix,7). It is thus typical of the Levites—and this fits perfectly into the entire character of the older Yahwism—that they sever all connections with their family, deny father and mother, brothers and children, in order wholeheartedly to serve Yahweh. The Levites do not form a tribe; on the contrary, they live as strangers outside the pale of every tribal or family organization. In the Book of Judges, too, a man of the tribe of Judah is expressly designated as a Levite: "And there was a young man out of Bethlehem-Judah of the family of Judah, who was a Levite, and he sojourned there." One thus became a Levite, not by heredity, but by choice, renouncing his family and joining Yahweh. There were also cases of parents dedicating a child to God. Samuel's mother, we are told, made a vow that the child which God would grant her should belong to Yahweh. Hence the Levites are also designated by the name of *Netunim* (wholly given). In one place we also find the expression *Shaul* ("ve-hu shaul le-Yahweh"—"he is lent to Yahweh"). Close to the Levites were the Nazirites *(Nezire Yahweh),* the faithful servants and champions of Yahweh. One became a Nazirite in the same manner as one became a Levite, *i.e.,* through a vow of the parents or by a personal vow. There were Nazirites for life and Nazirites for a fixed term.

In pre-Exilic Israel the Levites, Shaulites, and Nazirites played a role similar to that of the Christian monastic orders in the Middle Ages. They often—even demonstratively—separated themselves from the dominant official cult personnel of the large sanctuaries, and, with the utmost devotion, preserved and fostered the old Yahwistic traditions. In the Levites we also have the intellectual cadres which created the Yahwistic "ideology" and prepared the soil for the activity of the Prophets.

7. YAHWISM AND FOREIGN INFLUENCES

The beginning of the Yahweh faith in Israel coincides with the Exodus; it was therefore natural that various attempts should be made to find the source of Yahwism in the secret wisdom of the Egyptian priests. To be sure, Moses—according to Exodus—was reared in the royal court, and had an Egyptian upbringing. This Egyptian influence was stressed by Freud in his work on Jewish monotheism, published shortly before his death—*Der Mann Moses und die Monotheistische Religion* (1939). Together with other scholars, Freud emphasizes the fact that precisely in the 14th century B.C.E. a radical monotheistic reform was effected in the land of the Nile. King Amenhotep IV, or, as he was later called, Akhenaton, had abolished the cults of all the gods throughout the entire land of Egypt, and declared the sun-god, Aton, the only god to be served. We may conjecture therefrom, in the opinion of some scholars, that the monotheism of Moses had its roots in the Akhenaton reform and in the priestly circles where these new revolutionary ideas arose. Jewish monotheism, however, was not the beginning, but, as we shall see, the result of a long spiritual development that required centuries: it was the mature fruition of age-old struggles for a more exalted religious life. The Akhenaton reform was no more than an episode, the effect of which was entirely obliterated after the death of the royal reformer. With Moses, on the other hand, there begins a development which suffered no break in the course of centuries. Moses would undoubtedly have met with little success had it occurred to him to bring to his brethren, groaning under the yoke of Pharaoh's "rigorous labor," a new religious doctrine based on the speculations of Egyptian priests. No connection whatsoever can be established between the monotheism of Akhenaton and Yahwism in its older form. Akhenaton's reforms were completely devoid of socio-ethical content, whereas it was precisely this element that, as we have seen, played a dominant role in the rise of the Mosaic religion. In Yahwism there lived and worked dynamic forces of an altogether different quality, and it was that which gave the Jewish faith, as we shall see, its world-historic significance. Certainly there had penetrated into the Jewish religion, and into the religious ritual, Egyptian, Babylonian, Canaanite, and other influences. That is altogether natural; and it is a strange fact, and one which testifies to the spiritual independence of Israel in the biblical period, that so few traces of foreign influence in the Jewish religion can be established.

II. RELIGIOUS LIFE IN ISRAEL IN THE TIME OF THE JUDGES AND KINGS

1. FOLK RELIGION

It is necessary to observe that this outline of the original Yahwism indicates only the highest peaks of religious life in Israel in olden times. We have intentionally relegated to the background the very important lowest levels of the religious practice, in order to bring out more prominently those characteristic traits which had already, in the oldest time, distinguished the Yahweh faith and endowed it with such extraordinary dynamics. However, a strongly idealized and one-sided picture is obtained precisely for that reason. We have seen only the holy of holies. It is now necessary to delve deeper, and become acquainted with those forms of religious life and experience in Israel which were more prevalent, and in a large measure also typical of the other Semitic peoples.

Strict monotheism was definitely not among the principles of original Yahwism. Traces of an earlier stage in which even the loyal Yahweh worshipper did not deny the existence of other deities are preserved in biblical literature. Just as Yahweh is the God of Israel, Chemosh is the God of Moab (Judges xi, 24). When Laban makes a covenant with Jacob, the gods of both are invoked as guarantors and witnesses: "The God of Abraham and the God of Nahor... judge betwixt us." Yahweh, however, is not only the God of the people of Israel, but also master of the land of Israel, which is often referred to as the land of Yahweh.

David complains, when he is forced to flee from Saul: "For they have driven me out this day from abiding in the inheritance of Yahweh, saying, Go serve other gods." Even in the comparatively later parts of the Bible Yahweh is referred to as the ruler over all gods (Elohe ha-Elohim; God of gods): "For Yahweh is a great God, and a great King above all gods" (Psalms xcv).

Actually, no one doubts the existence of practical polytheism in Israel. There is reason to assume that, indeed, after the Jews had occupied Palestine, polytheistic tendencies in Israel, under the influence of the older Canaanite population, were considerably strengthened. The cult of Baal was especially widespread, Baal being the chief god of the Canaanites and the symbol of the Canaanite-Phoenician civilization, not only in the oldest time but even in the period of the Kings. The Bible recalls frequently how the people and its leaders became backsliders, forgot Yahweh, and served other gods. In Samaria and Jerusalem there were temples for Baal, for Astarte and other deities. At the entrance to the Temple in Jerusalem there were figures of horses and chariots, consecrated to the sun, which were not removed and destroyed until the reign of Josiah. The books of Judges and Kings are filled with stories of "idol worship." True, the authors of these books consider the worship of "strange" gods treason toward, and backsliding from, the faith of Yahweh. There can, however, be no doubt that this representation is, historically, entirely unjustified. The worship of various gods was an entirely normal phenomenon among the neighbors of Israel and was at least tolerated also in Israel. The struggle against the "strange" gods did not begin until the 9th century B.C.E., in the time of Elijah, and was not successfully completed until after the Babylonian captivity.

As late as the time of the Kings, the belief in all kinds of spirits and apparitions was widespread among the people. It formed not only an element of folklore, but played an important role in the reli-

gious cult. In Jerusalem incense was burned, as late as the time of Hezekiah, to a
bronze serpent *(Nehushtan)* which Moses
was reported to have made as a charm to
ward off the poisonous snakes in the wilderness. The Bible retains other remnants of
the serpent cult. The name *Seraphim* (ser-
pents) serves as a designation for angels;
in the story of the Garden of Eden, too, the
serpent plays the role of a divine being. In
several passages there is mention of sacrifices which the Jews were wont to offer
to demons. In the ritual of the scapegoat
this popular belief was legalized through
Yahwism. Traces of mythological motifs
are clearly evident in many biblical passages. In Genesis, for example, we are told
of the sons of Elohim who cohabited with
the daughters of men and the issue of these
unions were "the mighty men that were
of old, the men of renown." To these
mythological motifs belong, no doubt, the
Cherubim of the Garden of Eden, Levia-
than, and other legendary creatures mentioned in the Bible.

2.   MAGIC AND THE BELIEF IN SPIRITS

As among other Semitic peoples, so also
in Israel, magic and soothsaying occupied
a very important place. Magic ceremonies,
blessings and imprecations, the art of the
interpretation of dreams, and other methods of divining the future, are employed
not only by the common people, but also
in leading circles. The technique of magic
plays a very great role even in the miracles
of the prophets. The authors of the biblical books do not deny entirely the efficacy
of the art of magic. They merely attempt
to prove that the prophets of Yahweh over-
shadow with their art and wisdom the
famed wizards of Egypt. Among the "legal"
methods of divining the future, there were,
first of all, the "inquiring into the Urim"
by the priests, and the "inquiring of the
Lord" by the prophets. Dreams, too, were
among the accepted and recognized devices.
Before the battle of Gilboa Saul attempts
to discern the will of Yahweh, but "Yahweh
answered him not, neither by dreams, nor

by Urim, nor by prophets." When Saul does
not obtain an answer from God, he turns
as a last resort to a woman diviner and implores her to bring up the ghost of Samuel
the Prophet. The art of invoking and ques-
tioning the spirits of the deceased *(Ob* and
Yideoni), however, was strongly opposed
in Yahwistic circles. In Hosea there is mention of a device for divining the future
through a certain technique of "asking
counsel at their stock and seeking declaration from their staff." Very widespread
among the people, as is proved by archaeological finds, were various amulets and
charms; the art of "warding off" diseases
was also widely practiced.

Yet, although the Yahweh faith was by
no means free from the forms of magic
thought, and although the technique of
magic played a very prominent role both in
the wonder-working of the prophets and
in the sacrificial cult of the priests, Yahwism
in principle strongly opposed magic in all
its forms, especially because the wizards
(and witches were even more widely accepted), soothsayers, etc., performed their
miracles not in the name of Yahweh, but
through the mastery of spirits and other
powers. The entire art of magic and soothsaying was thus severely prohibited at a very
early date.

3.   THE CULT OF THE DEAD AND THE IDEAS CONCERNING LIFE AFTER DEATH

The very fact that early Yahwism was
not strictly monotheistic, liberated it in a
large measure from that sphere of beliefs
and ceremonies which we today usually
designate as "superstition." The people did
not renounce it, but associated it with
other divine beings and spirits; it thus had
no relationship to the worship of Yahweh.
The same is true of that important sphere
of religious beliefs and customs which occupied such a central place in the life and
thought of the peoples of the ancient Orient
and primarily of the Egyptians—the cult of
the dead. It has often been remarked that
there is almost no mention anywhere in
the Bible either of the after-life or of the

rites bound up with the cult of the dead. In later times the men of the Talmud, in their polemics with the Sadducees, sought various bases of support in the Torah for the belief in the immortality of the soul and the resurrection of the dead. Some modern scholars have even sought to deduce therefrom that the entire problem of life after death did not interest ancient Israel. This is unquestionably greatly exaggerated. It is true that the cult of the dead did not dominate the religious life in Israel, but it is just as true that the people and even the most rigid adherents of Yahweh believed in a life after death. The story of the witch of Endor who brought up the ghost of Samuel from the grave, is particularly instructive in this detail. The witch designates the spirit of Samuel by the name of Elohim. When Saul asks: "What form is he of?" the witch replies: "An old man cometh up; and he is covered with a robe." Thus one can recognize the ghost of the deceased by his appearance and garb. The departed ones are generally displeased when their rest is disturbed; Samuel complains to Saul: "Why hast thou disquieted me, to bring me up?" Usually it is assumed that the spirit of the deceased is found where his body rests. Mother Rachel weeps from her grave when her children are led away into captivity: "A voice was heard in Ramah, lamentation, and bitter weeping; Rahel weeping for her children, refused to be comforted for her children, because they were not" (Jeremiah xxxi, 15). The rulers and warriors, particularly those who fell in battle, descend into their graves clad in their armor (Ezekiel xxxii, 27). The sepulchers of celebrated personalities are therefore accounted holy places.

It is considered a great misfortune and a divine punishment not to be buried decently ("burial of an ass"); for which reason it is a great merit to inter the deceased "unto his fathers." Relatives also make provision to place in the grave of the departed one whatever he needed when alive. Archaeological discoveries show that the Israelites, too, were accustomed, like other peoples, to provide the deceased with vessels, victuals, and the like. However, we do not find in the Bible any traces of what is usually referred to as ancestor worship. Nowhere in biblical literature are the dead considered powerful, divine beings; on the contrary, they themselves need the care of the living. The dead person must be given "his due," and it is considered of great importance to be interred in a family plot and not among strangers. Jacob and Joseph who died in Egypt ask before their death that their bones be brought back to Canaan.

Many beliefs and customs bound up with the cult of the dead were not acceptable to the adherents of strict Yahwism. The prophets opposed not only necromancy, but also and primarily the sacrifices and offerings to the dead. Yahwism intentionally ignored, and as far as possible fought against, everything that had any relationship to the cult of the dead, because that originally belonged to the sphere of other divine beings. Only in the land of the living may one praise and serve Yahweh: "For the nether-world cannot praise Thee, Death cannot celebrate Thee; they that go down into the pit cannot hope for Thy truth" (Isaiah xxxviii, 18).

Life in Sheol is no more than an existence of shadows. The real existence of the individual after death is assured, according to the Yahwistic tradition, through the children who perpetuate the name of the departed. Should a man die childless and leave a wife, it is the duty of his brother to marry the widow, and the first child who is born of the marriage bears the name of the deceased: "And it shall be, that the first-born that she beareth shall succeed in the name of his brother, that his name be not blotted out of Israel." He who has no children, may assure the memory of his name through a monument or an inscription in the sanctuary, and, above all, through good deeds (Isaiah lvi, 5).

4. IMAGES AND SANCTUARIES

The worship of images, too, was a widespread practice in Israel and Judah. In the principal temples of Beth-el and Dan "golden calves" were worshipped (this was later an expression of derision for the images in the form of a bull, symbol of prowess and fertility among the Western-Semitic peoples). A colorful and, in many details, very informative description of a Yahweh sanctuary in the earlier times is found in Judges XVII-XVIII, in the story of Micah. "The man Micah had a house of God, and he consecrated one of his sons, who became his priest." In the Micah sanctuary there was also a Yahweh image which the mother of Micah had contributed. Later Micah engaged a Levite who performed the functions of a priest. For his services the Levite received his lodging, clothing, and ten silver shekels a year. Micah's house of God was thus a private sanctuary; the Levite worked for a wage, and his master undoubtedly derived an income from the offerings and sacrifices which visitors used to bring. Most interesting is the episode later narrated: the children of Dan in those times had not as yet received "all their inheritance" in Israel, and, seeking a place of settlement, the homeless and embittered children of Dan came upon Micah's sanctuary. The wanderers take away the holy cult objects and haul the priest away with them: "And these went into Micah's house and fetched the carved image, the ephod and the teraphim and the molten image. Then said the priest unto them, what do ye? And they said unto him, Hold thy peace, lay thine hand upon thy mouth and go with us, and be to us a father and a priest; is it better for thee to be a priest unto the house of one man, or that thou be a priest unto a tribe and a family in Israel?" From that time on Micah's image of Yahweh stands in the sanctuary of the tribe of Dan. The robbing and stealing of images of the deities was evidently not a rare phenomenon in ancient Israel. Rachel, too, took her father Laban's teraphim (small household images), when she fled from her home with Jacob.

The most important sanctuaries of Yahweh, as well as the holy places of the Canaanite gods, were found on high places (*bamot*). The high hills and mountains were considered the abodes of the gods. To that category belonged Mount Sinai, Mount Gerizim, the Temple Mount in Jerusalem, and others. Among the most important objects of worship were also the sacred trees near the sanctuaries, as, for example, Elon Moreh at Shechem, Abraham's terebinth in Hebron (the trees of Mamre), the tree in Beer Sheba consecrated to Yahweh El Olam, and others. An altogether legal cult object in ancient times was the Mazzebah (a stone-pillar) found near every sanctuary. The Mazzebah in the sanctuary of Beth-el had been erected, according to an old tradition, by the patriarch Jacob, in the place where Yahweh appeared to him in a dream.

These practices were later considered as pagan customs introduced into Israel under the influence of the Canaanites. Thus the sternly puritanic author of Deuteronomy xii exhorts: "Ye shall utterly destroy all the places wherein the nations which ye shall possess served their gods upon the high mountains, and upon the hills, and under every green tree: And ye shall overthrow their altars, and break their pillars, and burn their groves with fire; and ye shall throw down the graven images of their gods, and destroy the names of them out of that place."

5. THE YAHWEH CULT AND AGRICULTURAL LIFE

The Israelites were an agricultural people, a fact which determined in a decisive manner both the forms of their daily life and their entire religious thought and feeling. True, the Yahweh cult was originally bound up with the desert, but Yahweh was never a god of the wilderness in the actual sense, and His devotees were always recruited, as we have already seen, from the elements that used to come from the more cultivated areas. For that reason Yahwism adapted itself rapidly to the agricultural life of Canaan. Yahweh sends the rain in its season, blesses the soil so that it yields its fruit, and takes care of everything the farmer needs; for Yahweh created man to till the soil. The major Jewish holidays were adapted to the rhythm of agriculture. The Feast of Unleavened Bread (Matzot) is celebrated at the beginning of the harvest, when the farmer brings an offering to God from the first fruits of the soil; the Feast of Weeks (Shabuot) is the festival of the end of the harvest, and Succot, or the Festival of the Ingathering, as it was called in ancient times, is celebrated when the farm year is ended and the fruit is gathered from the vineyards. On the great festivals the people gather in the sanctuaries to "appear before God," and the farmers bring thither their offerings of the harvest and the first fruit of the womb of the herd. The first fruit and tithes were in the earlier times not given to the priests, but were used for sacred meals in the sanctuaries. Feasting and rejoicing before God was the central moment in religious life in ancient Israel. The free-will offerings and the thank-offerings (Todot) were consumed by the donors and invited guests (Keruim); the priests would receive only a small portion of the flesh. To invite guests to the sacrificial meal or generally to open wide the door for the hungry was considered an obligation. A portion of the flesh of the sacrifice was probably even left for the birds and animals. The donor would let it be known ("And offer a sacrifice of thanksgiving with leaven, and proclaim free-will offerings and publish them" Amos iv, 5) that all were invited to come to the sacred repast. An example of such a solemn invitation is contained in Ezekiel xxxix, 17: "Thus saith the Lord Yahweh: Speak unto every feathered fowl and to every beast of the field: Assemble yourselves, and come; gather yourselves on every side to My sacrifice that I do sacrifice for you, even a great sacrifice upon the mountains of Israel, that ye may eat flesh and drink blood." At public or royal celebrations it was the custom to distribute gifts to the entire people. During the great popular feast which King David gave when he brought the ark to Jerusalem, he distributed to all the people "both to men and women, to every one a cake of bread, and a cake made in a pan, and a sweet cake." A trace of these ancient sacred meals is still preserved in the custom to begin the Seder, the festive Passover meal, with these words: "This is the bread of affliction which our fathers ate in Egypt: whoever is hungry come and eat; whoever is in need celebrate Passover with us."

The system of sacrifices described in the so-called Priestly Code gives an unclear and erroneous picture of the actual role of the sacrificial cult in Israel. The Priestly Code concerns itself for the most part with the public cult in the central sanctuary which had primarily a national significance. In the daily life of the individual the sacrifice played an entirely different role, as can be seen from the accounts in the historical books, Judges, Samuel, Kings, and especially in the laws of Deuteronomy, which were intended principally for the common people. Deuteronomy particularly emphasizes the social function of the sacrifices, tithes, etc. In the Holy Days especially the poor and the homeless were to participate in the general rejoicing:

> And thou shalt rejoice before the Lord thy God, thou, and thy son, and thy daughter, and thy manservant, and thy maidservant, and the Levite that is within thy gates, and the stranger, and the fatherless, and the widow, that are among you, in the place which the Lord thy God hath chosen to place his name there.

It is now known that among other peoples, too, the sacrifice served an important social function. The folk customs observed by the Arabs in modern Palestine, as described by S. I. Curtiss in his work *Primitive Semitic Religion Today,* are especially illuminating:

> . . . A young woman belonging to a Moslem family . . . fell ill. A sheep was killed at the door, the flesh was cooked, and it was given to the poor. This is the most meritorious use which could be made of vows.

The author properly points to the relationship between the modern practice and the biblical tradition:

There is an allusion to such a use of vows in feeding the poor in Ps. xxii, 25, 26: "I will fully pay my vows before them that fear him; the miserable shall eat and be satisfied." This language is perfectly clear in the light of customs in the disposition of vows today; the miserably poor often eat of the sacrificial meals, served in connection with vows, and are satisfied.

The sacred meals had a very important social function. They introduced into the grey and hard work-a-day life of the peasant an element of joy bound up with an exalted religious emotion. The festivals were also the occasions at which people would meet, make acquaintances, dance, and enjoy themselves. Partaking of a meal in the sanctuary created a holy bond between God and the faithful; one ate, indeed, at God's table and "beheld" God. With the sacred repast there was also bound up the conception of a *sacra familia,* a holy family. As the brothers and sisters are seated together at the father's table, so in like manner are all those who sit at the holy table of Yahweh one family, brothers and sisters. The making of covenants between individuals or between peoples and tribes was, for that reason, accompanied by a sacrifice and a sacred meal. Thence the biblical expression, a Covenant of Salt.

6. RELIGIO-ETHICAL MOTIFS IN THE LIFE OF THE PEOPLE

The ethical element, as we have seen, occupied from the very beginning an important place in the Yahweh faith. That, however, is merely one aspect of the nature of Yahweh. In many of the earlier biblical narratives we see Yahweh in a more primitive form; here the acts of Yahweh are not always determined by ethical motives, and His anger may be assuaged through the sweet savour (Reah ha-Nihoah) of a sacrifice. Thus David says to Saul: "If it be Yahweh that hath stirred thee up against me, let Him accept an offering." Yahweh Himself at times even urges men to do evil. Yahweh moves David to number the people of Israel (II Samuel xxiv). He hardens the heart of Pharaoh that he may show His

signs, and puts a lying spirit into the mouths of the prophets of Ahab. In the earlier time no conflict with Yahweh's socio-ethical character had yet been noted in these traits of divine caprice. The innocent sufferings of people first become a problem with the prophets. On the other hand, the feeling of collective solidarity and responsibility is strong in the most ancient time. Yahwism, however, introduced into the primitive concepts of collective solidarity a new, ethically ennobled social element. Of primary importance is the institution of the right of asylum. Yahweh intercedes, at times even directly, in behalf of the defenseless and takes revenge for innocently shed blood that "crieth unto Him from the ground." As a consequence, the assembly of Yahweh takes over the function of an avenger with reference to those beyond the pale of the associations of families; it aids impoverished farmers to redeem themselves from debt, and persecutes the murderers of the stranger. In the story of the Concubine of Gibeah (Judges xix, xx) we have an example of how the "Congregation of Yahweh" used to take over the function of an avenger in exceptional cases. In Gibeah of Benjamin a vile deed was wrought, "the like of which had not been heard of in Israel." The concubine of a defenseless Levite was violated:

> Then all the children of Israel went out, and the congregation was gathered together as one man ... unto the Lord in Mizpeh ... and the tribes of Israel sent men through all the tribes of Benjamin, saying, what wickedness is this that is done among you? Now therefore deliver us the men, the children of Belial, that we may put them to death, and put away evil from Israel.

When the Benjamites refuse to carry out this command because it was contrary to the principles of the ancient clan solidarity, the assembled people resolve to start a war against Benjamin. In this story of Gibeah there appear rather prominently the two contrasting tendencies in the social life of ancient Israel: the tribal organizations with their ancient concept of solidarity and their political particularism, and the Assembly of

Yahweh with its religio-national discipline which accepts as a central duty the "putting away of evil from Israel."

There is an important parallel in the fact that the Delphic Amphictyony in Greece adopted similar responsibilities to those of the Yahweh Assembly or the Assembly of the Twelve Tribes of Israel. According to the Greek writer Aeschines the Delphic Amphictyony imposed on its members a series of obligations which had to be carried out in times of peace as well as in times of war:

Our forefathers swore not to destroy any amphictyonic town, nor to cut off the drinking water, neither in war nor in peace, and if any transgress in this regard, to march against him and destroy his town.

We can thus see what an important role these religious-political bodies played in establishing new concepts of justice and moral duty.

This religio-national attitude is inherent also in the origin of the rite of the broken heifer (Deuteronomy xxi). If a man be found slain in the field, and it be not known who had smitten him, it is incumbent upon the city that is nearest to the slain man to bring a sacrifice so as to wipe out the guilt. The elders of the community on that occasion offer the solemn declaration: "Our hands have not shed this blood, neither have our eyes seen it. Forgive Thy people Israel, whom Thou, Yahweh, hast redeemed, and suffer not innocent blood to remain in the midst of Thy people Israel." A deep chasm lies between the ancient institution of blood revenge, that acts only when a crime is committed against one's own members of the family, and the higher sense of duty which asserts that the community bears the moral responsibility for all crimes committed within its environs. How deeply rooted the sense of national responsibility already was in Israel in the ancient period is shown by the conduct of Uriah the Hittite when Joab dispatched him from the field of battle on a mission to Jerusalem. Uriah did not go down to his house, but slept with the rest of the soldiers at the door of the king's house. When David asks him why he did not go down to his house, Uriah answers:

The ark, and Israel, and Judah, abide in booths, and my lord Joab, and the servants of my lord, are encamped in the open fields; shall I then go into my house, to eat and drink, and to lie with my wife? (II Samuel xi, 11).

Yahwism created the organic national unity which by far transcended the bounds of the primitive union of clans and tribes. At the same time this national unity almost never coincided with the political unity in the form of the kingdom. Moreover, even in the time of the Kings the Israelites went to war not for king or country, but "for our people and for our God." The Assembly of Yahweh preserved its independence also in the time of the Kings and became the basis upon which arose the prophetic movement which gave the Jewish faith its world-historic significance.

III THE PROPHETS

1. ECONOMIC AND POLITICAL CHANGES IN ISRAEL AND JUDAH

Yahwism, at least during the period of the Judges and the United Monarchy, had, as we have seen, not completely dominated religious life in Israel. Side by side with Yahweh other gods were worshipped and the cult ritual in the sanctuaries of Yahweh itself was influenced to a large extent by the practices of the older Canaanite Baal cult. Yahwism, however, from its very beginning contained the seeds which were destined, under appropriate conditions, to develop and to produce entirely new forms of religious life. This development was stimulated by the socio-economic changes introduced into the life of Israel and Judah through the establishment of the monarchy and the flowering of an urban and money economy. The first kings successfully concluded the difficult wars which the people had in the course of generations waged against the Canaanites and Philistines. Israel had now become master in the land. An element of social unrest was introduced by the bureaucratic apparatus of the royal administration which was ambitious to occupy more and more the place of both the ancient tribal organizations and of the People's Assembly. In addition the kings aspired to set the tone of religious life. The Temple in Jerusalem was no more than a royal chapel, where the king appointed the priests and often determined even the character of the religious service. An even stronger upheaval was introduced into the life of the people by the changes in the economy, which violently accentuated the social cleavages and upset the foundations of the ancient tribal and clan organizations and the traditional moral concepts of the people. The problems of national independence and political unity no longer occupied the center of political and spiritual life, as had been the case in the time of the Judges and the United Monarchy. That position was now occupied by the problems of internal life and social justice. Even in moments of national peril, which in earlier times strengthened the sense of national unity, there was now a further accentuation of the social tensions.

The socio-economic and political ferment that had gathered in Israel and Judah was still not sufficient in itself to produce a new faith. History is replete with such social conflicts; there is not a land or a people that has not in the course of its history experienced severe social and political crises. A people may fight for economic and political rights; social and economic improvements may be attained by "realistic" means without social "illusions" and without Messianic utopias. Social and political crises prepare the soil and create the appropriate psychological situation for new ideas and new truths. In order for this possibility to become a reality, however, a stimulus from without is in most cases necessary. New ideas are not born in a day; an appropriate atmosphere is needed, a circle of men who occupy themselves with "problems," with illusions and utopias. Max Weber rightly points to the role of such circles of "doctrinaires" at the rise of new

religious movements. As we have already seen, the Levites were the champions of the older Yahwism; their mission was now taken over by the prophets, the doctrinaires of the new monotheistic Yahweh movement.

2. PROPHETS OF SALVATION AND PROPHETS OF DOOM

In the earlier period the prophets, or "seers," as they were then called, occupied themselves mainly with "private practice." People came to the prophet to seek aid and counsel in difficult personal situations as well as in matters relating to the community. The prophet healed the sick, divined the future and revealed things hidden, and he had the power to curse and bless. For his counsels and blessings the prophet received compensation. Prophecy was thus a profession that provided a livelihood. The more prominent prophets occupied themselves mainly with public affairs; they functioned in the royal court and participated in the deliberations of the public institutions of the people. Their fundamental distinction, however, was their service for a clientele on request. They waited for the client and placed themselves at his service. The prophet gave his blessing and uttered his formula for a fee. These functions of the older "seers" evoked no protest; they were accepted as unquestioningly as is the practice of the physician or lawyer of today. A typical example of a "seer" who worked for a fee is given in the story of Balaam, the son of Beor. Out of fear of the people of Israel, it is narrated in the Pentateuch, Balak, king of Moab, sent his messengers to the famed seer, asking him to come to Moab to curse the people of Israel: "For I know that he whom thou blessest is blessed, and he whom thou cursest is cursed; come now, therefore, I pray thee, and curse me the people of Israel. Everything that thou shalt request I shall give thee." In Israel, too, we meet many such prophets "that cry: Peace [bestow a blessing], when their teeth have anything to bite." In contrast to these popular prophets or "false prophets," as they are often called in the Bible, who remained true to the traditions of the old seers and diviners, the disciples of Elijah, the "true prophets," broke entirely with private practice and refused to accept gifts, even when they had occasion to aid with blessing or counsel. Prophecy thus assumed a new social function. The "true prophet" did not wait for his client and did not prophesy at the request of others, but came of his own accord, uncalled, driven by his moral sense, and said what his conscience impelled him to say. He did not speak at the request of human beings, but at the behest of God. Hence the entirely different tone and content of the new prophecy. The private client, who came to the seer or wonder-worker and paid for his visit, did not want to hear a dark prophecy; he waited for words of peace and salvation. The so-called false prophets are for that reason generally prophets of peace and salvation (Jeremiah xxviii). The leaders of the religious and social opposition, that is, the prophets of truth, felt themselves sent by God to reprove the people and its leaders; they therefore constantly foretell catastrophe and doom as God's punishment for the sins of Israel.

The prophets of doom were simultaneously heirs of the ancient Yahwistic tradition and radical reformers of the religious belief of their time. They continued the work of the Levites, of those who forsook their home in order to observe the commandments of Yahweh, introducing, however, a new spirit into the ancient faith of Yahweh. Whereas the Levites were wont to renounce their home, the prophets of the school of Elijah renounce everything that the world could give man, in order to serve Yahweh alone. The prophets had no relationship whatsoever to the official Yahweh cult; they did not share in the offerings and sacrifices brought into the sanctuaries of Yahweh, and even declined to accept gifts from individuals. Absolute material independence, both with reference to worldly rulers and priests as well as to

all matters touching the religious cult, was the sign of the "true prophets."

3. THE PROPHETS AND THE CULTURAL LIFE

In the center of the religious thought of the 9th century B.C.E. stands the question of the value of that which we usually call civilization. Israel had since the time of Solomon come into close contact with the more advanced civilizations of Egypt and Tyre. Commerce flourished, "and silver was as abundant in Jerusalem as stones, and cedars of Lebanon like unto carob trees." The splendor of Samaria in the time of the Omri dynasty was certainly not inferior to the splendor of Jerusalem in the time of Solomon. The new mode of life also carried over to the religious cult. In all the larger centers splendid and costly temples were built, adorned with cult objects of every description and images of gold and silver. A marked Phoenician influence was felt not only in Northern Israel but even in the Temple of Solomon in Jerusalem. This was only one side of the picture. On the other side the negative shadows of cultural life were in evidence: poverty among the masses of the people, oppression of the peasants, social corruption, and, in addition, all the other moral defects and evils which are particularly prominent against the resplendent background of material prosperity possessed only by a small circle of the upper classes.

For the prophets and the groups close to them the answer was clear: Yahweh did not desire all this; the entire evil of the world resulted from the fact that men travelled a false path. The prophetic movement was dominated by violent opposition toward everything related to the higher cultural life and particularly everything connected with wealth and might. One of the leaders of revolutionary Yahwism in Israel during the time of Ahab was the founder of the order of Rechabites, Jonadab, the son of Rechab. The Rechabites drank no wine, built no houses, and were not even allowed to till the soil, but lived in tents like shepherds (Jeremiah xxxv). The Nazirites, too,

faces: and they said, Yahweh, he is the God; Yahweh, he is the God. (I Kings, xviii, 38, 39.)

The prophetic demand to serve Yahweh alone was the result not of philosophical speculation, but of a tremendous revolutionary tension and a religio-ethical fanaticism. The life of the Yahweh zealots was completely permeated by the struggle for their faith. In the history of their people, as in the history of the world, they saw the fulfillment of the will of Yahweh and, for that reason, could not permit any other power to oppose the plans of Yahweh and destroy the moral order of the world. Whether the prophets of the school of Elijah entirely denied the existence of other divine beings cannot be definitely established. It is certain, at any rate, that Yahweh was for them the creator of the world and the only God whom Israel ought to serve.

5. SOCIAL AND RELIGIOUS REFORMS

The activity of Elijah led to political-religious revolutions in Israel (843 B.C.E.) and in Judah (837 B.C.E.), and to the elimination—at least for the time being—of the Baal cult. The socio-economic and religious demands of the prophets are contained in the so-called Book of the Covenant (Exodus xx-xxiv), a collection of laws which were put into effect, as some scholars assume, during these revolutions. The strong puritan tendency which dominated the prophetic movement is clearly shown in the first injunctions of the Book of the Covenant:

> Ye shall not make with me gods of silver, neither shall ye make unto you gods of gold. An altar of earth thou shalt make unto me, and shalt sacrifice thereon thy burnt offerings, and thy peace offerings . . . in all places where I record my name I will come unto thee and bless thee. [The Hebrew text should probably read "tazkir" instead of "azkir" and should be translated—"In all places where thou causest my name to be mentioned."] And if thou wilt make me an altar of stone, thou shalt not build it of hewn stone (Exodus xx, 23-25).

Yahweh does not desire splendid sanctuaries with images of silver and gold; the altar was to be as plain as possible, of simple stones or a little earth. Holy places and temples are actually superfluous, because "in every place where thou causest My name to be mentioned, I will come unto thee and bless thee."

The struggle of the prophets, as we see, was waged not merely against the worship of other gods, but also against the "Canaanite" forms of the Yahweh cult. The sharpest protest was evoked in the prophetic circles by the practice of sacred prostitution which was so widespread in the Western Semitic world, and which we encounter also in Israel and Judah (Kedeshot). Sexual transgressions, according to the narratives of the Pentateuch, caused the destruction of Sodom, the bloody conflict between the sons of Jacob and the men of Shechem, as well as the tragedy of the "concubine of Gibeah." As Max Weber rightly shows, the acutely negative attitude of Yahwism toward bodily nakedness ought to be regarded as a consequence of the prophetic reaction to the practice of sacred prostitution and sexual depravity generally. There is an echo of these almost ascetic moods in Yahwistic groups in the story of Samson and Delilah —a Nazirite, a warrior, must shun women— and, in a milder form, in the story of the Garden of Eden. Eve was to blame for the original sin which was committed by Adam and later caused the human species so much misery and suffering.

The most important social injunctions of the Book of the Covenant are bound up with the Sabbath idea. In the oldest biblical text the Sabbath is almost always mentioned together with the festival of the new moon. Some scholars conjecture that the Sabbath had been originally the day of the full moon, and was celebrated on the fifteenth of the month. No substantial proof of this conjecture has thus far been found. In the Book of the Covenant, the institution of the Sabbath already has a social aspect. Yahweh enjoins rest for the seventh day " . . . that thine ox and thine ass may have rest, and the son of thy handmaid, and the stranger may be refreshed." It is thus a day of rest for the toiler and the beast of burden. A parallel to the seven-day week with the rest-day on the Sabbath is the seven-year cycle which also ends in a Sabbatical year or year of release. In this seventh year the crop of the field may not be harvested, but left fallow for all: "That the poor of thy people may eat thereof, and what they leave the beast of the field shall eat." The injunction concerning the liberation of the slaves also belongs to the cycle of Sabbath laws: "If thou buy a Hebrew servant, six years he shall serve; and in the seventh he shall go out free." Typical of the Sabbath laws is not only the regard for the laborers, but also the concern for the beast of burden, and even for the animals of the field. The ideal order which is supposed to have prevailed during the time of the Garden of Eden is again realized in the Sabbath and in the year of release. All social differences disappear among the people; the right of private property in land is abolished, and even cattle and beasts enjoy the renewal of the world order. Later, in Talmudic literature, the holy Sabbath was seen as a foreshadowing of the Messianic era, and one waited for the time which would be completely Sabbath ("leyom she-kulo Shabbat").

Had the Sabbath been merely a protective law for the benefit of the laborer, it would have remained no more than an historic episode. The proletarian elements, slaves and day laborers, never occupied a position in Jewish life important enough to explain the extraordinary role of the Sabbath. The Sabbath merely as a day of physical relaxation was, at any rate, not indispensable in the lands of the Diaspora, where it often hindered the Jews in their economic activity. The festival of the new moon, for example, which, at least in the earlier biblical period, had been precisely as important a festival as the Sabbath, in time lost all significance whatsoever in Jewish life. The prohibition against interest on loans, an important social protective law, reiterated so many times in the Pentateuch, was in time actually abolished.

That the Sabbath had an altogether different destiny and was, in modified form, even taken over by the Christian and the Islamic world is due to its profoundly religious and emotional content. Not merely the need for physical relaxation, but mainly the need to divest oneself of all worldliness, to free oneself, one day a week, from all material cares and to transport oneself to the ideal atmosphere of Paradise and the End of Days; the need to become a renewed man, to become a Jew with an exalted soul (neshamah yeterah) — it was these yearnings which created the Sabbath, and sustained it throughout history.

6. LITERARY PROPHETS

Prophecy attained its highest peak in the words of the prophets of the 8th to the 6th centuries B.C.E. The fact that beginning with Amos the words of the prophets were spread and preserved in writing is evidence of the commencement of a new period in Jewish history. The words of the earlier prophets, Elijah and Elisha, had not been preserved in written form. Their disciples had left considerable rich biographical and historical material which is, however, entirely anonymous. The time of oral prophecy was now gone. In the Books of Amos, Hosea, and Isaiah, there appear the first literary personalities in Israel, poets and thinkers of an individual style and individual ideological coloration.

The bitter struggle against the oppression of the poor and defenseless, particularly of strangers, orphans, and widows, is one of the main themes in the prophetic writings. The social question had in time become still more aggravated through the growth of the landless and propertyless element (gerim), both in the villages and in the cities. In Israel and Judah there appeared an agrarian question, and along with it there arose ideas and plans which sought to protect the small farmer, and to effect a just redistribution of the soil and a restoration of his ancestors' possessions.

The demands for social justice, the words of reproof against the upper strata of the

that any attempt to convey in form and image the power and grandeur of Yahweh is blasphemy. The Creator of the world cannot be represented through something created by human hands.

9. RELIGIOUS INDIVIDUALISM AND MESSIANIC HOPES

The prophets did not possess any organized power behind them, although their moral influence was extraordinarily great. Some prophets gathered around them groups of disciples; in general, however, they waged their struggle against a world of enemies all alone. Jeremiah complains that he has become "a man of strife and a man of contention to the whole earth. I have not lent, neither have men lent to me; yet every one of them doth curse me." No wonder then that the prophets also became the creators of religious individualism. No more will the old adage hold true, says Jeremiah: "The fathers have eaten sour grapes, and the children's teeth are set on edge." The prophet of the Diaspora, Ezekiel, dwells in greater detail on the problem of personal responsibility and reward. This idea of personal accountability and personal contact with God later led to spiritual conflicts and to a profound revolution in the world of religious ideas in Judaism.

The destiny of the community, and the future of the people of Israel, however, remained the chief preoccupation of the prophets. The words of reproof and the prophecies of doom relate both to the present and to the immediate future; but God's punishment is no more than a transitional stage which is to usher in the new era. The disciples of Elijah and Elisha sought their ideal in the distant past, in the happy period of Paradise. The vision of the literary prophets, on the other hand, addresses itself more to the future, to the time of the End of Days. The prophets had little faith in political reforms; they did not believe that external changes of forms of government were likely to introduce any considerable improvement into the life of the people. A radical change of the social order

would become possible when man would change, when he would acquire a new heart. The task of the prophets is therefore primarily educational; he must teach the people the knowledge of God (*daat Yahweh*), the will and commandments of Yahweh.

At the center of their hopes lies the concept of the Messianic era, with the coming of which God will make a new covenant with the people of Israel. The people will abide by the covenant, because "I will put my law in their inward parts, and write it in their hearts" (Jeremiah xxxi, 33), and its terms will encompass not only Israel, but all living creatures upon earth: "And in that day will I make a covenant for them with the beasts of the field, and with the fowls of heaven, and with the creeping things of the ground; and I will break the bow and the sword and the battle out of the earth" (Hoseah ii, 18). . . . The new covenant will bring eternal peace and the dominion of righteousness upon earth. Classic are the Messianic prophecies of Isaiah; the divinely anointed king of the future will

> . . . with righteousness judge the poor, and reprove with equity for the meek of the earth; and he shall smite the earth with the rod of his mouth, and with the breath of his lips shall he slay the wicked . . . And the wolf shall dwell with the lamb, and the leopard shall lie down with the kid; and the calf and the young lion and the fatling together; and a little child shall lead them. And the cow and the bear shall feed; their young ones shall lie down together; and the lion shall eat straw like the ox (Isaiah xi, 4-8) .

10. THE JOSIAH-REFORM

Under the influence of the prophets a radical reform of the entire social and religious life was effected during the reign of King Josiah (639-609 B.C.E.). The program of this great reform movement is contained, according to the opinion of most biblical scholars, in the Book of Deuteronomy. In addition to a series of enactments intended to benefit the impoverished farmers—such as the prohibition of usury, the law concerning the year of release, etc.—the laws of Deuteronomy are predominantly intended to protect the slave, the Levite (who had no inheritance), the stranger, the orphan, and the widow. The social reforms are governed by a religious motif dominating the entire Book of Deuteronomy: all that Israel possesses—whether it be the individual or the community—he owes, not to his own prowess, but to the blessing of Yahweh. The law-giver insists repeatedly that it was God who had granted the land unto the people and had given it "great and goodly cities, which thou didst not build, and houses full of good things, which thou didst not fill, and cisterns hewn out, which thou didst not hew, vineyards and olive trees, which thou didst not plant" (Deuteronomy vi, 10, 11). The authors of the Book of Deuteronomy know that the complacent life often brings about the forgetting of God, and they therefore warn:

> Beware . . . when thy herds and thy flocks multiply, and thy silver and thy gold is multiplied, and all that thou hast is multiplied; Then thine heart be lifted up, and thou forget the Lord thy God, which brought thee forth out of the land of Egypt, from the house of bondage. . . . And thou say in thine heart; My power and the might of mine hand hath gotten me this wealth. But thou shalt remember the Lord thy God, for it is he that giveth thee power to get wealth (Deuteronomy VIII, 11-18).

The moral lesson which the legislator draws therefrom is: Set aside from Yahweh's bounty a portion for the poor, help your fellow-man when he is in need, and let it not be difficult for you to obey God's commands.

The religious reforms of the Book of Deuteronomy—the strict prohibition of all kinds of images, and the elimination of local sanctuaries—had a far-reaching effect on the development of Jewish history. The account in II Kings xxii, xxiii relates how all the sanctuaries and altars in the provinces and in Jerusalem were destroyed, and how the Temple, "the only chosen place where Yahweh caused his name to rest," was cleansed of all strange cults and images. The centralization of the sacrificial cult had, primarily, a political-national objective. During the time of Josiah a great portion of Northern Israel had been reunited with Judah, and the destruction of the local sanctuaries, the sites of the old tribal particularism, had as its purpose the strengthening of national unity. But the abolition of all the sanctuaries—except the Temple in Jerusalem—would not have been possible had the prophets not prepared the ground for it in advance. From now on the one God had but one Holy Place, and the Yahweh faith cleansed itself not only of the image cult, but also, to a large extent, of the sacrificial cult, for the provincial population had little opportunity to come to Jerusalem. The Josiah reforms thus prepared the ground for the cultivation of new, spiritual forms of religious worship.

IV. THE RELIGIOUS COMMUNITY

1. THE PERIOD OF THE BABYLONIAN CAPTIVITY AND THE SECOND COMMONWEALTH

The downfall of the kingdom of Judah in 586 B.C.E. marks the end of the classic period in the history of the Jewish people and the Jewish faith, and initiates the epic of Jewish life in the Diaspora. People, religion, land, and state, had in the course of centuries formed an organic unity. It is true that the prophets had long since gone beyond, in theory at least, the narrow boundaries of land and state; but it was only within the framework of a free, politically independent commonwealth that they had been able to function. The state had now fallen; the upper classes had been exiled to Babylon; some had voluntarily left Judah; and in the country there had remained only the lowest strata of the peasant population. The Jews had now become not merely a people without a state, but also a people without a country. True, the children of Judah were not the only people in exile. Mass deportation of conquered peoples was a common phenomenon from the time of the Assyrian emperor, Tiglath Pileser III (745-727 B.C.E.); the Jews, however, were the only people to survive exile. That had been no mere accident. Prophetic universalism and the belief in the one God, the master of the universe, played a tremendous role in this outcome. The exiles took along with them the belief that Yahweh would not forsake them in the strange land, but deliver them again from dispersion, even as he had once redeemed their forefathers from Egypt. But that faith had to be given a concrete content, such as forms of a religious cult, which would constantly remind the individual of his ties with the past and with the national community. Therein lay the historic achievement of the colony of exiles in Babylon.

The time of the Babylonian captivity and the Second Commonwealth is by general consent designated as the period of *Judaism*. It is, beyond any doubt, correct to assume that with the Babylonian captivity there begins an altogether new chapter in the history of the Jewish religion; and since Jerusalem and the province of Judah were, during the Second Commonwealth, the center of the life of the people, no essential objection can be raised against the term. However, the word Judasim has, with the majority of non-Jewish scholars, a particular connotation. The conflicts between traditional Jewry and Pauline Christianity, coupled with the bitter attacks on the Pharisees and Scribes in the New Testament, have greatly influenced the opinion of Christian scholars concerning the historic role and value of Judaism. It is customary to contrast the Torah and the so-called religious legalism of the post-Exilic period with the ethical monotheism of the prophets and their opposition to the ancient cult. As has already been shown by several Anglo-American scholars (notably R. Travers Herford and George Foot Moore), scientific research, in its evaluation of Judaism, must not yield blindly to the testimony of biased witnesses, and such, no doubt, were the authors of the ancient Christian writings. The time of the Babylonian captivity and of the Second Commonwealth cannot by any means be designated as a period of spiritual decline. Precisely in this epoch there were created the institutions and forms of a highly spiritualized religious life. Not until the period of the Second Commonwealth did alien cults and images finally disappear in Judah, and the "worship of the heart" (*Abodah she-be-leb*), for which the Prophets had fought so long, become a reality. The religious world of ideas, too, was greatly enriched during the Second Commonwealth. Such important biblical books as Isaiah xl-lxvi, Psalms, Job, and others, were created after the downfall of the kingdom of Judah. Indications of an intense spiritual life at the close of the Second Commonwealth were the rise and development of the various religious parties and sects in Palestine, such as the Sadducees, Pharisees, Essenes, Christians, etc.

2. THE SYNAGOGUE

It is not the temple, but the "little sanctuary," as the synagogue is called by Ezekiel, which is characteristic of the period of the Second Commonwealth. The exiles in Babylon had already been confronted by the question: How can God be worshipped in a foreign land, where no altar may be erected and no sacrifices offered? The only possible answer was: New forms of religious worship must be created, without altars and sacrifices. Everything had been prepared ideologically, as we have already seen, by the prophets and the Josiah reform; and thus there arose in Babylon the Meeting Place (*Bet Moed*), where the service of the Temple was superseded by the reading of the Torah and by prayers.

The prayer houses did not disappear even after the rebuilding of the Temple. On the contrary, they became more and more popular and widespread, not only in the Diaspora, but even in Judah and Jerusalem. The service in the Temple acquired more and more a symbolic-national significance. The sacrifices were offered in behalf of the entire people and expenses were defrayed by the half-shekel poll-tax. The remotest Jewish communities considered it their duty to send the shekel tax annually to Jerusalem. The custom of celebrating the great festivals in the Holy City was also of great national significance. The actual religious life, however, was enacted in the synagogues, where the people used to assemble every Sabbath, and later also on market days, on Mondays and Thursdays. There, in the synagogue, the individual had greater opportunities for religious experience. As is evident from several passages in Josephus and the Talmud, the services in the synagogue often included the partaking of sacred meals. In the decrees of Julius Caesar in behalf of the Jewish communities in the Diaspora, such communal meals are expressly mentioned. The social function of the sacrificial cult thus also passed to the synagogue. In a modified form these sacred meals are preserved in the custom of Kiddush from which, according to the opinion of many scholars, the Christian Eucharist is derived.

The synagogue became in time the center of social life. In the synagogues the Jewish courts (*Bet Din*) were convened; all kinds of meetings and councils were held there; likewise public and, frequently, private celebrations (marriages, circumcisions, etc.). All social welfare activities, the distribution of charity, etc., were also connected with the synagogue. Strangers would often find lodging and food there. Of no lesser importance was the function of the synagogue as an educational institution for adults and youth. On Sabbaths and festivals the Torah was read in public, translated, and interpreted. Particular attention was given to the education of the young. "Almost at the time when they are still in their swaddling clothes," says Philo, "the children are taught by their parents and teachers the laws of the Torah and the customs of the oral tradition."

"We place the greatest emphasis," says Josephus Flavius, "on the training of our children." In another passage the same author says: "It is easier for every one of us to repeat by heart the laws of the Torah than to tell our own names." At the end of the Second Commonwealth a well developed public school system was already functioning "in every province and in every town for children of the ages of six to seven" (Talmud Babli, Baba Batra, 21). The education of children was also, in the main, connected with the synagogue, although there were also many private teachers. In the smaller communities, one and the same person would often perform the functions of teacher, beadle, and precentor.

It is hardly possible for us today to evaluate the colossal revolutionary effect which the synagogue, through the introduction of a popular religious service without sacrifices and priests, had upon Jewish life. And it was no mere accident that the Jewish synagogue became a model for Christian and Islamic houses of worship. The most important quality of the synagogue had been, from the very outset, its thoroughly democratic character. Every small Jewish community could, with the modest means at its disposal, build a synagogue; in case of need, a religious service could be held in a private home. The synagogue, moreover, did not call for a cult personnel; every Jew could read the Torah and conduct a service. In contrast to the Temple, every humble Jew could enter the synagogue in his secular garments, without specific "consecrations"; and could pour out his heart before his Maker without the aid and mediation of the "servants of the sanctuary" and the "servants of the altar." Whereas the bringing of a sacrifice had not been accessible to all for material reasons, the entry into the synagogue was bound up with no difficulties whatsoever.

The synagogue service and the reading of the Torah were often coupled with discussions of biblical readings, frequently passing over to discussions of contemporary happenings and needs. A learned Jew would interpret the biblical portion to the people and add various Agadic passages. This "discoursing" in the synagogue was entirely unrestricted, and even visiting strangers had the opportunity of participating. As is seen from the New Testament,

Jesus and his disciples would frequently make use of the synagogue pulpit. Gradually, a separate class of scribes and teachers was formed, a class which was responsible for the most significant achievement of the Jewish people during the Second Commonwealth.

3. SCRIBES, LEVITES, AND PRIESTS

The synagogue raised enormously the prestige of the teachers and scribes of the Torah. In contrast to the Temple priests, these synagogue leaders did not belong to any cult personnel, received no fee for their work as teachers of the Torah, and might thus from the point of view of social status, be compared to the prophets. Even during the time of the Mishnah it was not customary to derive a livelihood from teaching the Torah. In the pre-Exilic period the Torah had been vested, particularly so far as questions of ritual were concerned, in the hands of the priests, and it was to them that people would come with religious problems and, at times, also with civil cases. The priests, however, could not, by their very character, adapt themselves to the position of teachers of the Torah; they remained primarily functionaries of the sacrificial cult. In time, the priests began to look upon the synagogues and the teachers of the Torah as their competitors, and thus there arose the conflict between priests and scribes, Sadducees and Pharisees—a schism which continued throughout the entire period of the Second Commonwealth.

There were, moreover, socio-economic conflicts which further widened the chasm between the priestly aristocracy and the class of the scribes. The social status of the priests had, thanks largely to the support of the Persian rulers, risen considerably during the time of the Second Commonwealth. Their material income, too, had increased. Jerusalem was now the only holy city where Jews were allowed to offer sacrifices; and not only from Judah, but from all Jewish communities throughout the world, there streamed in the shekel tax

and free-will offerings for the Temple. The priestly aristocracy associated itself more and more closely with the secular nobility, and there was formed a more or less uniform stratum of secular and secularized men of aristocracy and wealth. Among the step-children of the Temple was the lower cult personnel—the Levites—always living in want. In a Talmudic text, dating from the close of the Second Commonwealth, we encounter various accusations against the aristocratic priestly families: "Woe is me because of the family of Ishmael, the son of Phoebus; woe is me because of their fists, because they are high priests and their children are bursars, and their sons-in-law are overseers, and their slaves beat the people with clubs." A cry of woe rises against another family of high priests: "Open, ye portals of the Temple, and let Johanan, the son of Narbai, enter, he who is the disciple of the pampered ones, and let him stuff his belly with holy flesh" (Talmud Babli, Pesahim, 57).

The history of the Jewish religion in the ancient period is a constant struggle against the official representatives of the religious cult. Thus it was in the time of the Kings, and thus it was also in the period of the Second Commonwealth. The struggle was now waged by the Scribes and the Levites who fell heirs to the spiritual legacy of the ancient Levites and prophets. According to I Chronicles (ii, 55), the scribes derive their origin from the Kenites and Rechabites. The Levites, too, occupied themselves with the interpretation and explanation of the Torah (Nehemiah viii, 9). The Pentateuch still preserves a tradition testifying to the sharp conflict between the Levites and the Priests in the Persian period: the story of the rebellion of Korah and his congregation against Aaron, the High Priest (Numbers xvi, 3). "Ye take too much upon you," cry Korah and his associates, "seeing all the congregation are holy, everyone of them and the Lord is among them; wherefore then lift ye up yourselves above the congregation of the Lord?" As we know from the Book of Chronicles, the sons of

Korah were singers in the Temple. Many psalms are thus ascribed to the "sons of Korah." The resentment of Korah and his associates has a twofold significance: first, it is a protest against the claims of the priests to rule over the people; second—and this is particularly significant—it enjoins the entire people to be as holy as the priests, because all Israel is a holy people and a kingdom of priests.

4. PHARISEES AND SADDUCEES

In the time of the Hasmoneans there appear in Judah two parties, the Pharisees and the Sadducees, which for generations wage a struggle for power and for the spiritual domination of the people. The Sadducees were the party of the secularized priestly aristocracy, whereas the popular party of the Pharisees continued the tradition of the scribes and Levites. Josephus Flavius stresses the great spiritual influence exerted by the Pharisees upon the people. At the same time, the Pharisees are far from being "men of the people," and they even separate themselves from the common peasant, the *Am ha-Arets,* by their strict observance of all the laws of ritual purity. Particularly characteristic of the Pharisees is their observance of the laws concerning the tithe, which even brought them into conflict with the peasant population of Judah and, primarily, of Galilee. In the Mishnah there is a whole tractate *(Demai),* which concerns itself with the question: What is the ruling, when one is not sure whether a certain farmer had paid the tithe? The Pharisees were actually not so much a political party as a religious order with a strong social tendency; its mission was to turn Israel into a holy people. The separation from the folk of the land was not an aim in itself; on the contrary, its purpose was to set before the people a living example of pious conduct. The members of the order of the Pharisees, who took upon themselves the strict observance of the ritual commandments, designated themselves by the name of *Haberim*: during the great festivals, when the people used to gather in Jerusalem, all Jews were, according to a saying in the Talmud, *haberim*—"all Israel are comrades." Such private religious associations, brotherhoods and orders are typical of the entire period of the Second Commonwealth. The religious life was being transferred from the great sanctuary and from the public place to the synagogue, to the religious congregation and association. In the Persian period we meet the associations of the "God-fearing" and the "Haredim" (those who tremble at the word of Yahweh). During the revolt of the Hasmonaeans the order of the Hasidim plays an important role; at the close of the Second Commonwealth the order of the Essenes is active as well as the Christian brotherhood, the disciples of John the Baptist, and others.

This is, we may note, a phenomenon not limited to Judah alone. The conquests of the Assyrian and Babylonian rulers had led to the decline of a large number of national states. Then came the Persian, Greek, and Roman world empires, which obliterated all the ancient boundaries of states and kingdoms. The ancient national deities, too, lost their attachment to a national soil. Religion and state became two distinct worlds, not only for Jews, but for the majority of other peoples as well. Religious syncretism, the blending and merging of all kinds of deities and cults, had thus become a characteristic feature of the Hellenic-Roman period. Added to this was the development of large metropolitan centers with strongly mixed populations, where emigrants of various nations and cults met and mingled. A soil suitable for the rise of all kinds of religious-mystical associations and brotherhoods had thus been created. The ancient world of the gods had been destroyed, and the peoples now sought new forms of belief and life.

And yet the Jewish religious communities in those times were unique in regard to their organizational forms, their ritual, and their religious outlook. The Jews had not only religious ceremonies, but also

to that same time: and at that time thy people shall be delivered, every one that shall be found written in the book. And many of them that sleep in the dust of the earth shall awake, some to everlasting life, and some to shame and everlasting contempt (Daniel xii, 1-2).

The belief in the resurrection was among the most important points of conflict between the Sadducees and the Pharisees. Here, too, social motives had undoubtedly played a great role. True, it cannot be said that the problem of a life after death is without interest for those groups which have no complaint to make against their fate. The cult of the dead in Egypt, which was fostered precisely by the ruling spheres, proves quite the contrary. It is, however, true that the problem assumes an altogether different aspect when it becomes bound up with the idea of making restitution for the injustice and evil prevailing in the world. The Pharisaic belief in the hereafter and in the resurrection had precisely this end in view, and prepared the Jew ideologically for the belief in the advent of the Kingdom of Heaven which would put an end to the domination of evil on earth.

7. UNIVERSALISM

The religion of the Pharisees, too, had not limited itself to the sphere of a national faith. The God of Israel was, indeed, the master of the universe and the father of all mankind. The hopes of the prophets that a time would come when all men would serve one God, "When Yahweh will be one and His name one" (Zechariah xiv, 9), is also found in Talmudic literature. We are dealing here not merely with casual homilies, but with an earnest faith that has also found expression in the liturgy. Thrice daily the Jew implores God to perfect the world under His rule, so that all children of flesh shall call upon His name. The prayer "Now, therefore, impose thine Awe," included in the High Holy Day service, should be specially mentioned here. In this liturgical passage Jews pray "that the entire world form one band to do thy will

with a perfect heart." It is, moreover, also incumbent upon *all* men to observe at least the "Seven Commandments for the descendants of Noah." As among the prophets, we note also among the Pharisees a constant conflict between the national and universal motifs. The Pharisees have recourse to all methods, in order to separate the Jews from the surrounding world; at the same time they conduct an intense religious propaganda within the non-Jewish population, so that a considerable portion of the Jewish communities in the Diaspora come to consist of proselytes. In addition to the many proselytes there were also great numbers of half-converts, who would observe only a part of the Jewish precepts. Flavius writes: "There is not a city or a people, where there had not penetrated our customs of the observance of the Sabbath, the kindling of lights, fasting, and also many of our dietary laws."

Although there was considerable difference of opinion among the Pharisees regarding the practical results of religious propaganda among the non-Jews, they never abandoned the basic belief that the Jewish faith was in substance a faith for all peoples, and that the Torah would eventually be a light and inspiration for the entire world. It is especially significant that both the Greek-educated Philo and the Talmud emphasize the fact that the sacrifices in the Temple were offered not only in the name of the people of Israel but "on behalf of all the human race." Rabbi Johanan, one of the most important of the Talmudic authorities, who lived in Palestine after the downfall of the Jewish state, expressed the significance of the Temple for the non-Jews in the following words: "Woe to the peoples of the world who have suffered loss, but know not what they have lost. For as long as the Temple existed the altar served to atone for their sins; now who will atone for their sins?" This idea of universalism is given similar emphasis in Jewish mysticism concerning the Kingdom of God, which had a particularly strong influence on liturgical poetry. This influence is strikingly illustrated in the following excerpt from the Jewish New Year's services:

> Our God and God of our fathers, reign thou in thy glory over the whole universe, and be exalted above all the earth in thine honor, and shine forth in the splendor and excellence of thy might upon all the inhabitants of thy world, that whatsoever hath been made may know that thou hast made it, and whatsoever hath been created may understand that thou hast created it.

It is therefore not to be wondered at that Philo gives voice to the following complaint:

> And therefore it astonishes me to see that some people venture to accuse of inhumanity the nation which has shown so profound a sense of fellowship and good will to all men everywhere, by using its prayers and festivals and first-fruit offerings as a means of supplication for the human race in general and of making its homage to the truly existent God in the name of those who have evaded the service which it was their duty to give, as well as of itself.

By the close of the Second Commonwealth Judaism actually became a world religion with a strong urge toward expansion. But the strict Jewish ritual constituted a great obstacle; for the majority of non-Jews it was too much of a burden. Judaism, therefore, continued to be primarily the religion of the Jewish people, which had already long been something more than a people. Since the Babylonian exile Jews have been a religious community and a world people.

There was hardly another people in antiquity which struggled as valiantly and heroically for its country and political freedom as did the Jews. At the same time, it was the only people to manifest the miracle of existence without land and state. The history of the Jewish religion is a constant process of spiritualization. The religious life gradually frees itself of all worldly associations, of priests and sanctuaries, of sacrifices and altars, and, to a great extent, of state and land, too. When, for the second time, catastrophe overtook the nation, when Jerusalem and the Temple were destroyed again, the people was already prepared to withstand the difficult tests of a second exile. The *Shekinah* now accompanied the people on all its wanderings, and the individual Jew could worship God everywhere and without intermediaries. The religious development did not cease even now, but the Bible and the Talmud (the Oral Torah of the Pharisees) remained, throughout the Middle Ages and into the modern period, the foundation of the religious life of the Jewish people.

BIBLIOGRAPHY

WILLIAM F. ALBRIGHT, *Archaeology and the Religion of Israel.* Baltimore, 1942.

ALBRECHT ALT, *Die Urspruenge des israelitischen Rechts.* Leipzig, 1934.

LEO BAECK, *The Essence of Judaism.* New York, 1936.

SALO W. BARON, *A Social and Religious History of the Jews.* 3 vols., New York, 1937.

ADOLF BUECHLER, *Studies in Sin and Atonement in the Rabbinic Literature of the First Century.* London, 1928.

Cambridge Ancient History. 12 vols., 1923-1939.

A. CAUSSE, *Du groupe ethnique à la Communauté religieuse.* Paris, 1937.

LOUIS FINKELSTEIN, *The Pharisees.* 2 vols. Philadelphia, 1938.

L. GINZBERG, *Mekomah shel ha-Halakah be-Hokmat Yisrael.* Jerusalem, 1931.

LOUIS GINZBERG, *The Palestinian Talmud.* New York. 1941.

HUGO GRESSMANN, *Der Messias.* Goettingen, 1929.

R. TRAVERS HERFORD, *The Pharisees.* London, 1924.

R. TRAVERS HERFORD, *Judaism in the New Testament Period.* London, 1928.

YEHEZKEL KAUFMAN, *Toledot ha-Emunah ha-Yisreelit* (The History of Religion in Israel). 4 vols., Tel Aviv, 1937-1942.

RUDOLF KITTEL, *Geschichte des Volkes Israel.* 3 vols., Stuttgart, 1923-1929.

ADOLPHE LODS, *Israel.* New York, 1932.

ADOLPHE LODS, *The Prophets and the Rise of Judaism.* New York, 1937.

ABRAM MENES, *Die sozialpolitische Analyse der Urgeschichte.* In "Zeitschrift fuer die Alttestamentliche Wissenschaft," xliii, 1925.

ABRAM MENES, *Die vorexilischen Gesetze Israels.* Giessen, 1928.

EDUARD MEYER, *Die Israeliten und ihre Nachbarstaemme.* Halle, 1906.

GEORGE FOOT MOORE, *Judaism in the First Centuries of the Christian Era.* 3 vols., Cambridge, 1927-1930.

JULIAN MORGENSTERN, *Amos Studies.* Cincinnati, 1941.

S. MOWINCKEL, *Psalmenstudien.* 6 vols., 1921-1924.

W. O. E. OESTERLEY and T. H. ROBINSON, *Hebrew Religion: Its Origin and Development.* New York, 1937.

J. PEDERSEN, *Israel—its Life and Culture.* London, 1926.

HANS SCHMIDT, *Die Thronfahrt Yahwehs.* Tuebingen, 1927.

EMIL SCHUERER, *Geschichte des juedischen Volkes im Zeitalter Jesu Christi.* 4th ed. 3 vols., Leipzig, 1901-1911.

CHAIM TCHERNOWITZ, *Toledoth ha-Halakah* (History of Hebrew Law). 3 vols., New York, 1935-1943.

MAX WEBER, *Gesammelte Aufsaetze zur Religionssoziologie.* Vol. III: *Das antike Judentum.* Tuebingen, 1920-1921.

JULIUS WELLHAUSEN, *Israelitische und juedische Geschichte.* 4th ed., Berlin, 1901.

JULIUS WELLHAUSEN, *Prolegomena zur Geschichte Israels.* Berlin, 1883.

SOLOMON ZEITLIN, *The Sadducees and the Pharisees.* 1936.

THE HISTORY OF JEWISH RELIGIOUS THOUGHT

A. Steinberg

INTRODUCTION

Many of the questions about which religious thought revolves have also been, from the earliest times, the essential questions to which philosophy has sought the answers. However, the basic approaches of religion and philosophy toward these questions are entirely different. Whereas the primary postulate of philosophic speculation is the absolute independence and autonomy of reason, the basis of religious thought is *the word of God*. The convergence of interest of these two schools of metaphysical thinking far from closing the breach between them, has usually resulted in estrangement and antagonism. This will explain why the treasures of Jewish culture, in accordance with their strictly religious character, contain so little of the type of reasoning to which the Greek word "philosophy" has been applied. Instead, Jewish thought has concentrated on religious speculation.

It is true that at various times and in various lands, especially in Western Europe in modern times, we find a great number of individual Jews prominent in the field of philosophy. But these men, however deep their own roots in the Jewish spiritual past, devoted themselves to a line of thinking which had very little in common with the intrinsic development of Jewish thought. Very often, in order to turn to philosophy, the Jew had to step out of his background. This was true in the case of Spinoza. Regardless of the fact that he was greatly influenced by such Jewish thinkers as Maimonides (Rambam), Gersonides (Levi ben Gershon) and Hasdai Crescas, he was nevertheless a link in the chain which continued the Cartesianism of modern times rather than the philosophical trends of the Middle Ages. It is significant that whereas Descartes prepared the field for an independent French philosophy, and Leibniz (who took up the thread of modern philosophical tradition where Spinoza had left it off) became the father of a specific German philosophical school of thought, Spinoza exerted but slight influence on the Jewish way of thinking.

However, without continuity there can be no history, and especially no history of human speculation. No isolated episodes, however important, can take its place. The history of Jewish religious thought is therefore the only basis for understanding the historical development of the typical Jewish outlook on life.

At first glance, it may seem that even the development of the rationalistic aspect of Jewish religious thought lacked continuity. There is a series of distinct flourishing periods, separated one from another by centuries: the Prophetic era, the Hellenistic phase, the Jewish-Arabic renaissance, the period of modern Jewish-religious thought, each period having not only a specific geographic center but to some extent its own language (Hebrew, Greek, Arabic and German). This very fact would seem to indicate that these stages in Jewish rationalistic religious thought did not result from any immanent process of development but were due to outside influences. Closer study, however, shows that despite these historical pauses, that is, despite the intervals of decline in Jewish theological speculation and the influence exerted on Jewish thought by the outside world, its development runs parallel with the development of Jewish spiritual life as a whole. The earmark of the development of Jewish religious thought is the influence which its basic ideas exert on later stages, and in this regard the evolution of Jewish thought is the best example of an immanent development. The teachings of the Prophets, and the Bible which is the testimony of these teachings, were and are the classic norm for all Jewish thinkers—from Philo of Alexandria down to our own contemporaries.

Incidentally, no matter in what tongue they wrote and spoke, almost all these men knew the Bible in the original. Influences from without always had the effect of stirring Jewish religious thought to profounder introspection. When universalistic Jewish monotheism was confronted with Hellenistic universalism, it reacted with an interpretation of the "Ionian wisdom"—Greek philosophy—in a Mosaic spirit. This need for a sharp demarcation line between Jewish monotheism and its cultural environment grew even more acute with the rise of rigid Moslemic monotheism. Even the so-called deism, the philosophical monotheism of the 18th century, could not but have a similar effect on Jewish religious thinking. In other words, we find that whenever Jewish religious thought meets another world-view displaying certain common fundamentals, it makes a new effort to strengthen its traditional foundation. Herein lie the roots of the intrinsic antagonism between the positive-religious and the philosophical way of thinking. A negative substantiation of this is the fact that there is no specific "anti-Christian" phase in the history of Jewish religious thinking, unless we choose to view certain currents of Jewish mysticism in that light. It is very likely that Christian metaphysics was viewed as mere heresy by medieval Jewish thinkers. We can say that the magnificent creative epochs in Jewish rationalistic thought were not periods of spiritual dependence but periods of determined struggle against the dangers of such dependence; and the periods of decline simply represented intervals of spiritual tranquillity and consolidation when the outside world did not threaten Jewish religious thought—interludes of serenity which prepared the rising generation for a resumption of the struggle against external onslaughts.

It would still be an error to assume that Jewish religious thought has been either apologetic or has repeated persistently—in all languages and under all historic conditions—the traditional and eternally-graven *word of God*. Had this been the case, its history would not have been one of living development but merely one of mechanical reproduction. Though bound by the sanctity of tradition, Jewish religious thinkers very early felt free to seek in the holy text meanings to satisfy their own spiritual needs, and to interpret them in accordance with reason. It was this attitude which enabled the orthodox seeker after knowledge to accept, in principle, the influence of foreign metaphysical fundamentals — whether formulated by the Greek Plato, the Arabian ibn Roshd or the German Kant—and so to assimilate them that they eventually became an organic part of the Jewish outlook on life. Thus, very often Jewish religious thinking was strong enough to exert an influence in *its* turn on the world about it: on Hellenistic philosophy, on Islam and even on certain forms of Christianity. The immense spiritual wealth garnered through the long centuries of its existence, not only from within but from the world surrounding it, explains why to this very day it holds much more than a mere historic interest for metaphysical research.

I. THE CLASSICAL ERA

The basic principles of Jewish religious thought were clearly formulated between the 9th and 5th centuries B.C.E. During this period, the Hebrew literature of Palestine first began to formulate an original Jewish philosophy of life; and, simultaneously, there emerged a number of eminent personalities who were the heralds and bearers of the new outlook—the so-called Book Prophets (Amos, Hosea, Isaiah, and others, up to the time of Ezra). The early prophets who have left us the heritage of their own words unquestionably did not plough virgin soil; they leaned upon an older tradition. However, they did not accept this religious tradition unquestioningly; they submitted it to sharp critical scrutiny, thus extracting the valuable kernel from the ancient popular beliefs and discarding the empty shell. Despite the fact that they were not formal "thinkers" in the accepted sense of the word, and regarded the conclusions at which they arrived as divine revelations and not as their own spiritual accomplishments, "the word of God" as expressed through their lips is nevertheless so logical and so realistic in its congruence with the political, social and cultural conditions of their time, that, especially from a non-religious standpoint, these men emerge as metaphysicians, moralists and philosophers in the classical, non-Jewish sense.

Even today after the considerable achievements in the field of biblical criticism it is still difficult to point out with certainty the new ideas introduced by the prophets into the Jewish outlook on life. We are also unable to circumscribe with accuracy those portions of the Bible (especially in its first part, the Pentateuch) which bear the undeniable stamp of the prophetic and, particularly, "Deuteronomic" influence. It is equally difficult to isolate the individual contributions of any prophet. Despite these limitations of our knowledge, the spiritual world of the prophets rises as a firm structure with an individual style, a system both clear and transparent with regard both to itself and later developments.

The three cornerstones of this structure are: God, His Commandments, and Man. This is clearly brought out in the older parts of the Pentateuch in which a strong prophetic influence is discernible. The first word of God to man is a commandment, and because the first man transgressed this commandment he was expelled from the Garden of Eden. God's commandments, however, are not the product of the arbitrary will of an autocrat; indeed, the reverse is true. They are an expression of the eternal laws of the divine order of things, and as such they apply even to the Creator Himself. Thus Abraham could ask of God: "Shall not the Judge of all the earth do right?"

The entire history of the world beginning with Adam, through the catastrophes of the Flood, the dispersion of mankind, etc., are explained and made clear in terms of these relations between God and man. These principles are especially applicable to the history of Israel. It was to the children of Abraham, Isaac and Jacob that God's teachings and commandments were revealed. God, the Torah (God's teachings) and the people of Israel are therefore the three fundamentals of the prophetic doctrine as preached to Israel by the Prophets.

"Hear the word of the Lord, ye children of Israel," exclaims Hosea, the prophet of the 8th century B.C.E., "for the Lord hath a controversy with the inhabitants of the land, because there is no truth, nor mercy, nor knowledge of God in the land." And further:

"Seeing thou hast forgotten the law of thy God, I will also forget thy children" (Hosea IV, 1 and 6).

Here we have not only the three cornerstones—God, Torah, Israel—but also a very clear idea of the inter-relationship ascribed to them in the prophetic teachings. The people of Israel is bound to God through the Torah. As long as Israel does not *forget* its teachings but pursues its way in truth and righteousness, God concerns himself with the welfare of His people and its land. But the moment Israel disturbs this harmony, God sits in judgment upon Israel (see Isaiah III, 13-15 and Jeremiah XXV, 31). Even here, God is bound by His own code of laws and wishes to remain ever just; even though His verdict is harsh, His final words —as can be seen from the entire book of

Hosea—are love, mercy and kindness. This highly complicated metaphysical-ethical formula for the explanation (the diagnosis as well as the prognosis) of the events taking place in and around Palestine bears witness to the heights attained in the "knowledge of God" at the beginning of the Prophetic era. It also casts a light upon the array of basic problems which preoccupied contemporary Jewish spiritual thinkers. There was one question of general concern: how is one to conceive the nature of the world if its primary function is to serve as a home of justice for the nations and men? This was the question from which all Jewish spiritual contemplation developed in an ever-widening spiral.

Several centuries later, when Greek philosophy was grappling with the problem of the nature of the world—that is, how to encompass this problem in one single idea—Jewish monotheism evolved this answer in its search for the one common element inherent in all phenomena of the universe: all creation is one entity inasmuch as everything which exists is the creation of one God. Therefore, since the world and all that is in it, including man, is the creation of God, Who is the creator of heaven and earth and at the same time the Giver of the Torah—the teachings about man's conduct, about truth and falsehood, about good and justice and evil and injustice—it follows that conduct conflicting with the Holy Commandments is equivalent to transgression against universal order and defiance of the Lord of creation. Whereas Greek philosophy traced the principles of right and justice to the laws of nature, the prophets of Israel took the contrary stand, and transformed the natural world into a means of realizing the laws of justice and order. With them metaphysical monism assumed the form of ethical monotheism. This prophetic doctrine is most perfectly expressed in the words of Isaiah (Isaiah XLII, 5-6):

"Thus saith God the Lord, he that created the heavens, and stretched them out; he that spread forth the earth, and that which cometh out of it; he that giveth breath unto the people upon it, and spirit to them that walk therein:

"I the Lord have called thee in righteousness, and will hold thine hand, and will keep thee, and give thee for a covenant of the people, for a light of the Gentiles" (see also Isaiah XLV, 18 and XLIX, 8).

The word "thee" toward the end of the passage refers both to the prophet and the people. This double address is due to the fact that the advancement of ethical monotheism did not merely deepen the concept of God and the teleological world-view, according to which the world was created for man to live in and man was created to live in probity and justice; parallel with this the role of the people of Israel and the prophet's conception of himself and his own mission had assumed a new aspect in prophetic doctrine. The more clearly there emerged the idea that all living beings were *God's creatures,* the more difficult it became to understand why only the children of Israel were bound to God through His commandments. The answer is implied in the above-quoted passage of Isaiah: the people of Israel are to the other peoples of the world what the prophet is to his own people; just as he is the corporeal manifestation of God's *covenant* with the children of Israel, so is it Israel's mission in turn to be a *light* for the rest of the world (see Isaiah XLIII, 1; XLIV, 1).

The earliest, primitive Jewish concept of the relationship between God and man undoubtedly bore a strong resemblance to the prevalent religious beliefs of the neighboring Oriental peoples. The fact that from these primitive and particularist ideas there could eventually develop the ethically-cast universalism of the prophets—with their idea of a God who is one universal God and of a people whose mission it is to disseminate this *awareness of God,* together with social justice and harmony among peoples — can undoubtedly be ascribed to a peculiar appreciation of historical values by the people of Israel, even as far back as the pre-Prophetic era, presumably in consonance with its own individual historical experiences. At any rate, from the very first the prophets held strictly to historical tradition, and their empirical proofs are, more often than not, based on history. Thus, for instance, the Exodus from Egypt furnished them with one of their chief arguments for the justification of God's charges against His wayward people:

"Hear this word that the Lord hath spoken against you, O children of Israel, against the whole family which I brought up from the land of Egypt, saying,

"You only have I known of all the families of the earth; therefore I will punish you for all your iniquities" (Amos III, 1-2; see also Amos II, 9-10, and Hosea II, 17; XII, 13-14; XIII, 4-5).

Although the "Torah" of the prophets is not quite identical with our Pentateuch, they are both based on *Hukkim* and *Mishpatim* (statutes and laws), as well as on facts at the time generally accepted as based on history. We are given the *mathematics of history*, specific time chronology, as for instance the *forty years* of the sojourn in the desert (Amos V, 25). On such a basis, the *knowledge of God* assumed a historical character and, since God is the God of the world, as a consequence it also assumed a universal-historical character. *To know God* now became the equivalent of knowing the history of the world, from the *six days of Creation* till the current period with its outlook on a future along the lines of God's world-historical plan. In this framework the people of Israel is a *family* among all other *families,* created by the same Creator and all descending from Adam, the first man, who was the only creature to be made in the image of God. If God's will manifested itself most clearly in the annals of Israel, if Israel was rendered worthy of recognizing the true God, His intentions and His commandments, this, too, was but an expression of God's will. Just as the Lord designates His prophets without consulting the wishes of those He chooses (Jeremiah I, 4-10) so did He *recognize* the fitness of Abraham and his family to seal a historical *bond* with the Creator of the Universe (Genesis XVIII, 19). Therefore this bond or *covenant* is a privi-

lege, and it also imposes a burden—a burden of strict responsibility toward the Divine partner who had shown man *what is good* (Micah VI, 8) and toward all the rest of God's creatures. For the Lord made a covenant with Israel, as well as with all the rest of creation, an *everlasting covenant* (Isaiah XXIV, 5; LV, 4; Ezekiel XXXVII, 26 and Genesis IX, 16; XVII, 7) and at the end of time all the earth "shall be full of the knowledge of the Lord, as the waters cover the sea," and equally blessed shall be "Egypt my people, and Assyria the work of my hands, and Israel mine inheritance" (Isaiah XI, 9; XIX, 24-25).

Simultaneously with the development of the idea that made Israel God's collective messenger to the world (Deuteronomy XXVI, 18-19 and Isaiah XLIX, 1-7) the prophets deepened the idea of personal mission and responsibility of the individual as such. According to prophetic theism, the ultimate in absolute perfection is possessed only by God, the holy, just and mighty Judge of the world; the nearest approximation to this perfection is vested in the prophet through whose lips God speaks (Isaiah VI, 6-7; Jeremiah V, 14, 23, 29; Deuteronomy XVIII, 16-18). But all God-fearing men, whoever they may be, have it within their power to come close to God just as have the prophets: "But the word is very nigh unto thee, in thy mouth, and in thy heart, that thou mayest do it" (Deuteronomy XXX, 14). Whether due to universal cultural-historical causes or the independent development of the prophetic spirit, the fact remains that as we follow the prophets further in their growth, we find them ever more insistent on the personal self-awareness, and together with this the emphasis on individual ethical responsibility in general. It is, therefore, not by mere chance that Jeremiah, the most subjective of all the prophets, formulated the theory which is the basis of all ethical teachings, including the a-religious: *i.e.,* the individual must bear the responsibility for his own destiny, and must not rely either on the *merits of his forebears* or on the chance that his own deeds, either meritorious or blameworthy, are only trivial episodes in the life of the community, of his people, of mankind, or of the world as a whole. "In those days they shall say no more," Jeremiah tells us, "The fathers have eaten a sour grape, and the children's teeth are set on edge. But every one shall die for his own iniquity: every man that eateth the sour grape, his teeth shall be set on edge" (Jeremiah XXXI, 29-30 and Lamentations v, 7).

It was this idea that formed the basis of Ezekiel's entire philosophy. By his time, the period of the Babylonian Exile, Jewish thought had delved so deeply into these main problems that the previous thesis— that the bearer of moral responsibility is the community as a whole, and the new antithesis, that the real bearer of moral responsibility is the individual—resulted in a synthesis: the true religious-ethical ideal, the perfect human or *Messiah* who will redeem mankind "at the end of time," is an individual who bears moral responsibility for all men, as described in the Book of Isaiah (LIII, 11): "He shall see of the travail of his soul, *and* shall be satisfied: by his knowledge shall my righteous servant justify many; for he shall bear their iniquities." Several centuries later Christianity sought to use this as a support for the extreme-individualistic doctrine of redemption.

In the 5th century B.C.E., after Ezra's reform, when the Torah began to govern Jewish individual and public life, Jewish religious thought was able to bring about a deepening of personal morality alongside of personal piety. The Book of Psalms is the finest monument of this form of piety, characteristic of the period of transition when Jewish thought was just emerging from its classical stage toward its first encounters with Hellenism. Even Jeremiah was already not merely a passive instrument of God; he frequently engaged in dialogues with the Almighty (XIV, 11-14; compare this with the primitive dialogue-form of Amos VII, 4-6 and VIII, 1-2). In Psalms we return again to the monologue—this time not addressed by God to a human audience but on the contrary addressed by His devotees to Him (see Psalms x). And the pious man had many

things to discuss, questions to ask, doubts which pursued him, and even objections to the ways of the Lord; all of which he poured forth in the form of personal prayers. If God is just "and God has authority," he demands an explanation for the injustice implicit in the fact that often "the wicked are at ease," whereas men of virtue who "are pure of heart" are plagued (LXXIII, 1-12). Jewish thought was now confronted with problems regarding the theodicean philosophy, which underlies the entire Book of Job. The absorption in individual creative thinking and in personal piety with its belief that God watched over each of his creatures, led by natural stages to a freer and more conscious consideration of God's world (see the celebrated Chapter CIV of Psalms and Job, XXXVIII) and to a deeper human understanding. Such books as Proverbs and Ben Sira indicate clearly that concurrently with the intensification of theological speculation, the Jews were developing psychological generalizations and their practical application, particularly in the field of pedagogy. There is no question that, from ancient times to the Hellenistic period, Jewish sages drew on many non-Jewish sources but never deviating from their elementary thesis that "fear of God" is the beginning of all wisdom and that the ultimate aim of wisdom is the "nearness of God" (Proverbs I, 7; IX, 10; Ben-Sira I, 1; Psalms LXXIII, 28). External influences, even as far back as the era of the Prophets, can probably account for the introduction of the mystical element in Jewish religious thinking (see Isaiah VI; Ezekiel I, X, etc.; Zechariah v, etc.) and its later blossoming forth more extensively in the Apocrypha. The story of Jewish mysticism, however, is the concern of another part of this volume. Characteristic of Jewish thought and of the true prophetic spirit is, on the contrary, the doctrine of eschatology—concerned with the "end of time," the final stage, or the consummation of the pre-Messianic phases of universal history. This is most strikingly illustrated in the Book of Daniel and in Ezekiel's vision of the "dry bones" and Gog and Magog.

II. FROM HELLENISM TO THE MIDDLE AGES

By the end of the 4th century B.C.E. the foundations of Jewish monotheism had been so firmly established that, without fear for its future independence, it could welcome contact with Greek ideas and the achievements of the Greek philosophers. (Traces of this can even be found in the Bible—in its final books, *The Writings*). However divergent the opinions may be concerning the time of composition, the internal structure and meaning of the book Ecclesiastes, it must be conceded that it reflects a phase of Jewish thought distinguished by the assimilation of ideas which had their birth in the Hellenic world and not in Western Asia or Northern Africa. The gist of this book is nevertheless not the skepticism and pessimism of the "vanity of vanities" outlook on life, set against a background of Greek cosmology—according to which laws of nature impose an eternal repetitive cycle on events. Its intention is to show that acceptance of a materialistic (Democritic or Epicurean) outlook as the final and definitive basis of a world-view inevitably connotes the acceptance of blind chance as dominating the world, that man's life (both individual and historical) is purposeless and meaningless and that there is essentially no difference between knowledge and ignorance, good and evil, and consequently, between "man and animal." The moral implied here is that too much philosophizing is not good: ". . . God is in heaven, and thou upon earth; therefore let thy words be few" (Ecclesiastes, v, 2).

Thus the initial Jewish reaction to Greek philosophy expressed itself in profound polemics, a sort of *reductio ad absurdum*. But Greek philosophy was multi-faceted and, in addition to those abstractions which were offensive to the Jewish concept of life, it possessed many features with which Jewish thought could accord, as, for instance, the Stoic interpretation. Because of this, Jewish thinkers began to translate and thereby transfer Greek concepts and terms into Hebrew. The hypostatization of *wisdom* in Proverbs VIII, 22-31 (see also I, 20-33; IX, 1) is probably a translation of the Greek *sophia*. Even the Pharisaic theories of immortality and their attempts to link up the idea of personal moral responsibility with that of freedom of will probably did not develop entirely without Greek influence. The rapprochement between Jewish and Greek reasoning increased with the introduction of Greek concepts as well as the Greek language into the literature of the Jews.

On the eve of the rise of Christianity, the countries bordering on the Mediterranean had so far succumbed to Hellenistic influence that it could almost be said of them: "And the whole earth was of one language, and of one speech" (Genesis XI, 1). The restoration of the unity of mankind—one of the basic conceptions of Israel's prophets —was, according to the Holy Scripture, a continuation of the state of man in the Garden of Eden. However, the delusory reversion of mankind to its pristine youth during the Hellenistic period seemed to Jewish thinkers a mockery rather than the realization of the visions of the prophets. Although united superficially, the world—both in its cosmic attitude as well as in its individual and social morality—was now in a state of greater chaos and confusion than ever before. Despite this, Hellenized Jews joined non-Jews in attaching more importance to form than to content. Jewish thinkers were now confronted with the task of so interpreting the inherited Jewish tradition, that the contemporary cultural world could immediately grasp the essential difference between pure universalism and the superficial pseudo-universalism or cosmopolitanism of the Hellenized world. The most effective weapons they had for attacking this syncretism were those furnished by their opponents, the Greek philosophers' methods of reasoning. Thus even then philosophy became the handmaiden of theology, if not for its own benefit, then undoubtedly for the benefit of religious thought not only among the Jews but also among Christians and Moslems at a later period.

The foremost Jewish thinker of the Hellenistic period was Philo of Alexandria. The way had been prepared for him gradually since the 3rd century B.C.E. Already in the Septuagint (the first Greek translation of the Bible), the biblical anthropomorphisms had often been interpreted in an abstract sense, in accordance with the requirements of consistent, logical reasoning (see, for instance, the Septuagint translation of Exodus XXIV, 10). In the apocryphal *Wisdom of Solomon,* which probably antedates Philo's writings by a hundred years, the dualism of body and soul, of matter and spirit, is brought out in clear-cut Platonic fashion (as for instance, I, 4; VII, 1-6). At the same time, *wisdom* is endowed with the significance of a spiritual substance which unites the human soul with God and thus renders it immortal (chapters II-III). A closer examination of this *wisdom* reveals that this is merely a Greek (more accurately, a Stoic) metamorphosis of the old Jewish divine Torah, or "God's word."

A similar work is the so-called IV Maccabees (believed to have been written by an older contemporary of Philo) wherein the deeds of the Jewish heroes merely serve as a historic illustration of the ethical principle that man's virtues can master his lusts and passions ("affects"). Though one of the fundamentals of Stoicism, this reasoning accorded in principle with that of traditional Jewish morals; but whereas the Stoic wanted to destroy man's "affects," ascetic tendencies are alien to the Jewish author of this fourth Maccabean book and he contents himself with the moderate control of mind over animal instincts within the limits of Jewish law. The derivation of ethical precepts and metaphysical principles from the wealth of Jewish law and historical records, and their interpretation in an allegorical form—as parables and symbols of profound ideas and purposes—began to manifest itself in the Judaeo-Hellenistic literature as early as the middle of the 2nd century B.C.E. (Letter of Aristeas; Aristobulus). Here, too, the Jewish thinkers of Alexandria had much to learn from the Stoics who often sought philosophical truths in the naive tales of old Greek mythology. Simultaneously, there flourished in Palestine a school of Bible-commentators, the fathers of the "Oral Torah" who, by means of rational interpretations, did as much for the further development of the Jewish religious outlook as the prophets had done in their time through prophetic inspiration. Accordingly, it may be assumed that this method of allegorical biblical interpretation which is the most striking characteristic of Philo's approach had its inception in the Jewish as well as in the Greek "Midrash." From the concrete results of his work, it is apparent that the Jewish thinker of the 1st century C.E. was a deeply conscious Jew who, like many Jews of that generation, wished to disseminate the Torah among the peoples of the world, and was not an epigone of Greek philosophy among the barely Hellenized Oriental *barbarians.*

For this very reason, Philo's work in the field of Jewish thought was doomed to remain an isolated phase. His primary purpose was to emphasize the transcendentality or supramundaneity of the one God who is, therefore, not only immaterial, but beyond any quality of the spirit as possessed by man. This concept, which was perhaps too abstract for the average Jew, was no novelty to the leading representatives of the idea of ethical monotheism who, from the very first, had adopted the formula: "Who *is* like unto thee" (Exodus XV, 11; Psalms XXXV, 10; LXXI, 19; LXXXVI, 8; LXXXIX, 6, 8; CXIII, 5-6, Lamentations III, 37 or Isaiah LV, 8-9 and particularly XLVI, 5). The more profound interpretation of these words perforce remained far beyond the grasp of the plain people with their naive, anthropomorphic conceptions about the Creator, while to the thinkers of the people they constituted self-evident truths.

The very doctrine of ecstatic union with God which made Philo a predecessor of neo-Platonism and, as some will have it, a typical representative of mysticism, is really only an exemplification of prophetic inspiration. Even the passage in Genesis (XII, 1): "Get thee out of thy country, and from thy kindred, and from thy father's house" Philo considered a hint, in line with a pattern of metaphysical exegesis of the meaning of true prophecy: when God orders Abraham to leave his country, He means Abraham to become a prophet, to *discard* his body, which is earth and dust, his senses, which are his property, his father's home, which is the human brain, and even his own ego, since man cannot be at one with his Creator unless he divests himself of his own conscious "I" (*Legum Allegoria* III, 40; and *Quis Rerum Divinarum Heres,* 69-70). This metaphysical theory of prophecy is not entirely at variance with the deductions that can be made from various Bible-stories concerning the ecstasy of the prophets. The same can be said of Philo's greatest cultural-historical contribution, his doctrine of Logos. "The word" or Logos, which becomes an independent entity for Philo—a mediator between God and the world or, more accurately, between the Creator and the created —is again only a generalization based on the Bible, in which God's will is realized mainly by the word, as for instance, in Psalms (XXXIII, 9): "He spake, and it was *done;* he commanded, and it stood fast." "He spoke, and it came to pass" was, from the very first chapters of Genesis, an established formula. On the basis of such premises of religious thought, Philo advanced a step further in logical thinking and found in the biblical images and tales hints of various metaphysical, ethical and psychological theories which had long since been evolved in Greece. In methods and principles this was about as much as tradition-bound Jewish speculation could gain from contact with alien philosophical sources. Though Philo did not lay the foundation for a new Jewish philosophy, he did succeed in fructifying the Hellenistic-Roman world with the spirit of Jewish universalism, and thus helped to crystallize the Christian belief—the most widespread and universal faith up to the present time.

Whereas the superficial Hellenization of Jewish religious thought was a fleeting episode in its history, the main line of its development was along the broad highway of the Oral Torah—a natural sequence to the more ancient *Written Torah*. The Mishnah, Gemara, and Midrash are the literary monuments of this development. True, not one of the hundreds of great men whose names have been immortalized in this literature can be compared to a Philo as far as systematic speculation in the metaphysical field is concerned. If, among the great teachers of the Halakah and the Agada there were such great thinkers—and many of the aphorisms and parables of Rabbi Gamaliel the Second, Rabbi Akiba, Rabbi Simeon ben Johai, Resh Lakish, etc. quoted in the Talmud would justify such a conclusion—it nevertheless is obvious that they must have kept their systematic speculations secret. It was their principle never to speak openly about metaphysical problems, such as the nature of God (*Maase Merkabah*—literally, Divine Chariot), the Creation of the world (*Maase Bereshit*) and its infinity in space and time (see: *"Ein Dorshin"* — *Mishnah Hagigah* II, 1). The Jewish great men felt a mistrust of every attempt at logical rationalization of faith; this mistrust was given additional impetus by the fact that at about this time Christianity began to put forth religious dogmas patterned after the structure of philosophical thought. Philo Judaeus thus became an authority in the Church and was for many centuries forgotten by his own people. Whenever a Tanna (one of the authors of the Mishnah) felt a need to offer logical proof of the existence of God, he did so for the sake of a controversy with an idol-worshipper or atheist, according to the precept set down by Rabbi Eliezer: "Know whatever answer to give to the unbeliever" (*Sayings of the Fathers* II, 19).

Still, it cannot be said that the centuries between the conclusion of the Bible and the completion of the Mishnah were sterile. Though they produced less original Jewish thought than had the Classical Period, they were distinguished by a far greater maturity and precision of expression; by a superior versatility in the art of conveying abstract principles and especially ethical concepts in sharply defined formulas; by greater adept-ness in the application of logical lines of thinking, as, for instance, arriving at clear classifications, consistent divisions, cor-rect argumentation, etc. The keen minds of the sages of *Halakah* (Law) enabled them to deal with all problems which came before them. It was only after long and careful re-flection that Hillel was able to produce his famous summarization of Jewish ethics: "Do not unto another that which is repugnant to you" (Talmud Babli, Sabbath 31 A). That this was not an isolated conclusion can be seen from other aphorisms which are as-cribed both to Hillel and to his followers: "Love thy fellow-creatures and bring them nigh to the *Torah*," says Hillel (Sayings of the Fathers, I, 12). The very use of the new term "creatures" for the concept of man, and the conviction that love for one's fel-low-men is primarily a concern for man's spiritual elevation, *i.e.*, to bring him nearer the source of truth, justice and righteous-ness, indicates how far the teachings of the prophets had advanced in the preceding centuries in their view of life's meaning and the ultimate aim of history—from an ideal it had become a practical norm of daily life. This went hand in hand with the wide-spread recognition that man must possess freedom of choice in order to participate actively in the realization of the universal-historical ideal. Rabbi Akiba's laconic formulation of the basic principle of the Jewish outlook: "Everything is foreseen, yet freedom of choice is given"—for man to do good or evil—(Sayings of the Fathers III, 19) which was based on two passages in Deuteronomy (XXX, 15 and 19); and Rabbi Hananiah's like precept: "Everything lies in the hands of God except the fear of God" (Berakot 33 B)—since fear of God is up to man himself—both testify to the thorough consideration given by Talmudical sages to the problem of man's freedom of will, and to the antinomy between human freedom and Divine power which later challenged so many Jewish and non-Jewish minds.

For Jewish thought, from then on, the freedom of man to follow his good or his evil impulses became a sort of dogma; and, though "reward and punishment" in this life as well as after death play an important role in determining man's *free will*, the Tal-mud evolved a clearly defined religious-ethical concept of "virtue for virtue's sake" and strongly emphasized the idea that the "recompense of virtue is virtue" (Ben Azzai, Sayings of the Fathers, IV, 2; Antigonus, ibid. 1, 3; Rabbi Zadok, ibid. IV, 5).

The belief in another world where the soul is to reap the reward for its deeds on earth, lay at the very foundation of the theodicean motive, from ancient times on. In the Talmudic era, this belief assumed almost the form of a dogma. However, the voluntarism and activism in Jewish thought, characteristic of it from its very inception, prevented this theory from ever becoming petrified. The idea of an *after world* and the *future which is to come* are sometimes in-tended to mean "that world where the vir-tuous will bask in Divine glory" and the evil ones will burn in the fires of Hell. Sometimes, again, they simply imply "the days of the Messiah," *i.e.*, the eschatological finale of the world, in the prophetic sense. This double meaning would seem a further proof that Jewish thought never ceased to concern itself with the universal-historical role of the Jewish people. According to the Talmudic concept *Shekinah* (a new term for "God's *nearness*") itself is in need of "redemption"—how much more, therefore, must it be a concern of all mankind. On the basis of the Torah and perhaps remotely influenced by the ideas of Graeco-Roman Stoicism in accordance with this viewpoint, the Talmud evolved theories of universal human right founded on natural law. Many of the prayers which were composed during the Talmudic era breathe forth this universalist spirit. We find, for instance, the following passage in one of the Rosh Hashanah and Yom Kippur prayers: "And all creatures shall bow unto Thee and they shall all make an alliance in order to ful-fill Thy will wholeheartedly." The prayer "Aleinu," ascribed to that great figure of the Babylonian Amoraim, Rab, deals with the perfection of the world and expresses the hope that soon "every creature will call on Thy name" and "all inhabitants of the world will recognize and know that every knee must bend before Thee and every tongue swear to Thee" (see also Isaiah XLV, 23).

If, since the close of its Classical Period, Jewish religious thought has not developed much in depth, it can be said to have so expanded its range that, just before the Middle Ages, there was no other course for a Jewish thinker to take than either to desert "the house of his fathers" or to concentrate entirely on the solution of those problems which are the essential basis of Jewish religious culture itself. This became the foremost task of the so-called "Jewish religious philosophers" of the Middle Ages.

III. THE JEWISH-ARABIC RENAISSANCE

The most important event in history and, therefore, also in the spiritual development of the Jews, at the beginning of the Middle Ages, was the advent of Islam. It almost seemed as though there were a repetition of what had happened some thousand years earlier when Hellenistic culture began to spread. Precisely as in that time, the neighboring non-Jewish world began to embrace universalism, with this difference, that now the monotheistic idea was the focal point in world culture. Jewish thought was compelled to recognize in it a spiritual kinship, and inevitably there sprang up the crucial question: does the traditional Jewish world-view possess intrinsic justification for its special existence, or is not the fact that the one and only God had manifested Himself to other peoples of the world outside of Jewish history, a downright contradiction of its essential meaning and spirit? In other words, is not the entire "Sinaitic revelation" threatened with extinction once it can be shown that man's own reason will naturally lead him to conclusions approximating those set forth in the Holy Scripture?

This question became particularly acute for Jewish religious thought in the 9th cen-

tury, after Islam had assimilated the old Hellenistic heritage with its philosophical elements and produced the Kalam, an independent school dealing with the metaphysical fundamentals of the new faith. A number of the adherents of the new school exalted the rationality of the Islamic fundamentals and commandments. Whereas in the Hellenistic period Jewish religious thought had had to contend with any number of philosophical trends, it now found itself defied by a single school of thought—in itself profoundly religious—which demanded an accounting in the name of reason. Under such a stimulus, it now became the all-absorbing task of traditional Jewish thought to achieve clarity as to the nature of Judaism and reason within the framework of Jewish tradition itself. What was done in this respect by the most original Jewish thinker of the Oriental-Islamic period (Saadia Gaon, born 892 in Egypt) set the tone for the entire period of Jewish-Arabic renaissance. If not for him, it is questionable whether the Jewish element, in this period of joint cultural development, could have had the strength to preserve its independence.

Saadia is frequently referred to as the "father of the Jewish philosophy of religion." But, taken in the modern sense, this term presupposes a free, philosophical approach to the phenomenon of religion itself. It was, however, the intention of Saadia, who was the head of the Yeshibah in Babylonian Sura, to prove in his book *Emunot ve-Deot* (Doctrines and Religious Beliefs), written in Arabic (ca. 933), that actually there is only one faith revealed by the Lord—the Jewish faith, and this faith demands that its followers apprehend its truths also by means of reason. Even in the other faiths man has produced for himself, Saadia contended, there are vital metaphysical and ethical elements identical with those found in God's Torah and in the words of His prophets. In his polemics against Parseeism, Jewish agnosticism and the Christian dogma of the Holy Trinity, Saadia's weapons were those of pure logic; he went a step further and declared that the rationality of the Torah was proof of its divine character. Nevertheless, in the introduction to his main work, he states that no speculation by man can lay the basis for the discovery of pure truth as firmly as, by the grace of God, it is found in the Torah. And, moreover, not every man is a born thinker. Saadia then comes back to the ancient maxim that "the beginning of all wisdom is the fear of God." This establishment of the reciprocal relationship between faith and knowledge, between revealed truth and man-discovered truth, was transmitted about two hundred and fifty years later by Maimonides to Christian Scholasticism and was even current during the period of 18th century enlightenment.

Saadia also exerted a considerable influence on subsequent thought by his doctrine that tradition, flowing uninterruptedly through generations, is the chief source of knowledge that is also in accordance with reason. On this he posed his argument that if not for the constantly nurtured Jewish traditional concept of the divine source of the Torah, the truth about the one and only Creator would be left hanging in the air, not to speak of the belief in the redemption of the world "at the end of time." As for the precepts set down in the Torah, the real basis of Jewish faith, the moral commandments, are rational, while the other commandments are to be observed simply because they are God's commandments and their *raison d'être* is hidden from us. In other words, reason itself teaches us that not everything about us is or can be open to full comprehension. In later theological speculation, this difference between comprehensible and incomprehensible precepts became classic.

Saadia's conclusions concerning the rational basis of the Jewish religion were influenced by Islamic philosophy and by religious currents in Judaism itself.

The traditional Jewish world was greatly shaken by the rise of the Karaites who had produced, half a century before Saadia, a thinker of the stature of Benjamin Nahavendi. About the same time there appeared a Jewish heretic, Hivi al Balkhi by name, whose book criticizing the Torah was based on the internal contradictions he believed he had discovered in the Pentateuch. Saadia devoted an entire volume to polemicizing against him. An older contemporary of Saadia, Isaac Israeli (born ca. 850 C.E.) made a deliberate effort to strengthen Jewish faith by applying the principles of Greek philosophy, and attempted to harmonize the Jewish doctrine of the Creation of the world with the neo-Platonic theories of emanation. Israeli's chief aim is clearly reflected in his definition of philosophy as an attempt to have man approximate God as far as possible. Like his medical treatises, his philosophical works were intended for all readers, regardless of creed. However, they exercised a greater influence on the Christian scholastic world than on Jewish theology. At about the same time there appeared on the scene the Jewish thinker David al-Mukammas who also displayed a leaning toward neo-Platonism and argued that God's attributes, such as life, power, wisdom, do not really reveal another divine facet—He is one in perfect unity—but, in ever new details, they exclude any imperfection from His nature. Even Saadia came close to the conclusion that God's attributes can have only a negative significance—a thought which runs through Philo's works and which later became a pivotal idea in the theology of Maimonides.

For several generations after Saadia, a number of Geonim grappled with the solution of certain perplexing problems springing from the strictly monotheistic outlook. There is, for instance, the Gaon of Pumbedita, Hai ben Sherira, whose reply to the question—How can man be said to have free will if God knows in advance how his creatures will act?—was as follows: God's vision of the future covers not only actual occurrences but even what might happen were man's will to go in another direction; divine prescience is therefore no hindrance to man's choice. In devious ways this doctrine reached the Jesuits in Spain, and Leibniz still gave it serious consideration.

Eighteen years before the death of Hai Gaon in 1038, Solomon ibn Gabirol was born (1020) in Spain, the western outpost of Moslem culture. He was both poet and thinker, and heralded a resurgence in Jewish-religious thought. At that time the nature of the problems confronting Jewish thought became clear and definite. The central question was this: how is it possible, on the basis of reason, to include in one concept the absoluteness of God with the relativity of the temporal spatial world? The more firmly the monotheists stood by their theories of the absolute, transcendental character of the infinite Creator, the more difficult they found it to explain the finite and limited nature of His world; the more supramundane God appeared, the less the world seemed to be the work of His hands. In order to surmount this intellectual obstacle, ibn Gabirol built up a firm bridge resting on the theory of *Emanation*. However, his approach was altogether independent of those of his predecessors whether Jewish, Arab or Greek. In his greatest work, *Fons Vitae* (Source of Life), a title based on a phrase in Jeremiah II, 13; XVII, 13, and in Psalms XXXVI, 10, he developed an original doctrine about *matter* and *form* and, eight hundred years before Hegel and six hundred years before Spinoza, substituted for the theory of real being and of the chain of real causes and effects, a logical "world-process" wherein *form* in all its manifestations, phases and changes is the final result of varying degrees of *matter*. With him matter itself became a logically necessary premise, and with the spiritualization of all life, the creative and driving forces in nature were transformed into the multi-ramified streams of a single dynamic force, the force of Divine Will. Ibn Gabirol's voluntaristic panlogism, which displays a close affinity with various forms of pantheism, greatly influenced the development of European metaphysics. But among Jewish thinkers it was never accepted *in toto* and did not become a model for other thinkers, principally, perhaps, for the reason that it would make it difficult to find a way to the actual history of the Jewish people and therefore likewise to the concrete forms of Jewish religious life. However, one point of Gabirol's system was eventually incorporated as a vital component of the living Jewish tradition, *i.e.*, the thought that God is more than eternal, not only because He always was and always will be, but because, generally speaking, He is outside of time, a concept, incidentally, which figures prominently in Spinoza's system. Ibn Gabirol expressed this thought in many variations in a separate religious hymn of praise, the *Keter Malkut* (Royal Crown) which to this day is read on the eve of the Day of Atonement. Similar liturgical poetic echoes are found in the *Shir ha-Yihud* of Judah Hasid (12-13th century in Regensburg, Germany) where we read for instance the following verse: "Chance and Time exist not in Thee; Thou holdest in Thy hand the order of the ages." The same formulas are to be found in the hymns of the Middle Ages, *Adon Olam* and *Yigdal*, both distinguished by abstract and dialectical verses, as for instance: "He is the first, and yet there is no beginning to His firstness," or "He is and yet there is no 'when' for His being."

Such highly abstract concepts could become rooted in daily religious life only after a number of thinkers had accepted them and then disseminated them among the educated elements of the people. Even then, the essence of neo-Platonism and its direct product, Islamic mysticism (especially of the *Brothers of Purity*) would undoubtedly never have become an organic component of Jewish religious thought, had not a school which undertook to discover the most profound concept of God in the Holy Scriptures arisen simultaneously in Spain. The foremost figures of this movement were Abraham bar Hiyya, the Prince (ca. 1136), who revived the use of Hebrew in Jewish religious philosophical literature; Joseph ben Jacob ibn Zaddik of Cordova (d. 1149) who, in his famous work *Olam Katon* (Microcosmos), resuscitated the theory that man, as the "image of God," incorporates in his own *ens* the Almighty's world in its entirety, a theory which had been fully developed 150 years earlier in southern Italy by Sabbatai Donnolo in his commentary on the *Sefer Yetsirah*; and finally, by Bahya ibn Pakuda of Saragossa, surnamed the Judge (a contemporary of ibn Gabirol) whose book *Hobot ha-Lebabot* (Duties of the Heart), written originally in Arabic, rapidly became popular in Judah ibn Tibbon's Hebrew translation. In this galaxy of great men may also be included Abraham ibn Ezra (d.1167) who was inclined to interpret the relationship between God and the world in a pantheistic spirit (see, on the one hand, his exegesis on the concept of "man in God's image," Genesis 1, 26-27, and, on the other, the formula which is repeated throughout *Shir ha-Yihud*: "Thou art in everything"). The fact that a work like *Hobot ha-Lebabot* could become widely popular indicates what great strides Jewish religious thought had made from the times of Saadia, especially among the Jews of Spain. Abstract thinking became a sort of religious-ethical duty, a divine command and, as a natural consequence of this, logical reflection gained impetus. For instance, we may note the way Bahya undertakes to prove the impossibility of the existence of more than one Creator of the world: "If we are to believe that there is more than one Creator, we must assume that the substance of each is different. It then follows that, owing to this difference or disparity, they are independent of one another. But that which is independent is finite and that which is finite must have an end; that which comes to an end is a composite entity which must have been created; and everything which is created must have a creator. It thus follows that the proponent of the theory that the world may have had more than one Creator must of necessity arrive at the conclusion that the Creator Himself was created—but we have commenced with the presumption that He is eternal, the Cause of all causes and the Beginning of all beginnings. Thus, He is One, as we are told in Nehemiah ix, 6: "Thou, *even* thou, *art* Lord alone." This argument is the fourth in a series of seven proving the unity of God which appear in the seventh section of *Shaar ha-Yihud*, at the beginning of *The Duties of the Heart*.

But the development of metaphysical thought, even in religious tradition, brings with it a threat of spiritual division and is usually a symptom of a sort of internal crisis. Although the Jewish thinkers in the Islamic world of the 12th century were still following the course set by Saadia and were considering Judaism as the only revealed religion, the concept of faith was nevertheless no more than an abstract idea to them, bringing them ever closer to the non-Jewish adherents of monotheism. If at first their aim had been to establish a rational foundation for their inherited positive faith—in opposition to other positive religions and especially Islam—gradually, as time went on, this became an end-in-itself, all else became subordinated and revolved about this foundation to the exclusion of interest in the positive features of Judaism and especially its social-historic elements. Once more as in the days of early Christianity, there is a resurgence of a strong individualistic tendency, the inevitable result of the fact that the ultimate problems of Jewish life and thought were as a matter of fact posited by outstanding individuals, each treating them in his own peculiar way and colored by his individual development and training. As early as the 11th century, Solomon ibn Gabirol had erected a system of thought which was almost entirely divorced from the Jewish classical historico-philosophical system. And even in his ethics of the knowledge of God, Bahya projects the figure of an isolated individual, face to face with the Creator, as though the Jew could dispense with his real social environment—the Jewish nation. The perils of this a-social and hence anti-social tendency in Jewish religious speculation were felt more strongly by the poet in Judah ha-Levi (ca. 1080-1140) and, spurred by an intense spirit of disapproval, he undertook to lead Jewish religious thought back to its original prophetic roots, aiming thereby not only to rekindle its religious intensity but to render it completely Jewish in spirit.

The historical phenomenon of "prophecy" had long been the concern of both Arabic and Jewish thought. However, up to the time of Judah ha-Levi it had been propounded as a special sort of metaphysical-psychological question: attempts were made to explain in various ways how a man of flesh and blood could share God's knowledge, since only God can prevision the future of the world to the end of time. It was the Jewish thinker of Toledo who was the first and the only one to accord this problem —the phenomenon of prophecy—the greatest importance in his world-view and who pictured the supernatural in life in such a fashion as to make prophecy seem a most natural and fitting manifestation. The basis upon which he built his theory was the doctrine of the prophets themselves, their fundamental formula: the prophet is to the Jews what the Jews are to the peoples around them. Thus the question of the possibility of prophecy automatically took on the character of the historico-philosophical query: what must be the state of the world if the Jewish people is to fulfill its mission in accordance with that which its prophets have themselves experienced, known and foretold? Whereas the prophets had been content simply to proclaim the fundamental principles of their philosophy in the categoric form of God's word, Judah ha-Levi, as a son of his philosophically-schooled generation, felt the need to justify the prophetic doctrine—that is, to differentiate it from other forms of monotheism, especially that form which was a direct outgrowth of Greek philosophy. A similar polemical attitude toward philosophy now became recognizable among the orthodox elements of Islam (Al-Gazali). In disputing with the "philosophers" and their "faith," it was not Judah ha-Levi's aim to minimize rational reflection in favor of blind belief; on the contrary, he sought to clear the field systematically for profounder and more concrete knowledge which could absorb the prophetic conception of universal history, a conception whose heirs and guardians, until the coming of the Messiah are, according to Jewish tradition,

the people of the Torah (see, for example, Judah ibn Tibbon's Hebrew text of the *Kuzari* I, 4 and IV, 13). Judah ha-Levi thus arrives at the conclusion that besides having the essential attributes of man (character, soul and reason), the Jew, the "keeper of the Torah," is, in addition, endowed with the special ability to "apprehend the divine":

Courtesy Jewish Theological Seminary

MANUSCRIPT PAGE OF "KUZARI"
BY JUDAH HA-LEVI

this was another way of saying that only from such material could "prophets" be molded (see *Kuzari* II, 14 ff). Side by side with this Jewish-metaphysical anthropology, Judah ha-Levi outlined a geographical and philological theory whereby he showed that Palestine and Hebrew were the land and language of the true knowledge of God and prophecy, just as the people of Israel are "the people of God" (ibid II, 8-10; IV, 26 referring to *Sefer Yetsirah*). It is clear that God, referred to here, is not an abstract concept and that, for this reason, there is a sharp demarcation between the "God of Abraham and the God of Aristotle" (ibid, IV, 15).

Since this abstract-philosophical monotheism constituted the common ground upon which Jewish religious thinkers met those of Islam, the whole purpose of Judah ha-Levi's thought was directed toward undermining this common basis and setting up a chasm between them.

Judah ha-Levi marks the most critical point in the development of the complicated relations between Jewish tradition and philosophic thought. It seemed that a complete break between them was unavoidable. That it did not occur was primarily due to the rise of a *Jewish Aristotelianism* and especially to its most important representative, the Rambam (Moses ben Maimon, Maimonides, 1135-1204). In speaking of the history of Jewish religious thought, the use of such concepts as Stoicism, neo-Platonism or Aristotelianism is not to be taken to signify systematic schools of philosophy based on clearly self-centralized systems of thought, as was the case in the general history of philosophy. Jewish religious thought was less independent of tradition than was even that of the Moslems. Not one of the Jewish religious thinkers ventured to oppose the authority of the Torah; and if some of them undertook to interpret the nature of the universe in the spirit of neo-Platonic *emanation,* while others chose to cling to Aristotle's cosmological dynamism and teleology, both schools were convinced that their respective interpretations were in accord with the spirit of the Holy Scriptures. However, this period of close cultural contact with the surrounding world demanded a conclusive rational accounting of the Jewish concept of monotheism. Even the romantic Judah ha-Levi built up a "fence" around metaphysical speculation with the methods of rational speculation. It was thus that Judah ha-Levi's younger contemporary, Maimonides, the great systematizer of the Halakah, realized that the only way to arrive at a decision in the matter of the merits of Judaism and reason was to confront Jewish

tradition with the foremost philosophical system of the time—Aristotelianism—in order to establish once and for all that unless reason goes hand in hand with the tenets of the Torah, it contradicts itself. Maimonides did not seek the approval of Greek philosophy for the Torah, but emulated Philo in seeking to hitch Greek speculation to the *Merkabah,* the heavenly chariot of Divine Grace (*Shekinah*).

Chronologically as well as from the standpoint of contents, the work which formed a link between the *Kuzari* of Judah ha-Levi and the *More Nebukim* (Guide for the Perplexed) of Maimonides was the *Emunah Ramah* (Sublime Faith) of Abraham ibn Daud, Rabad I, whose work was originally written, as were the aforementioned two, in Arabic. Like Judah ha-Levi, Rabad came from Toledo. He died in 1180, a martyr for his faith, about ten years before the completion of Maimonides' metaphysical life-work. Whether or not Maimonides was familiar with the work of his predecessor, who is often referred to as the "first Jewish Aristotelian," is still a moot question; but there can be no doubt that both were motivated by the same desire—to allow of no compromises with Aristotelianism but to assimilate it and Greek philosophy in general to such an extent as to put an end to the independent influence they exerted on Jewish thought, and the consequent threat it held for prophetic monotheism. In this respect, both resemble Judah ha-Levi, although their attitudes toward "Greek learning" are basically different. Whereas Judah ha-Levi completely rejected philosophy, Maimonides and ibn Daud wanted to see it absorbed by Judaism. Ibn Daud summed this up most cogently: "The ultimate end of philosophy is the deed," *i.e.,* traditional Jewish conduct. For this reason he was at odds with ibn Gabirol, about whom he wrote that "his book displays a tendency to use philosophy in such a way that all peoples should partake of it, while the Jewish people is not set apart therein as a separate matter." Nevertheless, contrary to Judah ha-Levi, the author of these words hoped to see Jews restored to "the strength to bear two torches—in the right hand the light of Jewish tradition and in the left, the light of reason." As a supporting illustration, he points to the confusion that prevailed among educated Jews in his own circle. By means of his system of thought, Maimonides hoped to end this confusion and chaos in the Arabicized Jewish religious thought of the second half of the 12th century.

The world of Maimonides can be viewed from two aspects, the outer and the inner. Observed from the outer aspect of general philosophy, it presents the typical general picture of medieval Aristotelianism, with its partial absorption of neo-Platonist elements, the only difference being that the controlling power is not Aristotle's "First Mover" in His majestic eternal immutability, but a divine, all-powerful Will, simultaneously King and Ruler, Who is concerned with the conduct of the world, Whose providence reaches even unto the individual and Who sanctions exceptions in the eternal order of natural events, since all that exists is His doing. In brief, this is Aristotle's world, where generous room has been found for the God of the Jewish Torah. An altogether different picture emerges from an internal examination of Maimonides' system. It is at once apparent that here we find ourselves within the borders of the ancient, purely-Jewish religious tradition which stretches without interruption from biblical times and the days of the Talmud to the period of Saadia and his followers, even to Judah ha-Levi. But again there is a difference; the ancient Jewish heritage and outlook are now dominated by a systematic order and an atmosphere of speculative, or better still, terminological clarity, which are all indicative of the Greek classical spirit. It is no longer Judaized Aristotelianism but rather, Hellenized Judaism. The very fact that all the elements of Maimonides' system summed up into a harmonious whole is evidence that the basic aim of the Jewish thought of the Middle Ages—in its striving to preserve its historical independence with regard to non-Jewish monotheism—was to achieve a synthesis which should embrace the scientific elements of the surrounding culture wherever they did not contradict the Jewish religious tradition.

The point at which Maimonides dissented from the philosopher (Aristotle) was the question whether God's world is eternal or the result of creation. Aristotle contended that the world is just as eternal in time as is its "First Mover," while according to the Torah, life commences with *"Bereshit Bara"* (In the beginning God created). However, since there is no logical argument for either the thesis or the antithesis and the human mind is here confronted with what is now termed an "antinomy," Maimonides concludes that logical reasoning itself compels us, in this metaphysical basic problem, to rely upon the truth revealed in the Torah, and not upon logic and argumentation.

"Is then our whole Torah," he wrote, "less worthy than their empty phrases? If Aristotle may invoke the opinions of the Sabians, why may we not base ours on the words of Moses and Abraham and all that follows therefrom?" His advice therefore was that in dealing with this difficult question, man must ever "suspect his own reason" and follow the tradition of the "two prophets" who are the pillars on which humankind with its beliefs and peoples rest (*More*, II, 23). In the terminology of modern philosophy, this may be described as "critical irrationalism." It is the method of acknowledging super-rational sources of wisdom only when the object lies outside the realm of rational apprehension. Maimonides never questioned the existence of such "objects" and certainly not of the most exalted of them —God. In a most radical manner, Maimonides sets out to prove the ancient Jewish idea of "God's oneness" by showing that He is the perfection of unity and uniqueness and that His attributes must therefore all be negative; when we speak, for instance, of God's infinite wisdom or goodness, we can mean only that any form of finiteness or ignorance or evil is not applicable in His case.

"The more emphasis man lays on the

negative in connection with God, the nearer he approaches to the concept of God and to Him, praised be His name," declares Maimonides (ibid. I, 59). It is best not to speak about His essence at all, as we are told in Psalms: "Fitting praise for Thee is silence" (I, 59 and 50). If we are to speak of divine attributes, they must be found exclusively in the "character and quality of His acts"; attributes and acts which we humans must seek to emulate and which may be indicated as God's "ways" (ibid. I, 54). Thus the theosophy of Maimonides leads to the fundamental principle of his ethical system. If, despite its closeness to neo-Platonic mysticism, his theosophy is thoroughly impregnated with the Torah, so his system of ethics, regardless of the echo of Aristotle to be found therein, is essentially Jewish, especially in the so-called *Eight Chapters*.

Like Aristotle, Maimonides regarded it as man's supreme aim to strive for the cognition of God and the approach to Him. This God, however, is not Aristotle's God, but the "God of Abraham." Moreover, to Maimonides, the greatest nearness to God is attained not by abstract metaphysical reflection, but by prophecy, a concept which in this form is essentially alien to Greek philosophy. In his teachings about prophecy, Maimonides comes closest to a number of Arabian thinkers (Al Farabi, et al.) and, more particularly, to his Jewish predecessors—ibn Daud and Judah ha-Levi. It was Maimonides' conviction that to be a philosopher one must be virtuous himself, and in order to be a prophet, one must be something even more than a philosopher: side by side with logic, there must be the highest form of intuition and only when all these elements are at hand, can the miracle of Divine Revelation come to pass (ibid. II, 36). The "Master of all wise men" and the "father of the prophets," Moses, is, however, unique in history, since his Torah is one, and God, from whom Moses received the Torah, is the One and Only God (ibid. II, 39). It therefore follows that unique in its kind and hallowed is also the people of Israel; unique in its kind and hallowed, is even its tongue, Hebrew, a "holy tongue" (ibid. III, 8).

This was the metaphysical background against which Maimonides codified his Jewish religious dogma (in his commentaries on the Mishnah, from which is taken the "Ani Maamin" — credo — of the prayer-books, and in the first book of his Halakah codex "Mishneh Torah"). Maimonides' greatest contribution to the history of Jewish and even non-Jewish religious thought was especially the systematic and logical order he introduced into these studies. The great Christian scholars of the 13th century—an Albertus Magnus, a Thomas Aquinas or a Duns Scotus—discovered in Maimonides' *Doctor Perplexorum* (the Latin title of *More Nebukim*) a classic example of positive faith which fits in harmoniously with universal knowledge and learning. At the same time Maimonides' system represents the point where the paths of Christian Church and traditional Judaism meet for the last time and then part again—a logical inevitability once it has been granted that regarding its fundamental truth positive faith can permit no compromise on the basis of merely human knowledge. His insistence on the "oneness" of God, the Creator's absolute unity, supramundaneity, incorporeality, etc. was applied by Catholic teachers to the church dogma of the Trinity and the Man-God. It was only in comparatively recent times that even the non-Jewish world began to appreciate how much more stress Maimonides had laid on wisdom and logic than on the irrational element.

Maimonides' religious-philosophical system represented a milestone between two eras of Jewish thought. It marked a departure from which there set in a period of critical analysis of naive traditionalism. With his older contemporary, the Arabian Aristotelian ibn Roshd (Averroes), Maimonides shared the theory that metaphysical speculation is beyond the grasp of the masses and can only serve to deflect the man of no or little education from the path of piety.

Nevertheless Maimonides' entire system evinces an impulse to a differentiation in the traditional attitude of the Jewish masses toward their spiritual heritage. His very vindication of the sources of truth—knowledge and faith—in matters regarding the national outlook on life was in itself enough to rouse discussion as to their respective prerogatives. For instance, to what extent is an abstract, metaphysical interpretation of the Torah justified? Or, may one, as a pietist, discover in the accounts of the sacrifices, etc., merely a concession on the part of the Torah to more primitive habits, upon their flight from Egypt? (see *"More"* III, 35 and 46). In general, is not such "heresy" the result of absorption in "secular" studies? These, and similar questions, stirred the Jewish world and for several centuries were the shibboleths of sharp controversies. The great number of commentaries on the *"More Nebukim"* (from Shem-Tob ibn Falaquera, Joseph Caspi and Moses ben Joshua of Narbonne in the 13th and 14th centuries down to the *Gibeat ha-More* of Solomon ben Joshua Maimon at the close of the 18th century) testifies how deep and multifarious Maimonides' influence on Jewish religious thought has been. Ever since, every Jewish thinker has first had to determine for himself whether he is with Maimonides or against him. In the latter case, he has had to decide whether to follow the path back to ancient tradition or to go forward along the road of critical reason. The conflicts which arose as to the borderline between faith and knowledge awakened in the Jewish world such an awareness of metaphysical and scientific problems in general that, alongside with Hebrew translations of Jewish philosophical studies originally written in Arabic, Jewish scholars at the end of the 12th and during the 13th centuries translated more and more works of non-Jewish thinkers and scholars, from Aristotle to Averroes. For the first time in Jewish history, the "holy tongue" became a language of philosophy and science and endowed them thereby with a measure of "holiness."

IV. BETWEEN THE MIDDLE AGES AND MODERN TIMES

In the history of Jewish religious thought, the Middle Ages are, in the first place, the period in which a clear contrast is drawn between prophetic-biblical monotheism and all the other forms of belief in One God which did not directly cling to the Jewish historical tradition. At that period, this second category was primarily represented by Arabic philosophy. The 12th century, when Maimonides lived, is also the period when the center of Jewish national life began to shift more and more from Islamic lands to those of Christendom. However great the dangers that thus threatened the very survival of the Jewish people, as far as Jewish monotheism was concerned, it escaped therewith the peril that might have faced it. Only in the purely emotional spheres, Christian mysticism may have exerted a certain measure of influence on Jews. Thus it probably was not a matter of chance that in the 13th century, when Latin, the language of philosophy and science was also mastered by a considerable number of Jewish scholars, a new form of Jewish mysticism came to light, the Kabbala. Just as the Rambam (Maimonides) was the symbol and representative of the previous century, so Ramban (Moses ben Nahman, 1195-1270), one of the Fathers of Kabbala in Spain, became one of the outstanding figures of the next period. Nevertheless, the development of philosophical thought, from Saadia to Maimonides, continued to hold sway for several centuries, even under these changed conditions. The history of thought has its own immanent logic. Incompletely answered questions demand solutions, even though the circumstances giving rise to the problem have long since disappeared. Even at the very threshold of modern times, we thus find Jewish sages and scholars who prefer to follow old traditional paths and still try to build up metaphysical bases for the Jewish world-view along the lines of the old Hellenic-Arabic ways of reasoning. Regardless of the rich quality of their minds and their spiritual scope, these men are essentially still futilely engaged in settling old accounts for people who are long gone.

Among the tendencies of Jewish thought in the post-Maimonides era, the one most violently opposed by the zealots of tradition was allegorism, that form of metaphysical commentary familiar to us from Hellenistic times and now allegedly sanctioned by Maimonides himself. The interpretation of the Pentateuch tales in the allegorical-metaphysical sense was carried so far that Abraham, for instance, was translated into the concept of "form" and Sarah became "matter." The foremost figure of this movement was Levi ben Abraham ben Hayim or Ralbah of Southern France (d. ca. 1315). His contemporaries in Italy were Zerahiah ben Shealtiel Hen of Rome and Hillel ben Samuel of Verona, the author of *Tagmule ha-Nefesh,* a book in which the doctrine of reward and punishment in the after-life is treated in a strictly rationalistic manner, in the spirit of Maimonides. It is of historic significance that, in his polemics with Averroes, Hillel has recourse to a Christian source (a Latin tract of Thomas Aquinas). The new Catholic speculation now becomes an object of spiritual assimilation on the part of Jewish thinkers, as had once been Greek and, later, Arabic philosophy; with this difference, however, that Christian speculation was itself now in a great measure the result of the assimilation-process which had been greatly stimulated by essentially Jewish methods and thought.

Isaac Albalag's doctrine of the "twofold" truth—paralleling that of the Christian Averroists of the 13th century — now becomes historically comprehensible. This Jewish thinker, who lived either in Southern France or Northern Spain, developed the thesis that the spirit of philosophy and prophecy are diametrically opposed; in philosophy even concrete reality is apprehended conceptually, while in prophecy even concepts are apprehended concretely. From this, he infers that the truth of rational reflection and the truth of prophetic Torah have nothing in common—a thing may be true from the philosophical standpoint and yet may seem entirely false from the standpoint of faith and belief. Thus, Maimonides who wished to make concessions to both knowledge and faith, actually did injustice to both of them. This dual radicalism, which sacrificed the highest principle of the spirit—the one and only truth—in order to defend knowledge against faith and faith against knowledge, was symptomatic of the confusion then existing in Jewish religious thinking. The systems of Levi ben Gershon, Ralbag (1288-1344) and of Hasdai Crescas (ca. 1340-1410) attempted to overcome this confusion by a resorting to ancient metaphysics in the spirit of a changing world.

The system developed by Ralbag and especially evident in his work *Milhamot Adonai* (Wars of the Lord) is partly pattern-

Courtesy Jewish Theological Seminary

TITLE PAGE OF "MILHAMOT HA SHEM"
(THE WARS OF THE LORD)

BY LEVI BEN GERSHON; RIVA DI TRENTO, 1560

ed after Maimonides, but whereas Maimonides regarded the orthodox Aristotelianism of Averroes as offensive from the Jewish standpoint, Ralbag attempted to improve on Maimonides in the rationalistic spirit of classical Arabic Aristotelianism. At almost every point where Maimonides diverged from ibn Roshd's Aristotelianism, we find Ralbag in the opposite camp, commencing with his discussion of divine attributes. The essence of God is not such as to preclude any positive predicate; first, He is pure thought, as asserted by Aristotle; unity and being in their turn are inseparable from the essence of substance, hence it is a contradiction only for the analyzing reason to comprehend the One God's essence, in an aggregate of attributes such as thought, unity, existence, etc. (*Milhamot*, III, 3). Furthermore, Ralbag could not agree with Maimonides that the world was created *ex nihilo,* and held that on this point the Torah was on his side. He claimed that there existed a primordial substance without which even the Supreme Form, Divine Thought, could not have shaped anything. This primordial substance, he declared, was only the pure *potentiality* of being. It would be false to assume from this that the world is eternal and not the work of God. Here we hear in Ralbag's work again the echo of Jewish tradition; not only was the world *created* but "with every instant God renews His *Maase Bereshit* (creation)." The antinomy between creation and the eternity of the world leads to the concept of "eternal creation." With this is linked an entirely new concept of time: God is outside of time; time applies only to the world; viewed from within, the world renews itself every instant; viewed from the divine aspect, its very temporality, eternal in nature, is the conceptual substratum of all divine creation. It would thus seem that creative thought and time are correlative, and Ralbag substitutes them for the Aristotelian-scholastic formula of primordial form and primordial matter (*Milhamot,* VI, 1). Thus a cornerstone for the classical idealism of modern times was laid by a Jewish religious philosopher of the 14th century.

Typical of Ralbag's system are the indications of a new phase in the history of human thought. God is the Supreme Thought and hence the basic laws of thought apply to Him, too. His providence dwells in the wisdom, harmony and purposefulness which govern the universe. Hence it cannot affect the accidental nature of concrete individual existence. In this, too, Ralbag clashed with Maimonides (ibid. III, 2 and 4). For Ralbag, this did away with what constituted a mystery for Maimonides, how to reconcile man's free will with God's foreknowledge of everything that every man of flesh and blood would ever do.

As a student of astrology, categorically rejected by Maimonides, Ralbag so interpreted it that nature emerged as an organic entity ruled by its own immutable laws. Ralbag even attempted to explain miracles and prophecy according to natural laws. Most significant are his conclusions about immortality, since they are based on the premise that acquired or cognitive reason (according to Aristotle, the "immortal" in man) is a continuous ever-developing thought-process which constantly transcends itself (see *Milhamot* I, 13)—approximately the same axiom as that evolved by modern apperceptive psychology.

The advent in the Jewish world of the sage of Avignon (the Christian world knew him as Gersonides), whose scientific works were translated into Latin at papal behest and were said to have exerted great influence on Kepler, was tardy rather than premature. Aside from his influence on the youthful Spinoza of the 17th century, we may regard Ralbag as the final link of a broken chain. Even the philosopher Hasdai Crescas, the second great Jewish systematizer of the 14th century, who was born some four years before the death of Ralbag, followed a system entirely opposed to that of his older contemporary. The Chief Rabbi of Aragon, who lost his only son during the persecutions of 1391, hearkened back to the period preceding that of Maimonides and adopted approximately the attitude of Judah ha-Levi in his approach toward philosophy. His cry

MANUSCRIPT PAGE OF "OR ADONAI" (THE LIGHT OF THE LORD)

was: Torah, not philosophy! Following the method established by his 12th century predecessor, Crescas, at the beginning of the 15th, fought philosophy with its own weapons; and, since at that time philosophy and Aristotelianism were almost identical, Crescas turned his weapons against the antiquated Aristotelian metaphysics and thus unwittingly furthered the development of European thought.

Crescas' anti-Aristotelian system was carefully grounded. First, he attacked the scholastic theory of *matter,* asserting that even without form primordial matter is an *ens.* In other words, it is *matter* in the physical sense; where material substances do not exist there is vacuity, emptiness of space characterized merely by extension. Space is thus unbounded, infinite, just as are time and number. Thus, Crescas erected his framework in which the modern view of nature was to be set. Galileo, Bruno and especially Newton, meet, in very important details, with the arguments advanced by Crescas at the beginning of the 15th century, in his work *Light of God* (Or Adonai 1, 2). Just as for the rabbi of the 15th century, so for Newton infinity of space was the natural symbol of God's omnipresence. Actually, this thought is an ancient Jewish heritage: *Hu mekomo shel olam* (He is the world's space. Cf. Maimonides' *More* 1, 70). In the light of these arguments, the question of the Creation assumed a new aspect: if space, time and number are infinite, it must be assumed in principle that the chain of causes is also infinite, and it does not therefore necessarily follow that there must be a First Mover, Aristotle's God. If there is a logically necessary correlation between the world and God, it is because everything that exists can also be conceived as non-existent; consequently the world cannot have any real validity, unless there is some source whose existence is not only possible but absolutely essential, and that source is God, the only stable basis of being and existence. Thus, God is the only cause of the world's existence, its only guarantee of continuity from eternity to eternity (*Or Adonai* III, 1), a

point of spiritual agreement between **Crescas** and the older Kalam on the one hand and all the later proponents of the so-called "ontological argument" on the other.

Crescas' theories here have points of contact with those of his opponent, Ralbag, since with the latter the world's dependence upon God takes also an almost transcendental character. However, Crescas feels that, according to the Torah, we must assume that the world was created in time. Thereby he did not succumb to the philosophical heresy of advocating "double truth" (one for the philosophers and another for theologians) since the *time* he had in mind was not strictly that which man's ordinary language conveys.

A consistent opponent of Aristotelian rationalism, Crescas, together with Judah ha-Levi, is the foremost exponent of Jewish anti-intellectualism. In all his teachings about God, man's essence, immortality and "punishment and reward," he stresses the point that will and emotion, not intellect, are predominant and all-important. Supreme among God's attributes is His benevolence, His desire to create and do good; the joy engendered by His goodness becomes God's love for His creatures. The greatest height to which man can aspire is the love of God: "Thou shalt love the Lord thy God" is consequently a greater deed of merit than cognition of Him. And, since this is taught us by the Torah, and its commandments aim at evoking and fostering this emotion in man, the Torah towers far above all philosophical speculation. If man is immortal, his heart—"the love of God"—must be preserved even more than his intelligence. True paradise is to feel eternally this love of God (ibid. II, 6). Reward and punishment presented a particularly complex problem for Crescas since he was a stern determinist in his attitude toward natural philosophy. He had this to say about man's freedom of will: despite the fact that man's deeds are the natural consequence of a series of all kinds of causes, his own volitions are a vital link in that chain; should he incline toward evil ways, there will be an immediate and direct consequence, as though he had touched glowing iron (ibid. II, 5).

It is characteristic of this period which produced the Marranos, that the author of *Or Adonai* also wrote polemics in Spanish against Christian dogma. There is even a somewhat polemic undertone in Crescas' emphasis on the "love" element in classical Judaism; the same applies to his complicated doctrine of divine attributes which, according to him, stand in their multiplicity in the same close relation with God's indefinable essence, as light with a lighting substance (ibid. I, 3). His chief purpose was to strengthen Judaism in a positive fashion, even though it might occasionally be with a thought or argument from the works of a Thomas Aquinas (as, for instance, in his doctrine of *Creatio ex Nihilo*).

In general, now there began to manifest itself in the sphere of Jewish thought a conservative tendency and a trend toward mysticism. As early as 1360, Meir ibn Aldabi declared war on philosophy in his *Shebile Emunah*, The Paths of Faith. Whatever merit there might be in the systems of Plato and Aristotle he ascribed to the fact that they were disciples of Jewish sages. Aldabi and his younger contemporaries, Rashbaz (Simon ben Zemah Duran, 1361-1444) and Shem-Tob ben Joseph ibn Shem-Tob (d. ca. 1440), often resorted to Kabbala, especially in their doctrine of the soul. In his work *Magen Abot*, Rashbaz aimed his polemics especially at Paul the Apostle. Even Efodi (Profiat Duran), the famous commentator of Maimonides' *More*, published two tracts against the Christian dogmas of the Trinity and the Man-God. In order to rescue the vestiges of philosophical tradition among the Sephardim, ibn Shem-Tob's son, Joseph ben Shem-Tob (d. 1460), the author of *Kebod Elohim*, set out to prove that it was possible to be an Aristotelian and, at the same time, even more pious than Maimonides. Nevertheless, his own son, Shem-Tob ben Joseph (d. 1489) had the courage to write a comprehensive commentary on Maimonides' *More*. This was approximately four years prior to the expulsion from Spain. The two Sephardic thinkers who were fated to end their days in exile—Isaac Abravanel (1437-1508) whose name is so closely linked with the catastrophe of Spain, and Isaac ben Moses Arama (1420-1493), the Baal Akedah (thus called because of his popular Bible commentary)—are the symbolic figures of the conservative-mystic leanings of the period. Although thoroughly versed in philosophical literature Arama wrote *Hazut Kashah* in which he excoriated all ventures into the field of philosophical speculation, and the insolence of philosophy toward true faith, he compared to the temerity of the servant Hagar in setting herself up against her mistress Sarah, the wife of Abraham the Patriarch. Isaac Abravanel was just as harsh in his condemnation, and laid the blame for the Expulsion at the door of philosophy, just as the Kabbalist ibn Shem-Tob had previously held it responsible for mass conversion to Catholicism. In his commentary on *More Nebukim*, as well as in his own writings *Mifalot Elohim* (The Works of God) and *Rosh Amanah* (Foundation of Faith), Abravanel not only challenged Maimonides' theories about prophecy and miracles but also strove to refute Crescas' views of the Creation.

It is highly characteristic that to this last Jewish thinker of Spain, the very idea of Jewish dogmaticism was offensive. Following Maimonides, Albalag, Crescas and Rashbaz attempted to establish their own systems of Jewish dogma. Somewhat later, their disciple Joseph Albo (d. 1444) published his work *Ikkarim* (Principles). Just as with Rashbaz, his three fundamental principles are the three fundamental premises which the essential concept of a divinely revealed faith demands as a logical necessity: there is a God in the world; He reveals His wishes or Torah to man; He rewards him according to his deeds, since therein the actual importance of His Torah manifests itself (*Ikkarim* I, 10 and 13). In the tree of dogma, these three principles form the main "roots" from which spring any number of other "stems," each a different "shoot," displaying individual "strains" or dominating prin-

שתהיה ההצלחה האנושית נתלת בעיון ובמעשה כמו סבאר התילוסו בספר הנפש והיו הדעות האמתיות והמעשיס ה
המשובחיס או אשר סיושב על נכון מצד השכל האנושי להיות שכל האדם לוחה מהשיג הדבריס על חמיתתם כמו שי
שיבא חמייב בהכרח שימצא דבר הוא למעלה מהשכל האנושי שבל האנושי על ידו יונבלו המעשיס המשובחי ויושבלו הדעות הא
האמתיות בענין שלא יהיה בהס שוס ספק כלל וזה לא יהיה אלא בהישרה אלהית וע'כ היה ראוי ומחויב על כל האדם
להכיר דת הדת האלהית המישרת לזה מזולתה מן הדתיות וזה לא יתכן אלא בידיעת העיקרי שאי אפשר שתמצא דת הדת האלהי
אלתם והיא היתה כוונת החבור הזה לבאר העיקריס ההכרחיס לדת האלהית כמה הס ובעבור זה נקרח שמו ספר ה
העיקריס ויחלק להקדמה וד'מאמריס :

ההקדמה היא להודיע ההברח המביא לחבר הספר והח
באר בה נודל מעלת החקירה הנבלת בזה הספ'
והחקירה מדאוי שיסבו בו דרך כלל נית

וסרע בה פסוק והי נועס : **המאמר הא'** ויחקור מעיקרי הדתן כמה הס נאי אלו הס וההבדל
שיש בין הדתות האלהיות והיימוסיות
עקרי הדת הניימסית ויבאר ניש לדתנות עיקריס כוללים ונקריס מיוחדיס ושהעיקרי הכוללי לדתיות האלהית הס ג'
שהס מציאות השם · נתורה מן השמיס · ושכר ועוגש · ויבאר שיס תחת אלו עקריס אחריס נתליס בהס ומתעצפיס
מהס ויבאר במה במה תוכר הדת האלהית מן הדת המזוייפת המתדמה בהאלהית :

המאמר הב' כביאור העקר הראשון שהוא מציאות השם והעקריס הנתלים בו ומסתעפים ממנו :
המאמר הג' כביאור עיקר הב' שהוא תורה מן השמיס והעקריס הנתליס בו ומסתעפים ממנ :
המאמר הד' כביאור עיקר הג' שהוא שכר ועונש והעקריס המסתעפים ממנו והדכרי הנתליס בו :
המאמר הא' בחקירה מעיקרי הדתות כמה הס ויחלק אל שנה ועשריס פ'רקים :

פרק א' יודיע בו הקוצר שיש בחקירה על העיקריס לדתיות ויאמ'שיש שס עיקרי כוללי וחלקי'לכל דת ודת ויכנה
על הר'מבס ז'ל שמנה ביאת המשיח מעיקרי תור' מ'שה וכן יקשה על האומרי'שאחד העגול עיקר לתור מ'שה
פרק ב' ויבאר בו מי היא המכחיש דבר מן העקריס שיקרא כופר ומי הוא המכחיש אותס ולא יקרא כופר ויבאר
שאין ראוי שימנו ביאת המשיח ולא חדוש העולס עיקריס לתורת מ'שה כמו שחובי רבים :
פרק ג' יבאר על מה זה יפול מלת עיקר ויחקור על היינ עיקרי שהניח הר'מבס ז'ל אס המסבר ההוא הוא מהדקדק
אם לאו ויחקור ג'כ על עיקרים אחריס שהנינח לדת האלהית ויבאר מהס שוס מספר מהס מתחדך :
פרק ד' יבאר בו שהעיקריס הכוללים לדת האלהית הס ג'שהם כמו אבות והם מציאות השם ותורה מן השמי'
ושכר ועונש ומפתחת אלו שרשוס אחריס מסתעפים מהס ונקליס בהס ואל כי לכך היה ברכות ל'ה שלש
שהם מלכיות וברונות ומופרית כנגד הג'עקרי הללו ונא'שבל העיקרי שמנה הר'מבס ז'ל הס מסתעפים
מן הג'אבות הללו :
פרק ה' יבאר בו הכרח מציאות דת טבעית לקיום המין האנושי ויבאר שהיא לבדה לא תספיק לקיום הקבון המ
המדיני כאלת המצא דת אחרת ניבאר הברח מציאות השוטפ כמדינה או המלך :
פרק ו' יברע שהיא ראוי שתמצא תורה אלהית להיות להיישיר האנשיס אל מי'מול ההצלחה האנושית

Courtesy Jewish Theological Seminary

א ג'

PAGE OF TEXT OF "IKKARIM" (PRINCIPLES)
BY JOSEPH ALBO; SONCINO, 1485

ciples. With these are linked the "branches" of religion, that is, the specific commandments. Although every religion which regards itself as "divine" must incorporate these three basic "general dogmas," this is not necessarily proof that every faith which accepts them is revealed of God. Thus, neither Islam nor Christianity can qualify as pure, divine religion, since the only revelation made by God to man after Adam, Noah and Abraham, was through the Torah at Sinai. Although, in his philosophy of history, Albo closely approaches the materialistic naturalism of ibn Khaldun (see *Ikkarim* I, 25), he has no doubt whatever as to the special spiritual destiny of Israel in the world's history. Everywhere in his book, which is patterned after Latin scholastic works, one feels the anti-Catholic spirit (see III, 25) which filled him during the famous disputation at Tortosa (1413); and still, by the end of that century the whole problem of fundamental dogmas lost all *raison d'être* for Sephardic Jews. Abravanel contended that faith once granted demanded absolute faith in every letter of the Torah, without distinguishing between "roots" and "branches," between principles and corollaries (see especially *Rosh Amanah*). The Sephardic thinker and leader had now concentrated most of his attention on the consideration of a problem completely outside the sphere of philosophy—he was preoccupied with mystical calculations of the year of the Messiah's arrival. Later, at the beginning of the 17th century, distant Poland produced two commentators on Albo's *Ikkarim*, Jacob Koppelman of Brisk and Gedaliah ben Solomon of Lublin (author of *Sharashim ve-Anafim*, Roots and Branches).

By the end of the Middle Ages, Spain shared with Southern France the distinction of being practically the last outpost where the tradition of Jewish-Arabic philosophy was still influential in the midst of the new Christian world. Just on the eve of modern times, these traditions found a new refuge in Italy, where Christian-humanism was then flourishing. The direct Jewish thinkers to spring up in Italy beginning with Hillel of Verona, had been pupils of the Sephardic sages. It was not until the 15th century that the field of Jewish research in Italy produced figures of more or less original stature. First among these were: that savant in Christian, Greek, Arabic and Jewish philosophical literature, Judah ben Jehiel of Mantua, better known by his Italian cognomen of Messer Leon (ca. 1440-1490), and the friend of the Florentine Platonist Pico della Mirandola, Elijah Delmedigo (ca. 1460-1497) who translated Hebrew and Arabic philosophical works into Latin and, leaning on Averroes, attempted to find a golden midway between pious rationalism and Kabbalistic mysticism in his book *Behinat ha-Dat,* Scrutiny of Religion. But the most eminent among the Jewish thinkers of Italy was a pure Sephardi, the son of Isaac Abravanel, Judah Abravanel or Leo Hebraeus (ca. 1460-1530) in whose *Dialoghi di Amore,* Dialogues of Love, written in Italian, or possibly originally in Spanish, the spiritual influence of his old and his new home are evident to an equal degree. Though Leo Hebraeus still employed Aristotelian scholastic concepts, he nevertheless managed to introduce into his work a Platonic spirit, then experiencing a revival in Italy. Like his father before him, he espoused the theory that the *cosmos* was created by the One and only God and *in time* (*bizman*); but with him it is, in the best Platonic manner, a single organism, held together by the love of God toward His creation, a love which permeated the world from end to end, binding all its parts and drawing man and all creation back to God. He, the all-Powerful One, is the God not only of truth and justice, but also of beauty. Attempts have been made to trace the influence of Crescas, Solomon ibn Gabirol and the Kabbala in this work of Judah Abravanel. At any rate, it is clear that its author was the product of a generation which was on the road to a new era. Significant in this respect is the fact that his "discourses" rapidly gained favor in the Christian world, whereas they met with no response among the traditionally religious Jews.

The philosophic-scientific works of Joseph Solomon Delmedigo (1591-1655), the great-grandson of Elijah Delmedigo, have but a symptomatic significance in the history of Jewish religious thought. In his youth a pupil of Galileo, Yashar of Candia, as Joseph Solomon Delmedigo was called among Jews, oscillated between Kabbala and rationalism, between tradition and modern science. Born in Crete, fate cast him as far as Lithuania, and a number of his works first saw the light of day in Holland where, a few decades later, there was to burgeon forth Spinoza's *Amor Dei Intellectualis*, Intellectual Love of God.

In Spinoza's system, traditional Jewish speculation left its confines which had remained steadfast during the Middle Ages. The tide of the times broke down one barrier after another, even in the neighboring Christian world. For the first time in its history, Jewish religious thought was compelled to ask what purpose it had to fulfill in a world which sees its holiest possession neither in tradition nor in this or that positive faith nor even in disbelief, but in transhistorical reason.

V. THE PERIOD OF PURE REASON

The periods of Humanism, of the Renaissance, and of the Reformation gradually widened the spiritual horizon of Western Europe. In place of the Catholic outlook which had previously united all of educated Christendom, there arose now a new world-view. This world-view gradually liberated itself from any bonds with a definite theological tradition and sought its roots in the universal spirit of man, on the basis of experimental natural science and under the strict control of impartial reason. Arguments stressing the inviolability of tradition or prescribed opinions were no longer regarded as valid. The "chain of tradition" had, however, always been the prevailing factor in Jewish religious thought. Now, in the new era when reason took precedence over all else, Jewish religious speculation had only three possible roads open: to point out and emphasize the purely rational elements in Jewish tradition and thereby forever renounce its right to an individual historical existence apart, or, on the contrary, to delve more deeply than ever before into the treasures and hidden mysteries of the Jewish spiritual past; the third choice was to seek some middle course between Judaism and pure human reason. The first course was followed by a few isolated individuals who divorced themselves completely from the Jewish community (the classic example here being Spinoza). The second course had been followed as early as the 16th century by the large majority of the more educated among the Jewish masses who, contrary to the tendency of the individualistically-minded thinkers, cut themselves away ever more sharply from the surrounding non-Jewish world. The third course open to Jewish religious thought, to follow with the spirit of the time, was taken by the Haskalah.

From the time immediately after the expulsion from Spain almost to the end of the 18th century, Jewish religious speculation was dominated by the advocates of theoretical and practical Kabbala (together with the Messianism which had now become an integral part of Kabbala) and by the adherents of the strict rabbinic tradition. At that time, the reign of the Kabbala spread wherever Sephardic influence prevailed—from the Near East as far west as Holland. Parallel with it was the ascetic *Musar* (moralist) literature. The 16th and 17th century Messianism was the spiritual offspring of the Kabbala, but in the 18th century it degenerated into the Frankist movement, simultaneously encouraging the revival of mysticism in the form of the Hassidic movement. Rabbinical learning regarded these new spiritual currents with reserve, but on the whole accepted the Kabbala tradition and especially the newly-risen Zohar tradition.

To such great Halakah scholars in Poland (which now had become the center of rabbinical learning) as Solomon Luria, "Rashal" (1510-1573) and Joel Sirkes, "Bach" (d. ca. 1640), Kabbala represented *true wisdom.* It was far more significant for the further development of Jewish specula- tion that among leading Ashkenazic rabbis of Poland there were many for whom the attitude of reserve toward the Kabbala was not merely a matter of choice but a result of their adherence to the pre-Kabbalist school of Spain, primarily that of Maimon- ides. Moses Isserles, "Rama" (1520-1572), who first introduced the *Shulhan Aruk* (code book for ritual and legislative ques- tions) in Poland, was also the author of a work purporting to interpret the command- ments of the Torah in the light of Maimon- ides' teachings. Thus, in the 18th century, Maimonides' *More Nebukim* was still an important factor in the life of the Ashken- azic orthodoxy. Whereas in the case of the Lithuanian Solomon Maimon (1754-1800) the *More* served only to arouse his interest in general problems of philosophy which ultimately led him away from the Jewish world, for the German Moses Mendelssohn (1729-1786) it opened a completely new horizon and he saw therein a new path for Judaism to tread, leading directly to the Haskalah period in the history of Jewish religious thought.

When the time came to make an about- face toward the surrounding non-Jewish world, German Jewry became the van- guard and, for that reason, the qualified heirs of the Sephardic culture. Enthu- siasts of the Haskalah compared the Ash- kenazic thinker Moses Dessau or Ramba- man, as they called Moses Mendelssohn, to Moses ben Maimon of Cordova. Both dreamed of terminating the conflict be- tween Torah and Reason. But, whereas the Torah remained the old one, the prestige of Reason, commencing with the 12th century, had greatly risen. As it gained in impor- tance, it grew less and less tolerant of rivalry in the field of metaphysics.

The method of the rationalist era was to argue that if the Torah teaches us about metaphysical matters—God, freedom, im- mortality, etc.—whatever is not in accord- ance with pure reason, is false; if, on the other hand, its teachings coincide with those of Reason, it is superfluous. Mendelssohn favored this approach. His first metaphys- ical works, *Ueber die Evidenz in meta- physischen Wissenschaften* (1764), *Phaedon* (1767), and others, appeal to human reason as such and do not seek their support in Jewish sources, although their themes were the positive attributes of God, especially His absolute moral perfection, the question of an after-life and other such topics which had heretofore been regarded by orthodox Jew- ish thinkers as the basic principles of the Jewish religion.

In seeking a reply to the question: Why is the Torah necessary at all if reason need have no recourse to it? Mendelssohn finally came to the conclusion (particularly in *Jerusalem oder ueber religioese Macht und Judentum,* 1783) that, in contrast to the mystical Christian faith, Judaism is a system of practical commandments and "Ceremon- ial" laws imposing no obligation to "be- lieve" in a metaphysical premise. The pur- pose here is to educate an entire people to a point where it will be capable of compre- hending "the eternal truths of Reason" (*Jerusalem,* II). In his *Tractatus Theolo- gico-Politicus,* Spinoza had already pointed out that Moses' Torah was not a system of dogmas but a code of laws. Judah ha-Levi, long before and from a different standpoint, had been very insistent on the *Mitsvot Maasiot.* A sharp opponent of Spinoza's pantheism and a warm admirer of the great poet Judah ha-Levi, Mendelssohn employed modern *heresies* in order to strengthen the structure of the Jewish tradition of the Mid- dle Ages. It is interesting to note that al- ready at the beginning of the 18th century, David Nieto (d. 1728), the Sephardic rabbi of London, who was wrongly suspected of leaning toward Spinoza's pantheism wrote *Kuzari Helek Sheni* (Second Kuzari) in his own defense, patterning his work after the model of Judah ha-Levi.

Mendelssohn's effort to divorce ethical monotheism from the Torah and make the former the common property of all man- kind while at the same time declaring the Jews to be the sole owners of God's Torah, was in sharp conflict with his own meta-physical conviction that God's absolute goodness belongs to all men, Jews and non-Jews alike. If it is true that all Jewish *mitsvot* "remind and stimulate to reflect on the eternal truths of Reason" (*Jerusalem,* II), why were only the Jewish people worthy to receive the Sinai revelation? The answer to this was Mendelssohn's philosophy of history which, in sharp contrast to the current optimism of the times, testified that in the field of historic reality Jewish rationalistic universalism had its own experience after all. Man, declared Mendelssohn, is a naturally reasoning creature and yet permits himself to be led astray; it was therefore necessary that there should spring up a group of people whose particular task it was "through the fact of its very existence, so to speak, to disseminate among the rest of mankind healthy and unadulterated ideas" (ibid.). This group is the Jewish people, "a kingdom of priests." This was the seed from which there later sprang the *mission*-theory of the Reform movement.

Not ten years had passed after Mendelssohn's death, when his followers began to interpret his *mission* theory in complete opposition to his original intentions. The Kantian scholar, Lazarus Bendavid (1762-1832), held that if Jews had any contribution to offer to modern times it was through the tidings that they were prepared to follow the path of "pure reason" (Immanuel Kant's *Pure Reason*) and convert their "church beliefs," *i.e.,* their synagogue faith, into a pure philosophic "religious faith." In Mendelssohn's terminology, this meant capitulation to the "unification system," or to a would-be universalist and, actually, a Jewish-Protestant syncretism. Whereas individual Jewish thinkers of the 17th century had striven to separate themselves from Judaism, now it was quite the contrary: isolated thinkers were making efforts to wrest it from the spiritual perils besetting it on all sides through the rising flood of rationalism. Since post-Kantian German idealism left room in its system for transcendental reason certain Jewish philosophers found

that this offered them new opportunity to ground their ancestral faith in the spirit of the times. In this connection, two names in particular must be mentioned: Salomo Ludwig Steinheim (ca. 1789-1866) and the Hegelian scholar, Samuel Hirsch (1815-1889).

In his four-volume work *Die Offenbarung nach dem Lehrbegriff der Synagoge,* 1835-65 (Revelation According to the Teachings of the Synagogue), Steinheim postulated that critical reason must avow its inability to find a bridge between itself and empirical reality, whether in the matter of daily experience or in the actual revelation of religious truth. The reaction against Kant's "critical idealism," which was evident at the end of the 18th century and led Solomon Maimon to his "critical skepticism," was used by Steinheim for the purpose of reinforcing anew traditional anti-rationalism. Our knowledge of the existence of God, freedom of the will and immortality of the soul, is much more accurate than our knowledge of natural laws and, therefore, "the faith of the synagogue" is "an exact science." However, we owe this science not to reason but to God's revelation. The philosophical foundations on which Samuel Hirsch, Steinheim's younger contemporary, sought to strengthen Jewish faith were much deeper. He published his *Religious Philosophy of the Jews* in 1842 when only 27 years old. However his application of Hegel's dialectic method ran so counter to German Jewry's general trend to retain only the smallest possible vestige of Judaism, that they declared his system sheer impudent "heresy." In contrast to Hegel, Hirsch maintained that religion is not merely an element in the development of Absolute Spirit but that precisely within religion and, more concretely, within the Jewish religion, this spirit reveals itself in its genuine essence. Thanks to his original synthesis of Hegel's theories of human self-consciousness and Fichte's doctrine of the creative force of human freedom, Hirsch outlines a scheme of universal history with the people of Israel at its center, as in Judah ha-Levi's

Kuzari. Idolatrous cultures were characterized by a passive piety which granted nature's sway over man's free will; on the contrary Judaism, the religion of active will, placed man above nature. As soon as this active religious devotion became rooted in the Jewish people, miracles and prophets became superfluous; the time had now arrived to draw all of mankind into the Jewish-religious cultural sphere. This originally was, and continued to remain, the purpose of Christianity—to lead man from idolatry to God. As long as this task has not been fulfilled, Israel remains the living embodiment of the idea that man has been created to be his Creator's refulgence in nature, to be a "free man" and to be the Creator's free "first-born son." Since the beginning of the Christian era, the only miracle in the natural world has been the survival of Israel who is the suffering but, nevertheless—or more precisely, therefore,—the chosen "servant of God" (according to Isaiah, XLI et seq., especially LIII). Modern philosophy, from Descartes to Hegel, is not just "universalist" at all but specifically and definitely Christian. For this reason, it is still half-way to its goal and has still far to go to attain its real mission—to lead the Christian peoples to the threshold of the Messianic era.

With Hirsch, Mendelssohn's *mission* theory thus became a sharp weapon of self-defense for Judaism. In general, however, the *mission* theory of the Jewish Reform movement of the 19th century was inclined to drift along with the tide of compromise. *Religion des Geistes* by Solomon Formstecher (1808-1889), which appeared one year before Hirsch's book and was based on Schelling's philosophy, stressed the ethical side of Judaism in contrast to the aesthetic tendency of every sort of natural religion and set out to prove that in the Reformation, Christianity had moved in the direction of the Jewish spirit. Whereas Hirsch maintained that even when the Messiah arrived, the world would need the Jewish people and for this reason it must return to Palestine, Formstecher contended that the disappearance of Jewish political independence was a step forward in universal history and, therefore, on philosophical grounds, he became the apologist of the Diaspora as well as all manner of reforms which may eventually bring about a closer contact between Jewry and the rest of the world. Another disciple of Schelling, Meir Heinrich Landauer (1808-1841) sought ideological contact with Catholicism through the medium of Kabbalist doctrine and through the interpretation of the Torah in the light of the triadic theory. In so doing he based his arguments on the variations of God's name in the Torah (Adonai, Elohim, etc.). Although friendly toward Schelling's romantic philosophy, Landauer's older contemporary, the Rabbi of Hamburg, Isaac Bernays (1792-1849), leaned toward a strict traditionalism. At the same time, in Italy, Samuel David Luzzatto or Shadal (1800-1865) had formulated much more sharply than Formstecher and without any thought of compromise, the contrast between the intellectual-aesthetic (and therefore non-Jewish) and the emotional-ethical (the Jewish) factor in human history. The former factor, that is the Hellenic, he designated as *Atticism* which he considered the eternal opposite of *Abrahamism* which was the essential basis and meaning of Israel's eternal existence.

Together with a galaxy of more or less traditionally-minded German-speaking Jewish savants (Nachman Krochmal, Solomon Judah Rapoport, known as "Shir," Zunz, Geiger, Graetz, etc.), Shadal belongs among the founders of the new *Wissenschaft des Judentums* which also included the history of Jewish religious thought. All of them fervent adherents of objective scholarship and of unalloyed historical truth, these modern Jewish scholars differ sharply in their subjective basic outlooks, and this, in turn, determined the special place of each of them in the evolution of modern Judaism. At a time when Abraham Geiger (1810-1874), who inspired the Jewish Reform movement, regarded the scientific approach to the historical evolution of Judaism as a means by which he could demonstrate its need and justification for adapting itself to the changed times; at a time when even Nachman Krochmal (1785-1840) in his *Emunah Zerufah* (Pure Faith), which was published posthumously (1851) and accorded by Zunz the honorary title of *More Nebuke ha-Zeman,* "The Guide for the Perplexed of Our Times," had placed greatest emphasis on the vicissitudes in the history of the Jewish religious spirit, Shadal and his peers were resolved to elaborate most clearly whatever, in their opinion, was absolute and eternal in Judaism.

In his *Nineteen Letters on Judaism* (1836) and shortly thereafter, in *Horeb* (1837), Samson Raphael Hirsch (1808-1888), the father of modern orthodoxy in Western Europe, came out with the following maxim: "The Torah is as undeniable a fact as heaven and earth, *i.e.,* its decrees and commandments are as immutable as the laws of nature since the object of both is to *hallow* human life and impart true joy ('the joy of life') without which life can have no meaning."

If it was the hope of this pious rabbi of Germany to revive the traditional Jewish way of life in Jewish hearts, two other Jewish thinkers of the 19th century, Joseph Salvador (1796-1873) in France and Elijah Benamozegh (1822-1900) in Italy, were also engaged in defining the universal-historical worth of Israel's perpetuity. In Salvador's work, *Paris, Rome, Jerusalem* (1860), the link connecting Moses Mendelssohn's *Jerusalem* with Moses Hess' *Rome and Jerusalem* (1862), the old mission theory is concretely formulated: Judaism is the universal faith of the future which will effect complete harmony between Catholic orthodoxy and the ideas of the French Revolution. Benamozegh was less optimistic and therefore closer in spirit to his countryman Shadal. In his works, written partially in French (*Morale juive et morale chrétienne,* 1867, and *Israel et l'Humanité,* 1885), the rabbi and Kabbalist of Leghorn sharply contrasted the non-Jewish world outlook which recognizes moral behavior essentially between individuals only, and "Hebraism" with its original

feeling for brotherhood between peoples: only because of this, is Israel the "priest" among the peoples of the earth and must so remain until the redemption of all mankind. The emphasis placed on the ethical aspect of Jewish monotheism evoked a revival of interest in the prophets. In a treatise, *Les Prophètes d'Israel,* one of Salvador's admirers in France, James Darmesteter (1850-1894), declared that "a bond between prophetic ethics and science" is the only possible conclusion to the course of religious development (1891). In England at the same time Israel Abrahams (1858-1925), found that the genuine substance of Jewish spiritual history "no matter how many changes the abstract conceptions of Judaism may have undergone" was always the "Jewish moral code which was evolved from the noblest of ideals" (1891). On the basis of emphasis laid on the ethical-universalist element in the Jewish religion, Claude G. Montefiore (1858-1938), together with Abrahams, the founder of liberal Judaism in England, preached a "theism" which was to become a Jewish-Christian faith, although its theoretician himself realized that the new "truth" would prove "too Christain for its Jewish critics and too Jewish for the Christian critics (Introduction to *The Synoptic Gospels,* 1909). For this reason it was truly astounding that another Jewish thinker of almost the same generation, Moritz Lazarus of Germany (1824-1903), at the end of his life published a work *Die Ethik des Judentums* (Vol. I, 1898, Vol. II, 1911) in which he clearly pointed out the progress made by Jewish religious morals in the post-prophetic and, especially, in the Talmudic era. He reaches the same conclusions as the author of *Horeb,* that the meaning of all Jewish *mitsvot* is "the hallowing of life."

Hermann (Ezekiel) Cohen's (1842-1918) *Die Religion der Vernunft aus den Quellen des Judentums,* 1919, represents a magnificent synthesis of all the main tendencies and motives in Jewish religious thought in Western Europe since Mendelssohn. The rationality of Judaism, the bond between religion and ethics, the universal role of the prophets and their Messianism, the significance of the continuous development of Jewish spiritual tradition from oldest times to the present era, the question of the Jewish mission, the opposition to all forms of pantheism and naturalism, all of these elements which we find scattered or assembled in various combinations and expressed more or less clearly by various Jewish religious thinkers, were utilized by Cohen as essential cornerstones in the structure of his philosophic system. What Maimonides was in regard to his predecessors, Cohen was in regard to the Jewish thinkers of the early 19th century; Kant together with Plato represented for him what Aristotle had been for Maimonides. At first Cohen, as was the case with many Jewish religious thinkers before him, turned toward philosophy in general. For him, God was that concept, that idea which combined within a single realm of creative reason "the nature of natural science" and the moral order of the universe; or, expressed differently, that concept which postulated the possibility of realizing the highest ethical ideal, the ideal of social justice among united mankind. Cohen's system was in the tradition of Kant; his logic was that of "pure" cognition; his ethics, that of "pure" will; his aesthetics, a doctrine of "pure" feeling. This idea of "purity" bears the stamp of Kant and expresses the "autonomy" of reason, its independence from any other factor, whether empirical or superempirical. In the course of these several decades, however, the purity of Kant's transcendental idealism became fused, in Cohen's thought, with the Jewish "holy Scriptures," as well as with the entire structure of commentaries and philosophical speculation reared upon them during some two thousand years. It now became "purity," "holiness." The motto of Cohen's final work was Akiba's famous exclamation (Talmud Babli, Yoma, 85): "Praise be to you, Israel! Who purifies you and for whom do you purify yourself? It is your Father in Heaven."

If under transcendentalism the basic sense of "purity" is the idea that the tasks of theoretical as well as practical reason are endless, exactly so genuinely-Jewish holiness, man's striving to be worthy of "the image of God" which he bears in his individual lineaments, has essentially the same purpose. This Cohen came to see toward the end of his life. As a simple creature of flesh and blood, burdened with the realization of his moral guilt, and a constant prey to the weakness of the flesh and of social ills, man cannot exist without "love of God," without the religious feeling which binds God to him and him to God, and hence, to his fellow men, the "other one" (see *Religion der Vernunft,* especially chapters VII-X). This knowledge we acquire through "reason"; and whatever reason dictates in this connection has been taught from the very beginning by the "Jewish source"—the Bible and its qualified commentaries in the entire history of Jewish religious thought.

Cohen's spiritual development is typical of the entire era. It would seem that the Age of Reason gained its highest triumph at the beginning of the 20th century. And yet there began to manifest itself a yearning for those "sources" belonging to a former period and to other lands, sources which the scientific mind of the 19th century had heretofore accorded merely an objective, historical interest.

VI. RECENT TRENDS

The spiritual crisis which, at the end of the 19th century, became apparent in the intensification of social and political contrasts all over the world, also brought in its wake a regrouping of the creative forces in all spheres of Jewish cultural life, even in the closely circumscribed field still left for Jewish religious thought. The spirit of religious rationalism which had at first inspired the Haskalah began to disappear gradually, and to assume, especially in Eastern Europe, a purely secular character—whether a-religious or even anti-religious—in a well-nigh sheer national-Jewish form. Jewish thought now became nationalistic, humanitarian, socialistic; insofar as it remained religious it seemed to be dormant and lifeless. Only the decadence of rationalism and intellectualism in Europe called forth a "revaluation of values" also among the Jews. While a number of Jewish thinkers opposed Jewish "spirituality" in general (Micah Joseph Berdyczewski, and others) or still sought to interpret it in the spirit of evolutionism as a means to biological ends—the preservation of Jewish national life (Ahad ha-Am, Simon Dubnow)—there were indications that the apparently dried up spring of traditional speculation was capable of again gushing forth as it had in previous periods.

It was highly characteristic of the mood of the times that this revival was stimulated by an aesthetic interest in the Jewish believer, the Hasid, the man of faith who remained unaffected by the course of historical events, who got along without philosophical deliberations and was content with aphoristic gems of Hasidic "Torah." At first the object of a romantically nostalgic literature (J. L. Peretz, and others), the religiously devout soon drew the attention of the Jewish thinker to that world of speculation in which personal piety had long found refuge. It was principally Hillel Zeitlin who undertook in Eastern Europe to make the world of Hasidism better comprehensible to the Jew of modern times. However the development of religious thought, insofar as it has found expression in recent Yiddish and Hebrew literature, will be treated in another place. In Western Europe it was Martin Buber (b. 1878) who set out to familiarize the outside world with the ideas of Hasidism. In the course of his labors Buber emerged as an original thinker who considered Hasidism as a necessary element in the religious world-view in general, and all the more so, in Judaism. If at first he regarded himself a mystic, he later came to the conclusion that mysticism which seeks, through "nearness to God", to submerge and efface man's individual character, is essentially anti-religious and, therefore, non-Jewish. In his book *Ich und Du* (1923), written under the influence of German idealism and even more under the influence of Henri Bergson, he says that at the core of

the world unfolded to us by natural science there lies a profounder world of genuinely *real* being. He describes it by means of the concept *relationship*: only through the completely personal relationship between "I" and "Thou" is this revealed, and it depends upon "me" always and everywhere to find and hear "thy" voice. The beast and the plant emit this voice (an echo of Hasidic panpsychism); but above all, it is God, who speaks eternally to the people of Israel. His voice and speech are the Holy Scriptures and also the entire created world. Only occasionally was the individual deemed worthy to hear this voice from the depths: "One does not find God by remaining in the world; one does not find God by going outside the world; whoever, heart and soul, goes out to his 'thee' finds Him who cannot be sought ... " "The eternal voice sweeps on—when that is all." And yet the meaning of all history is that the world becomes God's realm "Malkut Shaddai," as one of Buber's last works is entitled.

Whether this semi-rational, semi-mystical conception of the world is Hasidism's legitimate heir is a question per se; at all events Buber became the center of a circle of his own Hasidim. Such circles and little groups were in general symptomatic of the postwar revival of Jewish religious thought in Western Europe.

Parallel with these partly supra-scientific, partly anti-scientific trends which became particularly strong during the great upheavals of the period after World War I, there once more rose to the surface of Jewish religious thought the older major West-European trends: neo-orthodoxy and Liberal or Reformed Judaism. Among the exponents of these trends may be mentioned Jacob Rosenheim who, in his *Orientierung im juedischen Geistesleben der Gegenwart* (1920), seeks to shield Judaism from the rationalism of Herman Cohen's variety and the irrationalists of Buber's school; likewise Isaac Breuer (b. 1883) whose object it was to entrench the ancient Jewish ideal of "God's governance over the united people of Israel" with the aid of modern theology. Breuer, incidentally, was the author of a *New Kuzari*.

The more liberal-minded Judaism of that period is most clearly expounded by the German rabbi, Leo Baeck (b. 1873), in his book *Das Wesen des Judentums* (new edition, 1926). According to him, Judaism is first of all, a "religion of deeds," ethical in essence and therefore "classical" in form in contrast to Christianity which is thoroughly "romantic"; and at that—one must distinguish between the eternal essence of Judaism and the chaff, which cannot withstand the test of time.

This is 19th century relativism which on the one hand inspired the Jewish Reform movement and, on the other, promoted the scientific investigation of the history of Jewish culture, a study which now, in the period of recent spiritual confusion, once more has focussed on an investigation of the history of Jewish religious thought and especially on the epoch of its Jewish-Arabic Renaissance. Among the liberal religious thinkers belongs David Koigen (1879-1933), the author of *The Moral God* (1922) which summons Judaism to bring the universal development of religion to its last and highest level.

The most eminent figure among the religious thinkers of this period, Franz Rosenzweig (1886-1929), cannot be classified as either an orthodox or as a religious liberal; he also cannot be bracketed as either a rationalist or its contrary, an anti-rationalist, since his *Star of Redemption* (1921) is an organic synthesis of the most diverse shades of thought which one-sidedly dominated the majority of his contemporaries. In his Jewish-religious world-view, Rosenzweig is closely connected with both Cohen and Buber: with the former, in his striving not to overlook the "two thousand year old history of philosophy" but to transcend it; and with his friend Buber, because he, too, sought to find something more in Judaism than merely the "knowledge" of God. To Rosenzweig this "something more" represents neither more nor less than the true "redemption" of the people of Israel, of all mankind and of

God's entire world. To him the "star of redemption" is symbolized by the star of David — two triangles intercrossing, each representing only half of the truth, from below to the top — toward God, from above downward — toward the world. Only when intertwined in one "pattern" do these triangles radiate as a star, which is God's "visage," that is, his "eternal truth" (*Star of Redemption* III, "the Gate"). "He is the One Who plants eternal life among us," among us Jews, and among us human beings, in whose midst we, the children of the "eternal people" live. Is this a knowledge? Is this a Faith? "We make Faith"—replies Rosenzweig, the exponent of a would-be new school of rationalism—"entirely as the content of knowledge, but of knowledge of a sort that has at its base a fundamental concept of faith" (ib. II, Introduction: "The Probabilities of Living to Witness a Miracle"). These words clearly echo the magnificent Jewish philosophical speculations of the Middle Ages. Rosenzweig's "sources" however, are even more ancient: the Bible, Talmud, Midrash, the Prayer-Book and even the "Passover Haggadah." His book rings with the "words of God":

"He hath shewed thee, O man, what is good; and what doth the Lord require of thee, but to do justly, and to love mercy, and to walk humbly with thy God."

This is just the passage which Hermann Cohen declared to be the *leitmotif* of every religious thought (cf. *Religion der Vernunft*, Introduction III, 15 and chapter XVII at the end).

A sign of this disturbed epoch is the fact that even the Russian language, which had formerly been with Jews as a rule a language of religious indifference — now became a means of expressing pious thoughts. On the eve of World War I, Baruch Stolpner (d. 1937), the "Jewish Socrates" among Russia's thinkers, barely mustered sufficient courage to become like them a "God-seeker" but quickly repented his effort to unite Marxism with faith. After the Russian Revolution, the former "Slavophile," M. Gershenzon (1869-1923) suddenly discovered that the Bible is an inexhaustible source of profoundest wisdom. A year before his death, in a treatise entitled *The Destiny of the Jewish People,* he unfolded the religious significance of the biblical "Thou-hast-chosen-us" idea. Even Leo Shestov-Schwartzman (1866-1938) the "Nietzsche of Russia," former exponent of metaphysical "rootlessness," at the end of his life put the Bible and the God of Abraham over against philosophy. Another Russian émigré, M. Hirschkopf, in his book *What is the Meaning of Life?* (1926) attempted to establish a connection between Jewish faith and modern natural science.

From the end of the 18th century German became the language of Jewish learning and, of course, of Jewish religious-philosophical literature. This spiritual hegemony of German-Jewry lasted through almost the entire 19th century. The cultural rise of Eastern European Jewry, with the consequent development of a many-sided and valuable Yiddish and Hebrew literature, together with the growth of large Jewish communities in the English-speaking countries, led to the creation of a rich Jewish literature in Hebrew, Yiddish and English. At present Jewish life and Jewish thought are reflected mainly in these three languages.

The newest tendencies in Jewish religious thought, insofar as they are expressed in Hebrew, Yiddish and English, are discussed elsewhere in this work.

BIBLIOGRAPHY

I. ABRAHAMS, *Some Permanent Values in Judaism.* 1924.

I. ABRAHAMS, E. R. BEVAN and CH. SINGER, *The Legacy of Israel.* 1927.

S. W. BARON, edit., *Essays on Maimonides.* 1941.

J. BLUVSTEIN, Hebrew translation of Gabirol's *Fons Vitae.* 1926.

A. CAUSSE, *Les "pauvres" d'Israel.* 1922.

JAKOB GUTTMANN, *Die Scholastik des dreizehnten Jahrhunderts in ihren Beziehungen zum Judentum.* 1902.

JULIUS GUTTMANN, *Die Philosophie des Judentums.* 1933.

P. HEINISCH, *Griechische Philosophie im Alten Testament.* 1913-1914.

G. HOELSCHER, *Geschichte der israelitischen und juedischen Religion.* 1922.

I. HUSIK, *A History of Jewish Mediaeval Philosophy.* 2nd ed. 1930.

M. JOEL, *Zur Genesis der Lehre Spinozas.* 1871.

D. KAUFMANN, *Geschichte der Attributenlehre in der juedischen Religionsphilosophie des Mittelalters von Saadia bis Maimuni.* 1877.

A. LEWKOWITZ, *Das Judentum und die geistigen Stroemungen des XIX. Jahrhunderts.* 1935.

A. LODS, *Des prophètes à Jésus.* 1935.

M. LOEHR, *Sozialismus und Individualismus im Alten Testament.* 1906.

A. MARMORSTEIN, *The Old-Rabbinic Doctrine of God.* 1927.

G. F. MOORE, *Judaism in the First Centuries of the Christian Era.* 1927-1930.

S. MUNK, *Mélanges de philosophie juive et arabe.* 1859.

D. NEUMARK, *Essays in Jewish Philosophy.* 1929.

D. NEUMARK, *Geschichte der juedischen Philosophie des Mittelalters, nach Problemen dargestellt.* 1907-1928.

E. PACE, *Ideas of God in Israel.* 1924.

H. W. ROBINSON, *Religious Ideas of the Old Testament.* 1913.

C. ROTH, *The Jewish Contribution to Civilization,* ch. VII, by Leon Roth. 1938.

L. ROTH, *Spinoza, Descartes, Maimonides.* 1924.

S. SCHECHTER, *Some Aspects of Rabbinic Theology.* 1909.

W. R. SMITH-CHEYNE, *Prophets of Israel,* 1895.

L. STRAUSS, *Philosophie und Gesetz, Beitraege zum Verstaendnis Maimunis und seiner Vorlaeufer.* 1935.

M. WAXMAN, *A History of Jewish Literature,* Vols. I-IV. New York, 1938-1941.

M. WIENER, *Juedische Religion im Zeitalter der Emanzipation.* 1934.

H. A. WOLFSON, *Cresca's Critique of Maimonides.* Cambridge, 1929.

D. NEUMARK, תולדות הפילוסופיה בישראל, Vol. I, New York-Warsaw, 1921.

S. BERNFELD, דעת אלהים, תולדות הפלוסופיא הדתית בישראל. Warsaw, 1897.

JEWISH MYSTICISM AND KABBALA

Gershom G. Scholem

Jewish mysticism is the sum-total of all religious trends in Judaism which seek to attain, by way of contemplation and illumination, religious knowledge outside the reach of reason. On the whole, these trends endeavor to remain within the framework of historic Judaism and seek, insofar as possible, to avoid conflict with it. Jewish mysticism presents, in bold contours, a thoroughly organic development which clearly reveals definite phases of the history of the Jewish religion, and especially of the religion of the plain man. Altogether, the history of Jewish mysticism covers the period of the last 2,000 years, although the Kabbala, in the limited meaning of the term, dates only from the 12th century. Its unique development may be divided into six periods:

First period: The Merkabah mysticism with its center in the Orient (first millennium);

Second period: German Hasidism with its center in Germany, primarily around 1150-1300; however, its influence extended up to the 16th century;

Third period: The rise and development of the Kabbala proper with its center in Spain, from 1200 to the Expulsion (1492);

Fourth period: The later Kabbala with its center in Palestine, 1500-1650;

Fifth period: The Sabbatian movement, ca. 1665-1800;

Sixth period: Hasidism in the countries of Eastern Europe, since 1750.

Although connecting links bind together the last four periods, the Sabbatian and Hasidic movements are not treated in detail in the present article, and the reader must be referred to the pertinent essays. They cannot, however, be omitted in an evaluation of the general character of Jewish mysticism.

I.   GENERAL CHARACTERISTICS

In its development, the movement of Jewish mysticism was characterized by an ever-growing tendency to become a social and national factor. This tendency was not discernible in the first period; however, it reached various degrees of clarity in the second and third periods, and later, in the last three stages, it revealed itself in particuarly sharp and bold dialectics. There is here a thoroughly original development, in which everything conforms to the internal logic of the history of the Jewish religion. On the other hand, it is clear that non-Jewish environmental influences were at work in all periods, but it was an error on the part of Jewish historiography, especially in the 19th century, to place the emphasis mainly on these external influences. The truth is that notwithstanding external influences Jewish mysticism in every period has an unmistakably original complexion. Even more, among the religious trends of post-exilic Judaism the Kabbala is the one which, rooted in religious motives, has obtained the deepest hold on large masses and has continued capable of dominating them. This may be explained by the peculiar character of Jewish mysticism in the Middle Ages, when it was at odds with the rationalistic trends which emerged clearly in the Jewish philosophy of the 12th and 13th centuries. Both movements—the rationalistic philosophies and the Kabbala—had a clearly aristocratic character; they pretended to offer their doctrines to the privileged élite. But, by its very origin, the Kabbala had deep roots in the folk religion and, as long as it was a truly religious power, it stood in the most intimate contact with the national mythos—the religion of the simple folk. But there is still another paradox here: the religious experiences and the piety of the people are expressed in the Kabbala in the language of religious ideology, often employing the conceptual and linguistic vocabulary of the philosophers. But in contrast to the rationalistic enlightenment of the philosophers, the mental processes of the Kabbala are fixed by mythical imagery to a much greater degree than we should expect on the basis of its external form and of its intricate and singular speculations. Myth and mysticism maintain an altogether intimate relationship in this movement. Myth, which in its classic forms and manifestations has been opposed by Judaism, or at least suppressed and relegated to the background, frequently comes to the fore with an almost elementary force in the varieties of mystic thought and is ever and again revealed as a prominent force in Judaism. Of special interest from this point of view are many Kabbalists who attempt to blend the thought-patterns of primitive myth with the strict monotheism of Judaism. In certain periods of Jewish mysticism, mainly since the expulsion from Spain, these efforts produced a particularly important result: the Kabbala appears as a power which in essence revolutionizes the Jewish mind. True, in the minds of the Kabbalists themselves the new and the old often became reconciled; frequently enough the Kabbalists regarded themselves as the conservative representatives of the old religious authority, whereas in reality their influence was rather in the opposite direction.

Where the Kabbalists knew that their ideas were revolutionary from the standpoint of rabbinic Judaism, they came close to a mystical "heresy" and to a conflict with the "official" Judaism of their day which hardly could be concealed.

The fact that mysticism, while teaching the ascent to God and religious intuition, nevertheless held on to its connection with both the classic forms of the Jewish faith and with the folk religion, explains the following characteristic phenomena:

First: Notwithstanding the entire mystical character of the system, it pretends to be the true tradition, "Kabbala," handed down secretly from generation to generation since the Creation. This assertion takes on all kinds of mythical forms; the Kabbala is supposed to be the knowledge communicated by the angel Raziel to Adam, then again it is supposed to be the very essence of the Oral Law revealed to Moses on Mount Sinai; at times the Kabbala bases its claim to authenticity on a long chain of tradition. It is noteworthy that nowhere among Jews, not even among the philosophers, were so many new ideas brought out as among the Kabbalists, who constantly insisted that they merely communicated the knowledge which they had handed down to them from previous generations as "Kabbala," tradition. Incidentally, definite Messianic concepts were here at work. We constantly encounter the idea that real, perfect knowledge will not be given to the world at large until the days of the Messiah, but that already on the eve of redemption it may be written down or communicated to disciples. Since many great Kabbalists were certain of the impending redemption, they found in this idea of Messianism sufficient ground to explain all those new elements in their teachings which did not harmonize with that which had been "handed down and accepted." In the majority of cases, moreover, the new appeared as a commentary on the old, although it did not always emanate from interpreting the old. The more daring an idea, the more firmly was it presented as belonging to the primeval religious tradition now restored to its original clarity because of the impending redemption. This thought was widespread both among the Kabbalists of Spain and Safed and the theoreticians of Sabbatianism.

Second: the very strong connection with the religion of the simple folk explains the intimate contact between mysticism and magic which may be observed in all the six periods of Jewish mysticism. Mysticism seldom differs completely from magic; in the history of Jewish mysticism particularly such a differentiation has almost never taken place. In all periods the Kabbala is bound up with a more or less popular or learned magic. That which since the 14th century has gone by the name of practical Kabbala (*Kabbala Maasit*) is no more than magic which has taken in old and new elements. In many cases it is but little related to the religious quests of the mystics. Even where the Kabbalists have developed a theory of such magic (as, for instance, in the book, *Berit Menuhah,* of the 14th century), the essential content, the material of the magic, is in most cases entirely independent of the Kabbalists' specific ideas. At any rate, the so-called *practical* Kabbala is much older than the *theoretical,* even where the latter is directed toward practical interests, namely, to point the way Godward.

Each of the six periods of Jewish mysticism has worked out a special language and a specific realm of ideas which make it possible to distinguish clearly and sharply each period from all the others. For all that, the legacy of the older periods persists in the later epochs, and it is constantly modified and kept alive in new combinations. This often very rich and quite complex religious terminology is not the least reason which makes it so difficult to understand the infinitely rich literature of Jewish mysticism, particularly of the last four periods.

II. RISE OF JEWISH MYSTICISM

We may surmise that Jewish mysticism emerged in the century prior to the destruction of the Second Temple. The details of these beginnings have not as yet been clarified. Many hypotheses have been advanced,

as well as many fictions—but entirely without foundation—among them the often emphasized role of the Essenes, but it may be said with certainty that the rise of Jewish mysticism is bound up with two factors:

First: the crystallization of the classic forms of Pharisaic-Rabbinic Judaism. The rigid contours of this system had the effect of making it easy for the new religious impulses seeking expression within the framework of Judaism to be directed into mystic channels, *i.e.* into an interpretation of the traditional content of religion in the mystical spirit.

Second: of significance also was the profoundly religious fermentation in the non-Jewish world of the period which resulted in the collapse of the older pagan religions, and often expressed itself under mystic slogans (the so-called syncretism). There is undoubtedly a connection between the beginnings of Jewish mysticism and the religious world of syncretism, as, for example, in the imagery of *Adam Kadmon* (primordial man) as a spiritual force of particular significance, in the journeyings of the soul into Heaven, and in the more or less personified and independently considered attributes or qualities of the Godhead.

In Judaism itself the mystical development also proceeds from two points: a) from the desire for deeper absorption in the study of the Scriptures; b) from the desire for inivividual experience of the Divine actions. The first quest leads to the widening of the boundaries and the importance of the Torah, which is considered not as a law for the Jewish people, but as the mystic law of the universe. As bases for such an interpretation of the Bible there were the first chapter of Genesis, the question of the reasons for the commandments (*Taame Torah*), the verses, especially in the Book of Proverbs, about Divine wisdom which was identified with the Torah, and finally the vision of the prophet Ezekiel concerning the Merkabah (the Divine Chariot), the bearer of God's throne of glory.

The second quest brought about new forms in place of the ancient prophetic ones, particularly the vision of the Merkabah and the Apocalyptic revelations of the End of Days. Because the dogmatic content of the Jewish religion had not yet found an unambiguous formulation, the question whether these oldest mystic ways of thought were orthodox or less orthodox, is not of such importance as Christian scholars have assumed. Much later, alongside of Rabbinic Judaism which takes ever-sharper shape, there are to be found still other currents of Judaism; and it is not always possible to determine the boundaries clearly.

III. THE MERKABAH MYSTICISM

In a certain measure, this form of Jewish mysticism has been clearly discernible since the 1st century. In a particularly long de-

Courtesy Jewish Theological Seminary

MANUSCRIPT PAGE OF "HEKALOT" (HEAVENLY PALACES)

velopment, it has passed through two stages: an older and a later. In the older stage its most important exponents were the Tannaim of Palestine. The fellowship of Johanan ben Zakkai and his disciples, Akiba and other sages of the period of the Mishnah, is well-known. Around them emerge the anonymous groups of the pseudo-epigraphic books (Enoch, Apocalypse of Abraham). Also, in the time of the Amoraim, especially in the 3rd and 4th centuries, we discern a number of great Talmudic authorities as representatives of mystical ideas (Joshua ben Levi, Resh Lakish, and particularly Rab). With Rab mystic speculation in the 3rd century came to Babylonia, where it endured for a long time and had a vigorous development. In the later stage on the other hand, from the 5th century on, the leaders of the movement are lost in an anonymous group, or hide behind the distinguished names of older authorities. Complete written works from the first stage are not extant (unless the Sefer Yetsirah belongs to that period), but in the Talmud and in the Midrashim we have scattered fragments and allusions to the ancient mysticism. We possess an entire literature of this later stage which is, however, connected with the older one in a single chain of development, and which has preserved many a fine ancient tradition. Included in this literature are the so-called Hekalot books (Hekalot Rabbati, Hekalot Zutrati, Maseket Hekalot), and later Midrashim related to them (in particular Otiyot de-Rabbi Akiba, Pirke de-Rabbi Eliezer, Midrash Konen). Most of these books were probably compiled in Babylonia; they contain, however, an abundance of Palestinian material. At any rate, the religious movement reflected in them developed in the Orient.

This movement had a very definite character. The object was not so much to construct a theology, a mystic theory, as it was to evoke and describe definite mystical experiences. It was also preoccupied with speculations concerning the creation of the world (Maase Bereshit). Its literature was chiefly concerned with describing in pictorial detail the throne of glory. The purpose is to show the elect—who are worthy of the privilege—the way through all the heavens and the celestial palaces (Hekalot) to God's holy throne. Having arrived before the throne of glory, in the world of the Merkabah, the soul receives instructions and revelations concerning those matters that have interested these mystics more than all else: about the Kingdom of the divine throne conceived as God's place from which he creates and governs the world; about the cosmos, about angels and demons, and also about the Messianic End of Days. To one branch in the Merkabah mysticism there was added, as particularly holy knowledge, the so-called Shiur Komah, i.e., the revelation of the stature of God, as He manifests himself in His majesty as the creator of worlds on His holy throne. All these things have a definitely mythical character, even where they are based on verses of the Bible. The speculations concerning Shiur Komah evoked an intense opposition on the part of latter-day Jewish theologians (Saadia Gaon, Maimonides). At the same time, however, it is evident that the bearers of these ideas had a definite attitude toward historic reality; they were even more indifferent to it than were the theologians of the contemporary Rabbinic Judaism, namely, the masters of the Agada. The tribulations of the times, the persecutions on the part of the Church, since the 4th century, directed the religious interest of these mystics with an especial intensity toward the higher world of the Merkabah, toward the prehistory of the cosmogony, or toward the post-Messianic period. The genuinely historic world is entirely lost here. It is regrettable that, from the sources extant, we cannot derive any clear ideas concerning the social background of the propounders of the later stage of the Merkabah mysticism. They betrayed very little interest in man himself as such; their gaze was turned entirely to God and to his resplendent world, the Merkabah.

The Merkabah mystics were ecstatics; their ideal was the ascetic who, by fasting and self-absorption, prepares his soul for the ecstatic ascent to the world of Divine Glory. This ascent, the exaltation of the soul, which in the writings of the later stage is called *Yeridah le-Merkabah* (Descending to the Merkabah), is the center of everything. In the imagery of this ascent of the soul, in the degrees through which it passes in the process, in the dangers connected with it, the Merkabah mysticism is close to the Gnostic trends in the religion of Antiquity in its final stages.

The circumstance that this mysticism limits its knowledge to a small circle of the consecrated, and that it appears as a doctrine of mystery, as a sort of Jewish mystery religion, places it among the religious movements of that period which seized wide circles (Heinrich Graetz, Leopold Zunz, and Philipp Bloch assumed that the *Hekalot* mysticism dates from a later time, and see in it traces of Islamic influence; this, however, cannot be proved. This "Jewish Gnosis" was already completely formulated prior to the 7th century in all of its important aspects).

This Jewish form of Gnosis is differentiated from its Christian and pagan counterparts in that the image of God is clearer than the image of man, the exponent of this mysticism. Non-Jewish Gnosis creates a chasm between the true "good" God of the soul and the righteous God, the "Creator of the World," the Lord of the Cosmos, Whom it relegates to a lower place as the "God of the Jews." The *Hekalot* texts do not know of such a mystic dualism. They strive to develop a strictly monotheistic form of the Gnosis, in which the "God of Israel" is also the true God of the mystics. In their conception of God the following points are particularly characteristic: He is the Holy King; the attributes of sovereignty belonging to the Exalted, Infinite and Holy God dominate the mood of the mystics; there do not exist for them those divine qualities which manifest love *(Ahabah)*, mercy *(Hesed)*, etc. The visions beheld, the songs and adorations heard by the ecstatic before God's throne of glory, and set down (especially in the book *Hekalot Rabbati)*, strong-

ly reflect this attitude. The holiness of God is experienced not in its moral interpretation, but in the direct awe and fear which hover around the Divine. The mystic of the *Hekalot* texts has a genuine religious experience only of a God who is conceived in terms of sovereignty. In his highest ecstasy, when he is divested of all materiality, the mystic stands before Him in his complete individuality as a creature bowing before the sovereignty of his King. This strictly monotheistic mysticism knows of no blending of the human individuality with God, of no fusion of the Divine and the human. Its interpretation of the ecstatic experience admits of no pantheistic element. It is the emperor-mysticism of the later Antiquity and the early Middle Ages, the glorification of God as the Cosmocrator, the Lord of the Universe, which here dominate the religious mood. The influence of the Merkabah mystic is evident in certain parts of the liturgy and in the religious poetry of the *payetanim* (liturgical poets). From these circles there has come down the text of the *Kedushah* (sanctification) in the *Yotser* of the morning service, of weekday and Sabbath. Some of the hymns in the books of *Hekalot* were admitted into the *Mahzor* (festival prayer book), as for example, the prayer, *Ha-Aderet ve-ha-Emunah le-Hai Olamim,* of the Yom Kippur liturgy. Mystical tendencies of a contrasting kind which, however, have not found organized expressions in a movement like the *Yorede Merkabah* (those who descend into the Merkabah), occur in the older and later Agada; here one notes the formulation of the idea of the Shekinah characteristic of the Midrash Agada. The Shekinah is that phase of God's nature inherent in the creation, which may be grasped by man, *i.e.* God's immanence in the universe. In the later Midrash the personification of the Shekinah grows ever clearer, even as the incarnation of the Divine attributes of mercy or of justice had been in an earlier day. But it is not as yet bound up with the conception of God as the absolutely transcendental, as the holy King who stands above the universe, as conceived by the Merkabah mystics.

However, there were also circles which occupied themselves with gnostic speculations in a much more intense manner, as may be seen from the orthodox Jewish Gnosis of the books of *Hekalot*. We have no substantial sources of information on these groups; however, remnants of such traditions and ideas have come down to the Kabbalists of the Middle Ages (as, for instance, in the *Sefer ha-Bahir*).

A particular form of mystical speculation is also represented by the *Sefer Yetsirah*, which is rather closely connected with the Merkabah literature, at least linguistically, and was written probably between the 3rd and 6th centuries. This is the first attempt at theological speculation in Hebrew. Its solemn, often strangely indefinite formulations, have seemingly sprung from mystic reflections. Because of its multifarious meanings, both philosophers and Kabbalists could find a prop in it in the Middle Ages. The book deals with the elements of the universe, which it identifies with the ten elementary and primordial numbers, called *Sefirot,* and the twenty-two letters of the Hebrew alphabet. In them live the mysterious forces through whose convergence the various combinations (*Tserufim*) of the creation *(Yetsirah)* came into being. These are the "thirty-two secret paths of wisdom" through which God has created all that exists. In brief texts the author clarifies the meaning of every letter in accordance with its function in the three manifestations of the *Yetsirah* known to him: man, the universe, and the rhythmic flow of time through the course of the year. Here ideas of the late Hellenistic mysticism are apparently combined with originally Jewish conceptions of the mysteries of letters and language.

IV. THE GERMAN HASIDISM

After reaching its highest peak, the Merkabah mysticism crossed over from the Orient to Southern Italy (ca. 8th century), and thence to France and Germany. In those countries there existed several circles which occupied themselves with it and studied it as an esoteric doctrine. Subsequently, particularly in Germany, it became interlinked with later elements: influences of the theology of Saadia Gaon, partly some neo-Platonic ideas (particularly as found in the writings of Abraham ibn Ezra and Abraham bar Hiya); a prayer mysticism which sought mysteries and mystical allusions in the accepted liturgical texts, *Gematrias, i.e.* the calculations of the numerical value of biblical words, etc. These elements, however, attained real significance only after they had been accepted and elaborated by a new religious movement. The exponents of this

Courtesy Jewish Theological Seminary

TITLE PAGE OF "SEFER HASIDIM"
(THE BOOK OF THE DEVOUT)

movement were the German Hasidim, primarily of the 12th and 13th centuries, who for a long time subsequently exercised a profound influence on the spiritual life of the German Jews. Their outstanding figure was Judah the Hasid (second half of the 12th century) and their most important literary representative was his disciple, Eleazar of Worms. The most important document of the movement is the *Sefer Hasidim,* which provides a deep glimpse into the actual life of a Jewish community in all its manifestations. The life of the German Jews of the period is described in the book in strong, realistic strokes, even though presented under the sign of a supreme idea. There is absent here that dogmatic, Halakic or even idyllic veil found in other works of Rabbinic literature.

Mysticism appears here in an entirely new form although it seeks to preserve thoroughly the ancient heritage. There is almost no doubt that the movement was called forth by the calamities of the Crusades. On the horizon of Jewish mysticism there arose entirely new ideas about God and man.

The three most important series of ideas relating to the religious life of man are the reflections on the essence of Hasidut and the moral ideal of the Hasid (devout, pious) on penance and its discipline, and also on the mysticism of prayer. A new type of personality is drawn as the ideal: the monastic ascetic of the Middle Ages in Jewish form. The ideal man and the true exponent of the mystical wisdom is no longer the ecstatic, but the Hasid. Three things above all others go to make the true Hasid as he appears before us in the *Book of the Devout:* ascetic renunciation of the things of this world; complete serenity of mind; and an altruism pushed to the uttermost extremes. Behind all this is a thoroughly pessimistic view of life. The true Hasid is no longer the guardian of the keys of the mysteries of the Merkabah world, but the humble man, the ascetic who deprives himself of his own ego. F. Baer has given us an excellent description of the social background and the natural law concepts and reform ideas connected with it (*Zion,* Vol. III, 1938, pp. 1-50), and he also explains the relationship of this outlook to the religious and socio-ethical ideas current in the Christian world of those times. Eleazar of Worms, at the beginning of his great book, *Rokeah,* has simply codified as law the most extreme moral ideals of Hasidism as well as the new laws of penance. The contrast to Maimonides' slightly older *Mishneh Torah* is very characteristic: there, at the beginning of the new codification of the *Halakah,* we find a metaphysical chapter which is entirely foreign to the ancient

Halakah, whereas here we encounter an equally new socio-ethical and ascetic chapter. The Hasid knows that in the proper situation the natural right of equity (דיני שמים) takes precedence over the positive right of the *Halakah* (דיני תורה) But, as a matter of principle, these puritanic Hasidim also avoid every conflict with the *Halakah.* By observing this cardinal rule of Hasidism as an ethical extremism, applied to oneself rather than one's fellowman, one attains the state of loving God. Man's love of God is drawn in strongly erotic images. Penance, earlier held in but little esteem by the mystics, is here emphasized with great intensity and according to principles strongly influenced by Christian sources. Specific gradations and methods of penance for specific sins are introduced. Hasidic Jews thus become known far and wide for their high achievements by penance or by particularly outlandish acts, such as sitting on ants or rolling in snow. Prayer is conceived as a mysterious act whereby contact with mysterious forces is established. The ecstatic prayer of the ancient Merkabah mystic is shoved into the background by prayer which is much more magically colored. Magic generally occupies an important position in the preoccupations of the Hasidim. The Hasid is represented as one who needs nothing for himself, but who is at the same time master of all hidden powers. All these elements spilled over far beyond the confines of Hasidism and were for a long time active in subsequent Judaism. Eschatological interest is also prominent in the rich literature of Hasidism: the hereafter, what is, in essence, the reward for the righteous and the martyrs in heaven and in the Messianic time, and the question of reward and punishment in general. With these matters, which were not dogmatically fixed, the piety of the people was much more concerned than the majority of great theologians would admit. The lamentable conditions of the time of persecutions deeply influenced the imagination of the mystics.

The God of these mystics also manifests new traits. The rationalism of Saadia Gaon and the new mystic ideas of the Hasidim immediately came into conflict with the ancient Merkabah mysticism. God's ubiquity now plays a great role side by side with the absolute spirituality and infinity of God. Unobtrusively, this assumes the character of God's immanence in the universe. God is the most revealed and the most hidden; the nearest and the remotest. Hasidism approaches God altogether differently from the way He was approached in the earlier period.

Eleazar of Worms says: "God is everywhere and sees both the good and the wicked. Therefore, when you pray, have the proper attitude of mind. And for that reason the beginning of all benedictions is 'Blessed art Thou, O Lord' even as a man addresses his friend." This very feeling of intimacy is altogether new. God's immanence is often emphasized in an altogether pantheistic manner. The author of the *Hymn of Unity* which expressed Saadia Gaon's theology in passionate verses, sings: "All is in Thee, and Thou art in All. Thou encirclest All, and Thou fillest All. When All came to be, Thou Wert in All. Before All had come into being, Thou Wert All. And when All had come into being, Thou filledst All." Another said: "All is in Him, and He sees All. For He is All-seeing, although He hath no eyes, for in His very self doth He see all."

Added thereto we find a peculiar hidden Torah: the mysteries of Godhead and its "glory," the hidden secret of the *Cherub* seated upon the Throne of Glory, the mystery of the Throne of Glory itself and of the arch-images of the creation in the universe, all this constitutes the content of the theosophical speculations of the Hasidim. A rather naive mythology is here awkwardly linked with mystical experiences and ideas. The Shekinah is here identified with the revelation of God upon the Throne of Glory, but also with the God who is immanent in the world.

V. THE SEPHARDIC KABBALA

With the end of the 12th century there appeared for the first time upon the scene a mystic movement of still greater significance, its exponents designating themselves as masters of the Kabbala (possessors of the true mystic tradition), the masters of wisdom, faith, and service. The movement first appeared in Provence and Catalonia; however, an analysis of some of its oldest texts (particularly that of the *Sefer ha-Bahir*) reveals that it had existed earlier and had gone through a long process of development, notably in non-learned circles in France, which had been reached by various older traditions directly from the Orient and later also from Hasidic circles. It included also fragments of ancient Gnostic writings which expressed fantastic mythological ideas concerning God and His powers. So far as its original elements may be extracted, the older Kabbala does not bear a particularly orthodox character, and some orthodox leaders considered parts of the *Sefer ha-Bahir* as downright heresy. It was not until the second half of the 12th century, when they began to be linked up with neo-Platonic philosophical doctrines, that these ideas acquired significance. In this new association they developed rapidly, according to their various trends, in the Spanish Kabbala of the 13th and 14th centuries. This development took place in the Christian Occident, with the religious life of which the movement had a more intimate contact than under Moslemic influence. Here, in an atmosphere of religious strife brought about by the struggle of the Catholic Church against the Catharists of Provence, we encounter the first stages of the Kabbalistic movement in the 12th century. It succeeded in attracting to itself several distinguished orthodox Talmudists, since which time the Kabbala always appeared in orthodox garb, carrying out its historical function in this form. Toward the 13th century it crossed over to Spain. Centers of the Kabbala arose in the little town of Gerona, in Burgos, Toledo, and other places. Gerona played the most important rôle; here the theories and basic notions of the Provençal Kabbalist, Isaac the Blind, were developed in various phases. A rich mystical literature grew up.

ספר הזהר

PAGE OF TEXT OF "ZOHAR" (BRIGHTNESS); CREMONA, 1560

Nahmanides, the most important religious authority in Spain between 1230 and 1270, openly championed the Kabbala. In his time and in the generation which followed him the number of Kabbalists in Spain grew steadily. Attempts to develop mysticism in the direction of rationalistic speculation and to effect a compromise with contemporary philosophy (Azriel ben Solomon, Isaac ibn Latif) are found side by side with other tendencies which admit myths and mythical ideas, seeking to mould them after their pattern (the brothers Isaac and Jacob ha-Cohen, Todros Abulafia, and Moses of Burgos). Many great Kabbalists (as, for example, Isaac the Blind) were regarded as the bearers of Divine inspiration who were privileged to experience the Revelation of Elijah; still others (as Jacob ben Joshua ha-Cohen of Segovia) explicitly stated that their ideas had been revealed to them from on high. The theory and practice of a mysticism aspiring to a restoration of prophecy and to a new religious revelation, crystallized most clearly in the personality of Abraham Abulafia (b. 1240 in Saragossa), who was "awakened" in 1270 in Barcelona and who later was widely active in Italy and Sicily. It was he who most clearly developed a form of Kabbala which taught a systematic absorption in thought as preparation for ecstatic states and revelations. There is some evidence that he had contact also with non-Jewish mystics. His disciples later merged his theory of absorption and meditation with the other trends in the Kabbala.

That the non-learned were also affected by the new movement is attested by such incidents as the "awakening" of an unlearned craftsman in Avila in 1295. In Castile these various trends found their most effective synthesis in the second half of the 13th century in the writings of Joseph Gikatila and Moses de Leon. The latter, or an anonymous disciple of his circle, is the chief author of the *Zohar* (ca. 1280), the most important work of Spanish Kabbala. In this book, which purports to be a *Midrash* of Simeon ben Yohai and his associates and disciples, the doctrine of the Castilian Kabbalists was transmitted not so much theoretically as by means of all sorts of homilies and expositions. The *Zohar* is the most important document of a mythical reaction in Medieval Jewry. Before it had become recognized in wider circles as holy writing, many developments took place in the Kabbala of the 14th century, among them the famous dispute with philosophy occupying the most prominent place. Here we clearly discern the conflict between pantheistic and theistic tendencies. The Kabbala, always seeking to continue the line of the *Zohar* and to pass beyond it, finally appeared in its most radical form in the books of *Peliah* and *Kanah*. These latter works contain a severe criticism of Talmudic Judaism and exalt mysticism as the sole content of Judaism.

F. Baer in his *History of the Jews in Christian Spain* was the first to define clearly the function of the Kabbala with reference to Spanish Jewry since 1250. The Kabbalists had become a spiritual force in Jewry, because they appeared not merely as mystics, but also as ideologists of the folk religion. The Kabbala directed its efforts against the secularization of Judaism and the tendency to make of it an abstraction, as the rationalist philosophers of the time had tended to do; in this the Kabbala saw a peril to the preservation of Judaism. In the changes that were taking place in the condition of the Jews of Spain since the Christian kingdoms had completed the conquest of the peninsula, there existed the social background for the rise of the Kabbala as an historical factor. In such works as the *Zohar* and the books of *Peliah* and *Kanah*, the Kabbala most clearly proves to be a "work of national romanticism and mystic-ascetic reform" (Baer). It seeks to satisfy the religious interests of the type of Jew which alone could persevere under the new conditions. Originally preoccupied with very few problems (theosophy, the mysticism of prayer, inquiry into the motives of some commandments of the Torah which are particularly incomprehensible), it gradually broadened its scope and took in more and more spheres of Jewish religious life into its mystical interpretation. In its struggle against enlightenment Kabbala considered itself a conservative force, as the representative of tradition; nevertheless at the same time it often developed an entirely new conception of Judaism and its values. Of greatest significance for its ascendancy was its ability to illumine, through its tenets, precisely those areas with which the rationalistic philosophy could not cope, namely the plight of the Jewish people in the Diaspora, and the entire complex of the Halakah (see below). The thin stratum of affluent Jews interested in political intrigue and tax-gathering evidently did not consider the Kabbalists as their representatives. Conversely, however, the Kabbala voiced the moods and feelings of the poor Talmudic scholars and the pious plain man, whom the Kabbalistic ideas had taken from the domain of history to a path of its own, namely: to meditate not so much on the Messianic End of Days but rather on the genesis of all worlds. This flight from history is characteristic of the Spanish Kabbala; it is primarily interested in a cosmogony, and certain Kabbalists are vitally concerned with former worlds (*Olamot she-neherbu*). For a characterization of the world-view of the older Kabbala the following points ought to be emphasized in detail; to be sure, they are variously treated in the several systems, but on the whole they are all alike, if not in the solutions, at least in the question.

1) *Mystical Symbolism.* The Universe, as a whole and in its various component parts, may not be grasped through the intellect alone, but only symbolically. This means that no matter what weight and significance everything existing may have, another reality is visible through it, and that reality can not be expressed *per se* and may only be conceived as a symbol. All the principal works of the Kabbalists strain to fathom the symbolic character of all aspects of the universe and life which were of interest to the Medieval Jew. This mystical symbolism differs in the following respect from the allegorism which was precisely at that time accepted by the philosophers: in these sym-

bols it does not seek any metaphysical or moral ideas which might just as well take form and be expressed by themselves, but the very mysteries of the Divine life found in Creation; mysteries which cannot be articulated and are not "ideas."

2) Consonant with this is the conception of the Torah as perceived by the Kabbalists entirely through this symbolism. This conception is expressed most strikingly in three ways: the Torah is conceived as a living organism, in which God's name is revealed as the primary principle of all creation. Just as an organism lives and appears uniform in all its limbs, so does God's name appear in the Torah—the Ineffable Name—as the primary element of every manifestation. The Torah is thus not something inanimate and static; in every word, every verse and every "limb," there glow innumerable "lights" and mysteries. In addition, there is the conception of the Torah as the sumtotal of the laws which dominate all hidden occurences of the Cosmos. Everything that is historical in it is an allusion to the eternal life process of the world which is nothing else but the life of the Divinity as it unfolds and reveals itself. Finally in the *Zohar* there appears for the first time the theory concerning the four different methods of interpreting the Torah, which are derived from Christian exegetics. For the interpretation of the Torah four ways may be resorted to, and all of them have meaning: *Peshat*—the simple meaning of the word; *Derash*—the exposition of the *Agada*; *Remez*—the allegoric and philosophical meaning; and *Sod*—the mystic and symbolic meaning of the word. Their initials are combined in the word *PaRDeS*, and they are the mysterious Pardes (Paradise) in which the Kabbalist is absorbed by his speculations. In these ideas there is a trace of mystical criticism of the Holy Writ. The *Zohar* says: If Torah really contained in it no more than what the adherents of the simple *Peshat* seek to find therein, we should ourselves be able to make a better Torah. Radical Kabbalists, as *e.g.* the author of *Raya Mehemna* in the *Zohar,* and several of his followers in the 14th century,

strongly attacked the adherents of the simple *Peshat* and rational allegorism, and sought again and again to reduce both of these tendencies *ad absurdum*.

3) Of central significance is the new theosophical conception of God, formulated by the Kabbalists, through which they intended to rescue the living God of the pious masses from the abstract conception of the Deity which the philosophers had fashioned for themselves. The new God of the Kabbalists, who in reality should be but the old living God of the beginning of things and Sinai revelation, and man who faces Him—these are the two foci of Kabbalistic speculation. The Kabbalists differentiate between God in His pure character, which they call *En-Sof* (Endless), and God in his manifestation, as the creator and Lord of the Universe. For many Kabbalists God, who is entirely impersonal as the *En-Sof*, acquires personality only when He is considered in the perspective of creation. God the Creator of the world is the living God of religion, the God of Israel. He manifests himself in the different aspects of attributes which the Kabbala calls *Sefirot*, a term found in the *Sefer Yetsirah* but which here takes on an entirely new significance. The *Sefirot* represent the waves of the hidden life of the Godhead as it streams from the depths of the *En-Sof* to the Creation. Every single one of the *Sefirot*, whose reality may only be conceived in symbols, has no end of names. Especially popular and characteristic is the list composed by the Kabbalists of the Gerona school:

1. *Keter Elyon*, the "supreme crown" of God or the Primordial Will;
2. *Hokmah*, the "wisdom" or primordial idea of God;
3. *Binah*, the intellect, which wells forth as a river from the primordial source of Wisdom;
4. *Hesed*, the "love" or mercy of God;
5. *Geburah*, or *Din*, the sphere of Divine power chiefly manifested as the power of strict judgment and punishment;
6. *Rahamim*, the "compassion" of God, to which falls the task of mediating between the two preceding Sefirot (the term *Tiferet*, "beauty," is used only very rarely);
7. *Netsah*, the "lasting endurance" of God;
8. *Hod*, the "majesty" of God;
9. *Yesod*, the "basis" or "foundation" of all active forces in God;
10. *Malkut*, the "Kingship" of God.

From *Yesod*, the foundation of all worlds, there well forth the creative forces of the Divine life into the last *Sefirah*, which the Kabbalists identify with the *Shekinah* of the *Midrash* and which is usually described in the *Zohar* as the *Keneset Israel*, the mystical archetype of Israel as a community. In it all the hidden powers of God are united, and it also represents God's Being in all that is created. As they unfold themselves organically, these ten "powers of God" form the *Ilan* or World Tree of the *Sefirot*.

Numberless symbols are to be found in the Kabbala expressing this mysterious world under all sorts of aspects. First of all God manifests Himself in the *Sefirot* as the Primordial Man, the *Adam Kadmon*, the spiritual Image and Form, in Whose pattern earthly man is created. From this point of view it becomes clear why the Kabbalists always advocated and defended the idea of the anthropomorphic representation of God. The Torah nowhere speaks of the hidden God, but rather of the living God, who reveals Himself. But of the God who sits on the Throne of Glory of the Merkabah as the *Adam Kadmon*, one may speak in physical and anthropomorphic symbols. Here, too, the Kabbalists appear as the determined theoretical defenders of the conception which the simple folk had concerning God. The many contradictions and logical difficulties inherent in the conception of the *Sefirot* served as stimuli further to develop these theosophic speculations concerning God. Of especial significance in this connection was the question of the interrelationship of the *Sefirot* and of their unity in the very essence of God. It is true that in the description of this world of Divine emanations or powers we find, in part, much of the ancient mythology. Efforts were made to harmonize it with strict monotheism, but this was by no means always successful. Certainly the living God of the folk religion is never as orthodox as the God of the philosophers, who is reduced to abstract concepts.

4) The Creation and the world process were conceived by the Kabbalists as being the hidden life-process of the Godhead itself externally revealed. For this reason the *Sefirot* function also in them. The Divine light descends many degrees, thus bringing into view the Creation; but in the interior of the Creation there remains a radiation of those primordial forces which alone gives the world its symbolic splendor. In this world-view there are found parallel motives more theistic and more pantheistic; in the system of one Kabbalist the former have the upper hand, in the system of another the latter may take precedence. No ultimate agreement had been reached in the conflict. We find strictly theistic formulations of the Kabbala in the theories of Joseph ibn Wakkar (ca. 1330); on the other hand David ben Abraham ha-Laban (somewhat earlier) is severely pantheistic *(Sefer Masoret ha-Berit)*. The *Zohar* vacillates between the two currents; its formulations tend, however, to develop a more theistic thesis concerning the relation between God and the universe. Remarkable is the theory, often expressed since Nahmanides, that the world-process wholly fails to follow strict natural laws but is a continuation of hidden miracles *(nissim nistarim)* which renew themselves continually. At every moment God is not only the last member of a long chain of causes *(Sibbat Kol ha-Sibbot)* but also the direct cause of every state and every happening.

5) Man here appears in a direct relationship to God, a relationship impaired only by sin. The essence of sin and of evil in general is isolation, that independent existence which has severed itself from God. The true man, *i.e.,* the true Jew, is the "master of creation" in a very definite sense. Upon him depends the undisturbed functioning of the world-process, whose regulator, and in a more mechanistic conception often its actual manipulator, he is; the very life of the world is reflected in him; he himself is a *microcosmos,* an *Olam Katon;* and because he is connected with everything, he can also affect everything. By observing the Torah, by submitting to the hidden life law of the *Cosmos* contained therein, man places himself in a direct relationship to God. This is the hidden meaning of the commandments— to release an impulse in the right place or to prevent a disturbing circumstance by keeping away from a transgression. Because everything in the life of the Jew acquired significance for the entire world, the Kabbalists were able to set up an ideology of the Halakah which for a long time functioned among Jews. This ideology is completely developed in the later part of the *Zohar,* the *Raya Mehemna.* In the *Keneset Israel,* the Jewish *Ecclesia,* which patterns its life in accordance with the hidden rhythm of the world order, there resides the *Shekinah* itself, in whom this world order is personified as the law of Divine life. This mystical anthropology is also distinguished as characteristically Jewish by its positive evaluation of the sexual life. No matter how prominent the ascetic tendencies of this mysticism may be, nowhere is sexual asceticism taught as a principle. Per contra, a definitely holy mystery is seen in the process of procreation (Nahmanides, *Iggeret ha-Kodesh*).

6) Consonant with this is the mystical psychology, with its attendant theory expounded by the *Zohar* concerning the intuitive mystical power of the human soul *(nishmata kadisha)* which is the bearer of the profoundest religious knowledge. In this deepest stratum of the soul, into which the highest *Sefirot* radiate, man is united with God: in passing we may note that here we have a mystical interpretation of the gnosiology of the medieval Aristotelians. The mystical power of the soul can become active only in the ever-growing realization of religious values.

7) The supreme religious value which the Spanish Kabbala places at the heart of its mysticism and ethics is *Devekut,* the continued attachment or adherence to God, that direct relationship which has here almost entirely taken the place of the ecstatic experience. Although definitely an act of *Histaklut* (contemplation), *Devekut* does not call for an a-normal state of mind. On the contrary, as Nahmanides already said, true *Devekut* is realizable precisely in the life of the individual within his community; thus it can preserve a social tone. All the other values of the moral system of the Kabbala are set in relation to this highest ideal. These are fear of God, love of God, purity of thought, chastity, charity, study of the Torah, penitence, and prayer, considered by the *Zohar* as the most important meritorious acts. This is the mystical apotheosis of the virtues of the poor and the devotee, which presents, socio-ethically, a very characteristic picture. The glorification of poverty as a religious value is in harmony with this and makes its appearance for the first time in Rabbinical Judaism in the *Zohar* (Baer is of the opinion that there is present here the influence of the Franciscan movement). The poor people are "the broken vessels of the Holy One, Blessed be He" (מאנין תבירין דקודשא בריך הוא). The *Shekinah* itself is "poor." The *Zaddik* (just) of the *Zohar* is the man who, through prayer and absorption in the Torah, has realized the *Devekut* with God. It is interesting, however, that he is considered above all as observing a specially conspicuous sexual chastity, although he need not be a complete ascetic. It is surely no coincidence that among the values glorified by the Kabbalists those of an inellectual character are almost entirely absent (except the study of the Torah). In their ethical teachings directed toward the activity of the will, the Kabbalists are also seen as the ideological exponents of a folk religion.

8) In the Sephardic Kabbala eschatological ideas are also of special significance, and here, too, it was precisely not so much the ideas concerning the Messianic era as those dealing with the life of the soul in the hereafter. Under all possible forms and through all kinds of variations was manifested the belief in the transmigration of the soul, the *Gilgul.* The theory of *Gilgul* is one of reward and punishment which runs counter to the ancient Jewish theory of punishment in Gehenna. Both motifs are found parallel in the *Zohar* where *Gilgul* figures as a punishment for definite sins only. Later Kabbalists of the 14th century entirely eliminated the Gehenna and its punishment from Jewish theology and considered the *Gilgul* as a universal world law under which man is always given reward or punishment for his deeds in a new *Gilgul.* The essence of the reward for the righteous in the other world is an intensification of the *Devekut* which they have attained in this world.

Thus, set in a mystical light, there crystallizes in the Kabbala a complete worldview of Judaism. But beyond some individual attempts, particularly in the second half of the 13th century, the Kabbalists generally did not seek to influence the daily life of the Jewish community. The most militant representative of this Kabbala, which was also to be socio-reformist in nature, was the author of that part of the *Zohar,* called *Raya Mehemna.* Most of the other Kabbalists also pretended to be the possessors of the true ideology of Jewish life; however, they did nothing toward its realization. This is manifested by the absence, in the *Musar* literature of the period, of any real propaganda for the Kabbala and of any mystical tendencies; however, an important exception is the work of Bahya ben Asher, of the 13th century.

VI. THE KABBALA AFTER THE EXPULSION FROM SPAIN

With the expulsion of the Jews from Spain this condition underwent a basic change. The old cultural world of the rationalists collapsed entirely amid the catastrophes of the persecutions and expulsions; the Kabbala remained the only living religious force in Judaism. It now began to

פרדס רמונים עם פרי מגדים ספרים עסגרדים:

ספר
פֵּרדס רימונים

אשר נטע ונטל החסיד והקדוש המקובל
האלקי כמהֹ"ורר משה קורדאירוֹזל מנכת
תוכב מקום אשר עמד אדח קדש הוא והאיֹ
לעולס. נטך ספיר ויהלוס כנר חיי עולס
לסעולים · ויך כלכבון סרשיו · פרן ופהנ
פרומיו · נאה דרומיו ויפה חדומיו · זך
ונכהיר · כעגס הסמים לטוסר · ונונה אור
וזוהר · צדיקיס יכאו בו · ויאבלו פרי קדש
הילוליס לה'. וה 'וכבנו לטלות לספר אור יקר
אשר און נוקר המאור הנדול כפירו הוזר
כלפיסו והגניהו כרוב טיון   הם"ר ינקק
' כנהם"ר משולם זל איש פוזנא

פה   קֹק   קראקא

אשר תחת ממשל' אדונינו מלך וינחונד סלוסי
ירוס הנונו · סם כתחלכו המלאכה וכנמרת
תחת השר פלשאפפסקי זרה כבפר נאונו
דנוחר   בסכת אתר אדני
י כאֹ'נאטיב לאלף הסספיֹ:

פי ינקק כנהם"ר אהרן זל מפרונסטיץ

TITLE PAGE OF "PARDES RIMMONIM" (THE GARDEN OF POMEGRANATES)
BY MOSES CORDOVERO; CRACOW, 1592

penetrate into the community's life which opened before it, ripe to absorb its teachings. The *Zohar* was accepted among the masses of the people as a sacred book on a par with the Bible and the Talmud. Throughout the 16th century there swept a religious ferment, and under the impact of the Spanish catastrophe the entire nature of the Kabbala underwent a great change. The most important factor in this process was the merging of the Kabbala and Messianism, which was prosecuted with great intensity (see *Messianic Movements after the Expulsion from Spain*). This gave the Kabbala a uniquely social impetus, and assured its preponderance in Jewish life for several centuries. At first an attempt was made to preserve the older form of the Kabbalistic systems, often without relation to the Messianic-mystical propaganda conducted originally in Italy and Palestine. When the direct hopes for the redemption had failed of fulfilment, Messianism changed its character and transfered its influence to deeper spheres of religious life; the very theories of the Kabbala became permeated with the Messianic spirit. This process took place first of all in the new religious center of Jewry which crystallized in 1530 in Safed, in Upper Galilee. While the Kabbala which flowered in Italy came under the influence of the Platonic philosophy of the Renaissance, the new Kabbala in Safed was almost entirely free from such influences. Here in a tiny area there lived together a great number of Kabbalists whose religious emotions had been profoundly stirred; among them Joseph Karo, Solomon Alkabetz, Abraham Galanti, David ibn Zimra, Eliezer Azikri and, chiefly, the three main pillars of the new movement: Moses Cordovero (1522-1570), Isaac Luria (later known far and wide under the name of Ari—initials of Adonenu R. Isaac, 1534-1572), and his most distinguished disciple, Hayim Vital (1543-1620).

In Cordovero the Kabbala found the best exponent of its ideology (cf. his *Pardes Rimmonim, Shiur Komah,* and *Elimah*); in Luria, its leading religious figure as well as the creator of the new mythos of the Kab-

bala; and in Vital, its strongest literary exponent (the extensive literature of the so-called Kitbe ha-Ari was written mainly by Hayim Vital: *Ets Hayim, Sefer ha-Kavvanot, Shemonah Shearim*).

Courtesy Jewish Theological Seminary
TITLE PAGE OF "ETS HAYIM" (THE TREE OF LIFE) BY HAYIM VITAL; KORETZ, 1672

In Safed religious fellowships were formed; not only did they conduct mystical ceremonies at their assemblies, but they preached mysticism to larger circles. Here, too, were born the classic *Musar* books of the new Kabbala which did much more to carry the Kabbala to the people than the scholarly works of Moses Cordovero and Hayim Vital. The most important books of this kind are: Cordovero's *Tomer Deborah* (where the ten *Sefirot* are interpreted as the rungs of a ladder for the moral protection of man), Elijah de Vidas' *Reshit Hokmah,* Eliezer Azikri's *Sefer Haredim,* and Hayim Vital's *Shaare Kedushah.* These were the beginnings of an extensive popular literature dominated by the Kabbala and which became a characteristic feature of Jewish life up to the end of the 18th century. A profound influence was exerted by the book of Isaiah Hurwitz, *Shene Luhot ha-Berit,* usually called *Shelah* among the Ashkenazim; and much later by the anonymous book *Hemdat Yamim,* among the Sephardim. Partly because of this literature, and partly through the propaganda by religious circles which had arisen in Italy under the influence of the new religious movement, the ideas of the Kabbalists of Safed penetrated into all the lands of the Dispersion: Persia, Yemen, as well as Morocco, Turkey, Italy, Poland, and Germany. Beginning with 1625 the ideas of the *Ari* occupied the first place. Not only the ideas, but also a wealth of customs spread by the Kabbalists for mystical reasons, took root in all the communities. Almost all of these customs pointed to the fact that the life of the communities had fallen more and more under the influence of ascetic principles: *e.g.,* the fasting of the first-born males on the eve of Passover, the keeping of the vigil on the nights ushering in *Shabuot* and *Hoshana Rabbah.* The day of *Hoshana Rabbah* was converted from a happy festival into a day of penitence which really concluded the Day of Atonement. The last day of every month, the eve of the New Moon, became a Day of Atonement in miniature; a midnight service was introduced to mourn for the destruction of Jerusalem; and many other similar innovations. The liturgy and the order of the service, always a vital mirror of the religious life, were profoundly influenced by the mystics. Many prayers, both for the individual and the community, found their way into the prayer books, as, for example, the hymn of *Leka Dodi* by Solomon Alkabetz in the Friday evening service. The mystical meaning of the prayer was here emphasized, the theory of the *Kavvanot, i.e.,* the mystical meditations during prayer.

Both in its theoretical conceptions and its practical institutions this new Kabbala was wholly dependent on the central idea of redemption. One may actually speak about the infiltration of the Messianic ideas into all strata of Jewish life. The essence of Diaspora and redemption, these were central themes which the Kabbalists proclaimed anew. In this respect they represent splendidly the historic position of the Jewish masses from the 16th to the 18th century.

Among these ideas there revolved the mystical conception created by Isaac Luria and elaborated by his disciples. The three key words of the Lurian Kabbala are: *Tsimtsum, Shebirah,* and *Tikkun.*

Tsimtsum (contraction), the self-limitation of God, is the theory which teaches the doctrine that the act of Genesis was not God's emergence from His concealment, not an emanation (as in the older Kabbala), but a withdrawal of God into Himself, whereby room was created for the world process. Thus in essence, from its very beginning, creation is a form of exile, for God, as it were, goes into exile and withdraws from the center of His Being into a deeper concealment. It was not until then that He caused the *Sefirot* to emanate from Him. The *Tsimtsum* is repeated with each new stage of creation. Viewed dialectically the world process stems from a clash between the powers which stream back in every *Tsimtsum* to their source and those which emanate from it; these powers are symbolized as *Meorot,* luminaries.

Shebirah (*Shebirat ha-Kelim,* Breaking of the Vessels), is the theory concerning the rise of evil. The vessels (*Kelim*) could not endure the plenitude of Divine light which radiated into them, and they broke (*Shebirah*). Because of that circumstance the world did not develop according to the original plan of Creation; to a certain extent everything is misplaced and distorted and nothing is where it ought to be. Sparks (*Nitsotsot*) of the Divine light-stream fell into the abyss and were caught by the powers of darkness who turned them into Husks (*Kelipot*) at the fringe of the Divine luminaries. The

Shebirah, the breaking of the vessels, is the most important event in the drama of the universe but it is conceived primarily as a process of the Divine life-stream itself. All worlds, down to the earthly world itself, crystallized according to the laws which dominated the course of the *Shebirah.*

Facing this "break-up," there stands as a third element the healing or restoration of the primordially planned order of all things in their relation to God. This is the meaning of the *Tikkun* (Improvement, Restoration), which is the essentially positive content of the world process. The *En-Sof* itself has radiated new luminaries which penetrate with healing powers into the disordered state of things. But certain central functions of *Tikkun* were left to the discretion of human beings and it is they who have the most important task of human life in this world.

All acts of human beings, all study and prayer, have as their aim the bringing down of the *Tikkun. Tikkun* is thus a mystico-Messianic concept. When all things have been redeemed from the defilement which they received through the breaking of the vessels, the redemption shall have come. Each religious act performs a definite function in the *Tikkun* of the inner worlds, and the Kabbala of Luria has assigned to every *mitsvah* its own function.

This is the frame in which Luria's theory of Judaism is set. It is manifested as a great mystery of the Galut (Exile) and the Redemption. For the theory of the *Shebirah* means only that, in essence, everything is in exile. And the Kabbalists were able to explain that the historic exile of the Jewish people was at the same time the most important symbol of that condition of the universe, with the entire creation in bondage. Diaspora and Redemption thus acquire a cosmic-mythical background that explains the tremendous attraction which these ideas exercised especially from the 16th to the 18th century. Again, in another leading principle of the new Kabbala, this motif comes to the fore: the evolution from the concept of the migration of the souls to that of the exile of the souls, an evolution

now going on with great momentum. The intensive propaganda of the Kabbalists carried this idea to wide circles of the people where prior to the 16th century it had no perceptible hold. Not merely the world as a whole must be redeemed; because its orderliness has been disturbed, every soul must toil in many transmigrations and forms of existence to cleanse itself of the defilement introduced into it by the sin of Adam. The severest punishment which can befall a man is the lot of the "naked soul" *(neshamot artilaot)* for which there is predestined neither punishment in Gehenna nor incarnation in a new metamorphosis. Thus the destiny of the people is shifted from history into psychology. The existence of the straying souls, which find no resting place anywhere, is the frightening symbol of all the evil of the Diaspora.

Under the influence of the Safed movement the Kabbalists designated not merely limited circles of the Kabbalists but the entire people as carriers of the mystical Messianism, which is concentrated in the conception of the *Tikkun.* The ascetic who concentrates in his personality the Messianic ideas, and whose yearning is aimed at perfecting the world, is put forth as the ideal type of man, especially as proclaimed in the *Musar* books of the Kabbala. This accumulated energy burst forth with particular force in the Sabbatian movement (cf. the article on *Messianic Movements*).

After the downfall of Sabbatianism in the 18th century there were left only two paths for the Kabbala: either to abandon the people and seek afresh the way to a mystery religion for a small circle, or to carry the Lurian Sabbatian Kabbala into the heart of the people, while seeking at the same time to eliminate the dangerous and revolutionary element from Messianism. The first path was taken by the orthodox Kabbalists who in the 18th century had their two large centers in the Brody conventicle and in the Bet-El Yeshibah in Jerusalem, which survives to this day. Among the Kabbalists of Jerusalem there existed for a long time (until ca. 1800) a secret society whose members were bound to one another not by a material but by a spiritual communism. To this day the influence of this later-day center in Jerusalem extends over the Jews of the Orient. The Hasidic movement chose the second path, and converted the Kabbala into a system of ethics, thus turning it into a socio-reformist factor. In Hasidism the ideas of the mystics in popular form again reached the widest circles of the people.

Characteristic of these tendencies is the Kabbalistic system of *Habad* (as formulated in *Tanya* of Shneur Zalman of Liady), in which the theosophy of the Kabbalists almost passes into a well-nigh modern system of mystic psychology. The influence of the mysticism of *Habad* can be seen also in the writings of the late Chief Rabbi of Palestine, Abraham Isaac Kook *(Orot ha-Kodesh)*, the last original exponent of Jewish mysticism.

BIBLIOGRAPHY

J. ABELSON, *Jewish Mysticism*. London, 1913.

S. A. HORODEZKY, תורת האר"י in כנסת Vol. III, 1938.

S. A. HORODEZKY, מאה שנים של פרישות ומוסר in התקופה Vol. XXII, 1924.

G. SCHOLEM, *Bibliographia Kabbalistica*. Leipzig, 1927.

G. SCHOLEM, *Kabbala,* in Encyclopaedia Judaica, Vol. IX. Berlin, 1932.

G. SCHOLEM, *Major Trends in Jewish Mysticism*. Jerusalem, 1941.

E. TCHERIKOVER, *Di komune fun yerushelaimer mekubbolim in 18tn yorhundert.* In Historishe Shriftn fun Yivo, Vol. II, 1937.

M. WAXMAN, *A History of Jewish Literature,* Vol. I. 1938, Vol. II, 1943, New York.

MESSIANIC MOVEMENTS UP TO THE END OF THE MIDDLE AGES

A. Steinberg

INTRODUCTION

Among the characteristic phenomena of Jewish history, perhaps the most remarkable is the succession of great popular movements — recurring periodically from the pre-Christian era to the 18th century — whose sole aim is the hastening of the time when the supra-historic Messianic ideal would, in accordance with the words of the ancient prophets, be realized. The general conditions which call forth these Messianic movements change from century to century; changes occur in the scope, the content and the driving force of the ideal. At times the entire people is caught up in it; at other times only a single community is affected; at times the movement spreads through all strata of the people; at other times the poorest elements alone make it their cause, so that it acquires a revolutionary character. But beyond these variations, all popular Jewish Messianic movements are marked by one unifying aim: they invariably seek to hasten the fulfillment of Jewish history and, therefore, of human history in general. Parallel with this, the yearning for the "End of Days" always projects the post-historic dream in the form of the ideal personality. Although the aim of every Messianic movement has always been the redemption of the people of Israel and of the world in a universalist sense, the specific problems of every given period were invariably reflected in the picture of the redeemer. Hence, even he whose personality incarnated the ultimate redemption, changed in consonance with the spirit of the age which brought him forth. Nevertheless, he, too — whether he existed only in the imagination of the people or was a demonstrable historic reality — never ceased to be the messenger of God, elected and anointed by Him, and, therefore, a "Messiah."

The king of the Jews had from of old been a "Messiah of the Lord," God's anointed, worthy of bearing the crown of the people, in particular if he had also been of the House of David. The High Priest, too, naturally laid claim to the distinction. Under the Hasmonaean dynasty the anointed King and the Messiah Priest were united in a single person. But it was the Hasmonaean period which witnessed the deepest disappointments both in the socio-political and the spiritual fields; that same period, therefore, gave birth to the concept that those who stood at the head of the people and ruled it in the name of God, could merit their claim only if they added to the ideal qualities of King and Priest, those of the prophet or, at least, of the kind of man who was the ideal of the prophets. Only such a chosen man, "anointed of the Lord," would — in accordance with this view — be capable of rescuing the people from its political, social, and spiritual misery, and of bringing it nearer to the "End of Days," of universal peace, absolute justice and perfect piety which an Isaiah, a Micah, and a Jeremiah had prophesied. Of the three personalities who were thus merged into one, the first two, because of the burden of historic sin weighing upon them, had been relegated to the background, while the ideal man of the prophets became primary in importance; although a prince of the Davidic dynasty, the Messiah of the future was to be "a poor man, riding upon an ass"; and, although elected to fill the whole world with holiness, he nevertheless was to remain God's simple "servant."

Such was the will and demand of the masses who yearned for redemption, not in behalf of this or that group, but for the benefit of all the people. The destiny of the redeemer, and the destiny of the entire world—such was the view of the believers who prepared the soil for the first Messianic movement in Jewish history—depended on whether he would find in himself the power to fulfill here and now that which had centuries before been foreseen and foretold in Divine prophecy. Should the fulfilment prove to be impossible in a natural manner, it would come about miraculously—only a strong enough faith was needed. A vast Apocalyptic literature spread and elaborated these thoughts and dreams; ancient saints were resurrected—at least in the writings of these dreamers—and they testified that the "true redeemer," the righteous one, chosen by God, would soon appear and renew the whole world with a "new covenant" (according to Jeremiah xxxi, 30). Already in the Book of Daniel (vii, 13-14), there is talk of a "Son of Man" (*Bar Enash*), who would unite all the kingdoms of the world under the sovereign rule of God. The Book of Enoch of the 1st century B.C.E. was inspired by the same Messianic-theocratic ideal; the same influence is apparent in a series of other works which are spiritually related to the Essenes. For this widespread longing to blossom into a genuine folk movement, there was wanting only the tangible "Son of Man," who would take upon himself the supra-historic mission in consonance with the Messianic ideal. That which the times demanded came to pass; such a "Son of Man" soon appeared. Indeed, he appeared again and again; and since none of these "Sons of Men" had more than a temporary success with the Jewish people, they all fall, in the Jewish tradition, under the concept of "False Messiah"—a parallel to the "False Prophet."

I. MESSIANIC MOVEMENTS UNDER ROMAN AND BYZANTINE RULE

In the last century B.C.E., the Messianic element in Judaism assumed the status of an independent spiritual factor in Palestine. A century later it began to develop as an independent belief which severed itself gradually from its Jewish soil in order to dominate the world. But with that the history of Jewish Messianism was by no means concluded; it continued to develop out of its ancient prophetic roots, in conscious contrast to non-Jewish Messianism which functioned in the outside world under the Greek name of Christianity (the Greek "Christos" is a translation of the Hebrew "Mashiah"). This world-historic movement was at the outset a typically Jewish popular movement; it rose shortly before the collapse of the Jerusalem aristocracy, against whose nearsighted politics and moral depravity it was directed; and it parted company with other similar movements in Jewish life only in one respect: while other Zealots believed that the first step toward the redemption was the liberation from Roman domination, the Messianists held that the hour had struck for the realization of the highest Jewish ideal, *i.e.*, for the initiation of God's rule, the Kingdom of Heaven, throughout the world. They therefore pinned their hopes upon the great miracle of spiritual world revolution, and not upon a physical triumph over a few Roman legions. Their "King," Jesus, was neither a hero of the battlefield nor a diplomat of the courts; he was a popular preacher, a "rabbi" (see this Jewish word in the Greek text: the Gospel according to

St. John I, 38; xx, 16 etc.), a wonderworker and a healer, as were the oldest prophets. But the general movement also produced, in the first half of the 1st century C.E., claimants to the crown of the Messiah who were closer to the other type of popular liberator. There had appeared in Palestine, for example, a Jew by the name of Theudas who gathered round him several hundred people, intending to lead them in a struggle against the Romans. He had boasted that he would repeat in the middle of the Jordan the miracle of the Red Sea. His ideal was apparently neither a hero of the post-biblical period nor even of the prophetic age; it was Moses, the "Father of the Prophets." The same sources also tell of a Palestinian "redeemer" of about the same period who was to have come from Egypt and who was to have gathered a multitude of Jews "in the wilderness." Even if the second story is merely an episode detached from the previous narrative, it has an importance of its own: we learn from it that the Messianic movement had already drawn into its sphere the Jews of the Diaspora. These attempts to hasten the redemption were drowned in blood by the Roman authorities. The Messianists whose attitude toward the world of reality, to *Olam ha-Zeh* (this world), was one of great disdain, certainly regarded redeemers of Theudas' caliber as "false Messiahs" and "false prophets." And to Jews, who even after the catastrophe in Palestine continued to believe in the coming redemption, all these Messianists whose "righteous redeemer" belonged only to the past, were for that very reason *Minim,* that is, heretics and schismatics. Into the *Amidah* prayer (the eighteen benedictions), which is the most eloquent monument in the Jewish liturgy to the Messianic movement of that day (see, for example, the first benediction: "And bringeth a Redeemer"; the eighth benediction: "Redeem us Speedily"; the eleventh: "Blow a great Trumpet"; the twelfth: "Do Thou Reign over us Alone," etc.), there was inserted a special impreca-

tion against the *Minim* (in later prayer-books: *Malshinim,* denouncers).

The depth of the chasm between the Jewish Messianists, who lived in the hope of the future, and the Christ-Messianists, who deified the "Son of Man," Jesus, and the story of his suffering, became particularly clear in the 2nd century C.E., when a new Jewish redemptive movement arose in Palestine. At its center stood Bar Kochba and Rabbi Akiba, the latter being the purest incarnation of the Jewish idea of *Kiddush ha-Shem* (Sanctification of the Name). The most noteworthy element in this movement, which soon assumed the character of a military uprising against the power of the Emperor Hadrian, was the fact that its leader became not the representative of the spirit, but of physical might, and that Rabbi Akiba himself, in spite of the opposition of some of the sages, proclaimed Bar Kochba as a Messiah. The very essence of Jewish Messianism, it appears, militated against any kind of aristocracy, even against that of the spirit. Whether the aim of the Bar Kochba rebellion (132-135) included, beyond the liberation of Palestine and the people of Israel, the redemption of the world, remains unclear. But Rabbi Akiba's life and martyrdom testify definitely to his Messianic concepts which were faithful in the last detail to the prophetic program of "the End of Days." In his person the Oral Law (interpretation of the Torah) merged with the ancient prophetic spirit and, far from representing the close of a supposedly antiquated legal tradition, as the followers of Paul thought, it became—thanks to Akiba's Messianic impulse—the natural heir of the true eschatological hope, namely that of the "End of Days." The Messianists, whose orientation was based mainly on the past, *i.e.,* the Christians, would not acknowledge this fact. Thenceforth, Judaism and Christianity part company for ever.

Three hundred years later, when Christianity had itself become a worldly power, and began to translate its hostility toward the Jewish tradition into action, it called forth a new attempt on the part of Jewish Messianism to realize its program. Thus we hear that in the time of Theodosius II, there appeared on the island of Crete a Messiah by the name of Moses (ca. 440); he also attempted to repeat the miracle of the earlier Moses, promising he would lead the Jews back to Palestine across the Mediterranean Sea as if it were dry land. A multitude of the faithful was drowned, and in the history of the Church the incident is cited as a new evidence of Jewish tenacity. Less than three centuries passed and Jewish Messianism was again embodied in a living personality: this time it was a refugee from Byzantium, Serenus, who aroused the entire Jewish world from Syria and Babylonia as far as Spain. In a number of details this popular movement was reminiscent of the beginnings of Christianity. The devotees of the new "Messiah" wanted to ease the yoke of the law for the masses (mainly those laws which had been instituted by the Talmud); the movement was grounded in the belief that the world-political crisis of that time, *i.e.,* the conflict between Christian "Edom" (Rome, Byzantium) and "Ishmael" (Islam), would be the transition to Messianic days. As had happened eight hundred years earlier, an Apocalyptic literature appeared. In the apocryphal work of that period, *Nistarot de-Rabbi Simeon ben Yohai,* the dramatic denouement of world history is envisaged as occuring in three separate acts: first a pre-Messiah *(Mashiah ben Joseph)* would restore the Jews to Palestine and rebuild the Temple; this however, would end in a new catastrophe, because a mighty king, Armilus, would drive the Jewish people into a wilderness; not until its sins shall have been entirely washed away by these last calamities would the true and righteous redeemer *(Mashiah ben David)* appear. In this wise Jewish Messianism anticipated possible failure for which it prepared comfort. Thereby it also confirmed anew, in the spirit of ancient prophecy, the belief that the restoration of a free Jewish state in Palestine was not of itself the last guarantee

of complete redemption. Already near the end of the 4th century, when the Byzantine Emperor, Julian the Apostate, had manifested the desire to effect a restoration of Jewish Palestine (362), the Jewish people showed that the spirit in which such a "redemption" was carried out was by far more important than the redemption itself, and Julian's offer touched no Messianic chord within the people.

II.   MESSIANIC MOVEMENTS UNDER ISLAMIC RULE

Christianity had from the outset been, and always remained, the belief in the first and only "Messiah"; Islam had originally been the religion of the last "Prophet." While Jewish Messianism, therefore, found itself in permanent conflict with the Church, and always strove to convince it that the true Messiah was yet to come, no such difference divided it from Islam, toward which it could remain neutral. One trend in Islam, the Shiites, had already, toward the end of the 7th century—and that under the influence of a Jew who had embraced the new faith—entered the stream of Messianism by its anticipation of a second coming of Mohammed at the "End of Days." Thus, in the Islamic world, too, occasion was given to the Jews to testify to their own Messianic tradition.

We encounter the first Jewish Messianic movement in the Moslem world approximately at the beginning of the 8th century. Its central figure is the Persian Jew, Abu Isa, or Isaac Obadiah, an illiterate man of the masses who nevertheless felt called upon to proclaim the coming of the Messiah. He preached an ascetic morality, bade his followers devote themselves to prayer as much as possible, and was also prepared to take up arms for the redemption. The universalistic element in his Jewish Messianism found expression in his assertion that not alone Mohammed, but Jesus, too, was for him a true prophet, sent by God to the heathen peoples. After he had fallen in battle against a Moslem army, his devotees announced that he lived on, and one of his disciples, Yudghan, the Paul of Abu Isa, evolved an entire system whose main principles were man's freedom of will and the rejection of all anthropomorphisms with reference to God. This Messianic sect, having crystallized into a system, was to branch out in later times, and we find traces of it in the region of Damascus as late as the 10th century. The travels of Eldad ha-Dani toward the close of the 9th century are evidently bound up with this flowering of Jewish Messianism in the Orient. His mission was to establish contact with the "lost ten tribes": it was clear that without them perfect redemption was impossible.

The close of the 10th century was a time of world unrest. The year 1000 was, in the belief of many Christians, to open the Millennium; Jesus was to descend anew from Heaven. Although divided between Christian and Moslem, the religious world of that day was, nevertheless, united in its ancient Jewish and, ergo, Messianic roots. From the depth of Central Europe the "men of Rhenus" (Jews of the Rhine Valley) inquire of the scholars of the Holy Land whether they should get themselves ready for the "End of Days." According to the computations of Saadia Gaon (in the first half of the 10th century), the time was at hand. The caliph of the Fatimite dynasty, al-Hakim (996-1021), began to look upon himself as a sort of Messiah. Three faiths simultaneously anticipated the same miracle. Jewish Messianism, however, proved to be the most patient: if the miracle did not occur when it was awaited, it would come a century later—that, at least, was the mood of the Jews among the Moslem peoples; and so in the 12th century Messianic movements blazed forth anew among them. The most powerful was kindled (ca. 1155) in Persia, the country which had witnessed a similar phenomenon three and a half centuries earlier. Its effects were felt as far as Baghdad, perhaps because this "Messiah" was a former pupil of the Yeshibah of that city. To his name, David Alroy, was added the epithet Menahem, i.e., the Comforter. Primarily he wanted to comfort the "Mourners of Zion," little groups of pious ascetics, who, in the period of the Crusades, had brooded on the question: When will the people of Israel, the party chiefly concerned, intervene in the conflict for Palestine between Christians and Moslems? When this "Messiah" had, like his predecessors, been sacrificed on the altar of his idea, remnants of the "Menahemist" movement continued to endure. About twenty years after the death of the "Comforter," David Alroy, there appeared in Yemen an illiterate Jew who regarded himself as the herald of the coming redeemer. No less a personality than Maimonides warned his contemporaries (in his *Epistle to Yemen*) against the temptation to follow all kinds of illiterate dreamers who promised to perform miracles with the power of the Holy Spirit. Nevertheless, it was precisely Maimonides who included the constant expectation of the Messiah among the Thirteen Articles of the Jewish faith; and another Jewish thinker of that day, Abraham bar Hiya, attempted in his *Megillat ha-Megalleh* (The Scroll of the Revealer), to compute the time of the apocalypse of human history. A typical representative of this Messianic 12th century was also Judah ha-Levi. Jewish Messianism, more clearly than heretofore, recognized itself in the subjective form of "patient impatience," according to the twelfth of the Thirteen Articles of Faith: "Even if the Messiah shall tarry, I shall wait for him every day."

III. MESSIANIC MOVEMENTS DURING THE CHRISTIAN MIDDLE AGES

While Jewish Messianic movements in the Orient, and particularly under Mohammedanism, frequently assumed an aggressive and even a military-revolutionary character, they were, in consonance with the general living conditions of the Jews, much more passive in Christian medieval Europe. They find expression partly in a yearning to return to the Orient and partly in polemics against the pseudo-Messianism of the non-Jewish environment. Even these polemics were evoked by an assault of the stronger party. Thus, at the close of the 9th century, the Bishop of Lyons, Amulo, charged the Jews not only with the denial of the true Messiah, *i.e.*, Jesus, but also with the erroneous conception of the two Messiahs (ben Joseph and ben David). It is evident therefrom that the Messianic conception as set forth, for example, in the apocryphal *Nistarot* of Simeon ben Yohai, had spread as far as France. In general there must have existed Jewish circles where the yearning for the Messiah was especially cultivated. This is indicated by a contemporary document, the Midrash, *Tanna debe Eliyahu*, dating from the 10th century, which speaks repeatedly of the coming of Elijah, who would announce the approach of the righteous redeemer. During the persecutions in connection with the first Crusade (end of 11th century), Jews of Central Europe took to the road. Many refugees arrived in Constantinople, and soon the rumor spread among them that the Ten Tribes and the Jews of the Khazar countries were marching from the fabled "Hills of Darkness" and would precede the Christians in the conquest of the Holy Land. Already some ten years earlier a "Messiah" had appeared in Southern France, only to encounter the same bitter fate as many earlier Messianic pretenders. During the course of the 12th century, while Jewish Messianism flourished mostly in Moslem lands, it provided in the Christian Occident the main theme for the oral and written disputes between Jews and Christians. From the same period dates Joseph Kimhi's *Sefer ha-Berit,* in which the internal contradictions of the Jesus story are presented. Joseph's son, David Kimhi (d. ca. 1235), puts this query to the Christians: How can they view Jesus as the true Messiah, when they know from the prophets of Israel that his main mission was to be the creation of permanent peace on earth, whereof no sign was evident? The same arguments are presented by the Jewish group during the celebrated disputations which took place in Barcelona (1263) and again in the Tortosa debates (1413).

This strongly polemical attitude toward non-Jewish Messianism, *i.e.*, toward Christianity, was a symptom of the readiness on the part of the Jewish masses in the Christian Middle Ages to receive with enthusiasm every announcement concerning the "End." Indeed, less than twenty-five years before Nahmanides' dispute with the Christians in Barcelona, the "righteous redeemer" had been impatiently awaited in all Jewish communities, simply because the year 1240, according to Jewish chronology, opened the sixth millennium, with which, a Talmudic dictum states, the period of the redemption was to begin. When the invasion of Mongolian tribes a year later crossed the German frontiers, a rumor spread among Christians that this was a result of a Jewish Messianic plot. There followed a wave of anti-Jewish persecutions; one of its motifs, then as always, was the tenacious "heresy" of the Jews, *i.e.*, their belief in a Messiah who was yet to come, rather than in one who had already lived on earth more than a thousand years before.

If the unrest which marked the middle of the 13th century was a Messianic movement without a "Messiah" (at any rate we have no knowledge of "leaders"), there appeared, toward the end of the same century, several "redeemers" who, per contra, attracted very few followers. The most significant personality among the new claimants to the Messianic crown was Abraham Abulafia, who in 1284 had proclaimed himself in Italy as the redeemer. Some time earlier he had proposed merging the Jewish faith with the Christian; the "arrogance" of this proposal, which he presented to Pope Nicholas III, nearly cost him his life. His end is unknown, but after his disappearance, disciples of his continued to prophesy about the "End." Almost simultaneously with Abulafia a Messiah appeared in Avila (Spain), an illiterate, who denounced the "non-believers" as Abulafia had earlier denounced the men of learning. The leading rabbis of the day, headed by

Solomon ben Adret, were bitter opponents of the new Messianic tendencies; there are reasons to believe that these tendencies, too, had a definitely anti-aristocratic character. Nonetheless, a century later, according to the report of a Christian divine who participated in the Tortosa debate, the Spanish community brought forth another false Messiah. From the 13th century on the Kabbala introduced a new element into Jewish Messianism. It was the main source from which Abraham Abulafia drew his inspiration for the belief in his universal mission of the redemption.

BIBLIOGRAPHY

The history of the Jewish Messianic movements is treated in the general literature on Jewish history, the history of Christianity, and religion in general. The most important special works are:

JULIUS H. GREENSTONE, *The Messiah Idea in Jewish History*. 1906.

HUGO GRESSMANN, *Der Messias*. 1929.

JOSEPH KLAUSNER, *Yeshu ha-Notzri*. 1922.

JOSEPH KLAUSNER, *Ha-Raayon ha-Mashihi be-Yisrael*. 1927.

EDUARD MEYER, *Ursprung und Anfaenge des Christentums*. 1920-1923.

EMIL SCHUERER, *Geschichte des juedischen Volkes im Zeitalter Jesu Christi*. 4th ed., 1901-1911.

ABBA HILLEL SILVER, *A History of Messianic Speculation in Israel*. 1927.

MESSIANIC MOVEMENTS AFTER THE EXPULSION FROM SPAIN

Gershom G. Scholem

After the expulsion from Spain the character of the Messianic movements underwent a marked change. The older movements of this sort among Jews in the Middle Ages had had no essential relationship to the Kabbala; and the Kabbala on the other hand had stood quite apart from Apocalyptic thought. What distinguishes Messianism since 1500 is the mystical imagery common to its chief representatives, whence all Messianic ideas acquired a peculiar intensity. All these movements reflected the tribulations and persecutions of their period, as well as the popular conceptions of the Messiah and the redemption which were current among the masses in the ghettos. They also incorporated, to an ever-increasing degree, elements of the Kabbala.

In the year 1500, shortly after the Expulsion, there emerged among the Marranos in Spain a restless Messianism of a completely popular and unsophisticated character. Several Marranos, among them Inez, the daughter of Juan Estevan of Herrera, arose as prophets, "were taken up to Heaven," and there received the tidings that soon deliverance would come for the Marranos, and that they would be taken back to Palestine (cf. Baer in "Zion," v., 1933). According to the records of the Inquisition the movement was current exclusively among "little people," whose conceptions of the redemption were extremely naive but as yet entirely without Christian admixture. The prophetess of Herrera was burned in 1502. At about the same time a Messianic unrest swept over the "unconverted" Jews. In particular it was the Spanish exiles who

considered the Expulsion of 1492 as the beginning of the "birth-throes of the Messiah," much as had been the case when Constantinople was taken by the Turks.

There began a lively propaganda of spiritual preparation for the impending redemption. The years 1496-1498 saw the appearance of three important works from the pen of Isaac Abravanel: *Mayene ha-Yeshuah* (The Fountains of Salvation), *Yeshuot Meshiho* (The Salvation of his Anointed One), and *Mashmia Yeshuah* (The Announcer of Salvation), containing a definitive codification of the Messianic doctrine of Medieval Judaism as well as the passwords and signs which were adopted in the Messianic propaganda of the next generation. He intimated that the Messiah had already been born prior to the Expulsion, *i.e.* in 1491. Abravanel thought that the deliverance would come either in 1503 or in 1531. For him the Messianic myth had a purely political character. It is otherwise, however, in the Apocalyptic works of the Kabbalists of that time; for them the political redemption was bound up with the world order as a whole.

Between 1500 and 1502 there arose in Venice the German Kabbalist, Asher Lemmlein, who initiated a penitential movement among Italian and German Jews. In the words of a contemporary, he "brought to deep repentance the majority of Jews in Christian lands"; indeed, in later times the year 1500 was remembered by Italian Jews as "the year of repentance." Asher did not proclaim himself the Messiah, but the harbinger of the impending redemption, which, it appears, he awaited in 1503, as predicted by Abravanel. For a period of over thirty years these penitential and redemptive currents ran unchecked. The Kabbalists in Italy and Salonica, and, above all, a group of apocalyptic mystics in Jerusalem, carried on an intense Messianic propaganda. An anonymous author in Italy wrote (ca. 1500) *Kaf-ha-Ketoret* (Ms., Paris), a commentary on the Psalms, which finds in every word of the Psalms an allusion to the Messiah; to this writer the Psalms as a whole were the battle-hymns of the final war of the Messiah. At the same time there arose the legend of the Spanish Kabbalist, Joseph della Reyna, who reputedly, even before the Expulsion, had attempted to bring about the redemption. By magic incantations he prevailed over *Sammael* (Satan) and bound him in chains, only to be overcome in turn by the guile of his adversary (later, in the propaganda of the followers of Sabbatai Zebi, this legend achieved considerable popularity). The Kabbalists insisted that redemption should be hastened not only by penitence and mortification of the flesh, but by the use of magic.

Particularly intense was the propaganda conducted by Abraham ben Eliezer ha-Levi, an exile from Spain, who, after many wanderings through Italy, Turkey, and Egypt, at long last arrived in Jerusalem, where he lived from ca. 1515 to 1530. He linked the ideas of Abravanel with those of the Kabbalists, wrote commentaries on all Hebrew books connected with the Messianic idea and made vivid apocalyptic commentaries on the events of his time. Like others of his type he was hostile toward the Christians and friendly to the Turks. He believed that Catholicism was about to fall, and in a great pastoral letter from Jerusalem (1526) he hailed Luther's Reformation as the beginning of the end of Christianity. He awaited the redemption in 1531. Many manuscript copies of his work were circulated in Christian countries.

Whereas, in Abraham ha-Levi's apocalyptic teachings, the Kabbala is bound up with political passion, Apocalyptics appear directly as political action in the bizarre figures of David Reubeni and Solomon Molko (his baptismal name was Diego Pires). The latter's activities were entirely devoted to the Messianic movement. The activities of David Reubeni are very doubtful and as a matter of fact actually unclear. He was probably a German Jew, as Aescoli has shown through an analysis of the Hebrew terminology in Reubeni's diary, remnants of which are extant. He appeared in 1524 in Italy, purportedly as an emissary of the Jewish kingdom of Habor in Arabia. He wanted the Pope to unite the Christian world and the allegedly "independent" Jewish tribes in a war for the conquest of Palestine; and in 1525 he actually left Rome for Portugal with a papal commendation in order to proceed with his mystical mission. David Reubeni's appearance awakened the Marrano, Diego Pires (born ca. 1500), a man of high culture and strong mystical leanings, who possibly, even before this, had studied the teachings of Judaism in secret. He had himself circumcised, immediately thereafter had visions from Heaven, and on the advice of Reubeni, fled from Portugal. He proceeded to Italy, where, it appears, he became absorbed in the study of the Kabbala; later he seems to have sojourned for a short while in Turkey (among the Kabbalists gathered around Joseph Taitatsak in Salonica)—his journey to Palestine is probably legendary—and later, from 1528 till 1532, was active again in Italy (Sonne, in *Annuario*, Rome 1534). He apparently worked hand in hand with Reubeni, although the true background and the details of their activity are unknown to us. Reubeni always posed as a military leader, declaring that he understood nothing in matters of learning and religion; at the same time he led the life of a strict ascetic.

Molko, on the other hand, was absorbed heart and soul in the Apocalyptic Kabbala, and he caused a great stir among the Italian Jews. He had his mystical sermons printed in Salonica (1529). They are permeated through and through by the spirit of Messianic propaganda, but they establish the year of redemption as no earlier than 1540.

Molko was primarily active in Venice, where Reubeni simultaneously endeavored to persuade the Republic to conclude a military treaty with the Jews whom he represented. Molko was for a considerable time also in Rome, where he evidently made no little impression on Pope Clement VII. Toward the end of 1532 both Reubeni and Molko left for Regensburg on a mission to see Charles V. After a brief conversation the Emperor had both of them arrested. Molko, as a Marrano who had returned to Judaism, was handed over to the Inquisition and, at the close of 1532 or early in 1533, was burned at Mantua. Reubeni vanished in the prisons of Spain. Molko's death for the Sanctification of the Name (Kiddush ha-Shem) made a great impression on the Jews of that time. Among the Jews of Italy he had ardent devotees as well as bitter opponents of his apocalyptic politics. Apparently Reubeni and Molko had actually hoped that precisely in those times of the "birth-throes of the Messiah" they would be able to bring about political action for the return of the Jews to Palestine. It is worth noting that they based their political activity on an anti-Turkish alliance.

It would seem that the struggle for the re-establishment of the Semikah institution—the rite of ordination—was not unconnected with apocalyptic politics of this type. In 1538 the Palestinian scholars of Safed and Jerusalem were drawn into the conflict. Jacob Berab zealously sought to restore the Sanhedrin in the then flourishing city of Safed and made efforts to prove that it was both permissible and possible to do so. True, the motives for the re-establishment of the Sanhedrin were of a secondary nature: an authoritative body was needed, so to speak, to provide Marranos who were willing to return to Judaism with means for doing penance; but it is possible that Berab had also in mind the impending redemption.

After 1540 the lively Messianic agitation cooled off. In its place came a deeper change in the religious world of Jewry, issuing from the new Kabbala of Safed. Messianism was built into the very core of the new system, and underwent an essential change of character. In the system of the Kabbalists of Safed, and more particularly in that of Luria (Ari), which became dominant in the 17th century, the essence of the redemption consists not so much in the liberation from the yoke of the exile and the restoration of Israel's political grandeur as in the internal transformation of the very nature of the world. When all things will have returned, in essence, to their original status, and when the process of Tikkun (perfection or restoration of the world) will have been completed, the Messiah will have come. The political redemption, and everything which the national legend had associated with it, are no more than external symbols for a cosmic process that takes place within the world.

Messianism thus acquired a specifically spiritualistic and mystical flavor, although there was no evidence of a conflict with the traditional politico-national content of the Messianic idea. Messianic activity in the now growing Kabbalistic circles meant the living of a life of seclusion and penance in order to hasten the advent of the "world of Tikkun" which had been anticipated to come before long. But it is characteristic that precisely in the long period during which the Kabbala of Safed had been struggling for domination over the Diaspora, there had taken place no sharp outburst of Messianism. On the other hand, there is no doubt that among wide circles there had simultaneously gone on a particularly profound readiness for the release of Messianic forces. It is true that the disciples of Luria (Isaac Luria, d. 1572) considered that he might be the Messiah. Also in the legend concerning him, which crystallized early, there occurred the idea that he was to be the Messiah, but there was no intimation that he himself laid claim to it. It is no wonder that after the Kabbala of Luria with its trend toward the cosmic redemption had taken hold of Jewry (since approximately 1625), less than a generation elapsed before this latent Messianism broke out violently in the Sabbatai Zebi movement. The great sufferings of Polish Jewry during the Chmielnicki massacres of 1648 and the wretched condition of large Jewish masses in Oriental lands furnished the background for the eruption. This, however, is not the complete explanation. Despite profound differences in the living conditions of Jews and of certain classes of Jews in various countries, the Sabbatian movement swept the entire Jewish community along in its wake; its historic effect was unique among movements of this kind.

The history of Sabbatai Zebi, the center of the new movement, can be told here only in brief. Its details are still not sufficiently clarified, and it is full of romantic and legendary elements that are too often accepted as history. Sabbatai Zebi was born probably in the year 1625 in Smyrna on *Tisheah be-Ab* (the ninth day of Ab), the fast-day commemorating the anniversary of the destruction of the Temple (it seems that

SABBATAI ZEBI

for numerological reasons, 1626 was later accepted as the year of his birth). His father, a small merchant, had apparently intended him for the rabbinate, and in his youth Sabbatai became absorbed in the Kabbala. The historicity of the reports first appearing in 1665, that as far back as 1648 his Mes-

siahship came to be revealed, is highly dubious. Similarly, there is little authenticity in the information concerning his life and wanderings in Turkey until approximately 1662. The narratives contradict each other. One thing is certain—his conduct was quite strange, his actions often aroused resentment, and in the oldest report extant about him he is simply considered a sick man. There it is told (and this is entirely confirmed by Sabbatai Zebi's own words) that for many years in succession he had suffered from alternating states of depression and exaltation. He was thus what modern psychiatry calls manic-depressive, and that in itself would sufficiently explain his character. He himself confessed to one of his devotees in Aleppo that in these moods he would commit acts which appeared incomprehensible to him in normal state. Around the year 1662 he appeared in Jerusalem, where he continued his strange manner of living. He did not, however, make any particular impression at the time. On the whole he seems to have been of a passive nature, never assuming an active role; he seems to have always been propelled and guided by others.

The driving genius of the movement was Abraham Nathan Benjamin of Gaza (usually referred to as *Nathan ha-Azati, i.e.* Nathan of Gaza), the son of Elisha Ashkenazi, a scholar who had come from Germany. Early in 1665 Nathan of Gaza proclaimed to his fellow-citizens that he had been exalted to the level of the Holy Spirit; that he could discern men's sins at a glance, and could reveal to each one the hidden root of his soul and his peculiar *Tikkun* (means of achieving perfection). Sabbatai Zebi was in Egypt at the time, on a mission from the community of Jerusalem, but the Kabbalists who were gathered about the wealthy banker, Raphael Joseph Chelebi, were as yet ignorant of his Messianic aspirations. It is, therefore, difficult to determine how much truth there is in the romantic story of Sarah, the "bride of the Messiah," whom he is supposed to have brought from Leghorn, because she had announced that she had been destined for the Messiah. It appears that not until Sabbatai Zebi had arrived in Gaza on his way back to Jerusalem, did Nathan call him the Messiah and convince him of his mission. The reports

NATHAN OF GAZA

concerning his Messiahship had spread from Gaza. But at the outset the narrators marveled more at the spirit of prophecy which had awakened in Nathan of Gaza than at the Messianic aspirations of Sabbatai Zebi.

Nathan, who was still quite young, is shown by his writings which are still extant, to have possessed a thoroughly original mind; seemingly fully convinced of his prophetic mission. He kindled a passionate enthusiasm for Sabbatai Zebi and became the heart of the new Messianic propaganda. From Gaza Nathan sent forth throughout the world a series of epistles prophesying that toward the end of 1666 the redemption would come. Since some apocalyptically-minded Christians of the time were proclaiming Christ's advent for that year, these Jewish tidings found a strong echo in the Christian world. In the summer of 1665, Sabbatai Zebi went from Jerusalem via Aleppo (where he was enthusiastically re-

ceived and where many joined him) to Smyrna, his native city. Here a great flame of Messianic enthusiasm blazed up, and lasted from September, 1665 to the end of the year. The news of this event spread rapidly through all the scattered communities. Aaron Lapapa, the rabbi of Smyrna, who would not recognize Sabbatai Zebi as the Messiah, was deposed, and the "faithful," as the adherents of Sabbatai Zebi called themselves, appointed in his place one of their own. Sabbatai Zebi began to introduce innovations into the religious life of the communities, although these were at first very minor in character. Nathan, who remained in Gaza, was showered from all sides with petitions for methods of doing penance and the like.

In Smyrna, in Istambul and in many other communities, particularly the Sephardic, conditions approached real mass psy-

SABBATAI ZEBI SEATED ON THE MESSIANIC THRONE
Title-page of *Tikkun;* Amsterdam, 1566

choses. Everywhere "prophets" appeared, among them frequently women and children, who confirmed ecstatically the Messiahship of Sabbatai Zebi. Everywhere the communities observed fasts, with rigid self-castigations, frequently giving way to joyous feasts and celebrations. All the old, accepted evidence of Messiahship was dispensed with. Nathan announced that the redemption would be realized when Jews would accept Sabbatai Zebi even without miracles, and one is astounded to see how readily the masses accepted his word. The "believers" persecuted the skeptics who were then a negligible minority, as testified by one of them, Jacob Sasportas. For a time the Turkish administration was apparently

bribed into non-interference, but in January, 1666, Sabbatai Zebi was brought before the Grand-Vizier in Istambul. He was thrown into prison and kept there until the spring, and then transferred to the fortress of Kum-Kalle on the Asiatic side of the Dardanelles, remaining there from the Passover until the beginning of Elul (September). It would appear that bribes made the conditions of his imprisonment easier. The "faithful" named the fortress *Migdal Oz* (Tower of Strength), and here the Messianic outburst reached its peak. From all parts of the world emissaries streamed in, presenting themselves before Sabbatai Zebi in order to honor him as Messiah the King. Samuel Primo, Sabbatai Zebi's secretary,

FOLLOWERS OF SABBATAI ZEBI IN SALONICA PERFORMING PENANCE
IN EXPECTATION OF REDEMPTION
From an engraving of 1701

sent out grandiloquent broadsides to the world in the name of the Messiah. Nathan prophesied in great detail concerning the impending redemption. This propaganda

bis, philosophers and thinkers, issued letters expressing their faith in the Messiah. When the sons of the celebrated rabbi of Lemberg, David ha-Levi (author of *Taz*, a col-

SABBATAI ZEBI, IN PRISON AT ABYDOS, TURKEY, RECEIVES HOMAGE OF HIS FOLLOWERS
From an engraving of 1701

seized the broad masses of the people, who for the first time were filled once more with a sense of approaching freedom. From Yemen, Morocco, Holland, Germany, Poland and other lands there are records that Jews suspended their business activities; many converted their possessions into cash so as to be ready at any moment to answer the call. Even the Christian world looked on with keen astonishment at the extraordinary excitement among the Jews.

And not Kabbalists alone, but great rab-

lection of glosses to the *Shulhan Aruk*), came to Sabbatai Zebi, they found him reading the book *Tsok ha-Ittim*, a description of the tribulations of 1648. All were anticipating the denouement of the drama, when the Sultan of Turkey would voluntarily surrender his royal crown to Sabbatai Zebi, as Nathan had prophesied. At the command of Sabbatai Zebi and Nathan of Gaza, the fast of the Ninth of Ab was converted almost everywhere into a festival. A prayer, *Ha-Noten Teshuah* (prayer for the welfare of a King), was introduced into the liturgy, for the special benefit of Messiah the King, Sabbatai Zebi. He, on the other hand, went on abrogating ever more commandments of the Torah, because in the new world, in the world of *Tikkun,* they would have no validity. Paraphrasing the blessing, "Blessed art Thou, O Lord, who loosest the bound," he introduced the blasphemous benediction "Blessed art Thou, O Lord, who permittest the forbidden," *Issurim* (things forbidden) being a play on the word *Assurim* (the bound).

During these months Sabbatai Zebi was evidently in a sustained mood of exaltation, but he took little part in the actual movement. He engaged primarily in an embittered dispute with the Polish Kabbalist, Nehemiah Cohen, who demanded of him proofs from the Kabbala that he really was the Messiah. The disastrous outcome of this dispute determined the larger issue. The Polish Kabbalist, feeling that he had been deceived, converted to Islam and denounced Sabbatai Zebi and his followers before the government as rebels. The Sultan summoned Sabbatai Zebi to his court in Adrianople. On September 16, 1666, Sabbatai Zebi was received by the Sultan, and there his exaltation collapsed. He denied that he had ever claimed to be the Messiah. Following the counsel of a Jewish apostate in the Sultan's retinue he donned a turban as a sign of his acceptance of Islam.

The report of the conversion of the Messiah was a crushing blow to the Jews. The Jews of Turkey trembled lest they be tried as rebels. In many communities harsh penances were introduced in self-purification from the sin of Sabbatianism. But the power of this Messianic outburst was without parallel in all previous Messianic movements. The catastrophic turn of events was not sufficient to cause everything to return to former conditions. After Sabbatai Zebi's conversion there arose in many countries a considerable "heretical" Sabbatian movement which strove to preserve the new awareness of the impending redemption in spite of historic reality. The fact that this lasted in many countries for two generations, and in certain regions survived until the period of the French Revolution, shows how deep-rooted the Messianic urge was among the wide masses of the people.

To justify the continuation of Sabbatai Zebi's Messianic mission, a new ideological foundation was needed for the paradoxical phenomenon of an apostate Messiah. The new theory, which in the course of time went through all kinds of transformations, provided the slogan for the conflict which, partly concealed, partly overt, was bound to arise between the world of traditional Judaism and the new movement. Nathan of Gaza, Michael Cardozo, and many other theoreticians, labored to demonstrate that such a conflict, *i.e.,* between the redemption, already realized in spirit, and the external world, was inevitable, but that it would be only temporary. It would hardly be possible to understand how these ideas, so repugnant to Jewish orthodoxy, could produce such effect as they did, if we did not bear in mind the strong Marrano element in Sephardic Jewry. All Sabbatian theories are based on the premise that the Messiah must for a certain time abide in the state of a Marrano. That which the Marranos had done under compulsion, namely, go over to an alien religion, the Sabbatian Messiah would do voluntarily in order to fulfill his mission.

Out of this paradox, clearly destructive and "heretical" in character, there developed among certain groups a purely Sabbatian interpretation of Judaism with all its dialectical consequences, a new Kabbalistic theory whose heretical nature was soon sensed by the representatives of the old rabbinic orthodoxy (cf. Scholem in *Keneset,* II, 1938; *Mitsvah ha-Baah ba-averah*). Before long the Sabbatians came to be mercilessly persecuted in many places. True, the movement was not thereby eradicated, but it was forced into hiding; and in the form of an underground sect, concealing itself from the outside world, it contributed considerably—and this especially in European lands—to the inner forces which made for the destruction of the old Ghetto. Usually in Jewish historic literature all manner of charges are cast against the Sabbatians, but modern scholarship has little reason to acquiesce in the verdict of full guilt. The attacks levelled against the Sabbatians by their orthodox contemporaries, simply prove that there had begun to emerge a group which was the harbinger of a new Jewish consciousness. Historically viewed, the Sabbatians were the forerunners of a new era in Jewish life. But, since the time was not ripe for the formulation of a suitable ideology, the Sabbatians sought to express themselves in a paradoxical, and in part actually nihilistic re-interpretation of the foundations of the former Kabbala. Very early the movement developed two wings, one moderate, the other extreme. The latter was characterized by a more or less nihilistic mood. True, the moderate wing also held that the apostasy of the Messiah was a necessary element in the redemption, but on the whole it was eager to retain, almost without modification, the entire world of traditional Judaism. A great many of the Kabbalists of the period between 1666 and 1720 belonged to this moderate group, which attracted many distinguished scholars.

Rigid piety, complete seclusion and severe asceticism went hand in hand with the certain consciousness that the time of cosmic redemption, of the *Tikkun* of the Universe, was at hand. Sabbatai Zebi's conversion was only a mystic device to overcome the sinister forces within their realm. But as against this, the radical Sabbatians believed that since Sabbatai Zebi had announced his Messiahship the older Judaism had been abolished and superseded by a new, Messianic Judaism, whose positive content would not be revealed until the return of Sabbatai Zebi from his "place of defilement." Instead of the "inferior" study of the Torah, with its more "material" character (*Torah de-Beriah*), there would arise a mystic-spiritual type of learning (*Torah de-Atsilut*). Some circles proceeded to assert that it was now a virtue to abolish com-

pletely—and even to violate—the religious values of the *Torah de-Beriah*.

After his apostasy, Sabbatai Zebi apparently still considered himself the Messiah, his ideas coinciding largely with those of the extremists. He lived as half-Turk, half-Jew in Adrianople and other places, but was finally banished to Dulcinia, Albania, where he died on the eve of the Day of Atonement, 1675. Many of his adherents, who looked upon his death as a mere "retirement" *(heelem),* still awaited his return; some believed this would happen forty years after his conversion, others forty years after his death. Until the latter date (approximately 1715 or 1716) the Sabbatian propaganda was carried on vigorously in many countries. But very little of its literature was printed. Nathan of Gaza traveled extensively throughout Italy and the Balkan Peninsula from 1667 until his death early in 1680. He never returned to Palestine. He preached the new "faith" but did not himself emulate Sabbatai Zebi. Influential Sabbatians, even of the radical wing, became rabbis in important communities; such were Samuel Primo, Sabbatai Zebi's former secretary, in Adrianople; Hayim Alfandari in Constantinople; Benjamin Cohen in Reggio; and Solomon Ayllon in London and Amsterdam.

The strongest influence upon the moderate groups was exercised by Abraham Miguel Cardozo (killed in 1706), a former Marrano who, while still in Spain, had studied medicine and Christian theology and introduced into Sabbatianism a very peculiar system of a Marrano Kabbala. For many years he wandered through Turkey. He carried on a bitter struggle against the radical group which professed to see in Sabbatai Zebi, particularly after his death, an incarnation of the Deity. In the history of Sabbatianism there were repeated, in new forms, and under modified historic conditions, many phenomena of the ideological development of ancient Christianity. In 1683 a large group of radical Sabbatians went over to Islam in imitation of the Messiah whom they had exalted to Godship.

Sabbatai Zebi's brother-in-law, Jacob Querido and, after him, Querido's own son, Berechiah, and other leaders of the sect, were accepted by the extremists as incarnations of Sabbatai Zebi. From these extremists sprang the sect of *Doenmeh,* or Faithful, in Salonica and Smyrna, which existed as a closed group, and about whose religious life little was known until the first World War. We now have reason to believe that it wielded considerable influence on the Young Turk movement. Externally, the *Doenmeh* conducted themselves as Moslems; but they considered themselves Jews, although of the anti-Rabbinic school. In the 18th century the *Doenmeh* were still in contact with the Sabbatians who had remained Jews.

There continued to appear new prophets, who expressed Sabbatian ideas more or less in Kabbalistic garb. Some called themselves precursors of the Messiah *(Messiah ben Joseph)*; others regarded Sabbatai Zebi as the *Messiah ben Joseph* and themselves as the true *Messiah ben David.* Such prophets were, for example, the well-known poet, Daniel Miguel de Barrios, in Amsterdam, also a former Marrano, who fervently preached Cardozo's ideas (ca. 1674); Joseph ben Zur in Marrakesh, Morocco (1677), who considered himself the *Messiah ben Joseph;* originally an illiterate he had received "Divine Revelation," particularly concerning the true order of the Hebrew alphabet which he rearranged in such manner as to obtain a propaganda text for Sabbatai Zebi; Daniel Bonafoux in Smyrna; Heshel Zoref in Wilno, who was also "awakened" in 1666 and was widely accepted until his death in 1721; Mordecai Mokiah (preacher) of Eisenstadt (ca. 1680), who made a strong impression on the communities of Austria, Germany and Italy; he considered himself the true Messiah come to complete Sabbatai Zebi's mission, and toyed with the idea of a mystic transition to Christianity but never carried it out. He announced that Sabbatai Zebi himself could not complete the redemption, because of his wealth. The Messiah, on the other hand, must be poor, even as he, Mordecai, was poor. There were, further, Mordecai Ashkenazi (active in Modena, 1696-1701), and Loebele Prossnitz, or Prostitz, in Moravia (since 1702), both of whom contended that the souls of certain departed mystics had visited them and made revelations in the spirit of Sabbatianism. Almost all of these prophets were originally simple men who became worthy of the "privilege of awakening." Around 1700, Sabbatai Zebi's return was expected at any moment in Sabbatian circles, and a strong movement toward Palestine set in. There is hardly any doubt that the large group which proceeded to Jerusalem in 1700 under the leadership of Judah Hasid and Hayim Malak, and which perished almost completely, consisted to a large extent of various shades of Sabbatians. Hayim Malak had for a long time been the leader of the Polish extremist Sabbatians, and already at the beginning of the 18th century he had appeared in semi-public disputations in Vienna to defend his point of view.

In the 18th century the movement became weaker in the Orient, but its impress was still felt everywhere. The great ritual work, *Hemdat Yamim,* written in Jerusalem by an indubitable anonymous Sabbatian (but not, as was generally accepted, by Nathan of Gaza himself), became, precisely in the middle of the 18th century, very popular among the Sephardic Jews. In Europe, however, the movement spread among Ashkenazic Jews, and through its secret propaganda won many adherents. In Lithuania, the center of Talmudic scholarship, it could gain no foothold; but made inroads among some centers of the Jewish West, such as Mannheim, Fuerth, Lissa, Berlin, Prague, and many Moravian and East-Galician communities. In the main there were three strata which sustained the movement: 1) rich court Jews who had connections with the world outside of the ghetto; 2) people deeply versed in Talmud and Kabbala, for whom the old Jewish religious world had fallen apart: their views are best represented in the mystic works of Jonathan Eibeschuetz; and 3) obscure people belonging to the lowest strata of the ghetto. For these last, as for the over-intellectualized scholars, Sabbatianism issued the call to a nihilistic revolt against ghetto Judaism in general.

A long-suppressed urge to life often finds futile expression in degenerated forms. Reliable testimony concerning the conduct of the radical Sabbatians, now emerging into the light, indicates identical traits everywhere, whether in Mannheim or Zolkiew; fanatical asceticism which, as often as not, turns into secret licentiousness. People who fervently studied the Talmud all day long felt a secret impulse to trample on its prohibitions in the night. Such a nihilistic mood spread particularly in Podolia, among the disciples of Hayim Malak. In the year 1725, in Prague and in many other communities, the Great Anathema was pronounced upon the groups of Sabbatians flourishing there. At the same time the opinion persisted that Jonathan Eibeschuetz, the first to sign the *Herem* (Anathema), himself belonged to the sect. When, shortly afterwards, the celebrated poet, Moses Hayim Luzzatto, announced to the world that he had been granted the privilege of experiencing Divine Revelation, he was savagely persecuted by the orthodox, although he was by no means a Sabbatian. The recently published correspondence (1937, ed. by S. Ginsburg) between Luzzatto and his group, casts a clear light on the religious passions of the time; but it also proves that Luzzatto cannot be included among the pseudo-Messiahs. Yet, essentially, there is little difference between his mystic conception of the redemption and the philosophy of the Sabbatians.

In the year 1751 a great sensation was created when a number of prominent rabbis began to denounce as a Sabbatian Jonathan Eibeschuetz, then chief rabbi of Hamburg; their accusations were based on the texts of amulets issued by him; actually these texts could not be otherwise interpreted. While Eibeschuetz and his defenders declared contemptuously that there

were no more Sabbatians, the final convulsion of the movement, known as Frankism, was making itself felt in Podolia, where the sect had maintained contact with the center in Salonica. The history of Frankism must

JACOB FRANK

be traced back in part to the ardent desire for emancipation prevalent in some circles of the ghetto, and in part to the extraordinary figure of the founder of the movement for whom it is difficult to find a parallel in the history of the Jewish religion. Jacob Frank, who was born in 1726 in the Podolian village of Korolowka, was by his inmost nature a despot, without a conscience, depraved and pathologically vicious. It was perhaps this diabolism which fascinated his followers to such a degree that his influence upon many of them endured even after his death. It appears that Frank was descended from the Sabbatian sect; in any case, he passed part of his youth among the *Doenmeh* of Istambul, Smyrna and Salonica. Toward the end of 1755 he returned to Podolia, called to leadership by the local Sabbatians. His following contained a number of unimportant rabbis; it consisted, in the main, of plain people, alert and energetic, but largely illiterates. The area in which Frankism took root was more or less identical with the birthplace of Hasidism. After a group of Frankists had been caught, together with their leader, in a scandalous orgy, and a new *Herem* had been proclaimed against the Sabbatians in 1756, the orthodox rabbis began to persecute the Frankists to the full extent of their authority.

At the command of Bishop Dombrowski, to whom the Frankists turned for protection against the orthodox leaders, a disputation between the Sabbatians (who now called themselves Anti-Talmudists) and the rabbis took place in June, 1757, at Kamenetz-Podolsk, in the episcopal residence. The bishop issued a decree for the burning of the Talmud, justifying the Sabbatians whose practice it was to make public only those points of their ideology which could easily be given a Christian appearance. Their true faith they kept hidden. It is certain that they considered Frank the incarnation of Sabbatai Zebi and, therefore, in accordance with the ideology of the Salonican sect, the incarnation of God. With the sudden death of Bishop Dombrowski there came a turn in the fortune of the Jews. Frank fled to Turkey, where he officially embraced Islam. His followers in Podolia appealed to the Archbishop of Lemberg against persecution by the Jews; they asked for admission to the Catholic Church and demanded that a public debate with the "Talmudists" be arranged. They also declared themselves ready (it appears, under the pressure of the Jesuits) to accuse the Jews of using Christian blood. Frank returned from Turkey, and the great debate took place in Lemberg, lasting from July till September, 1759. It was the last great religious disputation in which Jews were compelled to participate—this time on the initiative of Jews. After the end of the debate, Frank and a large number of his followers in Podolia embraced Catholicism. The leader declared that it was necessary to pass through all religions in turn so as to reach the true freedom of redemption

by the systematic rejection of all laws and customs. He thus preached a religion that may be called nihilism on a mystical basis. The greater part of his adherents, especially those outside of Podolia, nevertheless did not embrace Christianity; but they viewed rabbinic Judaism merely as a mask behind which they practiced their religion; just as the baptized Frankists, too, considered their Christianity nothing more than a disguise. Between 1759 and 1761 approximately a thousand Frankists became converts. Many of them left for Warsaw where, as Catholic citizens, they soon attained important economic positions. But soon after Frank's apostasy the Inquisition began to suspect him of disloyalty to Christianity. In 1760 he was sentenced to life imprisonment in the fortress of Czenstochowa. There he succeeded in gathering round himself a circle of his devoted followers. When the Russians captured the fortress in 1763, they released Frank. He left for Bruenn where he lived until 1786 under the title of Baron, posing as a great nobleman; later he left for Offenbach near Frankfort. There he gathered round himself many hundreds of Polish Frankists. He maintained a court with the gifts of his devotees, the converted and the unconverted, who remained passionately attached to him until his death. Externally he led a strictly Catholic life, but in his sayings (which have reached us in the Polish language) he still preached the mystical conversion of the world. He died December 10, 1791.

After his death, the leadership of the sect was taken over by his daughter, Eva. But her hold on the Frankists declined, she fell into material want, and the court in Offenbach, which had once aroused the awe and wonder of its contemporaries, ceased to exist. Eva Frank died in 1816. Those Frankists who had accepted Catholicism existed, at least until 1840, as a closed sect; but they took an important part in the political and social life of Poland. The groups which remained Jewish—there were many such on the territory of the Hapsburg monarchy, in Bohemia, Moravia and Hungary—merged their mystic ideas with those of the Haskalah and became, in many

EVA FRANK, DAUGHTER OF JACOB

places, important adherents of the first "Berlin enlightenment." They were called "Shebsen" (from "Sabbatai"; Jews did not employ the term Frankists). The orthodox Jews persecuted them, barred them from communal positions and in 1799 proclaimed the *Herem* against them.

In Prague there existed an active group of Sabbatians, led by Jonas Wehle, concerning which we have considerable authentic information. It consisted in the main of well-to-do and even rich people who, whenever possible, would send their children to the court of Offenbach. It was only in the twenties of the 19th century that this group dissolved. From among those Sabbatians who had remained Jews, are descended a number of prominent personalities, like the Austrian democratic statesman, Fischhof, the philosopher of language, Mauthner, and Louis D. Brandeis, equally famous as a jurist and Jewish leader. Writers on the Haskalah have almost wholly ignored the connection between the "heretical" Sabbatians and the early Haskalah; and the largest part of the documents relating to the Sabbatai Zebi movement in the 19th century have been lost or were, often enough, intentionally destroyed. There is, however, no doubt that the mystical Messianism of the Sabbatians helped in large measure to prepare the ground for the transformation which took place in the ghetto during the period of the Emancipation.

BIBLIOGRAPHY

M. BALABAN, לתולדות התנועה הפראנקית, Vols. I - II. Tel-Aviv, 1934-1935.

ARON FREIMANN, עניני שבתי צבי. Berlin, 1912.

DAVID KAHANA, תולדות המקובלים השבתאים והחסידים, 2 Vols. Odessa, 1913-1914.

JOSEPH KASTEIN, *The Messiah of Ismir*, 1931.

A. KRAUSHAAR, *Frank i Frankisci polscy*, 2 Vols. Cracow, 1895.

S. ROSANES, דברי ימי ישראל בתוגרמה, Vol. IV. Sofia, 1935.

G. SCHOLEM, *Major Trends in Jewish Mysticism*. Jerusalem, 1941.

CH. WIRSZUBSKI, האידיאולוגיה השבתאית של המרת המשיח. In Zion, Vol. III, 1938.

V. ZACEK, *Zwei Beitraege zur Geschichte des Frankismus in den boehmischen Laendern*. In Jahrbuch fuer Geschichte der Juden in der Czechoslovakischen Republik, Vol. IX, 1938.

THE JEWISH POPULATION OF THE WORLD

Arthur Ruppin

I. IN THE PAST

There exist no precise statistical data on the number of Jews in ancient times or in the Middle Ages. The figures we do have are all estimates and therefore of limited value.

In past ages the Jewish population of the world underwent very sharp fluctuations. In the year 70 of the Common Era, when the Jewish State ceased to exist, the number of Jews totaled about 4,500,000. In the following centuries it declined, reaching its lowest level, 1,500,000, at the end of the 15th century, at the time of the expulsion and mass conversions of the Spanish Jews. This number remained almost stationary during the 16th and 17th centuries; there were approximately 2,500,000 Jews in the later part of the 18th century. In the course of the 19th century the number rose rapidly and increased to about 10,500,000 at the begin-ning of the 20th century. By the end of 1939, the Jewish population of the world was estimated at 16,648,000.

Already in the 6th century B.C.E., the Jewish population was no longer confined exclusively to Palestine. Considerable numbers of Jews lived in Egypt, Mesopotamia and Syria. A letter of Herod Agrippa I, dating from the 1st century of the Common Era, mentions the following as countries in which Jews lived: Egypt, Phoenicia, Syria, Coelesyria, Cilicia, Asia Minor up to Bythynia and the Black Sea, Greece, Cyprus, Crete and Mesopotamia. In the year 70, according to various estimates, only 1,000,000 Jews lived in Palestine, the remaining 3,500,000 being dispersed over Western Asia and North Africa. Jewish communities were also in existence during the same period in Rome and Byzantium.

In the first millennium of the Common Era, the Jews migrated from North Africa and Italy to Spain, France, Germany and England. From Babylonia, Asia Minor and Byzantium they found their way to the Balkan Peninsula and the Slav countries. Nevertheless, up to approximately the year 1000, the majority of the Jews still lived in the countries of North Africa and Western Asia. It was only beginning with the 11th century that the center of gravity of the Jewish population was shifted to Europe, particularly to Spain, where Jews settled in great numbers. There they assumed the cultural hegemony among world Jewry which had previously been held by the Jews of Babylonia. At the time of the Spanish exodus in 1492, the world's Jewish population of 1,500,000 was distributed almost equally between the Oriental countries on the one hand and Spain and the rest of Europe on the other. This proportion remained almost unchanged until the end of the 17th century. The ensuing accelerated natural increase of European Jewry resulted in its substantial numerical superiority. It is since that time that, geographically, the Jews changed from an Oriental into a predominantly European population.

The position of the Jews deteriorated in France, England and Germany in the wake of the Crusades and especially after the so-called Black Death plague in 1349. Driven from those countries, the Jews turned towards Eastern Europe where they were welcomed by the rulers of Poland. From then on Poland grew to be the cultural and numerical center of world Jewry. With the disappearance of Spain as a Jewish center following the expulsion of 1492, Jewish cultural hegemony passed over to Polish Jewry which retained it for three centuries.

The slow natural increase of the Jews in the Middle Ages and up to the 18th century was parallel with the similar slow increase of the general population. The primitive standards of hygiene prevailing during this period were responsible for an exceedingly high mortality rate, especially among infants. Hygienic conditions were worst in the congested and enclosed fortified cities; the Jews, the overwhelming majority of whom lived in such cities, suffered even more than the Gentiles. The period was one in which the urban centers were regarded as graveyards of the population. In the 19th century, when improvement in hygienic and economic conditions led to a decline in the mortality rate, especially in infant mortality, the proportion of European Jewry in relation to other Jewish populations grew rapidly. About the year 1850 the Jewish population of the world numbered approximately 4,750,000, of which 72% lived in Eastern Europe, 14.5% in Western Europe, 1.5% in America and only 12% in the Oriental countries.

Beginning in the '80's of the 19th century the distribution of the Jews in the world became greatly modified as a result of mass emigration from Eastern Europe to the Western and Central European countries, the United States and other overseas regions (Canada, South America, South Africa, etc.) and, after the First World War, to Palestine. From 1881 to 1939 some 5,000,000 Jews left their native lands in Eastern Europe, thereby reducing the ratio of the Jews in Eastern Europe in relation to world Jewry from 75% to 44.9%. The percentage of Western and Central European Jewry in relation to the Jewish population of the world remained almost stationary, while in the United States and other overseas countries the ratio of the Jewish population to world Jewry increased enormously—from 3.5% in 1880 to 33.4% in 1939.

II. JEWISH POPULATION UP TO 1939

1. NUMBER OF JEWS IN VARIOUS COUNTRIES

It is difficult to give the exact number of Jews at any particular time on the basis of official census data, for these reasons:

a. In certain countries, *e.g.* Iran, Yemen, Brazil, a census in the proper meaning of the term has never been taken.

b. In many other countries, such as England, France, Belgium, the United States, Argentina, etc., the official census contains no indication of the religion of the inhabitants.

c. Official censuses are not taken simultaneously in all countries.

In order to ascertain Jewish population figures in every country as of the end of 1939, it is therefore necessary to qualify the available census figures by estimates which take into account the natural increment and the changes due to migration since the last census. The estimates thus obtained are quoted in column 7 of the following tables. The figures in columns 3 and 5 are usually the figures of the last official census; an asterisk indicates that they are based on estimates.

NUMBER AND DISTRIBUTION OF THE JEWS

Country	General Population		Jewish Population			Estimated Number of Jews (at the end of 1939)
	Year	Number	Year	Number	Percent	
1	*2*	*3*	*4*	*5*	*6*	*7*
I. Europe						
1. Poland	1931	32,183,500	1931	3,113,933	9.8	3,300,000
2. European Russia						
a. Ukraine	1939	30,960,221	1939	1,532,827	4.9	1,530,000
b. White Russia	1939	5,567,976	1939	375,124	6.7	375,000
c. Rest of European Russia	1939	95,990,930	1939	892,220	0.9	920,000
Total		132,519,127		2,800,171		2,825,000
3. Romania	1930	18,052,896	1930	758,226	4.2	800,000
4. Hungary	1930	8,688,319	1930	444,567	5.1	403,000
5. Germany incl. the Saar Basin	1933	65,988,491	1933	503,720	0.8	215,000
6. Czechoslovakia:						
a. Bohemia	1930	7,109,376	1930	76,031	1.1 }	80,000
b. Moravia and Silesia	1930	3,565,010	1930	41,250	1.2 }	
c. Slovakia	1930	3,329,793	1930	136,737	4.1	135,000
d. Carpatho-Ruthenia	1930	725,357	1930	102,542	14.1	100,000
Total		14,729,536		356,830	2.4	315,000
7. Great Britain & N. Ireland	1931	46,189,445	1931	300,000	0.6	390,000
8. France	1936	41,905,968	1935	260,000	0.6	300,000
9. Austria	1934	6,760,233	1934	191,481	2.8	55,000
10. Lithuania, excl. the Memel District	1923	2,028,971	1923	155,126	7.6	155,000
11. Netherlands	1930	7,935,565	1930	111,917	1.4	140,000
12. Latvia	1935	1,950,502	1935	93,479	4.8	95,000
13. Greece	1928	6,204,684	1928	72,791	1.2	75,000
14. Yugoslavia	1931	13,934,038	1931	68,405	0.5	75,000
15. Belgium	1930	8,092,004	1931	60,000*	0.7	90,000
16. European Turkey	1935	1,266,132	1927	51,726	3.9	50,000
17. Italy	1936	42,527,561	1931	47,825	0.1	57,000
18. Bulgaria	1934	6,090,215	1934	48,398	0.8	50,000
19. Switzerland	1930	4,066,400	1930	17,973	0.4	20,000
20. Sweden	1930	6,141,571	1930	6,653	0.1	10,000
21. Danzig	1929	407,517	1929	10,448	2.4	2,000
22. Denmark	1935	3,706,349	1930	5,690	0.2	7,000
23. Estonia	1934	1,126,413	1934	4,566	0.4	5,000
24. Eire	1936	2,965,854	1926	3,686	0.1	5,000
25. Spain	1930	23,563,867	1930	4,000*	0.0	5,000
26. Rhodes	1934	56,754	1930	3,886	7.1	4,000
27. Portugal	1930	6,825,883	1931	1,200*	0.0	3,000
28. Memel District	1936	150,893	1936	3,000*	2.0	3,000
29. Luxembourg	1930	299,993	1935	3,144	0.7	3,000
30. Finland	1930	3,667,067	1937	1,755	0.1	2,000
31. Norway	1930	2,814,194	1930	1,359	0.1	2,000
32. Gibraltar	1931	21,372	1931	866	4.7	1,000
					Total in Europe	9,462,000

According to Latest Available Census Figures

NUMBER AND DISTRIBUTION OF THE JEWS—(cont'd)

		According to Latest Available Census Figures				
	General Population		Jewish Population			Estimated Number of Jews (at the end of 1939)
Country	Year	Number	Year	Number	Percent	
1	2	3	4	5	6	7
II. America (North and South)						
1. United States	1940	131,669,275	1937	4,770,000*	3.7	4,870,000
2. Argentina	1935	12,402,068*	1934	300,000	2.0	350,000
3. Canada	1941	11,506,655	1941	170,241	1.5	170,000
4. Brazil	1930	40,273,000	1935	50,000*	0.1	80,000
5. Uruguay	1931	1,903,083	1935	20,000*	0.5	25,000
6. Mexico	1930	16,522,722	1935	20,000*	0.1	20,000
7. Cuba	1931	3,962,344	1933	7,800*	0.2	10,000
8. Chile	1930	4,287,445	1935	9,000*	0.2	15,000
9. Colombia	1928	7,851,000	1935	3,000*	0.0	4,000
10. Peru	1936	6,500,000*	1935	2,500*	0.0	3,000
11. British Guiana	1931	310,933	1925	1,786*	0.6	2,000
12. Jamaica	1935	1,121,823*	1935	2,000*	0.2	2,000
13. Dutch Guiana (Surinam)	1935	231,489	1934	800*	0.4	1,000
14. Curaçao	1935	79,395	1933	566	0.7	1,000
15. Paraguay	1935	926,580*	1935	1,000*	0.1	1,000
16. Venezuela	1926	3,026,878	1926	882	0.0	1,000
17. Other American Countries						1,000
Total in North & South America						5,556,000
III. Asia						
1. Palestine	1931	1,035,154	1931	175,006	16.9	475,000
2. Asiatic U.S.S.R.	1939	37,269,983	1939	221,000	0.4	235,000
3. Iraq	1935	3,561,000	1935	90,970	2.8	100,000
4. Iran	1935	15,000,000*	1935	50,000	0.3	50,000
5. Syria and Lebanon	1935	3,630,000	1932	16,588	0.5	15,000
6. Yemen	1935	1,000,000*	1935	50,000	5.0	50,000
7. Asiatic Turkey	1935	14,935,000	1927	30,146	0.2	25,000
8. India	1931	352,837,778	1931	24,141	0.0	25,000
9. China	1936	422,707,868*	1935	9,000*	0.0	9,000
10. Manchukuo	1934	30,504,689*	1934	8,000*	0.0	8,000
11. Afghanistan	1935	7,000,000*	1935	5,000*	0.0	5,000
12. Aden	1931	48,338	1931	4,000*	8.8	5,000
13. The Philippines	1935	13,264,000	1934	500*	0.0	1,000
14. Japan	1935	99,354,281	1930	2,000*	0.0	2,000
15. Straits Settlements	1931	1,114,018	1931	1,000*	0.1	1,000
16. Dutch East Indies	1930	60,727,233	1930	1,095	0.0	1,000
17. French Indo-China	1936	23,030,000*	1936	1,000*	0.0	1,000
Total in Asia						1,008,000
IV. Africa						
1. French Morocco	1936	6,242,706	1936	161,312	2.5	170,000
2. Spanish Morocco & Tangier	1934	855,202*	1934	19,918	2.3	25,000
3. Algeria	1936	7,234,684	1931	110,127	1.5	120,000
4. Union of South Africa	1936	9,588,665	1936	90,645	0.9	95,000
5. Tunisia	1936	2,608,313	1936	59,485	2.3	70.000
6. Egypt	1937	15,904,525	1937	62,953	0.4	70,000
7a. Tripolitania) Libya 7b. Cyrenaica)	1938	888,401	1938	30,046	3.5	30,000
8. Abyssinia	1935	5,500,000*	1935	10,000	0.2	10,000
9. Southern Rhodesia	1935	1,289,000*	1935	2,500	0.2	3,000
10. Other countries						1,000
Total in Africa						594,000
V. Australia						
1. Australia	1933	6,629,839	1933	23,553	0.4	25,000
2. New Zealand	1936	1,573,810	1936	2,655	0.2	3,000
Total in Australia						28,000
Total in the world						16,648,000

2. NUMBER OF JEWS IN EACH CONTINENT

The distribution of the Jewish population by continents was as follows (as of the end of 1939):

	Number	Percent
Europe	9,462,000	56.8%
America (North & South)	5,556,000	33.4%
Asia	1,008,000	6.1%
Africa	594,000	3.5%
Australia and New Zealand	28,000	0.2%
	16,648,000	100 %

3. COUNTRIES WITH THE LARGEST JEWISH POPULATION

The following countries had the largest Jewish population (at the end of 1939):

United States of America	4,870,000
Poland	3,300,000
Soviet Union (European and Asiatic parts)	3,060,000
Romania	800,000
Palestine	475,000
Hungary	403,000
Great Britain and Northern Ireland	390,000
Argentina	350,000
Czechoslovakia	315,000
France	300,000

All other countries had less than 300,000 Jews each. The first three countries together harbored two-thirds of the world's Jewish population.

4. DENSITY OF JEWISH POPULATION IN INDIVIDUAL COUNTRIES

Column 6 of the table "Number and Distribution of the Jews," gives the percentage of Jews among the general population of each country according to the latest census or estimate. With the exception of Palestine, where the Jews constituted 16.9% according to the 1931 census and some 30% according to estimates as of the end of 1939,

and with the further exception of Carpatho-Ruthenia with its 14.1% and of Eastern Poland with its 14.0% of Jews, the Jewish ratio in every other country is below 10% and in most countries a good deal less. In the countries of Eastern Europe, Aden and Gibraltar (two urban areas) and in the Island of Rhodes, the Jews constitute 4% to 10% of the population; in Danzig, the Memel District, the United States, Argentina, Iraq, Yemen, Tunisia and Tripolitania 2% to 5%. In all other countries they constitute less than 2% and even less than 1%. In Spain, Portugal, India, China, Manchukuo, Japan, the Philippine Islands, Dutch East Indies and French Indo-China the Jewish population is practically insignificant, the number of Jews in these countries being less than 1 to every 1000 inhabitants.

Within the individual countries the Jews are by no means evenly distributed. In Soviet Russia, for example, the Jews constituted toward the end of 1939 the following percentages of the general population in the different areas:

White Russia	6.7%
Ukraine	4.9%
Rest of European Russia	0.9%
Asiatic Russia	0.7%

In those parts of Poland which previously belonged to Russia, the proportion of Jews in the general population amounted to 14%; the smallest percentage was in the former Prussian provinces of Posen and Western Prussia, where it remained under 0.7%.

In Czechoslovakia, in the Carpatho-Ruthenian district, the Jews constituted 14.1% of the general population, in Slovakia 4.1% and in Bohemia, Moravia and Silesia only 1.1% to 1.2%.

In the United States, 84.2% of the Jewish population was concentrated in 1937 in nine states, namely: New York, New Jersey, Connecticut, Massachusetts, Pennsylvania, Maryland, Illinois, Michigan and Ohio. In the state of New York the Jews constituted 16.7% of the population and in New York City with its approximately 2,000,000 Jews, 28% of the total population. The remaining states taken together account for only 15.8% of the total Jewish population of the country; in most of these states they constitute less than 1% of the general population.

5. ECONOMIC AND CULTURAL ASPECTS OF JEWISH DISPERSION

The dispersion of the Jews among so many countries exerted a profound influence on their economic and cultural life. Since they represent everywhere only a comparatively small minority, the Jews are able to exert only a very minor influence on the economic structure and the cultural conditions of the countries in which they live. They have to accept conditions as they find them and adapt themselves to the new environment. From the East the Jews came to Europe as traders and artisans in specific fields and on the whole they retained these traditional occupations. The character and scope of their economic activity, however, were determined by the economic and legal conditions of the countries in which they lived. The same is true in the cultural sphere. Although, since the 14th century, the existence of the separate urban districts (ghettos) hampered the contact between Jews and non-Jews in Western and Central Europe, such contact was never completely disrupted and was fully resumed after the abolition of the ghetto. In the case of the Jews this led to their adoption of the languages of the countries in which they lived. This was true even in Eastern Europe into which the Jews, at the time of their immigration in the 14th century, had brought a new language based on German, with the admixture of numerous Slavisms and Hebraisms. This is the Yiddish of the present day. The knowledge of the languages of their respective countries and the introduction of compulsory primary education necessarily familiarized the Jews with the literature and culture of the country and diverted them from traditional Jewish culture. The dispersion of the Jews among different nations thus determines the culture which they adopt, creating the type of the French Jew, British Jew, American Jew, etc.

Approximately 52% of world Jewry lived in agrarian countries, *i.e.* in countries where over two-thirds of the population derived their livelihood from agriculture; 37% of the Jews lived in industrial countries which had less than one-third of agricultural population. In the last decades Jewish mass migration led the Jews from agrarian into semi-agrarian and industrial countries, with the result that they shifted from retail business and trades to wholesale commerce and industries, and at the same time moved from villages and townships to large urban centers.

With regard to the cultural level of the countries in which the Jews lived, their approximate distribution was as follows (as of end of 1939) in terms of their percentage among world Jewry:

A. Western and Central Europe 12.1%
B. North America and
             British Dominions 31.1%
C. South and Central America 3.1%
D. Eastern Europe, the Balkan
          States and Asiatic Russia 45.9%
E. Oriental countries 7.8%

In 1870 there were barely 20% and in 1900 only 24.5% of world Jewry in the first two of the above-mentioned zones, but by 1939 these countries contained 43.2% of the Jewish population of the globe. Bearing in mind that since the First World War Eastern Europe and the Oriental countries made great forward strides in their industrial, educational and general cultural conditions, we find that the movement of Jews into the more industrialized areas proceeded at an ever-increasing rate.

6. LINGUISTIC DISTRIBUTION

The mass migrations of the Jews in recent years were mostly directed toward the

English speaking countries. The distribution of the Jews among the various linguistic spheres is shown in the table below, in which the countries where several languages are spoken are classified according to the official language of the country or according to the language of the majority of its population.

MAJOR LINGUISTIC SPHERES OF JEWISH DISPERSION

Linguistic Spheres	Number of Jews	Percentage of World Jewry
1. Slav languages:		
Polish	3,300,000	
Russian (European & Asiatic Russia)	3,060,000	
Other Slav languages (Czech, Slovak, Serbian, Bulgarian, etc.)	450,000	
Total in Slav areas	6,810,000	41.0%
2. English	5,553,000	33.3%
3. Arabic	1,090,000	6.6%

It will be seen that 41.0% of world Jewry lived in the Slavic countries and 33.3% in English speaking countries. The language zones referred to above denote, of course, the languages of the countries in which the Jews lived, not the language spoken by the Jews themselves. In most Western countries, for example England, Germany, Holland, etc., the language of the country was the mother-tongue of the local Jewish population. In other countries the situation was different; in Poland, for example, in 1931 some 80% of the Jewish community spoke Yiddish and only 11.8% Polish.

In the United States, the second and third generation of immigrant families have adopted English as their mother-tongue, whereas the immigrants themselves still hold on to the language which they spoke in their homelands; this is especially true of Yiddish, which is also the mother-tongue of the Jews in Poland, Romania, Carpatho-Ruthenia, and Russia, as well as of the first generation of Jewish immigrants in the overseas countries.

Hebrew, which had practically ceased to exist as a living tongue until its resuscitation in Palestine towards the end of the 19th century, occupies a special category. Due to the establishment of a Hebrew system of education, the language has spread among the Jews in Palestine, and partly even in Eastern Europe. (In 1931, 7.9% of the Polish Jews gave Hebrew as their mother-tongue.) By virtue of an ordinance of the Palestine Administration issued in 1920, Hebrew is recognized as one of the official languages of the country, along with English and Arabic.

7. URBANIZATION

One's occupation predetermines to a large extent one's domicile. Coming as traders and artisans from the Oriental countries to Europe, the Jews settled wherever they had a chance to do business, i.e. in the cities, which since the early Middle Ages served as markets for the exchange of commodities.

Whether the Jews settled in all urban localities, including the smallest, or only in the larger commercial centers, depended on the economic development and the communication facilities. In countries like those in Eastern Europe where transport facilities were poor and where every minor region was in need of a local market, the Jews were able to find a livelihood even in the smallest townships. In countries with better transport facilities, where goods could be dispatched without difficulty to considerable distances, the Jews from the outset preferred the centers of traffic, from which points they pursued their commercial activity over a large area. Owing to the fact that roads were in a very poor condition throughout the Middle Ages—and partly even in modern times—so that it was chiefly the waterways which were used for freight traffic, the Jews preferred to establish their domicile in towns situated on navigable rivers. In their migrations to European countries they almost invariably followed the course of the rivers, such as the Rhine, the Danube, the Elbe or the Dnieper.

The development of communications in the 19th century enormously facilitated the transport of goods in Central Europe. As a result the small towns lost their value as commercial centers and trade became more and more concentrated in the large cities. As a consequence the Jews found it necessary to transfer their residence from the provincial towns into the larger cities. This trend is a general phenomenon of the modern epoch, especially since the industries established in the large cities began to attract masses of workers from the villages and towns. Among the Jews, however, this process of migration into the cities manifested itself earlier and more intensely than among the rest of the population. In some countries, for example in Germany, it led to the complete disappearance of hundreds of Jewish communities in small towns.

In the countries which had attained a high degree of economic development in the 19th and 20th centuries, as was the case in the United States, Jewish immigrants as a general rule avoided the small towns and settled in the large cities.

In some countries of Eastern Europe, for example Poland and Carpatho-Ruthenia, the reverse was the case. The Jews came to Poland in the 14th century in large numbers and found business opportunities even in the smallest townships. In those times there was no non-Jewish class of traders in Poland who could seriously compete with the Jews. The latter were even able to take root in the villages. There were a great many villages but comparatively few towns in Poland in the 18th century, and thus in Eastern Galicia the village Jews constituted 27% and in Western Galicia even 43% of the entire Jewish population of the country.

The character of the Polish township was very different from that of towns in Germany and other countries of Central and Western Europe, where the towns were built according to plan, provided with squares and paved streets and surrounded by walls. In Poland, however, when the Jews were driven from the larger cities by the municipal authorities, they settled on land belonging to large landowners. Such settlements were without plan or design. The occupations of the inhabitants (commerce and trade) gave an urban character to these settlements, although externally they were hardly distinguishable from the villages. In these townships a great number of the Polish Jews lived until late in the 19th century. (Market towns with large Jewish populations were similarly created in Germany in the 17th century on lands belonging to individual feudal lords in Hesse and Baden who permitted the Jews expelled by the municipalities to settle within their domains.) In the last fifty years, especially since the First World War, the improvement of roads and means of transportation led to a rapid economic decline of these townships, and a large part of the Jewish inhabitants migrated into the cities.

The above factors account for the larger percentage of town-dwellers among the Jews than among non-Jews in all countries as is indicated by the following table:

PERCENTAGE OF TOWN-DWELLERS

Country	Year	Among Jews	Among Non-Jews
Germany	1933	84.5%	49.5%
Poland	1931	76.4%	22.1%
Romania	1930	69.0%	18.0%
Latvia	1935	92.6%	33.6%

Czechoslovakia offers a striking example of substantial difference in the percentages of town-dwellers among the Jews within the same country dependent on the economic development of the respective areas. In that country (in 1930), in the highly developed provinces of Bohemia and Moravia-Silesia, the Jewish urban population amounted to 83.4% and 85.2% respectively, as compared

with only 44.6% in the economically backward Carpatho-Ruthenia.*

8. DEGREE OF URBANIZATION

On the whole it is possible to divide the
countries in which the Jews live into three
categories, according to the degree of urbanization of the respective Jewish communities.

a. Those countries into which the Jews
immigrated only when the countries in
question had already achieved a high standard of economic development. Here we find
no Jewish settlements, or very few, in the
villages and townlets of the countryside.
The best example is provided by the United
States, where 86% of the entire Jewish population in 1937 was concentrated in cities
with 100,000 inhabitants or more, compared with 10.7% in towns with a population of from 10,000 to 100,000 and
only 3.4% in localities with less than
10,000 inhabitants. Another example is
Canada where 68.8% of the Jewish population in 1941 lived in the three largest centers of the country, Montreal, Toronto and
Winnipeg. In Britain, France and Belgium,
where immigration was responsible for the
major part of the Jewish population during
the last fifty years, there were only individual cases of Jews living in the villages and
small towns.

b. The second category comprises the
countries of Central Europe in which the
Jews have lived for centuries. Here between
15% and 20% of the Jewish population is
generally found in the villages and townlets. Included in this category are:

---

*The distinction between the terms village and town
is due to administrative or historical factors which
differ in the individual countries. A comparison between one country and another might be misleading if
it is based merely on the distinction of terminology. In
Germany and Hungary all communities which have
over 10,000 inhabitants are regarded as towns; in Bohemia, Moravia and Carpatho-Ruthenia, all communities with 5,000 inhabitants. As for the rest, the administrative classification as town or village is here accepted for lack of other data.

Bohemia, with 16.6% of the Jews living
in localities with a population of under 5,000 (1930);

Moravia-Silesia, with 14.8% of the Jews
living in localities with a population
of under 5,000 (1930);

Hungary, with 20.6% of the Jews living
in localities with a population of
under 10,000 (1930);

Germany, with 15.5% of the Jews living
in localities with a population of
under 10,000 (1933).

Most of the Oriental countries also belong in the same category. Although these
countries are greatly retarded in their economic development as compared to the countries of Central and Eastern Europe, the
lack of legal security, particularly felt by
the Jews in the villages, caused them to
settle almost exclusively in the towns, pre-
ferably in the larger centers. In Tunisia
25,399 or 45.2% of all native Jews lived in
the capital, Tunis, in 1931. In French Morocco, out of its 161,000 native Jews, 75,098
or 46.8% lived in 1936 in the three largest
centers, Casablanca, Marrakesh and Fez,
where they constituted 15.1%, 13.5% and
7.3% respectively, of the population of
these cities. In Iraq over 90% of the Jews
live in the cities of Baghdad, Basra and
Mosul. In Egypt 93% of the Jewish community were concentrated in 1927 in Alexandria and Cairo, while the villages were
practically devoid of Jews. The same is true
of Syria and Iran. Palestine is an exception,
insofar as systematic agricultural colonization in the course of the last fifty years has
made it possible for some 24% of the Jewish population to live in agricultural settlements, some of which number over 10,000
inhabitants and possess important municipal privileges.

c. The third category comprises mainly
the countries which belonged to Poland before 1772 and the adjacent territories of Russia, Romania, Hungary and
Carpatho-Ruthenia. In these countries a
large percentage of the Jews previously

lived in villages and townships. During the first decades of the 20th century, although there was a strong Jewish migration to the larger urban centers, nevertheless there still remained from 20% to 30% of the Jewish population in localities with less than 5,000 inhabitants.

9. PREFERENCE FOR LARGE CITIES

The preference of the Jews for the larger centers can be seen from the figures quoted below for Germany and the United States, which show that the percentage of Jews in the population grew in proportion to the size of the cities.

PERCENTAGE OF JEWS AMONG THE POPULATION

Category of Town	In Germany (1933)	In U.S.A. (1937)
Principal cities (in U.S.A.— New York)	3.8%	10.9%
Other cities with over 100,000 inhabitants	1.2%	
Towns with 50,000 to 100,000 inhabitants	0.7%	2.8%
Towns with 25,000 (in Germany, 20,000) to 50,000 inhabitants	0.6%	
Towns with 10,000 to 25,000 (in Germany, to 20,000) inhabitants	0.4%	1.2%
Places with less than 10,000 inhabitants	0.2%	0.2%
Percentage of Jews in the entire country	0.8%	3.7%

The percentage of Jews among the population of the principal cities was greatly in excess of their percentage among the general population of the country.

The concentration of hundreds of thousands of Jews in a single city (in New York as many as 2,000,000) had no parallel in the Middle Ages. In those days the largest and most renowned Jewish communities, such as Prague and Frankfort, numbered no more than a few thousand persons.

It was only during the golden era of the Jews in Spain that Granada and Toledo had a considerably larger Jewish popula-

tion, and in the East, Baghdad, Smyrna, Constantinople and Salonika. In 1927 there were 22 cities in Europe and America each with a population of over one million. Altogether they had 52,000,000 inhabitants, including 4,500,000 Jews, or 8.7%. Of the total Jewish population in the world 27% lived in those great centers. Their percentage was largest in Warsaw (30.1%) and New York (28%) and smallest in Hamburg (1.5%), Glasgow (1.5%), Birmingham (0.6%) and Barcelona (0.3%). In these 22 cities the percentage of Jews in relation to the general population was 8.7%, approximately four times greater than the percentage of Jews in the general European population, 2.5%, and in America, 1.9%. Such a degree of concentration in centers inhabited by millions of people finds no counterpart among any other ethnic group.

Compared with New York and its 2,000,000 Jews, the other urban Jewish communities remain very far behind. In 1939 there were, in addition to New York, 19 cities in the world with over 100,000 Jews each. First among them was Chicago, Warsaw, Moscow and Philadelphia with 300,000 to 400,000 Jews each; followed by Lodz, Budapest, Paris, London and Leningrad with some 200,000 Jews each; Odessa, Kiev, Tel Aviv, Buenos-Aires with approximately 150,000 each; and Berlin, Boston, Cleveland, Los Angeles and Kharkov with 100,000 to 150,000 Jews each.

As has been said previously, the Jews preceded the non-Jews in their migration to the big cities. Since the end of the 19th century, however, the non-Jews followed the example of the Jews and even surpassed them in tempo. This was due to the fact that the mechanization and intensification of farming created a large labor surplus in the villages, while the rapid development of urban industries, particularly in the large cities, at the same time opened a new market for labor. As a consequence we find that the percentage of Jews among the urban population, which was steadily growing until the end of the 19th century, became stationary or even decreased thereafter.

10. EVOLUTION OF THE GHETTO

When in the Middle Ages the Jews settled in their own quarter in each town, it was because they felt more secure when they were together and because they were in this way enabled to observe their traditions and customs unmolested. (It was only at a later stage that this voluntary separation assumed a legal compulsory character.) In modern times similar circumstances led to a similar concentration of the Jews. The masses of Jewish immigrants arriving in overseas countries, with whose language and customs they were not familiar, preferred to live among members of their own people, at least in the first period of their stay in the new country. In this respect they were not different from immigrants of other nations, such as the Chinese, Syrians, Italians and Poles who also have their own districts in New York. Usually the growth of the "ghetto" begins with the settlement of the first immigrants in a part of the town to which they are attracted by its cheap rents and its proximity to places of work. The immigrants who follow after them settle in the immediate neighborhood of the first pioneers. A "ghetto" thus arises which is distinguished throughout by its bad housing conditions, since most of the immigrants are people without resources who have to content themselves with the poorest and cheapest dwellings.

It is true that this "ghetto" serves only for the first generation of immigrants. Every ambitious immigrant dreams of moving to another district as quickly as possible. In New York, for example, there is a constant shifting from the proletarian neighborhood of the East Side to the middle-class districts (predominantly Jewish) of Brooklyn and the Bronx, and from these to the more desirable areas. This shifting of the residence of the Jewish immigrant sometimes takes place during the lifetime of the first generation, in which

case it is a significant evidence of the rapid economic advancement of the immigrant. In most cases, however, the transition takes place only in the second or third generation. Since the restriction of immigration, the number of Jews living on New York's East Side is continuously declining, because the Jews whose circumstances improve move elsewhere and new immigrants do not arrive in sufficient numbers to take their place. The Jewish population in the "better" districts is, on the other hand, steadily growing.

The "ghetto" has a twofold significance for the Jewish people. In the first place it paves the way for the Jewish immigrant to self-supporting economic activity in his new homeland. Were he compelled to start from the outset in an alien environment, without a knowledge of the language and customs of the country, it would lead to a good deal of friction and difficulty. Owing to the fact that he begins his new life among his own people, he has time to become gradually acquainted with the language and customs of the new country, thus becoming much better equipped to start his economic career. This, of course, is on the assumption that at first the immigrant stays within the Jewish economic sphere, as for example the garment workers in New York, who work exclusively for Jewish employers. The second consequence is that the "ghetto" permits the Jew to continue his traditional cultural life with only slight modifications, thus saving him from the necessity of immediate assimilation. In this sense the "ghetto" discharges a socially useful function, since the sudden transition from a particular social environment into a very different one often has a damaging effect on character and ethical behavior, absolving the individual from his old traditions without immediately tying him to the traditions of his new surroundings. The "ghetto," in substituting a gradual adaptation for a sudden plunge, helps to mitigate the harmful effects of the change.

Whereas in the overseas countries the

"ghettos" often have as much as 80% to 90% of Jewish inhabitants, the percentage of the Jews is usually less in the Jewish districts of the European cities. The largest Jewish district in Europe was in Warsaw (Nalevki) which, it is true, owed its origin not to new immigration but to the fact that in the old times Jews were permitted to settle there, while other parts of the city were barred to them. In the same way Jewish districts grew up in many other towns of Eastern Europe. The same was true of Amsterdam and Prague. New immigration was responsible for the Jewish districts in London (Whitechapel), Paris (the neighborhood of the Rue de Rivoli and Belleville), Berlin (Grenadierstrasse), Vienna (Leopoldstadt). The Jewish character of the last named "ghettos" reposed in the fact that these districts had proportionately a much larger percentage of Jews than the rest of the town. In 1923, the Jews constituted 10.8% of the population of Vienna, but 38.5% of the population of Leopoldstadt. Similarly there were 4.3% of Jews in the whole of Berlin, but 10.5% in the district Berlin Mitte; 7% in the whole of Prague, but 39.3% in the district Josefstadt, and 16.4% in the Altstadt.

In the Oriental countries, the medieval ghetto (mellah), separated by walls from the rest of the town, survives in some places to the present day. In the North African countries, for example in Algeria, all legislation confining the Jews to the ghetto was abolished long ago, but the poor Jewish population remains there; only the more prosperous Jews move to other quarters.

The natural consequence of the concentration of the Jews in specific urban districts is that other areas have very few or no Jews at all. The outlying suburbs in particular have often almost no Jewish inhabitants; this is true even in the case of suburbs of cities with a large Jewish population.

11. EFFECT OF LARGE CITIES ON JEWISH LIFE

The shifting of large masses of Jews from the villages and townlets to the bigger urban centers had not only a geographical significance, but also a far-reaching effect on their social life. In the villages and townships the population is much more conservative in its mode of life than in the large centers, which are much more receptive to new ideas and more prepared to give up old customs. Spiritual or political revolutions never emanated from small communities, but always originated in the large cities. As far as the Jews are concerned, the effect of their migration to the big urban centers may be summarized as follows:

a. The active communal life, which previously characterized the Jewish communities and which impelled the individual to subordinate his own interests to those of the community, was weakened or dissolved entirely. In the large city the community no longer has sufficient control over the individual to prevent him from going his own way—a road which almost always led him away from traditional Judaism.

b. In the large city the Jew has easier access to higher schools and universities, and consequently finds more opportunity to enter the liberal professions.

c. Birth-control is much more commonly practised in the large cities, especially among educated classes, than in the villages and provincial townships. The concentration of the Jews in large centers is thus one of the causes of their lower birth-rate.

d. Social intercourse with non-Jews is easier in the large cities and tends to encourage intermarriage.

e. Religious indifference is more prevalent in the large cities. This tends to the alienation of the Jews, also, from their religious traditions, resulting in their adoption of the typical characteristics of large city life.

Under the influence of the urban environment of the large centers, Jewry, which up to the 18th century constituted a culturally and socially homogenous entity, split into different classes.

SOURCES

The data for the figures given in the table "Number and Distribution of the Jews" are mainly drawn from the following sources:

Statistical Yearbook of the League of Nations, Geneva.

The Statesman's Yearbook, London.

The American Jewish Year Book, Philadelphia.

The English-Jewish Year Book, London.

L. ZINGER, *Dos Banaite Folk,* U.S.S.R., 1941. (The Soviet census, however, does not contain any reference to the religion of the inhabitants of the Soviet Union, but merely to their nationality, as indicated by the individual citizen.)

The data regarding the Jewish population in Yemen are based on information supplied by Yemenite Jews in Jerusalem, and on the estimates of British officials in Aden.

THE ECONOMIC AND SOCIAL DEVELOPMENT
OF THE JEWISH PEOPLE

(FROM THE BEGINNING OF THE 19TH CENTURY UP TO THE SECOND WORLD WAR)

Jacob Lestschinsky

I. ECONOMIC DEVELOPMENT

1. INTRODUCTION

At the beginning of the 19th century the overwhelming majority of Jews lived in villages and provincial townships under Slav or Turkish rule. With the exception of a small upper stratum, they engaged in small shopkeeping and petty trade, leading a life of poverty and degradation. Theirs was an existence of complete cultural isolation from the surrounding world, a ghetto existence of disfranchised pariahs. For them there was not even the dream of freedom in the Diaspora; there was only the hope of a miraculous liberation through the advent of the Messiah.

During the 19th century, this compact and almost homogeneous middle-class mass became transformed into an occupationally and socially differentiated people, divided into groups and classes closely interwoven with those of the non-Jewish environment. Jews often reached foremost places in the economic life of the countries in which they lived, and gained access to the most important and responsible positions in the surrounding social and political world. Parallel with this phenomenon was the concentration of large Jewish masses, not only in specific geographical areas, but also in specific fields of economy. Equipped as they were with traditional age-old experience in certain pursuits the Jewish masses, aroused from their ghetto slumber, showed an intense eagerness for a free existence and an enormous capacity for social and cultural progress. Thus the 19th century witnessed the growth of the two basic movements of the Jewish people: assimilation in all its varieties and the Jewish national movement in its manifold guises. Although, from the political point of view, the two movements were not simultaneous but successive, they were in fact closely connected and interrelated in everyday life. This evolution was due, of course, not to the economic factor alone, but to a multitude of external and internal influences which often produced a contradictory effect; while they promoted the economic incorporation, and even the cultural assimilation of the Jews, at the same time they stimulated Jewish national sentiments and aspirations.

In general terms the 19th and the beginning of the 20th century up to the First

World War, may be described as a period of continuous rise of the Jews in the economic as well as in the political and cultural sense. This process, it is true, was interrupted by intervals of stagnation and decline, but taken as a whole this period of Jewish history in the Diaspora must be regarded as one of the brightest and as an epoch of great and important achievements in various fields.

The technical and industrial revolution of the 19th century changed the face of the world, shifted the center of economic life from the rural to the urban sphere and, generally speaking, made the urban classes the dynamic factors of human history. At the same time industrial capitalism produced the most favorable conditions for the oldest of the urban peoples, the Jews. It opened large possibilities for its accumulated financial and trading abilities and experience.

After centuries of wandering as an alien, urban people among firmly settled, deeply rooted farming populations, the Jews finally found themselves in the urban atmosphere of the 19th century, in the dynamic world of capitalism and industrialism. Their former occupations which, during the centuries, had alienated them from the surrounding agrarian peoples, became elevated to the rank of highly respected and valued functions in the life of the nations. The descendants of the upper classes of the feudal epoch, who looked down with contempt and derision on the traders and brokers, were now compelled to lean on these very traders and brokers in order to save the remnants of their fortunes and privileges. A certain fusion was thus effected between the feudal lords who had to climb down a few steps from their noble perch and the families of high finance who were ascending the golden ladder to the exclusive heights of the titled nobility. True enough, it was not easy for Jews to become elevated to the ranks of the nobility, and only few Jewish families achieved that distinction. However, through conversion and mixed marriages, wealthy Jews were able to shake off the last vestige of the "Yellow Badge" (which all Jews were compelled to wear in some countries in the Middle Ages), and the children and grandchildren of ghetto Jews became eligible for admission to Court and to the exclusive circles of society.

It was impossible to incorporate the more prominent families of the moneyed Jewish classes into the surrounding new society without proclaiming the principle of the equal worth and, consequently, the equal status of all men. This principle, an indispensable precondition of the new bourgeois society of which the *homo economicus* was the central figure, necessarily led to equality of status for the Jews. The predominance of these liberal principles was so strong in the 19th century that even in countries where the Jews were as yet very far from political emancipation, those strata which were most active in capitalist progress were exempted from the general status of the Jewish community and accorded special privileges. In Czarist Russia Jewish "guild" merchants, holders of academic degrees and certain categories of artisans received civil and economic equality of status while the Jewish masses were left in a position of legal inferiority.

This revolution in the concept of the value of man had a tremendous influence on the self-awareness of the Jewish masses. It had a similar influence on their attitude towards the countries in which they had lived for centuries but where they were barely tolerated aliens. For the first time during their long exile they felt at home, enjoying equal rights to work, to create, and to take part in political life. When "trader" and "merchant" ceased to be derogatory and abusive terms, their historical synonym—the Jew—was able to discard his "Yellow Badge" and sit down at the same table with the non-Jewish members of the class to which he belonged.

In the domain of the feudal lord or landed nobleman, as well as in the peasant village —those closed and segregated primitive economic organizations—the Jew could be useful. He could temporarily discharge a specific social function to the advantage or disadvantage of one or another class; yet he could never become an organic member of these social formations, and still less identical with either of them. The nobleman was too highly placed to permit of an intimate and human intercourse with him. The peasant was too inferior to make it worthwhile for the Jew to descend to his low level, especially when it was possible to remain aloof while continuing to be useful to him. Having a place in neither of these two basic classes of feudal society, the Jew squeezed himself in between them. This intermediate position between the two classes necessarily led to the Jew remaining an alien element not only socially, but politically and culturally. Even where urban life became established in medieval society, it was based not on the individual, but on the collective principle of corporations and guilds; in other words, of closed communities. For the Jew it was fundamentally impossible to merge with the majority population, which had erected bars and restrictions even between its own individual communities and corporations, to say nothing of alien elements. He could only seek protection, and even that not as an individual who would be lost in the alien environment, but as a community.

The rapidly growing urban classes of the majority populations opened their ranks to their Jewish class partners, especially since the latter were not only better suited for the economic dynamism of the capitalist system, but because they possessed more "grease" for the wheels of the capitalist machine, *i.e.* more liquid capital. Compared with the total national wealth, Jewish capital everywhere represented only a negligible percentage. From the point of view of liquid capital (the active role of which became incomparably more important than its absolute amount) the accumulated Jewish capital was, however, very substantial. Much greater still was the role of the Jews in devising and organizing the ways and means of attracting the scattered small savings of the masses of the population and converting them into large and powerful accumulations

of capital; in other words, into those instruments of finance which in the second part of the 19th century acquired a tremendous power over the entire life of the countries.

2. ECONOMIC PROGRESS IN VARIOUS COUNTRIES

The influence of the Jews in the evolution of capitalism differed widely in individual countries. In this respect these countries may be divided into the following three major groups:

1. Western Europe and the United States, where Jewish immigrants found a very high degree of capitalist development, and where they occupied an important place side by side with the business classes of the majority populations, without attaining a dominant position;

2. Central Europe (Germany, Austria, Hungary, Czechoslovakia), where the Jews in the 18th and partly in the 19th century were almost the only owners of liquid capital. In these countries they played an important pioneering part in the first stages of capitalist evolution, occupying a considerable and almost dominant place in what may be characterized as the nerve-centers and most important fields of capitalist evolution, such as banking, export and import trade, etc. These countries had a relatively larger number of Jews than the countries of the first group. It was not large enough, however, to play a predominating part even in those fields for which it was best adapted as a result of its earlier experience. In Germany, for example, the Jews never constituted more than 20% to 22% of the population engaged in commerce;

3. The countries of Eastern Europe (Russia, Poland, Lithuania, Latvia, Romania) in which compact Jewish masses lived for centuries, holding almost a monopoly in a large part of commerce and industrial activity. In these countries, even up to the 1920's, capitalism was only in its beginnings and needed the constant support of the State to enable it to outgrow its first stages, and the general population remained little affected by capitalist evolution. In these countries the Jews were not only the pioneers of com-

merce and industrial initiative, but in many branches of trade and in many industries almost the only founders and owners of enterprises. The situation became considerably modified in the period after the First World War.

We may now examine very briefly the role of the Jews in the capitalist evolution of a few of the countries of the above-mentioned three groups.

A. England: At the beginning of the 19th century Great Britain had only few Jews, perhaps some 10,000. It was only in the first quarter of that century that a considerable immigration of German Jews set in. In the 17th and 18th centuries Jewish immigration into England primarily consisted of Sephardic Jews coming from the Netherlands where they had acquired good connections in the financial world of that epoch. Individual Jews were already taking part to a certain extent in the financial life of London in the 18th century, but they played a minor role. Jewish influence began to grow only when one of the Rothschilds settled in Britain in 1798. At that time England already had sufficient accumulated capital to begin to look for foreign investments. Jews played a prominent part in assuring for Great Britain the control of foreign markets through the medium of British capital. In the first half of the 19th century the banking firm of Rothschild granted forty-four foreign loans to twenty countries (Prussia, France, Russia, Brazil, Greece, etc.) to an aggregate amount of over £130,000,000— in those times an exceedingly large sum. The Rothschilds loaned money mostly for railway construction, in which they were themselves largely interested, and which was a lucrative business at the time. The House of Rothschild played an important part in the redemption of the shares of the Suez Canal by Disraeli.

On the whole, however, Jews never played a dominant part in the credit machinery of the British Isles. Apart from the Rothschilds, several other important Jewish banking enterprises, among them the firms of Samuel Montague, Samuel & Co., Ham-

bro's Bank, Sassoon & Co., etc., were founded in Britain in the course of the 19th century. Certain Jewish banks played a prominent part in British foreign trade, others in the oil industry, like the famous Shell Company, or in the chemical industry, led for many years by Sir Alfred Mond (later Lord Melchett). The majority of British Jewish bankers are of German origin. Among these firms, which linked Germany with England and later with America, the banking firm of Speyer played an important part. Natives of Frankfort, the Speyers, at the end of the 18th century, were ten or twelve times richer than the Rothschilds. They had three banks—in Germany, England and the United States—and rendered great services to Germany by connecting her with the biggest world markets at a time when she was still industrially a backward country.

To sum up, notwithstanding the prominent part of Jews in the development of the British money market, of British foreign trade and partly also of individual British industries, the Jewish share remains very modest compared with the immense economic wealth of Great Britain. Jews, for example, are very little represented in the largest five joint-stock banks (the Big Five) whose deposits amounted in 1930 to over 85% of all bank deposits in Britain. On the other hand Jews play a prominent part in British chain and department stores, and they occupy a dominant position in the ready-made garment industry which was created and developed by Jewish immigrants and which remains in Jewish hands up to the present.

B. The United States: The role of Jews in the leading and vital spheres of economic life in the United States is still less important than in England. The Jews came to America in the first half of the 19th century, for the most part—and this refers even to the German Jews—without any resources. As far as Jews themselves are concerned, they have achieved a very important standing in America, but measured against the phenomenal development of the country, they occupy only a third-rate or fourth-rate position. It is true that in comparison to immigrants of other nationalities who came to the United States in the last sixty years, particularly the Slavs and Italians, the percentage of immigrants who achieved success in the economic, social or cultural spheres was much higher among the Jews. They were unable, however, to reach the very summits of the commanding economic positions.

In the banking business even the most important Jewish-owned firms—such as the firms of Kuhn, Loeb & Co., the Seligmans, etc.—play a modest part. Out of the 420 directors of the 19 largest New York banks which are members of the New York Clearing House, in 1933 only 30, or 7%, were Jews, though the Jews in New York constitute 28% of the population. Jews are inconspicuous in these dominating centers of finance not only as executives, but even as ordinary employees. Of the 919 members of the New York Stock Exchange in 1933, 148 were Jews, or about 16%. Even in the insurance business the role of the Jews is relatively small. It is true that they supply a large percentage of insurance agents, but they do not occupy leading positions in the business.

In the U.S.A., as in Europe, Jews are only slightly represented in the iron and steel industry, but are in the majority in the scrap-iron trade. 90% of junk dealers are Jews; New York firms alone have an annual turnover of more than $500,000,000. The automobile industry has three Jewish manufacturers of some importance, but they produce together less than half of the output of Ford alone. There are no Jews in the coal industry in the U.S.A. and even among the distributors of coal they represent hardly 10%. In the largest chemical enterprises there are practically no Jews at all, either among the owners, the executives or the employees. The railways have only one big Jewish proprietor. Although Jews are only feebly represented in heavy industry and finance, they predominate in many commodities-producing industries. The Amer-

ican clothing industry, for example, which with its annual output of over $3,000,000,000 in 1935, is among the most important industries of the country, is predominantly in Jewish hands. But this refers only to the employers. Some thirty years ago, the large majority of the workers in this industry was also Jewish. At present the Jewish needle-workers represent 25% to 30% of those employed in the needle trades in New York. The number of persons employed in that industry has increased very considerably during the last few decades; it is thus possible that the absolute number of Jews employed in the clothing industry has not decreased although their relative share has decreased.

Jews play an important part in the retail business in large cities. It is estimated that 75% of the textile retail stores are owned by Jews, whereas only 16% to 18% of the textile industries are in Jewish hands. We have here the recurring traditional phenomenon of Jews controlling the smaller enterprises, while the larger firms are owned by non-Jews. The situation is the same in the furniture and shoe industries; although Jews own a large number of enterprises, they control a proportionately much smaller share of the output, since they are mostly owners of small factories.

(A more detailed study of the economic evolution of the Jews in the United States is given separately.)

C. Germany : Jews played a very important part in the economic life of Germany. As early as the 18th century many Jews in Germany owned very large fortunes in the form of liquid capital which could be easily invested into business, and which constituted the greater part of the entire liquid capital available in Germany at the time.

In 1725, 17 out of 563 Jewish taxpayers in Hamburg possessed more than 100,000 florins each. These seventeen represented 53.3% of the entire Jewish wealth in the city; at the same time there were masses of poor Jews in Hamburg, many of whom were unable to find work even as stevedores at the docks. In the year 1800 in Frankfort-on-

Main, with its Jewish population of 600 families, 43% of the entire Jewish capital was owned by 60 families who controlled the only 12 important Jewish firms in the city. Nearly all of them later became banking enterprises of world fame, such as the Speyers, Rothschilds, Seligmans, Oppenheimers, etc. The first velvet factory in Prussia was founded in 1730 by the *Schutzjude* ("protected" or privileged Jew) Prager. The Ephraim family played a very prominent part in the middle of the 18th century as suppliers of merchandise, bankers and manufacturers. The first bulletin of the Berlin stock exchange (1804) listed five Jewish names among its nine signatories, although at the time Jews did not even have the right of residence in Berlin. Between 1801 and 1808, the Bavarian Government borrowed 8,500,000 florins (over 80% of the entire loan) from the Jews Seligman, Wertheimer and Strassburger. Out of the shares of the Bavarian Mortgage Bank, which amounted in 1835 to about 10,000,000 guldens, over 6,000,000, or 63%, belonged to Jews, including the Seligmans (who were by that time already raised to the nobility and bore the name von Eichthal), Rothschild, Jacob Hirsch, etc. Of the 2,406 shares of the *Rheinische Bahn-Gesellschaft* (Rhine Railway Company), over two-thirds were owned by Jews in 1837. On the other hand, no less than one-quarter of Prussian Jewry were at the same time peddlers who seldom eked out even a bare existence. Almost 40% of the Jewish population were impoverished small shopkeepers; 20% were domestic servants and artisans. Even in the epoch of the Revolution of 1848, after fifty years of progress, not more than 3% or 4% of the Jews were of the upper class, captains of industry and financiers. About 25% of the Jews belonged to the middle class, and some 70% comprised the lower middle classes and wage-earners. A considerable Jewish emigration from the German countries to America, where it laid the foundation of the future Jewish community in the United States, took place in that period.

The most important period of social ascendancy for German Jewry began after the Franco-Prussian War (1870-71), when Germany embarked on a course of rapid industrialization and began to occupy a prominent place in world commerce. In this phenomenal growth of Germany's economic, political, and even cultural power, the Jews had a major share, both in quantity and quality. The class of big capitalists among the Jews trebled; the middle classes also grew in numbers and acquired greater weight and influence. A Jewish intelligentsia came into existence and achieved so prominent a rank in German literature, art and science, that on the occasion of a public debate in 1912 many people asserted that the Jews were dominating the cultural life of the German people. Werner Sombart, the leading economist of the period, and Richard Avenarius, the famous philosopher, suggested that the Jews should voluntarily withdraw from the too prominent positions they occupied in order not to be so conspicuous and to avoid irritating the nationalistic ambitions of the "genuine" Germans.

D. Russia: Quite different was the situation of the Jews in Eastern Europe where they lived in compact masses, and where the surrounding population remained essentially rural until the very end of the 19th century. Even there the Jews played an outstanding part in the key branches of economic activity. However, as a general rule they occupied the middle and lowest positions on the economic scale.

We shall begin at the top of the social pyramid.

Jews played the most important part in railway construction in Russia and Poland in the 19th century, and it may be assumed that not less than three-quarters of all railways were built by Jewish contractors. The Poliakoffs, Kronenbergs, Nathansons, the bankers Efrosi & Co., Rafalovich, the Günzburgs, etc., were the most prominent railway builders in the second half of the 19th century. Russia possessed no capital of her own for railway construction. It was necessary to secure long-term foreign loans, and of all strata of the Russian population the Jews had the most suitable connections abroad and were best adapted for the purpose. The French Jewish firm, Pereira Frères, and the German Jewish firms, Bleichroeder, Sulzbach and others had, through the medium of the Russian Jewish bankers, a very great share in the construction of the Russian and Polish railways.

Jews laid the basis and promoted the further development of Russian and Polish banking. The banking firm Stieglitz, which was the first prominent banking concern in Russia (in St. Petersburg) played the pioneering role. Its founder was a baptized German Jew. In 1859 the Günzburgs opened their bank in St. Petersburg, which very soon began to develop a ramified activity in various directions. The bank of Meyer & Co. was opened in 1861. A comprehensive banking activity was pursued at the same time by the Wawelbergs, the Kronenbergs and the Fraenkels in Warsaw. In Odessa the Efrosi Bank played an important part in the grain export trade. A decade later, the Poliakoffs founded the Moscow Agrarian Bank, the Don Agrarian Bank, the Azov-Don Bank in St. Petersburg, the Moscow International Bank and others. In the time of Finance Minister Witte, towards the end of the 19th century, Jews obtained a larger access to economic activity, and their participation in the banking business and in Russia's foreign trade increasingly gained in importance. In 1916, among the 70 members of the boards of the 14 largest joint-stock banks in St. Petersburg, 28 were Jews. But Jews still had no right of residence in that city.

As early as 1844, a Jew, Brodsky, bought a sugar factory. Since then the participation of Jews in the sugar industry—and still more in the export of sugar—grew from year to year. It may be said that Jews were the first to find foreign markets for the sugar produced in Russia and Poland. The following figures give evidence of the share of the Jews in this industry, which began on the estates of the big Russian landlords and landed aristocracy. Within her 1914 frontiers, Russia had 300 sugar factories, of

which 100 were owned by Jews. Among the 743 members of the boards of the sugar producing companies and their 253 directors, 283 and 83 (38% and about 33%) respectively, were Jews.

E. Poland : With regard to the role of the Jews in the economic life of Poland, A. Surowiecki, author of the book, *On the Decline of Trade and Industry in Poland* (1810), writes: "It is solely to the Jews that Poland has to be thankful for the rescue of her commerce and industry. The smallest sum becomes converted in their hands into an inexhaustible source of life and activity, and, if necessary, twenty will put their heads together to provide the capital which keeps industry going."

Of the 2,843 Polish visitors who attended the Leipzig Fair in the years 1766 to 1796, 2,374, or more than 83%, were Jews. The first sugar factory in the Russian-occupied part of Poland was founded by a Jew, Epstein; this family produced several big bankers and industrialists. Of 175 large commercial firms which existed in Brody in 1827, 163, or 93%, were Jewish. Among 1,441 large firms registered in Galicia in 1820, 1,172, or 81%, were Jewish. The Jewish share in the textile industry of Lodz, the largest textile center of Poland, kept continuously increasing. This progress can be seen from the official "List of Mills and Factories" published in 1910. Out of 17 factories with more than 25 workers each before 1860, only 2, or 12%, were Jewish. But of the 156 factories established between 1880 and 1900, we find no less than 106, or 68%, owned by Jews. In 1931, over 77% of the textile manufacturers in the city of Lodz were Jews. In the same year Jews in the whole of Poland constituted almost 69% of all manufacturers; 88% of all sawmills were of Jewish ownership. In 1937, 76% of all canned food factories and the entire export of these products was controlled by Jews. In the same period 90% of the textile export trade in Poland was in Jewish hands. But in Poland Jews were not only manufacturers, they were also workers. In 1931, Warsaw and Lodz had 121,462 Jewish manual workers and wage earners; in 1939 their number exceeded 150,000.

As regards other countries with a substantial Jewish population, it may be said on the whole that the general situation of Poland also applies to Hungary and Romania. What has been said of Germany is equally true of former Austria, and the outline given of Britain fits the case of France to a sufficient degree.

II. CHANGES AFTER FIRST WORLD WAR

1. GENERAL CAUSES

The evolution which we have described is characteristic of the economic progress of the Jews in the course of the entire 19th century and in the first part of the 20th century up to the First World War.

Jewish life entered into an entirely new epoch after the First World War, although its characteristic features became clearly manifest only in the years preceding the Second World War. The First World War may be considered as the turning-point, because its results, whether economic or political, were in the last analysis responsible for the radical change which brought an abrupt end to the course of the economic evolution of the Jews. Instead of the integration of the Jews into the general economic organization of the country, they began to be eliminated; instead of being drawn into the ambit of the general evolution in a number of countries, the Jews were slowly squeezed out. The degree to which Jews were eliminated from the economic and social life depended on the extent of maturity and preparedness of the elements and classes which would have to take over Jewish functions.

The important economic positions theretofore filled by the Jews had not been taken away or acquired from anyone else. The Jews created these positions themselves, with tireless energy and great talent, often literally out of nothing. But this activity had taken place in an arena belonging to other peoples, to communities with a social organization of their own and which admitted the Jews only as aliens. Although the Jews felt by now that they were organically integrated into the countries in which they lived—indeed for most of them these countries were their native soil—this was by no means accepted by the surrounding non-Jewish populations. As soon as the latter became mature enough to shoulder the functions previously performed by Jews, their hostility to the no longer irreplaceable alien became even stronger. This finally culminated in the ostracism of the Jews, a development which in the 1930's became characteristic of almost every country in Eastern and Central Europe, except in the Soviet Union.

The formula given above is by no means exhaustive. Political, economic, social and other factors play a very important part in the anti-Semitic policies of the governments and political parties supporting and inspiring such policies.

2. SOCIAL AND POLITICAL DEVELOPMENTS IN VARIOUS COUNTRIES

From the viewpoint of their economic development or structure, we can divide the countries of the world into three major zones, each possessing a separate type of economic organization and, as a concomitant, a different attitude toward the Jews. The three groups are:

1. Countries which are based on the system of free enterprise, and where State ownership in industry and the intervention of the State in economic life is at a minimum;

2. Countries in which private ownership and private initiative in economic matters are entirely eliminated and which consequently have no free competition and no economic antagonism among the various groups of the population;

3. Countries which are characterized by the co-existence of private and State economy and in which free competition is accompanied by State intervention such as price regulation, registration of foreign trade and so on. Here the State intervenes into many domains of economic life; however, the existence of a free market economy is permitted. There is no economic liber-

alism but no planned economy either; the intervention of the State is oriented toward extreme economic nationalism.

The first group of countries, such as Great Britain, the Netherlands, Belgium, France, the United States, Australia, the South American republics, etc., comprises on the one hand highly industrialized countries with a corresponding political influence in the world and large colonial possessions playing an important part as sources of raw material and as markets for industrial products, and on the other hand colonial or semi-colonial countries with a very sparse population and specific conditions of expansion. Economic nationalism and the trend towards economic self-sufficiency are here least represented, and international trade plays a very great part in the life of these countries.

The position of the Jews in all these countries remains almost the same as in the liberal 19th century.

The second (Soviet) group of countries without free competition and private economy, has no class antagonism and no economic competition among national groups. Hence there is no Jewish problem, although there are still many special features of the social and economic evolution of the Jewish population.

In the Soviet Union Jews can be found in every field of activity. However, as a consequence of the urban character of the Jewish people and its entire historical evolution, there is a strong concentration of Jews in the liberal professions. According to the 1926 census, they constituted 26% of the physicians, but less than 0.5% of coal miners; among college professors they constituted nearly 30%, as compared with some 1.5% among railroad workers. Out of every 100 employees, the Jews had 37.9 factory and shop workers and 62.1 clerks and kindred workers; the non-Jews 59.8 and 40.2, respectively. The comprehensive and universal integration of the Jews into the social organization of the country has brought the Jewish social structure much nearer to that of the general population, but there

still remains a rather profound difference between them. The figures quoted refer only to the urban population. If we take the entire population of the country, the difference becomes much more pronounced. Since 1926, a very great economic transformation has taken place in Russia, due to the industrialization and collectivization of the country. This could not fail to have its effect, as will be pointed out later, on the economic and social evolution of Russian Jewry.

The third group of countries comprises, on the one hand, economically highly developed countries (such as Germany or Austria) without adequate power to enable them to exploit to the full their economic and industrial capacity; on the other hand, agrarian and semi-agrarian countries (e.g. Poland, Romania, Hungary, Lithuania, Latvia) whose tardy industrial development has been cramped from the very outset into the narrow confines of poor and limited domestic markets. The world markets are controlled by powerful empires with which the above countries, even Germany, could not compete. All these countries took recourse to autarchy, to economic self-sufficiency and extreme nationalism. They sought to protect their home markets from foreign competition and to assure for themselves a maximum domestic output of the products and raw materials they required. Naturally, they attempted also to eliminate from the economic life of the country itself all competitors who sought a share of the already narrow and limited possibilities of existence.

The countries of this type are politically dominated by the middle classes with their narrow ideas and limited horizons and the extremely nationalistic intelligentsia. They oscillate between free and managed economy. These middle classes found a temporary solution of their problems in the expropriation of the Jewish minority and the removal of Jewish competition in trade and the liberal professions.

The decade preceeding the Second World War in these countries witnessed the isolation and elimination of the Jewish populations from economic life. In different localities this process took on different forms and scope, from complete elimination in Germany to the ousting of the Jews from central positions in the economic front—such as in the spheres of credit and foreign trade —in Latvia and Lithuania. In this respect Poland, Romania and Hungary assumed an intermediate position.

It has already been remarked that it would be an error to explain the entire trend towards elimination of the Jews, peculiar to the countries of the third group, solely by the economic nationalism which we have described. Apart from Germany, where the conditions were quite specific, in the other countries of this group we find a series of other causes and factors leading to the organized elimination of the Jews from economic life. It is worth while to mention some of these causes.

Two developments after the First World War radically changed the economic and political position of the nearly 6,000,000 Jews in the countries of Central and Eastern Europe which we have classified as belonging to the third group.

A. *The Disintegration of the two Largest Multi-national Empires (Russia and Austria)*: The national independence of the small states created after the First World War confronted the Jewish population with an entirely new problem. Under the Hapsburgs and Romanoffs the Jews performed the function of a connecting link between the advanced, industrialized sections of the empires and the backward agrarian subject peoples. As a go-between group, the Jews were naturally concentrated in the towns and engaged in urban occupations. In scores of towns in Poland, Lithuania, Latvia and Romania, they constituted the majority of the entire population, or the largest of the individual national groups. Even where a developed local industry attracted large non-Jewish masses the Jews represented a very considerable percentage of the population, and in the better and more remunerative occupations, such as the liberal pro-

fessions and commerce, their percentage was much higher than in the population of the country or even among the town-dwellers. The non-Jewish majority of the local population was concentrated chiefly in the villages and engaged in the menial and lower paid urban occupations. When this majority became the ruling nationality in the new independent states, it rapidly began, with the aid of the State, to make up for its lost opportunities. It created its own classes of officials, merchants and artisans; in fine, its own urban population. This process began as a natural evolution before the First World War. With the growth of culture and industry in each area, its urban population also grew through the influx of villagers into the towns. These new non-Jewish town dwellers increasingly produced elements which not only aspired to a place in commerce and in the liberal professions, but were also more or less able to compete with the Jews. The industrial development in these areas was not sufficient to absorb the rapid natural increase of either the Jewish or the non-Jewish populations. The continued process of emigration relieved the situation, however, by absorbing a considerable part of the natural increase of the Jews, in Russia as well as in Austria. The emigration of non-Jews was comparatively smaller, and the rural population found outlets in the towns, not only in the growing industries, but also in commerce and other urban pursuits.

As a result the Jews were losing ground. However, their situation was not hopeless because emigration on the one hand and industrial development on the other made up for the ground lost. The more the non-Jews became absorbed in commerce and in the liberal professions, the more the Jews took to manual work. For some sections of the Jewish population this process meant a material come-down since it was more lucrative to be engaged in trade than to work as a factory hand or as a laborer on a farm. However, viewed from the angle of the social position of the Jewish people as a whole, the process of proletarization meant not decline but progress, since it made the economic structure of the Jews more stable.

An entirely new situation arose in these countries after the First World War. Subjected provinces of Austria, Hungary and Czarist Russia became independent states. The national emancipation of the non-Jewish majority population speeded up the cultural and social progress. The migration of rural elements into the towns became more intense. Before the war, it was mostly the poorest people from the village who went to the towns to seek work as factory hands, laborers, etc. Now, even the son of the rich peasant migrated into the city. The agrarian reform considerably improved the position of the peasants in several countries and it became an almost ordinary phenomenon to see children of peasants attending high schools or even colleges. In Lithuania and Latvia children of peasants constituted 40% of all university students. The situation was similar in Czechoslovakia. In Poland and Romania the percentage of peasant children in the universities was much lower, varying between 9% and 10%, but it was still higher than before the First World War. Besides, the percentage of such children in high schools and in the higher type of primary schools was very substantial even in these countries.

There was a demand for large numbers of new civil servants in the newly created States. In Lithuania, a little country which before becoming an independent state had some 2,500 officials, there were about 32,000 after her emancipation. Latvia had up to 35,000 officials. In Poland 470,000 persons were public servants. In order to supply this need the governments encouraged the influx of village children into the higher schools and universities.

However, although the trend towards urban occupation took on the size of a mass movement among the majority group, the Jewish population would nevertheless have adapted itself to the new conditions. But a factor came into play which led to a situation in which the powers of resistance of the Jewish masses proved to be inadequate.

That factor was the intervention of the State, which was dominated exclusively by the majority group and which possessed an immense influence on economic life, since it controlled the instruments of credit and taxation and regulated import and export activities. This State apparatus was not only placed at the service of the majority elements which organized themselves for the purpose of competing with the ethnic minorities, particularly the Jews, but moreover directly assumed the charge of wresting from the ethnic minorities, again especially the Jews, as many of their economic positions as possible.

In Poland and in Lithuania, in Romania, Latvia and Hungary, it became an everyday affair for the state banks to grant large credits to businessmen belonging to the majority group, even when their enterprises were only of recent origin and their future quite uncertain. At the same time credit was refused to old, solidly established Jewish firms. Import licenses and foreign currency were readily given to the "national" importer, but refused to the "alien." The method became pure arbitrariness when it was applied to the assessment of taxes; while the taxpayers belonging to the ruling nationality were very often treated leniently, the "alien" was squeezed without mercy. Still more dangerous for the position and interests of the Jewish population was the direct struggle of the State machinery against it. This does not refer to the formal laws directed against the Jews. Such legislation was introduced only in Hungary and, in a camouflaged form, in Romania. What is referred to are the activities of the State in the economic field such as nationalization of entire branches of industry, trade or commerce. In many countries the State became the largest employer and the largest customer. But Jews were excluded from these economic activities. They were not only barred from the State and municipal offices, but also from State-owned or controlled enterprises. Not everywhere and not in every case was State control established for nationalist purposes, but the result always remained the same; the State enterprises became accessible only to members of the majority nation.

A few figures will illustrate the scope of these processes. According to a statement made (in 1935) by the Prime Minister in the Polish Diet, no less than 37% of the entire national income came through the channels of public services and enterprises. Jews contributed a great deal to that national income, but of the gigantic sums spent by the public hand—some 10 billion zlotys in 1929 and 5.5 billion in 1933—they received nothing. The value of the economic enterprises of the Polish State amounted in 1935 to 14.8 billion zlotys, in other words, to over one-fifth of the entire national capital. No less than 38.5% of all wages and salaries in Poland were paid to the personnel of the State enterprises and offices, which represented 30% of all wage-earners. No less than 47% of all clerical workers in the country were in the services of the State or of the municipalities. These positions were barred not only to the Jews, but also to the other minorities—Ukrainians, White Russians, Germans. If we take into consideration only the national Polish element among the officials and employees, we find that not less than 75% of Poles in clerical occupations were employed in public offices and enterprises. The Polish State controlled 55% of the metallurgic enterprises, 47% of forests, 39% of the timber export, 35% of the banks, 31% of the grain export, 29.3% of harvesting machinery, 25% of the chemical industry, etc. The State owned up to 2,000 enterprises, including 46 sawmills, 51 printing plants, 11 brick kilns, apart from the monopolistic enterprises, such as tobacco, sugar, salt, alcohol, etc. Some 25% of the entire turnover of the country passed through the public enterprises. We hardly need add that this 25% of the national turnover was lost entirely for the Jews and, to a lesser extent, also for the other national minorities. In the public enterprises Jews were not employed even as unskilled labor.

As an example of the fatal effect of this nationalization on the position of the Jews of every class we may cite the tobacco monopoly. The tobacco industry in Poland was created by Jews. Not only the owner of the factories, the suppliers of raw material and the dealers, but also the workers and the employees were Jews. But since the State monopolized the tobacco industry, it dismissed Jewish employees and workers and even licensed Jewish tobacco retailers on a large scale. The tobacco licenses were withdrawn in 1938 from all Jews, save a few hundred wounded Jewish war veterans. It will not be far afield to assume that the tobacco industry provided a livelihood for some 10,000 Jews (or 40,000 persons, if we include their families).

The extent to which the State controlled the credit system of the countries mentioned will be best seen from the figures relating to deposits and credits. In 1936, 79% of all deposits in Poland were concentrated in the State banking institutions. In 1933, 69% of all credits granted in Poland emanated from the State banks. Subsequently the position of the State became still stronger. The importance of these facts lies, of course, not in what they meant to a few Jewish bankers, but in their effect on the position of thousands of Jewish employees. Of incomparably greater significance, however, is the fact that the entire credit machinery of the State was placed at the disposal of the Polish traders and artisans with the avowed purpose of facilitating their competition against the Jews.

How the screw of taxation was employed in the services of nationalist interests will be seen from the following figures. Trade and commerce, which were over 50% in Jewish hands contributed between 33% and 35% of the entire State revenue from taxation, although they supplied only from 16% to 18% of the national income.

Similar conditions with minor variations prevailed in Lithuania, Latvia, Romania and Hungary. In all these countries a large part of the economic life was controlled by the State, that is, by the majority nationality, and the power of the State was everywhere widely exploited for the purpose of ousting the national minorities, particularly the Jews, from the economic life. Without going into detailed data concerning the situation in Lithuania and Latvia, it may be said that a very considerable middle class originating from the peasant population was literally conjured up in the course of the twenty years between 1919 and 1939. In Latvia a law was enacted permitting the Government to take possession of any private enterprise whenever such expropriation was found to be in the interest of the State. In the years 1937 and 1938 the Latvian Government took over all larger Jewish and German enterprises, such as chocolate, textile, metal and machine factories. In all these cases not only were the Jewish owners removed, but also the Jewish directors, clerks and workers. Almost the entire foreign trade in these two countries was placed in the hands of specially created "cooperatives" which actually were nothing but agencies of the State. They purchased milk, butter, flax, pork, beef, anything that could be exported, and delivered it to the State warehouses in the cities. Needless to say, these cooperatives, which completely eliminated Jewish traders and salesmen in these fields, did not have any Jewish employees, members or agents.

In addition to the direct effect of this intervention of the State in the economic life of the country, it had a consequence which was, perhaps, no less important. In all the above-mentioned countries the economic activity of the State had become the best trade school for the non-Jewish middle classes. Thousands, and perhaps tens of thousands, of these people were leaving their position in State enterprises and opening their own private enterprises and shops and thus becoming dangerous competitors to Jewish traders and shopkeepers.

B. Suspended Emigration: The second factor which had a most unfavorable effect on the position of the Jewish masses in these countries was the cessation of the overseas emigration from Europe. The emigration of millions of villagers from Poland, Lithuania, Latvia, Romania and Hungary in the decades before 1914 served to counterbalance the natural increase of the rural population and to slow down the shift of the population from the overcrowded villages to the growing cities. The emigration of hundreds of thousands of Jews, on the other hand, served to reduce competition in the "Jewish" occupations and to limit the movement of Jewish youth from the provincial townships to the big industries which before the First World War provided a labor market for the non-Jewish village youth.

The increasing difficulty of emigration to countries overseas, at first curtailed and later almost entirely suspended, tremendously swelled the population surplus in the above-mentioned countries, particularly in the villages. Poland, for example, in the years 1895 to 1913 provided an annual average of 140,000 emigrants, but in the years 1924 to 1934 an annual average of only 49,000. At the end of the 19th century, Poland had within her pre-war frontiers a population of 25,000,000, increased by 1938 to nearly 35,000,000. In all the countries with which we are concerned, the result of the population increase was a mighty, elemental rush of large peasant masses towards every sort of urban livelihood from the lowest to the highest. This movement of rural masses into the towns was in many countries, particularly in Lithuania and Latvia, encouraged by the governments as part of their nationalistic programs aiming at the supplanting of the national minorities by the majority people, drawn from the population of the countryside.

3. THE THIRD REICH

The systematic economic and physical extermination of the Jews in the Third Reich —Germany, Austria, the Sudeten Provinces —in the years before and during the Second World War cannot be dealt with in this article. This is a matter for future studies. We shall confine ourselves to the period up to 1939.

In the beginning of 1933 these countries harbored some 750,000 Jews, of whom 525,000 lived in Germany, 200,000 in Austria, and about 25,000 in the Sudeten area. Towards the summer of 1939 Greater Germany (including Austria and the Sudeten area) had around 350,000 Jews. Of the other 400,-000 Jews 350,000 left the country, the natural deficit—increase in death rate, fall in birth rate, together with the victims of Nazi persecutions—making up the rest of some 50,000.

In Germany and Austria, of the 35,000 Jews engaged in the liberal professions, some 4,000 physicians and some 3,000 lawyers were permitted to practice until the end of 1938. In 1938, shortly before the war, this permission was withdrawn and the last vestige of a Jewish intellectual class disappeared. More than a half of the Jewish members of the liberal professions left Germany.

Jewish trade was almost completely liquidated by the end of 1938. Out of 80,000 Jewish commercial enterprises in pre-Hitler Germany, only some 9,000 were in existence in November 1938, including 3,667 in Berlin. By the end of December 1938, all Jewish retail shops were either closed or compelled to become "Aryanized." The wholesale enterprises were permitted to continue for the time being, mainly because they worked for foreign markets. But it was only a question of a few months until they, too, were entirely liquidated. But before then Jewish industry had practically ceased to exist. The very large industrial enterprises, such as Orenstein and Koppel (locomotive works), Hirsch-Kupfer (copper refineries), Ullstein and Mosse (publishing) and many others were "Aryanized" in the first year of the Hitler regime. In the last months of 1938 the axe fell on the clothing factories and stores, the fur trade, the diamond industry and a few others which had been permitted to exist until enough trained "Aryan" successors were available.

The banner-bearers of the German "National Revolution"—the bourgeoisie and the intelligentsia—substituted for the social expropriation of the capitalist classes the nationalistic expropriation of the Jews in favor of a small section of the German capitalist middle class.

III. SOCIAL DIFFERENTIATION

Even the medieval ghetto possessed its rich and poor, with a stratum of a middle class between the two extremes. All strata of ghetto Jewry, however, belonged almost entirely to one and the same occupational group—the trading class in its manifold variations. This fact often obliterated the social differences, especially since financial ups and downs, due to external causes as well as to individual factors, were a very frequent phenomenon in Jewish trade. It is in the nature of trade in general that the interval between sudden losses and unexpected gain is less than in all other fields of economic activity. The occupational and social homogeneity of the Jewish economic structure, until the end of the 18th century, prevented the social differentiation which was characteristic of the other peoples. Even inheritance of capital or property was therefore of less importance in Jewish life. Large Jewish fortunes seldom survived for more than a few generations, and Jewish capital shunned investment in real estate.

A one-class people—that is how we may characterize the Jews of the Middle Ages and up to the end of the 18th century. The small percentage of artisans—at the utmost 18% or 20%—changed the professional aspect of the Jewish population very little. These Jewish artisans belonged, moreover, to a few specific trades, such as tailors, furriers, butchers, bakers, shoemakers and jewelers. Towards the end of the 18th century various other trades appeared among the Jews, depending on the place where they lived and their standards of life, chiefly, however, on the density of the Jewish population. The greater the size of the Jewish community, the more it became necessary for its members to go in for manual work and the more rapidly grew the number of Jewish artisans and unskilled laborers. However, even at the end of the 18th and at the beginning of the 19th century we may still speak of the Jews as a group without marked class division, consisting of a large mass of middlemen, headed, *inter alia,* by a small group of money-lenders and all sorts of rich merchants. It must be added that in Central and Western Europe those rural Jewish elements were absent which in Eastern Europe possessed small gardens or cows in addition to their taverns or shops. The percentage of Jewish artisans in the West was only half as large and the Jewish working class, which appeared in the dense Jewish communities in Poland as early as the 18th century, did not exist in the West at all. Here the trading class in the literal sense of the term represented more than 80% of all Jews. This lent particular emphasis to the commercial functions of the Jews in the countries in which they lived.

In the course of the 19th century, however, there was a very great and rapid change in the occupational and social structure of the Jewish people, as shown by the figures quoted in the table below. And since the evolution of the surrounding non-Jewish population was towards commercialization and industrialization, the chasm between Jews and non-Jews diminished. In countries with a highly developed urban culture that chasm is less wide than in agrarian countries. However, it exists, manifesting itself in the occupational differentiation as well as in the social grouping of Jews and non-Jews.

We have no data regarding the occupational and social division of the Jews in all countries of the world. In a few highly important countries, such as the United States, such data are generally non-existent. However, on the strength of estimates, we can obtain an approximate picture of the social composition of the Jews a century ago and at the present time. The following figures are based on such estimates.

In the year 1825 the occupational distribution of the Jews was approximately as follows:

1. Innkeepers, farm tenants, leaseholders 30%
2. Traders and middlemen   30 "
3. Artisans   18 "
4. Farmers   1 "
5. Religious and ritual occupations   3 "
6. Undetermined occupations   18 "
                                         ——————
                                         100%

In 1939 the figures were as follows:

1. Commerce and Banking   40%
2. Industry and Trade   35 "
3. Professional and Civil Service   5 "
4. Agriculture   4 "
5. Domestic Service and Unskilled Labor   3 "
6. Undetermined Occupations   13 "
                                         ——————
                                         100%

We thus find that of the Jews gainfully employed in 1939, 47% consisted of those (groups 2-5) occupied in industry, trades and as unskilled labor.

The process of proletarization was developing hand in hand with the differentiation and productivization of the Jewish masses in the big Jewish communities. In the course of the 19th century an industrial labor class came into being among the Jewries in Eastern Europe and partly also in Central Europe.

In the large and overcrowded Jewish communities of Poland and the Ukraine, Jewish weavers appeared towards the end of the 18th and at the beginning of the 19th century. The number of journeymen employed by Jewish artisans, as well as the duration of the average period during which they remained wage workers, also increased to a certain extent. A similar increase took place in the number of employees in Jewish businesses and the average length of their service in a salaried position without going over into the group of small proprietors. The number of Jewish domestic servants increased with the growth of the Jewish middle classes which could afford the luxury of keeping servants. On the other hand, there was already a considerable natural increase of the Jewish population which, coupled with the political persecutions at the beginning of the 19th century, brought into the towns tens of thousands of impoverished Jews from the villages, thus supplying new contingents of domestic servants, journeymen and apprentices, and still more of pauperized elements suitable only for unskilled work. All these wage-earning elements, however, represented in the first quarter of the 19th century no more than 20% of the entire Jewish population.

The social and occupational differentiation among the Jewish masses reached a high point towards the end of the 19th century. Large numbers of Jews gained access to industries, both as employers and workers. Jewish artisanship extended to many new branches. The number of Jews in the liberal professions expanded and became a substantial group. The class of temporary day laborers made way for a permanent working class. By the time the Jews became integrated into the general economic life of the liberal countries they were already differentiated not only into rich and poor, but into economic classes with specific social and psychological characteristics.

A few examples will illustrate this thesis: In the large textile center of Lodz, Poland, Jews constituted no less than 80% among the wholesale merchants of the city, according to the census of 1931. Of the 31 largest factories, each employing over 500 workers, 8 belonged to Jews in 1929; moreover, these 8 factories employed 19,666 workers out of a total of 36,822, or 53% of all factory workers of this group. The rich Jewish merchants and manufacturers, who occupied the very forefront of the economic life of the city, were extremely conspicuous. At the same time the proletarian elements among the Jews of Lodz, factory workers, home workers and white-collar employees, represented, according to the census of 1931, 53% of all gainfully employed Jews. If to these purely proletarian elements we add the artisans and the petty shopkeepers who employed no hired workers, we find a Jewish "poverty base" comprising nearly 90% of the entire Jewish population of Lodz.

The figures given above are confirmed by the grouping of the taxpayers of this Jewish community. In 1930, 53% of the Jewish population earned incomes so low as to be exempted from the Jewish Community tax. Less than 10 zlotys* were paid by 23%. A total of 76% of the community was thus in the pauper class. To complete the picture of the lower strata of the Jewish

population in Lodz it may be added that 40% had to depend on charity in order to be able to have ritual food at Passover; and that up to two-thirds of all Jewish manual workers earned less than 20 zlotys a week.

The Jewish community in Berlin before Hitler was the most prosperous in Germany. Nevertheless, out of 40,135 taxpayers in 1913 (assessed on the basis of their income in 1912) only 1,559, or 4%, of the total had an annual income of more than 50,000 marks (at that time about $12.000). Less than 2,400 marks, not much more than the average subsistence level, was earned by 11,272 or 28.1% of all Jewish taxpayers. If we consider those who earned between 2,400 and 3,600 marks as belonging to the lower middle class—which was the case in Germany in 1912—we find another 7,534 Jewish taxpayers at the bottom of the pyramid, totalling, together with the former group, 18,806 or 46% of all Jewish taxpayers. We must, however, add those who had an annual income of less than 1,200 marks and who were therefore exempted from paying taxes. We thus find that the poor classes accounted for nearly two-thirds of the Jewish community in Berlin. Turning to the data for 1925, we find that persons with an annual income of between 1,200 and 3,600 marks constituted 51.5% of all Jewish taxpayers, while those with an annual income exceeding 50,000 marks constituted only 1.2% of the total. Adding those whose income was less than 1,200 marks to the first group, we find that apart from a very small group of rich people, almost three-quarters of the Jewish population of Berlin lived in poor circumstances or made merely a bare livelihood.

We shall deal more fully later with the social differentiation of the Jews all over the world. Here we wish only to stress to what extent the picture is distorted by the conspicuous place the Jewish bourgeoisie occupied within the ranks of the bourgeoisie in general. It is true that the Jewish upper class played an outstanding part in the economic spheres in which it functioned, but it constituted only a negligible percent-

*The official exchange rate of a zloty was at that time about 19 cents.

age of the entire Jewish population, among which the base of the social pyramid was often no narrower than among the surrounding non-Jewish peoples.

IV. OCCUPATIONAL AND SOCIAL DISTRIBUTION

1. OCCUPATIONAL DISTRIBUTION

A. *Jews in Agriculture*: Paradoxical as this may sound, Jewish agriculture is a product of the last century—the same century which was an epoch of commercialization and industrialization for all other peoples. It must be admitted that the trend towards agriculture among the Jews is as yet very feeble in comparison with their traditional preference for industrial and urban pursuits. Millions of Jews have been drawn into trades and industries, but only a few hundred thousands all over the world have settled on the land. However, in an industrial age and for a people driven away from the soil for untold centuries, the Jewish effort to return to agriculture is remarkable in itself. It cannot be assumed that the entire tendency to return to the soil was merely the result of ideological propaganda or of the pressure of extraneous authorities. A considerable number of Jews turned to agriculture voluntarily.

TABLE 1
NUMBER OF JEWS DEPENDING ON AGRICULTURE

Country	Year of Census or Estimate	Number	Percentage of the total Jewish Population
U.S.S.R.	1939	125,000	4.2
Poland	1931	134,965	4.3
United States	1937	100,000	2.2
Romania	1930	43,145	5.7
Czechoslovakia	1931	31,697	8.9
Hungary	1930	12,976	2.9
Argentina	1935	14,677	5.8
Palestine	1936	56,000	15.0
Lithuania	1937	6,000	3.8
Germany	1933	5,124	1.0
Canada	1931	2,188	1.3
Other countries	1937	5,000	—
Total:		**536,772**	

Table 1 shows the number of Jews whose livelihoods were drawn from agriculture in its various forms. In the Russian agricultural settlements the Jewish "colonist" represented a type far different from that of a Jewish farmer in the United States. The Jewish colonist in Argentina differed widely from his fellow colonist in Poland, just as in Palestine he was far ahead of the poor and backward Jewish peasant in Carpatho-Ruthenia. Yet all of them had one trait in common: the soil was the major source of their existence. Our table shows that in 1939, 536,772 Jews derived their livelihood from agriculture. The largest number of Jewish farmers was found in countries with compact Jewish communities.

At the beginning of the Bolshevik revolution, some 50,000 Jews earned their livelihood from agriculture, primarily in the Jewish colonies in the south of Russia, in the provinces of Kherson and Yekaterinoslav. In 1932 some 250,000 Jews were dependent on agriculture in Russia, including over 100,000 in the two provinces mentioned and in the Crimea, over 100,000 in the vicinity of urban localities, some 7,000 to 8,000 in Birobidjan, and some 10,000 among the Jews of the Caucasus. We hardly need add that these figures refer to cultivators who till the soil themselves, without the aid of hired labor.

Small farmers, aided only by their families, constituted also the overwhelming majority of Jewish farmers in Poland. According to the census of 1931, of the 22,103 Jewish homesteads in Poland 8,233, no less than 37.2% possessed less than 2 hectares (approximately 5 acres) of land; 6,094, or 27.6% possessed between 2 and 5 hectares. Small cultivators thus represented a total of 64.9% of all Jewish farms. Very large farms, with over 50 hectares of land, numbered only 770, or 3.5% of the total of Jewish holdings. Of the 22,103 Jewish farms, only 4,335, or 19.6%, employed hired labor. Over 80% of the Jewish farmers worked by themselves, with the aid of their families. Even in Hungary, which not long before had had a considerable number of big Jewish landowners, the proletarian elements in 1930 represented 31.4% of all Jews dependent on agriculture. Together with Jewish small-holders and tenants of farms of less than 5 hectares, the small farmers and farm workers represented in 1930 no less than 40.2% of all Jews engaged in agriculture. It is true that in the same year the percentage of land-lords owning over 110 hectares each amounted to 13.3% among the Jewish agri-culturists, as compared with scarcely 0.3% among the non-Jewish landowners. But the large Jewish farms in Hungary were grad-ually expropriated by the Government and divided into small holdings, which was not the case with the holdings of Magyar mag-nates. The number of Jews who possessed estates of over 1,000 hectares thus amounted in 1920 to 137, but in 1930 to only 54, whereas of the 661 non-Jewish owners of large estates 525, or 80%, preserved their estates. In the last years before the Sec-ond World War Jews lost all their land. In Romania and Czechoslovakia (primarily in Carpatho-Ruthenia) the overwhelming ma-jority of Jewish agriculturists were poor peasants.

B. *Occupational Structure of the Jews not Engaged in Agriculture*: The tables 2a and 2b contain data on the occupational structure among Jews and non-Jews in nine countries about which we possess official statistics. Almost all data refer to the early 1930's, except for the Soviet Union, regard-ing which figures are available only for 1926, and for Palestine, with reference to which the estimated figures for 1937 are utilized. The tables embrace a Jewish population of over 9,000,000, more than half of all Jews on the eve of the Second World War. They may, therefore, be taken as typical of the entire Jewish people. Let us examine the data referring to the Jews without reference to the non-Jewish populations. We find that the percentage of gainfully employed Jews in manufacturing industries is somewhat higher than the percentage in trade and commerce.

Palestine shows the highest percentage of industrially engaged Jews. Poland occu-pied the second place, with more than 45% engaged in industry.

The more compact the Jewish popula-tion of a given country, the higher the per-centage of industrially employed Jews. This is natural. In countries with a large number of Jews, their natural rate of increase is more rapid than the growth of possibilities for their absorption into trade and com-merce. Jews who emigrate to a new country naturally gravitate to their traditional trad-ing pursuits. It is only when Jewish immi-gration assumes large enough proportions that the newcomers turn to manual work.

A second general rule may be formulated on the basis of the tables given. The more industrialized a country, the smaller the percentage of the Jewish population en-gaged in the country's industrial activities. This is explained primarily by the fact that it was precisely the economically backward countries which had the largest Jewish populations. On the other hand, the highly developed countries offered more oppor-tunities for the commercial pursuits to which the Jews traditionally gravitated.

Let us now briefly compare the occupa-tional composition among Jews and non-Jews, bearing in mind that this comparison refers to the general population, except for those engaged in agricultural occupation.

A most striking difference between Jews and non-Jews is observable in trade and commerce. The percentage among the Jews thus occupied was almost three times larger than the percentage among non-Jews. Tak-ing into account the changes up to 1939 among the Jewish populations and the cor-responding strata of the non-Jewish popu-lations, we shall be justified in estimating the maximum ratio as only 2.5 to 1. Simul-taneously we shall find that the percentage of the population employed in public serv-ices and liberal professions is nearly 1.5 times higher among the non-Jews than among the Jews. The evolution of the ur-ban populations leads to a certain degree of equalization of the occupational struc-ture of Jews and non-Jews. We shall see later that the difference in the social composition

TABLE 2A

OCCUPATIONAL DISTRIBUTION (NOT INCLUDING AGRICULTURE)

A. JEWS

Country	Year of Census	Total	NUMBER OF GAINFULLY EMPLOYED PERSONS						
			Industry and Trades	Commerce and Credit	Communications and Transport	Public Service and Liberal Professions	Domestic and Personal Service	Non-labor Income	Others
Poland	1931	1,114,453	505,870	425,641	38,822	68,111	36,357	28,995	10,657
%		100.0	45.4	38.2	3.5	6.1	3.3	2.6	0.9
U. S. S. R:	1926	929,600	386,400	220,900	30,700	162,900	.....	70,400	58,300
%		100.0	41.5	23.8	3.3	17.5		7.6	6.3
Ukraine	1926	542,875	238,205	131,437	18,950	76,651	.....	38,149	39,483
%		100.0	43.9	24.2	3.5	14.1		7.0	7.3
Central Russia	1926	269,100	89,800	65,700	7,100	73,200	.....	21,400	11,900
%		100.0	33.4	24.4	2.6	27.2		8.0	4.4
White Russia	1926	117,778	58,357	23,829	4,710	13,040	.....	10,941	6,901
%		100.0	49.6	20.2	4.0	11.1		9.3	5.8
Germany	1933	297,261	55,655	147,804	988	27,953	3,920	60,941	.....
%		100.0	18.7	49.8	0.3	9.4	1.3	20.5	
Romania	1930	305,000	106,000	157,000	8,000	9,000	.....	.....	*25,000
%		100.0	34.8	51.5	2.6	2.9			8.2
Hungary	1930	207,295	67,879	95,844	4,126	17,354	3,128	15,420	3,544
%		100.0	32.8	46.2	2.0	8.4	1.5	7.4	1.7
Czechoslovakia:	1930	152,543	33,807	71,082	3,339	12,669	2,643	27,138	1,635
%		100.0	22.9	46.7	2.2	8.3	1.7	17.8	1.1
Slovakia and Carpatho-Ruthenia	1930	83,333	20,671	38,577	2,420	6,900	2,050	11,191	1,524
%		100.0	24.8	46.2	2.9	8.3	2.5	13.4	1.8
Bohemia, Moravia and Silesia	1930	69,010	15,136	32,505	919	5,799	593	15,947	111
%		100.0	19.0	47.1	1.3	8.4	0.9	23.1	0.2
Palestine	1937	151,800	50,500	27,000	9,500	22,300	8,500	.....	**14,000
%		100.0	38.3	20.5	7.2	16.9	6.5		10.6
Canada	1931	61,087	20,364	25,852	1,755	3,469	3,660	.....	**7,987
%		100.0	33.3	39.0	2.9	5.7	6.0		13.1
Latvia	1930	40,717	11,838	20,021	903	5,298	838	.....	1,819
%		100.0	29.1	49.2	2.2	13.0	2.0		4.5
Total		3,239,600	1,238,300	1,189,100	98,100	329,100	59,100	202,900	123,000
%		100.0	38.2	36.7	3.0	10.2	1.8	6.3	3.8

*Includes domestic service and income not derived from work.

**Includes persons living on income not derived from work.

404 of 460

TABLE 2B

OCCUPATIONAL DISTRIBUTION (NOT INCLUDING AGRICULTURE)

B. NON-JEWS

Country	Year of Census	Total	NUMBER OF GAINFULLY EMPLOYED PERSONS						
			Industry and Trades	Commerce and Credit	Communications and Transport	Public Service and Liberal Professions	Domestic and Personal Service	Non-labor Income	Others
Poland	1931	4,139,511	2,031,799	387,602	301,715	497,848	440,843	382,053	97,671
%		100.0	49.0	9.3	7.3	12.0	10.9	9.2	2.3
U. S. S. R.	1926	12,794,500	4,983,300	1,005,300	1,382,000	2,059,900		1,792,200	1,571,800
%		100.0	38.9	7.9	10.8	16.1		14.0	12.3
Ukraine	1926	2,155,416	900,763	120,549	225,575	326,026		255,278	347,235
%		100.0	41.7	5.6	10.5	15.2		10.9	16.1
Central Russia	1926	10,441,000	4,030,900	876,300	1,130,900	1,689,100		1,523,500	1,190,300
%		100.0	38.6	8.4	10.8	16.2		14.6	11.4
White Russia	1926	198,019	51,695	8,371	25,561	44,811		33,585	34,256
%		100.0	26.1	4.2	12.9	22.6		16.9	17.3
Germany	1933	28,477,584	12,997,327	4,299,779	1,551,003	2,374,297	1,494,563	5,760,615	
%		100.0	45.6	15.1	5.5	8.3	5.3	20.2	
Romania	1930	2,494,000	1,184,000	451,000	252,000	335,000			*272,001
%		100.0	47.5	18.1	10.1	13.4			10.9
Hungary	1930	1,719,474	850,865	171,446	106,900	178,458	199,075	154,020	58,710
%		100.0	49.5	10.0	6.2	10.4	11.6	8.9	3.4
Czechoslovakia:	1930	4,821,415	2,490,295	488,045	286,813	324,504	334,582	792,123	105,053
%		100.0	51.7	10.1	6.0	6.7	6.9	16.4	2.2
Slovakia and Carpatho-Ruthenia	1930	620,927	256,215	45,716	49,882	69,061	68,903	95,079	36,071
%		100.0	41.3	7.4	8.0	11.1	11.1	15.3	5.8
Bohemia, Moravia and Silesia	1930	4,200,488	2,234,080	442,329	236,931	255,443	265,679	697,044	68,982
%		100.0	53.2	10.5	5.8	6.0	6.3	16.6	1.6
Palestine	1931	91,870	26,986	17,614	12,864	14,117	6,748		**13,541
%		100.0	29.4	19.2	14.0	15.4	7.3		14.7
Canada	1931	2,642,598	716,450	327,631	298,522	274,598	353,368		**671,848
%		100.0	27.1	12.4	11.3	10.4	13.4		25.4
Latvia	1930	370,253	152,084	43,614	39,427	66,705	38,746		**29,677
%		100.0	41.1	11.8	10.6	17.0	10.5		8.0
Total		57,551,000	25,433,100	7,192,000	4,231,300	6,125,400	2,867,900	8,881,000	2,820,300
%		100.0	44.2	12.5	7.3	10.7	5.0	15.4	4.9

*Includes domestic service and income not derived from work..
**Includes persons living on income not derived from work.

of the Jewish and non-Jewish populations is due not only to the difference in their occupational structure.

C. *The Participation of the Jews in Economic Life*: The participation of the Jews in the economic life of the European nations continually decreased especially during the first decades of the 20th century. In the years preceding the Second World War, in almost all the countries of Europe the percentage of the Jews among the population was on the decline, because of the decrease in the natural increment and their larger emigration as compared with non-Jews. Further, the percentage of Jews among the urban populations declined,—with a few exceptions—even more rapidly, since the influx of non-Jewish villagers into the towns was much greater than the influx of Jews. In addition, every non-Jewish peasant or farm laborer migrating to the town abandoned his former economic function and increased the percentage of non-Jews occupied in industries or trade and commerce,

whereas the Jewish artisan or trader shifting from the small towns to the larger urban centers usually retained his former occupation, so that the change did not affect the occupational structure of the Jewish population. This process of the steady decline in the relative number of Jews in urban occupations is in part only a statistical fiction. However, it was often accompanied by a real shrinkage of the economic opportunities open to the Jews; especially when the policy of eliminating the Jews was deliberately organized and enforced by the authorities of the State, as has been previously described. The decrease of the Jewish share was not always the same in every field of economic activity. It was most pronounced in trade and commerce, where the influx of non-Jewish elements sometimes assumed the character of a veritable invasion, accentuated by the policies of the State.

TABLE 3

RATIO OF JEWS PER EVERY 100 GAINFULLY EMPLOYED PERSONS

Country	Year of Census	In all Branches exc. Agricult.	Industry and Trades	Commerce and Credit	Communications and Transp.	Public Service and Liberal Profes.	Domestic and Personal Service
Poland	1921	25.3	22.2	62.2	10.2	12.4	16.7
"	1931	21.2	19.9	52.3	11.4	12.0	7.6
Germany	1895	1.7	0.6	7.5	0.1	1.5	—
"	1910	1.3	0.6	5.9	0.1	1.6	—
"	1933	1.0	0.4	3.3	0.1	1.2	0.3
Hungary	1920	13.0	8.8	40.6	5.7	10.3	2.4
"	1930	10.8	7.4	35.8	3.7	8.9	1.5
Czechoslovakia	1921	3.4	1.6	16.6	1.4	4.0	1.1
"	1930	3.1	1.3	12.7	1.2	3.8	0.8
Slovakia and Carp. Russia	1921	12.0	8.3	54.9	4.0	10.1	3.4
	1930	11.8	7.5	45.9	4.6	9.1	2.9
Bohemia, Moravia and Silesia	1921	1.9	0.7	9.5	0.8	2.5	0.4
	1930	1.6	0.6	6.8	0.4	2.2	0.2
Canada	1921	1.9	2.3	5.1	0.5	0.9	0.5
"	1931	2.3	2.7	6.8	0.6	1.2	1.0

Table 3 gives us an idea of the decrease of the Jewish share in the urban fields of economic activity. (In agriculture the Jewish share was less than 1% in every country and therefore figures on agriculture are not given). We find that in all countries, except Canada—a typical country of immigration —the share of the Jews decreased in every economic branch, but most markedly in trade and commerce. The percentage of Jews in German trade and commerce decreased between 1895 and 1933 from 7.5% to 3.3%. Between 1920 and 1930 the Jewish share in Hungarian trade and commerce fell from 40.6% to 35.8%. In the course of a single decade the Jewish share in trade and commerce declined in Poland by one-sixth and in Czechoslovakia by one-fourth.

It must be remembered that all these figures refer to periods when the falling off of the Jewish share in trade and commerce was the result chiefly of a continuous growth of the non-Jewish trading elements. The organized and systematic elimination of the Jews by planned intervention of the State began only in the 1930's and its effects are not apparent in our tables. Incomplete private investigations carried out in Poland revealed a much more rapid rate of relative

JEWS AND NON-JEWS IN POLISH COMMERCE AND INDUSTRY IN 1921 AND 1931

	JEWS		NON-JEWS	
	percentage among		percentage among	
	All gainfully employed Jews	All gainfully employed persons	All gainfully employed non-Jews	All gainfully employed persons
Commerce				
1921	39.4	62.2	8.2	37.8
1931	38.2	52.3	9.3	47.7
Industry				
1921	36.6	22.2	42.8	77.8
1931	45.4	19.9	49.0	80.1

decline of the Jewish share in trade and commerce, although the total number of Jewish tradesmen and merchants remained almost unchanged.

The Jewish share in industrial activity also dropped in all European countries, but this was due only to the rapid increase of non-Jewish elements in this field and by no means to a falling off of the number of industrially employed Jews. On the contrary there was even an increase of Jews in industry, primarily in small industry.

This phenomenon can be best illustrated by a few figures with regard to Poland in the years 1921-1931. The number of Jews occupied in trade and commerce amounted in 1921 to 324,936 and in 1931 to 425,641, an increase of over 30%. Non-Jews were occupied in trade and commerce to a total of 197,754 in 1921 and 387,608 in 1931, an increase of 96%, or three times the increase among Jews. The number of Jews occupied in industries was in 1921—324,524; in 1931 —505,870, an increase of 64%. The number of gainfully employed non-Jews in manufacturing and mechanical industries was: in 1921—1,139,718; in 1931—2,031,799, an increase of over 90%.

We have very little data concerning the occupational structure of the Jews in the Asiatic and African countries, except for Palestine and South Africa. The table below shows the occupations of the native Jews and non-Jews in the city of Tripoli in North Africa. It will be observed that the occupational structure in 1931 resembled that of any Eastern European city. Almost a third of the Jewish population was engaged in trade and commerce; almost a half were artisans and craftsmen.

OCCUPATIONAL DISTRIBUTION OF THE JEWS IN TRIPOLI IN 1931

	JEWS	%	NON-JEWS	%
Artisans and Craftsmen	2,130	46.2	7,373	58.9
Trade and Commerce	1,465	46.2	1,663	13.3
Communications and Transport	142	3.1	1,022	8.2
Public Services and Professions	369	8.0	2,144	17.1
Domestic Service	506	11.0	318	2.5
	4,612	100.0	12,520	100.0

TABLE 4

SOCIAL DISTRIBUTION OF GAINFULLY EMPLOYED JEWS AND NON-JEWS IN VAROUS COUNTRIES

(exclusive of agriculture)

Country	Year of Census	JEWS					NON-JEWS				
		Total number	Employers & Independent Workers	White-collar employees	Manual workers	Not specified	Total Number	Employers & Independent Workers	White-collar employees	Manual workers	Not specified
Poland %	1931	1,114,453 100.0	693,160 62.2	91,168 8.2	299,181 26.8	30,944 2.8	4,139,511 100.0	753,666 18.2	546,964 13.2	2,449,876 59.2	389,005 9.4
U.S.S.R. %	1926	929,753 100.0	361,800 38.9	305,800 32.9	177,100 19.1	85,053 9.1	12,794,500 100.0	2,233,800 17.5	3,971,900 31.0	4,811,100 37.6	1,177,700 13.9
Ukraine %	1926	542,875 100.0	230,515 42.5	148,818 27.4	118,064 21.7	45,478 8.4	2,155,426 100.0	324,277 15.1	656,002 30.4	874,759 40.6	300,388 13.9
Central Russia[1] %	1926	269,100 100.0	75,000 27.9	132,400 49.2	34,200 12.7	27,500 10.2	10,441,000 100.0	1,885,300 18.0	3,244,800 31.1	3,871,500 37.1	1,439,400 13.8
White Russia %	1926	117,778 100.0	56,297 47.8	24,651 20.9	24,876 21.1	11,954 10.2	198,079 100.0	24,307 12.3	71,107 35.9	64,813 32.7	37,852 19.1
Germany %	1933	297,261 100.0	128,036 43.1	85,056 28.6	23,228 7.8	60,941 20.5	28,477,584 100.0	3,703,657 13.0	5,399,285 19.0	13,614,027 47.8	5,760,615 20.2
Hungary %	1930	207,295 100.0	72,470 35.0	52,548 25.3	66,857 32.3	15,420 7.4	1,719,474 100.0	283,017 16.4	189,272 11.0	1,093,115 63.6	154,070 9.0
Czechoslovakia %	1930	152,343 100.0	64,275 42.2	42,944 28.2	17,986 11.8	27,138 17.8	4,821,415 100.0	590,252 12.2	866,281 18.0	2,572,759 53.4	792,123 16.4
Slovakia and Carp. Ruthenia %	1930	83,333 100.0	38,978 46.8	19,146 23.0	14,018 16.8	11,191 13.4	620,927 100.0	81,935 13.2	122,149 19.7	321,764 51.8	95,079 15.3
Bohemia, Moravia and Silesia %	1930	69,010 100.0	25,297 36.7	23,798 34.5	3,968 5.7	15,947 23.1	4,200,488 100.0	508,317 12.1	744,132 17.7	2,250,995 53.6	697,044 16.6
Palestine[2] %	1937	164,800 100.0	53,800 32.6	75,000 45.5	22,000 13.4	14,000 8.5	— —	— —	— —	— —	— —
Total %		2,865,905 100.0	1,373,500 47.9	652,500 22.8	606,400 21.2	233,400 8.1	51,952,500 100.0	7,564,400 14.6	10,973,700 21.1	24,540,900 47.2	8,873,500 17.1

[1] All Soviet Republics, except Ukraine and White Russia
[2] Including agriculture (estimate)

2. SOCIAL DISTRIBUTION

Table 4 shows the social composition of the nearly 3,000,000 gainfully employed Jews and the 52,000,000 non-Jews in a number of countries. In spite of the fact that the social differentiation among the Jews had progressed considerably and that in the six countries referred to 44% of the gainfully employed were salaried and wage workers, there still remains a very great difference between Jews and gentiles. Among the latter the proportion of employees is over 68% of all who were gainfully employed, which is 1.5 times as high as among the Jews. If we bear in mind the changes which have taken place in the Soviet Union since 1926 and the fact that the number of Jewish wage-workers grew considerably in Poland in the years before the Second World War, we shall probably be not far afield in assuming that in the countries in question approximately 50% of the Jewish labor force were employees in 1939. In the United States and other countries of immigration the percentage of wage workers and salaried employees was certainly not less.

A second phenomenon, revealed by Table 4, is that the number of independent workers and employers is more than three times larger among the Jews than among the gentile population. This indicates that the middle-class character of the Jewish masses has not disappeared. The fact that Jews were engaged in trade and commerce to a much greater extent than non-Jews also accounts for the greater percentage of independent proprietors among the former. Of every 100 persons engaged in trade and commerce, 84.1% in the case of the Jews and only 49% of the other ethnic groups were proprietors of business establishments. Thus Jews are not only strongly represented in trade and commerce, which generally have a high percentage of small proprietors, but the percentage of tiny enterprises among them, even in this field, is much greater than among the non-Jews (93.6% among the Jews, 87% among the gentiles). The same situation prevails in industry.

In individual countries conditions differ, but everywhere without exception the percentage of independent businessmen is higher among the Jews than among non-Jews.

Omitting the Soviet Union with its special conditions, the highest ratio of Jewish employees, according to our table, was to be found in Palestine, namely 58.9% of the Jewish labor force. Hungary came next with 57.6%.

The numerical relation between manual workers and white-collar employees among Jews in Soviet Russia in 1929 can be seen from the fact that the white-collar workers constituted the following percentage of the total of Jewish employees:

In Moscow 78.2
In Leningrad 68.1
In Ukraine 55.7
In White Russia 46.3

Apart from the fact that the percentage of employees (wage workers as well as white-collar employees) is considerably less among the Jews than among the non-Jews, we find that the composition of the proletarian strata themselves among the Jews differs from that among the Gentiles. In the first place the Jews have almost no farm workers who constitute quite a prominent element among the other populations. Our table, therefore, does not include agriculture, in order to make the comparison between the Jews and non-Jews more closely approximate the actual conditions. The lowest stratum of the urban proletariat—domestic servants—is much smaller among the Jews than among the non-Jews. Generally speaking the town girl will more willingly accept factory work, even at a lesser wage, than employment in domestic service. Among the Jews this phenomenon is much more pronounced. The following table shows (in percentage) the distribution of employees, Jews and non-Jews.

	salaried employees	*workers*
Among Jews	51.8	48.2
Among non-Jews	30.9	69.1

Among the Jews, the white-collar employees form the bulk of all workers: among non-Jews it is the manual worker who represents the large majority. In the case of the Jews the term "white-collar employee" actually refers to personnel employed in private enterprise; in the case of the non-Jews it includes state and municipal officials. As regards the wage workers, in the case of the Jews these are mostly artisans or workers in very small private enterprises, whereas among the non-Jews they are for the most part employed in large and medium-sized private and State factories.

These general characteristics are based on data concerning a limited number of countries. Nevertheless, on the whole, they are true of the Jews all over the world. In the United States two-thirds of the Jewish workers—estimated between 1,000,000 and 1,100,000—consist of white-collar workers. Of the 350,000 or 400,000 Jewish workers employed in trade and industry, at least two-thirds are in the clothing industry, which still includes a large number of small and very small enterprises. American-born Jews show a higher percentage of metal workers than immigrant Jews. The latter stick more stubbornly to the traditional Jewish trades, for the reason that it is easier for them to find work in industries which are almost entirely in the hands of Jewish employers. It is also easier to learn a trade among one's own kin and fellow townsmen.

A genuine revolution in the economic existence of the Jewish people has taken place in Soviet Russia, where the number of Jewish manual workers has increased considerably. However, even in the Soviet Union a very large percentage of the Jewish working class is (or at least was in 1936-1937) still employed in the traditional Jewish trades. Of all Jewish industrial workers (excluding those in the building trades), a considerable number was employed in the four "Jewish" branches, namely the needle, leather, printing and food industries: in the Ukraine 39.5%, in White Russia 45.7%.

If, on the other hand, we take manifestly

"non-Jewish" industries such as coal and ore mining, metallurgy, chemical industry, we obtain a very different picture. Employment in these branches was represented in the Ukraine in the same period (in percentage of the total number of Jewish workers) as follows: in Ukraine 6.6%, in White Russia 5.4%.

Jewish workers entered the Soviet metal industry in large numbers. According to the figures of 1935 and 1936, it employed over 50,000 Jews. It may be assumed, nevertheless, that a large percentage of Jewish proletarians remained in the traditional Jewish industries. In 1929 Jews were represented in the trade unions of White Russia as follows:

Trade Unions	Percentage of Jewish membership
Needle Workers	86.2
Leather Workers	73.4
Printing Trade	70.5
Metal Workers	37.8
Railway Workers	1.4
Post Office and Telegraph	3.7

The traditional Jewish industries in the Soviet Union, however, lost many of their traditional features. They became mechanized and concentrated. It is true that these industries are still smaller in size and scope than the metal plants or mining industries. There are scores of factories employing up to 1,000 or even 2,000 Jewish workers, but the Jews still constitute a larger percentage of the personnel in the smaller factories than in the larger plants. Data are available concerning the percentage of Jewish workers in 52 larger factories (with over 100 workers) in White Russia. The percentage of Jews among their personnel amounted in 1929 to:

Factories with	Number of Factories	Total number of Workers	Jewish Workers	
			Number	Percentage
100- 200 workers	14	2,285	1,197	52.4
200- 500 workers	18	5,649	2,535	44.9
500-1000 workers	13	9,323	3,943	42.3
1000-2000 workers	7	10,639	3,264	30.7
Total :	52	27,896	10,939	39.2

We thus see that in the larger factories Jewish labor constitutes less than one-third, as against one-half in the smaller enterprises. From the same statistics we learn, nevertheless, that a good deal of Jewish labor is already employed in large factories. On the average there are no less than 210 Jewish workers per enterprise. We may add some figures about 26 factories in the Ukraine which had over 100 Jewish workers each. These 26 factories had in the aggregate 18,643 Jewish workers, making an average of 717 Jewish workers per factory. Ten of these factories together employed 13,550 Jewish workers, an average of 1,355 Jewish workers per enterprise.

The figures just quoted refer to the years 1929 to 1930, and they do not embrace all Jewish workers. The process of concentration no doubt made considerable progress in the later years. We may thus assume that in the Soviet Union there is by now a relatively high percentage of Jews in the very large enterprises.

Unlike the other countries dealt with in this article, Soviet Russia—in the period from the early 'thirties to the outbreak of the war—underwent profound economic changes of a structural character. These changes affected deeply the Jewish population of the Soviet Union. Specific data from the census of 1939 on the occupational and social structure of the individual ethnic groups in the USSR, have not been published as yet. But on the basis of L. Zinger's book* and of data published in Soviet-Yiddish newspapers, an approximate picture of the social structure of Soviet Jewry as it was on the eve of the war can be presented.

The fundamental changes which took place in the years from 1926 to 1939 can be characterized thus:

a. The process of agrarization which had reached its peak in the years 1932-1933 and had provided some 250,000 Jews with a livelihood, was not only halted in the later years but a process of retrogression set in. In the years 1932 to 1939 there was in Russia an

*Dos banaite folk (Yiddish, Moscow 1941.)

immense movement from country to town and it caught up a good part of the Jewish population which is, by tradition, less bound to the soil than the non-Jewish population. According to Zinger, on the eve of the Second World War only 25,000 families derived their livelihood from agriculture, this would make up about 125,000 persons, on the assumption that there were five persons per family in the Jewish "Kolkhozes."

In 1939 these 25,000 families were distributed as follows:

Crimea	5,000
Ukraine	15,500
Birobidjan	3,000
Caucasus and Central Asian provinces	1,500
	25,000

b. The number of Jews in the higher, and especially in the middle educational institutions increased considerably, and the number of Jews in the professions also increased greatly. True, the number of students among the non-Jewish population grew even more, so that the ratio of Jews among the students of the USSR somewhat decreased. In the school-year 1927-1928 there were 23,405 Jewish college and university students in the whole of Russia— 14.4% of all the students; in 1935 there were 61,384 Jewish students, or 13.3%.** It must be taken into consideration however, that a larger percentage of Jewish than of non-Jewish students complete their studies and thus join the ranks of the professional men and women. It can be thus assumed that although Jews constituted 13% of the students, or approximately seven times their percentage in the population, they made up at least 15% of all persons engaged in the professions, that is, more than eight times their percentage in the population.

Here are some characteristic data on the number of Jews in the professions (from Zinger's book, p. 106):

**The National Policy of the All-Russian Communist Party: Statistical Data (in Russian), Moscow, 1930; Cultural Progress in the USSR (in Russian), Moscow, 1936.

Technical personnel		60,000
Engineers, architects, constructors		25,000
Elementary and high-school teachers		46,000
Journalists, librarians, cultural workers		30,000
Medical personnel (technicians, nurses, etc.)		31,000
Physicians		21,000
Art workers		17,000
Professors and scientists		7,000
Agronomists and agro-technicians		2,000
Total		239,000

At most, only a half of these 239,000 Jews occupied academic positions, but they all belong, as far as classification is concerned, to the professions. It is extremely interesting to note that whereas in all other countries the number of Jews engaged in medicine and law comprise the vast majority of Jews in the professions, in Russia—in keeping with its general development—the first place goes to industrial technicians.

c. The category of those engaged in private enterprises (especially storekeepers), which in 1926 comprised some 25% of all gainfully employed Jews, has now completely disappeared. This does not mean that these elements really changed their occupations; instead of selling in their own stores, they now sell in government stores. Socially the difference is great, but occupationally there is none.

In consequence of the economic changes, it can be assumed that the distribution of the gainfully employed Soviet Jews was in 1939 approximately as follows:

	Number	Percentage
1. Officials and civil government employees	430,000	33.1
2. Professions	240,000	18.5
3. Factory and shop workers	280,000	21.6
4. Artisans	180,000	13.7
5. Agriculture	80,000	6.2
6. Miscellaneous	90,000	6.9
Total	1,300,000	100.0

Manual workers thus constitute 41.5% of all gainfully employed Jews in the USSR. This is a smaller percentage than was true of the Jews in pre-war Poland. This is understandable since in Soviet Russia the Jews have an incomparably better chance of achieving a higher economic position

than in most European countries. And, of course, the professions and the positions of officials are not only more remunerative but also socially higher, if we take into consideration the specific character of the Soviet regime in which officialdom plays such an important part. That Jews availed themselves of these favorable circumstances in the Soviet Union to a high extent is indicated by the considerable number of Jews in the first two categories, especially, in the second category in the above table, the liberal professions. In no country in the world have Jews ever had such a large percentage of professional men and women. The same can be said of the number and percentage of Jewish public servants.

3. THE JEWISH WORKING CLASS

Let us now see what is the number of Jewish workers in the world and what proportion of the Jewish people it represents.

There were in the years 1935-1939 over 2,900,000 Jewish workers throughout the world, which represented about 44% of all gainfully employed Jews. The geographical distribution of these working masses will be seen from the following table:

JEWISH WORKERS THROUGHOUT THE WORLD
(in 1935-1939)

U.S.A.	1,000,000
U.S.S.R.	950,000
Poland	450,000
Hungary	120,000
Palestine	120,000
Romania	100,000
Czechoslovakia	55,000
Great Britain	50,000
France	50,000
Argentina	50,000
Diverse countries	50,000
Total	2,995,000

The characteristic features of the structure of the Jewish working class are as follows: first, Jewish agricultural labor is almost completely absent; second, white-collar employees represent a much higher percentage of the working class than among the non-Jews; third, the lowest group of urban labor, namely, domestics, occupy a much smaller place than among the non-Jewish population; fourth, Jewish industrial labor is concentrated in branches which have a more manifestly artisan character, in other words, in smaller enterprises; fifth, among the Jewish workers women represent a much smaller percentage than among the non-Jews, due to the fact that the percentage of Jewish women leaving the factory, store or office after marriage is greater than among non-Jewish women. On the other hand, the percentage of youth is much higher among the Jewish than among the non-Jewish workers, because more adult Jewish workers prefer to become independent businessmen than is the case among non-Jews.

These characteristic features of the Jewish proletariat differ in the various countries. On the whole these features are present everywhere. They are present even in the Soviet Union where the situation is fundamentally different from the rest of the world. Tradition is a potent element. It is not only a result of the past, but a factor for the future. Just as there were few Jewish farmers before the Russian Revolution, there is still an inconsequential number of Jews occupied in agriculture as compared with the Slavs. Similarly, the concentration of large numbers of Russian Jews in commerce before the Revolution is reflected in the number of Jews employed in Soviet commercial and trading apparatus. In trades, too, the Jews, having before the Revolution represented a larger percentage of artisans than the non-Jews, now show a higher percentage of members of the "artels" (artisans' productive cooperatives). The so-called Jewish trades, such as tailoring, shoemaking, cabinet-making, etc., have been, indeed, mechanized and combined into larger units, but the new factories thus created are still of a much smaller size than the giant Soviet metal works or mining enterprises.

It is, of course, impossible to compare the Jewish proletariat of the Soviet Union with that of Poland, where, before the Second World War, these specific characteristics found their strongest expression. Nor can we compare the Jewish proletariat

in the United States with that of the Soviet Union or Poland. The American Jewish working class occupies an intermediate position. It is employed in mechanized and large-sized enterprises to a greater degree than was the case in Poland, but less than in the Soviet Union. Nevertheless, it is possible to trace many resemblances between the Jewish workers in all these countries. All the groups of Jewish workers with which we have just dealt show with particular clearness the first three of the national characteristic traits: the negligible number of agricultural elements, the high percentage of salaried employees, and the very small number of domestic servants.

Naturally, what is dealt with here is only the occupational and social structure of the Jewish working class; not its pecuniary position or its standard of living. That theme does not belong to the scope of the present study.

4. PARTICIPATION IN VARIOUS ECONOMIC AND SOCIAL GROUPS

Up to this point we have analyzed the structure of the Jewish population and compared it with that of the non-Jews. We may now briefly deal with the importance and influence of the Jews in various economic spheres and within different social classes.

Table 5 contains data pertaining to the few countries for which exact census figures are available. The table does not give total figures for all these countries combined, since there are vast differences between them. Computed totals would only blur the actual picture.

The percentage of self-employed and employers among Jews is generally greater in countries with a greater density of Jews than in other places. In White Russia, for example, 69.8% of those who were businessmen or employers in 1926 were Jews; this was nine times greater than their percentage in the total population. The corresponding figures for Poland and Carpatho-Ruthenia are 47.9% (5 times greater) and 32.2% (3 times greater). In the countries with small Jewish populations (in most

TABLE 5

PARTICIPATION OF JEWS IN VARIOUS GROUPS

Country	Year of Census	In All Branches* % of Jews			In Industry % of Jews			In Commerce % of Jews			In Professions and Public Service - % of Jews		
		Self Employed	White collar employees	Manual workers	Self Employed	White collar employees	Manual workers	Self Employed	White collar employees	Manual workers	Self Employed	White collar employees	Manual workers
Poland	1931	47.9	14.3	10.9	35.6	19.7	12.9	65.4	30.3	23.1	43.7	10.3	5.1
U. S. S. R.	1926	13.9	7.1	3.6	11.4	8.3	4.4	25.4	13.9	8.1	13.3	7.1	3.6
Ukraine	1926	41.5	18.5	11.9	34.9	19.2	13.3	65.7	40.0	31.7	30.5	18.4	10.7
Central Russia	1926	3.8	3.9	0.9	2.9	4.6	1.2	7.4	7.3	2.5	6.9	4.1	1.2
White Russia	1926	69.8	26.7	27.7	65.7	45.2	39.6	89.2	56.9	51.6	35.7	21.2	31.2
Germany	1933	3.3	1.6	0.2	1.3	1.4	0.2	5.5	3.0	0.3	6.0	0.8	0.3
Hungary	1930	20.4	21.7	5.8	10.6	33.0	4.8	41.9	47.7	24.4	34.2	7.4	3.1
Czechoslovakia	1930	9.8	4.7	0.7	4.6	3.5	0.5	16.8	12.1	3.1	14.9	2.8	1.1
Carpatho-Ruthenia	1930	32.2	13.6	4.2	16.0	13.9	4.0	57.3	40.6	16.6	29.6	7.4	3.7
Bohemia, Moravia and Silesia	1930	4.7	3.1	0.2	1.8	2.5	0.1	8.2	7.8	1.0	10.6	1.5	0.5

*Except Agriculture.

cases highly developed countries), the percentage of Jews is not very high even among those self-employed. In Germany, for example, it amounted to 3.3%, only 3.5 times as much as the Jewish percentage of the total population. When we examine the figures relating specially to trade and commerce, we find a great increase of the Jewish share in every social group occupied in these fields, particularly, however, among the self-employed and white-collar employees. The Jews in Poland thus represented the following percentage (in 1931) in the different categories:

1. Independent proprietors : general, 47.9%; trade and commerce, 65.4%; industry, 35.6%; liberal professions and public services, 43.7%.

2. White-collar employees : general, 14.3%; trade and commerce, 30.3%; industry, 19.7%; liberal professions and public services, 10.3%.

3. Manual workers : general, 10.9%; trade and commerce, 23.1%; industry, 12.9%; liberal professions and public services, only 5.1%.

The group "Public Services and Liberal Professions" does not present the actual picture, since it combines two spheres in which the share of the Jews is very different. The ratio of the Jews in the liberal professions was very high in many countries, whereas among public servants Jews always represented, even in the best of times, an insignificant percentage. In Prussia in 1925 the Jews constituted 26.6% of all lawyers; 15.51% of all physicians; 14.79% of all dentists; 12.88% of all writers, but only 0.11%

of post-office employees, 0.04% of railway officials, 0.38% of the officials of the administration, 0.9% of the officials of the educational services, and 1.2% of the personnel of the public health services.

The same phenomenon could be observed in every country. In 1931 the Jews constituted in Poland 66.2% of all private medical practitioners, but only 16.5% of the medical staffs of hospitals. It must be added that almost all these Jews worked in Jewish and not in general medical institutions. While in 1931 Jews were still represented in the State or municipal hospitals in Poland, in later years they were dismissed. In other professions in Poland in 1931 Jews were represented as follows: 53% of all lawyers, but less than 1% of judges and public prosecutors; among 39,300 persons employed by the Polish post offices there were only 307 Jews or 0.7%; of 194,171 railway employees there were only 700 Jews or 0.3%; of 69,815 municipal officials and workers there were only 1,804 Jews or 2.6%.

Similar conditions existed in Hungary. According to the census of 1930, Jews represented 49.2% of all lawyers, but only 1.8% of judges and public prosecutors. They constituted 54.5% of all medical practitioners, but only 16.2% of the medical staffs of the public hospitals. Among scientists, writers and poets the Jews represented 25.7%. Among editors and journalists, 31.7%, but among teachers in academic institutions only 3.4%, and among teachers in the secondary schools, only 6.4%.

BIBLIOGRAPHY

Official statistical publications of various countries.

Deutsche Hochschulstatistik, 1910-1930.

PAUL EMDEN, *Money Powers of Europe*. London, 1937.

ENCYCLOPAEDIA JUDAICA, *Finanz und Bankwesen*. Berlin.

LEO GOLDHAMMER, *Die Juden Wiens*. Wien, 1929.

JACOB LESTSCHINSKY, *The Development of the Jewish People During the Last 100 Years* (Yiddish). "Shriftn far Ekonomik un Statistik." Vilna, 1928.

JACOB LESTSCHINSKY, *Die Umsiedlung und Umschichtung des juedischen Volkes im Laufe des letzten Jahrhunderts*, "Weltwirtschaftliches Archiv." Kiel, 1929-1930.

JACOB LESTSCHINSKY, *Das wirtschaftliche Schicksal des deutschen Judentums*. Berlin, 1932.

JACOB LESTSCHINSKY, *Das juedische Volk im neuen Europa*. Prague, 1934.

A. MARCUS, *Die wirtschaftliche Krise der deutschen Juden*. Berlin, 1931.

WERNER SOMBART, *Die Juden und das Wirtschaftsleben*. Leipzig, 1911.

Statystyka Szkolnictwa. Warsaw, 1926-1938.

JACOB THON, *Die Juden in Oesterreich*.

KURT ZIELENZIGER, *Juden in der deutschen Wirtschaft*. Berlin, 1930.

Yidishe Ekonomik. Vilna, 1937-1938.

THE ECONOMIC DEVELOPMENT OF THE JEWS IN THE UNITED STATES

Jacob Lestschinsky

I. MAIN FACTORS IN THE ECONOMIC DEVELOPMENT OF AMERICAN JEWRY

Three fundamental factors shaped the socio-economic character of American Jewry:

a) The economic and cultural traditions which the Jewish immigrants brought with them to the new land;

b) The economic evolution of America during the period of the great Jewish immigration;

c) The economic and cultural traditions of the non-Jewish groups of immigrants who came here from the same European countries as the Jews, and who, in one way or another, were also linked with them in this country.

No immigrant group comes to a new land empty-handed. Besides material goods it also brings along social and cultural values, traditions, habits, skills. This applies not only to individual economic and technical experiences and abilities, but to the group as a whole, and plays an important part in the shaping of the destiny of the immigrant groups, especially in the case of the first and second generations. True enough it is the new environment, the stage and tempo of its economic development, that ultimately determines the lot of the immigrant. There is no doubt, however, that various national groups with their individual social and cultural heritages are differently prepared and suited both for the utilization of the new conditions and for adjustment to the economic development.

Immigrants came to America from many lands and comprised representatives of many nations. They came from very backward agrarian countries and from semi-agrarian as well as highly developed industrial countries. Since the Jews have been an urban people for many centuries and for a long time engaged in commerce and other urban occupations, they are particularly quick to orient themselves in new conditions, to learn new languages, and to recognize the potential opportunities of the new land. For the same reason the Jew is mentally more alert, more energetic, more resilient and more enterprising. This is especially true of the Jews in comparison with the non-Jews of the backward lands of Eastern and Southern Europe.

The pioneers of Jewish immigration into America—the Sephardic Jews and the Marranos—belonged almost exclusively to the commercial class, and, to a large extent, to its upper stratum. The second group of Jewish immigrants—the German Jews—also consisted almost entirely of commercial elements; in their old home only about 10% of the German Jews were artisans. These two immigrant groups were able to adapt themselves quickly and easily to the new conditions of life and to attain advanced economic positions.

Much more difficult was the lot of the great masses of Jewish immigrants who came to America from Eastern Europe. The first wave of immigrants (1870-1900) consisted of artisans, unskilled workers, and in large measure of economically declassed elements and of unskilled youth who had just left the *Heder* (elementary Jewish school) or *Yeshibah* (Talmudic college) and had no experience or training in economic life. They were not children of peasants or workers, as was the case with the majority of non-Jewish immigrants, but sons of storekeepers and peddlers, brokers and middlemen, and people of no fixed economic class *(luftmenschen)* who were still living in the atmosphere of the traditional Jewish townlet with its synagogues and study-houses.

These people were compelled at first to toil under all sorts of hardships in the sweatshops or to eke out a meager livelihood as pushcart peddlers. Among these there were many who had had a thorough Jewish education. This education was of little practical use to them, but the agility of mind they had acquired made it easier for them to learn English and to understand the laws and customs of the new land. Thus among this first generation of immigrants there was already a sizable contingent which contrived, after enduring real hardships for a decade or so, to leave the sweatshops or pushcarts and open stores or factories. There were some who managed, with traditional Jewish perseverance, to study medicine, dentistry or law at night, after a hard day's work. But during this period (the last quarter of the 19th century) such groups were the exception rather than the rule. In general the Jewish population in the American cities consisted primarily of manual workers and also of some small businessmen. However, favorable conditions were already established and the moment was ripe for a transition to other occupations.

The second large wave of Jewish immigrants—from 1900 to 1925—consisted in large measure of artisans and skilled workers. According to the official statistics almost 70% of all gainfully employed Jewish immigrants during this period were skilled artisans or workers, as compared with 20% among the entire European immigration. This, however, does not mean that there were not among this 70% many with commercial traditions and experience. Many Jewish artisans in Europe produced goods for the local market and sold them directly to the local population. This was especially true of the trades in which more than two-thirds of all Jewish artisans were engaged: tailors, cap and hat makers, shoemakers and carpenters. There were many among them with sufficient ability to adapt themselves to the tempo of economic development in the new land and to avail themselves of its possibilities and opportunities.

It must also be noted—and this is a fact of great importance—that a considerable percentage of immigrants who came here in the first quarter of the 20th century had participated in the revolutionary movement in Czarist Russia and Poland. Hence they brought with them to America not only progressive social and political ideas, but also greater aspirations and a broader outlook. They were unafraid of life and people, and accustomed to getting along with others; they were also more daring and imaginative than the average immigrant. Their dynamic energy—often carried over from public affairs to private business enterprises—affected the entire community of Jewish immigrants.

Here is a characterization of the Jewish immigrants by Niels Carpenter, who wrote on the life of the immigrants. After stressing the fact that Jews are almost wholly unrepresented in agriculture and in heavy industry and preponderantly represented in trade and commerce and in clerical occupations, he goes on to say: "It does seem that they bring with them to this country at least a disposition to take up certain occupations and in many cases they probably already have a specific training for the vocations which they adopt in America.'"

Subjective factors, however, are not enough to enable an ethnic group in a new land fully to utilize its experiences and skills. Fortunately, from 1870 to 1940, the main period of Jewish immigration, there prevailed in the United States almost ideal objective conditions for the utilization of these accumulated energies of the Jews.

The enormous growth of the population and of the cities, and the high standard of living of the masses created an intensive and ever-growing demand for those economic activities which in Eastern Europe lay traditionally in Jewish hands. These activities included commerce, small industry, production and distribution of consumer goods, handicraft and the liberal professions. In America, these traditional "Jewish" economic activities reached unprecedented dimensions and intensity due to the gigantic scope of American economic development.

tremendous increase in the number of those engaged in the so-called Jewish occupations, surpassing the increase in the number of those in agriculture and even in industry.

In 1870 the population of the United States was 38,558,371 and in 1940 it was 131 million, three-and-a-half times greater. The urban population was proportionately as follows: in 1870—25.7% and in 1940—56.5%, somewhat more than double.

An analysis of the table on occupational distribution and the growth of each occupational group reveals that the number of

TABLE 1

NUMBER AND PERCENTAGE OF ALL GAINFUL WORKERS BY OCCUPATIONAL CATEGORIES*

Group	1870	1940	1940 over 1870
Agriculture, forestry and fishing	5,973,183 47.6%	9,542,467 18.0%	3,569,284 60.0%
Manufacturing and mechanical industries	3,463,781 27.7%	13,864,875 26.3%	10,401,004 300.3%
Extraction of minerals	169,499 1.4%	1,140,199 2.2%	970,700 572.7%
Transportation and communication	403,274 3.2%	4,874,206 9.2%	4,470,932 1,108.7%
Trade	573,574 4.6%	7,277,574 13.8%	6,704,000 1,168.8%
Public service	70,367 0.6%	1,518,257 2.9%	1,447,800 2,057.6%
Professional service	332,179 2.7%	3,583,322 6.8%	3,251,143 978.7%
Domestic and personal service	1,208,142 9.7%	5,412,803 10.3%	4,204,661 348.0%
Clerical occupations	311,889 2.5%	5,521,297 10.5%	5,209,408 1,670.3%
Total	12,505,888 100.0%	52,735,000 100.0%	40,229,112 327.7%

*H. Dewey Anderson and Percy Davidson, *Occupational Trends in the United States*, 1942, pp. 16-17.

Table 1 shows the economic development of the United States during the period 1870-1940 and provides a key to the understanding of the changes which the Jewish immigrants underwent. This period witnessed a

those occupied in agriculture—formerly the most important branch of economic activity—increased by only 60%, only one-sixth the rate of increase of the general population. This in itself implies a revolution in the economic life of the country. The United States is not only self-sufficient agriculturally, but even has a considerable surplus for export. Yet this vast production is accomplished with only 60% more man-power than was required in 1870 when the population was less than one-third of the 1940 figure.

The figures on the growth of the number of those engaged in industry are even more remarkable. Here the increase almost coincides with the growth of the population, although the United States now produces vastly more industrial commodities than it did in 1870. The proportion of the population engaged in industrial production diminished from 27.7% in 1870 to 26.3% in 1940. This change took place primarily from 1900 to 1940, the period in which American technology developed with colossal rapidity. In 1900, 31.1% of all those gainfully employed were occupied in industry, but in 1940 only 26.3% were so employed.

Passing from the production to the service and distribution branches of economic life, i.e., to those branches in which European Jews were mainly engaged and for which they were consequently most readily suited, we find that the picture undergoes a complete change. If we omit communication and transportation—since Jews were hardly represented in these activities—and consider trade and commerce, in which the Jews play a prominent role, we see that the number of persons engaged in this field of economic activity was twelve times as high. The actual numbers are striking; from 1870 to 1940 there was an increase of more than 6,700,000 in trade and commerce. It would have been inconceivable if, in the face of such a tremendous development of the apparatus of distribution, the immigrant Jews with their centuries-old traditions in trade and commerce, with their experience and skill in this field, had not availed themselves of this exceedingly favorable situation and had failed to move into this area of economic activity. Naturally it was not easy for immigrants, even if they possessed an urban background and an ability for adapta-

tion, to enter the commercial field. In such a field some knowledge of the language is essential, a certain amount of capital is required, and a measure of experience in the consumer-market and knowledge of the desires and tastes of the customer are important. The lack of these requirements explains the fact that in the first three or four decades of mass-immigration most of the new Jewish immigrants were compelled to work in the sweatshops or to return to pushcart peddling.

In this period the number of employees in public service multiplied twenty-one times. In Europe, even in countries with democratic regimes, the Jews had very little access to such employment. Nor did the Jewish immigrant find in the United States unlimited opportunities for such employment, but he found some employment commensurate with his proportion in the population.

In the same period, from 1870 to 1940, the number of those engaged in the professional service increased over ten times, an addition of over 3,251,143 new positions. It was only natural that among the Jews, with their special leaning toward this sphere of economic activity, there were many who took part in this development. In most cases they entered the fields of medicine and law, in which individual ability and enterprise are a decisive factor.

The growth of the class of white-collar workers was also enormous. It multiplied eighteen times, an increase of more than 5,000,000 clerical workers in the seventy year period. In proportion to the entire population this increase was fourfold, from 2.5% to 10.5%. These figures include only the white-collar workers in private enterprise. With the addition of those employed in public service the figure rises to 13.4%. This colossal growth of the white-collar class diverted Jewish youth from the garment factories in which their parents worked to employment in department stores and offices.

A third factor helped to expedite the rise of the Jewish artisan and worker to higher occupations and to higher social positions. With the immigration of East European Jews into America there came millions of non-Jews from the same countries, but with wholly different traditions and skills. Magyars, Czechs, Slovaks, Ruthenians, Ukrainians, Poles, Lithuanians, Latvians, White Russians, Serbs, Bulgars—millions of peasants poured into America. In their native countries they had been accustomed to see the Jew as merchant, storekeeper, doctor, lawyer, pharmacist. A large number of these peasant immigrants settled in the large cities in the United States.

From 1820 to 1930, 13,944,454 immigrants came to America from Eastern and Southern Europe, from countries which were in the main agricultural. Of these some 3,000,000 were Italians, and the rest, some 11,000,000, came from Slavic lands with compact masses of Jews engaged in urban occupations. Of these approximately 14,000,000 immigrants, according to Davie, only 69,729—a bare 0.5%—came from 1820 to 1870; 13,874,725, or 99.5%,[2] came during the sixty year period from 1870 to 1930. This was also the period of Jewish mass-immigration when some 3,000,000 Jews emigrated from Slavic countries.

Carpenter cites the following figures[3]: According to the census of 1870 there were in America 4,936,618 European-born persons; of these 4,815,171 (97.5%) came from Northern and Western Europe and only 2.5% from the other parts of Europe. In 1920, of 11,882,053 European-born persons in the United States only 5,516,202 (46.5%) came from Northern and Western Europe. Some three-quarters of these immigrants settled in the large cities. Carpenter goes on to say: "It is clear that the immigrant is settled most heavily in the cities. When the several urban areas are grouped according to size, it appears that, in general, the larger the city, the greater the relative number of immigrants and their children within it."[4] It is needless to add that most of the Jewish immigrants settled in the large cities.

As to the direct effect of the non-Jewish immigrants on the economic position of the Jews, especially the German Jews, we may quote Rudolph Glanz. He writes (with ample evidence to substantiate his thesis): "Their common old country, their past connections, the same causes which led to their emigration, their simultaneous arrival here, the possibility of communication in the same language, German—all this led to good-neighbor relationships between Jews and Germans on the new continent. Both Germans and Jews—like all recent immigrants—were still tied with many threads to their old home. This led also to economic ties."[5]

A question which must be left open is whether the large immigration of non-Jews affected the tempo and scope of Jewish emigration from the same lands. It is an accepted fact that the Jews were the pioneers of emigration from the Slavic lands to America. This does not preclude the possibility that in a later stage the non-Jewish emigration from these countries affected the extent of Jewish emigration. It is sufficient to stroll through the Polish districts of Chicago, Detroit, Buffalo, where there are some 800,000 Poles, and where the stores, especially those of the middle and large type, are almost exclusively Jewish, to realize that many a Jewish storekeeper in Poland would probably have hesitated to exchange his business for work in an American sweatshop if he had not been persuaded by a relative or friend that he might open up a similar business in the Polish section of Chicago, Detroit or Buffalo and feel almost as if he were at home.

In any case there can be no doubt that the concentration of non-Jewish immigrants in separate sections of the city speeded up considerably the transition of Jewish workers to trades, professions, and clerical occupations. Among the Jewish owners of businesses in the Polish districts in the above-mentioned cities there is a substantial percentage of former workers.

Naturally, the children of the Slavic immigrants, although on the whole they remain in the same districts and are engaged in the same occupations as their fathers, are not so closely bound to the Jews who are their parents' fellow-countrymen. In all likelihood the third generation severs these ties completely. This is also true of the American-born Jews. Here, too, the second and especially the third generation are no longer dependent on the ties which were carried over from Europe. The second and third generation Jew with English as his mother-tongue and adequately educated, knows his country and is aware of its economic potentialities and opportunities. He therefore takes his chances in the large field of American business and enterprise. In consequence a greater occupational and more thorough-going social differentiation takes place among the Jewish population; the geographical expansion also widens.

II.   OCCUPATIONAL AND SOCIAL DISTRIBUTION OF AMERICAN JEWRY

There are, unfortunately, no official data on the occupational distribution of the Jewish population in America. The census questionnaire does not contain any questions on nationality or religion. Hence the following figures are only approximations. They are based on unofficial investigations in various small, medium-sized and large Jewish communities and on estimates often arrived at indirectly (as for example, from the assumption that in 1900 in a number of cities, almost all those registered according to country of origin as Poles and Russians, were really Jews). We must utilize such data because no more authentic statistics are available and because, in the final analysis, we are not concerned so much with mathematical precision as with the general picture of the occupational structure of the Jewish population and its social differentiation. The available data, despite shortcomings, are sufficient for this purpose.

B. Weinstein, one of the pioneers of the Jewish labor movement in the United States, reports as follows regarding the early Jewish immigrants from Eastern Europe.[6]

"Fortunate were those who brought knowledge of a craft with them from the old country. Tailors, carpenters and other skilled workers were able to procure jobs easily. The majority of the Jewish immigrants without any vocational training and experience, however, consisted of non-workers." He goes on to say: "The committees and their friends would take the 'green' immigrants into their shops and would teach them a craft. Many immigrants would hire themselves out for hard labor at the docks, on the railroads, and in the large factories."[7]

Dr. B. Hoffman, in his history of the cloakmakers' union, has this to say regarding the heterogeneous character of the overwhelming majority of Jewish immigrants who came here during the first ten to fifteen years of the Jewish mass-immigration:

"Former Talmudic students, clerks, insurance agents, teachers, bookkeepers, storekeepers, merchants, would-be intellectuals, now became cloakmakers. On the whole they constituted an element devoid of discipline and inclined toward individualism, but also more capable, more alert, and more restless, and also more impatient, than the average immigrant."[8]

All these people eagerly accepted the most difficult jobs on their arrival, but from the beginning they sought an opportunity to liberate themselves from such hard labor. And hard labor it was. We cannot discuss here the conditions of work which prevailed at the end of the 19th and at the beginning of the 20th centuries in America in general and especially in the so-called Jewish economic fields. The hours were unbearably long, the hygienic conditions were intolerable, the wages were low, and the attitude of the "boss" was one of contempt and irresponsibility. All this militated against keeping the Jewish immigrant in shop or factory.

We can assume that at first—up to 1890— the large majority of the East-European Jews in the United States were manual workers. The German Jews, who by now were almost all American-born, had achieved considerable economic success. At the end of the 'eighties I. Markens wrote:

"In the cities of New York and Brooklyn

there are 4,000 retail and 300 wholesale butchers, one-half of whom are Hebrews, including several millionaires and many whose wealth is represented by six figures. They employ in this business an army of 6,000 men, and their annual trade is $25,-000,000. The abattoir of Schwarzschild & Sulzberger occupies an entire block and they employ 500 men. Joseph Stern's establishment covers half a block.

"The manufacture of hats and caps, the importation and manufacture of hides and leather, furs, laces and embroideries, artificial flowers and feathers is largely controlled by the Hebrews, while the wine and liquor trade is one of the most extensive in which they are engaged. It is estimated that the Hebrew capital represented on the New York Cotton Exchange is not far from $6,000,000 ...

"The holdings of real estate by the Hebrews of New York, is estimated at $150,-000,000. Five-eights of the transfers in real estate, in the city of New York, are for their account."[9]

The same author goes on to enumerate large Jewish wholesale firms of clothing, diamonds, cigars, etc. with a total annual turnover of 248 million dollars.

Let us try to draw a picture of the occupational distribution of Jews in the United States at the beginning of the 20th century, using the city of Boston as an example.[10] On the basis of the census which registers Russians and Poles as separate groups, and bearing in mind that at least 90% of them were Jews, we get the following table:

Occupational Structure of the Jews in Boston in 1900

	Number	Percent.
Gainfully employed	10,834	100.0
Agriculture & fishing	42	0.4
Manufacturing & mechanical industries	5,712	52.7
Trade & clerical occupations	3,845	35.5
Domestic & personal service	751	6.9
Professions	259	2.4
Transportation & communication	207	1.9
Other	18	0.2

Somewhat different results are arrived at by Nathan Goldberg[11]. On the assumption that the Russians of the 1900 census in fifteen cities each with a population exceeding 250,000 were all Jews, he reaches the following figures regarding 150,000 Jews ("Russians"):

Occupational Distribution of Russian Jews in Cities with 250,000 *Inhabitants or More*

	Number	Percent.
Manufacturing & mechanical industries	89,748	59.6
Trade & commerce	31,047	20.6
Domestic & personal service	12,138	8.0
Clerical occupations	10,016	6.7
Professions	3,958	2.6
Transportation	2,613	1.7
Agriculture, fishing, forestry, mining	698	0.5
Public service	476	0.3
Total	150,694	100.0

The difference between the two preceding tables is not as great as would appear at first glance. A number of those listed under the heading "Clerical occupations" in the Goldberg table were actually engaged in "Trade and commerce." It must also be noted that the Goldberg table deals with such cities as New York, Detroit and Chicago, where the number of Jewish factory workers was particularly great. We must reach the conclusion that in 1900 approximately 25% or 30% of all Jews gainfully employed were engaged in trade and commerce, and between 50% and 55% were engaged in manufacturing and mechanical industries.

It is clear from the following data that as early as 1900, the East-European Jews began to go over from factory-work to trade and commerce. There may be some doubt as to whether all the Russian and Polish inhabitants of New York in 1900 may be counted as Jews. There is no doubt, however, that whatever Russians and Poles were in New York at the time, were employed as workers and not engaged in the liberal professions, and surely not in the wholesale business. According to the census there were in 1900 in New York 305 doctors, 217 lawyers, 75 dentists, 403 musicians and 4,562 wholesale merchants, all labelled "Russian" or "Polish." We can take it for granted with a fair degree of certainty that they were almost all Russian and Polish Jews. This already suggests the considerable change in status the Russian and Polish Jewish immigrants underwent since the 'seventies and 'eighties of the preceeding century.

On the other hand, however, we see that more than half of the Jewish population in the United States was at that time still engaged in industry, the majority undoubtedly workers and clerks. There was, of course, a considerable number of Jewish manufacturers even among the East European Jews, not to speak of the German Jews.

We have dealt at length with the two most important branches of activity—commerce and industry—since in varying proportions they always embrace from three-fourths to four-fifths of all gainfully employed Jews. Two other groups in the above tables merit fuller consideration—the liberal professions and the clerks. Somewhat later these groups play an important part in Jewish life in the United States. In 1900 only some 2.5% of Jews were engaged in the liberal professions, a figure which recurs in all our data—the data on Boston and fifteen other large cities as well as New York. The same holds for the clerks who in 1900 constituted some 6% or 7% of all Jews gainfully employed.

Let us now examine the figures for recent years. Here the material at our disposal is fuller and more reliable[12].

Occupational Distribution in Several Cities (1935-38) in Percent

City	No. of Gainfully Employed	Trade	Indus.	Profs.
Trenton	3,061	59.0	13.3	12.3
Passaic	4,370	43.2	22.5	12.3
Pittsburgh	25,000	60.4	13.8	9.5
Chicago	......	44.4	35.5	8.5
New London	597	54.5	16.2	13.7
Norwich	620	50.8	22.7	9.4
Stamford	1,540	52.4	15.0	12.5
New Orleans	2,590	48.6	14.5	12.5

Before analyzing this table it may be worthwhile to consider some more detailed data on the occupational structure of the Jews in several additional cities.

Occupational Structure of Gainfully Employed Jews in Detroit[13] (1935)

	Number	Percent.
Trade	15,850	54.1
Manufacturing	6,653	23.3
Professions	2,884	9.5
Domestic & personal service	2,910	9.6
Transportation & communication	627	2.2
Public service	257	0.9
Agriculture & unspecified	118	0.4
	29,299	100.0

The occupational distribution of Jews in New York, the largest Jewish community in the world, was somewhat different than in the cities previously mentioned.

Occupational Distribution of Jews in New York (1933) in percent[14]

Occupation	Percent.
Trade	30.5
Clerical occupations	21.6
Manufacturing & mechanical industries	30.6
Professions	7.4
Domestic & personal service	5.3
Transport & communication	3.7
Public service	0.9
	100.0

In this table clerks are listed separately. In order to draw a comparison between this and the previous table we must separate the clerks engaged in trade—two-thirds; and in industry—one-third. Thus some 45% of New York Jews are engaged in trade and some 37% to 38% in industry.

What conclusions can we draw from these tables? The highest percentage of Jews engaged in trade was in Pittsburgh—over 60% of all those gainfully employed; the smallest percentage was in Passaic—over 43%. Local factors are of course largely responsible for the fluctuation, but it is certain that in general the proportion of Jews engaged in trade is very high, much higher than among the population as a whole. We can assume that on the average the number of Jews engaged in trade in the entire country is no less than 50%, perhaps somewhat higher. This means that there are two-and-a-half times as many persons among Jews in trade (including the addition of two-thirds of the clerks, as per table 1) as there are among the population as a whole. This percentage is twice as high as the figure prevailing among Jews at the beginning of the century—one of the most characteristic and important aspects of the economic evolution of American Jewry in the last four decades.

The percentage of those engaged in industry was the highest among the Jews of New York—37-38%; Chicago was second with 35%; and Detroit was third with 23%. This is quite natural; the larger the city the greater the proportion of employees in industry. In all other cities the percentage of persons among Jews engaged in industry fluctuates from the minimum of somewhat over 13% in Trenton to the maximum of almost 23% in Norwich. Since almost half of all the Jews in America are concentrated in the two largest cities, New York and Chicago, and since the percentage among Jews of those engaged in industry exceeds 35%, and in the other cities the average is about 20%, we may infer that in the entire country approximately 28% of those gainfully employed among Jews are engaged in industry. This coincides with the percentage of those engaged in industry among the population as a whole.

The third group of occupations to be considered is that of the liberal professions. Here New York has the lowest percentage, 7.4%, and New London, the smallest of all the above-mentioned Jewish communities, has the largest percentage, 13.7%. It is an established fact that in the smaller cities the percentage of those engaged in the liberal professions and in trade is higher than in the larger cities. The tables make this plain. On the basis of the data in the above tables we can assume that the percentage among Jews of those engaged in the liberal professions amounts to approximately 10%.

On the basis of the preceding data we can set up a table which might give us a concrete picture of the occupational structure of the Jewish population in America and might tell us to what extent it differs from that of the non-Jewish population.

Occupational Structure among Jews and Non-Jews in the United States

Occupation	Gainfully Employed (percentage)	
	Jews	Gen. Pop.
Trade	50.0	20.8*
Industry	28.0	32.0
Professions	10.0	6.8
Domestic & personal service	6.0	10.3
Transportation & communication	2.5	9.2
Agriculture	2.0	18.0
Public service	1.5	2.9
	100.0	100.0

This table requires no comment. It must, however, be emphasized again that the data on the Jews do not pretend to be mathematically exact, but do offer, in a large measure, a true reflection of the real situation.

The figures on the participation of Jews in various economic branches as compared with that of the population as a whole are particularly instructive. It is in this arena that a competitive struggle ensues and friction between national groups is engendered. The following table[15] refers to New York City.

Jews constitute over 28% of the population in New York, but, as the table reveals, in trade in general and in several of its branches, especially, Jewish participation is much higher, notably high in connection with goods designed for mass consumption.

Jewish participation in wholesale trade is somewhat less than it is in retail trade. As for the wage workers, the situation is reversed. This is due to the fact that in the retail trade more unskilled labor is employed. The percentage of Jewish-owned retail stores selling consumer goods such as furniture and clothing is very high—three

*This figure includes two-thirds of the clerks as per table I.

TABLE 2

DISTRIBUTION OF JEWISH GAINFUL WORKERS IN WHOLESALE AND RETAIL TRADE IN NEW YORK CITY (1937)

Trade Classification	ALL GAINFUL WORKERS			JEWISH GAINFUL WORKERS			Percent of		
	Total	Number of Employers	Number of Employees	Total	Number of Employers	Number of Employees	Jewish Gainful Workers of Total	Jewish Employers of Total	Jewish Employees of Total
Trade—Total	573,780	—	—	236,820	—	—	41.4	—	—
Trade—Wholesale & Retail	544,841	103,854	440,987	234,320	67,450	166,870	43.0	64.19	37.8
Retail Trade	334,848	90,122	244,728	163,500	60,150	103,350	48.8	68.7	42.3
Food Stores	108,761	48,461	60,385	63,150	35,050	28,100	58.2	72.5	46.6
General Merchandise Group	61,870	3,485	58,385	11,200	1,700	9,500	18.1	48.8	16.4
Apparel Group	54,419	9,675	44,744	43,500	8,400	35,100	80.0	86.8	78.5
Automotive Group	13,762	2,675	11,087	1,700	200	1,500	12.4	7.5	13.5
Furniture—Household Group	15,370	2,752	12,618	9,100	2,400	6,700	59.3	87.3	53.0
Lumber—Building, Hardware Group	10,851	3,391	7,460	5,350	2,150	3,200	49.3	63.5	42.8
Drinking Places	16,865	4,219	12,646	3,500	1,000	2,500	20.8	23.7	19.8
Drug Stores	13,890	3,468	10,422	8,800	2,300	6,500	63.3	66.3	62.3
Other Retail Stores	36,833	10,808	26,025	16,000	6,250	9,750	43.5	57.7	37.5
Second Hand Stores	2,247	1,188	1,059	1,200	700	500	53.5	59.0	47.2
Wholesale Trade	209,993	13,732	196,261	70,820	7,300	63,520	33.7	53.2	32.3
Advertising	12,000	—	—	2,500	—	—	20.8	—	—
Related Trade Services (Warehousing, etc.)	16,939	—	—	—	—	—	—	—	—

times that of the percentage of Jews in the population. The same is true of the number of Jewish-owned drug stores—a shade less than two-thirds. It is interesting to note that here we have the only instance where the percentage of Jewish owners and the percentage of Jewish workers coincide. Among the clothing-store owners the percentage of Jews is almost as high as among furniture-store owners and here, too, the percentage of workers is close to that of owners. In all other branches the percentage of workers is considerably lower than the percentage of owners.

As to whether this high representation of Jews in the selling of consumer goods is true only of the large cities we find a clear answer in the census of Jews in Stamford, an industrial city in which the Jews constitute 5% of the population. Here are the figures on Jewish participation in several branches of trade[16].

Type of Trade	Number	Jewish	Percent.
Large food markets	5	5	100.0
Children's clothing	5	5	100.0
Men's clothing	16	15	93.8
Various men's articles	15	13	86.6
Jewelry stores	15	13	86.6
Drug stores	5	4	80.0
Women's clothing	30	22	73.3
Women's hats	10	6	60.0
Shoe stores	19	10	52.6
Egg and dairy stores	9	5	55.5
Furniture and radio	25	14	56.0
Department stores	7	3	42.8

These figures are probably typical of many medium-sized and small cities, although the subject requires further investigation.

Let us discuss briefly the participation of Jews in industry in New York. We shall consider only those branches of industry in which Jews constitute more than half of all the owners. In 1937 this participation was as follows[17]:

Branch of Industry	Percentage of Jews Among Employers	Percentage of Jews Among Employees
Of all employed	61.2	33.5
Fur industry	94.3	80.7
Clothing industry	87.0	53.8
Textiles	57.5	13.7
Wood products	61.5	35.1
Paper products	56.5	21.8
Glass and glass products	50.8	36.5

Jewish participation in the liberal professions in 1937 was as follows:[18]

	Percentage
Lawyers and judges	65.7
Musicians and music teachers	58.7
Physicians	55.7
Dentists	64.0
Artists and sculptors	50.8
Actors	43.1
Writers, reporters, editors	37.8
Architects	34.2
Teachers	29.4
Engineers	29.4
Chemists	28.6
Professors	11.1

In all but one of these classifications the percentage of Jews is greater (in four cases more than double) or approximately equal to the Jewish percentage in the general population. In one branch only, "professors," Jewish representation is hardly one-third of this percentage. The reasons for this are well-known and need not be elaborated upon. At any rate, the small percentage of Jewish professors is surely not due to a dearth of Jewish scholars.

Here are some figures on Jewish participation in the liberal professions in Greater Cleveland where the Jews constitute 7.7% of the general population[19]:

	Percentage
Pharmacists	26.1
Lawyers	23.1
Physicians	20.8
Dentists	17.8
Architects	5.0
Teachers	4.7
Engineers	2.2

New York and Cleveland can be accepted as typical of Jewish participation in the liberal professions in the large cities. Let us cite some figures on such participation in a smaller town—Stamford[20]. Of 110 lawyers, 48 were Jews (43.6%); of 101 physicians, 18 were Jews (17.8%); of 51 dentists, 18 were Jews (35.3%). It should be recalled that Jews constitute 5% of the general population in Stamford.

While the general occupational structure is an important factor in itself, it does not present a complete picture of the economic status of a given population. To an extent a person's occupation determines his social status; a tradesman usually occupies a higher rank than does a farm-worker, and a member of the liberal professions is higher in the social scale than a tradesman. However, in order to draw valid conclusions from these figures, it is necessary to subject the data on large groups to closer examination. Modern society is too complicated and too differentiated to enable us to arrive at a concrete picture of a given population by means of an overall generalization. The manufacturer who employs 5,000 workers and the one who employs only five fall under the same heading in these general group statistics. This is also true of the storekeeper whose turnover amounts to millions and the one whose turnover is negligible.

Of each 100 persons engaged in trade as employers in New York in 1937, there were:

	Among Jews	Among Non-Jews
Retailers	89.2	78.5
Wholesalers	10.8	21.5

It is true, of course, that in the larger cities there are some retailers whose turnover and profit are larger than those of wholesalers. In 1943, for example, one of the large New York Jewish-owned department stores had a turnover of 166 million dollars with a net profit of $3,732,000. But such cases are rare; the small storekeepers who work from 12 to 15 hours a day and make only a meager living, are to be found in the tens of thousands. While the non-Jewish wholesalers number twice as many as the Jewish, still of the non-Jews only one-fifth figure among the wholesalers.

Outside of New York the percentage of wholesalers among Jews is larger. Of each 100 persons engaged in trade in Pittsburgh and Passaic there were[21]:

	Pittsburgh	Passaic
Retailers	82.3	82.4
Wholesalers	17.7	17.6

It is obvious, of course, that the large city offers greater opportunities for the small retailer than does the small city.

III. THE SOCIAL DIFFERENTIATION OF THE JEWISH POPULATION

We have thus far discussed the distribution of the Jewish population according to occupation. Since each occupation includes both employers and wage-earners it is important to determine this class-differentiation.

To begin with let us look at the 1940 census, which offers a picture of the class-differentiation of the general population in the United States[22].

Wage or salary workers	76.9
Employers and own-account workers	18.9
Unpaid family workers	2.8
New workers	1.4
Total	100.0

We thus see almost four-fifths of the entire working population consists of wage-earners, that is, of people who derive their livelihood from physical or intellectual work and not from capital. This class-differentiation is typical of all highly developed industrial and commercial countries. Unfortunately we have no data on the entire Jewish population in America and we must confine ourselves to partial investigations of a number of individual cities. This, as we have already noted, will give us a general picture of the class-differentiation of American Jews.

Of each 100 engaged in 1937 in retail trade in New York there were[23]:

	Among Jews	Among Non-Jews
Employers	36.8	18.0
Employees	63.2	82.0
Total	100.0	100.0

In Wholesale Trade

	Among Jews	Among Non-Jews
Employers	10.3	4.7
Employees	89.7	95.3
Total	100.0	100.0

In the Entire Trade

	Among Jews	Among Non-Jews
Owners	28.8	11.7
Employees	71.2	88.3
Total	100.0	100.0

Here we have a picture reminiscent of the Jewish position in all of the European countries, regardless of their varying economic evolution. Among Jews there is everywhere a greater percentage of self-employed than among non-Jews. In trade, as a whole, it is twice that of non-Jews.

But even among Jews over 70% of all those engaged in trade are workers and white-collar employees. Among non-Jews the figure is 90%.

Of each 100 persons engaged in industry in 1937, there were[24]:

	Among Jews	Among Non-Jews
Employers	8.8	3.0
Employees	91.2	97.0
Total	100.0	100.0

Let us now compare the class-differentiation among Jews and non-Jews in two industries: the clothing industry, in which Jews constitute a large percentage, and the metal industry, in which Jews constitute a small percentage.

Of each 100 persons engaged in the garment industry in New York there were:

	Among Jews	Among Non-Jews
Employers	7.5	1.4
Employees	92.5	98.6
Total	100.0	100.0

Of each 100 persons engaged in the metal industry in New York in 1935, there were:

	Among Jews	Among Non-Jews
Employers	13.8	5.0
Employees	86.2	95.0
Total	100.0	100.0

From these data on the class distribution of Jews and non-Jews we can draw the following conclusion: though class-differentiation among Jews is not as sharp as among non-Jews, it is nevertheless a marked differentiation. In trade, the working elements constitute over 70% and in industry over 90%. In view of the fact that approximately 80% of all Jews gainfully employed in New York are engaged in these two economic activities, it is possible to arrive at a fairly accurate conclusion as to the class-differentiation of the entire Jewish population in New York.

We possess data on another economic activity in which a considerable number of Jews is engaged: the restaurant business. Of 17,000 Jews engaged in the restaurant business, there were 6,300 (37.1%) owners and 10,700 (62.9%) workers. Among non-Jews, out of 65,885 engaged in this business, there were 3,134 (4.7%) owners and 62,751 (95.3%) workers.

We have no information on the hotel business, barber shops, laundries, dyeing and dry-cleaning and domestic service. Some 85,000 Jews were engaged in all these activities.

In general we can safely assert that approximately 75% of the Jewish population in New York belong to the working class. In the entire country, as shown previously, the figure is over 77%, but in New York, the largest city in the country, the percentage of employees is surely higher than the average in the entire country.

Outside of New York the percentage of employees among Jews is much smaller. But before we take up the rest of the country, we must consider the differentiation among the employees themselves. The working class is not homogenous; there is a difference between the highest paid skilled workers or officials or professionals on the one hand, and the unskilled worker or farm-hand, on the other. And between these two extremes there are several strata of workers differing as to wages and conditions of work. We cannot discuss here in detail the structure of the Jewish working class in the United States; we lack adequate statistical material for such an undertaking. But we do have enough data to determine the basic distribution of the Jewish working elements as compared with the non-Jewish population. One of the fundamental divisions is that between the white-collar workers and all other workers. The following table casts some light on this question:

The Social Structure of the Population in the United States and among Jews.[25]

Social groups	In the entire country in 1930	Pittsburgh (1938)	Detroit (1935)	San Francisco (1938)
			AMONG JEWS	
Proprietors, managers, officials	9.3%	22.3%	26.8%	30.7%
Professions	7.4	10.8	7.6	11.4
Clerks and kindred workers	20.5	42.7	39.1	40.3
All other workers	62.8	24.2	26.5	17.6
	100.0	100.0	100.0	100.0

Thus we see that wage-earners and salaried employees constitute:

In the entire country 83.3%

Among Jews in Pittsburgh 66.9

Among Jews in Detroit 65.6

Among Jews in San Francisco 57.8

Among Jews the percentage of employees is approximately one-fifth less than among non-Jews (in San Francisco it is even one-fourth less). But whereas among Jews the white-collar workers constitute two-thirds of all workers and the manual workers only one-third, among the entire population the reverse is true—three-quarters of all employees are manual workers and only one-fourth belong to the white-collar category. This is one of the basic characteristics of the Jewish working class. Another characteristic is that it has a negligible percentage of unskilled workers.

The following table shows the distribution of manual workers in various categories among Jews and in the country as a whole[26]:

Type of worker	In the entire country (1930)	Detroit (1935)	San Francisco (1938)
Skilled	16.2%	8.9%	5.6%
Semi-skilled	20.5	14.8	10.8
Unskilled	26.1	2.8	1.2
Total	62.8%	26.5%	17.6%

Among the entire population the unskilled workers constitute two-fifths of all workers, but among the Jews they constitute only one-tenth in Detroit and one-fifteenth in San Francisco. This is probably typical of all Jewish workers in America. A thorough investigation among Jewish and non-Jewish youth in New York (ranging in age from 16 to 24) disclosed that only 3% of Jewish youth were children of unskilled workers whereas among non-Jews there were 18%.[27]

The percentage of skilled workers in the entire population was somewhat more than one-fourth of all workers, whereas among Jews it was one-third in Pittsburgh and approximately one-third in San Francisco. This is also true of the semi-skilled workers; among Jews their percentage is higher than among non-Jews.

Data on class-differentiation among Jews in many other cities confirm the figures on the medium-sized communities. The percentage of workers in these cities varies from 55% to 65% of all those gainfully employed. In the very small communities the percentage of Jewish wage earners is small. Here is a table showing the occupations of Jewish youth in an unnamed community[28]:

	Number	Percentage
Entered father's business	31	22.14
Became owners of their own business	31	22.14
Became professionals	27	19.29
Without an occupation	16	11.43
Occupation unknown	6	4.29
White-collar workers	26	18.57
Manual workers	3	2.14
	140	100.0

Here the number of employees among Jews is only 20%, that is, one-third as much as in the medium-sized cities and one-fourth as much as in New York. However, it must be borne in mind that only some 1.7% of all American Jews live in small communities.

From the point of view of class differentiation we have three types of Jewish communities: New York with approximately 75% employees, medium-sized cities with some 60% and small Jewish communities with some 20%. We can thus conclude that in the entire country the workers among Jews constitute 62% to 63% of all those gainfully employed. This is approximately one-fifth less than is the case among the en-tire population. As for the differentiation within the working elements among Jews, manual workers constitute no more than one-third of all employees, and two-thirds belong most likely to the white-collar category.

A general survey of the occupational distribution of Jews in the United States reveals that it is similar to the occupational distribution of Jews as it existed before the war in most countries in Europe, except in Poland where the number of those engaged in industry and the crafts exceeded the number of those engaged in trade. Among American Jews, it is true, the percentage of those engaged in the liberal professions is somewhat higher than it was among the Jews in most European countries.

However, class-differentiation in America goes much deeper than it did in Europe. The percentage of workers in the United States among Jews is almost twice as large as it was in most European countries. In America the white-collar workers constitute a majority of Jewish workers, whereas in most of the European countries—except in Western Europe—the number of manual workers was greater than that of the professionals.

REFERENCES

1. NILES CARPENTER, *Immigrants and their Children*. New York, 1920, p. 287.

2. MAURICE R. DAVIE, *World Emigration*. New York, 1936, p. 53.

3. CARPENTER, *Op. cit.*, p. 78.

4. CARPENTER, *Op. cit.*, pp. 22-23.

5. RUDOLF GLANZ, *Yidn in dem Kulturkrais fun Daitshn in Amerike in di 80-er yorn* (Yiddish). "Yiwo-bleter," January-February, 1945, p. 86.

6. B. WEINSTEIN, *Yidishe Unions in Amerike* (Yiddish). New York, p. 44.

7. *Ibid.*, pp. 46-47.

8. B. HOFFMAN, *Fuftzig yor Cloakmaker Union* (Yiddish) . New York, 1936.

9. I. MARKENS, *The Hebrews in America*. 1888, pp. 156-158.

10. FREDERICK A. BUSHEC, *Ethnic Factors in the Population of Boston*. 1903.

11. N. GOLDBERG, *Occupational Patterns of American Jews*. "The Jewish Review," April, 1945, p. 11.

12. *Jewish Population Studies*. Conference on Jewish Relations. 1943, p. 189.

13. HENRY J. MEYER, *The Economic Structure of the Jewish Community in Detroit*. "Jewish Social Studies." April, 1940, p. 131.

14. MAURICE KARPF, *Jewish Community Organization in the United States*. New York, 1938, p. 14.

15. Manuscript. "Conference on Jewish Relations."

16. S. KOENIG, *The Socio-economic Structure of an American Jewish Community*. In "Jews in a Gentile World." New York, 1942, p. 200.

17. Manuscript. "Conference on Jewish Relations."

18. *Ibid.*

19. LEE J. LEVINGER, *Jews in the Professions in Ohio*. "Jewish Social Studies." October, 1940, p. 406.

20. S. KOENIG, *Op. cit.*, p. 212.

21. *Jewish Population Studies,* pp. 104, 133.

22. U. S. Bureau of the Census, 16th Census of the United States. 1940, *Population,* vol. III.

23. Manuscript "Conference on Jewish Relations."

24. *Ibid.*

25. MAURICE TAYLOR, *The Jewish Community of Pittsburgh.* 1941, p. 122.

26. *Ibid.*

27. NETTIE PAULINE MCGILL, *Some Characteristics of Jewish Youth in New York.* "Jewish Social Service Quarterly." December, 1937, xi, 1935.

28. D. G. MANDELBAUM, *A Study of the Jews of Urbana,* "Jewish Social Service Quarterly." December, 1935, p. 230.

JEWISH MIGRATIONS DURING THE LAST HUNDRED YEARS

L. Hersch

I. THE GROWTH OF MODERN JEWISH EMIGRATION

The hundred-year period from the 1840's to the 1940's was the epoch of the greatest migration in human history in general, as well as in the history of the Jewish people —a people with a long past of mass wanderings. For the Jews, as well as for other modern peoples, it was a period of all types of migration. Great masses of Jews left the villages and small towns to settle in the big cities. The Jewish population, originally a small town and village population, was transformed into a mainly urban population, and in the old countries of Jewish settlement there arose great Jewish centers such as Warsaw, Lodz, Budapest, Vienna, Berlin, Odessa, Kiev and Moscow, each of them with a Jewish population probably larger than that of Jerusalem under King Solomon. Within the boundaries of the old countries of settlement the Jews migrated from one region to another: for instance, from Alsace to France, from Poznan province to Germany, from Galicia to Austria, from Lithuania and White Russia to Poland and Southern Russia, from Central Russia (as a result of expulsions) to the former Pale of Settlement, and later, beginning with the First World War, from the former Pale of Settlement to Central Russia and Siberia. To these must be added the continental Jewish migrations in Europe, which usually moved from east to west, at first creating the Ashkenazic communities in Holland and England and later a numerous Jewish population in various Western European countries, with such great centers as the Jewish communities of London and Paris. The Jewish urban centers are discussed in the article *The Jewish Population of the World* in this volume; as for the other internal and continental Jewish migrations, available statistical data are scant, and are yet to be worked out systematically. Here we shall deal almost exclusively with the overseas migrations which, with the possible exception of the internal migrations to the cities, are by far the most important type of migrations in Jewish history.

1. THE THREE PERIODS OF EMIGRATION

The last hundred years of Jewish migrations can be divided into three great eras: the first, the German period, extended from the 1830's to the 1870's; the second, the East European period, covered the last quarter of the 19th and the first quarter of the 20th century; the third, the Central European period, began in 1925.

A. *The German Period:* During the German era Jewish emigration originated chiefly in Bavaria and the region of Poznan as well as in Bohemia, and was directed towards England, France and especially to the United States. It began in the 1830's and reached its climax in the 1840's and the early 1850's. This was likewise the era of the greatest non-Jewish emigration from Germany, where the industrial revolution and the agrarian crisis had brought misery and starvation to the peasants and artisans. Later both the Jewish and non-Jewish emigration from Germany subsided, and in the 1870's Jewish emigration from Germany stopped completely. Germany gradually became a country of immigration for Poles, Ukrainians and East-European Jews, and after the First World War Jewish immigration into Germany increased, a situation which prevailed until the advent of Nazism.

The German-Jewish emigrants to the United States were actually the forerunners of the later Jewish mass emigration from Eastern Europe. Judged by these later standards the Jewish emigration from Germany was not large, considering the relatively small number of German Jews. No general statistics of this migration exist, but it can be assumed that no less than 50,000 Jews left Germany in that period. As a result a number of small Jewish communities in Germany entirely disappeared, although this first wave of emigration had no destructive effect on the Jewish community in Germany as a whole.

B. *The East European Period:* The East European wave of Jewish emigration came almost exclusively from the former Russian empire, Galicia and Romania. The emigrants were chiefly Lithuanian, White Russian, Polish, and Romanian Jews, and at first the bulk of them, like the German-Jewish emigrants, went to the United States. Later, in much smaller numbers, they went to Argentina, Canada, South Africa and Palestine. Russia, which had just abolished serfdom (1861), was going through an economic upheaval marked by capitalist expansion, a grave agrarian crisis, and social and political struggles. Russian peasants by

the millions rushed to the endless expanses of Siberia; the village population of the western provinces of the empire, chiefly Poles and Lithuanians, began to emigrate to America (or Germany). The Jewish masses of these regions migrated in even larger numbers than did their gentile neighbors.

The 1880's marked an extraordinary upswing of emigration from all corners of Europe. The Jews, in addition, had the incentive of fleeing from the brutal wave of pogroms which was Russian czarism's answer to the revolutionary movement of the *Narodnaya Volya* that culminated in the assassination of Czar Alexander II in 1881. The great historic overseas emigration of East-European Jews now began. True, a handful of pioneers emigrated to Palestine and founded the first Jewish colonies there (*Rishon le-Zion, Zichron Yaakov, Rosh Pinah, Petach Tikvah*), while others, for example, the group *Am Olam*, hoped to establish socialist communes in America. But the mass of the people simply fled to America in order to earn a livelihood and to achieve a secure existence. From 1880 to 1900 more than 500,000 Jews emigrated to the United States. A small number of Jews went to other American countries and even to South Africa. But all this was only a beginning; the real Jewish mass emigration came later.

The period between 1900 and 1914 witnessed what was beyond doubt the greatest migration in Jewish history. During the ten years preceding the First World War some 1,500,000 Europeans left the shores of Europe annually to seek work and living space in North and South America, in South Africa and in Australia. Almost one-tenth of all these European emigrants were East European Jews who, like the overwhelming majority of the other overseas emigrants, went chiefly to the United States. In July, 1898, the United States initiated the practice of registering immigrants not only according to their countries of origin, but also according to their "race or people," the Jews being classified as

"Hebrew." * Thus, beginning with this date, we have systematic and detailed statistical data concerning Jewish immigration into the United States. Between 1899 and 1914, 1,486,000 Jews immigrated into the United States; of these 1,200,000 came between 1904 and 1914. During the same East European Jews who emigrated in the same period to England, France, Holland, Belgium, Switzerland, Scandinavia and other European countries, in the sixteen year period 1899-1914 nearly 2,000,000 Jews left Eastern Europe, a number equal in size to the population of Norway in

JEWISH AND GENERAL IMMIGRATION INTO THE UNITED STATES
FROM 1899 TO 1944

Fiscal Years*	Absolute Numbers		Percentage of Jewish Immigrants		Fiscal Years*	Absolute Numbers		Percentage of Jewish Immigrants
	Jews	Total				Jews	Total	
1899	37,415	311,715	12.0		1923	49,719	522,919	9.5
1900	60,764	448,572	13.5		1924	49,989	706,896	7.1
1901	58,098	487,918	11.9		1925	10,292	294,314	3.5
1902	57,688	648,743	8.9		1926	10,267	304,488	3.4
1903	76,203	857,046	8.9		1927	11,483	335,175	3.4
1904	106,236	812,870	13.1		1928	11,639	307,255	3.8
1905	129,910	1,026,499	12.7		1929	12,479	279,678	4.5
1906	153,748	1,100,735	14.0		1930	11,526	241,700	4.8
1907	149,182	1,285,349	11.6		1931	5,692	97,139	5.9
1908	103,387	782,870	13.2		1932	2,755	35,576	7.7
1909	57,551	751,786	7.7		1933	2,372	23,068	10.3
1910	84,260	1,041,570	8.1		1934	4,134	29,470	14.0
1911	91,223	878,587	10.4		1935	4,837	34,956	13.8
1912	80,595	838,172	9.6		1936	6,252	36,329	17.2
1913	101,330	1,197,892	8.5		1937	11,352	50,244	22.6
1914	138,051	1,218,480	11.3		1938	19,736	67,895	29.0
1915	26,497	326,700	8.1		1939	43,450	82,998	52.3
1916	15,108	298,826	5.1		1940	36,945	70,756	52.2
1917	17,342	295,403	5.9		1941	23,737	51,776	45.8
1918	3,672	110,618	3.3		1942	10,608	28,781	36.9
1919	3,055	141,132	2.2		1943	4,705	23,725	19.8
1920	14,292	430,001	3.3		1944	....	28,551	....
1921	119,036	805,228	14.8					
1922	53,524	309,556	17.3		Total	2,082,136	20,059,957	10.4

*From July 1st of the preceding year to June 30th of the year stated.

period Jewish emigration to Argentina and Canada also grew considerably; in the course of the ten years preceding the First World War almost 80,000 Jews immigrated into Argentina and more than 60,000 into Canada. A Jewish community of more than 50,000 persons was created in South Africa (47,000 according to the census of 1911; 59,000 in 1918). During the same period approximately 20,000 Jews emigrated to Palestine. Including no less than 250,000

*This classification was discontinued at the end of 1943, rendering unavailable official data on Jewish immigration into the United States beginning with that date.

those years. Three quarters of this great mass of people settled in the United States.

Of the immigrants in the United States, 1,066,000 came directly from Russia, 240,000 from Austria-Hungary, and 63,000 from Romania (these figures do not include those emigrants who, before coming to the United States, had settled in other countries—England, Canada, etc.). Assuming that the immigration to the United States represented five-sixths of the total Jewish overseas emigration and three-quarters of the total Jewish emigration, the following table is obtained for the sixteen years before the First World War:

JEWISH EMIGRATION FROM EASTERN EUROPE DURING 1899-1914

	From Russia	From Austria-Hungary	From Romania
Overseas	1,279,000	288,000	75,000
Total	**1,421,000**	**320,000**	**84,000**

The average annual figures of Jewish emigrants during the same period as compared with the Jewish population of the countries of emigration is shown in the following table (number of emigrants per 1,000 Jewish inhabitants):

number of Jews who took refuge in various European countries is unknown, but doubtless quite large. Thus, the total Jewish emigration in that twelve-month period amounted to from 200,000 to 250,000.

In spite of this extraordinary mass migra-

NUMBER OF JEWISH EMIGRANTS PER 1,000 JEWISH INHABITANTS
(Average number per year during 1899-1914)

	From Russia	From Austria-Hungary	From Romania
Emigrated to U. S. A.	13.0	7.2	14.7
Emigrated to other overseas countries	2.6	1.5	3.0
Emigrated to European countries	1.7	0.9	1.9
Total	**17.3**	**9.6**	**19.6**

Although Jewish emigration from Austria-Hungary reached high proportions, it was not as high as the emigration of other ethnic groups from the old Hapsburg empire. Emigration from the Russian empire and Romania, where the Jews lived in conditions reminiscent of medieval times, was twice as high as from Austria-Hungary and considerably higher than from the other ethnic groups. From July, 1905 to July, 1906, the year of the wave of pogroms by which czarism countered the revolution of October, 1905, Jewish emigration from Russia was twice the average for the years between 1899 and 1914. This was the culminating year in Jewish emigration: 154,000 Jews emigrated to the United States, 13,500 to Argentina, more than 7,000 to Canada, 3,500 to Palestine and a considerable number to South Africa. The

tion, which in a period of sixteen years shifted an average of 1.7% of the population every year, the Jewish population of the czarist empire (as well as of Russian Poland, White Russia, Lithuania and Ukraine) did not materially decrease for the reason that the same period was marked by a great natural increase of population among the Jews.

The First World War put an abrupt end to the great overseas migration, both Jewish and non-Jewish. A new period in East European Jewish migration began.

For the Russian Jews the period 1915-1920 was one of frequently tragic and arduous inland migrations from west to east. These were caused, in the first place, by the brutal expulsions of the Jewish population ordered by Russian military authorities from areas in the theatre of war operations;

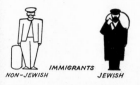

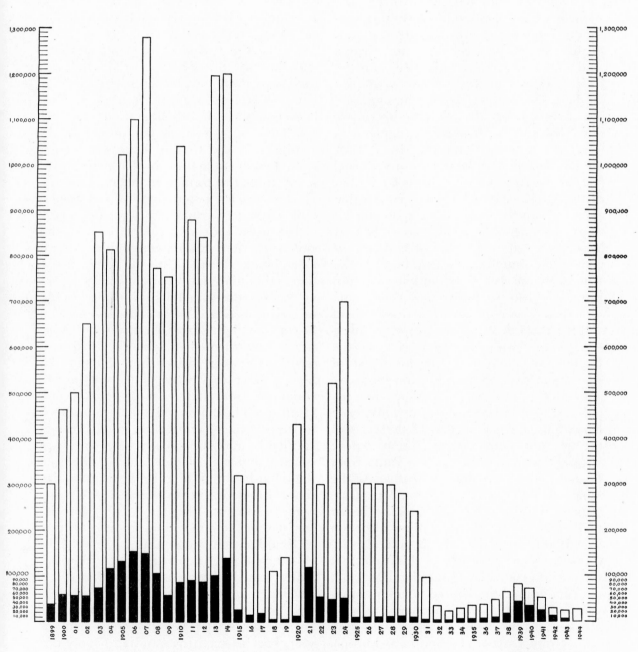

(*Chart by E. Schloss*)

THE IMMIGRATION CHART ABOVE SHOWS JEWISH IMMIGRATION (REPRESENTED BY THE BLACK PORTIONS)
IN RELATION TO THE TOTAL IMMIGRATION INTO THE UNITED STATES FROM 1899 TO 1944.

in other cases, they were merely flights or evacuations before the arrival of the enemy. The war—and later the Revolution—finally broke down the walls of the stifling Pale of Settlement and Jewish masses by the hundreds of thousands moved into the cities of Central Russia. Nevertheless, despite all the hardships and dangers involved, the overseas stream of emigration was not completely interrupted even during the war. In the six years between 1915 and 1920, a total of 80,000 Jews immigrated into the United States. But this was only a drop in the bucket as compared to the immigration before 1914 or to the considerably intensified desire of the masses to emigrate as a result of the devastation caused by the war, the Revolution and the terrors of the cruel pogroms during the time of the Civil War in the Ukraine. It is for these reasons that as soon as hostilities ended, Jewish emigration recommenced on an extraordinarily large scale. Large numbers of middle class people and intellectuals fled from Soviet Russia to the Far East and to Western Europe, chiefly to Berlin and Paris. Considerably greater masses went from Poland and Romania to Western Europe and overseas. The Jewish immigration into the United States, which in the fiscal year of 1920 (from June 30, 1919 to June 30, 1920), amounted to only 14,000, jumped to 119,-000 in the fiscal year of 1921. This was a figure almost equal to that of the years of the greatest Jewish immigration before 1914. Of this number 75,000 came from Poland and 18,000 from Romania. At the same time the emigration to Argentina, Canada, South Africa and Palestine began to increase. General emigration, although to a lesser extent than the Jewish, also increased. It was precisely at this time that the various countries of immigration, and, most important, the United States, promulgated a number of restrictive laws and soon almost entirely closed their gates to emigrants from Eastern and Southern Europe. Nevertheless, in the course of the first three years of the new immigration policy, from 1922 to 1924, about 153,000 Jews immi-

grated into the United States, or over 50,-000 every year. In other countries Jewish immigration during these years at first increased; between 1922 and 1924 nearly 30,000 Jews immigrated into Argentina, 11,500 into Canada and 28,000 into Palestine, etc. Following the further restriction of immigration into the United States in 1924 Jewish immigration fell to 10,000 a year and later to a much smaller number. So ended the period of free immigration and the East European period in the history of modern Jewish migrations.

C.   *The Central European Period:* The latest period of Jewish migrations was the result of the growth of fascism and anti-Semitism in the Central European countries. Jewish emigration in that period differed from the former in many respects: 1) The Jewish population of the Soviet Union, granted equal rights with the rest of the population and subject to the general restrictions against emigration, ceased to emigrate abroad. Thus the White Russian, Ukrainian and Central Russian Jews no longer constituted a part of the Jewish migrating masses. 2) Great masses of Jews began to emigrate from Germany and Austria to save themselves from the Nazi persecutions or were driven out of their old homes; later they were joined by Jewish emigrants from Italy, Czechoslovakia and Hungary. These new emigrants were added to the stream of emigration from Poland, Lithuania and Romania, where the reactionary and anti-Semitic forces were on the offensive. 3) While the Jewish populations of these countries were perhaps more eager to emigrate than the Russian Jews in szarist times, the most important countries of immigration were almost completely closed to them. In particular, the United States ceased to serve as the chief goal for Jewish emigration: in the period between 1925 and 1930 the United States received an average of 11,281 Jewish immigrants a year, but between 1931 and 1936 only the insignificant number of 4,340 a year. In the years preceding the Second World War the number of Jewish immigrants into the

JEWISH IMMIGRATION INTO VARIOUS COUNTRIES

Year	Canada	Argentina	Year	Canada	Argentina	South Africa	Brazil	Uruguay
1900	2,765	. . . .	1922	2,793	7,198	. . . .	. . . .	. . . .
1901	1,015	. . . .	1923	4,255	13,700	. . . .	. . . .	. . . .
1902	2,066	. . . .	1924	4,459	7,800	773	. . . .	. . . .
1903	3,727	. . . .	1925	4,014	6,920	1,353	2,624	. . . .
1904	7,715	4,000	1926	4,863	7,534	1,479	3,906	. . . .
1905	7,127	7,516	1927	4,766	5,584	1,752	5,167	771
1906	6,584	13,500	1928	3,848	6,812	2,293	4,055	1,500
1907	7,712	2,518	1929	4,164	5,986	2,788	5,610	2,000
1908	1,636	5,444	1930	3,421	7,805	1,881	3,558	1,600
1909	3,182	8,557	1931	649	3,553	885	1,940	1,250
1910	5,146	6,581	1932	772	1,801	676	2,049	765
1911	5,322	6,378	1933	943	1,962	745	3,317	500
1912	7,387	13,416	1934	624	2,215	1,123	4,010	1,205
1913	11,252	10,860	1935	880	3,169	1,078	1,759	560
1914	3,107	3,693	1936	619	4,261	3,330	3,450	1,262
1915	65	606	1937	584	4,178	954	2,003	1,530
1916	136	. . . .	1938	890	4,856	. . . .	530	3,115
1917	32	. . . .	1939	1,623	1,833	566	4,601	2,170
1918	22	. . . .	1940	626	932	. . . .	2,416	373
1919	116	280	1941	388	1,164	. . . .	1,500	639
1920	2,763	2,071	1942	270	192	. . . .	108	138
1921	8,404	4,095	1943	. . . .	. . . .	. . . .	11	. . . .
Total				132,732	188,970	21,676	52,614	19,378

United States sprang up suddenly to 19,736 in 1938, 43,450 in 1939 and 36,945 in 1940, to drop in 1941 to 23,737, in 1942 to 10,608, and in 1943 to 4,705.

But not only in the United States, indeed everywhere, immigration was placed under partial or almost complete restriction. Whereas as late as 1923, 14,000 Jews immigrated into Argentina, between 1925 and 1930 the yearly average was less than 7,000, between 1931 and 1935 around 2,500, over 4,000 between 1936 and 1938, and 1,000 on the average from 1939 to 1942. In 1921, 8,404 Jews immigrated into Canada; only half of this figure (4,219) immigrated into that country on the average each year between 1924 and 1930, and not even one-tenth (more than 700) on the average each year between 1931 and 1942. 4) The Jews who were compelled to emigrate were no longer able to choose their destination; they had to go where they would be admitted. Jews who sought to save themselves by emigration were ready to go to the end of the world. They suffered and struggled, got rid of their possessions for a song, begged for the chance to breathe the air of desert lands and to earn their daily bread by the heaviest toil. 5) Those who managed to obtain emigration permits went to countries whose names they had hardly heard of. Up to the time of this latest period, Jewish overseas emigration had been extremely concentrated; it was directed to only a few countries and about five-sixths of all Jewish overseas emigration went to the United States. Now Jewish emigration was more widely scattered than ever before in all of Jewish history. There is almost no country in the world in which Jewish emigrants have not sought admission. In addition to North America, Argentina and South Africa, small numbers of Jewish immigrants have been admitted to Mexico, Cuba, Brazil, Bolivia, Uruguay, Paraguay, Venezuela, Chile, Australia, New Zealand, China, Japan, etc., and this list does not include the Western European countries and the Near East. 6) Only one country, Palestine, remained for a long time open to substantial numbers of Jewish immigrants. When Hitler came to power the emigration to Palestine increased considerably. In 1933, 30,327 Jews immigrated into Palestine; in 1934, 42,359 and in 1935, 61,854. The German Jews not only constituted a large part of these immigrants (6,941 in 1934, 7,447 in 1935 and 8,180 in 1936), but brought large amounts of capital into the country, founded various enterprises and, at least temporarily, raised Palestine's capacity for receiving newcomers. As a result the number of Jewish immigrants from other countries, especially Poland, was greatly increased (18,000 Polish Jews came to Palestine in 1934 and 27,000 in 1935) and Palestine came to occupy first place among the various countries of Jewish immigration.

2. GENERAL SURVEY

It is not possible to give a detailed statistical summing up of the Jewish migrations in the last hundred years. The data from the countries of emigration are not exact as a rule; they are available only in a small number of countries and even there they cover only a relatively short period. The same is true for the European countries of immigration. The main source of information is supplied by the data from those countries into which immigration was controlled at the debarkation points and where Jewish immigrants were registered as Jewish. As has been said above, this was the case in the United States since July 1898. Since 1901 there have been official (although summary) statistics covering immigration into Canada, Palestine since June 1921, South Africa since 1924. All the other data concerning the various countries of immigration are based on estimates or have been collected by Jewish social organizations (ICA, HIAS). Taking all such sources into account, the following general survey can be given regarding Jewish migrations from the 1830's to the 1940's.

From this table it appears that in the course of the period covered more than 4,100,000 European Jews left their old

JEWISH EMIGRATION: 1830-1943

	To U. S. A.	To other Countries outside Europe	To Europe	Total
First Period (German) up to 1870	50,000	. . . .	10,000	60,000
Second Period (Eastern Europe)				
1881-1898	550,000	50,000	100,000	700,000
1899-1914	1,486,000	250,000	250,000	1,986,000
1915-1924	352,000	50,000	100,000	502,000
Total: 1881-1924	2,388,000	350,000	450,000	3,188,000
Third Period (Central European) 1925-1943	245,000	580,000	100,000	925,000
Grand total 1830-1943	2,683,000	930,000	560,000	4,173,000

homes; of these 3,600,000 emigrated overseas, and more than 550,000 to other countries in Europe (chiefly to England, Germany and France). About 2,700,000 emigrated to the United States and almost 1,000,000 to other overseas countries, including Palestine. Despite the fact that in the last period the gates of the United States were almost completely closed, nearly two-thirds of all Jewish emigrants (63%) or almost three-fourths (72%) of Jewish emigrants overseas went there in the last hundred years. Even during the "closed" period (1925-1943) nearly 245,000 Jews entered the United States. Among the other overseas countries Palestine in that period occupied the first place, with a total immigration of about 300,000 Jews; of these about 66,000 between 1925 and 1931, over 144,000 between 1932 and 1935; and nearly 90,000 between 1936 and 1943.

We shall not undertake to draw up even an approximate summary of the number of Jews who emigrated from the various countries; first, as mentioned above, because of the lack of statistical data concerning Jews in those countries; second, because the countries of origin of the Jewish immigrants are indicated by statistics only in the United States (although incomplete), in Palestine, and South Africa. But since the data concerning the countries of emigration for the Jewish immigrants into the United States embrace the period of the greatest Jewish migrations (after 1899) and account for almost half of all the Jewish migrants of the last hundred years, we shall analyze them in a separate chapter. As for Palestine, it can be observed that of its 279,000 Jewish immigrants in the sixteen years between 1922 and 1937, 120,000, or 43%, came from Poland. In the first years of that period the number of Polish immigrants, like the number of all immigrants, was smaller, but in proportion greater than in the later years when Jewish emigration from Germany to Palestine increased. The same is true of emigration to Palestine from other countries (except Yemen), as can be seen from the tables on succeeding pages.

For the period between 1934 and 1937, emigration from Germany constituted almost one-fifth of the total Jewish immigration into Palestine and in 1937 even more than one-third (34%). The situation was similar as regards South Africa, where the Jewish immigrants had previously come chiefly from Lithuania (especially from the Kovno region). During the period 1924 to 1932, the Lithuanian immigrants constituted 55.5% of all Jewish immigrants into South Africa. During the same period the Polish immigrants were 16% of the total, and the German immigrants only 0.6%. In 1933 the Lithuanian immigrants constituted less than one-third (32%) and in 1934 only one-fourth (26.6%) of the total Jewish immigration into South Africa, while the number of German-Jewish immigrants there rose suddenly to more than one-fourth (27%) in 1933 and in 1934 reached 40%; in that year more German Jews than Lithuanian Jews emigrated to South Africa. The ratio of Jewish immigrants from Germany to the United States rose even higher: during the period of free immigration (1899-1924) they constituted less than 1% (0.8%) of the total of Jewish immigrants (15,000 during the twenty-six-year period). After the introduction of the quota system which so sharply reduced Jewish emigration from Eastern Europe and after the victory of Nazism in Germany, the percentage of Jewish immigrants from Germany, and from Central Europe in general, increased very rapidly. In 1933 the percentage of German Jews among all Jewish emigrants to the United States was still insignificant (3.04%) but in 1934 the percentage was 43.2%, in 1935 34.8%, 52.53% in 1936 and 53.81% in 1940. It dropped in the subsequent years to an average of about 15%.

II. THE GREAT MIGRATION
(1899-1924)

1. ANALYSIS OF JEWISH EMIGRATION
TO THE UNITED STATES

As has been said, we possess detailed United States statistics for the period of

PALESTINE: JEWISH IMMIGRATION 1922-1943

Year	Total Immigration	Re-Emigration	Net Immigration
1922	7,844	1,503	6,341
1923	7,421	3,466	3,955
1924	12,856	2,037	10,819
1925	33,801	2,151	31,650
1926	13,081	7,365	5,716
1927	2,713	5,071	- 2,358
1928	2,178	2,168	10
1929	5,249	1,746	3,503
1930	4,944	1,636	3,308
1931	4,075	666	3,409
1932	9,553	. . . . . .	9,553
1933	30,327	. . . . . .	30,327
1934	42,359	. . . . . .	42,359
1935	61,854	396	61,458
1936	29,727	773	28,954
1937	10,536	889	9,647
1938	12,868	1,095	11,773
1939	16,405	1,019	15,386
1940	4,547	693	3,854
1941	3,647	426	3,221
1942	2,194	130	2,064
1943	8,507	. . . . . .	8,507
Total	**326,686**	**33,230**	**293,456**

PRINCIPAL COUNTRIES OF PREVIOUS RESIDENCE OF JEWISH IMMIGRANTS IN PALESTINE

	1934	1935	1936	1937	1938	1939	1940	1941	1942	1943	1944
Poland	18,028	27,291	11,596	3,636	3,269	1,759	878	357	376	1,999	822
Germany and Austria	7,869	8,408	8,761	3,601	6,753	9,490	791	91	128	96	488
Romania	2,031	3,596	1,444	314	48	424	940	783	78	173	3,944
Czechoslovakia	860	1,397	642	220	519	2,314	492	12	53	75	475
Lithuania	1,124	1,967	783	218	414	151	209	707	10	......	......
Latvia	759	1,042	507	110	160	94	70	6	......	......	......
France	......	......	544	89	129	105	44	6	......	......	......
Turkey	495	764	294	44	52	12	56	124	284	2,158	1,521
Yemen and Aden	1,964	1,425	754	337	334	148	19	42	231	2,421	1,822
Iraq	......	......	345	......	......	......	......	......	576	359	386
Greece	1,598	2,122	389	......	......	......	......	......	14	......	......
U. S. A.	1,171	1,638	357	172	94	36	8	3	......	......	......
Other Countries	6,480	12,204	3,311	1,795	1,156	1,872	1,060	1,516	444	1,226	5,206
Total	42,359	61,854	29,727	10,536	12,868	16,405	4,547	3,647	2,194	8,507	14,464

the greatest Jewish migration, comprising a mass of about 2,000,000 Jewish immigrants, almost one-half of the total Jewish emigration of the last hundred years. These statistics are only part of the general immigration statistics of the United States, which was also the most important immigration reservoir for the other European nations (if the Russian migrations to Siberia are excepted). Thus we have uniform comparative statistics concerning the Jewish and non-Jewish emigrants of various nations, and are able to discover which features of the Jewish immigration are general, and which are specifically Jewish. Of the forty-five year period (1899-1943) covered by United States immigration statistics, we shall discuss only the period of free immigration (1899-1924) during which about 1,838,000 Jews immigrated into the United States and especially the period of by far the greatest Jewish migration (1899-1914), during which 1,500,000 Jews came to the United States. We shall do this for three reasons: first, because this is the period of the greatest Jewish migration; second, because it was a period of *free* migration. The later years of regulated and restricted immigration created an artificial selection among the immigrants (both Jewish and non-Jewish), and created artificial similarities and differences that are more often reflections of United States legislation than characteristics of the migrating masses themselves. Third, because after 1933, as a result of restricted immigration, the United States statistics are less detailed than in the period of free immigration. However, we shall call attention to the important changes that took place later in comparison with the "classical" period of modern Jewish migrations.

The absolute numbers of Jewish immigrants into the United States fluctuated sharply from year to year, depending on the American economic situation and on the anti-Jewish persecutions in the countries of emigration, as well as in conformity with the general tendency towards increase in the period of 1899-1914, the effects of

the war, and the restriction of immigration. In the forty-five year period 1899-1943, the lowest figure of Jewish immigrants (2,372) was recorded in the fiscal year of 1933 and the highest (153,748) in the fiscal year of 1906. All in all, as to the absolute number of immigrants, the Jews occupy second place among the various classifications (1,486,000 for the period 1899-1914) since 1899; they follow the Italians who come first with 3,207,000 immigrants for the same period, and are ahead of the Poles (1,403,000), the Germans (1,047,000), and the British (623.000).

The percentage of Jews among the immigrants fluctuated from year to year, but much less than did their absolute numbers. For the entire period of 1899-1914 it varied between 14% in 1906 and 7.7% in 1909. During this period of the greatest Jewish migration the percentage of Jewish immigrants among all immigrants into the United States was on the average 10.9%, one Jew to about eight non-Jews. During the period between the two World Wars, the percentage of Jewish immigrants fluctuated quite violently—from 2.2% in 1919 to 52.3% in 1939. On the average during the 45 year period from 1899 to 1943 the Jews constituted 10.4% of the total immigration.

A. *Countries of Origin:* An analysis of Jewish immigration for the period 1899-1914 as to the countries of origin reveals that 92% of the entire immigration came directly from the Russian empire, Austria-Hungary and Romania. If we include the immigrants whose last residence was Great Britain and Canada, but almost all of whom originally had come from Eastern Europe, we reach the conclusion that 95% of the

PREVIOUS RESIDENCE OF JEWISH IMMIGRANTS IN THE UNITED STATES (1899-1914)

Country	Number	Percentage
Russia	1,066,000	71.7
Austria-Hungary	240,000	16.2
Romania	63,000	4.2
Great Britain	60,000	4.0
Canada	18,000	1.2
Germany	10,000	0.7

great immigration which created the present American Jewish community consisted of East European Jews. The United States immigration statistics for the years 1921-1924, which classified immigrants according to the post-war boundaries of the European countries of emigration, somewhat modify the picture. Of the 272,000 Jews who immigrated during those four years, 123,000 (45.3%) came from Poland; 44,000 (16%) from Russia; 38,000 (14%) from Romania (including Bessarabia); 7,600 (2.8%) from Czechoslovakia; 4,900 (1.8%) from Hungary; 3,900 (1.4%) from Austria; 4,300 (1.6%) from Germany; 6,100 (2.2%) from England; 17,000 (6.3%) from Canada. This means that 75.3% (or nearly 84% if we include the immigrants whose last residence was England or Canada) have come from Eastern Europe. After the restriction of immigration and especially after the advent of Nazism in Germany the picture radically changed. The main bulk of the Jewish immigration to the United States began to come from the countries of Central (and Western) Europe.

B. *Concentration in Large Cities:* It is interesting to note that despite the changes in the make-up of the mass of Jewish immigrants in the course of the last hundred years, the majority consistently concentrated in the large urban centers, especially in New York. The same tendency was also true of the non-Jewish immigrants. But the Jews concentrated in large cities to a much greater extent than the non-Jewish immigrants. Of the 1,486,000 Jewish immigrants in the period 1899-1914, 928,000 or somewhat less than two-thirds (62%) settled in New York. Earlier, the percentage of Jewish immigrants who settled in New York was doubtless larger. During the course of the period under consideration, the percentage kept decreasing: 1900—72%; 1910—62%; 1914—57%. But after the restriction of immigration, when entry preference was given to the nearest relatives of previous immigrants,

Courtesy Joint Distribution Committee

JEWISH REFUGEES ARRIVING IN NEW YORK FROM GERMANY, 1938

the proportion rose to 60% in 1931 and 1932 and 62% in the late '30's.

C. *Character of Jewish Immigration:* Another characteristic of Jewish immigration to the United States (as well as to other countries outside Europe) is that such immigration remained almost entirely permanent, very few Jewish immigrants returning to their countries of origin. It was only in 1908 that the United States government began to keep a record of emigration from the United States. From that date till 1943 the emigration of the foreign-born equalled approximaely one-third of the immigration (34.4%). Among Jewish immigrants, however, emigration amounted to only 4.6%; over 95% of the Jewish immigrants remained permanently settled. This difference is particularly great between the Jewish and non-Jewish immigrants from the East European countries: the proportion of re-emigrants among the Jews was one-fifth that of the Lithuanians, one-eighth that of the Poles, one-tenth that of the Russians and one-thirteenth that of the Hungarians and Romanians. In the years 1935-1937 when the total re-emigration from the United States amounted to 83% of the immigration within the same period, Jewish re-emigration amounted to only 4%.

Because a larger proportion of Jewish than of non-Jewish immigrants remained permanently in the United States, the Jews bulk larger in the net immigration (excess of immigration over re-emigration)

JEWISH AND NON-JEWISH RE-EMIGRATION FROM THE UNITED STATES

Years	Jewish Re-emigration		All Re-emigrants Per 100 Immigrants
	Number	Per 100 Jewish Imgr.	
1908-1914	46,838	7.1	30.8
1915-1920	3,470	4.3	56.6
1921-1924	1,986	0.7	25.8
1925-1943	4,913	3.5	38.9
1904-1943	57,207	4.6	34.4

than in the gross immigration. Thus between 1908 and 1924 the Jewish net immigration was 13.5% and for the nineteen-year period between 1925 and 1943, 13.3% of the total net immigration to the United States. In other words, there was during this period one Jewish immigrant for every seven non-Jewish immigrants who remained permanently settled in the United States. During the period 1908-1924 the Jews hold the first place as to the number of permanent immigrants (956,000), exceeding even Italians (with 945,000) and leaving far behind them the British (648,000) and the Germans (644,000).

2. COMPOSITION OF JEWISH IMMIGRATION

The permanent character of Jewish immigration determined the composition of the immigrant mass according to sex and age groups.

A. *Sex Groups:* Under free migration, the number of male emigrants is considerably larger than that of female emigrants, because males are usually gainfully employed, while a large number of women are economically dependent. Moreover, the more temporary the character of emigration, the less frequently do the emigrants take their wives and children with them; whereas the more permanent the emigration, the more frequently do the emigrants take their families along or bring them over later. From this we can infer that in the period of free migration, the percentage of women and children among Jewish immigrants was particularly large. This was actually the case in the period between 1899 and 1914. Of the total number of immigrants to America 68% were males and 32% females; among the Jewish immigrants there were 56% males and 44% females, so that 15% of all female immigration was Jewish. The difference between Jewish and non-Jewish immigrants from Eastern Europe in this regard was particularly great: among the Poles and Lithuanians, the females constituted only 33%; among the Hungarians, 31%; among the Ukrainians, 30%; among the Russians, 14%; among the Romanians, 13%. When immigration was restricted and preference was given to relatives of previous immigrants, the situation changed: the percentage of females not only rose abruptly, but soon began to exceed that of males (the de facto restriction of immigration caused by the war had a similar effect, but to a smaller extent). Among the Jewish immigrants the number of females exceeded 50% even during the period of 1921-1924 (54.5% females as against 45.5% males). Later it exceeded the percentage of males of nearly all other nationalities, especially of those upon whom the quota imposed greater restrictions. In the years between 1925 and 1927, the number of females amounted to 53% for the Poles, 61% for the Lithuanians, 55% for the Hungarians, 51% for the Russians, 59% for the Romanians, as against 54.5% for the Jews. During the years between 1935 and 1937, as a result of the administrative facilities granted to Jewish immigrants from Germany, the percentage of males among the Jews temporarily rose, and the percentage of females dropped to 46%, while for all other immigrants the percentage of females remained higher than that of males. However, in subsequent years the percentage of women among Jewish immigrants rose again and kept steadily rising from 48.1% in 1938 to 53.7% in 1943. (Among all immigrants the percentage of women was 55.9% in 1938 and 58.6% in 1943.)

B. *Age Distribution:* Similar phenomena can be found with regard to the age of the masses of Jewish immigrants as shown in the following table:

During the period of free migration (1899-1914) the percentage of children among the Jewish immigrants was twice as high as the percentage of children in the total number of immigrants, and larger than that among any other nationality. Almost one-fourth of all Jewish immigrants were less than fourteen years of age. The Jewish children at that time constituted 21.4% of all immigrant children, so that for every four non-Jewish children there was one Jewish child. The absolute number of Jewish children who emigrated during those sixteen years was 362,000, an average of more than 20,000 a year. The number of children in every hundred (24.4) Jewish immigrants greatly exceeded even the number in every hundred immigrants from Western Europe (17% for the Germans and 16% for the British), but in this respect the Jewish immigrants were particularly distinguished from the non-Jewish immigrants who came from the identical fatherlands. The proportion of children was slightly less than 10% for the Poles, 8% for the Lithuanians, 5% for the Russians and Ukrainians and 4% for the Romanians. The percentage of immigrants older than 45 was slightly higher among the Jews than the average (5.8% as against 5.2%); it was lower than among the West European immigrants, but much higher than among the East European ones. As a result, the percentage of adults among the Jews from 14 to 44 years of age (69.8%)

AGE COMPOSITION OF IMMIGRANTS IN THE UNITED STATES (IN PERCENTAGE)

Years	Under 14		14-44		45 and Older		Total	
	Jews	General	Jews	General	Jews	General	Jews	General
1899-1914	24.4	12.4	69.8	82.4	5.8	5.2	100.0	100.0
	Under 16		16-44					
1921-1924	29.6	18.5	57.7	72.3	12.7	9.1	100.0	100.0
1925-1927	22.7	16.0	54.1	74.6	23.2	9.3	100.0	100.0
1935-1936	18.0	19.4	65.3	64.5	16.7	16.2	100.0	100.0
1937-1938	17.1	15.0	65.4	69.3	17.4	15.7	100.0	100.0
1940-1941*	15.4	15.4	51.9	59.4	32.7	25.2	100.0	100.0
1942-1943	12.6	13.4	53.7	64.4	33.7	22.2	100.0	100.0

*In 1940-1941 the age classification was changed as follows: under 16, 16-45, 46 and older.

was considerably lower than in the total American immigration (82.4%). It was lower than among the immigrants of any other nationality; lower than among the West Europeans (73% for the British, 76% for the Germans) and much lower than among the other East Europeans. Thus the Jewish immigration mass had an individual age-group composition.

After the First World War there occurred a radical change in the Jewish age-groups, particularly since the beginning of the third period (1925). First, the percentage of children among Jewish immigrants dropped considerably, while, as a result of the quota system, it rose among all other nationalities. This phenomenon is chiefly explained by the great decline in the birth-rate among the East European Jews after the First World War. In other nationalities this decline was more gradual, and among the immigrants it was more than compensated for by the fact that since 1925 the non-Jewish immigration had a more permanent character than before. Moreover, after 1933, German Jews began to emigrate to an increasing extent; among them children were almost a rarity. In the last period before the Second World War Jewish immigration became Central European rather than East European. But whatever the explanation, the fact is that in recent years the percentage of children among Jewish immigrants was slightly less than the average: 12.6% among the Jews as against 13.4% for all the immigrants for 1942 and 1943. In the second place, until recently the percentage of older people constantly increased among the immigrants in general and among the Jews in particular. This was caused both by the United States legislation that favored the relatives of previous immigrants and by the "aging" of the Jewish population in Europe.

C. *Occupational Groupings:* The most striking element of Jewish immigration in the period of free migration was its occupational composition. Because the Jewish immigrants had a relatively greater percentage of dependent women and children, the percentage of Jewish immigrants not gainfully employed was of course particularly large. Until the end of free immigration this percentage was far higher than the average among immigrants into the United States, and exceeded the percentage of the similar class of immigrants from any other nation, even from Western Europe, where the percentage of such persons was very high. Here again, the Jewish immigrants radically differed from the non-Jewish East European immigrants. For the period 1899-1914, the proportion of dependents among Jews was 43%, as against 26% in the United States immigration as a whole; it was 39% for the British and Germans, 26% for the Hungarians, 23% for the Italians, 21% for the Poles, 18% for the Lithuanians, 14% for the Ukrainians and 12% for the Russians and Romanians. In the course of time the percentage of dependent persons both among Jews and the other nationalities grew considerably; the restriction of immigration resulted in increasing the percentage among the formerly only partly dependent East European immigrants. The difference between Jewish and non-Jewish immigrants into the United States considerably decreased also in this respect. The following table shows the number of economically dependent immigrants in the United States out of every hundred immigrants:

PERCENTAGE OF DEPENDENTS AMONG IMMIGRANTS IN THE U.S.A.

	1899-1914	1921-1924	1925-1927	1931-1932
Among Jews	43.3	54.5	57.0	65.0
In General	26.3	38.5	38.5	58.8

Unfortunately no occupational statistics of immigrants according to their nationalities are available since 1933, *i.e.,* for the period when Jewish emigration to the United States became predominantly of German origin.

From the previous observations concerning women and children, it can be deduced that the percentage of dependent Jewish immigrants in all likelihood decreased considerably since 1933, and that in this respect, too, the difference between the Jewish and the general immigration has diminished as compared with 1931-1932; it is even probable that in recent years this percentage has become smaller among Jews than among non-Jews.

The immigration statistics of the United States divide all occupations into three main categories: professionals, skilled workers and miscellaneous professions. The category of skilled workers includes artisans and industrial workers, as well as white collar employees. The group of miscellaneous professions comprises such varied occupations as agricultural laborers, unskilled workers and domestic servants on the one hand, and bankers, manufacturers, brokers and merchants on the other. Our analysis will be based on these official statistics.

were agricultural and unskilled workers, while the Jewish immigrants chiefly came from the cities and small towns of the former Russian Pale of Settlement, Galicia and Romania, and were for the most part artisans and skilled workers. From this it can be inferred that with regard to their occupational distribution the Jewish immigrants more closely resembled the immigrants from the industrialized West European countries than the non-Jewish East European immigrants. This was actually the case; skilled workers constituted 68% of all gainfully employed Jewish immigrants, as against 48% for the British and only 30% for the Germans; while they constituted barely 9% for the Hungarians, 7% for the Poles, 6% for the Russians and Lithuanians, less than 3% for the Romanians and only 2% for the Ukrainians.

OCCUPATIONAL DISTRIBUTION OF GAINFULLY EMPLOYED IMMIGRANTS IN THE UNITED STATES (IN PERCENTAGE)

	1899-1914		1921-1924		1925-1927		1931-1932	
	Jews	General	Jews	General	Jews	General	Jews	General
Liberal Professions	1.3	1.5	5.2	4.6	9.6	5.7	13.3	13.4
Skilled labor	68.2	20.2	41.4	30.5	47.8	29.6	40.0	30.0
Miscellaneous	30.5	78.3	53.4	64.9	42.6	64.7	46.7	56.6
	100.0	100.0	100.0	100.0	100.0	100.0	100.0	100.0

The figures covering the important period of 1899-1914 show that the occupational composition of the Jewish immigration was quite different from that of the immigrants as a whole. It is only in the professions that the proportion was approximately equal (only 1.5%); in the two other categories, comprising almost 99% of the total immigration, the Jews and immigrants as a whole figure in almost inverse ratio: among the Jews, over two-thirds of those gainfully employed belonged to the skilled trades, and less than one-third to the sundry other trades; while among the immigrants as a whole, only one-fifth of the gainfully employed immigrants belonged to the skilled trades and almost four-fifths to the miscellaneous. The reason for this is that the great majority of the non-Jewish immigrants came from villages where they

Later, when immigration was restricted, these differences between Jewish and non-Jewish immigrants decreased but never entirely disappeared. All in all, the Jews comprised a greater percentage of immigrants with skilled trades and a smaller percentage of immigrants with miscellaneous trades than did the immigration to the United States on the average.

A clear idea of the occupational composition of Jewish and non-Jewish immigrants is obtained when the various occupations indicated in the United States immigration statistics are regrouped and divided into the following five categories: 1) Agriculture; 2) Industry; 3) Commerce and transportation; 4) Professions; and 5) Unskilled labor and domestic service. For the period of free immigration the picture was as follows:

OCCUPATIONAL DISTRIBUTION OF JEWISH AND TOTAL IMMIGRATION INTO THE UNITED STATES (1899-1914)

	Number		Per 100 Gainfully Employed		Jews per 100 in Each Category
	Jews	General	Jews	General	
Agriculture	21,000	2,809,000	2.6	28.1	0.8
Industry	544.000	1,771,000	65.6	17.8	30.7
Commerce & transport	77,000	469,000	9.2	4.7	16.4
Liberal professions	11,000	152,000	1.3	1.5	7.4
Unskilled labor and domestic servants	177,000	4,777,000	21.3	47.8	3.7
	830,000	9,978,000	100.0	100.0	8.3

The specific occupational composition of the Jewish immigration stands out very clearly in this table. The ratio of Jewish agricultural workers to those in the total immigration is 1 to 11. The ratio of unskilled and domestic workers to those gainfully employed is one-fifth among Jewish immigrants, and one-half among all immigrants. But among the Jews the percentage of industrial workers is four times as great (two-thirds of the Jewish, and one-sixth of all the immigrants), and of persons engaged in commerce and transportation twice as large as among all the immigrants. Three-fourths of the Jewish immigration total were employed in industry and commerce, while three-fourths of all the mass of immigrants were employed in agricultural work, unskilled work and domestic service. It must be assumed that in reality the difference was even greater, because the Jewish immigrants who are listed as unskilled workers were to a great extent former petty traders, while among the non-Jewish immigrants they were chiefly former farm hands. Accordingly, the percentage of Jews among the immigrants varies extremely in the occupational groups. They represent

OCCUPATIONAL DISTRIBUTION OF GAINFULLY EMPLOYED IMMIGRANTS IN THE UNITED STATES (1899-1914):

	Agriculture	Industry	Trade and Transp.	Liberal Professions	Unskilled Labor, Dom. Servants	Total
Number (in thousands)						
Among:						
Jews	21	544	77	11	177	830
British	26	149	53	34	94	356
Germans	143	164	58	24	241	630
Italians	876	340	58	13	1,164	2,451
Poles	427	71	3	2	604	1,107
Ukrainians	109	5	0.3	0.2	105	219
Among all immigrants	2,809	1,771	469	152	4,777	9,977
IN PERCENTAGE						
Among:						
Jews	2.6	65.6	9.2	1.3	21.3	100
British	7.2	41.9	14.8	9.7	26.4	100
Germans	22.7	26.0	9.2	3.8	38.3	100
Italians	35.8	13.9	2.3	0.5	47.5	100
Poles	38.6	6.4	0.3	0.2	54.5	100
Ukrainians	49.8	2.1	0.1	0.1	48.0	100
Among all immigrants	28.1	17.8	4.7	1.5	47.8	100

less than 1% of the agricultural workers and less than 4% of the unskilled workers and domestic servants, but are one-sixth of all immigrants employed in trade and almost one-third (31%) of those employed in industry: for every two non-Jewish immigrants in industry there was one Jew.

The total number of Jews skilled in industry who immigrated into the United States between 1899 and 1914 exceeds half a million (544,000). No other group supplied an even remotely comparable number of such immigrants during that period; even the two groups that are next to the Jews according to the total in this class, the Italians (340,000) and the Germans (164,000), did not together supply as many as the Jews.

This immense mass of immigrants engaged in industry was unevenly divided among the various branches of industry, as can be seen from the following table:

needle industry, for each 100 non-Jewish immigrants there were 155 Jewish immigrants; among tailors alone, for each 100 non-Jews there were 216 Jews—twice as many Jewish tailors as all non-Jewish tailors taken together.

This does not mean that the Jews were inadequately represented in other industrial branches; on the contrary, they also occupied a prominent place among the immigrants in the great majority of the other branches of industry. It is sufficient to point out that the Jews numerically occupied the first place in 26 out of the 47 trades itemized in the United States immigration statistics up to the end of the period described. The table (p. 427) shows these trades, the number of Jewish immigrants employed in them, and their percentage of the immigrants in the period 1899-1914.

In eight of these trades the Jews constituted an absolute majority. These trades

DISTRIBUTION OF JEWISH IMMIGRANTS ENGAGED IN MANUFACTURING INDUSTRIES (1899-1914)

	Number	Of every 100 immigrants engaged in industry	Of every 100 gainfully employed
Needle trade	329,000	60.4	39.6
Building and lumber industry	80,000	14.7	9.6
Machine and metal industry	51,000	9.4	6.1
Food industry	39,000	7.1	4.7
Paper and leather industry	12,000	2.2	1.5
Textile industry	6,000	1.1	0.7
Graphic and art industry	6,000	1.1	0.7
Miscellaneous industry	22,000	4.1	2.7
TOTAL	545.000	100.0	65.6

Sixty percent of all these Jewish immigrants or 40% of all gainfully employed Jewish immigrants were engaged in the production of apparel (tailors, dressmakers, seamstresses, shoemakers, millinery workers, hatters, furriers). Those employed in the needle industry alone (tailors, dressmakers and seamstresses) constituted the absolute majority (51%) of all such Jewish immigrants and one-third of all the gainfully employed, so that out of every three wage-workers among the Jewish immigrants one was employed in the needle industry. Among all the immigrants employed in the

are: tailors, hatters, furriers, bookbinders, watchmakers, millinery workers, cigar and cigarette makers and tinsmiths. Of the 26 trades listed in which the Jews occupied the first place, in the case of 12 of them records began to be kept only in the course of the period described; before then the immigration of persons in these trades was not registered. The fact is that Jewish immigrants really imported these trades into the United States.

The restriction of immigration wrought deep changes in the occupational composition of the Jewish immigrant masses and to

Trades	Number of Jews	Percentage of Jews among all immigrants in the trade
Hat and capmakers*	6,000	79.8
Furriers*	5,000	75.0
Tailors	205,000	68.3
Bookbinders*	4,000	68.0
Watchmakers	6,000	60.2
Milliners*	6,000	60.0
Cigarmakers**	126	56.5
Tinsmiths	9,000	54.5
Tanners*	5,000	49.3
Undergarments	44,000	48.6
Turners	4,000	48.3
Upholsterers*	2,000	45.5
Jewelers	2,000	43.5
Painters and glaziers	22,000	43.4
Dressmakers (women)*	30,000	43.3
Photographers*	2,000	37.9
Saddle-makers	3,000	37.6
Locksmiths	13,000	34.2
Butchers	16,000	33.7
Metalworkers (exc. iron and steel)*	3,000	32.6
Printers	4,000	30.7
Bakers	15,000	26.7
Carpenters*	2,000	25.8
Building trade	47,000	24.2
Cigar-packers**	87	23.9
Blacksmiths	11,000	16.0

*Itemized since 1904.
**Itemized since 1911.

a great extent leveled the occupational differences between Jews and non-Jews. If we consider those employed in the garment trade (tailors, dressmakers, seamstresses) who in the period of free migration comprised one-third of all gainfully employed Jewish immigrants (33.6%), their ratio dropped to less than one-sixth in the years between 1925 and 1927 (15.5%), and to less than one-tenth (9.4%) in 1931-1932. The table below shows to what extent the occupational composition of the Jewish immigrants became similar to that of the non-Jewish.

Since it principally affected the immigrants from Eastern and Southern Europe more than those from Northern Europe, the restriction of immigration on the average lowered the percentage of agricultural and unskilled workers and raised that of industrial, commercial and professional occupations. Although the occupational composition of the Jewish and the general immigration into the United States thus became similar to a great extent, they were far from identical. Jewish immigration remained slightly agricultural as compared with general immigration. It remained less an immigration of unskilled workers (domestic servants in 1931-1932 represented 10.7% of the Jews and 20.1% of all gainfully employed immigrants) and much more an immigration of industrial and commercial elements; even the percentage of those employed in the needle trades remained four times higher among the Jews than among the non-Jews (9.4% of gainfully em-

DISTRIBUTION OF IMMIGRANTS IN THE U. S. A. ACCORDING TO GENERAL DIVISIONS OF INDUSTRY
(In percentage)

	1899—1914		1921—1924		1931—1932	
	Jews	General	Jews	General	Jews	General
Agriculture	2.6	28.1	3.0	12.5	3.6	12.7
Manufacturing	65.6	17.8	36.3	24.8	31.1	22.6
Trade and transportation	9.2	4.7	17.1	11.2	29.2	14.1
Liberal professions	1.3	1.5	5.4	4.9	13.3	13.4
Unskilled labor and domestic service	21.3	47.8	38.1	46.6	22.8	37.2

Courtesy Joint Distribution Committee

JEWISH WOMEN AND CHILDREN WAITING AT EUROPEAN PORT TO EMBARK FOR OVERSEAS

ployed Jewish immigrants and only 2.3% of non-Jews in 1931-1932). Jewish immigration has in general preserved its specific occupational character, although to a considerably smaller extent.

III.   CAUSES AND EFFECTS OF JEWISH MIGRATION

The industrial revolution that characterized the first period of capitalism brought almost complete ruin to the masses in the small-sized economic units such as the villages and towns; town-dwellers migrated to the cities, city-dwellers and town-dwellers migrated overseas. This movement took place in various countries, especially in Germany in the 1830's, 1840's and 1850's. Several decades later the same process took place in Russia, Galicia and Romania. The peasant and urban population began to emigrate in large numbers; and the Jewish population emigrated in great masses because its adjustment to the new economic system and its transition to new productive forms was made extremely difficult by special legal and administrative measures and by the complete boycott of Jewish man-power on the part of governments, non-Jewish employers and even a considerable number of Jewish capitalists. The workers and artisans belonging to the "Jewish" trades, in which were concentrated large Jewish working masses who worked not only for the Jews but largely for the sur-rounding non-Jewish population and who were particularly affected by the anti-Jew-ish boycott, were driven to emigrate even more urgently than the others. For that reason, the "Jewish" trades, principally tailoring, occupied an even greater place among the Jewish immigrants than they did in their old homes. In the years of anti-Semitic persecutions during the Russian pogroms and later during the Nazi per-secutions in Germany, Jewish emigration rose considerably, drawing in elements that normally are less inclined to emigrate. Emigration from villages, with peasants leaving their farms to be taken care of by their families during their absence, is often temporary; emigration from cities, in which the emigrants usually do not leave any en-terprises behind them, is almost always permanent. That reason alone would ac-count for the fact that Jewish emigration was more permanent than the emigration of other East European ethnic groups; in addition, the East and Central European Jews who had been suffering from discrim-ination and persecution were unwilling to return to their old homes. Temporary emigrants usually leave their families at home; permanent ones more often take them along or bring them over later. Therefore the percentage of women and children was larger among the Jewish em-igrants than among the non-Jewish, espe-cially those from Eastern Europe; for the same reason the percentage of economically dependent persons was particularly large among the Jews. And because of the one-sided occupational composition of Jewish

immigration and concentration in a few dominant trades, there was little chance for economic interdependence among them. A large mass of immigrants cannot go to an undeveloped country. In conditions of free migration they will go only to coun-tries with a large and rapidly increasing non-Jewish population, whose occupational composition is quite different from their own. Such a country was the United States (and later, though to a lesser extent, Argen-tina and Canada). The great Jewish emigra-tion of the free period actually went to these lands, only an insignificant part of it going to Palestine.

The most important results of the great Jewish migration can be summarized as follows:

a) The migrations of the last hundred years transformed the Jewish people—until then concentrated in Europe and around the Mediterranean basin—into a world people. At the same time, up to the eve of the Second World War, the Jewish people in Europe continued to increase numerically, since that was the period of the greatest natural increase among the Jews and the Jewish population in Europe did not decrease even in the period of the greatest Jewish emigration (1899-1914). Until the most recent times, emigration overseas did not mean the dispersion of the Jewish people. The immigrants were concentrated in a few countries, chiefly in the United States, where there arose a great, powerful and economically more prosperous Jewish community than in Eu-rope.

b) So far the great migration has failed to create a Jewish state or an autonomous territory inhabited by Jewish masses. But it has created a considerable settlement in Palestine which now numbers over 500,000 people, 30% of the total population of the country. Mention should also be made of the Soviet experiment in establishing an autonomous Jewish region in Birobidjan. At the present time it comprises 22,000 to 25,000 Jewish inhabitants.

c) The great migration transformed the

character of the Jewish population from a small-town into an urban, and to a large extent, even to a metropolitan population. About 85% of the Jewish population of the United States is settled in cities of more than 100,000 inhabitants. The same is true of Argentina and Canada. Even in Palestine, the majority of the Jews live in two big cities, Tel Aviv and Jerusalem. In New York the great migration created a Jewish community of approximately 2,000,000 persons, and in Chicago a community with more Jews than lived in pre-war Warsaw. The same is approximately true of the third greatest city in the United States, Philadelphia. The transformation of the Jewish masses into urban dwellers marks a real cultural revolution.

d) The mass emigration was a transition, on the one hand, from commerce to handicraft and industry, to a small extent also to agricultural labor; and, on the other hand, from the lower middle class to the salaried and wage-earning class.

e) There is no doubt that through emigration the more than 4,100,000 Jewish emigrants acquired for themselves and for their children incomparably more favorable material living conditions and im-measurably greater freedom and recognition of their human dignity than they would have acquired if they had remained in most of the countries of their origin.

f) The Jewish masses who remained in the old home countries greatly profited economically from the fact that more than 4,100,000 Jews had emigrated overseas. They profited either directly, thanks to the enormous sums of money that were sent by Jewish immigrants from America and Africa to their relatives and friends in Europe in the course of two generations; and indirectly, because emigration considerably eased the congestion, misery and bitter competition among the Jewish populations of Russia, Poland, Lithuania, Romania, etc.

g) But it is not only economically and as individuals that the Jews profited from the great emigration. Jewish social life in Eastern and Central Europe and in Palestine, the cultural movements and creative activity, the various institutions of social welfare,—all these were favorably affected by the material and moral support on the part of the organized forces of the new and prosperous Jewish communities in the countries of immigration.